THE FIRST EUROPE

JUSTINIAN AND HIS ATTENDANTS (MOSAIC OF A.D. 547 IN S. VITALE IN RAVENNA)

Note nimbus or halo on Christian emperor; dress of sixth century (cope, alb, etc.), later developed into vestments; monogram of Christ on soldiers' shields. Referred to page 116

THE FIRST EUROPE

A Study of the Establishment of
Medieval Christendom

A.D. 400—800

by

C. DELISLE BURNS

London
GEORGE ALLEN & UNWIN LTD

FIRST PUBLISHED IN 1947
SECOND IMPRESSION 1949

PRINTED IN GREAT BRITAIN
in 12-Point Bembo Type
BY UNWIN BROTHERS LIMITED
WOKING

TO

BARBARA and LAWRENCE HAMMOND
with gratitude and affection

PREFACE

The First Europe was that of the Middle Ages, the establishment of which is the subject of this book. It was the Europe of the united Christendom of the Latin Churches and of local lordships in continuous minor conflicts. The second Europe came into existence at the Renaissance and Reformation; and it has lasted almost until our own times. It was the Europe of independent Sovereign States, which were saved from extermination in mutual conflicts by expansion in the New World, the East and Africa. The third Europe does not yet exist.

For those who desire to make a third Europe of peace between nations and between social classes, and of well-being for the "plain people," the interest in the formation of the First Europe may be found partly in analogies between our position and that of our ancestors fifteen hundred years ago. They were at the beginning of a social transition in which slavery was transformed into serfdom, and an old unity, based upon a military dictatorship, was changed into the unity of western Christendom. In that time is to be found the real basis of modern democracy—the assumption that all human beings have an equal right to derive benefit from the social system and all adults an equal responsibility for its maintenance. This assumption is directly derived from the experience of the Christian Churches. The transition from the Roman Empire in A.D. 400 to medieval Europe in A.D. 800, was achieved by experiment and the invention of new social institutions. New moral standards and new conceptions of the moral worth of all human beings began at that time to dominate western Europe. The political and economic changes were less important than these, just as at present we are faced by moral problems more fundamental than the economic and political. Also, we know what it is to feel that the barbarians are at the gates. But the decay of an old civilization is less important

A*

than the creation of a new. And the four centuries dealt with in this book were ages of creation.

Another interest in this period may be derived from the survivals in contemporary society of functionaries and institutions of the early Middle Ages—for example, kings, bishops, churches and certain types of law. Also, about a thousand years ago in western Europe were to be found the beginnings of those rivalries which still obstruct the establishment of peace: for example, the long-standing rivalry between the peoples living to the East and the West of the Rhine, may be traced to the manner in which the so-called Holy Roman Empire came into existence. In that far past may be found the first traces of what is now called the "Axis," connecting Italy and Germany, and of the common Christian tradition of England and France. Indeed, it would be well if political theorists who now write about "the State," would study the problem, not of power but of *moral authority*, as it was in the last days of the Roman Empire in western Europe and in the new barbarian kingdoms. In the same period "nations" began to be the basis of State organization and not cities; different languages of equal cultural value arose beneath the superficial Latin of the learned caste, and a civilization developed which was dependent not upon one intellectual or cultural centre but upon interchange between many.

Between us and that first transition there lie both the experience of medieval Europe, which clearly was in continual development, and the second great transition which produced the wages system, industrial capitalism and Sovereign States. But the transition which produced the First Europe is still of interest, because it seems to have been the result of efforts to face problems as fundamental as our own. Then as now, a tradition of centuries seems to have been shattered by a *nomadism* which is to be found not merely in the wanderings of barbarian tribes, but also in the diversity of opinions and ways of life. In our day a certain nomadism of the mind, which divides society, and especially its more thoughtful members, into rival and sometimes hostile groups, is the sign of deeply-seated unrest. It seems to be due to causes very similar to those which operated in western Europe between A.D. 400 and A.D. 800. New experiences, new social ideals, new moral standards then appeared on the horizon, which could not be fitted into the traditional institutions or adjusted to the traditional ideals of conduct. Nomadism in any type of civilization is to be found where a great number of men and women are *déracinés*, having no recognized function in the community and no great interest in the continuance of the system into which they have been born. In our day widespread unemployment in the Democracies and the still more pernicious militarization by which the Dictatorships try to solve the problem, are signs of a fundamental social dislocation. Fifteen hundred years ago, in the last days of the Roman Empire in the West, slaves and poor farmers in flight from oppression, and the masses of men and women kept alive by gifts of food from the Public Authorities in the great cities, played their part in the dissolution of local religions and customs, which preceded the recognition of all human beings as members in the one community of Christendom. The nomadism of the mind in those centuries is to be found in the differences of opinion and purpose, expressed in their literature.

This book is concerned with the changes in the climate of opinion in western Europe between A.D. 400 and A.D. 800—in the so-called Dark Ages. During these centuries the First Europe was brought into existence by men and women working in circumstances much more difficult than our own, in the light of ideals which moved them, and with such little knowledge and ability as they possessed. It was a time of social transition. The dissolution of the social system of which the Roman Empire was the last defence, left western Europe a chaos out of which a new world was created. But much more attention has been paid by historians to the ruins of the Roman system than to the laying of the foundations of that Europe which we now inhabit. This book, on the other hand, definitely looks forward to medieval Europe and not backwards to the Roman Empire. It is not a chronicle of events. Such events and dates as are mentioned are used only to indicate the framework within which the action and thought of men were conducted during four centuries of transition. They built their world upon a new design, although they used for it material found among the ruins of the past. It is indeed ridiculous, historically, to treat medieval Europe as a mere interval of "Gothic" barbarism between Roman civilization and the Renaissance. But some of our greatest historians have made that mistake. Again, the ages called "dark" were times in which work was being done at foundations; or to change the metaphor, the new shoots hardly yet showed themselves above the surface. The cynic may indeed suppose with some justification that the "Dark Ages," like the "Dark Continent" of the nineteenth century, were called "dark" chiefly because most historians knew nothing about them.

In order to study the climate of opinion during a social transition, it is necessary to read the letters, treatises and chronicles produced at the time. On these alone this volume is based. Such a mass of learned works, chiefly in French and German, has been accumulated around the original documents, that the student is in danger of being lost in the ivy while he examines the building. Most of the documents are in Latin or Greek, in the great collections made by Migne and Mansi, in the *Monumenta Germaniae Historica* and in the *Corpus* of Latin ecclesiastical writers; but it will be clear from the references in the text that I owe a great debt to the scholars of France and Germany who have edited and annotated and written treatises on the original documents.

Almost all these documents have been available for the use of historians since the eighteenth century and have been used by Gibbon and other great scholars. But the same documents may contain material for the discussion of problems which were less familiar even twenty years ago than they are now; and, as Lord Acton said, the study of history should deal not with periods but with problems. The problem I have had chiefly in mind is the relation between armed force and moral authority in the art of government and in social organization generally, especially during a period of transition. With this is connected a study of the methods by which moral authority is acquired in new social relations. Mythology and the belief in magic had important effects upon the institutions of the First Europe. They take different forms in different ages; but they are not unknown even to-day as sources of social influence. Again, what at first sight appears to be a dissolution of moral standards is sometimes, as in western Europe after the fifth century, a sign of the growth of new ways of life and the establishment of new moral ideals.

The dates of the chroniclers and historians referred to in this book, and the general character of their works, are discussed in the appendices to Bury's edition of Gibbon; and some of the Latin treatises of the same dates are summarized in Laistner's *Thought and Letters in Western Europe, A.D. 500–900* (1931). Among the more recent studies of the period are Hodgkin, *Italy and her Invaders, A.D. 376–814* (1892–1899, 8 vols.), Fustel de Coulanges, *Institutions Politiques de L'Ancienne France* (6 vols., 2nd ed., 1904), Duchesne, *L'Histoire Ancienne de l'Eglise* (1911, 4 vols., Eng. trans. 1909–1925), the same author's *Les Premiers Temps de l'Etat Pontifical* (2nd ed., 1911) and Eric Caspar, *Geschichte des Papsttums* (1930–1934, 2 vols.).

In the text of this book English only is used, reference being made to other languages only when no satisfactory equivalent exists in English; because the book is intended, not for specialist scholars of the period, but for the ordinary reader who is interested in the problems of social transition. Obviously a study of the climate of opinion cannot be confined only to the discussion of social institutions. But this volume is so confined, in order that a further study may follow, which will deal with the changes in the moral standards and the philosophical views of the universe and of man in the early Middle Ages. In this volume, wherever it is indicated that the problem will be discussed "elsewhere," reference is made to a second volume not yet completed.

My own interest in the problem of social transition began more than thirty years ago when, after taking the Classical Tripos in the University of Cambridge, which gave me some slight knowledge of the Roman Empire, I spent four years in Rome and its neighbourhood, studying the use made of the ruins of that Empire in the early Christian basilicas, mosaics, inscriptions and other memorials.

These records of the first attempts to create medieval Europe have, no doubt, affected my views of the written documents of the period. It seems to me impossible to study the history of any period without some knowledge of the buildings and the plastic arts produced by the people of that time, and some appreciation of the customs and beliefs which serve to explain the form taken by the arts. In Rome also I studied medieval philosophy by attendance at Latin lectures and by myself maintaining "theses" in "disputations" in Latin—no doubt reminiscent of the "Letters of Obscure Men" and of Rabelais' problem: "Whether a chimera buzzing in empty space can eat second intentions." Again, the historian may find it useful to have some acquaintance with the districts familiar to the writers and men of action of the time he is studying. The geographical features of central and northern Italy, of France, eastern England and the Rhine country have not changed for more than a thousand years; and I have had the advantage of journeys in the Roman Campagna, Tuscany, Liguria, Lombardy and Venezia, and also of following the whole course of the Moselle and so appreciating the scenes which infused a little poetry into the lifeless verses of Ausonius. I know also the forests around Aachen, where Charles the Great hunted, and those north of Fulda, where St. Boniface founded his monastery "in the wilderness." The French part of my family came from the region round Bordeaux, where, in the fifth century, Ausonius and Paulinus of Nola held property, and where in the early ninth century Louis the Pious suffered education. From a knowledge of the coastal defences of 1940, in England to guard against Germanic invasion, I can appreciate the worries of the Count of the Saxon Shore (*Comes litoris Saxonici*); and the Roman forts under his jurisdiction, which I have seen at Anderida (Pevensey) and Burgh Castle on the Waveney, are as impressive even to-day as more recent defences. In reference to the problem, rather than the period, I worked in public offices between the years 1917 and 1934 in unimportant positions, but at certain specific difficulties of the first attempts at social reconstruction in our own day, after the war that was "to end war." First, as an official of the Central Government in England, in the Ministry of

Reconstruction and the Ministry of Labour; later, in the Central Office of the Labour Party, I learnt to appreciate such difficulties as a Roman official in the sixth century may have had to face. Again, in discussions with officials of the League of Nations at Geneva and of the Central Governments in Paris, Berlin, Vienna and Warsaw, I thought I was watching the establishment of the third Europe. Only after the "first barbarian kingdoms" collapsed in 1932 and 1934, as in the sixth century, did I turn back to the history of the first "black-out."

The first barbarian kingdoms of the sixth century failed because they were too closely copied from a model that had decayed. And clearly the settlement of 1919 failed because of *archaism*, not utopianism. The Peace Settlement of 1919 collapsed, not because those who supported it were moved by ideals which were too exalted for practical politics, but because both the idealists and the practical politicians were thinking in terms of Sovereign States—terms which belonged to the Renaissance and were archaic in the twentieth century, exactly as the conception of a centralized Empire was obsolete in the ninth century. The history of the "Dark Ages," however, shows how difficult it is for any age to escape from the ghosts that haunt the graves of the past.

My thanks are due first to the best of friends, J. L. Hammond and Barbara Hammond, who have read through the whole of my manuscript and made the most valuable criticisms and suggestions; and also to R. H. Tawney, who has done the same for some of the chapters. I was fortunate in having the assistance of historians who understand that the writing of history involves making moral judgements as well as recording facts. I thank also my wife for her labour in writing down a great part of the manuscript, and for carrying about the large volume of Mansi's *Concilia* and of the *Codex Theodosianus* in the edition of Gothofredus—no light labour. Thanks are also due to the Librarian of Dr. Williams's Library, Mr. Stephen K. Jones, who found for me some of the less easily traced passages; to my brother R. E. Burns for studying sections of late Latin and Greek documents with the long-suffering of the classical scholar when he reads anything later than Thucydides and Tacitus.

For assistance on special points I have to thank also my friends Count Guglielmo degli Alberti, Sir Eric Maclagan, Mr. M. P. Charlesworth and Miss J. M. C. Toynbee.

It need hardly be said that any judgements expressed upon persons and institutions are my own; and so are any mistakes which may have escaped the attention of my friends.

C. DELISLE BURNS

DORKING, *Martinmas* 1941

Owing to the death of my husband before the completion of the proof-reading some errors and omissions may have escaped notice. For these I must apologize. I should also like to express my thanks to those friends, and especially to my brother-in-law, R. E. Burns, who gave me valuable assistance in the final reading of the proofs.

M. DELISLE BURNS

CONTENTS

17

CONTENTS

ILLUSTRATIONS

MAPS

At end of book

21

ABBREVIATIONS

C.I.L.	*Corpus Inscriptionum Latinarum.*
Cod. Theod.	*Codex Theodosianus*, ed. Mommsen and Meyer.
C.S.E.L.	*Corpus Scriptorum Ecclesiasticorum Latinorum.*
H.E.	*Historia Ecclesiastica* (various authors).
Mansi	*Conciliorum Omnium Amplissima Collectio, etc.*, ed. Mansi.
M.G.H.	*Monumenta Germaniae Historica.*
Pat. Graec.	*Patrologia Graeca*, ed. Migne, Paris.
Pat. Lat.	*Patrologia Latina*, ed. Migne, Paris.
Script. R.G.	*Scriptores Rerum Germanicarum*, 8vo, reprints of texts in *M.G.H.*

CHAPTER I

INTRODUCTION

THE FORMATION OF THE FIRST EUROPE

The First Europe came into existence during the four hundred years from the beginning of the fifth century to the end of the eighth century of the Christian era. It included, geographically, the countries now known as France, England, Ireland and southern Scotland, western Germany, central and northern Italy and northern Spain. Its peoples spoke Germanic languages in the North and East, and variations of Latin in the South and West. They were socially united in a Christendom which excluded the older eastern forms of Christianity; but they were divided by local lordships. This First Europe was, indeed, dependent in its earlier years upon the older cultures of the Mediterranean, which had produced finally the Roman Empire; but it was a new type of civilization. Thus, the word Europe became, after the collapse of the Roman Empire in the West, more than a geographical expression; and it was used in the new sense for the first time in the ninth century, for example, by Nithard the ninth-century historian, when he wrote that Charles the Great at his death "had left all Europe in the greatest happiness."[1] Europe is thus distinguished, not only from other lands, but from the tradition of the Greek-speaking Churches and Empire, and from Islam. From that time Europe was "the West"—not merely a different place but a different spirit.

The Roman Empire had never been European or Western, in the modern sense of these words. It had always united the countries surrounding the eastern Mediterranean, from which it drew its

[1] Nithard, Hist. I: "Karolus . . . merito Magnus imperator ab omnibus nationibus vocatus . . . omnem Europem in summa bonitate reliquit." Nithard wrote between A.D. 841 and A.D. 843.

chief wealth, with the less developed countries of the West, including northern Gaul and Britain. And when, at the beginning of
the fourth century, first Diocletian and then Constantine removed
the central administration from Rome eastwards, it had become
obvious to Roman generals and lawyers, as well as to the adherents
of Christianity, that the real centre of the Empire lay at the junction
of Asia and Europe. The Roman Empire was based upon the
control of the trade routes in the basin of the Mediterranean. It
inherited the conquests of the Greek successors of Alexander in
Egypt, Syria and Asia Minor. And although it had also succeeded
to the conquests of the Roman Republic in the West, these were
of less importance, three centuries after Augustus, than the rich
and populous cities of what is now called the "Near East."

The civilization of the First Europe was quite distinct from the
Roman. It did not depend upon the Mediterranean. It was the
creation of the Latin Churches, and not of any one military or
civil power. Its intellectual centres were in northern France, the
Rhine country, England and northern Italy. Its architecture and
other plastic arts were original experiments to meet new needs. Its
music came out of popular songs. Its organizations of a learned
caste, the clergy, of monasteries and of the universities which were
later established, were new social inventions. Thus, the First Europe
of the so-called Middle Ages, was an original experiment in new
ways of living and thinking. Medieval civilization was more
primitive than the Roman in externals, because it lacked, for
example, baths and roads; and in culture it was more primitive,
because it lacked that natural intercourse between educated men
and women, which existed in the Roman villas and city mansions.
But in other aspects it was an advance upon Mediterranean civilization; for example, in its moral and religious ideals, in its community
of feeling between the rich and the poor and in its widespread
sense of social responsibility. If character and conduct in different
ages are to be compared, St. Francis was not more civilized than
Seneca, but he had wider and more subtle sympathies; and Abelard,
Aquinas and Occam were better thinkers than Cicero and Pliny,
although their observation and experience were more limited. The

greater philosophers of ancient Athens cannot be supposed to add credit to the Roman Empire, the culture and social organization of which retained few traces of their teaching in the fifth century of the Christian era. To avoid misunderstanding, therefore, it should be clearly stated that medieval civilization is regarded here as only a first stage in the development of a pattern of culture, whose later forms were the second Europe of the sixteenth to nineteenth centuries, and the third Europe now being established. To compare the Roman system at its best under the Antonines, or in its later years under Constantine or Theodosius the Great, with the First Europe in the days of Charles the Great, is like comparing a great river, losing itself in the sands at the end of its course, with a mountain torrent from which a still greater stream arises. Or again, to change the metaphor, the early history of the First Europe treats of the roots of that great tree which has now expanded into modern science, modern music and arts, and modern skill in government. But the roots of that tree, if exposed to the light of history, may not appear so attractive as the latest faded flowers of Greek and Roman culture.

Although medieval civilization, throughout its whole course until the Renaissance, and certainly in its first years, was more primitive than the Roman, its roots struck far deeper among all classes of the community; and it contained forces much more powerful than the Roman Empire had ever included. The doctrine and practice of the Christian Churches, based upon the belief that each human being had an immortal soul to be saved, and that all were in some sense equal as Christians—this was one of the most important influences in the formation of what is now known as democracy. Democracy as an ideal means a social system of liberty, equality and fraternity for all men, and not a system in which a few share freedom among themselves in order the better to control the rest. And democracy as a system of government, by which the ideal may be approached, means at least some control by the "plain people" over their rulers and agents and some right of public discussion concerning public policy. But even in this sense, the sources of some elements in the democratic tradition of to-day are to be found in the election of bishops in the earliest Christian Churches and in the meeting of bishops as representatives in Synods, rather than in ancient Athens or Rome.

The word "democracy" in Greek did not refer to slaves and women as members of the political community, although, as in the case of cattle, their owners and masters might care for them. On the other hand, the Athenians developed and the Roman Republic preserved the power to criticize and remove public authorities and the free discussion of public policy by all citizens. But neither criticism nor discussion survived in the Christian Churches; and the democracy of early Christianity had passed, before the fifth century, into a form of despotism under the control of the bishops and clergy. The democratic tendency of Christianity in medieval Europe survived only in the sacraments and ceremonies, which were equally shared by all, and in early Christian documents which served at times to support protests against despotism, political or clerical. Nevertheless, democracy in the modern sense of that word, did in fact arise within the Christian tradition and not elsewhere. Medieval civilization was also the source of the great European literatures and of modern European music and plastic arts. Even modern experimental science can be traced to the practices of magic, both sacred and secular, in the Middle Ages. But in social institutions the early years of the First Europe were still more important for the future. At that time the system of nation-States had its origin in the barbarian kingdoms which replaced the Roman provinces in the West. The Roman organization of Christian communities spread from Italy and Gaul into England, Ireland and Germany. The great monastic system of the West was established; and pilgrimage connected the common people of all Europe. These are the roots of the First Europe.

This book deals less with the disappearance of the ancient world than with the first signs of the new civilization, of which our own is the direct descendant. In order, therefore, to express the difference between the beginning and the end of the process which is to be studied, a short series of contrasts may be described.

The Contrast between A.D. 400 *and* A.D. 800

Of the most obvious institutions in A.D. 400 the Roman Empire is the best known. It was one system of government which included all the lands from northern Britain to the borders of Iraq, and from the Rhine and Danube to the Sahara. In A.D. 800, on the other hand, the same institution, still called the Roman Empire, included only part of the Balkan peninsula and of Turkey, within easy reach of its capital at Constantinople. But in western Europe separate kingdoms under Germanic chieftains were established in Gaul, then called western France, and Germany, then called eastern France, in Italy, in England and in northern Spain. The most striking feature of the change is the localization of government. Many different and independent centres of power and authority had taken the place of one; although all these countries were felt to be united against the outer world, as Latin Christendom. Africa north of the Sahara and southern Spain were ruled by Mohammedan Caliphs. In the East were unknown tribes; and in the West, the Ocean.

In A.D. 400 the Roman Emperors, who were Christian and Catholic, were legislating on doctrine and Church discipline, with the advice of bishops, who were themselves largely under the control of imperial officials. But by A.D. 800 there was an imperial Church, outside the surviving Roman Empire in the East, subject to the bishops of Rome, legislating for itself, and sometimes using the power of local kings for civil as well as ecclesiastical organization. A large part of western Europe was united again, but now by the organization of the Latin Churches, which had lost contact with the Christianity of the eastern Mediterranean. Less obvious, but more important than the great changes in political and ecclesiastical institutions, was the change in the system of production and distribution. In A.D. 400 the Roman Empire depended upon the organization of great cities—Rome, Constantinople, Alexandria, Carthage, Arles and the rest, whose populations obtained food and clothing from distant sources of supply. There was a trade in slaves, food-stuffs and raw materials throughout the Mediterranean basin, extending also to the Rhine country, northern Gaul and Britain,

A cultured, city-bred, rich class provided administrators for a single system of economic customs and political laws. By A.D. 800 all this had disappeared from western Europe. The great Roman cities were in ruins; and their diminished populations continually suffered from plague, famine or the raids of armed gangs. Trade between the East and the West of the Mediterranean basin had almost come to an end. The slave-trade hardly existed; and neither ships nor road traffic were able to carry raw materials and food-stuffs for long distances. Distribution, therefore, had become local. It was organized by local landowners, controlling serfs tied to the soil, but possessed of customary rights. The ruling class, except for a few of the higher clergy, consisted of ignorant, illiterate, country-bred "sportsmen," whose chief enjoyment, when not killing or robbing their neighbours, was hunting game in the forests. In the four centuries that followed the fifth, a great process of de-urbanization was taking place. The population was more evenly spread over the whole area of north-western Europe. Thus, medieval Europe was embodied in the primitive castles and the abbeys and not, at any rate in its first phase, in the houses or churches of merchants and craftsmen in the towns.

Again, in A.D. 400 the centres of intellectual activity, of the arts and of trade, were the sea-ports of the Mediterranean basin—Constantinople, Alexandria, Carthage, Arles and Rome. By the ninth century the centres of activity in the First Europe lay in the North-West—Paris, Tours, Fulda, and, in later years, Antwerp and London.[1] Thus the geographical setting for the new type of civilized life lay in countries on the border of the great ocean, which proved eventually to be, not the limit of the earth, but the pathway to a new world. Finally in A.D. 400 Christianity was a proselytizing religion, fighting long-established customs and beliefs of many different types; and Christianity itself, even among the more simple-minded western races, was divided into different sects—Arians, Donatists, Priscillianists and others. It was organized in local congregations or Churches, each independent of the other,

[1] The revival of Italian cities after the eleventh century introduces another problem—the contact of the West and the East after their severance.

but connected by a common literature and ritual, and by the Councils of bishops. Later, in A.D. 800, in western Europe Christianity had become Christendom. Everyone was assumed to be Christian and Catholic. The Latin Churches of the West had coalesced into one imperial Church controlled by a separate caste of clergy, monks and nuns, most of them celibates, under the government, at least in theory, of the bishops of Rome.

Romans and Germans

The contrast between A.D. 400 and A.D. 800 is startling. What is here attempted is to explain how and why the change occurred. In its earliest stages the change may be regarded as due to a conflict between a particular type of civilization and a particular type of barbarism. It is assumed in what follows that the "pattern of culture" called the Greek-Roman civilization, embodied in the late Roman Empire, was only one of many possible forms of civilized life. Not civilization in general, but only Roman civilization was in question in the fifth century, although most of the writers of that time thought of their own tradition as civilization itself. In the same way, some writers and speakers of to-day who lament the danger to "civilization," fail to perceive that an earlier pattern of culture may be replaced by a better. The Roman system was the last of the great predatory Empires based upon slavery; but it brought unity and extended culture throughout the countries in the basin of the Mediterranean. Its best products were regarded by eighteenth-century historians as standards for all civilized men; and they were therefore unable to understand or appreciate the new forms of civilization which took its place. But they were not wrong in supposing that any form of civilized life is better than any barbarism, although it is always difficult to distinguish the first signs of a new civilization from the barbarism by which it is surrounded.

This book is concerned with the transition from one type of civilization, the Roman, to another—the European. Any form of civilization is a complex of social relationships, more varied and more intricate than those of barbarism. Among civilized men and women opinions and tastes differ, and social customs are continually adjusted by individual experiment. Occupations are differentiated in what is called the division of labour, and the political and economic "interests" of the members of any community, and of different communities, are different and interdependent. In barbarism, on the other hand, all the members of the community are as far as possible alike in opinions, tastes, occupations and interests. Society is homogeneous. Established custom and belief control daily life and prevent variation. One man, or one caste of magicians or lords, provides the rules for thought and action. And therefore even in civilized communities the simplicity of barbarism has an attraction for minds weakened by personal distress or confused by social unrest, as it had for the Cynics in ancient Greece and the hermits of the third and fourth centuries of the Christian era.

Although civilization and barbarism are face to face, the chief purpose of our discussion is to show, not how an old civilization disappeared, but how a new civilization arose. Social relations change when a child becomes a man, when acquaintances become husband and wife, or when lovers use telephones instead of writing. When such changes occur, it is misleading to think of them as a decay or decline of an earlier system. It would be absurd to treat a change in social custom, such as the wearing of trousers instead of tunics in the fifth century, as a decay or decline of anything whatever. Biological metaphors applied to types of civilization or patterns of culture misrepresent the facts. Indeed, in times of social transition there is greater vitality among ordinary men and women than at other times, precisely because the displacement of ancient customs compels them to think and act for themselves. Again, the transition from a long-established social system to the crude beginning of a new Order, must not be rendered in terms of good and bad. French is not bad Latin. But from the fifth to the ninth century, when the transition from Latin to French was taking place, the finer qualities of the new language were not so easily perceived, especially by the educated, as the mummified elegance of the Latin of the vanished past. As in the history of language, so in that of the plastic arts, the splendid temples of ancient Rome were more magnificent than the Christian basilicas of the fourth century and their mosaic decoration. But in the study of the transition to a new type of civilization it is necessary to foresee in the colours of the mosaics the future development of the decoration of the Christian Churches in the glass of the cathedrals of Chartres and of York. Thus, the transition from the Roman system of civilization must not be regarded primarily as the spread of barbarism.

On the other hand, the barbarism by which the Roman system was faced in the fifth century, was not barbarism in general, but a particular form of it. It was the barbarism of the Gothic and Germanic tribes introduced at first into the heart of the Roman world as its defenders. Historians of the nineteenth century, however, were as mistaken in their estimate of Germanic barbarism as their predecessors had been in their view of Roman culture. By the later historians, the Germanic barbarians were taken to be pure-souled, loyal and valiant supplanters of an effete social and political system. This astonishing mistake was, no doubt, partly due to a misunderstanding of the prejudices of the Christian Fathers, partly to the Romantic Movement, but chiefly to the uncontrolled imagination of sedentary scholars. As it is clear from contemporary records, the Germanic barbarians, with a few noble exceptions, were drunken, lecherous, cowardly and quite untrustworthy, even among those for whom they professed friendship. They did not indeed suffer from such vices of luxury as may be due to fine clothes, baths and good cooking. Simplicity has its attractions, even when, as Sidonius Apollinaris says, it stinks.[1] But the Vandals in Africa in the fifth century showed that the so-called virtues of barbarians were largely due to their ignorance of the more subtle tastes of civilized men. And it is an absurdity to treat Theodoric the Ostrogoth or Clovis the Frank as examples of nobility or valour. The first, with his own hand, killed his guest; the second split open the skull of. a subordinate, when his back was turned. These men were savages. But the particular form of barbarism

[1] Felicemque libet vocare nasum, etc. (Carm. xxiii. 13). "Happy the nose which cannot smell a barbarian." This was written about A.D. 455 in Gaul.

which can be contrasted with the Roman type of civilization in the fifth century, was certainly Germanic. A great German historian has said that "the process of barbarization of the Roman Empire was a process of Germanization."[1] The barbarism, therefore, with which this book is concerned, is not barbarism in general, but only one type of it.

In very general terms, the characteristics of Roman civilization and of Germanic barbarism may be described as follows. Under the Roman system the relations between men, women and children were complicated and various. A long-established system of slavery had been somewhat modified, under Stoic and Christian influence, to the advantage of the slaves. But the slave population was large; and even soldiers had slaves. Legal rights of ownership, marriage, inheritance and trade were clearly defined; and an official administration made them effectual. The mechanisms of production and transport were well developed. Public buildings and aqueducts still remain to prove the existence of applied sciences of which barbarians are ignorant. The minor arts of clothing and the preparation of food were carried on in a characteristic form, as it is still evident in the Roman dress of the fifth century, which has served as a model for ecclesiastical costume and vestments surviving into modern times. The fine arts in the fifth century were superficial and derivative. Writers lived upon the pages of other writers, long since dead; and artists in the plastic arts spent their energies upon ornament rather than structure and function. But the fine arts had a recognized place in society.

Germanic barbarism, on the other hand, was the common characteristic of a number of disconnected small tribes, speaking dialects hardly yet developed into languages. Each of these tribes was as much, if not more, hostile to its neighbours than to the Roman Empire. The young men of these tribes, with some camp-followers, eagerly left the tribal settlements to seek booty or service in war under Roman commanders. They were simple folk, without

[1] Mommsen, *Romische Geschichte* (1885), Part v, bk. viii, ch. 4. The words in German are: "Die letzte Phäse des römischen Staats ist bezeichnet durch dessen Barbarisirung und speciell dessen Germanisirung." Eng. Trans. in Mommsen, *Provinces of the R.E.*, vol. i, p. 168.

any skill in agriculture, building or other useful arts, whose social relationships, as expressed in their legal customs, were troubled chiefly by personal violence, murder and stealing. That is to say, they were in that situation which sociologists describe as a transition from the pastoral to the agricultural stage of social development. In their entertainments and their religion, some customs and beliefs survived from a still earlier stage of social development—that of the hunters. Thus, even when the barbarians had entered into territories hitherto Roman, they preserved the pleasures of the chase and their belief in the magic of woods and sacred places. The members of a small barbarian community were, no doubt, more closely united in the simplicity of their minds, and in loyalty to their chieftains, than were the men and women of the more complex Roman city life. This may have been the basis of the idea of romantic historians that loyalty and honour were barbarian virtues. But any barbarian community faced two dangers. First, if it took service under one Roman general, it might be reduced to slavery by the victory of another; and, secondly, if it remained outside the Roman frontiers, it might suffer from the slave-raids which had been essential for many centuries before the fifth in order to supply the Roman world with cheap labour. No doubt, this is the basis for the idea that Germanic barbarians stood for "freedom." Tacitus wrote in the second century a brilliant political pamphlet on the "noble savage," the *Germania*. This attack upon the political opponents of Tacitus in Rome has been used, even in modern times, as evidence of the situation among the German tribes three hundred years after Tacitus wrote. But the Germanic barbarians were, like other barbarians, entangled in continually changing social situations, with their own defects and advantages. The same situations existed, in the main, among non-Germanic barbarians of the North, with whom the Roman populations came into contact—the Huns, the Avars, and the Slavs; but no Tacitus has made political capital out of these savages. Neither German nor other barbarians in the second or in the fifth century can be used by a modern historian as models of morality, with which to contrast the decadence of the Roman upper class. But the very simplicity of

B

the barbarian mind in a barbarian society has its uses, if a new step is to be made in the history of civilized life. At least a futile culture will be brought down to common earth.

The barbarian warriors and the tribes from which they came, were not opposed to Roman civilization, and certainly did not mean to destroy it. Indeed, they asked nothing better than to be allowed to share in its products—food, wealth, security and more refined pleasures. Barbarian warriors sought pay or booty; and in the later fifth century discovered that they could obtain more wealth by settling among a civilized population than by looting and moving from place to place. There were barbarian settlements within the Roman frontiers, and thousands of Germanic slaves there, before there were barbarian invasions. But even the barbarians who invaded Italy and Gaul did not attempt to destroy the Roman social system or the Roman Empire which maintained it. They desired only to plunder a building which was already falling into ruins. And on the other hand, the policy of the later Roman Emperors was that called "appeasement" in modern times. For example, the Visigoths and Burgundians were granted leave to retain their conquests, in the hope that they would not take any more. The Vandals were invited into Africa by a Roman General. The Ostrogoths, under Theodoric, conquered Italy with the acquiescence and perhaps the approval of the Roman Emperor at Constantinople. It is probably true, as was supposed at the time, that the Lombards entered Italy at the request of a Roman Exarch. And after "appeasement" had allowed the establishment of barbarian kingdoms in Gaul, Spain, Africa and Italy, Justinian's attempt in the sixth century to adopt the opposite policy proved to be quite futile. It came too late to save the Roman provinces in the West.

From the point of view of the governing class in the Roman Empire, there was no hostility to the Germanic barbarians. The Emperors and the Roman generals desired to use them. They welcomed them as soldiers, and found them useful and also decorative as slaves. The imperial Authorities, in fear of civil war, had forbidden men of senatorial rank to join the army, and were not eager to recruit the legions from the city populations, which had various other duties to perform in industry and transport. In consequence the majority of the Romanized city and country population in western Europe was demilitarized; and the best recruits for the armed forces were found among the barbarian tribes. Thus, in the fifth century, the word "soldier" (miles) was equivalent in meaning to the word "barbarian" (barbarus). The situation thus created may be regarded as an attempt to civilize the barbarians, by using them for the only services for which they were competent within the Roman system. But to the minds of men of the fifth century, to civilize meant to Romanize; and the barbarians themselves accepted this idea. The result was obvious. While it became more doubtful in what institution or persons moral authority was to be found, clearly armed force, and the wealth and power which it could obtain, fell more completely into the hands of the barbarians as the years went by. The barbarians were not only soldiers of the line and cavalry, but generals and even Emperors. The Emperor Justin, the uncle of the great Justinian, could neither read nor write. Here again, then, it must be repeated that the problem was not that of civilization in general, but of the Roman form of it. A similar problem in the modern world exists in Africa. Europeans desire to civilize the Africans; and the Africans desire to be civilized. But because both assume that the only form of civilization in question is the European, Europeans attempt to Europeanize the Africans. Some Europeans believe that Africans can be used only as cheap labour, exactly as Romans of the fifth century believed that Germanic barbarians could be useful only as slaves or soldiers. And, on the other hand, some Africans, in their attempt to escape from the pastoral and agricultural stages of social development into what they believe to be civilization, have contrived to become Europeanized. The result is satisfactory neither to Africans nor Europeans. As in the fifth century in western Europe, a particular type of civilization has not proved flexible enough to meet new strains and pressures. The Roman crisis has come to an end; and that in modern Africa has hardly begun. But it is still possible that modern European civilization will be more successful than the Roman in adapting itself to new experiences and alien influences.

From this point of view, the Middle Ages were centuries during which, after the failure to adjust the Roman system to the play of new forces, these forces built up a new kind of civilized life and culture in its first form.

The Process of Change

The process of adaptation by which the Roman system, and the barbarism with which it was confronted, gradually produced the First Europe, was continued for about four centuries. In its earliest stages the Roman governing class was still preserving, as culture, an obsolete aloofness from the real world. They wrote and perhaps also felt and thought in artificial imitation of "classical" authc. Virgil, Ovid and Livy themselves produced a faked pastoral poetry and a faked history; but Ausonius and Sidonius Apollinaris wrote verses which were fakes of the original fakes. The plastic arts also had become mere exercises in archaism. The system of government embodied ideas derived from political situations which had not existed for at least two hundred or perhaps four hundred years. At the same time the great majority of the population—about twenty million in western Europe—slaves, craftsmen and traders, who were maintaining the system by their labour, had no share in political influence or cultural expression. An artificial and irrelevant culture and a system of manual labour without any means of making its own contribution of intelligence or emotion to meet new issues, was hardly capable of internal transformation. Quite apart from difficulties due to external pressure, there was too little free movement of thought and emotion upwards or downwards between the social classes within the Roman system. Indeed, the problem of Roman civilization in the fifth century may be stated in more general terms. "To any vital and organic society its vocations are *structural* not accessory. Slave-based societies fail because there is too little interpenetration of culture with vocation. Culture is sustained in such societies, not by the significant and contributory vocational activity of those who share the culture, but by technical contributions of a slave-class or proletariat which is largely excluded from it. Where integration is satisfactory, a culture may indeed be known and recognized by its vocations, as we understand the Middle Ages or the culture of a long-vanished society by examining the memorials of craftmanship that its workers have left."[1] Already, then, in the fifth century the Roman system contained a division within itself, which was likely to prove fatal—the division between culture without function and function without culture.

It remains to be seen how the Christian Churches attempted to solve the difficulty. They had in their hands a new literature—a literature of power not of form; and they united members of all social classes by the use of the same ceremonies and sacraments. What was vital in the old order lay in the common ground beneath the fading flowers of culture. But after the establishment of barbarian kingdoms under Arian kings within the areas in western Europe which had hitherto been Roman, social changes came too quickly for the thought of the time. In the sixth century the control of government had passed into the hands of illiterate barbarian warriors; and they made use of members of the Roman governing classes and civil service, as officials and secretaries. Men like Cassiodorus, who served Theodoric the Ostrogoth, preserved Roman forms of government and the Latin language. But the letters of Cassiodorus and the version of his political ideas preserved in the *History of the Goths* by Jordanes, show that the ideas of the time were inadequate to promote the absorption of barbarians into civilized society. Cassiodorus himself ended his life as a monk in an Italy devastated by wandering bands of warriors. The Christian Churches had by that time undertaken the salvaging of civilization; but they too were led by men educated in the artificial culture of the past, and still dominated by the belief that the Roman Empire was eternal. Worse still, the dead hand of the past in the Old Testament hampered the growth of new forms of civilized life almost as much as did the survival of obsolete customs and ideals of government in the decaying Roman system. Hebrew kings and prophets of almost a thousand years before, in primitive Palestine, were accepted as models for Visigothic and Frankish warriors and their bishops. The result was archaism in the art of government.

[1] F. Clarke, *Education and Social Change*, 1940, p. 61.

Indeed, the Churches themselves might have perished of the disease of archaism, if they had not been severed from the Roman Empire and the eastern Mediterranean.

In the later sixth century all the Arian kingdoms had disappeared. New barbarian kingdoms, under Catholic kings, were established in Gaul and Spain. Western Europe became definitely Latin and the Empire at Constantinople definitely Greek. The two parts of the Christian world could no longer communicate freely in either tongue; and Rome regained as the Capital of the Latin Churches the prestige it had lost to Constantinople as the Capital of the Roman Empire. Then, after a brief period of about fifty years, during which the troops of the Roman Emperor at Constantinople subjected to his authority the Province of Africa, eastern Spain and parts of Italy, a new assault, by Mohammedans, destroyed the Roman and Christian tradition in Egypt, Africa and Spain. By the end of the seventh century the medieval rival of Latin Christianity, Islamic civilization, controlled most of the Mediterranean basin. This was a new type of civilization, which had arisen directly out of the barbarism of the desert, in contrast with the Germanic barbarism of the forest; and in its earlier forms, it owed nothing to the Greek and Roman tradition. It compelled the Latin Churches and the kingdoms in the West to face new dangers in which neither the Roman tradition nor the Hebrew Scriptures gave any guidance.

In north-western Europe, meantime, the kings of the Franks had come into increasingly closer co-operation with the bishops of Rome; and the Roman Church had extended its influence by missionary work, first in England and later, by the preaching of English missionaries, in Germany. The fading memories of Latin literature were preserved by a new learned caste, the clergy, united by custom and status across the frontiers of kingdoms, dukedoms and other lordships. But in the whole of the now distinguishable *First Europe* all men and women were united, whatever their status or function, in local communities and, at least by sentiment, across all political divisions. Medieval civilization had come into existence. After the centuries during which the seeds germinated in darkness, the first shoots of a new life began to appear above the surface. It is absurd to treat the great medieval abbeys and cathedral churches as either better or worse than the palaces and temples of ancient Rome. They are entirely different in character and purpose. But they may be taken as symbols of the social transformation, which was indeed due less to the conquests of kings than to the preaching of monks and bishops. The Roman system had, in fact, been unable to survive the strain put upon it; and what remained of its tradition had become merely part of the material for a new creation. But the creation of the First Europe cannot be understood as part of any necessary or inevitable process. It was the result partly of unconscious tendencies in men's minds, arising out of new dangers and new possibilities of initiative. It was in some degree due to a confused struggle for wealth and power, the results of which cannot be made intelligible by the application of any historical law or dialectic. But it was most clearly the result of new moral and social ideals. That is to say, men and women with insight and influence envisaged and sometimes realized new ways of life for individuals and communities. These men and women established the bases of that *moral authority* which conquest, plotting and the seizure of wealth and power could not provide.

The heroes of this story were Augustine in Africa, Pope Leo I and Epiphanius, bishop of Pavia, Isidore, bishop of Seville, Eligius in Gaul, Bede and Boniface; and not Theodoric or Clovis or Charles the Great. Historians who study chiefly political institutions, overestimate the importance of warriors and kings. But it is of little or no consequence which of two ruffians kills the other or secures a victory; and even hereditary magic counts for little in times when bastards and usurpers are more energetic and intelligent than those who have received their royal status from their fathers. In any case, it is always more important in law and administration to hold power than to seize it; and power cannot be held by force of arms, but only by some form of moral authority. For that reason alone it is impossible to understand either medieval or modern Europe without a study of the Christian Churches through which moral authority was infused into the political and economic institutions of the First Europe. Indeed, the whole history of these centuries may be read as an attempt, with many mistaken or fantastic results, but with increasing urgency, to find and establish a form of moral authority which could control or at least moderate the struggle for wealth and power.

Historians of Christianity, however, have been no less misleading than others, because they have overestimated the importance of disputes about doctrine. The most fundamental contribution to the progress of civilized life made by European Christendom, was not its cosmology nor its theory of the Deity, but its establishment of a community of feeling and experience among all men, women and children in western Europe, through sacraments, ceremonies, fasts and feasts and other religious customs. Medieval Europe was divided by a caste system in every locality and by the rivalry of independent lordships; but across these barriers *catholica fides* united the serf with his lord and the whole community in any one district with those of all others in the Latin Church, which claimed to be universal. *Catholica fides* had taken the place of that *fides Romana* which had been the moral basis of the Roman Empire; and neither was only a system of belief. The *fides Romana* was the credit or reliability inspired by the name of Rome. Men trusted the imperial system—indeed, as it turned out, they trusted it too much, because they believed that it was eternal. And when, in the four hundred years after the beginning of the fifth century, *catholica fides* was gradually taking the place of an older moral principle, it meant not only belief in doctrines but also the reliability of each person as a member of a single community, and the reliability of the Churches in the service of all their members. Thus schism and heresy were regarded not merely as disagreements about doctrine, but also as treacherous violations of the common allegiance. This was obviously important for the whole social system and not merely for ecclesiastical history. The central problem in a time of social transition, is clearly that of social cohesion—upon what principle it can be based, and what kinds of beliefs and customs are required in the majority of men and women, as a means of securing it. But the beliefs and customs required in any one place and time are obviously dependent upon the prevailing climate of opinion. The change in the climate of opinion between the fourth and the ninth centuries is the subject-matter with which this book is concerned. But throughout those centuries the central force of social cohesion remained *catholica fides*.

Sources of Information: the Historians

The material upon which the discussion is based, must necessarily be the original documents in Latin and Greek, written in the four centuries from the beginning of the fifth to the middle or end of the ninth. An immense amount, however, of historical study has been devoted to this period since the eighteenth century; and, therefore, something may be said first about the attitude adopted here to recent historians. It is well known that Gibbon and other writers of his time accepted the assumptions and standards of the late Renaissance. They thought of the centuries after the fourth as years of decay in civilization and growth in barbarism. They admired and preferred an era of benevolent despotism, supported by a small cultured class, in which they were themselves the leading examples of culture, controlling an almost unnoticed mass of illiterate and superstitious peasants and craftsmen. This was the kind of civilization which they studied in the history of the Roman Empire, the disappearance of which they regretted. It was therefore difficult for them to understand or appreciate the civilization of medieval Europe.

After them, in the nineteenth century, historians were divided into two opposing schools. One school, mainly French, tried to show that whatever was valuable in the civilization of the Middle Ages was derived from the Roman or rather Gallo-Roman tradition. These writers suffered from a survival of Renaissance archaism, which still dominates the French conception of "culture générale." On the other hand, another school, mainly German and English, tried to show that a pure and vigorous "race" from Germany originated the civilization of the First Europe. These historians suffered disastrously from the mythology of the "noble savage" and from the futilities of the Gothic Revival and the Romantic Movement. But the contrast between these two schools has been admirably described elsewhere; and the controversy is now of no interest.[1] It is far more important for the present purpose to recognize that no historian, ancient or modern, is an unprejudiced chronicler of colourless facts. All history is a statement of policy. All historians are affected by the climate of opinion of their own time and place. At best, they assume that the prejudices of their day are the only tests of goodness and truth. At worst, they reflect the ignorance concerning the lives of the majority in their own times, from which an academic circle always suffers.

Unfortunately most of those who write history pay no attention to metaphysics or philosophy; and are therefore unaware of the assumptions which underlie their approach to the problem and the results at which they arrive. The lack of training in metaphysics or even in the logic of evidence has peculiar results, especially on the moral judgements expressed or implied by historians. In some cases the historian takes sides in "battles long ago" and assumes that the distinction between his side and the other is the same as the distinction between good and evil.[2] It must be confessed that the situation is still worse when metaphysicians try to write history, as in the case of Hegel and Karl Marx; for they tend "to identify the limitations of their own intelligence with the necessary bounds of human reason."[3] That, however, is no excuse for the historians. None of those who have written on the period and problems with which this book is concerned can be safely read without plentiful doses of doubt.

No one can understand history if he reads only the historians. He must go directly to the sources—letters, poems, sermons and treatises—because these are the unconscious records of a climate of opinion; and the description of that climate by later historians is always affected by the time and place in which the historian is writing. Any historian is a dangerous guide. The better he is, the

---

[1] The best analysis of the contributions of scholars of the two schools is in the introduction to Vinogradoff's *Villainage in England*. There is also a short account of the controversy in Dopsch, *Social and Economic Foundations of European Civilization*.

[2] Thus Freeman in his *Norman Conquest* informs his readers that "we" were beaten at the battle of Hastings! But "in a few generations *we* led captive our conquerors" (*Norman Conquest*, Introd., p. 2). Not bad for an Anglo-Saxon freeman or "ceorl"! 	[3] F. H. Bradley.

harder it is to observe what he has omitted; and even a great historian, writing of his own time, as Tacitus or Thucydides did,
makes a selection of those facts and judgements which happen to
attract his attention. The historian who studies earlier ages is no less
limited, as in the case of Gibbon. The Roman Empire collapsed
because of its own weight: the foundations could not bear the
superstructure. But Gibbon underestimated the importance of the
foundations. He admired the temples, palaces and baths; and
listened far off with exultation to the tramp of legions. But he paid
little attention to slavery, militarism, centralization, depopulation
and the ignorance of Emperors, which eventually destroyed the
system. Still later ages have produced attempts at a "science" of
history, which explains the succession of events as due to inevitable
causes, either in a "dialectic" or in some form of inductive logic.
Clearly, every stage in the history of civilization may possibly be
pre-determined by that which preceded it. But the evidence available for each stage in the process is limited and defective. Therefore
no historian can feel certain that the available evidence provides
enough knowledge of the forces which have been most important.
The limits of historical knowledge are set, not by the nature of the
mind, but by the accident of survival among documents and other
records of the past. Defects in the evidence may be supplied by
imaginative genius; but nothing can justify the followers of Hegel
or of Marx in supposing that their masters discovered in the early
nineteenth century, with sublime disregard for the original evidence,
the final truth about historical development. It cannot be assumed
that the evidence available about the past in any age is enough to
provide certainty with regard to the future. It cannot be assumed
that the way of thinking adopted by any age or any group of the
enlightened, even in the nineteenth century, is the only correct way
of thinking of the past or of the future in all ages.

On the other hand, the logic of induction should produce a
certain hesitation with regard to general statements about historical
processes, which are based on the perception of some similarities or
analogies between social situations in different times and places.
Each stage of the development from barbarism to civilized life, in

each distinguishable tradition, is a complete "pattern of culture." Therefore it is dangerous to select from one social situation and to isolate from it any part of the pattern, for comparison with what appears to be a similar part in another "pattern."[1] For example, it is dangerous to compare the militarism of the late Roman Empire with the militarism of Prussia, without due regard to the fact that each is a part of a whole pattern of culture. It is dangerous to isolate marriage customs in one pattern of culture and to compare them, so isolated, with marriage customs in other times and places.

In any case, the evidence for the changes in the climate of opinion from the fifth to the ninth centuries is still largely the same as it was for the historians who wrote in the nineteenth century. But the documents which were available then, as they are now, must be read in the light of social crises and social forces of to-day, which were altogether beyond the experience and even the imagination of the last century. The sublime aloofness of the eighteenth-century scholars and the self-confidence of the nineteenth century can no longer be accepted by the historian. In the "Dark Ages" of to-day, the problem is not merely one of contending powers or of scrambles for power. The most fundamental problem is that of the source and function of moral authority. And any writer on social institutions who does not understand the distinction between social power and moral authority is likely to misrepresent the history of civilization. The study of certain forms of social power may involve only attention to facts—such facts as a blow on the head, or the cutting of throats. But the influence of a saintly or learned person cannot be understood without attention to what philosophers call "value." Beauty and goodness and truth may be illusions. Whether they are or not is a problem of metaphysics, with which the historian is not directly concerned. But it is quite certain that, without concentrating attention upon such "values," whether illusons or not, no history of civilization can be made intelligible.

Sources of Information: the Documents

A short review of the chief sources of information about the

[1] This has been admirably stated in Ruth Benedict's *Patterns of Culture*.

social institutions of the early Middle Ages will indicate the character of the evidence available. This book is not concerned with the detailed description of these social institutions, but with the climate of opinion in which they arose, and to which they gave a new character. Clearly, no social institutions are intelligible without some understanding of the cosmology and moral teaching of their day. But in this volume the larger problem of what may be called the philosophical climate, is not discussed. It will be necessary, nevertheless, to call attention, at certain points in the argument, to the prevailing belief in magic, to the efforts at finding explanations of good or bad fortune in the intervention of some Divine Person, and to the general belief that a store of truth existed in certain documents—the Bible and the Fathers—which had only to be drawn upon, and could not be added to by any further discovery. This clearly explains the tendency to look to the past, which is so obvious in the establishment of the new political, ecclesiastical and economic institutions of the First Europe. Similarly, without some understanding of the place of magic in primitive minds of all centuries, even the present, it is impossible to understand one important source of the influence of bishops or kings in the early Middle Ages. Also the majority in those times believed that good men and women lived after death above the sky, and bad ones below the earth. This was no metaphor, but quite literally their statement of "the Truth." But here the argument must be confined more strictly to the atmosphere immediately surrounding the old and the new social institutions.

The evidence is contained in chronicles, histories, poems, letters, laws and treatises. Of the chronicles some, like that of Prosper and those of the monastic writers of the eighth and ninth centuries, are bald records of events in chronological order. But even in these bald statements the selection of the events to be recorded indicates the climate of opinion familiar to the writers. The barest annals, for example, of the eighth and ninth centuries have a political purpose—generally "propaganda" for a king or for the clergy in a wicked world. It is suggestive also that they report the doings of kings, the appearance of comets, eclipses, floods, and in particular where the kings kept the feasts of Easter and Christmas. Of all the chronicles of this period, which fall short of history in the true sense, the most important is the so-called *Book of the Bishops* (*Liber Pontificalis*). In its earliest form this is a collection of traditions regarding the bishops of Rome, which were accepted by the Roman clergy in the fifth century. The list of bishops, from St. Peter onwards, and some of the details given about the building and decoration of churches, may have been based upon earlier records. But in any case the book is a political document. It is an argument maintaining the apostolic origin and unbroken tradition of the Church of the city of Rome. The later additions and versions of the book are quite obviously not colourless records of events, but statements of policy, leading directly to the establishment of the "temporal power" of the Papacy. This does not imply that the record of events is falsified; it means only that the authors had a keen eye for what was likely to be of advantage to the Roman clergy.

Of histories the most important in the early period, during the collapse of the Roman Empire, are those of Zosimus, Orosius, and some ecclesiastical historians. Each of the authors has a distinguishable political and ecclesiastical prejudice for which allowance must be duly made. The somewhat fantastic *History of the Goths* by Jordanes is clearly a political pamphlet in favour of assimilation between Romans and barbarians. After him, in the middle of the sixth century, comes Procopius—a great historian, with a definite and limited purpose of explaining the wars of Justinian, the futility of which can be well understood by anyone who can read between the lines of an official report. At the end of the sixth century there is the *History of the Franks* by Gregory of Tours—a confused account by a simple and honest man who seems to have hoped rather vaguely that there was some significance in the murderous brawls of kings and the ineffectual efforts of saints which he recorded. At the end of the period, in the early eighth century in northern England, there was a truly great historian—Bede. His *History of the English Church* contains much evidence of the prevailing belief in magic and visions, which was shared by the author. But it is a noble story, well told, with a deep appreciation of the fact that the problem of maintaining civilized life had not been solved.

The poems which have some bearing upon social institutions are those of Prudentius, in the early fifth century, of Venantius Fortunatus, in the late sixth century, and of Theodulf and his contemporaries, in the early ninth century. For the purpose of this book the interest in such poems is not literary. They are taken as indications of the climate of opinion, immediately affecting the establishment of the Christian Churches and of the new barbarian kingdoms. Both Prudentius and Venantius Fortunatus wrote beautiful popular hymns. But the latter and his successors in the ninth century also wrote incredibly bad verses, mostly about nothing at all, containing broken fragments of Virgil and Ovid. Even this, however, indicates the domination of the second-rate Latin literature which survived into the Middle Ages. If the much greater literature of ancient Greece had been available, even in translation, in the early Middle Ages, the history of the First Europe would have been very different. Medieval religion and morality would have been more robust, if Homer, and not Virgil, had guided Dante through hell.

The letters upon which the historian must depend are of three kinds—private correspondence, official despatches and ecclesiastical communications. Of the private letters the most useful are those of Sidonius Apollinaris in the fifth century and of Alcuin at the end of the eighth. Official despatches are such as the pompous platitudes of the *Variae* of Cassiodorus, in the sixth century, and some few letters of emperors and kings, usually contained in collections of Papal letters. Ecclesiastical communications are of two kinds. There are great numbers of letters of the Popes, of which the most important are those of Pope Leo I; the extraordinarily full and interesting collection of the letters of Gregory the Great; and the collection of Papal letters to the Frankish kings, known as the *Codex Carolinus*. Such documents must obviously be used with caution. They contain statements of "theory" relating to political and ecclesiastic authority, made at different dates and in entirely different circumstances. But the "theory" advocated is usually a mere excuse or cover for a particular policy. All the Papal letters, including those which deal with theological doctrine, were written in reference to a definite policy of the writer and definite political or ecclesiastical problems of the day. It may be possible to trace some continuity of belief or mental attitude between Leo I in the fifth century and Leo III in the ninth. But it is quite misleading to construct a single and consistent doctrine or policy out of phrases in the letters of different Popes who were in fact concerned, in these letters, with quite different practical problems. For example, the first barbarian invasions, the Lombard conquest of Italy and the substitution of the king of the Franks for the Emperor at Constantinople as Protector of the Roman Church, caused drastic changes in the policy of kings and bishops and therefore in the theory of the State and the Church.

Besides Papal letters, the most important material is to be found in the letters of St. Augustine and St. Jerome at the beginning of the fifth century, and those of St. Boniface at the beginning of the eighth. These letters contain the prejudices, as well as the noble aspirations, of vigorous minds at work in maintaining or extending the basic civilization of the First Europe. The Englishman, Boniface, wrote with a directness and clarity which does much to explain his skill in converting the German barbarians east of the Rhine from the worship of the gods of war to the service of Christ; and together with the letters of Alcuin, another Englishman, they serve to elucidate the distinction between the traditions of Christendom in England and France on the one hand, and those of Germany on the other, which existed throughout the Middle Ages and perhaps even later. The Christianity of Gaul and of England was established in defiance of "the Powers that be"; but the Christianity of Germany, in spite of the influence of Boniface and Alcuin, was established by armed force.

The texts of laws include, first, the great Theodosian law-books (*Codex Theodosianus*) of A.D. 438 and the so-called barbarian laws, most of which were written down in Latin in the seventh and eighth centuries. The most important of these latter are the laws of the Visigoths, some fragments of which belong to the sixth century, the laws of the Franks and Burgundians, and those of the

Lombards, which belong to the eighth century. These are the sources in which may be traced the beginnings of the medieval system of castes or social classes. In addition there are the Capitularies of Frankish kings and a few laws of English kings, which may be taken as evidence of the character of civil authority and its functions in the early Middle Ages. On the other hand the Canons of the Churches in the different provinces or kingdoms indicate the manner in which the medieval clergy was formed. The Canons of Carthage, of Toledo, of Arles and other synods in Gaul mark the first stage in the consolidation of Christendom; and the second stage, centralization under the bishops of Rome, is marked by the Latin version of Canons of universal application, first made available for the Roman Church by Dionysius the Little in the sixth century. This collection, with later additions, handed by Hadrian I to Charles the Great in A.D. 787, was the basis of the ecclesiastical law of Christendom in later times.

The documents for which the general term "treatise" is here used include both statements of political theory and practice and ecclesiastical works on the life of the Church and its members. The use of such treatises for the purpose of this book must obviously be quite different from the use made of letters and laws which deal with particular issues and immediate practical problems. The element of idealization in these treatises is stronger because the writers are as much concerned with what ought to be as with what is. The climate of opinion may be the same in all the documents of any one period or place; but clearly the creative imagination is more strongly at work in treatises which attempt to explain in general terms and in reference to fundamental causes the situation of the writer and his circle.

The most important of all the treatises is that on *The City of God* by St. Augustine. The first part of this treatise is an attempt to explain the position of the Christian Empire and the Christian Churches in the early years of the fifth century. The author assumed the existence of a supreme Roman Empire, and perhaps retained that assumption even on his deathbed in A.D. 430 when the Vandals were besieging the city in which he lay. He died only forty-six years before the Roman Empire disappeared from western Europe and Africa. But what he had assumed as a reality survived as a vision and helped to confuse the minds of medieval scholars and perhaps also some writers of later date, who are not skilled in distinguishing what really exists from what they would like to exist. But the importance of St. Augustine's treatise for the historian who is concerned with social institutions lies, not in his arguments, but in the emotional force with which he expressed them.

Other less important treatises are those of Ennodius—the *Panegyric* addressed to Theodoric the Ostrogoth in the sixth century; of Julian, bishop of Toledo—a violent pamphlet against the Franks; of commentators on the *Books of Kings*, which served as guidance in the establishment of the First European Kingdoms; and, in the ninth century, of Hincmar and Smaragdus. On the authority and functions of local rulers, theoretically subordinate, the letters of Fulgentius Ferrandus to Count Reginus in the sixth century, and of Paulinus of Aquileia to Count Henry of Friuli at the end of the eighth century, are indications of the service expected from military rulers in the Middle Ages. They were taught by the best of the clergy that their power should be used for the advantage of the poorest and weakest. These were the terms in which the moral authority of those in power was then expressed.

Ecclesiastical treatises include, first, the two works of Cassian on the life and teaching of the eastern Monks, which have had an immense effect on western monasticism. The *Rule* of St. Benedict must be taken, from this point of view, as a treatise on monasticism as an institution, which has had an influence on the history of civilization far greater than the collection of old laws made by his contemporary, the Emperor Justinian. At a slightly later date, at the end of the sixth century, the most important treatises are the *Pastoral Rule*, on the duties of bishops, and the *Morals*, or Commentary on the Book of Job, both by Gregory the Great. In the same period were written the *Lives of the Fathers* by Gregory of Tours and after them a series of other lives of saints written during the seventh, eighth and early ninth centuries. Of these perhaps the most important for the study of social institutions are those of St.

Eligius by St. Audoenus (Ouen) and the life of St. Remi by Hincmar.

General Characteristics

Some general characteristics of all these documents should be noted. In the first place almost all the writers were unable to distinguish between personal virtue and social justice. In other words, although the foundation of the First Europe involved the creation of new institutions, there was no general understanding that social institutions can, and if unjust should, be abolished, modified or consciously adapted to changing circumstances. Thus most of the writers of the period, who were all ecclesiastics, were concerned chiefly with telling their contemporaries to be virtuous or good men and women. To the slave-owner and the slave, to the king, the lord or the serf, they said that each ought to be a "good" slave-owner, slave, king, lord or serf. The moral assumption was that, if each fulfilled the duties of his station, justice would prevail. But these writers apparently did not understand that a man's "station" itself might involve injustice. It is clearly not "justice" that a slave-owner should be kind, if slavery itself is unjust; and although many writers of the period did perceive, as the Stoics had before them, that slavery was unjust, they certainly made no effort to abolish it. The prevailing belief that whatever existed and whatever happened was the will of God, prevented them from distinguishing between the good intentions of a virtuous man and right action in a just society. Like the modern advocates of "goodwill," as a means of removing social injustice, they failed to see that the fundamental problem was that of institutions. Any institution—a church or a state or a goose-club—is a series of acts relating certain persons, which follow a certain curve or pattern. That is to say, an institution exists in its "rules"; but keeping the rules may be useless, or even pernicious, if the rules themselves are futile or obsolete. A slave-owner who is kind to his slaves may be virtuous, if good intentions are the tests of virtue; but his acts are morally wrong, if nobody ought to own slaves. Again, all these writers suffer from archaism—the belief that the past contains the standards of moral and political conduct. The very fact that they all wrote in Latin tied them to the dead. They loitered about the tombs of a dead civilization and sometimes saw ghosts. But Latin as a language was itself dying during the four centuries before the ninth, although it retained an enfeebled vitality, as the dialect of a learned caste, for almost a thousand years after. Nevertheless this Latin was the instrument for the preservation of the civilized tradition and of the unity of the First Europe. The common use of Latin separated the Churches of the West from those of the East and western Christendom from Islam. Latin used in ritual and learning prevented the separation of the Germanic, Celtic and Slavonic peoples from the peoples of the South, whose languages grew out of Latin. And although Latin thus became only the language of a caste, the Latin Bible and other Latin documents were not deliberately kept from the people. The so-called "closed Bible" of the Middle Ages was due to the accident that the learned class never imagined that the common people could have time or ability to read and write in any form of civilization. Reading and writing were assumed to be the technique of a caste, just as ploughing was the technique of a ploughman.

The other form of archaism to be observed in all the writers of this period is the continual reference back to the past for guidance in moral conduct and public policy. At the end of the fourth century the principle of "ancient authority" was firmly established. And as civil disorder spread, the intelligence was more and more confined to commentary upon ancient texts, whether sacred or secular. In psychological terms, the *mnemé* or recording habit was more powerful than the *hormé* or impulse to original thought and action. The reference back to past experience was easier in a time of disorder than the effort required for new experiment or imaginative adventure. The climate of opinion thus formed was favourable to unadventurous persons, because these run for shelter to an established order if changes threaten. Therefore even the best minds of the Middle Ages were more concerned with the effort to realize an ancient ideal of conduct or policy than with the discovery of new and better ideals. On the other hand—here is a paradox—the very ages which could think of nothing better than copying the past, themselves broke with the past. The very writers who admired the Hebrew kings and the Roman Empire helped to create what had never hitherto existed—western Monasticism, the Latin Catholic Church and European kingships and lordships. The reason is that they knew much less about the past than they supposed. They had no conception of historical development, which would have indicated to them that the customs and beliefs of Hebrew tribes were primitive. Nor did they know that the Roman Empire was in its origin a temporary device of party politics and, in its later years, an ephemeral form of military dictatorship. Therefore, although they modelled their institutions upon those of the Hebrews and the Romans, they knew so little about either, that the copy was very different from the original. It should be recognized also that every writer in every age sees the facts and feels the "values" of his time in the light of imagination. There are no bare facts or final values to be discovered in history. Every event recorded or judgement made by the writers upon whom the historian depends is part of a greater whole, most of which is constructed by the creative imagination. That is to say, each fact and value is perceived in a particular setting. Nobody can see the whole of the world he inhabits or even the whole of his own life. The climate of opinion, therefore, affecting all the writers, to which reference is here made, must be conceived to be, at least in part, a poetic expression of their hopes and wishes.

The Uses of History

Before discussing in greater detail the formation of the First Europe, it may be well to note the relation between the problems of the present and those of the four centuries after the dissolution of the Roman Empire in the West. History has two uses. It is, on the one hand, a voyage backwards in time—an escape from the present. On the other hand, it is an appreciation of problems which are similar in the present and the past. It is an illusion, due to bad logic and worse metaphysics, to suppose that history can be useful only if it provides "scientific" generalizations based upon similarities between one age and another. The escape from the narrow limits of the time and place in which the historian writes into entirely different regions of thought and emotion is itself a necessary training for an educated man. Without that training no man can see the life of his own time in its true perspective. Without it he cannot protect himself against the illusion that the future is determined by the accidents of the present day and the passions of the living, because he cannot hear the greater voice of the multitudes who are dead and because he knows nothing of the debt he owes to their sufferings and their struggles.

History, as an escape from the present, like travel abroad, may indicate the position of contemporary village-politics in the larger world of space and time. From one point of view history dwarfs the present; but from another point of view, history indicates the true greatness of the present in the drama of human achievements, most of which lie in the future, beyond the horizon of to-day's experience.

On the other hand, there are many analogies between the social transition which occurred in western Europe after the dissolution of the Roman system and the transition which has been occurring in almost all parts of the world since the end of the nineteenth century. The differences between these two periods of transition are even greater than the likeness between them; and it is, therefore, not logical to conclude that, because Roman civilization gave place to medieval, modern civilization must necessarily follow a similar course. It is enough to note that under modern conditions, as compared with the situation in western Europe from the fourth to the ninth century, a far greater number of men and women are trained in scientific knowledge and scientific methods; that the applications of the sciences in medicine, engineering and other production, are far more extensive; that the same type of civilization is maintained in a far greater number of centres over the whole surface of the earth; and that communication between these centres is more rapid and intimate than it was between Rome and Constantinople in the fifth century. If modern powers of destruction are greater, so also is modern ability to reconstruct not merely material objects but social institutions.

In spite of great differences between the two periods, however, the similarities are striking. There is now, as there was then, an obvious contrast between a traditional civilization with inherited defects and a barbarism which is acceptable to the simple-minded or the brutal. In the two periods there is the same "nomadism" of the intellectuals among the civilized and the same simple trust in armed force among the barbarians. There is the same "failure of nerve" among the civilized, when they see that the traditional system has not abolished poverty or war; and the same simple belief among the "have nots"—the barbarians—that they can appropriate the results of civilization or the applications of science without adopting the process which has made them possible. This is a fundamental problem in the history of civilized life. Those who do not play a part in the establishment and maintenance of a particular type of civilization—who therefore look at it from the outside—see only its final results and cannot understand the nature of the methods by which alone those results have been attained. They imagine that the wealth and power incidental to civilized society can be merely transferred to themselves by conquest or revolution. Therefore they mistake the achievements of the past for the final expressions of truth, goodness and beauty—valid for all time. They repudiate or oppose free experiment and free criticism; and the representatives of the dead become an infallible authority for the living.

At the birth of the First Europe, new experience was entering into the Roman tradition. The poorer classes and the Germanic barbarians had been affected by Christianity. These people had something new to contribute. New ways of life and new moral standards were being introduced into the social system. The problem was whether the new wine could be preserved in the old bottles. Could the new forces, the new hopes and desires of men, find a place in the tradition of civilized life, without destroying the political, economic and cultural structure? The strain upon the Roman system was very great; and it came *from within*. Similarly, to-day the most important problem of social transition is caused by the entry into an old civilization of new powers, new hopes and new moral standards. To-day also the intellectuals are nomads, moving in small cliques from one encampment to another; and the "Powers that be" have lost their nerve. Attempts were made during all the four centuries of the Roman Empire to hold the system together. But most of these attempts were applications of force in support of a failing moral authority. The most urgent problem, therefore, hardly understood at the time, was the problem of the relation between wealth and power on the one hand, and moral authority on the other. While the wealth and power of the Roman Empire increased, its moral authority over its subjects and its agents gradually declined. There was a time when it seemed possible to provide a new form of moral authority for those who already possessed wealth and power. If that attempt had succeeded, slavery would have continued in Europe and Christianity would have disappeared. But in fact—and not by any necessity—the Christian tradition, which had in its earliest centuries neither wealth nor power behind it, proved to contain within itself a source of moral authority which could control—at a price—the uses of wealth and power. The Christian Churches survived the Roman Empire; and they transferred to barbarian kingdoms the moral authority which the possession of armed force could never have secured. But if it seemed at times that "the meek possessed the earth," in the process of establishing their influence they had lost their meekness. The same problem, whether and at what cost moral authority can control wealth and power, was left for future ages to solve in new terms. The problem is not—Who shall have power? but—How shall power be used? The purpose for which power is used, and at least some partial achievement of that purpose— these alone give moral authority to those who hold power.

But the existence of moral authority and its influence in history imply certain philosophical assumptions. These are briefly as follows. All men have certain tendencies or impulses which are stimulated when they become aware of something beautiful, something good in human conduct and character or something true in statements or judgements. Certain men and women, either as individuals or as agents of social institutions, have the ability to excite in others these tendencies or impulses so that their influence is accepted—all the more readily if they have neither wealth nor power of their own. Against such men and women the holders of wealth and power contend in vain. These men and women have moral authority.

The fundamental problem, therefore, with which this book is concerned is that of moral authority. This problem is most difficult to solve in times of transition, when an old political, economic and religious system loses its hold upon the imaginations of men, so that an increasing number are unwilling or unable to make an effort strong enough to maintain it. The process of transition is the discovery of a new social system which a sufficient number are willing to establish and maintain. But in the transition, so far at least as the history of the First Europe provides evidence, there is no clearly conceived and generally accepted alternative to the old order. Men tend to look back into the past, in the belief that they will there find the models for the architecture of the future. That is why the ghost of the Roman Empire haunted medieval Europe; and that is why the so-called "Renaissance" was, in so large a measure, a mere continuance of medievalism. There was a birth— a new spirit in thought and emotion; but as a "re-birth," the second Europe was half dead, of archaism, from its earliest years.

Medieval Europe is now dead and buried. Its ghost may yet haunt certain corners of the modern world. But it is assumed in this book that the First Europe, whose roots are to be studied here, has already flourished and died. Whatever lessons its history may contain for later ages, this one lesson at least is clear, that we can neither revive it nor reproduce it. Indeed the First Europe itself suffered from archaism. It established "infallible" authorities in Church and State and obstructed free criticism, because it believed blindly in what it had inherited from the past. It would be the merest folly, therefore, in a new social transition, even more fundamental and widespread than that of the early Middle Ages, to rely upon the past for the sources of moral authority which are required for the establishment of a new civilization in a third Europe.

This book, however, deals only with the beginning of medievalism. It is a study of the transition from one type of civilization to another, during which new social institutions were established in western Europe. But all social institutions are only relations between living men formed by their actions, their thoughts, their fears and hopes. About twelve or fourteen generations, between A.D. 400 and A.D. 800, worked at the foundations of the First Europe. Of these men and women the great majority could neither read nor write; but a few of them have left records of what they and others thought and felt. Before the play began, which is traditionally called the Middle Ages, the characters in the prologue move in a sort of mist, and many of them, therefore, attain a giant stature which was not in fact their own. But romance is not misleading unless it is mistaken for history. Romance is the record of fear and hope.

Two episodes have been taken as indications of the beginning and the end of the transition—the sack of Rome by Alaric in A.D. 410, and the proclamation of Charles the Great as "Emperor of the Romans" at St. Peter's in the Vatican in A.D. 800. Each of these episodes was enlarged in importance by the imagination. Alaric stole from Rome what was of no importance; but to men of the time his raid seemed to be a sign of the approaching end of all things. The laments for Rome were like the last sighs of a dying world. Four hundred years later, the shout that greeted Charles the Great as the Emperor of the Romans, was the infant's cry at the birth of the First Europe.

CHAPTER II

DISSOLUTION OF A SOCIAL SYSTEM

When Alaric and his Goths sacked Rome in the late summer of
A.D. 410, they were helped to find loot by thousands of their own
race who had been slaves in Roman households. This is the most
significant episode in what was merely a raid by a band of thieves.
Two years before, when the Goths had first blockaded Rome,
"almost all the slaves that were in Rome left the city day by day
and joined the barbarians to the number of forty thousand." These
are the words of the contemporary historian, Zosimus.[1] The Goths
had then been bought off with gold and silver, hastily accumulated,
and by the release, at their demand, of other slaves still held in the
city.

Barbarian warriors, looking for portable treasure, made common
cause with barbarian slaves who knew where it was to be found.
But no revolution was involved. The Goths desired nothing but
loot; and although some houses, especially that of Sallust, near the
gate at which the Goths were first admitted by their friends within
the city, were injured by fire, there was no wanton destruction or
slaughter. The raiders stayed in Rome only three days. They took
the gold and jewels of the rich, slew some who resisted their robbery, filled their waggons and burdened their horses with booty,
and went off.

The slaves who assisted them were not opposed to slavery, but
only to being slaves themselves; and they readily helped the raiders
to enslave their former masters and mistresses. The number of free
Roman citizens carried off for ransom or sale as slaves during the
raids by the Goths is indicated by an edict issued at Ravenna on

[1] Zosimus, *Hist.*, v, 42.

December 10th, 408. This says that barbarian savagery has reduced to slavery people of either sex and all ranks and ages. These are to be restored to freedom and to be allowed such food and clothing as charity can supply. But if the barbarians have sold them, the buyers should not be faced by complete loss of the money paid. Therefore, these slaves are either to make a payment for their liberty or to serve their new masters for five years. In order that the decree should be carried out, Christian priests of the local Churches and members of the local councils must approach the imperial officials in the matter.[1] That the captives of the Goths were of all ranks is most strikingly shown by the fact that one of those carried off from Rome in the raid of A.D. 410 was Galla Placidia, the half-sister of the reigning Emperor Honorius.

The confusion of the time produced a flood of refugees—the rich fleeing to Africa or the East; and scholars and clergy scattered in all directions. Thus Rufinus, the historian, took refuge at Messina in Sicily and watched the burning of Reggio across the Straits. "What place," he asks, "is there for the writer when all fear the weapons of the enemy, when under our eyes the cities and the fields are devastated, and some seek refuge even in the dangers of the sea, and not even exile is without its terrors? For under my own eyes, as I looked across the narrow straits dividing Sicily from Italy, which held off the barbarians, Reggio went up in flames."[2] The poorer manual workers in Rome who, together with the slaves, were by far the greater part of the population, are not mentioned by the historians; but evidently there was little resistance to the looting of the great houses and the public buildings. Alaric and his leading warriors, however, were Christians and showed respect particularly for the shrine of St. Peter and for those who had sought refuge there. They also left untouched the valuable ornaments and sacred vessels of the churches.

Earlier Raids

The situation is more clearly understood as a continuation of the

---

[1] *Cod. Theod. Constit. Sirmondianae*, No. 14.
[2] The account of the scene is in the Prologue to the translation of Origen's *Homilies on the Book of Numbers* (Origen, *Werke. Gr. Chr. Schr.*, Bd. 7, p. 1, 1921).

raids for loot during preceding years. After looting Greece, Alaric and his Goths had descended upon Italy and had been twice completely defeated, in A.D. 403 and A.D. 404, by the troops of the Emperor Honorius under Stilicho, a Roman general of Vandal descent who acted as chief minister. The first defeat occurred during the Easter festival of A.D. 403, when the troops of the Christian and Catholic Emperor took advantage of the fact that Alaric and his Goths, as good Christians, were commemorating the Resurrection. After the second defeat the poet, Claudian, wrote that Rome was finally saved:[1] and an inscription on an arch in Rome, in honour of Honorius, records "the extinction of the Gothic nation for all ages."[2] But Stilicho's troops were themselves almost entirely barbarians; and the Roman Authorities, evidently fearing the danger from those who sympathized with barbarian raiders, had the wives and children of Gothic mercenaries, living within the Roman cities, killed. This was regarded by the barbarians as an impious violation of faith by the Romans; and thousands of them, therefore, joined the forces of Alaric.[3] Meantime another and more terrifying body of Goths and other barbarians invaded Italy in A.D. 405. The alarm of the Roman Authorities and their appeal to their slaves are expressed in an Edict of April 17th, 406, issued from Ravenna, in the following words: "Against enemy invasion, not rank only, but efficiency must be considered; and although we believe that free men are moved by love of the fatherland, we appeal to slaves also, granting them, if they will serve in war, liberty and payment."[4] Under a pagan leader, Rhadagast (Radagaisus), whose warriors are said to have hated Christianity as much as they despised the Empire, an immense horde of barbarians from the North descended upon Italy and attempted to attack Florence. But they were surrounded by Stilicho's army on the hill of Fiesole and starved into submission. The contemporary Christian historian Orosius, rejoicing, as St. Augustine did, at the defeat of the pagans, wrote that so many thousands of these Goths were then taken as slaves "that they were sold at the price of the cheapest cattle" and were so weak that they

[1] Claudian, de Consulatu Stilichonis, ii, 130 sq.   [2] C.I.L., vi, 1196.
[3] Zosimus, Hist., v, 35.   [4] Cod. Theod., vii, 13, 16.

did not survive. The buyers, having saved on the purchase price, had the expense of burying them.[1]

Then followed the raids of the barbarians across the Rhine into Gaul. The Vandals, Suevi, Alans and Goths entered Gaul in A.D. 406 and Spain in A.D. 409. At about this time also Roman legions were withdrawn from Britain; and the south-east coast, which had been defended for many years by Roman troops and fleets under the Count of the Saxon Shore, lay open to invaders from Germany.

The next event of importance was the murder of Stilicho in A.D. 408, as the result of a palace plot. But already the policy of appeasement was in the air. The Emperor sought refuge behind the marshes at Ravenna; and even before that it had been proposed, in the Senate at Rome, that the barbarian invaders should be paid a sufficient sum to keep at least Italy safe, if the leader of the barbarians had no further territorial ambitions and would promise peace. One senator, Lampadius, is said to have opposed appeasement with the words—"This is not peace, but a pact of enslavement";[2] but he had to take refuge in a church from the anger of the supporters of appeasement. And when Alaric appeared before Rome in A.D. 408 he had received large reinforcements led by his wife's brother, Adolf, who was later his successor as king of the Goths.[3] Appeasement was adopted by the Senate and the Goths retired to raid other parts of Italy; but they returned in A.D. 410 and, as described above, sacked Rome.

The Social Situation

This "devastation of the city," as St. Augustine called it, was by no means a sign of the collapse of the Roman Empire. Indeed, for forty years after Alaric's death, the city was left undisturbed by barbarians. But the raid for loot by the combined action of nomad thieves and slaves of the same race was an important sign of the dissolution of an ancient society of rich slave-owners and multitudes

[1] Orosius, *Hist.*, vii, 37. See also Augustine, *De Civ. Dei.*, v, 23.
[2] "Non est ista pax, sed pactio servitutis." The whole story is in Zosimus, *Hist.*, v, 29.
[3] Adolf is given a Romanized name "Adolfus" by Gibbon and "Ataulfus" by other historians. The name is "Atta-ulfus" meaning "father wolf."

of slaves and workers who had no interest at all in the maintenance of the social system. All the great cities of the Roman Empire in the early fifth century included among their inhabitants a large majority of men and women of different races who were without roots in society, and for whom the small group of rich men who hired a foreign soldiery to defend their power, provided nothing but a bare subsistence and occasional entertainments. Chariot races and distributions of food for the greater part of the population were enough to keep the majority quiet, while the struggle for wealth and power went on above their heads.

For many centuries, before the beginning of the fifth, continual civil wars between those who were rich enough or reckless enough to aim at supreme power, had interfered with the system of production and trade which made the existence of the great cities possible. The corn-lands of Africa had displaced the fields of Italy and Gaul in the supply of necessities for the city populations; while in the Mediterranean a great trading system had developed, not unlike the so-called world-economy of the late nineteenth century, although on a smaller scale. And the social results were much the same in the fifth century as they were at the beginning of the industrial era. A small class of increasingly wealthy families enjoyed the luxuries of a civilization maintained by multitudes who had little or no share in the control of public policy or the distribution of private wealth.

In a slave society the majority are not deeply concerned about a change of masters. And the rich, as in other ages, either sought safety in flight, or came to terms with those who had military force, in order to save what they could of their property. No doubt, there were in every part of the Empire in the West some Roman commanders or civic authorities who attempted to withstand the barbarian newcomers. But most of those who had influence or military power were contending against rivals within the Roman Empire; and all were willing to use barbarian warriors against their opponents. It is certain, in any case, that there was no co-operation of the generals or the populations, within the Roman Empire, against the barbarians. And it is sufficiently clear that there was no feeling of responsibility for maintaining the system among the inhabitants of that Empire; while the central Authority, whose position will be described in the next chapter, was unable or unwilling to defend them. The result was wide-spread pillage and slaughter in all parts of Gaul, Spain, Africa and finally Britain. One lament has come down to us which describes the destruction in Gaul; but it is a cry of helpless victims. Orientius, a poet of the early fifth century, describes the invasion of Gaul in A.D. 406 as follows:[1]

See how swiftly death comes upon the whole world and how many peoples the violence of war has stricken. Nothing contrives to escape the hands of the barbarians—not the depths of the woods, nor the mountain heights, nor the strong swift rivers, nor the forts in the country, nor city walls; not the trackless sea, nor the lonely desert, nor the cellars, nor caves under the sullen rocks.[2] The cause of death for many was treachery; for many public lies; for many the betrayal of the State. Ambush did much; open war did much. Those not overcome by violence died of hunger. The unhappy mother fell with her child and husband; the lord went to slavery with his slaves. Some lay as food for the dogs; others were killed by the flames that licked their homes. In the villages and country houses, in the fields and in the countryside, on every road—death, sorrow, slaughter, fires and lamentation. All Gaul smoked in one great funeral pyre.

This passage is part of two books of verse, exhorting the reader to turn his eyes away from life to the existence after death. The blessings of life, the joys of the senses and the beauties of the world are described; and afterwards the sins which mislead men—lust, jealousy, avarice and the passion for fame.[3] Greed and drunkenness are contrasted with the joys of heaven, which are described in terms of golden roofs, jewelled columns and fields of sweet-smelling flowers. The reader is then urged to consider the ruin of the present world and the near prospect of his own death; and at the end the

[1] Orientius, *Commonitorium*, ii, 165 sqq. *C.S.E.I.*, vol. i (1888). Orientius is referred to, with Sedulius, by Venantius Fortunatus (*Life of St. Martin*, i, 14 17). Therefore probably he lived about A.D. 400–470.
[2] Cf. Lord Mottistone, House of Lords (*Times*, July 14, 1940): "As had been proved not far across the Channel, the troglodytes were doomed. The peoples who sought safety by digging deeper were doomed to extinction."
[3] Orientius, *Com.*, ii, 13.

author gives his own name—Orientius—asking for the prayers of the saints, that is to say, of the holy men of the Church.

A similar tone runs through the poem on "Divine Providence" which has sometimes been attributed to Prosper of Acquitaine.[1] In this poem, also, there is a description of the destruction wrought in Gaul by the Vandals and the Goths.[2] After saying that the fields and the crops and the cattle are all destroyed, the poet asks why, if this is a punishment from God, innocent children and devout men and women should perish or be driven into exile, and why the deceitful and avaricious should derive gain from it all. The reply is then given that God wills it and that difficulties are sent to try us. The loss of wealth and happiness is of no account, and we must pray for what is to come after death. A third short poem is that by an unknown poet, of "a husband to his wife."[3] In this poem, too, there is a description of the reversal of fortune—"the rich man who went in his carriage through the cities, now toiling on foot through the empty countryside; and he who had had ten tall ships on the sea, now steering by himself a small boat." "All things rush to their end: peace has left the earth and our death too is near." The poet says that he does not fear exile because the world is one house for all and God has made him a citizen of another fatherland.[4] Therefore he urges his wife to be a faithful comrade in the service of Christ "so that one spirit should animate them both."

The sense of helplessness expressed in these poems is even more important than the evidence they contain of disaster and ruin following the barbarian invasions. But it must be remembered that such poems are only fragments of a much larger literature and that they survive largely because they suited the mood of the copyists who preserved them in the eighth and ninth centuries. These copyists were themselves monks who had despaired of the

[1] Printed at the end of the works of Prosper in *Pat. Lat.*, vol. 51, col. 617 sq.
[2] *De Prov. Div.*, line 34. "Vandaliciis gladiis sternimus et Geticis."
[3] *Poema conjugis ad uxorem. Pat. Lat.*, 51, col. 611.
[4] *Poema Conjugis*, 97.

> "Non metuo exilium, mundus domus omnibus una est, . . .
>   Spes igitur sola Deus: quem credere vita est,
>   Qui patriae civem me dedit alterius."

world in their own day. The religious defeatism which survives in the literature of the early fifth century, therefore, must not be taken as proof that the whole western world was of the same opinion, or that nobody in those days could do anything more than devoutly wring his hands.

Divisions and Disorders

The success of barbarian raids, like that of Alaric, and of invasions, like that of the Vandals, was only a superficial symptom of the operation of forces which were testing the adaptability of the Roman system. These forces caused the distrust or disagreement which divided the inhabitants of the Roman Empire; for, even if barbarians who came from outside the frontiers had not threatened its destruction, the social system of the Empire was disintegrating under the pressure of new forces within its borders. Christians and pagans were opposed, and different groups of Christians still more violently hostile one to the other. Extreme contrasts between the few rich and the many poor and enslaved began to be felt more keenly. The powerful bureaucracy of the central Government was unable or unwilling to establish security of life and property among the majority. But all these differences and the social unrest which they caused were not signs of moral decadence; they were the results of a sporadic, unorganized vitality chiefly among the social classes which derived little benefit from the Empire.

New conceptions of the life worth living, new views of deity and of the universe, were struggling to find expression within the ancient system. And in the fifth century that system might have proved to be sufficiently adaptable. The Roman world had survived the transition from Republic to Empire. It had survived innumerable civil wars, and the introduction of many new forms of worship during the four hundred years of varying success and failure after Augustus. It had survived finally a great change in the position of the Emperor—the transformation of a Roman official into an oriental despot, under Diocletian and Constantine. It might have survived, even in the West, the new crisis of the early fifth century. But it did not. The forces it could not assimilate or reconcile must now be reviewed in greater detail. But it must not be assumed that these forces were either objectionable or necessarily destructive. Every living form of civilization contains a surplus of thought and emotion beyond what is required for its maintenance. And whether the forces of new thought and new moral ideals transform or destroy the established order, depends upon its flexibility. When the old formulation of customs and beliefs can be made to include new knowledge and new action on the horizon of inherited experience, the social transition from one form of civilized life to another is less destructive. But if the social system is rigid, its resistance to change increases the explosive force of the desire for private wealth and personal power among the unbalanced and the ignorant. Such desires dominated the minds of those who sought control of the Roman Dictatorship in the fifth century; and these desires were socially destructive. But they could have been controlled if a place had been found in the old order for new conceptions of the universe and new moral standards. In the early fifth century the problem was not envisaged as it would be in modern times, because the great majority of those who thought at all on such subjects were deeply affected by the sense of their own helplessness. This gave support to the belief in celestial Powers outside their control, which might serve to explain their fate.

Two Views of History

The two chief contemporary authorities for the account of the sack of Rome are Zosimus and Orosius; but both wrote propaganda rather than history, and neither was a witness of the event. Zosimus, a non-Christian writing in Greek, was chiefly moved by regret for the old gods and their worship; and he compares Athens, protected by Athena, and therefore not sacked by Alaric, with Rome, whose Christian God did not prevent the Christian Alaric from taking his plunder. Orosius, a Spanish priest, writing in Latin, was chiefly concerned to show that Christianity did no harm to Rome when Alaric plundered it. His book bears in its title the phrase "against the Pagans," and he draws a contrast between Rhadagast who failed to reach Rome, and Alaric who succeeded.

"By the ineffable judgement of God," he says, "it came to pass that two tribes of Goths with their two most powerful kings raged about the Roman provinces, of whom one was a Christian and nearer to the Roman, and, as the event proved, in fear of God, gentle in slaughter; the other a Pagan, a barbarian and truly a Scythian (Goth). . . . Wherefore God, the just governor of the human race, willed the pagan enemy to perish and the Christian to succeed."[1] This seems to mean that God prefers a robber and murderer who is a Christian and assists him in his efforts. Thus the sufferings of his victims are shown to be good for them, as a punishment for sin; while, fortunately, as Orosius remarks, "the blessed Innocent, the bishop of the city of Rome, like the just Lot withdrawn from among the Sodomites, by the hidden providence of God, was then staying in Ravenna."[2] Also Alaric and his men are said to have spared valuables which belonged to the basilica of Saint Peter—another blow to the pagans. Thus, behind the actual events in Rome, the historians of the day sought to discover the working of celestial Powers.[3] That was their chief interest. There was no agreement about the nature of these Powers, and still less about which among them was most powerful. But it was generally believed that something or somebody in the sky was at work in deciding what should happen. About fifty years before the sack of Rome, Ammianus Marcellinus, a soldier and a gentleman, explained in his history that these celestial Powers knew what was going to happen and could convey the knowledge, if they chose, to men.[4] And without understanding this attitude of mind in the early fifth century, it is impossible to explain either the events or the policies of that time.

The disagreement between pagan and Christian historians turned upon their moral judgement with regard to the action of divine

[1] Orosius, *Hist.*, vii, 37–8. The description of Alaric as "mitis in caede" is, to say the least, simple-minded, whether it means that he cut your throat quite gently, or, as Orosius probably intended, that he gently killed pagans only and not Christians.
[2] Ibid., 39, 2.
[3] Zosimus begins (i, 1) with reference to (θεία τινὶ προνοίᾳ) "some divine providence."
[4] Amm. Marcell., xxi, 1, 8. Fundamental forces (*substantiales potestates*) can be controlled by rites.

Powers. The facts were the same for both; but the mind of the time demanded an answer to the question whether the situation as a whole was better or worse. And both parties assumed that it was either better or worse because of the character and conduct of the gods. But on that issue the historians had obviously to rely, not upon the exact knowledge then available to them, but upon traditional beliefs with regard to forces or powers which lay beyond the horizon of their knowledge. Many forces, however, unknown to them are now within the horizon of exact knowledge; and therefore some of the operative causes in the dissolution of the social system in the fifth century, which they conceived vaguely in terms of celestial Powers, can now be explained in terms of exact knowledge. Within their horizon there was no knowledge of what is now called economic or political science or biology. They knew nothing of the causes of the rise and decline of prices, or of the action of bacteria in plagues. But precisely such forces were operating to effect the changes which they believed to be due to celestial Powers. The modern historian, therefore, has to rely upon incidental phrases, hints and suggestions, in the original authorities, for evidence of actual forces, of the importance of which they were almost entirely ignorant.

But allowance must also be made for the fact that other forces were at work in former times, which are still unknown in the twentieth century. These are no more mysterious than the action of bacteria seemed to be in the Middle Ages. Even Gibbon when he recorded the extension of plagues in the later Roman Empire knew no more about bacteria than Zosimus. There is no complete or final knowledge at any date. But to allow for the limits of the knowledge of historians even at the present day, does not imply belief in the existence of any force or factor which cannot be known in the future. For example, a further examination of graves or of the ruins of cities, may explain the nature and extent of the depopulation from which the Roman Empire suffered; or again, a greater understanding of psychology may explain the function of the "Spiritual Power" or of magical ceremonies used from the fifth to the ninth century. It would be unwise, therefore, at any date to accept the assumptions of either Christians or non-Christians in the fifth century about the existence and nature of celestial Powers as an explanation for what is, at the moment, unknown.[1] The increase of knowledge and the improvement of the moral judgement will, no doubt, in later years serve to explain more, but never all, of the history of the far past.

Works of Controversy

The public Authorities in the Roman Empire, from the Emperor downwards, were already committed to the support of some form of Christianity, and in general opposed the use of the traditional rites and ceremonies. For many years before Alaric sacked Rome, Christianity had been gaining ground. But some of the most highly educated and influential Romans still hoped that the old non-Christian rites would be allowed to survive. A striking example of this attitude is to be found in the appeals of the Senator Symmachus, Prefect of the City of Rome, A.D. 384 and Consul A.D. 391, to the Emperor Valentinian II. His first argument is that Rome had won her victories while the old rites were performed and that she had failed to resist barbarians under the Christian God. He writes—"Clearly Emperors may be found of either part and either opinion. The earlier followed the rites of their fathers; the latter did not abolish them. If the religion of the older Emperors is not an example to be followed, at least permit the compromise (*dissimulatio*) of the later Emperors to act as one. . . . Constantine followed the old ways and admired the founders of the temples; and while he himself adopted other rites, these older rites he kept for the Empire."[2] This first argument is based upon the policy of the past century since Constantine. But Symmachus then turns to

---

[1] Hodgkin, in his admirable book *Italy and her Invaders*, asserts that the disappearance of the Roman Empire in the West was due to the will of God. For other statements he scrupulously offers proofs, but not for this. Far be it from any historian to attempt to disprove the truth of a statement for which no proof is offered. This, however, is one of the examples of the way in which historians are led to make statements which are metaphysical, without even knowing that they are metaphysical.

[2] Symmachus, *Relationes*, Ep. lib. x, *M.G.H.*, Auct. Ant., vi, p. 280. "Si exemplum non facit religio veterum, faciat dissimulatio proximorum."

the more general argument that each city has a presiding deity, with whose rites the life of the city is intimately connected. Thus Symmachus writes—"Different cities have different gods"; and Rome herself is imagined as speaking for her own gods "who preserved her from Hannibal and the Gauls." "Therefore we ask peace for the gods of the fatherland." A third argument follows, that there is no sacred road to deity. Symmachus says: "Rightly that which all men worship is thought to be One only. We look to the same stars; the same sky is common to all. The same world holds us all. What does it matter by what wisdom each man seeks the truth? Not by one road only can so great a mystery be approached."[1] But the argument is evidently a despairing appeal to imperial Authority, to spare the remnants of a dying tradition.

A direct reply to Symmachus is in a letter of St. Ambrose, addressed to Valentinian II, then a young man and recently accepted as Emperor in the West.[2] In this letter the arguments of Symmachus are taken in order; and his actual words are sometimes quoted. On the first point, that Rome owed her success to her ancient rites, St. Ambrose argues that Rome has often been defeated while she used those rites. Jupiter even allowed the Gauls to come as far as the Capitol, where a goose defeated them: "Did Jupiter speak in a goose?" As for the argument, "there are many ways to approach the great mystery," Ambrose replies: "We know, by the voice of God, what is unknown to you," which means either that there is no mystery or that many ways may mislead. Symmachus, speaking for the weaker side, pleads for toleration; and Ambrose expresses the emotional certainty which has in all ages been the basis of the persecution of minorities. As for the request of Symmachus that the Vestal Virgins and the temples should be supported by imperial funds, Ambrose replies that the far greater number of Christian virgins do not ask for riches and that "the wealth of the Church is merely the income of the poor"—this implying a new

---

[1] Uno itinere non potest pervenire ad tam grande secretum. *Relat.*, *M.G.H.*, Auct. Ant., vi, p. 283. Compare the statement in F. H. Bradley's *Appearance and Reality* (1902), p. 7: "there is no calling or pursuit which is a private road to the Deity." [2] Ambrose, Ep. xviii, *Pat. Lat.*, vol. 16, col. 971.

conception of the functions of religious foundations.[1] The same argument is used as in the poem of Prudentius, to be referred to later, that Roman victories are "due to the Roman legions and not to the efficacy of Roman rites";[2] and as for the "Compromise of Constantine," it must not be taken as an expression of consent.[3] In any case the Emperor Valentinian should adhere to the decrees of his brother-Emperor, Theodosius.

The two poems of Prudentius "Against Symmachus" follow the same line of argument. The first of these begins with the statement that the author thought that Rome had been freed from its old diseases, but the plague still survives there. He then proceeds to cast doubt upon the powers, not the existence, of the traditional Roman gods. He complains that "whatever the earth or sea, the hills or rivers bring forth is made into gods"; and the services of these gods, like the banquets of Janus, grow from bad to worse. Then the gods of the underworld are reviewed; and all are shown to have been useless. After about six hundred hexameter lines, Prudentius comes to a more important point. He says that in fact, if one looks at the people of Rome, they are seen to be going in crowds, not to the temple of Jupiter, but to the Tomb in the Vatican and to be baptized at the Lateran.[4] It does not affect him, he says, that a small number of men with illustrious ancestors keep their eyes closed to what is happening. Even in the Senate the majority is Christian.

The second poem contains better argument. In this Prudentius first makes reference to the plea of Symmachus for the preservation of the altar of Victory: "Do you seek for the mistress of success in war? It is for each his own right hand and Almighty God"—not a woman with hair flying and bare feet.[5] He does not notice that by adding "Almighty God" to "one's own right hand" he is only using a new name for what the ancients had called by many other names. As for the argument that cities have their traditional gods

[1] Ambrose, ibid., section 16: Possessio ecclesiae sumptus est egenorum.
[2] Ibid., section 30: legionum gratia, non religionum potentia.
[3] Ibid., section 22: dissimulatio pro consensu interpretantes.
[4] Prudentius, *Contra Sym.*, i, 158.
[5] Ibid., ii, 35. Vincendi quaeris dominam? sua dextra cuique est et deus omnipotens.

and rites, this is precisely the same argument, used in later years, to maintain Christianity against innovations. Prudentius replies that if we can never break with the past, we should have to go back and live with primitive man in a cave.[1] Christianity is new—a revolution. But Rome survives; and "by Rome I mean the men who make the mind of the city."[2] "Whoever gives Venus the credit, takes from the unconquered legions and from Rome herself the palm of victory."[3] And yet Roman victories were due to the design of the Christian God. All the world has been made Roman to prepare it for the worship of Christ; and the services and labours under the Roman system will continue in the new dispensation.

This obviously is the poetic expression of confidence in victory over the old order. It is not valid argument. Prudentius was a poet—a Spaniard who admired the ancient achievements of Rome, but was more deeply moved by the sight of the Christian people of Rome thronging the great basilicas. Clearly the great majority in the City, as well as in the Senate and among the public Authorities, were Christian and cared nothing for "the ancient rites," which seemed to a cultured few to be essential to the survival of civilization.

Another attempt to find a basis for toleration and compromise is the *Saturnalia* of Macrobius, written about A.D. 400. This is a discussion of many different points of view affecting the social and religious problems of the times. The author evidently hoped for a religion which would acknowledge one Deity, symbolized as the Lord, the Sun, and allowing diverse rites to be practised under legal protection. The character in the dialogue named Evangelus (gospeller) does not maintain what would now be called a Christian view of social classes, but rather the inequality of men. The author is believed to have been Praetorian Prefect in Spain (A.D. 399) and Pro-consul of Africa (A.D. 410): he was probably not a Christian.

---

[1] Prudentius, *Contra Sym.*, ii, 289: redeamus ad antra.
[2] Ibid., ii, 443. Romam dico viros, quos mentem credimus urbis, non genium. . . .
[3] Ibid., ii, 553.

> Detrahit invictis legionibus et sua Romae
> Praemia diminuit, qui quidquid fortiter actum est
> Adscribit Veneri, palmam victoribus aufert.

C*

Learned laymen, however, were not to be found only among the non-Christians. If indeed the author of the *Quaestiones*, hitherto called "Ambrosiaster," was Hilarius, a Christian, who was twice Prefect of the City of Rome, his discussion *Against the Pagans* (Quaestio cxiv) is of great importance; because his work is the earliest now known in which the word "pagan" is consistently used to describe all varieties of non-Christians. Again, his knowledge of the Epistles and of the Old Testament, as well as his legal and administrative knowledge, give great weight to his treatment of texts from Scripture. In any case, the author was a Roman layman who was critical of the Roman clergy, as in his attack on the pride of the deacons of the Roman Church; and he was also evidently a friend of Damasus, bishop of Rome. His work indicates how completely the Bible had taken possession of the minds of devout Christians.[1]

Thus the controversy between the most cultured advocates of paganism and those of Christianity was fully developed in the later years of the fourth century. In spite of famines, defeats of Roman armies and invasions of the Empire by barbarians, the Christian Emperors seemed to be still part of the eternal order of things. It was into this atmosphere of Christian confidence in the new order that the news of the sack of Rome by Alaric came as warning of worse to follow.

The City of God

The most celebrated work in the controversy between non-Christians and Christians is St. Augustine's treatise on *The City of God*. This was a direct result of Alaric's sack of Rome in A.D. 410; and it was intended by the author to be a refutation of the "pagan" view that the sack of Rome was due to Christianity.[2] The twenty-two books of *The City of God* were written during thirteen years

[1] See Souter, *A Study of Ambrosiaster* (1905), and the Note by C. E. Turner in the *Journal of Theological Studies*, vol. vii, p. 284, on the word "paganus." In Ambrosiaster also is the word "paganitas." The writer of the *Quaestiones* is believed to be Decimus Hilarianus Hilarius, to whom some of the rescripts in the Theodosian law-books are addressed.

[2] Augustine, *Retract.*, ii, 69. Deorum falsorum multorumque cultores quos usitato nomine paganos vocamus in Christianam religionem referre conantes (i.e., eversionem Romae).

in the intervals of the busy life of the bishop of Hippo, whose energies were spent in preaching, in controversy with the Donatists, in political negotiation, and in the care of refugees and of the poor dependants of the Churches in his diocese. Augustine was fifty-nine when he began it; and he died at the age of seventy-six (A.D. 430), four years after it was finished, while the Vandals were besieging the city in which he lay. *The City of God*, therefore, must not be taken as the abstract theory of a dispassionate observer. It is an urgent appeal, addressed mainly to Christians, who had been disturbed by the obvious collapse of Roman power in the West; and its chief purpose is to express in terms of world-history, as Augustine understood it, the fundamental importance of the distinction between right and wrong.

Augustine was born and brought up in Africa, and knew Rome only as a visitor. Unlike Symmachus, he belonged, as a lawyer or lecturer, to the intellectuals of the middle classes, who were attracted in different directions by the many different Oriental philosophies and religions. His own preference had been for the Manichaeans and what is now called Neo-Platonism. Thus, even before accepting Christianity, Augustine was familiar with the theories of history, which contrasted the evil forces of "matter" and "the world" with the divine, conceived as morally good. The interest of *The City of God*, however, for the purpose here in view, is confined to its expression of a theory of social institutions affected by celestial Powers. But it is impossible to understand Augustine's conception of social institutions without reference to the general view of the universe, with which the last fourteen books are concerned. The first ten books were intended to be directly controversial; but the argument is, to say the least, obscure, and the conclusions neither clearly stated nor consistent. The treatise begins by attacking non-Christians for not being grateful because the sack of Rome (vastatio urbis) had been less destructive than it might have been. The barbarians had respect for the Christian basilicas. The sack of the city is said to have been one of the normal experiences of war; but what was exceptional in it was due to Christianity, namely the survival of most of the inhabitants and their sacred buildings. In

75

any case, Augustine continues, the sufferings of the Romans were punishments sent by God; and neither the loss of wealth, or of life or of honour, is of any importance to the Christian. In fact the Romans had only become worse, the more wealth and power they had acquired. Roman peace had been merely an opportunity for vice, which even misfortune could not cure.[1] This clearly implies, not a disproof of the assertion that the sack of Rome had been due to neglect of the ancient gods, but rather the doctrine that the Christian God had in fact designed the disaster for the moral benefit of those who suffered. In the next book Augustine argues that the older gods had given no guidance or support in the good life. The Romans suffered from a lust of conquest, which their gods had not corrected. The gods had even fought among themselves and had, therefore, taught the Romans civil war.[2] Indeed these gods may support the appetite for wealth and power, but have no concern with right and wrong. The philosophers and teachers of Greece and Rome were better than their gods, because they tried to stop the decay of morality. And "without justice what are kingdoms but great robber bands?"[3] The extension of the Roman Empire was not due to the gods whom the Romans worshipped, nor to their ceremonies, nor to the stars, but to the one God only, whom the Jews worshipped and whose service led them to success and wealth, until they sinned finally by killing Christ.[4] The success of the Romans, such as it was, was due to the virtues of their great men in earlier times; and even now, as Augustine says, when under his eyes the people of Carthage asserted that Rhadagast could not be conquered without the use of pagan ceremonies, he was in fact defeated and more than a hundred thousand of his army destroyed.[5] This shows that Christian Emperors have the blessing of God. Christians, however, do not call Constantine or Theodosius great, because they were successful, but only because they ruled justly and used their power to extend the worship of God.[6] This

---

[1] Neque enim in vestra securitate pacatam rem publicam, sed luxuriam quaeritis inpunitam, qui depravati rebus prosperis nec corrigi potuistis adversis. *Civ. Dei*, i, c. 33.　　　　　　　　　　　　　　　　　　　　　　　[2] *Civ. Dei*, ii, c. 25.

[3] Ibid., iv, c. 4. Remota iustitia quid sunt regna nisi magna latrocinia?

[4] Ibid., iv, c. 34.　　　　　[5] Ibid., v, 23.　　　　　[6] Ibid., v, 24, 25, 26.

concludes the argument of the first five books. The following five cast ridicule and doubt upon various pagan gods, and contain lengthy refutations of certain neo-Platonic theories. The purpose of the latter half of the argument is to show that pagan beliefs and non-Christian philosophies are useless for the life which is to come after death.

Augustine is by no means consistent. In one section he argues that wealth and power are not desirable; and as a good African he seems to have felt some resentment at the Roman destruction of Carthage.[1] But, on the other hand, he says that God allowed the Roman Empire to spread and the Jews to obtain wealth, which he regards as desirable. The still greater obstacle to consistency in his treatise is the confusion which gradually shows itself in his argument, between the statement that certain acts are morally right and the statement that they are willed by God. Thus, virtue and justice become for Augustine identified with the acceptance of his own cosmology. This leads him to exchange Cicero's definition of justice for one more consonant with the idea of a life after death; and as a social ideal he discards the idea of the community as a relationship in accordance with right or justice and substitutes the idea of a community as an agreement to pursue a certain purpose which, for Augustine, is life after death in heaven. Right action is thus distinguished from wrong as the action of the blessed contrasted with the damned. And the blessed are those chosen by God to be excepted from the general damnation of the whole human race, which was the natural effect of Adam's disobedience.[2] According to Augustine, the eternal torture of those not chosen is "not evil-doing on the part of God, who allows it by a just but unintelligible judgement," although it would be evil-doing in a man to hurt anyone else for revenge.[3] Thus, the last fourteen books of *The City of God* describe the division of God's chosen, who formed a city of God, from the rest of humanity. A history of the universe is drawn from the Hebrew Bible and legends. The civil war of

[1] *Civ. Dei*, xi, c. 30.
[2] Ibid., xxi, c. 12. Hinc est universa generis humani massa damnata.
[3] Ibid., xxi, c. 13. . . . sed non peccat Deus, qui iusto, quamvis occulto, iudicio fieri sinit.

angels in heaven is fully discussed; and Augustine's uncritical imagination plays about primitive man, whose sexual organs, he informs his readers, were under better control than those of later times.[1] Concerning the resurrection of bodies after the last judgement, when no one will be too fat or too thin, Augustine, like Thomas Aquinas, was somewhat troubled by the case of a man who had eaten human flesh, on the ground that there would not be enough "body" for both the cannibal and his victim. But he is comforted by repeating many times Christ's saying, "not a hair of your head shall perish."[2] The contrast between Christianity and Paganism, therefore, in *The City of God*, is not based upon critical reasoning. It is the expression of assumptions about the truth of Hebrew records and the validity of the moral judgements expressed in them, which would not be accepted by Augustine's opponents. Christianity, however, appears as an emotional acceptance of a new point of view with regard to the celestial Powers.

Both Christians and non-Christians agreed that such Powers existed; and the celestial Powers in which Christians trusted were indeed alien to the Roman tradition, but more definitely connected with a doctrine of moral right and wrong than were the gods of the pagans. The conceptions of right and wrong in the new doctrine were crude, and confused with oriental imagery relating to the events of history. But evidently the strength of the Christian position lay in the fact that it did in some way express the importance of that moral authority which was generally felt to be dissolving in the last days of the Roman Empire in the West. It is of great importance that the distinction between right and wrong should be seen to be quite different from the distinction between success and failure or strength and weakness. The collapse of the whole world, as all Christians believed, would make no difference at all to the distinction between right and wrong. The traditional description of another sort of world in which this truth was embodied,

---

[1] *Civ. Dei*, xiv, c. 26. He repeats the same theory in the treatise on *Marriage and Lust*.

[2] Ibid., xxii, c. 20; Aquinas, *Contra Gentes*, iv, 81. "Caro comesta resurget in eo in quo primo facit anima rationalis perfecta." Cannibals, according to Aquinas, have a share in their victims' bodies at the Resurrection.

must not be allowed to obscure the fact that a new form of moral judgement had now taken hold of thousands of simple folks, outside the circles of the philosophers. The whole weight of the argument in *The City of God* rests upon the belief in another world in which the dead are divided for ever—some living above the skies in happiness, and others beneath the earth in torture. And although Augustine expresses his admiration for the heroes of old Rome—Regulus, Scipio and the rest—these too are among the damned.[1] This belief, again, rests upon the acceptance of the Bible, not only as a record of historical facts, but also as a final authority on the estimate of moral values. Thus, the estimate of good and evil, and of right and wrong action, was confused with a statement of fact about heaven and hell. *The City of God* must be read as a whole. Its importance for those who read it in the dark days of the fifth and sixth centuries, lay in the fact that it gave them confidence and hope, while the Roman world collapsed around them. It was indeed a refusal to accept disaster and defeat as final. It was a call to endure suffering as only a trial through which right and justice might be at last established, not by our own strength, but by celestial Powers, and not in this, but in another world. Augustine did not appeal in *The City of God* for social or institutional reforms; and his moral standards, not indeed peculiar to himself, were crudely conceived. He condemned the pagan gods because their civil wars gave a bad example to man; but he saw no difficulty in the civil war of the angels, which implied at least weakness in the Christian God. He condemned Jupiter for his amorous adventures; but he showed no distaste for the unprovoked aggression of the Hebrews in their conquest of Palestine, or for the savage commands of their God, or for the cruelty involved in the tortures of hell.

About twenty years after the death of Augustine, Salvian, a

[1] Some non-Christian Romans, like Symmachus, must have felt as King Radbod of the Frisians is said to have felt in the early eighth century. The King, in the act of being baptized for his own salvation, enquired where his ancestors would be; and, on being told that they would lie for ever in hell, he withdrew from baptism, saying he would prefer to stay with his ancestors (*Annales Xantenses*). Dante in A.D. 1300 saw in hell Caesar, Seneca, Socrates, Plato and Aristotle—because they had not been baptized. But they were not tortured. Torture was reserved for the critic of Dictatorship, Brutus, in the tower storey of the medieval "Brown House" or Concentration Camp. See *Inferno*, iv, 123 sq. and xxxiv, 65.

priest of Marseilles, wrote a book on *The Government of God* which was an attempt to reply to those who said that the distress of the time proved that the events of history are not designed by a benevolent Providence. The book is much more reasonable and consistent than anything written by Augustine, and expresses a much more definite moral teaching than that of *The City of God*. But it has had much less influence, precisely because its argument depends upon a clear perception of facts and of moral values, whereas Augustine's work played upon an imagination which found relief in it from the normal difficulties of thought and emotion. In a period of childhood, like that of the First Europe, fairy tales are more effectual than social criticism. The argument of Salvian rests upon the assumption that the distress of the time— recognized to be more serious than Augustine or Orosius thought— was the direct result of God's desire to teach men to be just. "We deserve," writes Salvian, "what we have suffered, because of our evil-doing and the complacency which covers our crimes."[1] Then follows a review of the character of the barbarians, of "bacaudae" or riotous bands, the flight of Roman citizens, the injustice of judges, and the tyranny of the rich. This will provide evidence for the discussion later in this chapter. But perhaps the whole book, in spite of its directness and strength, can hardly be classed as a work of controversy, except in so far as it implies a criticism of the complacent admiration of the established order among the rich and powerful, who derived great benefits from its maintenance, and whose feelings are expressed by such writers as Rutilius Namatianus and Sidonius Apollinaris.

Churches and Temples

The opposition between Christians and non-Christians is not wholly expressed in controversy. It can be more clearly perceived in the contrast between the sacred buildings which they erected and used. More striking than any documents are the Christian basilicas of the fourth and fifth centuries in Rome, in Ravenna, and

---

[1] Salvian, *De Gub. Dei*, iv, 12. The book was published probably before A.D. 451, because the invasion of Gaul by Attila in that year is not mentioned.

other parts of Italy. The contrast between these buildings and the temples of the older religions is a clear indication of the character of the New Order. Prudentius, as it has been shown above, contrasted the empty temples with the crowded basilicas of the Lateran and the Vatican. In his hymn for Saints Peter and Paul he describes the splendour of their shrines. And it was to the Christian basilicas that men and women fled for safety from the marauding Goths under Alaric. But it is not merely because these buildings were popular that they are important for the argument here. The contrast of the two systems of religion is shown by the difference between the uses for which they were designed. A temple is a shrine for the statue of a god, to be looked at from outside. Worshippers at festivals gathered outside. The priest or priestess was a person of a certain family or of some social influence. On the other hand, the Christian basilica was designed to hold crowds; and the crowds were of all classes, rich and poor, strong and weak. They formed a single community. They gathered not merely for hymns, processions, and the central ceremony of the Eucharist, but also to hear instruction and exhortation in homilies and sermons. In the church or at its doors the poor received alms. And the officials of the Christian community—priests, bishops and deacons, were selected for their office by some kind of popular acclamation.

At the end of the fourth century no more temples were being built. But the great Christian basilicas, some of which had been built, or at least used, in the days of Constantine the Great, were being extended and adorned. In the Vatican the basilica of St. Peter was a centre for ceremonies and pilgrimage from the early days of the fourth century until the middle of the sixteenth century. The basilicas St. John in the Lateran, St. Paul's outside the Walls, St. Mary the Greater (*Basilica Liberiana*) and St. Sabina, are all of the fourth or early fifth century; although all have been remodelled. In these many places the Romans of the fifth century gathered and prayed, while the old social system fell into ruins. Significant, also, of the change were the mosaic decorations in the basilicas. In Rome those of the fifth century are on the triumphal arch of St. Paul's outside the Walls, on the entrance wall of St. Sabina and in St. Mary the Greater. But in Ravenna, where the fifth-century basilicas no longer survive, the most brilliant mosaics are those in the mausoleum of Galla Placidia (about A.D. 450), whose adventures and death were closely connected with the destruction of imperial authority in the West.

Opposing Attitudes

Whatever may be thought about the celestial Powers, the most important historical fact is that in the early fifth century, within the Roman Empire, there was complete disagreement about them. The two groups most definitely opposed are represented by Orosius and Zosimus. They have been called the Christians and the Pagans. But each of these two names obviously covers a very large number of different views of life and of the Powers which men believed they ought to propitiate. It is true, as Sir Samuel Dill has so admirably said, that those who shared in the traditional culture, both the Christians and the non-Christians, were able to enter into friendly communication. Ambrose could admire the scholarship of Symmachus, and Symmachus the vigour of Ambrose, as in the early fifth century Augustine, already a bishop, could enter into friendly controversy with the non-Christian Longinianus.[1] But the student of history will not be misled by literary politeness. The feelings of the great majority of Christians were certainly hostile to Paganism. And the non-Christians, not only among the rich senators, but also throughout the country districts, felt a deep hostility to the Christian suppression of ancient rites and the Christian disdain for traditional forms of reverence of the Divine. It is most important that the disagreements about beliefs and practices in religion disturbed all the communities of the Roman Empire, which was, in this matter, a house divided against itself. The dissolution of traditional religious belief weakened the reliance of men upon their neighbours, and therefore tended to undermine the traditional social system. The opposition between non-Christians

[1] Dill, *Roman Society in the Last Century of the Western Empire*, 2nd ed., 1921, p. 14 sq. This admirable book gives a full account of the culture and manners of the fifth century in western Europe.

and Christians in the early fifth century, therefore, must be treated as one of the chief causes for the dissolution of the Roman system of government and social organization.

The non-Christians included a highly educated society of rich men, still powerful in Rome and the other great cities, in spite of the fact that the Emperors adopted and supported Christianity. This group of rich and powerful men supported the traditional rituals by associating them with the long history of the success of Rome in the pursuit of wealth and power. Their chief strength lay in the memory of the past, while, for the Christians, the future in another world seemed more important. The memory of great Roman generals and statesmen was sufficient to prove to non-Christians that the established order depended upon the acceptance of traditional beliefs and customs. The heroes of the educated and richer classes were men who had established and maintained public authority. They were free men and not manual workers; but obviously Christianity had begun among the working classes; and the uneducated mass of slaves and artisans could hardly be expected to understand or to estimate correctly the value of a system which they did not establish or control.

Again, the non-Christians admired vigour and valour (*virtus*) which was effectual in controlling nature or governing men.[1] They thought of "manliness" as the basis of that great system of the administration of justice, which is implied in the work of the great jurists, and in Roman Law. Men and women, impressed with the value of the culture they had inherited and the order and civilization which their forefathers had established long before Christ had been heard of, naturally regarded the Christians as evil influences and regretted the official support of Christianity. The non-Christian aristocracy in the West was aware of the disturbances which followed disputes among Christians themselves. Such scenes, for example, as those which accompanied the struggle for the bishopric of Rome, between the supporters and opponents of Damasus, the bishop of Rome, in A.D. 366, must have contributed

[1] Vetus illa Romana virtus et sobria. So Ammianus Marcellinus (xv, 4, 3), referring to the road over the Cottian Alps.

to the mistrust of the new religion.[1] The attitude of the non-Christian wealthy or middle classes was like that of similar observers in German cities between 1918 and 1932, who heard with disgust of street-fighting between manual workers, under the leaders of various fascist, communist or socialist groups. The upper class in Roman cities can hardly have supposed that their power would pass within a few centuries to the successors of the leaders in such street brawls.

Again, non-Christians were aware of the contradiction involved in the Christian teaching with regard to public office, and in particular to military service. An imperial Edict forbad non-Christians to serve in the army or to hold public office.[2] But there was no agreement among Christian teachers concerning the fulfilment of public duties. On the one hand, Paulinus, bishop of Nola, speaking in the name of Christianity, advised the Christian against military service on the ground that it involved giving assistance to murder, and was unworthy of a follower of Christ;[3] on the other hand, Augustine, bishop of Hippo, a friend of Paulinus and a much more influential teacher, wrote: "I do not approve of killing others for the defence of one's own life, unless you are a soldier or an official acting, not for yourself, but in defence of others or of your city, if you so act under a lawfully given command and in a way proper to your office."[4] It is hardly strange that the opponents of Christianity should be distrustful of a religion which seemed to have no consistent teaching with regard to public service.

Again, the principle of toleration for diverse rituals and beliefs which was traditional in the Roman Empire, implied that those who took advantage of toleration should at least practise it towards others. Toleration does not logically permit the advocacy or the

---

[1] The supporters of the rival bishop were shut in and killed or maimed in the basilica, now S. Maria Maggiore, by the supporters of Damasus.

[2] *Cod. Theod.*, xvi, 10, 21 (Dec. 7, 416). Qui profano pagani ritus errore seu crimine polluuntur, hoc est gentiles, nec ad militiam admittantur nec administratoris vel iudicis honore decorentur.

[3] Paulinus, *Ep.*, xxv. Qui militat gladio mortis est minister . . . ideo dicit dominus: non potestis duobus dominis servire, scilicet uni deo et mammonae, Christo videlicet et Caesari, cum ipse Caesar Christi servus nunc studeat esse, ut aliquarum gentium rex esse mereatur.

[4] Augustine, *Ep. ad Publicolam.*, No. 47 in *C.S.E.L.* ii, pars 2, p. 135.

practice of intolerance. But the Christians denied that any other view of the universe or of virtue than their own was correct, and refused to perform symbolical acts of loyalty as trivial, in the opinion of pagans, as in modern times it would be to stand while a national anthem was played. Worse still, they seemed to expect and to approve a subversion of the established social order; for in one of their sacred books a hymn declared that their God had degraded those who had social influence and raised up the lower classes. As the Latin text had it—"Deposuit potentes de sede et exaltavit humiles"; and it must be remembered that the "potentes" were the governing classes of the Empire and the "humiles" were their dependants.

Non-Christians were also aware that Christians stood aloof from public affairs and supported what seemed to be social revolution only until they had obtained complete control of the central government under Theodosius. After that time they had supported the persecution, not only of pagans, but also of fellow-Christians who happened to be in a minority. And when Christian bishops had become imperial functionaries they were also opponents of any movement tending to social revolution. The pagans not unreasonably suspected that the desire of the Christians was to obtain power and that the policies they adopted were due chiefly to this.

A last, and most reasonable, ground for doubt about the new religion was the fact that the barbarians themselves, who were destroying the Empire, were Christians. That they were Arian heretics made no practical difference; for some Christian Emperors after Constantine had supported the Arians. The non-Christian must have felt that Christians in the Roman cities welcomed the destruction wrought by the Christian barbarians. They, no less than the Christians, remembered that before Constantine deserted Rome for an eastern capital, the Emperors had treated Christians as enemies of the commonwealth. Indeed Christianity itself might be only a passing phase in the long history of Eternal Rome.[1]

[1] St. Augustine (*Civ. Dei*, xxviii, 54) argued against a pagan theory that Christianity would last for only 365 years. This theory also asserted that St. Peter had won over Rome to Christianity by magical arts; and it is in this connection that St. Augustine makes the significant remark "non in Petrum credimus, sed in quem credidit Petrus."

But the non-Christians who feared the influence of the new religion were not all rich and powerful. In the country districts, as the word "pagan" (country-man) implies, there were thousands of simple men and women who desired only to continue the worship and propitiation of celestial Powers, which their forefathers had believed to be effectual. These made no theories about Deity. All they knew was that certain rituals at certain times would protect the crops or increase their flocks, or keep them secure against the dangers of flood or earthquake or other calamities. The suspicion, therefore, with which the new-fangled beliefs and practices of an eastern, and indeed partially Jewish religion was regarded, was sufficiently widespread throughout western Europe to divide the community.

On the other hand, the Christians might well be suspicious of the influence of those who stood for the traditional religion. It was only about a century since the last persecution; and the Christian Churches still maintained in their festivals and their writings the memory of official and popular hostility organized in the name of the very system which its supporters said had made Rome great. It was quite reasonable for those who now accepted beliefs and practices which had been bitterly persecuted, to fear a revival of what earlier Christians had suffered. The hatred of the Emperor Julian, who tried to revive Paganism, is an indication of fear surviving among Christian writers and preachers. Again, the Churches in the early fifth century were no longer small numbers of aliens in the Roman cities. They had their own organizations for mutual benefit under their own officials, the bishops, who could rival in force of character and, in some cases, in learning and culture, the representatives of the old order.

Further, the very fact that Christianity counted among its founders and first adherents men and women of the lower classes, slaves and manual workers, made the contrast between the new gospel and the old order the more obvious.[1] Christianity had more widely extended and more highly organized the equality of all

[1] In the *Octavius*, viii, of Minucius Felix, the non-Christians say of Christians, "qui de ultima faece collectis imperitioribus et mulieribus credulis . . . plebem instituunt."

brethren within each community or church, which had proved so attractive in the earlier mystery religions of the East. At certain times in the development of the ancient social system, the desire to disregard the barriers of caste or class had attracted the best men and women. The Stoics had thrown doubt on the institution of slavery; and although the Christian Churches made no attempt to abolish slavery, the equality of all human beings as "souls" was an assumption generally accepted in Christian society. The heroes of the Christian Church were not generals and statesmen, but martyrs or confessors who had been slaves or manual workers. Poor and humble folk had founded the Churches and suffered nobly, as well as some few among the rich, who despised riches. As Theodoret argues, servant girls and slaves among the Christians had shown a valour and constancy as great as that of the heroes of the non-Christian world.[1] Indeed it was with pride that St. John Chrysostom remarked that the Emperor himself prayed for the help of a tent-maker and a fisherman.[2] Christianity had not yet forgotten that its source was to be traced to the insight and character of manual workers, and not to the wisdom of the schools or the experience of rulers. The Christian bishops had not yet forgotten their responsibility for justice due to the weak and the poor.

Again, the Churches in the different cities and towns of the Empire were organized societies, independent of the social and political system, long before Constantine had sought to use their influence, by admitting them to power in the State. Three generations after Constantine, in the early fifth century, the Churches were still largely independent of the organization of local government. The Emperor was Christian; and his decrees supported the Churches and opposed Paganism. The bishops were therefore loyal to the Emperor and his direct representatives, rather than to the

---

[1] Theodoret, *Graec. Affect. Curatio*, lib. vii (Teubner edit., p. 217). Theodoret was probably thinking of the letter of the Church of Lyons (A.D. 177) to the Churches of Asia, preserved in Eusebius, *History of the Church*, in which the slave girl Blandina's suffering is described.

[2] St. John Chrysostom, Hom. in 2 Cor. xxvi, 5. τοῦ σκηνοποιοῦ καὶ τοῦ ἁλιέως προστατῶν καὶ τετελευτηκότων δεῖται ὁ τὸ διάδημα ἔχων. Pat. Gr., vol. 60, col. 582. "He that wears the crown beseeches the tent-maker and the fisherman, though dead, to be his patrons."

survival of republican forms in the Senate or in the municipal councils. The Churches themselves, by this time, were organized on an authoritarian basis. The bishops, once chosen, exerted absolute authority, or at any rate claimed to hold it, within the community formed by each local Church. The Churches were therefore no longer "democratic." Their members felt a natural sympathy for the dictatorship which governed, at any rate in theory, the Roman world. As it will be argued in a later chapter, Christianity in the West remained in this sense oriental. But the very fact that the Christians and their bishops naturally looked to the Emperor and not to the Senate, the municipal authorities or the oligarchy of rich men, which controlled parts of the western world, created another opposition of outlook between Christians and non-Christians.

Between the two opposing forces, which were later called Christian and Pagan, there were many mystical or religious groups of men and women who were regarded at the time as heretical Christians. An edict of May 30, A.D. 428, from the Emperors Theodosius II and Valentinian III, addressed to Florentius (*Praefectus Praetorio*), gives a list of Christian or almost Christian sects which were to have no right of meeting or praying in the Roman Empire. These are "Arians, Macedonians, Apollinarians, Novatians, Sabbatians, Eunomians, Valentinians, Montanists or Priscillianists, Fryges, Marcianists, Borborians, Messalians, Euchites or Enthusiasts, Donatists, Andians, Hydroparastates, Tascodrogites, Fotinians, Paulians, Marcellians, and those who have arrived at the lowest depths of crime—Manichaeans."[1] This is a sufficiently terrifying number of groups, seeking shelter under the common name of "Christian," who were to be suppressed and persecuted. The traditional religious tolerance of the earlier Roman Empire, which had excluded only "Christians," now changed, under the influence of rival groups of clergy and monks, into the *gleichshaltung* of an infallible Dictatorship. The Christians who had suffered persecution were not opposed to persecution, but only to being persecuted

---

[1] *Cod. Theod.*, xvi, 5, 65. The list is repeated with some additions in *Cod. Just.*, i, 5, 5.

themselves. And in the early fifth century, when the many different beliefs and customs which were later confused under the name of Paganism, no longer had any general appeal, the persecuting zeal of those Christians who happened to have influence was turned against their fellow Christians. As Ammianus Marcellinus remarks in reference to the struggles for power in the fourth century, "no beasts are more savagely hostile to men than Christians attacking their fellow-Christians."[1] This hostility, and the persecution it caused, helped in the general dissolution of the social system.

Again, the line between Christians and non-Christians was by no means so clearly defined as the advocates of either religion would have liked to suppose. Many, no doubt, were undecided from year to year which attitude to adopt. A decree of the Emperors in A.D. 381 refers to Christians who had returned to pagan practices.[2] All this would perhaps have made little difference in the earlier years of the Roman Empire; because the Roman system was always hospitable to foreign gods and foreign religious practices. Indeed, the Roman Church, even at a later date, carried on the tradition of ancient Rome in its acceptance of the heroes and the rituals of other religions. But in the fifth century religious passions ran high. Such passions were less violent in the West than in the East; but even in the West, when the minds of men were disturbed by their fear that the traditional system which they had inherited was being undermined, this fear led to suspicion and hatred of each man for those who differed from him. The mixture of diverse races, religions and economic interests which had been united by Rome, proved to be explosive; the system was being destroyed by disruptive forces without it; and one of these forces was religion.

The Poor

The second great force disturbing the Roman system was the opposition of interests between the poor, the manual workers and the slaves on the one hand, and the rich and powerful on the

[1] Amm. Marcell., *Hist.*, xxii, 5.
[2] *Cod. Theod.*, xvi, 7, 1 (2 May, 381). Gratian, Valentinian and Theodosius. His, qui ex Christianis pagani facti sunt.

other. The hopelessness of the poor and the irresponsibility of the rich showed that neither rich nor poor would make any effort to support the traditional system. The poor fled from estate to estate and even into the camps of the barbarian invaders; while the rich retired to any of their estates which they imagined would be safe. These two groups can be watched as they separate under the impact of barbarian invasions and leave the city-civilization of western Europe in ruins. The poorer free workers in the country-side, and the free artisans in the cities, were hardly different from the slaves, in power or social functions. The tax system destroyed the poor man. The State for generations had farmed out the tax-collection to the *publicani*. These men, throughout the Roman Empire, paid a fixed sum to the treasury and squeezed as much as they could from the defenceless peasantry. A tenth of the peasant's crops was the theoretical basis of what he owed; and even an exact computation of his debt would have borne hardly enough upon him, not only because of unfavourable harvests, but because of the incessant wars.

The poorer classes, both slaves and manual workers, had for some generations sought refuge in flight. Some fled from one estate to the other, seeking the protection of a more powerful, or perhaps more kindly, master; others fled to the cities where they might be lost among the mass of unemployed who were dependent upon public assistance. Others took refuge in the forests or the hills, and lived by brigandage; and some joined any marauding band of barbarians who would permit them to share the loot. The Theodosian law-books contain many decrees directed against fugitives and those who gave them shelter.[1] But the decrees are repeated year after year and are therefore proved to have been ineffectual. Indeed it was to the advantage of a powerful landowner or his agent to have more labour on his estate; and he could easily protect fugitives, both by such armed force as he himself might raise, and by his influence with the local officials of the Empire. But evidently the flight of men and women from one place to another, seeking

---

[1] *Cod. Theod.*, v, 17. Rescripts of Constantine (A.D. 332) and of Gratian, etc., in A.D. 386.

escape from oppression, must have reduced the productive powers of the old system.

When it became clear that the barbarians were not only marauders, willing to accept the assistance of fugitive slaves, as in the sack of Rome, but also powerful groups settled upon the land, the poor and the oppressed were all the more willing to seek protection from them. Salvian, the Marseilles priest, writing about fifty years after Alaric's invasion of Italy, says that in Gaul poor men sought liberty by escaping to the barbarians. It had evidently become clear to many that they had nothing to hope for from the Roman system. Salvian writes: "As with the outlaws, so it is with nearly all the poorer classes. . . . What else but liberty can these poor wretches desire, who suffer the pressure of continuous taxation, who are threatened always by endless requisitions, who desert their own homes lest they should be tortured in them, and seek exile lest they suffer punishment? The enemy are kinder to these than the tax-collectors. Experience proves it. They fly to the enemy to escape the weight of taxation. And this, although hard and inhuman, is less bitter if all suffer it equally."[1] And again: "Who calls the impoverished lower classes to a share in benefits? . . . And do we wonder if the Goths are not conquered by our men when Romans prefer to live among them than among us? And so, not only do our brethren refuse to fly from them to us, but they fly to them and leave us."[2] As for the poor who seek protection on the estates of the rich, "they suffer such a transformation as Circe worked—they are changed into cattle. For those whom the rich receive as strangers, they hold as their own men; and those who are free are turned into slaves. Do we wonder, then, if the barbarians enslave us, when our own brethren make us captive? Small wonder that there is devastation and the ruin of cities."[3]

In Rome and the greater cities of the Empire, thousands of the poorer manual workers, who were not slaves, had for centuries been dependent upon the distribution of bread by the public Authorities. The gift was called the *panis gradilis*, or "step-bread,"

[1] Salvian, *de Gub. Dei*, v, 7. Salvian was born about A.D. 400 and finished his book about A.D. 450.   [2] Ibid., v, 7.   [3] Ibid., v, 7.

because each householder who claimed a portion received it publicly at the steps of some official building in his district.[1] In the fifth century bacon and other food was added to the bread distributed. But three points about the distribution are worth notice. First, the beneficiaries were men without a master, that is to say, without roots in the social system. Secondly, the distribution was made to heads of families. The right to the bread depended upon the father's status. Therefore it was an advantage to the poor to have small families or none. Thirdly, the number of dependants upon public charity was always increasing; and by the fifth century the supplies available for distribution by imperial Authorities were becoming uncertain. Corn for Rome, for example, was often not obtainable, either because of bad harvests in Africa, or because of wars in different provinces. The water-supply and the baths of ancient Rome and of other great cities were also available for the poor, and the destruction of the Roman aqueducts during the barbarian invasions must have made the lives of the poor intolerable. But as the poor became more and more uncertain of support from the State, the Authorities of the Churches in all the great cities increased the distribution of food and clothing among the aged, the widows and other impoverished members of their own communities. This reason alone would be enough to explain the gradual transfer of dependants among the poor from the State to the Church. But the State had provided not only bread but circuses. And even in the fifth century the rich, who held public office, continued to pay large sums for public entertainment, in which the poor, no doubt, found some enjoyment. But although the influence of the Churches was generally opposed to the traditional entertainments, the clergy meantime was developing an elaborate ceremonial which provided an emotional substitute for the old circuses; with the additional advantage that the common people themselves played a part in the processions and other ceremonies of the Church, singing hymns, or electing bishops or receiving the Sacraments. They were no longer merely a cheering crowd of onlookers, but were partakers in the

---

[1] *Cod. Theod.*, xiv, 17. Section 2 requires that the bread shall be handed out from the steps and not from the bakeries (palam in gradibus, non clam a pistoribus).

"Communion of Saints." The general lowering of the standard of living, no doubt, diminished the sense of loss when the aqueducts and the baths were falling into ruin. The change, however, was very gradual; for at the end of the sixth century Pope Gregory remarked in a sermon that some of his congregation went to the baths. But the cities were falling into ruins: and no work of construction for public services continued except the building of churches.

Slavery and Depopulation

For some generations before the fifth century the population of the country districts in Italy and the West had been decreasing. The introduction of the labour of slaves working in gangs had driven out the independent farmers; and as the wars in the East no longer produced a sufficient supply of slaves for the large estates, the lack of agricultural produce in Italy was supplied by import from Egypt and Africa. This made it less necessary to have a working population in the country-side in Italy; and there was a drift to the towns such as always accompanies the exhaustion of an agricultural system. Further, the slave system depends upon a slave-trade in adults, because slaves are either unwilling or unable to rear children; and it does not pay a slave-owner to maintain the children of slaves for the eighteen or twenty years after birth, until they can become efficient instruments of production. Again, a slave system, at least for agriculture, does not employ a sufficient number of women to maintain the birth-rate; for women are useless for hard labour in fields.

For all these reasons, the Roman system of production in the West directly favoured depopulation. And a system which depended for its labour upon successful wars which brought in supplies of slaves, necessarily failed when the supply ceased. In the towns as well as in the country-side the same tendencies were at work. Countries to the East of Italy had supplied slaves in the early days of the Empire, when the slave-trade brought to the great cities of the West men and women already accustomed to slavery in their own countries, and many of them trained in domestic manufactures. But these, too, did not produce children; and depopulation was therefore rapid even in the great cities. Slaves were used increasingly for the supply of private pleasures for the rich, or public entertainment, as in gladiatorial shows. The wars in the East had supplied not only slaves but loot of all kinds; and new tastes for luxury and abnormal practices. The whole of society, throughout the Roman world, for the four centuries before Alaric sacked Rome, was therefore changing from within.

When the wars in the East no longer supported the slave-trade on which the Roman system depended, other and very different slaves began to come in from the wars in Gaul and Britain, on the Rhine and the Danube. These northern slaves were not accustomed to the highly developed slave-system of the Mediterranean countries and the East. They came from the forests, not from captured cities and cultivated fields. They were strong in body and restless under subjection, but without an independent culture of their own. The Germanic or Gothic slaves had another characteristic which made them entirely different from the slaves of earlier times. They had a community of race, and perhaps even of language or dialects and physical resemblances which made it easy for their masters to feel that they were a class apart. At an earlier date the Roman Authorities had thought of imposing a common dress or uniform upon all slaves, in order to keep them in their place. But the plan was never adopted because it was feared that the uniform would show to the slaves themselves how greatly they outnumbered their masters. In the fifth century the slaves in Rome and other great cities were still indistinguishable in dress from the poorer freedmen and artisans. But the northern slaves, with their fair hair and skins and sturdy bearing, were all of the same type, and felt their own numbers to be considerable. The sense of power created sympathy. In all the great cities, therefore, in the early fifth century, there were thousands of household slaves who had no place in society, few rights against their masters, and no feeling of respect or responsibility for the system which held them in its toils, but were conscious of their own common character. The eagerness with which many of them in Gaul welcomed the opportunities for release afforded by the barbarian invasions, is sufficient proof that the slave-system had a corroding influence in the Roman Empire. The thousands of slaves who flocked out of Rome to join the Goths under Alaric provide another indication of the desires of men and women who had no part in the society in which they lived. There was no slave-revolt or slave-war at that time. Nor can it be said that there was anything resembling a proletarian revolution. But the struggle for wealth and power which had continued in western Europe for more than two generations, since the establishment of military dictatorship as a system of government, now began to stir to its depths the ocean of dim feelings which are in the minds of the ignorant and oppressed.

An example of the general confusion is to be found in the activities of the gangs known as Bagaudae or Bacaudae. These were fugitive peasants, artisans and deserters from the army who robbed and plundered where they could, and as early as A.D. 285 had been so active that Maximian, Caesar under Diocletian, had been compelled to lead his army against them. He overcame them in the spring of A.D. 286. But again in A.D. 450, Salvian describes the position of these Bagaudae as if they were in continuous revolt. He says that they have been driven into revolt by taxation and the injustice of officials, and that those who have been despoiled and injured have begun to act as barbarians, because they were not allowed to be Romans. They have been forced to defend at least their lives, because they saw that they had already altogether lost their liberty.[1]

The Rich

In contrast with the slaves and the helpless population of poorer artisans and scattered peasantry, the rich, in all the great cities, were becoming more irresponsible and perhaps more complacent in their ignorance of the real situation. After the sack of Rome by Alaric, many fled to Africa; and St. Augustine reports that they seemed to be more interested in attending the theatres in Carthage than in news of the fate of Italy.[2] Those who had property in

---

[1] Salvian, de Gub. Dei, v, 6. Cf. Hodgkin, Italy, ii, 116.
[2] Aug., de Civ. Dei, i, 28.

Africa sought safety there, if they had sustained losses in Italy. They were, no doubt, not unlike the Irish landlords who had some property in England, to which they could retire during "the troubles" of 1920. For the majority of the richer landowners under the Roman system the preservation and enjoyment of their own personal riches was more important than any system of government. Similarly, about a generation later, Salvian describes the irresponsibility of the rich and their dependants who thronged to public entertainments in the Rhine country after their cities had been sacked.[1]

An account of a rich man's life during the barbarian invasion of Gaul is given in the *Eucharisticus*, by an unknown author who was the grandson of Ausonius, the rhetorician. The author wrote this "thanksgiving poem" in A.D. 459, when he was eighty-three; and he must therefore have been thirty-four years of age when Rome was sacked by Alaric. He had lived most of his life in or near Bordeaux, although he fled for a time from the Goths to Marseilles. He had a small estate at Marseilles and some property in Macedonia; but part of his wealth seems to have come to him, through his wife and father, in estates near Bordeaux. His life as a young man, before the Goths appeared, was precisely that of the wealthy in whose houses, as Salvian says, the slave-girls were merely unpaid prostitutes. The author of the *Eucharisticus* says of himself that he was prudent enough to check his passions by this rule:—to keep his reputation unstained by avoiding the affection of ladies, even though spontaneously offered, "but to be satisfied by servile amours in my own house; for I preferred to be guilty of a sin rather than of an offence in law, lest I might lose my good name. But I shall not be silent about this—one son I know was born to me at that time—though neither he then (since he soon died) nor any bastard of mine afterwards, was ever seen by me—when freedom might have more seriously injured me, if Thou, Christ, had not taken care of me."[2] Thus the good man is grateful to Christ for his complete irresponsibility with regard to his illegitimate children and their mothers. He goes on to describe how he then married a

---

[1] Salvian, *de Gub. Dei*, vi, 15.   [2] *Eucharisticus*, 164-175.

wife with property so that he was able to live in luxury, in "spacious apartments suited to meet the varying seasons of the year; table lavish, my servants many and young, the furniture abundant, and the plate valuable. My workmen skilled, my stables in the best condition, and stabling carriages."[1] And into this charming existence came the Gothic invasion! "And on me, above all, who had a second country in the East, in which I was an owner of great consequence, misfortune came . . . because my house, among all its luxuries, lacked only a Goth as a guest." This had the disastrous result that, because no personal influence protected it, "my house was given up to be pillaged by the retiring horde; for I know that certain of the Goths, most generously, strove to serve their hosts by protecting them."[2]

He proceeds to say how he then tried to make peace with the Goths, as many others prospered through their favour; and "when King Adolf commanded us to leave the city," the Goths stripped him of all his goods, and his house was burned. He was at Bazas when the Goths laid siege to it and tried to make terms for himself; and when the Goths quarrelled with their allies, the Alans, the siege was raised. He then thought of going to his estates in the East "where a large part of my mother's property still remained intact, and the extensive farms well manned by numerous serfs, though scattered, were not widely separated and even for a prodigal or careless lord might have furnished means abundant."[3] But he was unable to leave Gaul, mainly owing to his wife's unwillingness. He decided to become a monk—probably in order to avoid again the responsibility for a family. But, as he says, "through the counsel of the saints" (*consilio sanctorum*) he decided to live under a fixed rule and avoid "corrupt doctrines" (*dogmata prava*). His father had died during the first invasion of the Goths; and now his mother, his wife's mother and his wife also died. Two of his sons, one already a priest, having also died, he settled at Marseilles, "a city in which there were many saints dear to me, but only a small property, part of my family estate." He was reduced to poverty; but a Goth bought his small farm at Marseilles and he retired to

---

[1] *Eucharisticus*, 205–212.   [2] Ibid., 270–290.   [3] Ibid., 413–419.

live, apparently in dependence on a remaining wealthy son, at Bordeaux. The purpose of the whole poem is to thank Christ for having kept him alive and irresponsible for so many years!

The irresponsibility of the rich was not due to personal weakness but to the steady deterioration of their own security under the imperial Dictatorship. The struggle for power between Emperors and between higher officials of the Empire had no more obvious effect than the accumulation of wealth by those who were successful. Wealth, it seemed, could hire military force to defend those who could acquire and increase private fortunes. And those who were already rich might, by a private policy of appeasement, secure defenders and buy off marauders. But such a policy is doomed to failure when traditions are weakened and administration irregular. Even if, for a time, the rich can make armed men their servants, in the end these armed men will thrust the rich aside and divide the spoil among themselves. That has been the history of Fascism in Italy and of the Nazi Dictatorship in Germany; and it was the situation in the Roman Empire in the fifth century, wherever Rome had recruited its soldiers among the barbarians. A man of property in the cities, or one who held estates in agricultural areas, might any day become a victim of the cupidity of armed gangs or of those in control of the Empire or its provinces. But that is not the difficulty with which the documents of those days are most concerned.

The greatest pressure of the Roman system exerted upon the rich was the obligation to fulfil public functions as councillors (*curiales*) in the cities, and to supply troops from the men on their country estates. As the disturbances caused by invading hordes on the Rhine and in northern Italy increased, the demand for troops became more continuous. But, because the country-side in Italy, at least, and perhaps also in other parts of the Empire had been depopulated, it was found necessary by the imperial Authorities to call to service in their armies even artisans and slaves. No doubt, among the rich and educated in the early fifth century, a traditional admiration for the Roman Empire still continued to be felt. But the political situation in the West had been completely changed since Diocletian's division of the Empire and the establishment of the supreme power in Constantinople. The rich in the West, upon whom chiefly the burden rested of maintaining the system which protected their riches, gradually lost any sense of personal duty towards the oriental State. Indeed, the majority of them can hardly have had any knowledge of the intrigues and armed conflicts which decided who was to be their master.

The decrees which attempted to compel those who had municipal obligations (*curiales*), follow one another throughout the early fifth century. And each succeeding decree proves that those preceding it had been ineffectual. Men fled from taxation and the obligations of service, either, if they were rich enough, by obtaining entrance into the ranks of Senators of the Empire, or, if they had become impoverished, by seeking the protection of some powerful neighbour. Some descended far in the social scale and became workers on country estates, others joined the clergy.

The Emperors sought to compel those who had inherited obligations as *curiales* to return to their positions in the cities; because the diminution in the numbers of the city councillors always involved a decrease in public services and in the sources of taxation for the Empire; and, as the rescript of A.D. 341 says, "it is inconvenient for the State that the city councils should be weakened by not having enough members."[1] The whole of the first section of the twelfth book of the Theodosian law-books, consisting of one hundred and ninety-two rescripts or edicts, deals with city councillors (*curiales* or *decuriones*). The first imperial order is dated A.D. 313, and the last A.D. 436; and nearly all are concerned with preventing the members of municipal councils from escaping their obligations. One legal escape is allowed by a decree of A.D. 363, namely that the father of thirteen children may be freed from his civic obligations. The decrees of Honorius and Arcadius, the Emperors of the years 410 and 415, make it clear that the obligations

---

[1] *Cod. Theod.*, xii, i, 32 (Aug. 17th, A.D. 341). "Nam rei publicae incommodum est curias hominum paucitate languescere."

of *curiales* are to be enforced.[1] And in the *New Laws* of Majorian, a long decree of the year 458 continues the imperial complaint that the *curiales* are deserting their positions. This decree begins— "*Curiales*, as everyone knows, are the sinews of the State and the vitals of cities; and their council was rightly called of old a lesser Senate. But the injustice of officials, and the bribes paid to pliable tax-collectors, cause many to desert their native places, to despise the honour of their birth, and seek hiding-places on country estates, adding to their dishonour marriage with farm women and servant girls. So it comes about that the upper classes disappear in the cities; and some lose their status as free men by contact with the lower classes." These refugees are to be compelled to return to their duties as councillors; and "those who have tried to escape by joining the clergy, if they are still below the rank of deacon, should be forced back to their civil duties. . . . If, however, any of these is already a deacon, priest or bishop, he is to have no power of disposal over his property."[2]

The attempt to restrain the internal nomadism, which weakened the structure of the Empire, was based upon ideas of organization which were obsolete. The forces at work were too strong for imperial decrees to control them. The imperial Authorities tried to cure the symptoms of social dissolution without understanding their cause. But de-urbanization was inevitable in the general uncertainty of supplies and the decline of trade and agricultural production. The very forces which drove men "to hide on country estates" were in fact replacing the city civilization of the Roman Empire by the country civilization of the Middle Ages. The local community of an agricultural area was becoming the basis of a new social order.

The impoverishment of the cities, and therefore the undermining of the city civilization on which the Empire was based, was largely due to the pressure of taxation for the needs of the imperial system. But while some of the *curiales* were impoverished or driven to take refuge under the protection of more wealthy men, some were

[1] *Cod. Theod.*, xii, i, 178 (Jan. 21st, 415). "Omnes, qui curiali genere origine vel stirpe gignuntur, curiarum nexibus obligentur."   [2] *Nov. Majorian*, vii.

increasing their wealth and entering the rank of imperial Senators. Imperial legislation obstructed this movement upwards.[1] But it is quite clear that, while the poor were becoming poorer, the rich were becoming much more powerful. Thus, the members of the senatorial body could escape taxation by pressure upon imperial officials, and even control in their own interests the administration of justice. The "powerful" (*potentes*) could protect their dependants, as local lords could in the Middle Ages. The laws provide against attempts of "the powerful" to escape jurisdiction;[2] and forbid them to sit on the bench with the judge.[3] But evidently the same sort of pressure was being exerted by the rich landowner as that which continued well into the nineteenth century in England by the authority of justices of the peace. Again, the rich, seeking refuge themselves from the disturbances of the times, sometimes fortified their buildings in the country, and paid retainers who could defend them. They were thus helping to undermine the centralization of authority in the Roman Empire and, almost unconsciously, establishing independent local governments. Within the structure of the single, universal Empire they were planting the seeds of medieval lordships.

Of the rich in the towns, there is evidence, fifty years before Alaric sacked Rome, in the account given by Ammianus Marcellinus of the ostentation and the crowds of slaves by which the wealthy were surrounded.[4] Olympiodorus says that in Rome at the time of Alaric's invasion, the houses of the rich were like towns in themselves, with their baths and entertainment halls.[5] And from St. Jerome's letters we learn that the appetite for wealth and ostentation was to be found, not only among Christian ladies with jewelled prayer books, but even, as he says, in his own order—that is among the clergy. He wrote a bitter description of a deacon in Rome, carefully groomed and affected in his movements, who haunted

---

[1] *Cod. Theod.*, xii, i, 171 (A.D. 409). "Principales viri"—not allowed to leave their order until five years service is completed.

[2] Ibid., i, 16, 4 (A.D. 328, Constantine). Si quis potiorum. . . .

[3] Ibid., i, 20, 1 (A.D. 408, Honorius). Honorati . . . residendi cum iudice non habeant facultatem.

[4] Amm. Marcell., *Hist.*, xxviii, 4.

[5] Olymp., *ap. Phot.Myriobiblion, Pat. Graec.* vol. 103, col. 278.

the houses of rich ladies.[1] Thus we have, on the one hand, an increasingly powerful rich class of landowners on country estates, and an increasingly irresponsible and idle body of rich men and women in the cities. The appetite for private power among some rich men and the irresponsibility of others were potent causes of the ruin of the system from which they derived advantage.

The Barbarians

Into this old Roman world, hardly able to control the forces within its own borders, came the barbarians of the Germanic tribes, east of the Rhine and north of the Danube. The armed men under chieftains, who thus disturbed the communities of the Roman Empire, were themselves without settled homes, without roots in the soil, and without interest in the common labour which is the source of wealth, because they thought they could procure wealth more easily by plunder. To men of the older tradition the Goths seemed fitter to be slaves for sale than warriors. The Emperor Julian, in the year 363, when "his intimates tried to persuade him to attack the neighbouring Goths who were often deceitful and treacherous, replied that he was looking for a better enemy, and that the slave-traders could look after the Goths whom they offered for sale everywhere without distinction of rank."[2] And yet Goths and members of other savage tribes were not only recruited in bands under their leaders into the Roman forces, but as individuals often rose to important positions in the army and at Court. Such men had no real understanding of the old Roman tradition. There was always therefore the danger of treachery when a Roman army, including officers from among the tribes they were fighting, was in close contact with these tribes. In A.D. 354, for example, when the Emperor Constantius was on the Rhine, a guide was bribed to show him a ford "and the army might have crossed, had not a few men of that same race, who held military positions of high rank, informed their countrymen of the design, by secret messengers, as some thought. Suspicion fell upon Latimus, count

---

[1] Jerome, Ep., 22, c. 28. Rufinus declares, however, that Jerome was unfair to the clergy. [2] Amm. Marcell., Hist., xxii, 7, 8.

of the bodyguard, Agilo, tribune of the stables, and Scudilo, commander of the Targeteers, who were then highly regarded as having in their hands the defence of the State."[1]

The situation had become even more difficult by the end of the fourth century. That armed men, hired to defend the rich and the Roman system by which millions were held under the control of the rich, should make common cause with those of their own race who were slaves in Roman households, was but a natural development. This danger to society had been foreseen. Synesius, in his treatise on "The Supreme Power," had proposed the exclusion of non-Romans from political and military positions of influence, and had pointed out the danger of sympathy between men of the same race acting both as slaves and as soldiers. His treatise, in the form of a speech, was published in Constantinople about A.D. 400, and was addressed to the Emperor Arcadius.[2] He writes:—

First, let all be excluded from magistracies, and kept away from the privileges of the council, who are ashamed of all that has been sacred to the Romans from olden times, and has been so esteemed. Of a truth both Themis herself sacred to the Senate, and the god of our battle lore, must, I think, cover their faces when the man with leathern jerkin marches in command of those that wear the general's cloak, and whenever such an one divests himself of the sheepskin in which he was clad, to assume the toga, and enters the council chamber to deliberate on matters of State with the Roman magistrates, having a prominent seat perhaps next the consul, while the lawful men sit behind him. Then again, such as these, when they have gone a little way from the assembly, are again attired in their sheepskins, and once in company of their fellows, laugh the toga to scorn, and aver that they cannot even draw the sword in comfort with it. For my part I wonder at many other things, but not least at this over-absurd conduct. All this is in the face of the fact that every house, however humble, has a Scythian for a slave.[3] The butler, the cook, the water-carrier, all are Scythians, and as to retinue, the slaves who bend under the burden of the low couches on their shoulders that their masters may recline in the streets, these are all Scythians also; for it has been proved of old that theirs is the most useful race, and the fittest to serve the Romans. But that these fair-haired

[1] Amm. Marcell., *Hist.*, xiv, 10, 7, 8.
[2] See Bury's Appendix, p. 482, in Gibbon, vol. iii (ed. 1897).
[3] "Scythian" is the common name in Greek for "Goth."

men who arrange their locks like the Ereboeans should be slaves in private to the same men whom they govern in public, this is strange, and perhaps the most incredible feature of the spectacle; and I know not what sort of a thing the so-called "riddle" may be, if this is not one. In Gaul, Crixus and Spartacus practised the calling of arms in dishonour, in order to become the victims of the Roman populace in the arena; but, when they accepted and bore a grudge against the laws, they engaged in the so-called slave-war which became the most calamitous campaign of those which the Romans of that time encountered. Against these slaves they had every need of consuls, of praetors, and of the happy fortune of Pompey; for their city was nearly ravaged off the face of the earth. And yet those who revolted along with the Spartacus and Crixus, were not of the same race as they, nor of the same race as each other. Notwithstanding this, the fate which they shared in common furnished them with a pretext and made them of the same mind. It is, I suppose, in the nature of things that every slave is the enemy of his master once he has hopes of overcoming him. Is the case then the same with us also? Are we nourishing on an altogether greater scale the germs of untoward troubles? Remember that in our case there are not only two men, and those dishonoured individuals, heading a rebellion; but great pernicious armies, who, kinsmen of our own slaves, have by evil destiny poured into the Roman Empire and furnished generals of great repute both amongst themselves and amongst us. . . .[1]

The barbarians, both as soldiers under the Roman Empire, and as invaders, were divided into many different tribes under separate leaders. Some indeed had been induced to settle on empty lands within the Roman Empire. But the majority of the raiders who wandered about Gaul and Spain, and eventually reached Africa, were nomadic by inclination. They lived by loot and they destroyed what they could not steal. Some might take service for a time under a provincial leader or a Roman official; but they had no desire to enter into the productive system; for clearly that system still depended upon slavery; and slavery the barbarians would not accept, unless they had been overwhelmingly defeated.

The entry into the Roman system of this destructive force gradually reduced available supplies in agriculture and trade, and had an immediate effect, both in making poverty more widespread and in depopulation. In addition, all the barbarian tribes

[1] Synesius, *On Kingship*, trans. Fitzgerald, p. 135.

aimed chiefly at increasing their own wealth; and all were therefore open to bribery. They would serve any master; and each armed band could be bought and used to fight against other barbarians.[1] They were treacherous, drunken and violent in their passions; and even Salvian, who contrasts them favourably in some respects with those in control of the Roman system, writes that "the Saxons are savage, the Franks treacherous, the Gepids inhuman, the Huns lustful; and indeed the life of all the barbarian tribes is one long vice."[2]

Clearly the noble savage is a romantic myth. The Germanic and other barbarians who entered the Roman Empire either as soldiers for pay or as raiders for loot, were not more trustworthy or high-minded or chaste than the civilized populations over which they obtained control. But personal virtues or good intentions are of no importance for the argument here. It is useless to discuss whether the barbarians were more or less virtuous individually. The important point is that they did not understand, and therefore could not maintain or reform the complicated social system of the Roman Empire. Their simpler experience gave them no insight into the problems of social justice; and although some of them were trained as soldiers in the Roman armies, they had no knowledge of commerce, transport, law or civil administration. Their entry into the Empire therefore was inevitably disruptive.

General Character of the Early Fifth Century

From one point of view, the situation in the western parts of the Roman Empire in the first half of the fifth century was that of a society in dissolution. Everyone who could was saving himself. Those who had nothing to lose welcomed the control of any master who could offer them security. And the general decrease in the resources of civilized life spread a sense of futility over the normal interests of men. All this made it easy for the majority to accept, when they thought at all, the Christian conception that the whole world was soon to pass away. Clearly something more than

[1] Amm. Marcell., *Hist.*, xv, 530: fluxioris fidei et ubertate mercedis ad momentum omne versabiles.   [2] Salv., *de Gub. Dei*, iv. 41.

individual life was ending. Those who survived the widespread ruin could feel only anxiety for their fate and hope that their terrors would soon be removed. On the other hand, food and clothing and shelter were still worth working for, if they could be had. And, as at all times, the more energetic men and women managed to collect a certain amount of goods and services for their own advantage.

But while in theory, and perhaps in the belief of the majority the last age had come, and the Last Judgement was soon to occur, almost unconsciously the people of the fifth century were laying the foundations of a new social and political system—that of the European Middle Ages. Their Churches and kingdoms in the fifth century were not intended to survive for long. They were at the end of time, as far as they could tell; and yet they established the foundations of customs and beliefs which endured for more than a thousand years.

Looked at more closely, the changes which seem to be signs of dissolution can be seen to have had in them, even in the early fifth century, traces of new associations, new groupings, new moral ideals and new social institutions which were to become the established commonplaces of later centuries. In the first place, the struggle between Paganism and Christianity already showed in the fifth century that Christianity in the Churches was the only possible basis for a community in which all classes of society could work together. The traditional Paganism was, on the one hand, an upper-class survival and, on the other, a mere remnant of local rituals, different in every place and dividing rather than uniting the Roman world. But Christianity had a firmly established organization of its own, based upon the power of the bishops and uniting men and women of all classes and races. Here then were the first signs of the medieval Church.

Secondly, the supply of slaves was gradually decreasing; and the poor who had found no roots in the Roman system, were gradually establishing themselves as dependants with rights of their own on the estates of the rich and the powerful. Local lordships, at first Roman in origin, and later under barbarian control, were taking the place of the old imperial system. And the local lord served his own dependants as a ruler and judge and organizer of mutual defence against marauding bands or against powerful neighbours. These local lordships no longer looked to the imperial Court, either for actual power or moral prestige. And the fact that the lords of the land and the bishops of important cities could act both as protectors and judges of their people supported the general tendency towards a localization of authority. If it is noted further that the local lordships tended to become hereditary, with the inheritance of property, this may be taken as a forecast of the medieval system, known later as feudal. Finally, the wandering bands of armed men, taking service eventually under this or that king or duke—the barbarians organized in a primitive military system—were the forerunners of the knights and armed retainers of medieval dukes and kings. Thus the history of the fifth century is by no means only one of dissolution. If there is decay, it is the decay of a seed already beginning to throw out roots which will later support a great tree.

The Climate of Opinion

But the seeds would not have grown unless the soil of established custom had been ploughed up by material disasters and distresses in the minds of men. The sense of helplessness which was prevalent in western Europe in the early fifth century undermined that confidence in the established order which was the chief obstacle to the creation of a new system of civilization. But the feeling that one has no part to play in a tragedy which involves one's own house is not necessarily due to moral inertia or a failure of nerve. Indeed the divisions and disorders within the Roman Empire prove that great numbers of men and women were unwilling to make the effort required for the maintenance of the old order, not because they were not good enough to fulfil their civic duties, but because they were too good to be satisfied with a system from which so few derived benefit.

The mind of the time was uprooted—*déraciné*: it had become nomadic. A poet, quoted above, sang that exile was no evil, because the whole world was a single house; and the historian, Orosius, wrote that everywhere he went he was at home. Again, while the minds of men were freed from the restrictions of time and place, those who thought and felt deeply about the events of their day were in disagreement. Each sect among the Christians, each party among the pagans, went its own way; and so uncertain was the future, that the chief interest of poets and preachers was to discover some method by which they could acquire again the certainty of expectation which the collapse of the social system had destroyed. In a world which seemed to be united only by the overarching sky, all agreed to look upward. Some held that the future could be discovered from the study of the stars; and even some Christians—the followers of Priscillian—seemed to have been affected by this desire to discover a fixed law governing events. Others, also looking upwards, found there a personal Will which decided the issue; and these had the advantage over the star-gazers in their conviction that the fundamental issue was the conflict between good and evil. On the other hand, the disadvantage of a belief in a personal Will, as the chief cause of historical events, is that such a belief involves blind trust in what appear to be arbitrary decisions. The star-gazers were looking for a general law, not an imperial Decree. But the doubt about the future for the individual and the race at least set the mind free from the assumptions of the old order. The mind must become nomadic in order to search for a new settlement.

The dominant belief, however, by the middle of the fifth century was that the end of all things was near. The sudden death of thousands in war or in the famines following upon war, and the increased likelihood of premature death for each, made the end of individual life seem to be evidence of the near approach of the destruction of the universe. But this was an emotional reaction, not a rational conclusion. The death of individuals, and even the disappearance of nations, is no proof of the mortality of the race; and the failure of one system of civilization provides no evidence for the belief that civilization itself is in danger. But the belief that the end of all things is at hand has the great advantage of releasing the minds of men from too great a dependence upon the customs and beliefs of an established order. Even the faith, so vigorously expressed by St. Augustine, that there was a permanent existence in another world beyond the sky and beneath the earth, brought comfort to men and women who had been brought up to believe that the Roman Empire was eternal and saw it collapsing under their eyes. Thus the other-worldliness, by which the early Middle Ages were dominated, was itself an imaginative preconception which proved in practice useful for the creation of new institutions. These replaced the social system of the ancient world and provided the foundations for the First Europe.

Medieval institutions were established almost "in a fit of absence of mind," while what was permanent and eternal was transferred in the imagination from the universal Empire to the Kingdom in the skies. At any rate, the illusion of eternity was no longer applied to the Roman Empire. *Roma aeterna* became *Roma caelestis*: the eternal City of this world became the Heavenly City. And the practical problems of man on earth became for the imagination what they actually are—transitional adjustments to a changing situation. The disappearance of the belief in the eternity of the Roman system left men free to make social experiments. But unfortunately for them, and for later ages, the ghost of the Empire still survived in the magic of the name of Rome.

CHAPTER III

DECLINE OF MORAL AUTHORITY

The "Glory of the Romans," inscribed upon Roman coins, was derived partly from successful wars, partly from the moral authority of a system of law and public services. Power may be an instrument of moral authority, but cannot provide a substitute for it. Victory alone serves only to blind the victors and to paralyse their victims. Therefore, those who hold power by force of arms inevitably seek the support of moral and religious influences.

The fraud, the greed, the murderous violence by which Roman conquests were achieved, were forgotten when those who resisted were dead and those who yielded were enslaved. And when the Roman Republic, unable to control its treacherous and avaricious governors, passed from party politics to civil wars and bloody riots in Rome itself, the oligarchy of senators was eventually replaced by a military dictatorship. Julius Caesar is said to have secured a million slaves as the proceeds of adventure in Gaul; and he himself wrote a carefully falsified account of what he had done. He went to Gaul for loot, and not for the advancement of civilized life. The bitter comment of his contemporary, Cicero, brings out the contrast: "So long as our government depended, not upon injustice and violence, but upon service and kindliness, wars were waged to protect our allies or defend our honour; and their results were accompanied by mercy, or at least by no more force than was needed. . . . This city was not then the Empress, but the protector of the world. . . . Now there has come one after Sulla (Cicero does not name Julius Caesar) whose cause was impious and his victory scandalous and inhuman."[1] But the influence of unknown men who did not aim only at private wealth and personal power,

[1] Cicero, *Off*, ii, 8.

covered the tracks of blood and tears where Caesar had slaughtered men and burnt their poor homes. In the same way, in modern times, the first English who went to Africa took slaves to sell in the West Indies; but a later generation established a form of justice and liberty among the populations whom the slave traders had almost destroyed.[1]

Augustus began the establishment of a new Roman Empire upon the ruins left by civil wars; and mythology, in poetry and history, was enlisted to adorn the unseemly facts upon which the system rested. Under Augustus, Virgil appealed to the traditional religion; and Livy set himself to make propaganda, disguised as history, for the idea that Roman conquests made amends by their results for the looting and slaughter and treachery which were the means of obtaining victory. The falsification of history served to justify military dictatorship in the early years of the Christian era; and it has been used many times since, for example, by Machiavelli and his followers, to hide the ugly facts of the slave-system and the exploitation of the poor, which were the real bases of Roman peace.

The Roman Empire was not worse than the many other Empires which had preceded it. All had been formed by foreign conquest, undertaken for the sake of obtaining slaves and other loot. And all had been based upon the exploitation of the great majority of men and women by a few leaders of ability. Slavery, no doubt, is a step forward from the primitive slaughter of conquered peoples, such as the Hebrews are reported in their sacred books to have practised in their conquest of Palestine. But slavery itself was an insecure basis for production and the arts, because it assumed that great numbers of men and women can be treated as cattle; and it always had disastrous effects upon the moral stamina of those who maintained it. It must not be imagined, however, that the tribes which were conquered and enslaved by the Romans were any better morally or in their social institutions than their conquerors.

---

[1] In the days of the Republic Paulus Aemilius sold one hundred and fifty thousand slaves taken in Epirus, and Marius the same number, taken in Gaul. Augustus took forty-four thousand slaves after one campaign. And ninety-nine thousand Jews were sold as slaves after the sack of Jerusalem by Titus. See Wallon, *Histoire de l'Esclavage*, ii, 33 sq.

The use of armed force for the sake of obtaining loot and cheap labour was common among all peoples: the more efficient in the application of force and fraud were the more successful.

The civilizations which have arisen in slave societies have all disappeared. The Roman was the last of them in western Europe. But for many centuries the Roman Empire was, like others before it, an instrument of order in law and administration, and of certain forms of social justice. Its extent was great enough to bring together many diverse tribes, religions and types of culture; and for this reason, whatever the character of the forces which brought it into existence, and however unstable the foundations upon which it rested, the Roman Empire, during the first four centuries of the Christian era, maintained and developed a new form of civilized life. Great advances were made in the technique of agriculture and building. Social institutions were adjusted to meet the needs of a more humane and peaceful community. Roman peace gave security to large areas against invasion, and provided against violence and other crimes within its borders. The sufferings of slaves were reduced by law and administration, under the influence of Greek philosophy, when the great Roman jurists accepted the Stoics' teaching that slavery itself was not natural to man. And in the three centuries after Augustus civil wars, arising out of the impossibility of finding a rule of succession in a dictatorship, sometimes disturbed, but did not destroy, the commerce and intellectual intercourse of Roman civilization.

In the four centuries between Augustus and Alaric, the military dictatorship went through many changes. Soon after the death of Augustus the "secret" was discovered that an Emperor could be made elsewhere than at Rome by any band of soldiers reckless enough to make their favourite a candidate for the purple;[1] and for three centuries all attempts failed to solve the problem which is fundamental in dictatorships—the problem of succession. At one time the dictator would look round to find some competent person to succeed him, whom he could adopt; at another the dictator

---

[1] Evulgato imperii arcano, posse principem alibi quam Romae fieri. Tacitus, *Histories*, i, 4.

would try to pass on his power to his son. But the struggle for supreme power was always a struggle between small groups of armed men; and the majority of those who called themselves Roman citizens throughout the Empire, after the first century had neither interest nor influence in the choice of a ruler.

But the possession of power (*vis*), of which the Roman Empire had enough, was long recognized to be less important than the exercise of moral authority (*auctoritas*); and different methods were adopted during the four centuries after Augustus for the main-tenance and increase of this authority. In a very summary form, three stages may be distinguished in the methods by which the Roman Emperors before the fifth century endeavoured to fortify their moral authority. First, under Augustus and his immediate successors, the great civil wars were still so recent that dictatorship could be supported as the only practical method of maintaining peace. The *Pax Romana* meant not merely security against invasion but also peace among the Romans themselves. Again, the prestige of the old order was, in theory, transferred to Augustus as *Princeps*; and the moral authority of the Senate was supposed to be concen-trated in the hands of the Emperor. The ancient rites of Roman religion, connected with a community of peasants, were revived—perhaps in order to protect the authority of the Roman tradition from the danger of Orientalism.[1]

The second stage is marked by the efforts of the Antonines to infuse Greek, and especially Stoic, philosophy into the spirit of the Roman Empire. In this period the Emperor derived moral authority from the fact that he was a single and universal providence (*providentia*) in a cosmopolitan society. The principles of Roman juris-prudence in this period were given that appearance of universal application which has made it possible for Roman Law to survive the Roman Empire. But already moral authority was sought outside the Roman tradition; and the later Emperors of this period played with the possibility of reinforcing their moral authority by the use of Oriental religions.

[1] Under Augustus the worship of the Ruler as divine was deliberately begun, especially in the Provinces. See Beurlier, *Le Culte Impérial* (1891).

The third stage was reached under Diocletian, who was Emperor from A.D. 284 to A.D. 305. The Roman Empire then openly turned to the East for a mystical and moral reinforcement of its authority as a system of government. Diocletian seems to have hoped to establish an imperial Monotheism, using sun-worship, which had become widespread especially in the army under the influence of the religion of Mithras. The Emperor himself withdrew from the public gaze; and forms of Oriental ruler-worship took the place of the carefully considered simplicity of Augustus and the Antonines. From this point of view the policy of Constantine the Great in seeking the support of the Christian Churches merely transferred the source of moral authority for the Roman Empire from one Oriental religion to another. But the results of this transference proved to be revolutionary. The Emperor soon became involved in theological controversies; and although there was an anti-Christian reaction under Julian, and a tendency to support Arianism under other Emperors, by the beginning of the fifth century the moral authority of the Empire definitely depended upon "Orthodox" or "Catholic" Christianity. The Emperors were no longer "divine" in the old sense; but they reflected, in their own persons, the authority of Christ over law and government and, therefore, they had what was called in later ages divine right.

The attempt to give moral prestige to imperial authority by the use of religion was begun quite consciously under Augustus. The name "Augustus" was chosen, as Suetonius reports, by Octavianus, the nephew and heir of Julius Caesar, for its associations with augury, and as an alternative to the name "Romulus"; because, although Octavianus felt himself to be a new founder of Rome, he preferred a more impressive name than that of the first founder.[1] The name

---

[1] Suetonius: *Lives of Caesars, Augustus, c.* vii. Infanti cognomen Thurino inditum est, in memoriam maiorum originis: vel . . . Postea C. Caesaris, et deinde Augusti cognomen adsumsit: alterum, testamento maioris avunculi: alterum, Munatii Planci sententia: cum, quibusdam censentibus Romulum adpellari oportere, quasi et psum conditorem urbis, praevaluisset, ut Augustus potius vocaretur, non tantum novo, sed etiam ampliore cognomine, quod loca quoque religiosa, et in quibus augurato quid consecratur, augusta dicantur, ab auctu, vel ab avium gestu, gustuve, sicut etiam Ennius docet, scribens—

Augusto augurio postquam inclyta condita Roma est.

The *Mirabilia Romae*, a guide-book to the city of Rome, which was used in the early twelfth century, has another derivation. It says that "Augustus" is derived from "augere"—because Augustus "increased the Empire"!

"Augustus" continued throughout the centuries that followed to be the chief title of a reigning emperor. The edicts and letters of Emperors in the law-books of Theodosius and Justinian all begin by giving the title "Augustus" after the personal name of the emperor, without the word "Imperator." But even as late as the fourth century "Augustus" remained something more than a title. It was an adjective implying reverence, as in the thanksgiving of Ausonius, addressed to the Emperor Gratian, where Gratian is addressed as "Imperator Auguste" and "Auguste Iuvenis" and again as "Augustus Sanctitate."

A further expression of the nature of the prestige in the supreme authority is to be found in the use of such words as *providentia*, *clementia*, and *serenitas* to express the function which the Emperor performed in the Roman world.[1] He was the "providence," foresight or care, to which all his subjects were taught to look. He had the position of a divine providence. On inscriptions and on coins the imperial authority was thus held up to its subjects as a power of beneficence in all parts of the known world. That power was personal; and it was the power of one man,—never in practice a woman, until the early fifth century under Galla Placidia. And as the man was traditionally "divus" or divine, his associations with the celestial Powers were obviously much closer than those of ordinary mortals. The moral authority of the Emperor, therefore, and of the imperial system, was due in part to religious or philosophical conceptions, consciously used by the holders of power for maintaining their control.

The clearest sign of the connection of the Emperor with the celestial Powers is the nimbus or halo, which was later used in representations of Christ and later still in those of the Saints. The nimbus represents the sun. It belonged originally to the sun-god (*sol invictus*); and its use in representations of the Emperor is connected with early attempts to introduce Monotheism by means of sun-worship. There are coins and medallions still surviving which

---

[1] Charlesworth, *Harvard Theological Review*, xxix, 1936. *Providentia* and *Aeternitas* and *H.T.R.*, xxviii, 1935, *Ruler-Cult*. Also *The Virtues of a Roman Emperor*, Brit. Acad., 1937, for "*clementia*" and "*pietas*."

show the Emperor Antoninus Pius (A.D. 138–161) wearing a radiate nimbus.[1] After Diocletian this becomes more common. There are medallions showing the nimbus round the heads of the Emperor Constantine the Great, his wife Fausta,[2] Constantius, Constans, Valentinian I, Valens, Theodosius I, Arcadius, Honorius and Galla Placidia. The inscription *Gloria Romanorum* on some of these medallions and coins is clearly connected with the nimbus.

When the Empire became officially Christian, the worship of the Emperor ceased; and the nimbus was used in representations of Christ. The earliest known example of a saint represented with a nimbus is St. Lawrence on the tomb of Galla Placidia of about A.D. 450. In the mosaic of about A.D. 526 in the Church of SS. Cosmas and Damian in Rome, Christ "in glory" has a nimbus; but not St. Peter or St. Paul.[3] The nimbus still remained a sign of imperial majesty in the mosaics of Justinian and Theodora of about A.D. 547, in the church now called S. Vitale in Ravenna. But, by about A.D. 550, all the saints on the walls of Sant' Apollinare Nuovo wear the nimbus. The moral authority directly held by the Emperor in the fourth century had been transferred to Christ and the communion of saints by the middle of the sixth century. The sign of the sun-god now therefore belonged properly to Christ, who, in the hymn of Saint Ambrose, is "the true Sun."[4]

What is moral authority?

For four centuries a certain moral authority survived in the dictator of the moment, his representatives in the Empire and the institutions which held together in one community the peoples of many different races and languages in the Roman world. Moral authority, in this sense, is the influence which keeps most men's

---

[1] I am indebted to Miss Jocelyn Toynbee for all the details about the use of the nimbus. There is an altar, in the Capitoline Museum, Rome, of the third century, dedicated to Sol Sanctissimus, on which the sun-god is represented wearing the radiate nimbus.

[2] On the reverse of a gold medallion Fausta Augusta, wearing a halo, is seated on a throne holding a baby on her lap and surrounded by female figures and genii.

[3] See illustration facing page 224.

[4] "Diem, dies illuminans verusque sol, illabere."

actions within the limits of established custom, even when there is no external force operating upon them. This moral authority is embodied in the *mana*, or magic power, which resides in the priests and kings of primitive society. It is the force which binds men together under law; and whether based upon ignorance and superstition or upon a clear perception of moral values, it is the fundamental basis without which no system of government can stand. The success of Roman arms had, no doubt, contributed something to the moral authority of the imperial system, because simple men always imagine that God is on the winning side. The very fact of victory, therefore, even when obtained by treachery and murder, gives the sort of blessing to established Power which provides a primitive form of moral authority. When victory follows upon victory and the area and population increase over which the victors hold sway, the original belief that something more than human is on their side seems to receive confirmation. Occasional defeats and internal disorder are readily believed to be signs of divine displeasure; but the survival of the system itself, even after disaster and in spite of the obvious villainy in its representatives, seems to prove all the more forcibly that it is eternal.

Rome itself and, in its name, the Roman Empire, at the beginning of the fifth century, were believed to be "eternal" by everyone at that time who thought at all on such subjects. In four centuries the Roman Empire had become, for its victims and still more obviously for its beneficiaries, a part of the nature of things. Whether Fate or Fortune or the Gods or Rome itself, worshipped as a Goddess, was believed to be the cause of this eternity, no one really doubted that the history of human institutions had reached its final phase. Even the Christian writers of the fourth and earlier centuries thought of the Roman system as the last before the final dissolution of the world. The Christians had at first hoped for the destruction of the "new Babylon," which persecuted the Churches, before the final establishment of the Kingdom of God. And after the acceptance of imperial support by Christianity in the fourth century, all Christian writers agreed that no other form of political authority would exist on earth before the Last Judgement. As Lactantius wrote: "The problem itself shows that the fall and ruin of the world will shortly take place; except that while the city of Rome remains it appears that nothing of this kind is to be feared. But when that capital of the world shall have fallen, and shall have been set afire, which the Sibyls say shall come to pass, who can doubt that the end has now arrived for the affairs of men and the whole world? It is that city, that only, which still sustains all things; and the God of heaven is to be entreated by us and implored—if, indeed, his designs and decrees can be delayed—lest, sooner than we think, that detestable tyrant should come who will undertake so great a deed, and dig out that eye, by the destruction of which the world itself is about to fall."[1]

The very fact that the Roman system was believed to be either eternal or the last of all the ages, gave it a certain "sanctity." The word *sanctus* includes both a reference to magic powers and reference to moral authority. Thus from very early times a tribune or other public Authority was referred to as *sanctus*; and in later times the Emperor is addressed as *sanctissimus Imperator*.[2] Established public Authority, whatever its origin in fraud or violence, was regarded as, in some sense, divinely appointed; and therefore when Constantine accepted the assistance of the Christian Churches, no change was necessary in the traditional conceptions either of the old religions or of Christianity, in order to give him the prestige of divine authority.

For centuries the Roman Emperors had claimed to be themselves divine and, at death at least, to become actually Gods. They shared the worship directed towards the system under the title of the Goddess Rome herself. Deification of former Emperors reflected light upon the soldier who, having given sufficient bribes to his troops, could call himself Emperor, or upon the feeble descendant of some strong man. And yet the road to deification for many of the Emperors was death at the hands of their successors. The man who was treated as a God after his death had in fact often succumbed to something very different from worship. "In some instances a timely dose of poison or a judicious arrangement of the bed-clothes

---

[1] Lactantius, *Div. Instit.*, vii, 25.   [2] Pliny to Trajan: *Sanctissime Imperator.*

over the mouth had hastened his departure from a world in which his presence was no longer convenient."[1]

The word *sanctus* continued to be used, even under the Christian Emperors, to indicate the prestige or moral authority of an established order; and in the fifth century it had only just begun to imply that moral quality now suggested by the word "holy." The "Imperium Romanum" was *sanctum*, as the Emperor was *Sanctissimus*, long before the foundation of the so-called Holy Roman Empire. Gregory the Great at the end of the sixth century used the phrase "Holy Empire";[2] but the word *sanctum* expressed the moral authority of an established order rather than moral excellence in the modern sense. The Christian saints were originally called *beati* and not *sancti*; and holy men during their lifetime were referred to as *beatissimi*, although spiritual advisers having moral authority were sometimes called *sancti*.[3] The sacredness of imperial Authority at the beginning of the fifth century is expressed in the titles used for themselves by the Emperors in their decrees. These titles are generally either "our clemency" (as in an edict of A.D. 402) or "my eternity" (as in an edict of A.D. 405).[4] Everything connected with the Emperor is "sacred" (*sacrum*). The central office of the Empire is the *"sacrum palatium"*; control is in the hands of the "Controller of the sacred bedroom" (*Primicerius sacri cubiculi*); and the finance minister is "Count of the Sacred Largesses."[5]

Thus by an elaborate use of language with religious and traditional flavour, the military dictator was raised above the forces of criticism or discontent and was generally accepted as part of the natural or divine order of things. And thus the source of authority, which had, however vaguely, been felt in earlier times to be the choice or consent of the Roman people, was now believed to come directly from heaven. The change which had been skilfully designed by Augustus to undermine possible opposition among the older

[1] Hodgkin, *Italy*, i, p. 203.   [2] *Greg. Mag. Ep.*, v, 38. *M.G.H.*, *Sanctum Imperium*.
[3] As in the *Eucharisticus*, see above, Chapter ii. For the use of the word *Sanctus*, see H. Delahaye, *"Sanctus."*   [4] *Cod. Theod.*, xxiv, 17, 14, and xii, 1, 160.
[5] As in the *Notitia Dignitatum Romani Imperii*. This is a list of officials of the Empire in the East and the West, of which the existing versions probably date from about A.D. 400 with additions of later date.

families of Rome by connecting him with early Roman religion, began after Constantine to operate in favour of the conception of public authority which was common among the bishops of the Christian Churches. The divine right of whatever military dictator contrived to seize imperial authority rested ultimately upon the popular conception that the Emperor was indeed divine and that his Empire was sacred or holy. And the immense prestige of the established system in all parts of the Empire, derived from its association with the overarching heavens, was more than enough to hide from the beneficiaries, and even from its victims, the slavery, oppression and impoverishment of the majority which were among its essential characteristics.

So far the titles and the prestige of Roman Emperors might seem to be derived from the tradition of the early successors of Augustus and therefore of Rome itself. But clearly some eastern influence had already begun to affect the conception of authority within the Roman system long before Constantine. Diocletian was the first to introduce into the practice and conception of the supreme authority a frankly Oriental costume and ritual. The change that he brought upon the Roman system had two aspects. On the one hand he improved the centralized administration; and on the other, he increased the prestige or magic power of the Emperor by aloofness from the old Roman traditions and by the introduction of an Oriental pageantry at his Court. This same movement away from Roman traditions still reminiscent of the Republic, was continued and established as a permanent method of government by Constantine. When Constantine acknowledged, according to the traditional story, that his final overthrow of his rivals in the struggle for supreme power was due to the Christian religion—*Hoc signo vinces*—he added a new prestige to the old. From his time, as Orosius said, all Roman Emperors except Julian were Christian.[1]

No system of government, however, can derive all its moral authority from the magic of success or the glamour of ceremonies, titles and ostentatious wealth. Every established system derives part of its moral authority from the fact that those who submit to it

---

[1] Orosius, *Hist.*, vii, 28, 2.

derive some benefit from their submission. It is a modern conception that government should be carried on chiefly for the sake of the governed, a conception indeed partly due to the influence of Christianity in the Middle Ages. But at all times it has been felt that the ruler should provide some benefits for his subjects. And these benefits were undoubtedly enjoyed throughout the Roman Empire, at least until the fifth century. Aelius Aristides praised the Roman system under the Antonines for benefits which are still recognized to have been very great; and although the millions of slaves and impoverished artisans and peasants in all parts of the Empire could not read or write, and have left no record of their sufferings, they also, no doubt, felt some gratitude for the peace which was called Roman. The benefits which flowed from Roman roads, Roman law and civic administration were new to most of the world over which the early Emperors ruled. However dimly ordinary men may feel that they have a *right* to derive advantage from those who govern them, the moral authority of any system of government always depends in part upon the actual benefits which it is believed to confer. In practice conquest and the military power of those in control of a community are never enough to secure obedience or respect. Submission to power is all that is granted to a tyranny; and it is an insecure foundation for government. But when the distress invariably caused by war and the enslavement of the conquered begins to be forgotten, in a later generation, a system of government originally based upon fraud and violence may prove to be advantageous to the health and happiness of its subjects. That is why Colonial Government in modern times, originally based in many cases, as the Roman system was, upon fraud and violence, has come to be regarded as a trusteeship. Its moral authority therefore depends upon the general answer among its subjects to the question whether in practice its laws and administration are beneficial to them.

In the western parts of the Roman Empire, Roman force and ambition had overcome, not a higher civilization as in Greece and the East, but simpler tribal communities. Roman conquest was therefore able to introduce into Gaul and Spain and Britain a more highly developed system than they had hitherto possessed. For this reason the peoples of the West, at the beginning of the fifth century, undoubtedly felt that they had derived great benefits from the Empire. Although western and north-western Europe had been used, as all the conquests of Rome had been, as a source for increasing the supply of slaves, it had been brought by the Empire into closer touch with the more highly civilized eastern Mediterranean. Commodities were interchanged, communication was frequent, and the small rich class in the cities increased their knowledge and extended the range and depth of their emotion by contact with Greek thought and eastern forms of religion. Such, in brief outline, were the real advantages from which, in part, the Roman system derived its moral authority. The social advantages which western Europe derived from the imperial system may be summarized therefore as follows. First, a fixed order of social classes, social functions and administrative officials was established throughout the Roman world. Each man and woman had a definite status recognized by others and maintained by public Authority. The whole of society throughout the Roman Empire rested upon the organization of cities. That is to say, those who held power in cities shared in their own districts the control of the whole Roman territory; and agriculture and other country pursuits were definitely subordinate to the needs of the city populations. This is in obvious contrast with the situation in medieval Europe, north of Italy, where those in power lived outside the cities and the life of the countryside dominated that of the small towns. Roman civilization was essentially a city civilization; and the advantage of established expectations among the men and women of plainly distinguished ranks or classes (*ordines*) clearly provided an opportunity for greater peace of mind and the enjoyment of amenities even among the victims of the system—the slaves and other manual workers.

The second great social advantage was the administration of justice in accordance with a well-considered system of Law. Roman Law throughout the Empire and the administration of justice at its best gave to all, on the one hand, a definite relation to public Authorities and, on the other, definite private rights and duties, affecting, for example, property, marriage, inheritance and contract. The Theodosian law-books, issued in the early fifth century, provided a collection of examples or patterns which still indicates, as it did to the men of those days, the general features of the Roman system of justice.

Again, trade and social intercourse in the Roman Empire depended upon the safety of transit and travel throughout the Mediterranean, which made the Empire one.[1] The greatest cities were sea-ports such as Constantinople, Alexandria and Carthage, or river-ports, having sea-ports closely connected with them, such as Rome, Arles and Ravenna. Until the fifth century, at any rate, piracy and warlike expeditions did not interfere with large-scale sea-borne commerce. Ships carried across the Mediterranean corn from Africa and Egypt to Italy and Constantinople, and brought the finer products of Oriental manufacture from Asia to Gaul and Spain. And with the transit of goods went the interchange of ideas and customs. Practical ideas, for example, in methods of building or of water-supply for cities were carried from land to land; and similar groups of devotees of new religions or new magical cults were formed in all parts of the Empire spreading mainly from the East and South to the North and West.

The feeling of respect and gratitude for the Roman system of government adorned with a magical brightness the city of Rome. A celestial light seemed to shine upon its temples and palaces—a light which did not entirely fade, even in the Middle Ages when they were in ruins. The *Gloria Romanorum*, inscribed on imperial coins, shone out from the city which had made a world, and gave moral authority to all that was Roman and to the name of Rome. The devotion to Rome itself was expressed in the early fifth century by two non-Christian poets, Claudian and Rutilius. Claudian was a native of Egypt; and Rutilius had his home in Gaul, probably near Toulouse. But both came to Rome with the devotion of pilgrims to a sacred place. Claudian wrote of Rome: "This is she who alone received those whom she conquered into her household, and cared for the whole human race under one common name, as

---

[1] See M. P. Charlesworth, *Trade Routes of the Roman Empire*, 2nd ed., 1926.

a mother not a mistress. She gave the name of citizen to those over whom she had power, and bound them far and wide in devotion. All of us are in debt to her for her lessons in the manners of peace."[1] Rutilius expresses in glowing terms the last sight of the glorious city when he left Rome on his return in A.D. 417 to his native land. His greatest admiration, however, is given, not to the external splendours of the city, but to the moral authority which Rome derived from her services to mankind. To Rome itself, Rutilius says: "That you have power is of less account than that you deserve to have it."[2] The service of that peace and justice which Rome maintained was to Rutilius the highest moral ideal; and for that reason he condemned as deserters the hermits and monks whom he saw living in the caves as he passed by sea from Italy to Gaul.[3]

Christian writers at the end of the fourth century and the beginning of the fifth, agreed with non-Christian in their admiration for the city of Rome. It was generally recognized by Christian apologists that the unity of diverse peoples and the peace between them which Rome had achieved, had been essential for the spread of Christianity. Even Orosius, an exceedingly foolish Spanish priest, recognized that he met friends everywhere by grace of the Roman Empire. But the city of Rome itself retained for Christians the magical influence due to the splendour of her buildings and the belief in her eternity. Rome had become Christian without losing in their eyes her ancient glory. St. Ambrose supported the imperial authority of Rome; but Ambrose had been an imperial official before he was a Christian bishop. Prudentius, the Christian poet of the early fifth century, however, was no less impressed by the dignity of Rome. And although he looked to the tombs of the martyrs rather than to the palaces and temples, it was in Rome that he found the highest expression of moral authority. Something of this feeling survived the collapse of Roman power in

[1] Claudian, *De Consulatu Stilichonis*, ii, 115. Claudian probably died about A.D. 408.   [2] "Quod regnas minus est quam quod regnare mereris."
[3] The fragment of the poem of Rutilius which now remains was preserved by the monks of St. Columban, an Irishman, at Bobbio, and rediscovered in a library by a Renaissance scholar. The monks preserved the attack upon monks, and the muse of history must have smiled when she handed the fragment to Papal Rome.

western Europe and the decline of the moral authority of the Roman system of law and justice. The city of Rome had an important influence, as will be explained in a later chapter, upon the formation of the medieval Papacy. But the magical power of the ghost of Rome among its ruins was very different from the moral authority which, in the early fifth century, was derived from a system of government.

Decline of Authority

The gradual decline of the moral authority of the Roman Empire must now be considered. This decline had begun about a century before Alaric entered Rome. The fact that the Emperor no longer used Rome as his capital, no doubt, weakened his authority; for the magic of Rome could not easily be carried off from the place even by a supreme ruler who continued to call himself "Roman." It was pointed out above that the Oriental pageantry introduced by Diocletian, and the inevitable influence of the East upon the "New Rome" established by Constantine, must have added something to the prestige of the Empire. On the other hand, the mere fact that Constantinople was a new foundation and contained none of the buildings or monuments which had made Rome sacred in the past, weakened the authority of the Emperor in Italy and in the West. When there were two Emperors reigning, the capital in the West was not Rome but first Milan and afterwards Ravenna. Indeed, when the Emperor Honorius entered Rome, if indeed he did, in A.D. 404, for a whole century Rome had been visited only three times by an Emperor.[1]

The magic associated with the name of Rome remained in the city itself. In the Middle Ages, when the Popes left Rome and the Papal Court resided for about seventy years at Avignon, the prestige of the Papacy gradually diminished, until it was found possible by a Pope to return to the Sacred City.[2] The magic of a place can be

[1] By Constantine, A.D. 312; Constantius, A.D. 357; Theodosius, A.D. 389. See Hodgkin, *Italy*, vol. 8, p. 300.

[2] In 1377 Gregory XI, a Frenchman, reached St. Peter's. Then began the connection between the Vatican as a Papal residence *outside* Rome, and the Papacy, which had hitherto been established at the Lateran.

used even in modern times. Thus the recent removal of the centre of British government in India from Calcutta to Delhi, and the effort to adorn the new capital with an Oriental magnificence, were clearly intended to reinforce the authority of the British Raj. In any case, the removal of the Emperor from Rome destroyed the roots of the system which Augustus had established in its connection with the historic Senate and the great families of the Roman tradition. The centre of authority was Constantinople, in spite of the theory that the two Emperors were equal; for no one could believe that an Emperor who sought refuge behind the marshes surrounding Ravenna had control of the western provinces through his own power, especially as Ravenna was chosen for a residence because of its connections by sea with Constantinople.

Another cause of the loss of prestige in the Empire in the West was the substitution of Greek for Latin as the language of the Court and of learning. When the capital of the Empire was moved eastwards, it became the centre of an eastern world already united in trade and in culture by the Greek language. The original language of the earliest Christian Churches was Greek; and the titles of the Church officials (bishop, priest, deacon) and the names of the ceremonies of the Church (baptism and Eucharist) were forms of Greek words. Constantinople was distinguished from old Rome because its chief public buildings were not Roman temples but Greek churches; and the keenest thought of the now Christian Empire was expressed in Greek. This in itself inevitably weakened in the West the hold which imperial authority had derived from what had hitherto been the universal language of Roman Law and administration; and, as it will be shown later, all the associations of the Roman tradition embodied in the use of Latin, especially in the Law, were taken over by the Church in the West from an imperial system which had become, in letter as well as in spirit, alien.

In the general decline of the moral authority of the Empire in the West the most obviously destructive influence was the gradual decrease in the advantages which all classes derived from the system. In the first place, Roman Law and Roman Order became ineffectual as the dictatorship of the Emperor became in practice weaker. Local governors and local judges twisted law and administration to suit their private interests. Criticism of official injustice became impossible as the supreme Authority was either more distant or more completely severed from the life of the majority of its subjects. Public administration was used for obtaining private wealth; and the rich landowners of any locality were able increasingly to exert pressure both upon imperial officials and upon the poorer classes who paid most of the taxes. The complaints of Salvian in the middle of the fifth century give sufficient proof that all except the very rich derived little enough advantage from the old system. But if further proof were needed the provisions of the Theodosian law-books against unjust judges and local governors under the control of a local aristocracy indicate that the central Authorities knew how badly the old system was working. For many years before the fifth century taxation had been exacted for the advantage of officials; and the property of the small landowners fell into the hands of the rich, as a result of the pressure upon them exerted by imperial agents or by the bailiffs of powerful senatorial families.

When the barbarian gangs began in the fifth century to loot towns in Italy, Gaul, Spain and Africa, it was quite obvious that no protection for the majority was to be had from the central Authorities of the Empire. The system had become useless to the majority of its subjects; and whatever advantage it might still have, accrued almost entirely to the rich landowners. Again, the breakdown of the Roman system involved also a disturbance of the traditional ranks or orders or classes in society. Rich men climbed into the senatorial order out of reach of taxation and obligations of public service. In the early days of the Empire the entry of freedmen into positions of power at Court had been at first resented; but by the fifth century it had become a commonplace that any barbarian soldier, whose cunning or luck served him well enough, might reach control not only of a city or province but of the central Government. And besides, among the Court officials of the new Christian Empire since the days of Constantine some of the most important were eunuchs in the palace. The very elevation of the Emperor himself above all his subjects tended to reduce them all to a mass within which the distinctions were of minor importance. And in those parts which were distant from the seat of central Authority, as it has been explained in the second chapter, men of the poorer classes were continually seeking refuge from oppression either by flight to the barbarians or by the acceptance of a servile position on the estates of rich landowners. Thus Roman Order was disturbed. The system of government was in dissolution; taxation no longer supported public services; and the courts no longer maintained an equal justice even for those who claimed to be Roman citizens.

Finally, the Mediterranean was no longer safe. After the Vandals had crossed into Africa from Spain in A.D. 429, sea-borne supplies from Africa to Italy were often interrupted; and in the next fifty years frequent sea-battles or warlike expeditions across the sea began the destruction of the unity of the Empire which had held together the shores of the Mediterranean.

The decline of the moral authority of the Roman Empire in the West may be made clearer by distinguishing between the stages through which it passed. In the early part of the fifth century under Honorius and his sister Placidia, the prestige of the Empire was maintained, so long as the military and civilian officials acted in the name of the Emperor and so long as barbarian warriors were his allies; but by the middle of the fifth century the situation in the West was considerably altered because an increasing number of Roman officials were already under the authority of barbarian kings, while the bishops who represented the Roman tradition attempted to give stability to the new barbarian kingdoms. A second stage was therefore reached when the great barbarian general Ricimer made and unmade Emperors; because this implied that the Empire itself had become merely a traditional decoration which might be used to cover the real power of a barbarian dictator. Ricimer's death in A.D. 472 was clearly the beginning of the last stage in the decline of the moral authority of the Emperor in the West, which disappeared when in A.D. 476 Romulus Augustulus was

PLATE 2.—MEDALLIONS AND COINS

A. (Referred to page 116, line 4) Reverse of bronze medallion of Fausta, wife of
Constantine the Great, with inscription PIETAS AUGUSTI (Paris).

B. (Referred to page 116, line 6) Reverse of gold medallion of Galla Placidia,
sister of Honorius, wearing a halo and seated on throne, with inscription
SALUS REIPUBLICAE/RV/COMOB/ (Paris).

C. (See page 116, line 4) Gold medallion of Constantius II (British Museum).
   obv. DN CONSTANTIUS MAX AUG—bust, helmeted, cuirassed, holding Victory
   and Spear.

   rev. GLORIAE ROMANORUM/SMN/—Constantinopolis seated on throne, her foot
   on a prow, holding Victory on globe in right hand and sceptre in left.

D. (Referred to page 448) Gold coin (called Mancus) of Offa of Mercia, copied
from Arab dinar, with inscription in Arabic.

E. (Referred to page 447) Merovingian coin of Limoges, issued by authority of
the Church (Ratio ecclesiae).

F. (Referred to page 448) Dernier of Charles the Great with title IMPERATOR
AUGUSTUS.

stripped of the purple and a barbarian king ruled Italy in his own name.

At each of the stages thus summarized both the actual success of Roman arms and the utility of the Roman system of government became more and more doubtful. And therefore the moral authority which had depended in the early Empire both upon success in arms and upon the advantages derived from the system by the majority of its subjects, was gradually lost. But the loss of moral authority in the older system of government was, from another point of view, merely a transference of moral authority to a new system of separate kingships.

First Stage in the Decline: Roman Generals

During the first period the prestige of the Roman Emperor survived almost by accident the inaction of the actual Emperor. The barbarians under Alaric, as well as those who invaded Gaul and Spain, still had a superstitious fear of the uncanny power of Rome. They might destroy cities and carry off loot; but they never thought of themselves as destroyers of the Empire itself. Indeed, Orosius tells us that Adolf, the brother-in-law and successor of Alaric, made a deliberate decision that he should preserve the Roman system. He took in marriage Galla Placidia, the half-sister of the reigning Roman Emperor, Honorius—the same lady who had been taken captive at the sack of Rome in A.D. 410. This is the account Orosius gives of his evidence for believing that the barbarian chief aimed at preserving what he calls "Romania":—

When I was at Bethlehem I heard a citizen of Narbonne who had served with distinction under Theodosius, and who was besides a wise and religious person, tell the most blessed Jerome that he had been on terms of the greatest intimacy with Adolf at Narbonne, and that he had frequently heard him say that in the first exuberance of his strength and spirits he had made this his most earnest desire: to obliterate the Roman name and make the whole Roman Empire the Empire of the Goths in fact and in name, so that in popular words what had been "Romania" should be "Gothia," and himself, Adolf, what once Caesar Augustus was. But when he had learnt by much experience that on the one hand the Goths could not obey laws because of their unbridled barbarism, and on the other that laws could not be abolished in a State, since without them no State can be a State, he had chosen to seek the glory for himself of restoring wholly and of strengthening the Roman name, by using the power of the Goths, and that he would be believed by later ages to be the author of a Roman restoration, since he had failed in his attempt at transformation.[1]

It will be noticed that, in the words of Orosius, "Romania" has not quite the same meaning as "Romanum Imperium." The Empire eventually disappeared; but Roman civilization did not. Indeed, in one sense, "Romania" is a good name for the whole social system of western Europe during the Middle Ages; and perhaps Orosius himself recognized that there was a distinction between the dictatorship of a Roman Emperor, which might be held responsible for the destructiveness of Roman arms, and on the other hand the civilization he called "Roman." He does not hesitate to criticize the past conquests of Rome; and at the same time he takes pride in the fact that wherever he goes he finds friends and fellow-citizens. In this sense he can call himself "Roman"; but the word "Roman" is thus already beginning to mean the unity of a civilization based upon the Church. These are his words: "The victories of Rome grow by the destruction of peoples and cities; and if you think it out, more harm than good has come from them. . . . See how happily Rome conquers and how unhappily everything outside of Rome is conquered . . . the happiness of one city is made of such a heap of misery that the whole world is turned upside down."[2] He refers to the ruins of Carthage, the desolation of Spain, the exploitation of Italy; and again in a later book he says that Spain has suffered from the Goths for only two years, but she has suffered from the Romans for two centuries.[3] On the other hand, Orosius says: "I go everywhere among friends; everywhere is my fatherland; everywhere my law and my religion—among Romans, a Roman; among Christians, a Christian; among men, a man."[4] The contrast could not be greater between the evils of

---

[1] Orosius, *Hist.*, vii, 43. (Trans., except for a few words, from Hodgkin, *Italy*, i, p. 402.) [2] Ibid., v, 1. [3] Ibid., vii, 41.
[4] Ibid., v, 2. Mihi . . . ubique patria, ubique lex et religio mea est; inter Romanos, Romanus; inter Christianos, Christianus; inter homines, homo.

imperial power and the unity of a civilized world which had learnt
to call itself Roman.

In the years immediately following the sack of Rome by Alaric,
five usurpers in the West challenged the authority of the Emperor
Honorius; and each was either defeated or brought to submission.
As Orosius says, first Constantine established himself as Emperor
in Britain in A.D. 407; and in A.D. 408 he and his troops had conquered Gaul and Spain; but in A.D. 411 he was defeated and slain.
Maximus was proclaimed Emperor in A.D. 409 in Spain against
Constantine; and when Orosius wrote he was wandering as an
exile among the barbarians. Attalus had been proclaimed Emperor
in Rome by Alaric himself in A.D. 409 and was restored in A.D. 414;
but in A.D. 416 he was surrendered to Honorius. Another of Alaric's
Emperors was Jovinus, and he too was surrendered to Honorius in
A.D. 416. Finally, Heraclian, Count of Africa, proclaimed himself
Emperor and invaded Italy; but he too was defeated and slain in
A.D. 413. The prestige of an Emperor was therefore still worth the
risk involved in claiming the title; but the authority of Honorius
survived. Orosius regards this as evidence of the divine blessing
bestowed upon the Emperor who not only held the Catholic Faith
but also gave unity to the Church in Africa by the decisions against
the Donatists made, under his authority, by the Tribune Marcellinus.[1]

The situation was hardly changed by the death of Honorius in
A.D. 423. Galla Placidia, his half-sister, had been married first to the
barbarian Adolf in A.D. 412, and secondly to Constantius, a Roman
general and conqueror of the usurper Constantine. But Constantius,
although proclaimed Augustus, when Placidia, his wife, was given
the title of Augusta, died suddenly in A.D. 421; and at the death of
Honorius, Placidia fled to the Court of the other Emperor in Constantinople. After an abortive attempt at making a certain Johannes
Emperor, the son of Placidia, Valentinian, at seven years of age,
was established as Emperor in the West by the forces of Theodosius II, then reigning in Constantinople.

In this first stage of the decay of Roman authority the significant
fact is the power of Roman generals acting under the authority of

---

[1] Orosius, *Hist.*, vii, 42, 16.

the Emperor Valentinian III and actually as servants of his mother, Galla Placidia. The situation just before Alaric sacked Rome was indeed not very different. Stilicho, the Vandal, had been the active force of the Roman Government under Honorius; and Constantius, the general of Honorius and later the husband of Placidia, had also been the real force behind the same inanimate Emperor. But after Placidia and her son had been endowed with the magic prestige of the names "Augusta" and "Augustus," the situation became even more obviously dependent upon the vigour and ability of officials. The two great men on whom the Empire in the West depended were Bonifacius, Count of Africa, and Aetius, Count of Italy. As Procopius wrote, about a century later: "There were two Roman generals, Aetius and Bonifacius, especially valiant men and in experience of many wars, inferior to none of that time at least. These two came to be at variance with regards to matters of State; but they attained to such a degree of high-mindedness and excellence in every respect that if one should call either of them the last of the Romans he would not err, so true was it that all the excellent qualities of the Romans were summed up in these two men."[1] But in the end the rivalry of these two men did more to undermine the moral authority of the Roman system than their administrative and military ability had done to maintain its failing strength. Bonifacius was the friend of St. Augustine, and received from him advice and instruction on the Christian duty of maintaining his public functions while adopting the form of asceticism then generally approved. Augustine wrote: "Do not think that nobody can please God who serves in the armed forces."[2] And in a later letter: "After the death of your first wife you wished to retire from administrative duties and become a monk. And what hindered you? Was it not the thought urged upon you by Alypius and myself, that even your public duties would greatly help the Churches of Christ, if you made this your only aim, so that they might be delivered from attacks of the barbarians? . . . You were to seek in this world nothing but the bare necessities of life for yourself and your family,

---

[1] Procopius, *Hist.*, iii, 3, 14. (The translation is from the Loeb edition.)
[2] Augustine, Ep., clxxxix. (*C.S.E.L.*, vol. 87, Pars iv, p. 133.)

and preserving the chastest continence in the midst of bodily armaments you might be more safely yet more strongly defended by spiritual arms."[1] In this letter Augustine complains that the Berbers have devastated Roman Africa while Boniface was absorbed in securing his own position.

The disappointment expressed by St. Augustine in the same letter at the second marriage of Bonifacius does not concern public policy; but his new wife was an Arian heretic, and therefore may have influenced his next step. Bonifacius seems to have believed that his position in Africa was being undermined by intrigue at the imperial Court; and he may have been suspected of such ambitions as many other Roman governors had had. In any case, the Count of Africa appealed to the Arian Vandals who had established themselves in Spain, to help him to secure his own position in Africa. It was clearly impossible for the Count to realize at that time the disastrous consequences. But in a few years the Vandals were fighting for their own purposes against Bonifacius himself. They had come over to Africa in A.D. 429; in A.D. 432 Bonifacius fled to Italy; and in A.D. 439 the Vandals had complete control of Roman Africa.[2] The effort of a Roman governor to secure himself against the policy of the central Authority of which he was the servant, had undermined the authority of the Empire in one of its most important provinces. Africa was the chief source from which the city of Rome drew its supplies of corn for public distribution; and after the Vandal conquest these supplies were cut off. Thousands of the poorer Romans therefore must have been made painfully aware of the weakness of the imperial Authority as an earthly Providence. Again, the Vandals were Arian heretics with their own clergy and their own Gothic bible. The Vandal kings persecuted the Catholic clergy of Africa when they were cut off from the Empire; and the prestige of the Empire was therefore further diminished by its failure to maintain the Churches to which the Emperors had been for so long devoted.

[1] Augustine, Ep., ccxx. (C.S.E.L., vol. 57, Ep. Pars iv, p. 433.) Trans. partly inexact from Hodgkin's *Italy*.

[2] It must be remembered that Africa in this sense does not include Egypt and Cyrenaica.

The other great figure of the time was Aetius, who for seventeen years maintained Roman authority in Gaul and Italy by continuous fighting and later by his influence at the Court of Galla Placidia and her son, the Emperor Valentinian III. During those years appeals were made for help against barbarians in the West to Aetius himself and not to the Roman Emperor. Appeals came from Britain and from Spain but no help was given; for, although Aetius was able to use some barbarians against others, his forces were evidently so unreliable or so weak that it was all he could do to maintain Roman authority in Gaul.

The position of Aetius in the eyes of the Roman population in western Europe is most clearly indicated in the chronicle of Idatius, bishop of Chaves (*Aquae Flaviae*) in Gallicia, that is north-western Spain.[1] He was born in A.D. 388 and became bishop in A.D. 427. His chronicle continues until A.D. 469; and he died in A.D. 474. In A.D. 400 he was in Egypt and Palestine where he conversed with St. Jerome; but in A.D. 402 he was in Gallicia again and lived there for the rest of his life. Thus he is a contemporary witness of the collapse of Roman authority in one of the most distant provinces of the West. He reports the entry of the barbarians, chiefly Vandals and Suevi, into Spain in A.D. 409. "The drunken violence of the barbarians throughout Spain, and a raging pestilence, scattered by tyranny and destroyed by the sword the wealth and stored resources of the cities; a dreadful famine spread so greatly that human flesh was eaten by men in the extremity of hunger: mothers also ate the bodies of their children, cut up and cooked. Wild beasts fed on the corpses of those killed by the sword, hunger and pestilence; they killed stronger men and, devouring their flesh, everywhere contrived the destruction of the human race. So by the raging in the whole world of the four plagues—the sword, hunger, pestilence and wild beasts—what was foretold by the Lord through his prophets is come to pass." He then describes the division of what is now Spain and Portugal between the Vandals, the Alans, and the Suevi. When he puts into his record the marriage of Adolf the Visigoth to Galla Placidia at Narbonne, he says that this fulfils the

---

[1] Idatius, *Chronicon. Pat. Lat.*, 51, col. 873 sq.

prophecy of Daniel—that the daughter of the King of the East would be united with the King of the North. He notes the passage of the Vandals into Africa, and in the following years mentions victories of Aetius over the Burgundians and the Visigoths in southern Gaul. In A.D. 431 he says that, because the Suevi once again violated the peace they had made with the people of Gallicia, he himself, bishop Idatius, undertook an embassy to Aetius. But evidently Aetius had no forces available for Spain, because in the following year Idatius says that Aetius won a victory over the Franks and made peace with them, and sent Count Censorius as a legate to the Suevi, Idatius himself returning with the Count to his own country.

During all this time the good bishop was concerned with the Manichean heresy in Spain, in connection with which Pope Leo the Great had written to Turribius, bishop of Astorga.[1] After noting the invasion of Italy by the Huns in A.D. 451, he writes of the quarrels in Spain between the Goths and the Suevi and the great defeat of the Suevi twelve miles outside Astorga. The results were again disastrous for the unfortunate population. Idatius writes that Theodoric, king of the Goths, sacked the city of Bracara and "a great number of Romans were taken as slaves, basilicas of the Saints destroyed, altars broken, virgins of God carried off but not violated, clergy reduced to extreme poverty and the whole people of both sexes with their children torn from sanctuary, the holy place filled with the filth of oxen, swine and camels, and the writings fulfilled about Jerusalem under the anger of heaven."[2]

The decay of moral authority in the central Government of the Empire is shown by the record in the chronicle of news from Rome. As Emperor follows Emperor in the years after the death of Valentinian III, Idatius notes the arrival of legates in Gallicia announcing the names of the new rulers; and apparently legates were sent from Spain to every new Emperor. But this was evidently only the futile survival of an ancient form. The most important events of the time in Spain were the struggles of barbarian bands, one against the other. The Roman Authorities still retained the

---

[1] See below, p. 528.   [2] Idatius, *Chron. Pat. Lat.*, 51, col. 885.

respect of those over whom Emperors had once ruled; but actual policy in the distant provinces was concerned merely with the adjustment of the quarrels of barbarians and protection for the population which was called "Roman" against the robbery and violence of the armed gangs under their barbarian kings.

The situation was less disastrous in Gaul after the first raids of the barbarians in A.D. 406. By the middle of the fifth century some barbarian kings and warriors had established themselves in control, of whom the most important were the Visigoths under their king Theodoric. But in A.D. 451 a new and more destructive invasion seemed about to begin. The Huns, under their king Attila assisted by other barbarian allies, advanced into Gaul and destroyed cities in the Rhine Valley and north-eastern France. They reached the walls of Orleans where the bishop Anianus inspired the defence while messengers were sent to Aetius. He was able to induce the Visigothic king to support the Roman authorities; and with the assistance of other barbarian troops he advanced against the Huns. Gaul was saved by the defeat of Attila in the battle of Châlons or the Mauriac Plain. As Jordanes writes: "On the side of the Romans such was the ability of the Patrician Aetius, on whom the commonwealth of the West then depended, that he was able to mobilize fighters from all sides and meet on equal terms the savage and countless multitudes of the enemy."[1]

But Attila had not given up all attempts of extracting loot from the Empire. He and his marauding bands entered Italy, destroyed some cities in the north and were believed to be about to descend upon Rome, as Alaric had done nearly fifty years before. The Roman authorities, thereupon, decided to send as an embassy to the Huns two senators and Leo, bishop of Rome. By the influence of Leo, according to one chronicle, and under the pressure of disease among his troops, according to another, Attila retreated from Italy to the Danube and there died.[2] The situation had changed

---

[1] Jordanes, *Getica*, ch. 26 sq. The whole battle is elaborately described in this passage.

[2] The Chronicle known as Prosper's mentions the influence of Leo; the Chronicle of Idatius makes no reference to it, but only to disease. Jordanes (chap. 42) suggests that the death of Alaric after his sack of Rome had an influence upon Attila.

in one important particular. The bishop of Rome had become much more powerful politically as well as in ecclesiastical affairs. This is but one of the many signs of a transfer of moral authority from the Empire to the Papacy which was taking place without attracting the attention of contemporary historians. Indeed, the Churches and their bishops did not yet adopt a single common policy with regard to the barbarian invasions. For example, at the time of Attila's advance into Italy, Maximus, bishop of Turin, delivered homilies to his people which express a form of religious defeatism.[1] He says in one homily that the invasions are signs of the end of the world but that David killed his enemy, not with arms, but by the spiritual sword which is the stone; and this stone which the builders rejected is Christ. Life is a trial (*experimentum*); death is not evil and the only means of repelling the ferocity of barbarians are prayer and fasting (*Hom.* 87). If prayer fails to achieve its object, that is because of sin (*Hom.* 92). Meantime Maximus is concerned at the evil habit of the rich in fleeing from danger (*Hom.* 91) and at the still more pernicious purchase of slaves and property which had come on to the market owing to barbarian looting (*Hom.* 96). "The money-maker always feeds upon another's misfortune . . . a father mourns a captive son and you take him as a slave. . . . Your excuse is that you bought them, when you take the poor man's ox or the widow's household goods. . . . Where did you get your Roman slaves? We know that they belong to our fellow citizens. . . . As a Christian and a citizen you should purchase only to restore what is taken from the rightful owners." Maximus is, therefore, not careless of social duties. Indeed his conception seems to be that, although as a bishop he is not concerned with armed force, the prayer of Christians should support the established order. Thus, either as supporters of defence against the barbarians or as preachers attacking the avarice and corruption which they felt to be the chief dangers of the old order, the bishops of the Latin Churches gradually increased their moral authority, as that of Emperors and their generals declined.

But the old game of politics went on. Aetius clearly believed

---

[1] Maximus of Turin, *Pat. Lat.*, 57. *Homilia*, 86 96.

that he was indispensable to the Emperor, as Stilicho had seemed to be to Honorius in the days of Alaric. Galla Placidia had died in A.D. 451 or A.D. 454. Aetius was negotiating for the marriage of his son with the daughter of the Emperor. The general had the real power; but evidently he dared not make himself Emperor. He aimed therefore at securing for his son the position which he could not attain for himself, as it was said Stilicho had done. But the jealousy of his rivals at Court was his undoing. The Emperor invited his chief minister to the Palace, and there with his own hands stabbed him to death. As Sidonius wrote: "The lunatic half-man slaughtered Aetius."[1] Three months after, in March 455, the Emperor himself was stabbed to death outside Rome by followers of the general. Thus ended the first stage in the decline of authority of the Empire in the West.

Second Stage: the Patrician Ricimer

The next stage was marked by the complete control of the Empire by a general in his own name, who condescended, however, to make his agent an Emperor. The few months that follow the death of Valentinian III may be regarded as an interlude. A rich old Senator, Petronius Maximus, was dressed in the imperial purple in Rome and in that same year the Vandals invaded Italy. At the news of their coming the old man was killed by his servants. Leo, bishop of Rome, went out to ward off the invaders from the South, as he had in the North when Attila threatened; but he failed. The Vandals entered Rome a few days after the death of the Emperor, and took what they wanted of the precious metals and other booty. Meantime in July of that year, A.D. 455, another rich nobleman, this time at Arles in Gaul, was proclaimed Emperor. Avitus, the new Emperor, went to Rome and ceremonies were held in the traditional manner; but the farce did not continue. Ricimer, a Count of the Empire, won a victory at sea over the Vandals and felt himself strong enough to put aside at once the

[1] Sid. Ap., *Panegyric of Avitus, Carm.*, iv, 359. Aetium Placidus nectavit semi-vir amens. And also in *Carm.*, vii, 305. Principis gladio lacrymabile fatum clauseret Aetius.

master whom he was supposed to have served. In September 456, the Emperor fled from Rome, was captured by Ricimer at Placentia, dethroned and immediately consecrated bishop. This was the recognized method in the fifth century for removing a man from politics.

Ricimer was now undisputed master of the Empire in the West, or rather, of all that remained of it in Italy and Gaul. He himself was a barbarian by birth—half Suevic, half Visigothic; and now for sixteen years he controlled and used the old imperial power, taking for himself the title of Patrician. It was the title that had been borne for twenty years by Aetius, and seems to have now come to mean Prime Minister.[1] Ricimer immediately made a young officer on his staff Emperor (A.D. 457). Majorian, the new Emperor, wrote from Ravenna to the Senate in Rome a letter which was preserved among the edicts of his reign. The significant sentences of this letter run as follows: "The Emperor Majorian Augustus to the Senate. You recognize, Senators, that I have been made Emperor by your election and the appointment of the army. May Divine Providence support the opinion of all and render fruitful our rule for your advantage and that of the public. Since I have ascended the throne not by my will but in the service of public interest, lest I should be thought to act in my own behalf alone or to be ungrateful to the Commonwealth to which I belong . . . we and our parent and patrician, Ricimer, will take watchful care of the military situation . . . and by the Divine Hand we wish you happiness and good fortune for many years, Senators of the Sacred Order."[2] In this document the Emperor has become little more than a ghostly shadow. It is mere pretence for him to write that the Senate and the army had any connection with his selection as Emperor. The real power was derived obviously from the Patrician, Ricimer. And in two years Majorian had ceased to be Emperor. He was put to death, apparently by the order of Ricimer, in May 460.

Some months later, in November 461, Ricimer proclaimed

[1] Hodgkin, *Italy*, ii, p. 406.
[2] Nov. Majorian I, January 11, 458. At the end, the inscription is "et manu divina . . . sanctissimi ordinis patres conscripti."

as Emperor a certain Libius Severus who died at Rome in August 465; and, according to Cassiodorus, some said that Ricimer had given him poison. But the Patrician never attempted to make himself Emperor, although he was continually engaged in wars for the defence of Italy and the remnants of the Empire in the West. Indeed, after the death of Severus there was no Emperor at all in the West until A.D. 467. It may be presumed that in theory the Emperor at Constantinople, Leo, was the acknowledged head of the Empire; but in fact Ricimer ruled, until Anthemius, a son-in-law of the new Emperor Marcian, was accepted by him as Emperor. A quarrel followed between the new Emperor and Ricimer; and Epiphanius, bishop of Pavia, was sent by Ricimer from Milan to the Emperor Anthemius in Rome to negotiate a peace. The Emperor is said to have assured the bishop that he would commit himself and the State entirely into his hands and grant to him the pardon which Ricimer himself would not have obtained.[1] In A.D. 472, however, Ricimer was again hostile to Anthemius; and in the early months of that year he proclaimed as Emperor the Roman Senator, Olybrius, who had married the daughter of Valentinian III. He then marched against Anthemius who was in Rome, entered the city, slew Anthemius in July A.D. 472, and on August 18th himself died suddenly of haemorrhage. This marks the end of the second stage in the decline of the moral authority of the Empire in the West. Ricimer had held power for sixteen years, made Emperors as he chose, but himself never troubled to claim the title. The prestige of an Augustus was evidently already of little account.

Third Stage: the End of the Empire

The last days of the Empire in the West ended with the final disappearance there of the very name of Augustus. Olybrius died at Rome in October 472. A puppet Emperor, Glycerius, was set up at Ravenna in March 473; and a new Emperor, Nepos, came from Constantinople to claim the title and power of an Augustus early in A.D. 474. His rival, Glycerius, was made a bishop in Dalmatia—another compulsory retirement from politics into the

---

[1] Ennodius, *Vita Epiphanii.*

Church; and Nepos, after being accepted in the outskirts of Rome as the new Emperor, reigned for fourteen months, until he was dethroned by a Roman general, Orestes. Nepos fled to Dalmatia in A.D. 475, where the ex-Emperor he had dethroned had been sent; and in August 475 Orestes proclaimed his own son Emperor, taking for himself the title of Patrician, which had now become the symbol of real power. The new Emperor, a boy of about fourteen, was named Romulus after a relative, and the title Augustus was modified by sarcasm into a diminutive Augustulus. Thus he bore the names both of the first and of the second founders of Rome. But in A.D. 476 a revolt of Roman troops against Orestes, under a barbarian leader, Odovacar, compelled Orestes to flee to Pavia. The followers of Odovacar captured and sacked Pavia. Orestes was killed and Romulus Augustulus, the last of the Emperors in the West, was summarily dethroned and kindly allowed to retire to a villa near Naples.

The only record of the new situation is in a fragment of the Greek historian, Malchus. He wrote: "When the Augustus, the son of Orestes, heard that Zeno, driving out Basiliscus, had again obtained possession of the Empire in the East, he compelled the Senate to send an embassy to make the following declaration to Zeno—that they had no desire for an Emperor of their own, but that a single one in common, holding sway over both territories, sufficed; that Odovacar had been chosen by them as fitted to safeguard their interests, because of his knowledge of civil and military affairs; and that they besought Zeno to bestow on Odovacar the dignity of Patrician and also the diocese of Italy."[1] Zeno is said to have replied that the Senate ought still to acknowledge their lawful Emperor Nepos; but nothing effectual was done to restore him to power. Odovacar was given the title of Patrician, and seems to have paid some sort of respect to the Emperor at Constantinople. But he neither claimed to be an Augustus himself, nor did he attempt to disguise his own power by choosing another to fill the place of Romulus Augustulus. Such was the end of the Roman Empire in the West.

[1] Malchus, *Hist.* (ed. Niebuhr), p. 235.

The situation, therefore, in western Europe at the close of the fifth century was this. The barbarian kingdoms established throughout all western Europe paid a nominal respect to the Emperor; but the only Emperor was at Constantinople—far away, and without any real influence upon the exercise of political or military authority west of the Adriatic. But the position of these kings will be discussed in a later chapter. So far as the Empire was concerned they were merely possible allies, more or less loyal, to be used on occasion, one against another, in a primitive sort of balance of power.

The Roman Empire remained. It had always been one Empire, even in the years, since Diocletian, when it had been administered by two Augusti. It is therefore misleading to speak of the "Empire of the West" or to suppose that anything fundamental had changed when there was no longer any other Emperor but the Augustus at Constantinople. The prestige, however, of the Roman name was no doubt greatly reduced by the fact that the Emperor and his Court at Constantinople were obviously more Greek and Oriental than Roman. For the nations in the West the Emperor had become a distant and almost mythical being in another world. The pomp and glory of Constantinople and the eastern world were known to the warriors and kings of the West; but the Emperors were as far removed from the daily experience of their subjects as the heavens seemed to be.

Roman Law survived in all the oldest provinces of western Europe; although probably in north-eastern Gaul and Britain Roman administration and law-courts had ceased to operate. The moral authority, however, of the only civilized system of justice which western Europe had known, naturally survived in the minds of men and women who no longer could look to a law-giver on earth. Thus almost by accident the moral authority which had belonged to an actual political system was transferred gradually to an imagined or mythical state of things, which was regarded partly as a memory of a better past and partly as the "natural law" of another world.

In the third place, the city of Rome itself retained some moral authority over men's minds in spite of the disappearance of a Roman Emperor from the West. Indeed in some ways Rome had increased prestige. For many years Ravenna, as the residence of the Emperor, had drawn to itself some of the culture and political ability of which Rome had been the centre. But there was no longer an imperial Court in any western city. Rome itself seemed to remain eternal in spite of the collapse of the imperial system in the West, and indeed, in a new age, it revived as a centre of moral authority under the influence of the Christian Church. The Roman Empire had lost Italy, Gaul, Britain, Spain and Africa; but in all these "Romania" still had a meaning. The language of culture, law and trade was still Roman; and the Churches which had grown up under the imperial system, being now cut off from the Empire, looked more eagerly to the old Rome, whose bishop was the only patriarch of the West and the most obvious heir of the moral authority which imperial Rome had once possessed.

General Conclusions: the Policy of Appeasement

The new situation in western Europe was indeed partly the result of a succession of events over which the imperial Authorities had little or no control. No doubt, the pressure of marauding bands far outside the Roman frontiers was one of the many causes of the raids by barbarians upon Roman territory. And military control over that territory by Goths, Vandals and other tribes was, no doubt, due in part to the accidents of war. But policy also, even if half-hearted and ill-conceived, played a part in the ultimate disappearance of the moral authority of the Roman Empire in the West. The policy of the imperial Authorities obviously had to take account of the weakness of the Empire in mere military force (*vis*); for the moral authority of a system of government (*auctoritas*) which lacks the power to defend itself is inevitably disregarded. Even the "providence" (*providentia*) of an Authority which is helpless to defend its subjects may well be doubted. But the lack of military forces to resist invasion or to prevent civil war was itself partly the result of policy. The Roman Empire had already for some centuries largely depended for its military forces upon recruits from barbarian tribes and upon barbarian allies (*federati*), that is to say, armed barbarian gangs under their own kings or dukes. The great landowners were still supposed to supply recruits from their own estates; but they were not eager to assist a distant Emperor by depleting their own labour resources; and besides, the Roman Emperors of the fourth century were willing to leave the local population of the cities and municipalities, which made up their Empire, unarmed and untrained to arms, partly for fear of civil war, partly in order to maintain normal manufacture and commerce. The result was that the military power of the Empire increasingly depended upon mercenaries; and the mercenaries were untrustworthy.

But there was another and more important aspect of imperial policy—appeasement. This was the method by which the central Authority of the Empire strove to protect itself by granting to any band of robbers sufficiently powerful the control of territory and population in those parts of the Empire which were distant or from which they could not easily be ejected. Thus, the Burgundians were allowed to settle in the territory on the upper reaches of the Rhone; the Visigoths entered into a treaty with the Empire for their settlement in Aquitaine; and the Franks were left in control of what is now north-eastern France and Belgium, on condition that they would assist the Roman Authorities against the invasions of other Germanic tribes. After the middle of the fifth century the policy of appeasement involved the actual use of barbarian tribes by Roman Authorities, as Count Bonifacius used the Vandals in Africa, and as the Emperor Zeno used the Ostrogothic king, Theodoric, against Odovacar in Italy.

The conceptions underlying a policy of appeasement seem to have been these. The barbarians admired the Roman Empire and would perhaps be willing to maintain it, if they were treated as friends. All, except the Franks, were Christians, and could therefore be supposed to respect the Christian Empire. Indeed, Constantine the Great had been actually accused of a love for barbarians; and the attempt at reaction against Christianity under his nephew, the Emperor Julian, was also partly a reaction against barbarian influences within the Empire. Again, the rich and powerful land-owners in the western provinces of the Empire evidently thought that they could make convenient terms with the barbarian armed bands. Most of the barbarian warriors and their kings wanted loot; and the rich could thus buy their friendship by parting with super-fluities. The mistake they made lay in supposing that the appetite for loot can ever be satisfied. Appeasement failed because the barbarians thought, not without some justification, that if the threat of violence could obtain so much, it could obtain all there was to have.

Another reason for appeasement was the belief of the Roman officials that they could civilize the barbarians by acting as their agents and advisers. Thus, many Romans of ability and high culture entered the service of barbarian kings who had settled with their warriors in Roman territory. But this aspect of the situation will be discussed in a later chapter. While the richer classes hoped to preserve their influence by friendship with the barbarians, the poor and the unemployed supported appeasement because they felt they had nothing to lose by changing masters. Indeed, as it has been shown in the preceding chapter, many poor men fled from Roman taxation and the oppression of the powerful to seek some form of liberty under the barbarians. Finally the bishops of the Latin Churches were divided in their conception of policy. Some, like Anianus of Orleans or Germanus of Auxerre on his visit to Britain, organized armed resistance. Others, like Maximus of Turin, trusted in prayer alone. These latter were only too willing to regard the defeat of imperial forces and the destruction of cities as blessings in disguise, because they were supposed to be methods employed by God for the moral improvement of His people. Religious defeatism therefore supported appeasement. But whatever its other effects, the policy of appeasement led directly to the collapse of the moral authority of the Roman Empire in the West.

The fact that barbarian kings derived prestige from the acqui-escence of the Roman Authorities in their control of a province damaged the moral authority of the Empire itself. Barbarian warriors did what they chose with property and persons in order to increase their own loot; and although some barbarians might be less objectionable than avaricious Roman officials, the provincials in other cases certainly suffered from the recurring wars of the barbarians among themselves, and from the oppression of primitive rulers. Wherever therefore the disorder increased, as in Spain and Africa, the prestige of the Empire, which seemed to acquiesce in the new situation, was diminished. A partial likeness to this situation may be found in contemporary India, wherever the extortion and violence of the agents of the less important Indian Princes within their own States seems to reflect upon the British Government's acquiescence in their power. For example, in one small State recently six thousand, out of a population of forty thousand, sought refuge in neighbouring territories; and in another, about twenty thousand peasants left their homes and fled for protection to a province in British India. The situation in India is obviously different from that of western Europe in the fifth century, because of the undoubted power of the British Government; but it provides some examples of the effect upon moral authority, when subordinate rulers are not controlled.

It was not unreasonable to admit the barbarians to share in the advantages of civilization, which both the Empire and the Catholic Churches had to offer. Roman civilization in its political and economic aspects, as well as in the new moral and religious tone it had acquired, might have survived the entry into it of barbarians already impressed by the majesty of Rome and already Christian, although heretical. Again, the actual policy adopted may have been due to unconscious awareness of their own limitations among the Roman rulers and their officials. They were probably, in fact, unable to imagine any other policy, and probably would in any case have been too inert and mentally conservative to carry out any other. But whatever explanations there may be of the policy of appeasement, it weakened the moral authority of the Empire in the West, because compromise was regarded by the barbarians as a sign of weakness. Worse still, it weakened the confidence in the Empire among those who lived within its borders. They saw that the imperial Authorities were willing to desert distant provinces in order to save themselves; and they naturally concluded that any subjects of the Emperor might become the next victims of his desire to buy off the barbarians in order to secure peace for himself.

A second aspect of policy, perhaps the result of the failure of appeasement in the West, was the gradual subordination—in terms of moral authority—of the western provinces to the imperial capital at Constantinople. Clearly the two greatest of the Christian Emperors before the fifth century, Constantine the Great and Theodosius I, had made the new Rome the capital of the whole Empire which then included Britain and Spain. The whole Roman world, which had now become the Christian world, looked to Constantinople. Indeed, Lactantius, writing in the early years of the reign of Constantine, regarded Diocletian's policy as pernicious, precisely because he divided the central Authority. "This man," he says, "by avarice partly, and partly by irresolute policy, undermined the Roman Empire because he chose three others to share the government with him. And thus, the Empire was divided into four, armed forces were increased, and each of the four rulers tried to maintain a larger army than any single Emperor had done in the past."[1] But complete centralization was impracticable; and the Empire of the early fifth century was ruled by two Emperors, theoretically equal. When Honorius died, as described above, the western provinces of the Empire proved to be unable to establish an Emperor of their own. First, Valentinian III with his mother Galla Placidia was sent with armed forces from Constantinople to take over the position of Emperor in the West; and having thus, at seven years of age, become theoretically the equal of his cousin the Emperor Theodosius II, he returned to Constantinople in A.D. 437 to marry Eudoxia, his cousin's daughter. Again, in A.D. 468, when Ricimer sought support from the Emperor in Constantinople, a rich nobleman, Anthemius, was sent from that city by the Emperor Leo to Rome as an Emperor. In a decree of March 19, 468, issued in the names of Leo and Anthemius jointly as Augusti, the Emperor Leo refers to his equal in the following terms: "The devout and victorious, always Augustus, our son

[1] Lactantius, *Mort. Persec.*, vii.

Anthemius holds full imperial power by the gift of the divine majesty and our creative act."[1]

When Ricimer besieged Anthemius in Rome, another rich man from Constantinople, Olybrius, was accepted as Emperor under the protection of Ricimer. Finally, in the general disorder which followed the death of Ricimer, another Emperor, Julius Nepos, was provided with armed forces and a title by the Emperor at Constantinople for acceptance in the West. The last flicker of moral authority in the Roman political system in the West died out when the letter of the Senate of the city of Rome, described above, acknowledged the Emperor at Constantinople as the supreme authority of the Roman world. From the position thus established, Justinian, in the sixth century, advanced to his attempted reconquest of the West.

As the authority of the Roman Empire in western Europe and the province of Africa declined, the authority of the bishops of the Catholic Churches increased. The provincials who had lost the protection of imperial officials turned increasingly to the bishops, either in order to prevent barbarian looting or to make terms with the thieves. The Churches of the western world were already powerful, popular organizations in the chief cities. The development of their power will be described in the next chapter. But here it may be noted that the effect of the transfer of moral authority from an organization for law and government to religious organizations for mutual assistance and the salvation of souls, inevitably changed the character of moral authority. The Churches had no armed force. The bishops of the fifth century were not warriors. And even where a bishop might organize or support armed resistance to barbarian robbers, the ultimate purpose was clearly not victory, but peace. Thus, the *Pax Romana*, which had been based upon conquest and subjection, was transformed, as an object of policy, into an entirely different kind of peace—not indeed clearly conceived or resolutely pursued, but more attractive to common folk than the march of the legions. The great majority had no wealth to lose and little enough liberty. What they feared was

[1] *Cod. Theod.*, ed. Mommsen and Meyer, vol. ii, p. 206.

death or slavery. And against these their chief protectors were the bishops. Some of the most capable of the bishops had been wealthy men and Roman officials; and the best of them had in mind the needs of the poor and unprotected. Their moral authority was therefore derived, not from the use of armed force, nor even from the success of their efforts, but from the general belief in the honesty of their motives. The "providence" of the Church, which was the providence of God, had taken the place of the providence of the Emperor. It is clear evidence of the fact that moral authority does not arise from the use of armed force, and may exist without it. But moral authority without armed force as its instrument is effectual only with those men and women who can be influenced by the appeal to moral principles.

It follows that the particular form of moral authority, which is adequate for a religious organization, may not be suitable or sufficient for the maintenance of law and administration. The transfer of moral authority from the imperial to the ecclesiastical system did not solve the fundamental problem. That problem concerned the nature of the particular kind of moral authority which is necessary for the maintenance of a stable and progressive community. And it is this problem which was continually recurring in the efforts to establish the First Europe. The moral authority of the bishops was largely affected by an other-worldliness which might have had disastrous effects upon the survival of any form of civilized life at all. Indeed, the influence of the bishops upon the barbarian warriors and kings might easily have led to a loss of the moral authority of the Churches themselves. To be careless of wealth and property may be justifiable, especially in the eyes of those who have none. But to be careless of human life and of the bare necessities of living, because of another world beyond the skies, does not promote confidence among common folk. Such carelessness is easily interpreted, either as a confession of incompetence in the organization of civilized life, or as a lack of interest in the sufferings of others. Those bishops who relied only upon prayer seemed willing to accept whatever happened without resistance. And this might easily be taken as proof of an inability to make the effort to resist. Those bishops, on the other hand, who believed that God could use the sword, had to face the dilemma that successful force could not establish the moral authority of a system of law and government, although no such system could exist without force. These bishops believed that Christianity did not imply inaction in face of the sufferings of others. Famine, disease, destruction, death and enslavement might indeed be in accordance with the will of God. But it might also be God's will that men and women should take action to avoid or resist such evils. With these problems was connected the difficulty that, although material needs might not save souls, no souls would be alive at all without the supply of some needs. It was in the midst of such practical problems that the Christian Churches found themselves in the latter half of the fifth century.

CHAPTER IV

THE DILEMMA OF THE CHURCHES

While the structure of the Roman Empire in western Europe was falling into ruin, another organization based, not upon conquest, but upon the free co-operation of individuals, was being established. This was the Christian Church. At the beginning of the fifth century Christianity was strongest in its local groups, organized as separate congregations or Churches, whose members in different parts of the Empire were still connected only by occasional visits of preachers and by common beliefs and rituals. For three centuries the Christian Churches had been increasing the number of their members, changing their methods of organization, and passing beyond the farthest frontiers ever reached by Roman arms.

A great change in the relation of the Churches to law and government had taken place about three generations before, under the Emperor Constantine; but the results of the change upon the social structure as a whole and upon the Churches and the Empire, were not yet clear at the beginning of the fifth century. The earliest literature of Christianity was that of an Oriental religion expressed in the language of Hellenism. The New Testament belongs to a time when Christians were small groups closely connected with Judaism, without responsibility for law or government, commerce or the social relations involved in marriage and the rearing of children. So far as the earliest Christian documents, therefore, are concerned, those who wrote them and read them in the first and second centuries of our era were not concerned with the problems of civilization as a whole. They either accepted the social situation without discussion, or opposed public Authorities which had begun to take note of them only as possibly dangerous to the established order.

The second group of Christian writings, following those of the

New Testament—the work of the early Fathers in the third and fourth centuries—expresses the same attitude of aloofness towards the problems of law and government. At the beginning of this period the most influential writers expressed the opinion that the true Christian should avoid those military and other public services by which "the World" was organized. The members of the Churches were still small groups in the midst of a surrounding society with its own ancient traditions, its many different religious practices and its suspicion of those who held aloof from the civic duties and ceremonies which were generally acceptable. With the recognition of Christianity by the Emperor Constantine another change occurred. Christian literature then began to include sermons, histories and treatises on the controversial points which divided those who called themselves Christian. But from the beginning of the fourth century, obviously the problem of the relation of the Churches to the economic and political institutions of the day had to be faced. Mere hostility was impossible. It was difficult to avoid responsibility for the actions of public Authorities which supported the bishops of the Church in the exercise of their functions. And although many devout Christians, no doubt, still felt that they were aliens in the Roman world, and although every Church remembered its martyrs whom the Roman Empire had persecuted, the gradual spread of Christianity among the rich and the powerful compelled the officials of the Churches to adopt new policies towards the established order.

In spite of the many changes in the Christian tradition which had occurred already, the Churches in the Roman Empire at the beginning of the fifth century still preserved among their members two distinct attitudes towards the social system within which they found themselves. On the one hand, Christians were conceived as in some way separated from the traditional order of things; and thus not responsible for the maintenance of public order or the organization of the supply of goods and services. On the other hand, Christians had been taught, even in the earliest times, to accept public Authorities as expressions of the divine Will. The Churches might therefore either go their own way, and leave the established order outside their purview; or they might use their influence to maintain the established order with whatever corrections of its defects their own tradition might suggest. The two attitudes had been inherited by the Christian Churches from the Jewish communities within which Christianity first arose. In the early years of the Christian era, in all the chief cities of the Roman Empire, Jewish communities were regarded, and regarded themselves, as outside the social and political system. Either as racial or religious associations they were granted by the Roman Authorities a certain internal autonomy. They had their own laws and customs, rituals and beliefs. But, on the other hand, individual Jews, and perhaps also some Jewish teachers, assisted in the maintenance of the political system under which they lived. They recognized obligations to the imperial Authorities who gave them the power to trade and to preserve their own manner of life, in peace. Thus aloofness, on the one hand, and loyalty to the established order, on the other, were characteristic of the Jewish communities in the Roman Empire. The early Christians accepted both attitudes; but their aloofness was greater than that of the Jews, because they believed that the whole social system would soon disappear; and their loyalty was uncertain because they were often persecuted.

Sometime before the fifth century Christianity was organized in small groups of men and women in the chief trading centres of the Roman Empire: and each Church was connected with others only by the visits of preachers and by the letters which passed between the Churches. The small Christian communities were in the position of other non-Roman and non-local religious groups which were organized as *Collegia*. They were generally associations of men and women with a similar outlook on life, who belonged to different classes of society, but were in the main manual workers, small tradesmen and slaves. These small communities within a great city might easily appear to the educated classes and to the officials of the Government to be secret societies with very dubious aims.[1] But by their own members such societies were, no doubt,

---

[1] Minucius Felix in the *Octavius* gives a very good impression of the suspicion aroused among non-Christians by the meetings of the "lower classes" for Christian worship or mutual benefit. See above, p. 86n.

regarded as the early Protestant groups among humble folk were regarded by their members at the Reformation, or even later during the growth of Nonconformity in England in the nineteenth century: and apart from purely religious organizations, examples of similar societies are to be found among the early trade unions. The members of such small groups find some compensation for the sense that they are without power in public affairs by a greater intensity of friendliness and mutual aid among themselves.

The Christian Churches, in addition to their purely religious functions, served as "benefit societies" for the support of members in need, as organizations for burial, and as opportunities for social intercourse. They elected their own elders or presbyters and their administrative officials—bishops and deacons (overseers and assist- ants)—thus forming even from the earliest times independent units of social life in the midst of the city-organizations of the Roman Empire. In such a position it was obviously natural for the Chris- tians to adopt very different attitudes to the outer world. The more enthusiastic of their members, impressed by the belief that the world would soon come to an end, held aloof from all contact with non-Christians. This attitude led to a refusal to take any part in the social or official life of the Empire. Such Christians would naturally refuse not only to make the sacrifices symbolic of loyalty to the established order but also to bear arms in its defence. They followed in general those texts of the New Testament which indicated that the true Christian should depart from the common ways of men, especially in marriage and begetting children, and should regard themselves as aliens in a hostile world.[1]

Their attitude was, no doubt, strengthened by the suspicions surrounding them and the persecutions under which so many suffered torture and death. It was the basis of the lives of hermits and monks who believed themselves to be the true followers of Christ's teaching. And the aloofness of these most fervent Christians created difficulties even within the Christian communities them-

[1] "My kingdom is not of this world" (John xviii, 36). "He that hath left his house, or parents, or brethren, or wife, or children for the kingdom of God's sake" (Luke xviii, 29). "The time is short: it remaineth, that they that have wives be as though they had none" (1 Cor. vii, 29).

selves. The early hermits and monks dispensed even with the ceremonies and sacraments of the Churches. Other Christians followed the tendencies expressed in such texts of the New Testament as that which commanded them "to give to Caesar the things that are Caesar's,"[1] or, in the letter to the Romans, asserted that the established authority "was ordained by God."[2] Christians who adopted this attitude might hold that it was their duty to support the law and government under which they lived, in so far as this support could be separated from a worship of divine Powers which they repudiated. And, no doubt, the officials of the different Churches who had charge of the common funds and of burial-places or meeting-places were naturally inclined to support the social system which gave them some kind of security. It must be remembered, however, that the two tendencies in the early Christian communities were themselves the sources of the two very different kinds of "texts" which are to be found in the New Testament. It is perhaps hardly necessary to note that the Christian Churches formed the New Testament, and not the New Testament the Christian Churches. In general the attitude of mind, or the sentiment, uniting the members of a Christian Church was more nearly what the pre-Christian world would have called a "philosophy" than what it would have called a religion. And as late as the fifth century Christianity is still referred to, even by Christian writers, as a "philosophy," because that word combined a reference to a "way of life" with a reference to certain views of the universe, and in particular of the celestial Powers.[3] The way of life uniting even the smallest Christian groups is expressed in the sentence "where two or three are gathered together in my name, there am I in the midst of them."[4] From the earliest times, and certainly as late as the fourth century, the "Christ of experience" was more important for the Christian Churches than the "Christ of history."

---

[1] Matt. xxii, 21.

[2] Rom. xiii, 1. See also Titus iii, 1; 1 Timothy ii, 1; and 1 Peter ii, 13.

[3] For example, St. John Chrysostom, preaching to the people of Antioch in A.D. 388, referring to Christian country-folk coming into the city for a feast-day, says: "These are our philosophers, and theirs is the best philosophy; for they show their virtue, not by their dress, but by their minds" (*Hom.* xix. *ad pop. Antioch.*).

[4] Matthew xviii, 20.

That is to say, the emotions aroused and the actions inspired by the teaching of Christ were the motive forces of Christianity, rather than a belief in any recorded occurrences. The experience of brethren who adopted the manner of life implied in mutual service and subordination to the universal Fatherhood of God, was the chief force which united the members of any one Christian Church and made them feel their fellowship with the members of distant Churches.

The memories of the martyrs and confessors of the times of persecution provided another force which promoted the unity of the Christian Churches. Lists of martyrs were kept and circulated from one Church to another; and public reading of the records of their lives and sufferings, besides memorial meetings at their burial places, served to consolidate the Churches. Their "Acta" and "Legenda" were no doubt affected from very early times by the imagination which became eventually, in the fifth and sixth centuries, sometimes fantastic in its adornment of a tale. But the Christian tradition in all the Churches was deeply affected by this new literature. Obviously the majority of Christians were more often influenced by the reading of the memorials of saints and martyrs than by the theological controversies with which the clergy and monks were more generally concerned. Again, it must not be imagined that the Churches, even in any one city, were already parts of one great organization. Different groups of Christians, organized as Churches with different bishops and elders, existed side by side; and the differences were in many cases not due to doctrine or discipline, but to different personalities—preachers, ascetics or bishops, who attracted a following. At the end of the fourth century, as Duchesne says, "Rome was full of little Churches. Not to speak of such remnants as there might be of old sects, such as Valentinians, Marcionites, Montanists, and Sabellians, the Novatian Church still continued to exist, governed by a series of bishops, who linked themselves on to the old episcopal succession from St. Peter to Fabian. The African Christians, . . . if Catholics, attended the same churches as the Catholics of Rome; but the Donatists were organized separately under bishops of their own country. . . .

There were also the Luciferians (followers of Lucifer of Cagliari) ... who had a bishop named Aurelius; but the most renowned personage of this party was a priest called Macarius, whose austerities were famous. . . . The police, stimulated by denunciations from the Lateran, made life hard for the schismatics."[1] Clearly, then, Christianity at the beginning of the fifth century was by no means a single and united movement. The quarrels of its adherents amongst themselves were as fierce as the opposition which all of them felt to non-Christian religions.

In spite of disagreements, however, all those who claimed to be Christian believed that they had adopted a new way of life and a conception of the universe fundamentally different from Paganism. The new moral ideal and the philosophy or general conception of the universe must be discussed elsewhere. But clearly they were the sources of the power which held Christian communities together. No economic or political changes can account for the extension of Christianity; because the enthusiasm and devotion of the members and officials of the Christian communities scattered about the Roman Empire had no direct reference to law and government, or to the problems of production and distribution. Again, from the earliest times the membership of the Christian Churches was held together, not only by a common outlook, but by certain rituals. All the Eastern religions in the Roman Empire had symbols of initiation; and in Christianity baptism continued to be recognized in the fifth century as a ritual accompanied by "sacramenta" or oaths and promises binding the new member of a Christian Church to avoid the ceremonies and theatrical performances of Paganism. The other great common ritual was that of the Eucharist.[2] The ceremonial meal of bread and wine had developed greatly from the simpler forms of early Christianity; and in the fifth century it was already the most significant of the ceremonies of the Churches.

But organized and traditional rituals in any community produce a class of officials who act in the name of all its members. Thus,

[1] Duchesne, *Early Hist. of Christian Church*, Eng. trans., vol. i, p. 366.
[2] For early Christian ideas see Loisy, *Les Mystères Paiens et le Mystère Chrétien* (1914).

the growth of the Christian rituals strengthened the influence of those who began to be called "the clergy"; and by the fifth century a fundamental difference already existed between the clergy and other members of the Christian Churches. Not only as controllers of the common funds and of the organization of Church property, but also as the chief actors in the ceremonies of the Church— bishops, priests and deacons had by that time taken control of whatever influence Christianity might have; and the separation of the clergy from other Christians, especially in ceremonies connected with the Eucharist, gradually made their position more like that of the priesthood in the "mystery" religions. It can hardly be doubted that in a society which believed very strongly in magic of one sort or another, the Christian rituals had gradually acquired some of the characteristics of magical ceremonies. Magic in this sense means the performance of traditional, generally symbolic acts, which are supposed to have effects such as purity from sin or salvation after death, of the reality of which no proof can be offered. Thus, the medieval practice of hanging some part of a vegetable round the neck in order to cure a tumour was clearly magic. And so were many of the cures for disease or for "sin" which were common in the mystery religions of the Roman world. The Christian Churches evolved their own magic.

A childish mind finds it difficult to distinguish between symbolical action and magical practice. A child may be unable to distinguish between the man who is playing the part and the part he is playing; and thus, no very clear line can be drawn by simple minds between the psychological effects of a ceremony or drama and the material or objective results of the action performed. Also, in "the climate of opinion" in which Christianity grew, there was widespread belief that magic could obtain what was desired, or discover the future.[1] Thus the early Christian rituals, which united the members of a Church, had acquired in very early times, and retained in the early fifth century, some elements of magic. Baptism and the Eucharist might be only symbolical of the entry into

[1] In Apuleius, *The Golden Ass*, there is evidence of this climate of opinion. See Thorndike, *History of Magic and Experimental Science* (1923), vol. i.

communion and the sharing of a common life of Christians; but in proportion as the officials of the Churches became a separate caste, the presbyter or elder naturally became more like the *sacerdos* or magic-worker of the older religions. The efficacy of magical rituals and objects with magical powers was not in dispute in those days. Both Christians and non-Christians generally agreed that celestial Powers could be induced to give help or knowledge, if the correct rituals were used. The only question was which kind of ritual was most effectual. And this climate of opinion, affecting the ceremonies of the Christian Churches, gave a new character to the "clergy." Thus bishops, deacons, priests and other subordinate officials were more and more separated from the general body of Christians. The clergy began to have a mind of its own. It was distinct from the laity and also from the more enthusiastic exponents of Christianity, the hermits, monks and nuns. Above all, the clergy began now to represent the Church itself. The bishops in particular became the embodiments of the common life of their Churches, and the only representatives of these Churches in their contacts with the officials of the Roman Empire. At the beginning of the fifth century individual bishops were the most prominent persons outside the official world, of whom the Roman authorities had to take account; and councils of bishops in the different provinces of the Empire laid down the rules that all Christians, and especially the clergy, had to follow.

In the many different cities (*civitates*) of the Roman Empire the tradition naturally differed as to the manner of selecting the bishop and the kind of person selected. But by the fifth century in all the great cities there had been established a recorded list of bishops, leading back to the days when Christianity first reached each city. In all cases the bishop had become the chief official of the Church or Churches in the city, and the natural representative of the Christian community there. When, therefore, the Christian community at last included the great majority of the inhabitants of the city, the bishop was in practice the most influential person in the district. He held a traditional power as judge or arbitrator among Christians, which was, indeed, only an extension among Christians of the old and still existing judicial or arbitral functions, in Jewish communities, of the Beth-din. In addition the bishop was recognized as judge by the imperial Authorities, as in the decree of Constantine, A.D. 318.[1] And in A.D. 333 the jurisdiction of bishops was recognized in civil suits, even if one of the litigants was unwilling to appear.[2] A later decree of A.D. 452 reads as follows: "The Emperor Valentinianus Augustus to Firminus, Praetorian Prefect and Patrician: There is dispute about the jurisdiction of bishops, and therefore we must make a decision by this law. When there is any case between clerics and it is convenient for the parties, let the bishop have the right to judge, but always after an arrangement has been made. This is also allowed by our authority with regard to the laity if they consent; but otherwise we do not allow bishops to be judges unless, as we have said, by agreement between the parties, because it is clear that bishops have no court under the laws or in any but religious cases according to the decrees of Arcadius and Honorius, which the Theodosian Book contains."[3]

The bishop was also the supreme controller of the property and other wealth of the local Church and was in the position of absolute authority over all the clergy of the district. Monks and hermits remained for some years, in the fifth century, either outside the control of the bishop, or only doubtfully under his jurisdiction. But for all practical purposes after this time "the Christian Church," in relation to political and military authorities, is the bishop, sometimes acting alone, sometimes with the bishops of Sees in the neighbourhood, acting in synods or councils.

In ritual, however, the division between the clergy and other Christians, which was characteristic of the social system in the First Europe, had hardly begun in the fifth century. The time was far distant when in a Christian church the clergy were to be enclosed in a chancel, within a screen, near an altar removed from the congregation and placed against a wall or other screen. In the fifth century the table for the commemorative meal in common had not yet become the altar for the "sacrifice of the Mass," as it did

---

[1] Cod. Theod., i, 27, 1. [2] Constitutio, Sirm., i (Mommsen, ed., p. 907).
[3] Nov. Valent., xxv, April 15, 452. De episcopali judicio.

later under the influence of Hebrew, Greek and Roman practices. The congregation stood on all sides of the table, as it still does in the older basilicas of Rome; and the officiating bishop or priest faced across the altar towards the majority of the people.[1] The clergy had no distinctive dress and no sacred vestments for ceremonial use, but wore the ordinary fashions of Roman citizens of the fifth and, later, of the sixth century, which became in the Middle Ages a ceremonial costume. As Celestine I, bishop of Rome (A.D. 422–432), wrote: "We, the clergy, are to be distinguished from the laity (*a plebe*) or others by doctrines, not clothing; by our manner of life, not of dress; by purity of mind, and not by adornment."[2] Also, as St. Jerome says, "the clergy should wear their hair short, but not with shaven crowns as the priests and votaries of Isis and Sarapis have it."[3] The language of ritual and sermons was the ordinary vulgar tongue, Latin in the West and Greek in the East.

On the other hand, the beginnings of sacerdotal celibacy in the Latin Churches in the early fifth century already threatened to produce the segregate caste of clergy peculiar to medieval Europe. The Greek Churches have never abandoned the maintenance of married priests, in spite of the extremes of asceticism among Eastern monks. In the Latin Churches, however, the much closer control over monasticism exercised by the bishops seems to have been secured at the cost of accepting for all the clergy that abstention from sexual intercourse which excited the enthusiasm of monastic reformers. So far as the Canons of the Latin Churches are concerned, the earliest rules against the marriage of deacons, priests or bishops seem to have been those of small local Councils of bishops in Spain and Gaul. Celibacy, or at least abstention from sexual intercourse by bishops and priests who were already married, was advocated by enthusiasts for many centuries before it was a rule to be enforced.[4]

Women had been excluded from the ritual services of the

[1] Augustine, *Sermo* 46, *de Verbo Domini*. Christus quotidie pascit. Mensa ipsius est illa in medio constituta. See Bingham, *Antiquities of the Christian Church* (ed. 1840), vol. ii, p. 432.   [2] Celestine I, Ep. ii, *ad Episcopos Gall.*, c. 1.
[3] Jerome, in *Ezek.* xliv.   [4] See Lea, *History of Sacerdotal Celibacy*, vol. i.

Churches by the Council of Laodicea in A.D. 352 (Canon xi). And from even earlier times it seems to have been generally felt that bishops and priests should not live an ordinary married life with their wives. The idea that sexual intercourse should be avoided was supported by references to the Levites in the Old Testament; and the praise of virginity was a commonplace. But it was not the general practice, even in the Latin Churches in the early fifth century, to refuse the priesthood to married men. A violent controversy, however, broke out among ecclesiastical writers when Vigilantius, a Spanish priest, maintained that the attempt to enforce celibacy on the clergy led to great evils. Unfortunately for his attempt to restrain the excesses of asceticism, Vigilantius also opposed the increasing use of relics, fasting and self-flagellation. He was attacked by St. Jerome in one of that saint's most abusive, ill-tempered and unreasonable diatribes, on the ground that to admit the marriage of the clergy was to open the way to the excesses of lust. But St. Jerome was on the winning side; and Innocent I, bishop of Rome, in A.D. 405, declared in a letter to bishops in Gaul that priests or deacons who were not celibate should be deprived of their offices. The chief difficulty seems to have been, not so much the continuance of ordinary marriage among the higher officials of the Church, as the attempt to reconcile a belief in the superior sanctity of the avoidance of sexual intercourse with the contradictory belief in the sanctity of marriage. But in practice, although bishops were generally compelled to live separately from their wives, the custom continued for many centuries after the fifth, even in the Latin Churches, that priests and deacons, as well as bishops, should be married. The separation of the clergy from other Christians, however, was promoted by the abhorrence of sexual intercourse, which was vigorously expressed by St. Jerome and St. Augustine. Both of these, in their old age, had reached—as they themselves confess—an abnormal intensity of feeling on the subject. Thus, the personal peculiarities of these two energetic and irrational old men reinforced the ascetic tradition. St. Jerome confesses that he had to retire to the desert because he found himself unable to control his feelings when he passed a pretty girl in the street;[1] and he argued against marriage on the ground that the wife might have to arrange a dinner-party at which dancers wearing very little might appear.[2] It is not strange that such a man should imagine that any form of sexual pleasure would lead to overwhelming and uncontrollable passions. As for St. Augustine, in his *Confessions*, he writes, first, that he lived with a concubine for over ten years, and then cast her off. But while waiting to be married to a young lady of fortune, he was unable to control his sexual impulse, and therefore lived with another concubine.[3] Even in the treatise *On Marriage and Lust*, in which he attempts to show that he is not opposed to marriage, he argues that there should be no pleasure derived from sexual intercourse.[4] Both Jerome and Augustine evidently suffered from the after-effects of the Manichean theory that there was something fundamentally evil in what they believed to be "the body" or "material flesh."

But the popular support for an enforced celibacy in the case, at least, of the higher clergy, was due less to asceticism than to the fear that the property and wealth of the Churches would pass into the hands of the families of the clergy, if the clergy were married. This is openly stated in later documents; but even in the fifth century the poorer Christians and the more devout clergy were afraid of the opportunities for enrichment which might fall into the hands of bishops and priests. An unmarried clergy would be likely to feel more acutely the influence of the members of their own order, and would be more easily controlled by councils of bishops. The attempt, however, of those who strove to enforce on the clergy the celibacy which was freely chosen by monks and nuns, tended, as far as it was successful, to separate bishops, priests and deacons from other Christians, and to make them a caste with opinions and interests of its own. This is the earliest sign of the medieval identification of the Church with the clergy, and of later clericalism.

---

[1] Jerome, *Adv. Vigilantium*, 16. *Pat. Lat.*, 23, "ne forma pulcherrima ad illicitos ducat amplexus."

[2] Ibid., *De perpet. Virginit. B. Mariae*, section 20. *Pat. Lat.*, 23, "tenuitate vestium nudae."   [3] Aug., *Conf.*, vi, 25.

[4] Ibid., *De Nuptiis et Concupiscentia*, *C.S.E.L.*, vol. 42, p. 215.

Imperial Policy

It is generally admitted that the last of the great official persecutions of Christianity was due to fear on the part of the Authorities.
It is said that, under Diocletian, Galerius inspired the final attack
upon Christianity; and later legends described how his persecution
of the Christians was punished by the disease from which he died.
When Constantine decided that he would seek the support of the
Christian God he may indeed have had the vision which later
writers described; he may have been influenced by his mother, who
was of "the lower class."[1] But much more probably he had in
mind the power and prestige of the Christian communities which
could be drawn upon, if he had the support of the Christian bishops.
In any case, his removal of the seat of government from Rome to
a city newly established and called by his name, certainly broke
the connection of the Empire with the traditional rites and the
established sources of imperial prestige. Rome was full of non-
Christian temples and priesthoods; and it was dominated by an
ancient aristocracy, which had long acted as a sort of opposition
within the imperial Dictatorship, and was committed by tradition
to non-Christian ideals. On the other hand, Constantinople, or
New Rome, was gradually filled with Christian churches. It had
no non-Christian past of any importance; and a new aristocracy,
arising in the Court of the Emperor himself, could hardly despise
the source of its wealth and prestige.

For almost a century after Constantine the Great had established
himself as the only Emperor of the Roman world, the Christian
Churches had been developing both in theory and practice their
new relations with the Government. The result at the beginning
of the fifth century may be shortly described as follows. In the
first place, the Roman Empire was a single, highly centralized
dictatorship; but the Christian Churches had grown up separately
in different cities or towns wherever missionaries had been successful. Therefore, when Constantine decided to seek the support
of organized Christianity, it was natural that he should desire the
members and officials of all the Churches within his Empire to be

---

[1] *Anon. Vales. Vita Constantini.* The writer says—"vilissima matre."

united in practice and belief. Christianity as a whole had rivals, not only in the traditional Roman and Greek forms of religion, but also in the religious movements, which like Christianity had entered the Empire from the East. Mithraism and Manichaeanism were probably the chief Oriental rivals of the Christian Churches; and there were many shades of belief and custom among small groups, which more or less approached what is now regarded as the Christian tradition. The chief difficulty of the Churches was, however, heresy. This meant division and disagreement, which weakened the forces from which Constantine proposed to draw his strength. It was therefore important for him to assimilate the organization of the Christian Churches to the unity of the Empire. He had, as an instrument of unity, the established custom that the bishops in different provinces should meet in councils, in order to state the rules which the members of their Churches should follow. These local councils bound together the Churches of different cities; and Constantine's first important act as patron of the new religion was to call the first general council of the bishops of the whole Roman world. This council met under the presidency of the Emperor at Nicaea in A.D. 325. The assembled bishops, of whom very few came from the West, decided to condemn the doctrine associated with the name of Arius; and this decision ruled out, at least for the moment, from the Churches of the Roman world the conception that Christ was in some way less divine than the Everlasting Father.[1] Constantine, at any rate, had the satisfaction of supposing that all the bishops within his Empire would be agreed upon doctrine. The Council also issued rules or canons which for the first time were intended to apply to all the Churches. In practice, however, the agreement reached at the Council of Nicaea did not diminish the number of sects or of Churches and bishops holding different views about the nature of Christianity. Constantine's son and successor, Constantius, was under the influence

---

[1] At the Council of Nicaea, there were about three hundred and eighteen bishops of whom about five came from the Latin Churches, and two priests representing the bishop of Rome. At the Council of Constantinople (in A.D. 381) there were three hundred and eighty-one bishops from the East and only one, a Spaniard, from the Latin Churches.

of Arian bishops; and so, later on, was the Emperor Valens. But in general the Emperors continued to attempt the enforcement of orthodoxy as defined at Nicaea. Their difficulties seem to have been greater in the East than in the West, largely, no doubt, because the bishops, clergy and monks in the East were more highly educated and more inclined to speculate and discuss the problems of the Divine Nature. This tendency of the eastern Churches to disunion, at times leading to bitter rivalry and murderous riots, may have brought into greater prominence the more accommodating spirit of the western or Latin Churches. The Emperors themselves, at certain times, might look to Old Rome as a source of unity in belief and practice such as they desired to see prevailing throughout their Empire. Thus in the imperial decree on Christian doctrine issued in February 380, the Roman tradition is definitely connected by imperial Authority with the Nicene Creed, and the attempt is made to secure, for those who accept this creed, the title of Catholic. The first part of the decree runs as follows:—

"The Augusti, Gratian, Valentinian and Theodosius: Edict to the people of Constantinople. We wish that all nations subject to the rule of our Clemency shall adhere to that religion which the divine apostle Peter handed to the Romans (as is sufficiently shown by its existence among them to this day), and which it is obvious that the pontiff Damasus follows as well as Peter, bishop of Alexandria, a man of apostolical holiness: so that according to the apostolic discipline and the doctrine of the Gospels we believe in one Deity of Father, Son and Holy Spirit, with equal majesty and merciful (*pia*) Trinity. We order those who obey this law to take the name of Catholic Christians: we pronounce all others to be mad and foolish, and we order that they shall bear the infamous name of heretics and shall not call their conventicles churches. These are to be punished by the divine vengeance first, and afterwards by our action which we have taken under the will of heaven."[1] Thus Catholic is made to mean, not merely universal as opposed to local, but also united as contrasted with diverse; and the Church in

---

[1] *Cod. Theod.*, xvi, 1, 2 (February 27, 380). It is not easy to find suitable English for the description of Deity—"parili majestate et pia Trinitate."

general, or the Church of the whole world from about this time, came to be regarded as more important, at any rate for the clergy, than the separate Churches of different districts.

The second great advantage which the Churches received from the Empire was an official repudiation of non-Christian rites and, by implication, of the worship of the Emperor as divine, which had hitherto been one of the unifying forces of the Empire. In later years—after Constantine—the temples were closed, the non-Christian priesthoods suppressed, and the funds which they drew from the State withdrawn. It is said that the Emperor Gratian, the pupil of Ausonius, was the first Emperor to refuse the title of Pontifex Maximus, which made him the head of the traditional priesthood of Rome. The days were still very distant when that same title could be adopted by the bishop of Rome. But obviously the bishops of the Christian Churches in the early fifth century had already obtained much greater influence and authority than had been possessed by any pre-Christian priesthood.

The third great benefit conferred by the Empire upon the Christian Churches was the elimination of all groups claiming to be Christian which did not submit to the discipline or accept the doctrine of the majority of bishops. The majority of bishops might be persuaded to move in one direction or another at different Councils; and the dissentients at any Council did not easily submit to the vote of the majority. These dissident groups were now called heretics; and they included chiefly Arians in the East and Priscillianists and Donatists in the West. As the men of the Middle Ages would have said, the "secular power" was the instrument of the "spiritual authority" of the bishops. But at the beginning of the fifth century it was still doubtful which doctrine and which discipline would be enforced by imperial Authority. Apart from the short period of revived religious antiquarianism under Julian, the successors of Constantine were by no means all of the same opinion about the nature of the Deity worshipped in Christianity. When Constantius, the son of Constantine, and Valens ruled, many Churches were controlled by Arian bishops. The issue, which will be discussed elsewhere, lay fundamentally in the conception of a man who was God. The Arians in general followed the Eastern or Semitic belief in God as a celestial Power aloof from human affairs; but the Hellenic tradition of hero-worship, and above all of the worship of Emperors in the Roman world, was so strong that the belief in Christ as God inevitably became Catholic and Roman. The tradition of the Roman Empire thus undoubtedly helped the Christian Churches in their opposition to the Arian heresy.

Another advantage which the Christian Churches may be reckoned to have received from the Empire is the right of asylum or sanctuary in the church building. This was an adaptation to the new Christian regime of the old right of sanctuary attached to certain non-Christian shrines and to contact with the statue of the Emperor. A powerful pursuer did not often hesitate to tear his victim from any altar; but in pre-Christian days, as in the Middle Ages, the fear of the magic of supernatural Powers might occasionally restrain the violence of personal hatred or political enmity.

One further point is important for estimating the relationship between the Churches and the Empire. The Empire had been from the beginning a dictatorship with the characteristics of all such forms of government—the suppression of criticism, the influence of a small group of persons in immediate contact with the dictator, who were selected by him as his advisers and agents, and finally, the use of secret agents or of spies and informers. In the earliest years of the imperial dictatorhip there had been a survival of criticism and even something approaching an official opposition among the older senatorial families in Rome.[1] But one effect of Constantine's removal of the seat of government from Rome was the reduction to impotence of the older forms of opposition. It is important, therefore, that the Churches, and especially their bishops, began at that time to fulfil some of the functions of criticism and opposition within the dictatorship. The Christian Emperors after Constantine continually attempted to prevent criticism and opposition from any bishops. They used exile and

[1] The position is explained in Boissier, *L'Opposition sous les Césars.*

imprisonment, even after the fifth century, to reduce recalcitrant bishops to obedience. But the Church had in fact increased its power and organization, at first in opposition to official persecutions and later independently of the civil and military Authorities. The tradition of independence, therefore, survived; and bishops who had a strong popular following, or exceptional moral influence, often defied and sometimes openly rebuked the civil Authorities and the Emperor himself. The example of Ambrose, as bishop of Milan, refusing to admit to the communion of the Church the Emperor Theodosius, remained throughout the centuries that followed an example of the function of the Church as an opposition under dictatorship. On the other hand, the influence of dictatorship in civil and military affairs supported a tendency to dictatorship within the Church. In the fifth century, and indeed throughout the Middle Ages, authority in the government of States and Churches was so ineffectual that an exaggerated value was placed upon obedience. Criticism was feared: opposition, if possible, suppressed. Thus, in the Churches, after the fourth century, bishops became more independent of the whole body of Christians in each Church, and more absolute in their control over persons and property. They naturally, therefore, supported dictatorship in the form of absolute monarchy as the only form of effectual government then conceivable.

The Latin Churches

In western Europe, in the fifth century and after, the aloofness, if not the opposition of the Churches, was increased by the gradual separation of the language and thought of the Latin-speaking world from those of the Greek-speaking Court and bishoprics dependent upon Constantinople. The old Roman language was that of the Churches of the West. And with the language went habits of thought and of emotion, which were associated with the traditions of Roman government, and were quite different from the Oriental attitude towards authority which found expression in the Greek of the eastern Churches. Thus even the accident of a linguistic difference in rituals, creeds, prayers and preaching, tended to support the position of the Latin Churches as an opposition. This separation of the moral authority of the bishops from the moral authority of even Christian Emperors, who might claim some ecclesiastical influence, made it easier for the bishops in the West to come into close contact with the leaders of the barbarian invasions, without appearing to be agents or advocates of the Roman system of government.

In the early fifth century, under the Emperor Honorius, the established situation in the relations between the Empire and the Churches in the West increased the prestige and power of both. The Emperor and his Court and many of his chief officials professed Christianity, and were regarded generally as responsible for the maintenance of that form of it which was called Catholic and Roman. The Churches, therefore, derived both the power to suppress opponents and the prestige of an official body from the Roman Empire. On the other hand, the influence of the Empire was maintained and extended by the bishops of the Church, especially when the barbarians had destroyed in any towns or territories the Roman military and administrative organization. By such means the moral authority of the Roman system of law survived long after there was any military force to maintain it. Again, the Churches contributed to the prestige of the Emperor and his Empire by their acceptance of his authority as divinely appointed, and by the widespread belief that the Roman Empire was the last established order upon earth before the final dissolution of all things.

Finally, the Latin Churches gained moral authority by the removal of the centre of government to Constantinople. The eighth-century legend, expressed in the "Donation of Constantine," that Pope Silvester had been left supreme authority over the Roman Empire in the West when Constantine removed the seat of government to "New Rome," is obviously fiction. But it is based on the indubitable fact that the bishop of Rome, after the seat of government had been fixed in Constantinople, gradually acquired prestige as the only apostolic patriarch among the Latin Churches. These Churches were obviously more independent of any civil or military authority than those of the eastern Mediterranean. And their independence gave them additional moral authority.

The Christian Churches and Civil Government

The problem of adjusting the traditions of Christianity and of the Empire was not easily solved. Within the Christian tradition the two different attitudes towards government, and the "world" generally, were equally strong. On the one hand, the monastic tradition, developed in Egypt and Syria, had spread to the provinces of the West. Thousands of men and women, who claimed to be in the truest sense Christian, left the cities and lived in deserted places or adopted a manner of life within the cities which separated them entirely from their fellows. The moral standards and the conception of the ideal life among such men and women will be discussed later. Here it is necessary only to note that their influence tended to weaken the Roman system of government and the development of normal civilized life. Hence the hostility to them expressed by Rutilius Namatianus.[1]

Among the most influential of Christians who adopted the attitude of aloofness towards the world was St. Jerome. His writings express most fully the fear of the normal relations of life, which drove men and women into solitude. He lamented, indeed, the downfall of Rome; but he showed no desire whatever to do anything to prevent it, and had no feeling of responsibility for the maintenance of the system upon which civilized life depended. His concern was with the salvation of his own soul after death and with the instruction of devout ladies—his followers—in the avoidance of marriage and of social intercourse. On the other hand, the tradition that Christians should maintain the authority of an established Government is represented by such writers as St. Ambrose and St. Augustine; and the Churches of the West found it increasingly impossible to refuse responsibility for the established order as their membership increased to include nearly all the inhabitants of each city, and as their properties increasingly required the protection of law.

[1] Rutilius Nam., de Reditu, i, 440.

In practice the two different attitudes affected the Churches chiefly in the selection of bishops. It was still the custom at the beginning of the fifth century that the bishop of a Church should be elected by all its members. Usually this election took place by a sort of acclamation in the chief church of the neighbourhood. And the name of a possible bishop would, no doubt, be suggested by the clergy, or even by the bishops of neighbouring Sees, who met for the election. Sometimes accident seems to have suggested the name of the bishop, as at the election of Ambrose to the bishopric of Milan, when a child is said to have cried out, "Ambrose is bishop."[1] Sometimes, indeed, there was violent controversy between the advocates of different candidates for the See. At the election of Damasus as bishop of Rome, for example, by a majority of the clergy and people, another candidate had already been elected in another church by a small number of clergy and people. After some fighting, the opponents of Damasus, who had barricaded themselves in the church now called Santa Maria Maggiore, were assaulted, stoned, and many of them slain by the supporters of Damasus. At a later date there is an interesting account of the election of a bishop after some disagreement as to the candidates, in a letter of Sidonius Apollinaris.[2] He writes as follows:—

I cannot delay an hour in letting you know of an event which must cause you the greatest pleasure, anxious as you were to learn what success attended the piety and firmness of our Metropolitan and Father in Christ, Patiens, upon the occasion of his visit to Châlons. He went to ordain a bishop of that town, where discipline had been imperilled after the retirement and subsequent death of the young bishop Paulus. Some of the provincial bishops formed his escort; others had preceded him. When the episcopal council met, it found that the opinion of the citizens was not unanimous, and that there existed private factions of the kind so ruinous to the public welfare. The presence of three candidates aggravated these evils. The first had no moral qualifications whatever, but only the privilege of ancient lineage, of which he made the most. The second was brought in on the applause of parasites, bribed to support him by the free run of a gourmand's table. The third had a

[1] Ambrose had not even been baptized, when thus selected.
[2] Sid. Apoll., Ep. iv, 25, trans. by Dalton, ii, p. 46. Letter to Domminulus of A.D. 470.

tacit understanding with his supporters that if he attained the object of his ambition, the plundering of the Church estates should be theirs. Seeing this, the holy Patiens and the holy Euphronius determined that no thought of odium or popularity should move them from the firmness and severity of the saner judgement. They communicated their intention to their fellow bishops in secret conclave assembled before they made it public. Then, with a complete disregard of the unruly crowd, they suddenly joined their hands upon the holy John, a man conspicuous for an honourable, humane and gentle life, and without the faintest suspicion of what they proposed, or the slightest desire for preferment. This John was first a Reader, and had been a server at the altar from his tender years. In course of time and strenuous duty he became archdeacon, in which office or rank his efficiency kept him back; they would not give him promotion because they did not wish to relieve him of functions he performed so well. Such was the man, a member only of the second order, on whom they laid their hands to the perplexity of the factions which had no acclamations ready for one never even put forward for the office, but dared not at the same time say anything against a man whom his own career acclaimed. So, to the stupefaction of the intriguers, the rage of bad citizens, and the delight of the good, without one dissentient voice, they two consecrated their new colleague.

The contrast in this case was that between saintliness and simony, not between aloofness from worldly affairs and practical ability. But clearly the bishop who would have control of the properties of the Church and the support of the needy, besides being practical, must also be honest. Not unnaturally, those who intrigued for a bishopric were suspected of having a desire for wealth and power. The majority, however, in every Church preferred a bishop who was capable as well as benevolent.

The two different attitudes of Christians towards the social order—opposition or acquiescence—may be perceived in the fifth century in the difference between the two different types of men selected as bishops. On the one hand, the devout and enthusiastic preferred to have as a bishop a man of saintly character from the monastic tradition of asceticism and aloofness from the world. On the other hand, the clergy, and perhaps the majority of those who were concerned with the administration of ecclesiastical property and its use in charity, or with the relation of the Church to the civil Authorities, preferred to have as their bishop a man of education, of wealth and social position, and of some administrative experience.

An example of the ascetic type of bishop is Saint Martin of Tours. He had been a soldier, but had retired as a hermit to a hut near Tours. His holiness attracted the people, who demanded that he should be elected as bishop of Tours. According to the writer of his life, Sulpicius Severus, some of the bishops who had been summoned for the election said that Martin was unsuitable because he had an undistinguished face, dirty clothes and untrimmed hair.[1] Martin was, however, elected; and his activities, according to his biographer, were largely concerned with destroying Paganism in his diocese. He died in A.D. 397. Another example of a bishop taken from the ascetic tradition is Paulinus of Nola. He had been a man of property in Gaul and a friend of Ausonius. He lived for some time in Barcelona and there married a wealthy lady; but both determined to give up their wealth and to retire to a small estate of his at Nola, near Naples, and there pay their devotions at the tomb of St. Felix. His home there he describes as a monastery;[2] and, apparently after the death of his wife, he was chosen bishop of Nola. There and at Fundi, where also he had property, he built and adorned churches in honour of St. Felix, the decoration of which he describes in detail in a letter to his friend Severus.[3] The churches were covered with paintings and verses, and in one of the many hymns which he wrote in honour of St. Felix he says that the decorations were planned to attract those "who had come for prayer and not for feasting."[4] He was bishop of Nola in A.D. 410 and continued to live there until he died at the age of seventy-eight in A.D. 431, apparently quite untouched by the political vicissitudes of Italy. He visited Rome occasionally for the feast-day of the bishop of Rome at the time; and in his letters he describes the devotional exercises which filled his time there. He does not seem to have been interested even in ecclesiastical affairs,

---

[1] Sulpicius Severus, *Vita S. Martini*, Section 9.
[2] Ep., v, 15.   [3] Ibid., xxxii.
[4] *Carm.*, xxvii, 398, "quos huc ad sancti justum Felicis honorem duxerit orandi studium, non cura bibendi."

for his mind was concentrated on the "inner life" as expressed in his famous apology to Ausonius: "Even so in these days also they who with pure hearts have adopted Christ are wont to live—not as beside themselves, nor out of savagery choosing to live in desert places; but because, turning their faces to the stars on high, contemplating God, and intent to scan the deep wells of truth, they love repose void of empty cares, and shun the din of public life, the bustle of affairs, and all concerns hostile to the gifts of heaven both by Christ's command and in desire for salvation."[1]

Evidently bishops like Martin and Paulinus belonged to the tradition of unworldly Christians who are not concerned with the difficult problems of law and government, trade and industry, or with the relation of the Church to such problems. Indeed, on the assumption, which was, no doubt, accepted by the majority of Christians in the fifth century, that the world was near its end, maintenance or destruction of the social system was of no account.

On the other hand, the majority of the bishops of the Churches in the West were men with administrative ability, who were willing to play a part in the control or direction of the social forces of the time. Such were St. Ambrose and St. Augustine, and the great majority of the bishops elected by the Church in Rome. In Gaul, where the Arian kings of the barbarians ruled during the fifth and sixth centuries, the bishops were generally men of ancient and wealthy Roman families, such as Sidonius Apollinaris, Simplicius, bishop of Autun, and Gregory of Tours.[2] Such men had not only the confidence of the majority of the population in their diocese, but were also able to exert an influence over the barbarians because of their greater knowledge, their obvious culture and the skill that many of them had acquired in the public services of the Roman Empire.

The position of the bishops in relation to the civil Authorities may be briefly summarized under three headings. They assisted the

[1] "Non inopes animi neque de feritate legentes
desertis habitare locis; sed in ardua versi."

[2] Greg. Tur., G.C., 76, Pat. Lat., 71, col. 883. Simplicius de stirpe nobili, valde dives in opibus saeculi nobilissimae conjugi sociatus . . . propter illam saeculi dignitatem . . . a populo eligitur.

civil Authority and were assisted by it in establishing greater unity of doctrine and practice among Christians. Secondly, the bishops often organized resistance against barbarian conquest or tyranny; and thirdly, when barbarian conquest was achieved, the bishop might act in favour of compromise or the adjustment of claims between contending barbarian warriors or between conquerors and conquered.

At the beginning of the fifth century an instance of the relation between the imperial Authorities and the bishops in Africa is to be found in the record of a discussion held in Carthage in A.D. 411 between Catholic and Donatist bishops under the presidency of the Roman Tribune, Marcellinus.[1] Thus, about six months after the sack of Rome by Alaric, the bishops of Africa were trusting to the imperial Authority to decide which of them should control the Churches. Among the Catholic bishops was the great Augustine himself. The presiding Tribune calls him to order when he attempts to evade answering a question.[2] On the other hand, the Donatist bishops declare that they cannot understand the sort of Latin spoken in Rome, and demand that their own African Latin should be used.

St. Augustine himself was in no doubt that the Church should expect from the civil Authorities the persecution of heretics; and his use of the phrase in the Gospel, "compel them to come in," was accepted for many generations after him to support the idea that Christ himself approved of persecution as a means of inducing heretics to conform.[3] This attitude of the bishops towards the civil Authority was, no doubt, common throughout the Roman world; and the function of persecutors in the name of Christianity was publicly accepted by the imperial Authorities and expressed in many sections of the Theodosian law-books. It was assumed that, as the bishops expected the civil Authorities to assist them, the

[1] The fullest account of the early days of this discussion is to be found in Mansi, *Concilia*, iv, 410 sq.; and a short summary of the rest of the discussion is in St. Augustine's works.

[2] Mansi, *Conc.*, iv, 241. Marcellinus to Augustine: "ad quaesita responde"; and again (col. 246), "Ad interrogata respondere dignare."

[3] The phrase is in Luke xiv, 23; and is obviously quite irrelevant in a discussion of persecution. The phrase is used as the title of a small book "Contrains les entrer," attacking St. Augustine and persecution, issued under a pseudonymn (Th. Brugge) by Bayle, about 1680. See Augustine, *Ep.* 93, 5, *C.S.E.L.*

bishops themselves would use their influence to support whatever Emperor happened to reign, by whatever fraud or violence he might have attained his position.

The most striking transformation, however, of the position of the Churches occurred during the barbarian invasions of Gaul and Italy in the fifth century, when many bishops of important Sees assisted or actually organized the defence against the invaders. During the earlier invasions of Gaul certain bishops undertook the duty of providing for the military defence of the citizens under their care. Sidonius Apollinaris, chosen as bishop of Averni (Clermont) in A.D. 471, was regarded as a leader of the defence of Auvergne against the Visigoths in A.D. 474. But in spite of a momentary truce, Auvergne in the following year was under the complete control of Euric, the king of the Visigoths; and the bishop, at first banished, suffered later from the hostility of Arian priests who had the support of the Visigothic king. Many bishops were thus compelled to accept the new Gothic rulers; and when their cities lost the defence or support of the Roman Empire, they remained representatives and advocates of Roman civilization at the Courts of the new kings.

When, however, the Huns under Attila were known to be approaching Gaul, the bishops in general seem to have made common cause with such Gothic rulers as were willing to combine with the Romans against the new invaders. Attila crossed the Rhine in A.D. 450 and first pillaged Trier. Bishops and priests were slaughtered at Tongres, Arras, Laon and Rheims; and Attila marched from Metz, where the bishop had not been killed, to Orleans. The bishop of Orleans, Ananius (St. Aignan), set out for Arles to ask for military help; and he secured it from Theodoric the Visigoth, whose forces relieved Orleans when the pillage of the city was already beginning. Attila was then approached by Lupus, bishop of Troyes, already seventy years old, who besought him to spare the people of that district. Lupus was granted his request; but he was taken by the Huns as a hostage in their retreat.

This same bishop, Lupus, is connected with an earlier resistance to barbarian invasion. He and Germanus, bishop of Auxerre, are said to have gone over from Gaul into Britain to counteract the influence of the British heretic Pelagius; and while they were in Britain the barbarians of the North together with the Saxons invaded the areas settled by the Romans. Germanus and Lupus are said to have encouraged the Britons to resist, to have baptized those in the British army who were not Christians, and soon after Easter, A.D. 430, to have devised the method by which the Britons routed their enemy. The two bishops had urged the Britons to make their stand in a narrow valley, and on the approach of the enemy to shout loudly three times "Alleluia"—which is said to have resulted in complete victory over the pagans.

In spite, however, of attempts at organizing resistance and at the "appeasement" of conquering barbarians, new barbarian kingdoms were established by the end of the fifth century in complete independence of the Roman Empire. The bishops had then to face a new situation. Political and military power were neither imperial nor Catholic. The population of *Romania* was subject to the rule of barbarians who were Arian heretics. The bishops, therefore, who alone still retained moral authority over this population, had to make some changes in the relations between the Churches and the kings. In most cases they sacrificed their connection with the Roman Empire in order to secure some justice and liberty for their own congregations. They acted as intermediaries between the subject Roman population and its barbarian rulers, urging wherever possible some consideration for the victims of the conquest. An example of work done by the bishops is to be found in the labours of St. Epiphanius, bishop of Pavia. When Ricimer desired to send an ambassador to Anthemius in Rome in A.D. 471, Epiphanius was chosen as a man who would be "respected by anyone who is Catholic and Roman";[1] and he made peace between them. At the time of Euric's accession to power at Toulouse, Ennodius says that the same bishop thought that friendship might be preserved between kings which could not be maintained by arms; he therefore went to Euric to persuade him "that he should not use the

---

[1] Ennodius, *Vita S. Epiphanii*: "Quem venerari possit quicumque, si est Catholicus et Romanus." See above, Chapter III, p. 140.

sword against the boundaries of the Empire lest the Lord of Heaven should be offended, and reminded him, as king, that there was a King above him who proclaimed peace."[1] Under Odovacar, Epiphanius secured a remission of taxes for his people and protested against the exactions of a royal officer. When Theodoric invaded Italy, Epiphanius met him at Milan and together with the bishop of Milan asked for an amnesty for those who had supported Odovacar. Theodoric is said to have told them in reply to look at the empty fields and vineyards of Liguria. The Burgundians had taken captive many thousands of the inhabitants of Liguria to sell as slaves at Lyons. Epiphanius and Victor, bishop of Turin, then went to Gundobad, king of the Burgundians, with money; and the king ordered his minister to release those who had been captured and to sell cheaply those who had fought. As a result, six thousand men and women were able to return to their own land. But when the bishop had led back this great army of ransomed slaves, they besought him to intercede for them against taxation; and he undertook the journey to Ravenna. On his return he caught a chill and, "owing to the lack of skill of the doctors," he died in A.D. 497.

A more famous example of the efforts of bishops to ward off barbarian invasion is the journey of the bishop of Rome, Leo I, to meet Attila in northern Italy in A.D. 452. Attila and his Huns were threatening to attack Rome when Leo, together with two senators from Rome, persuaded him to withdraw to the Danube. His success gave immense prestige to the bishop of Rome as a defender of the Roman Empire and a peacemaker. And in a letter written fifty years later by some eastern bishops to Pope Symmachus (about A.D. 510), the example of Leo is quoted as follows: "If your predecessor, the archbishop Leo, now among the Saints, thought it not unworthy of him to go himself to meet the barbarian Attila, that he might free from captivity of the body not Christians only but also Jews and pagans, surely your Holiness will be touched by the captivity of soul under which we are suffering."[2] This letter implies that Attila's success in Italy would have resulted in the reduction of thousands of the inhabitants to slavery; but it is not

---

[1] Ennodius, *Vita S. Epiphanii*.   [2] *Pat. Lat.*, 62, col. 63.

known how Leo contrived to persuade Attila to leave Italy, nor indeed whether Attila had not already decided to retire eastwards for strategic reasons. A few years afterwards, however, there was danger again. In A.D. 455, a raid of the Vandals from Africa approached Rome; and Leo went out with a procession of the Roman clergy to attempt to persuade the Vandal king Gaiseric not to sack the city. The Vandals, however, entered Rome and went off with much treasure. Leo had failed; but the bishop of Rome was evidently the only person in authority who faced the barbarians as an opponent.

During the barbarian invasions of the fifth century the bishops of the Catholic Church evidently stood as far as possible on the side of the Roman Empire, or at least in defence of those who had been Roman subjects. In all cases this position of the officials of the Church was rendered easier because the barbarian invaders were Arians and had with them Arian clergy who might prove to be dangerous rivals of the reigning bishops, and did in fact, at least in Africa, incite the new rulers to persecution of the Catholic clergy. Throughout the western world the bishops of the local Churches were men whose language and culture were Roman, and who were often men of wealth and power in the Roman world. They would naturally, therefore, look to the Roman Emperor as the true representative of divine authority in the political sphere. But the position of the bishop of Rome was even more intimately bound up with that of the Roman Emperor. Leo himself was in the closest possible touch with the Emperor Valentinian III and his devout mother, Galla Placidia.

In spite of the bishops, however, barbarian kingdoms took the place of the Roman Empire in the West; and the bishops therefore were compelled by the new situation to change their attitude towards political authority. It became necessary for them to recognize as in some sense legitimate the rule of barbarian kings; and their policy was directed to increasing their influence in the new situation. Under Arian kings, who were not violently anti-Catholic, the bishops retained their ecclesiastical and some of their civil powers. In Africa alone was there any opposition to the Catholic clergy. In Italy, when Odovacar made himself king in A.D. 476, the bishop of Rome, Simplicius, seems to have felt no difficulty in accepting such authority as the new Arian king might claim; but he still continued to communicate with the Emperor at Constantinople on the old basis, as a subject with his ruler. The discussions between Simplicius as bishop of Rome, and the authorities at Constantinople, both ecclesiastical and political, were concerned with doctrinal matters; but he wrote to the Emperor as an authority having some legitimate power in ecclesiastical matters.

When Theodoric took the place of Odovacar as king of the Goths in Italy, the Pope and the Catholic clergy of Italy were separated from the Emperor and the Eastern Church by disagreement on doctrine. And Theodoric in A.D. 498 heard the appeal of the Roman Church, as an arbitrator in the disputed election of that year for the bishopric. The king decided that Symmachus, who had been elected bishop of Rome on the same day as Laurentius, should hold the See; and thus an Arian barbarian king of Italy took action with the same sort of authority in deciding ecclesiastical disputes as to the succession in a Catholic bishopric, as might be granted by all the Churches to an Emperor. Within the boundaries of what had been the western parts of the Roman Empire the position of the bishops with regard to the civil and military authorities, who may be regarded as "the State," was ambiguous and experimental during the first stage of the transition from the Roman Empire to medieval Europe. All the bishops, and particularly the bishop of Rome, looked to the Emperor at Constantinople as the true representative of civil authority; but all were compelled by circumstances and by the policy of acquiescence, where Arian kings did not persecute, to establish a new relationship between the Church and the civil and military Authorities.

The extension of the Christian Church outside the boundaries of the Roman Empire created new problems. Originally the Christian communities had been small and select companies of men and women in the cities of the Empire; and Optatus, the bishop of Milevis in Numidia, had quite clearly written in about A.D. 370 that the Church is "within the Empire, not the Empire within the

Church." But missionary activity soon carried Christianity into regions hitherto untouched by Roman authority; and it was largely through the capture of slaves and the trade in slaves that Christianity was thus spread. The two most important examples of this extension of Christianity were the results of the work of Ulfilas among the Goths, and of St. Patrick among the Irish. The missionary work of Ulfilas led to the conversion of the Goths and Vandals. He worked as bishop in the lands near the Danube between A.D. 350 and A.D. 380; and translated the bible into Gothic, omitting the books of *Kings*, on the ground that they were too warlike; because he believed that the Goths were warlike enough already. But his own Christianity and his ordination as bishop were derived from bishops who held the Arian view of the Deity; and, therefore, almost by accident, the Goths and Vandals knew of Christianity only in its Arian version. If in addition, as seems to be the case, their Arian bishops and priests used the Gothic language in religious ceremonies, they were all the more separated from the Latin Christians over whom later their kings were to rule. Thus heresy, which the barbarians inherited, as Salvian says, through no fault of their own, led at a later date to political difficulties and affected very deeply the relations of the Latin Churches to the barbarian kingdoms of the fifth century. Arian or Gothic Christianity, after the conversion of the barbarians, entered the western parts of the Roman Empire as the religion of its conquerors. Their conversion, indeed, made it easier for Christians within the Empire to accept them as agents of Divine Providence, as it has already been shown in the quotations (in Chapter II) from Orosius, with reference to Alaric; but the ultimate effect of the work of Ulfilas was to disturb the Latin Churches rather than to extend the territories in which Christianity prevailed.

The work of St. Patrick had quite different effects. He was a Briton under the Roman government of Britain at the end of the fourth century, the son of a Christian deacon, who was a municipal councillor, and the grandson of a priest.[1] He was captured, probably on the coast of Glamorgan, by raiders from Ireland; there he lived

---

[1] *Patricii Confessio*, in *Pat. Lat.*, vol. 53, col. 801 sq.

for six years as a slave and, after his escape, he went back to Ireland to preach Christianity. His own Christianity was influenced chiefly by that current in Gaul[1] where he studied before returning to Ireland. The result of his activity and that of later missionaries was the development of a strong Christian movement in Ireland, dominated by monastic ideas and organization. Ireland had never been touched by the Roman Empire, and it was now won by the Latin Churches. But differences of practice in the keeping of Easter and in the wearing of the tonsure led in later years to controversy between those who maintained the Irish and the Roman traditions respectively. With the growth of Christianity in Ireland learning and the arts also grew; and from Ireland the people of Scotland and northern England eventually derived their Christianity. In this case at least the extension of Christianity was in no sense dependent upon the power or prestige of the Roman Empire. The relations between the bishops and kings of Ireland and northern Britain were therefore quite free of the difficulties that arose from loyalty to the Roman Empire in other parts of the western world.

The Latin Bishops and the Roman Empire

The establishment of organized authority in the Christian Churches before the political and military systems of medieval Europe arose, greatly increased the influence of the bishops in the social system which followed the disappearance of the Roman Empire in the West. The bishop of the congregation or Church in any city or town gradually acquired the authority of the civil as contrasted with the military officials of the Empire. And the bishop had the additional advantage of being in some sense chosen by local public opinion. He was generally a man already well-known in the district before he became bishop, and was not, like so many Roman officials, a stranger resident only for a time. Like the governor of a British Colony to-day, the Roman official in the last days of the Empire in the West had no intention of remaining in the district he governed. But the bishop belonged to his See. Again,

---

[1] This is implied in the *Confessio*, section 19, "*eram usque Gallias visitare fratres et ut viderem faciem sanctorum Domini mei.*"

the bishops of neighbouring Sees had begun even before the fourth century to meet in Synods and Councils, not only for the election of new bishops, but also to agree upon rules called canons by which their Churches should be governed. The bishops of the western Churches, therefore, were gradually building up in the fifth century a form of federal government which eventually, under the Metropolitans and the only patriarch in the West, the bishop of Rome, survived into the Middle Ages. The strength of the Churches, and especially of the bishops, as against kings and other civil authorities, lay in the much more efficient organization for unity on a scale larger than could be maintained in those days by military forces.

Again, the division of civil from military officials, begun by Diocletian and confirmed by Constantine, had accustomed the Roman world to a distinction between public functions—service, on the one hand, and power on the other. The civil Authorities, Praetorian Prefects and Vicars under them, had dealt with final appeals in the law-courts, the imperial post, public buildings, the *collegia* or public associations, the control of prices, the corn-supply and recruiting, and the organization of higher education. They had some theoretical superiority over the military commanders within their jurisdiction. But by the end of the fifth century the civil administration of the Empire in the West had broken down and the military organization had been "barbarized." The natural result was that the bishops as representatives of Roman culture took over the functions of the old *civil* authorities. They were already judges under the imperial decrees. They had care of the churches, which had become already the chief public buildings. They organized the relief of the indigent; and they supported whatever was left of education. Thus the connection between the Church and the School, which dominated the Middle Ages and still survives in England and her colonies, was the result of the accident that the barbarian rulers of the fifth century could neither read nor write. Hence also the connection of the Church with poor-relief and "public works" in the Middle Ages. There is nothing in the "nature of things" to decide whether Church or State shall control education or other public services; and what medieval writers took as the divine dispensation in dividing "spiritual" from "temporal" powers, was in fact only the effect of the Roman system of Diocletian.

The fact that all the bishops and the great majority of the Christian people in the West used Latin as their ordinary language, gave them an immense advantage over their barbarian conquerors. The different forms of Germanic or Gothic dialects, used by the barbarian warriors as well as by their Arian bishops and priests, divided one barbarian kingdom from another. And for the practical problems of administration and law, barbarian rulers were rendered less competent by the limitations of dialects, which had no means of expressing the complicated relationships of the more civilized Roman world. Indeed the barbarian kingdoms of the fifth century, as will be shown later, were compelled to have even their own traditional customs formulated in Latin. The Latin language, therefore, which was the common speech of western Europe as well as the language of the Christian literature and rituals of the West, united the subjects of the different barbarian kings and separated them both from their conquerors and from the Empire and the eastern Churches, whose language was Greek. In the fifth century Latin had not yet become the language of a caste and of traditional rituals, distinct from the language of common folk, as it was in the Middle Ages. But as early as the sixth century it was possible to note differences in the Latin of the different countries of western Europe and Africa, although Latin of some sort still remained the only adequate means of communication between educated men and women and between those who lived in different parts of western Europe.

Another important effect of the distinction between the Latin-speaking Churches and the barbarian kings and warriors was the final exclusion of the Arian heresy from western Europe. Undoubtedly the bishops of the West, quite apart from questions of doctrine, felt a natural hostility to bishops and priests who depended for their influence entirely upon invading barbarian kings. And probably the Latin bishops were greatly superior in general culture, and in their knowledge of affairs, to the clergy which followed in the train of barbarian armies. The efforts of the Catholic bishops

to convert Arians, as in the case of bishop Avitus and the Bur-
gundian king, were not merely attacks upon doctrinal differences.
There was also, no doubt, as there had been in the case of the
Donatists, a desire on the part of the Catholic bishops to strengthen
their own Churches by uniting in them all who claimed to be
Christian.

A general theory of the relation between the Church and the
State was already taking shape in the fifth century; but theory
then, as always, was only an attempt to express in more general
terms the character of a particular situation. Actual bishops had to
deal with actual kings; and they did so by letters or sermons or
commentaries upon sacred literature or past history. The letters, for
example, of Popes to Emperors arose out of particular difficulties;
and the general ideas concerning the relations of the Church and
the civil Authorities were gradually developed out of solutions of
these difficulties, adopted from time to time. But it would be
misleading to suppose that in the fifth and sixth centuries the
relations between the bishop of Rome and the Emperor at Constantinople were the most significant of the relations between the
Church and the "State" in western Europe. It would be still more
misleading to apply the ideas of bishops of Rome in the fifth or
eighth centuries to the relations of "spiritual" and "temporal"
powers, when the so-called Holy Roman Empire of German kings
was in existence. The controversies of the later Middle Ages in the
time of William of Occam did indeed turn upon the relationship
of Pope and Emperor; but that was a much later development,
which was largely due to the creation in A.D. 800 of a "play
Emperor" to whom the Pope could appeal.

Even in the fifth century, however, the letters of the bishops of
Rome provide most of the evidence for the attitude adopted by
bishops of the Church towards the civil Authorities. In each case
the position of the particular bishop and Emperor made a difference
to the theory expressed. But as the years passed in the fifth century,
the division between civil and sacerdotal authority became clearer.
Pope Leo I, the representative, as described above, of Roman
prestige in opposition to barbarism, wrote to the Emperor at

Constantinople that "human affairs cannot be safe unless the regal and sacerdotal authorities combine to defend the faith."[1] And in a later letter to a new Emperor he wrote that the Emperor's position is granted to him, not only to rule the world, but to defend the Church.[2] Again, Pope Gelasius (A.D. 492–496), who succeeded to the bishopric of Rome during a schism between the eastern and western Churches, spent most of his energy in asserting the supremacy of the Roman See within the Churches. But in a treatise he declares that, although Melchizedek had been both priest and king, since the time of Christ the priesthood had been divided from kingship, and bishops were dependent upon the Emperor for civil government.[3] The phrases of Leo and Gelasius were used in later centuries to support the medieval theory of "spiritual" and "temporal" powers; and they were so used, without regard to the context in which they had first appeared, and generally in ignorance of the political situation which had given rise to them. But the ideas and emotions drawn from traditional phrases are usually quite unlike the ideas and emotions which those phrases originally expressed. And, therefore, the preservation of a doctrine or of a theory often becomes merely the retention of a form of words whose meaning has become either unintelligible or at least quite different from that originally intended.

The fifth century left the Churches of the West more closely related among themselves and more dependent upon a policy of their own with regard to civil government and to armed force. The disappearance of imperial Authority in the West made the unity of the Latin Churches all the more striking; and the bishops as well as the clergy and laity under them were conscious of maintaining, not merely a common religious faith and moral standard, but also what remained of Roman culture. Finally, the bishops had a moral authority over clergy and laity which rested entirely upon their selection for their office and the services they performed, and did not depend upon any form of military force. Thus, in the tradition of the Churches, moral authority as the basis of govern-

---

[1] Leo I, Ep., lx. [2] Ibid., Ep., clvi.
[3] *Tomus de Anathematis vinculo. Pat. Lat.*, 59, col. 102.

ment and social organization was entirely unsupported by physical compulsion. On the other hand, the barbarian kings and their warriors obviously depended for their control over their subjects upon their military power. But although the conquest of new territory and the control of new populations might be secured by force of arms, this could not provide a basis of right or justice against any usurper or invader who might try his hand at displacing a former conqueror. Even the barbarian kings and their warriors, therefore, were compelled to look for some source of moral authority in support of their rule; and they found it in the Churches through their relationships with the Catholic bishops. Thus, the history of the barbarian kingdoms in western Europe and Africa during the fifth century is a proof of the dependence of even the crudest type of government upon moral authority rather than upon force.

General Conclusions

By the end of the fifth century the Latin Churches, so far as their dominant policy was concerned, had escaped from the dilemma of aloofness and acquiescence by generally accepting the policy of acquiescence. The conception that the true Christian ought to remain aloof from the business of life was preserved, as it will be explained later, in monasticism; but the great majority of the bishops of the Latin Churches accepted the necessity of supporting law and government, commerce, marriage and the applied arts. Aloofness had been natural in the communities of early Christianity, which had consisted largely of the poor and helpless. It was natural in later years, even among the rich, when the imperial dictatorship had withdrawn power and responsibility from them. But apart from a few eccentrics who sought to hasten their departure for another world, the majority of Christians seem to have felt that even a saint must have some food and clothing and shelter, and, if possible, security from murder or slavery. But this implied that the Christian should at least not put obstacles in the way of production, trade and government.

The responsible officials of the Churches were, therefore, driven by the decline of Roman authority to increase their support of such government as was possible. The decline in the power and moral authority of the Roman system in the West left the bishops and clergy of the Latin Churches without the support of the structure of law and government upon which the properties and civilized customs of the Christian communities had depended. If they had adopted as a policy the doctrine of aloofness from worldly affairs, the whole of western Europe would have returned to primitive barbarism. But instead they maintained for their own communities, which now included the majority of the inhabitants of the towns and cities, the Roman tradition of social organization, and Roman skill in the applied arts of building and agriculture. This involved the acceptance of the Roman principles which governed, among other matters, the holding of property and the use of armed force. It became clear, in the circumstances of the fifth century, that, for example, the use of armed force could not be considered morally right or wrong for Christians except as part of the general problem of the art of government. In actual administration it was impossible to isolate certain parts of the governmental system, and reject these while maintaining the rest. Justice in accordance with law was obviously impossible if any strong man could take what he desired without resistance. Whether or not armed force ought to be used clearly depended upon the nature of government, and could not be decided as an isolated problem of personal virtue.

To acquiesce, however, in the established methods of government involved in practice submission to the barbarian kings who had taken the place of Roman provincial governors. Thus, the Latin Churches were able to survive the Roman Empire in the West. But the new position of the bishops as subjects of independent kings, had several strange results. In the first place, authority was sought for their acquiescence in barbarian rule in certain passages of the Old and New Testament which seemed to support the doctrine of general acquiescence in any established order. Thus Christianity, which in its earliest years had seemed to imply, if not revolution, at least opposition to the established order, gradually

189

became one of the chief supports for any order that happened to be established. Secondly, the Christian communities had discovered for themselves the use of organization for the preservation of their properties and the support of their members. And they had also found the need for officials and for rules (canons) of admission to the community and exclusion from it. They had thus learnt in practice the art of government. They had now to extend their experience.

Finally, when the Latin Churches and their bishops found themselves under the military control of barbarian kings, their conceptions of government naturally remained the same as they had been under the Roman Empire. The barbarians had nothing new to offer either in law or in the applied arts of civilization. The Christian communities had no general principles of their own in such matters. The earliest Christianity was one among the mystery religions which offered to its adherents individual salvation. And it had no concern with the larger aspects of government, production and trade.[1] Therefore, in the fifth century the bishops derived their political and economic ideas from the Roman system. Acquiescence in the establishment of barbarian military power left most of the organization of social life—marriage, inheritance, trade, agriculture and building—what it had been before—that is to say, Roman. The bishops, therefore, in their policy of acquiescence, had the advantage of introducing among the barbarians whatever survived from Roman civilization. Thus, the Christian communities of the fifth and sixth centuries preserved and extended, amid the disorders of the time, the tradition of civilized life. And they did so, not as Christians, but as Romans. It has sometimes been said that Christianity brought civilization to medieval Europe; but it would be truer to say that civilization brought Christianity.

[1] The later effort to extract political principles from detached sentences, such as "Render unto Caesar . . ." could not supply a consistent social philosophy. As R. H. Tawney wrote: "The modern world is not seriously inconvenienced by rendering to God the things which are God's. They are not numerous, nor are they of the kind which it misses." *The Acquisitive Society*, p. 228 (1921).

CHAPTER V

BARBARIAN KINGS

At the end of the fifth century the whole of western Europe was ruled by barbarian kings. Their military force was entirely independent of the Roman Empire whose capital was Constantinople; and their moral authority had only the very slightest connection with the memory of an imperial ruler of the whole civilized world.

In Britain, if Gildas may be taken as an authority, local rulers in different parts of the island were as much engaged in mutual conflict as in resisting alien invasion.[1] If the story of Germanus and Lupus at the "Alleluia Victory" is true, the Church seems to have attempted, not merely to fight the British heresy of Pelagius, but also to unite the British kings against the invaders. These kings, of whom King Arthur is the legendary representative, were, however, swept aside before the end of the sixth century by Saxon and other marauding bands.

In northern France and Belgium the kings of the Franks had control; but in the early fifth century they were still non-Christian and, among the barbarians, the least influenced by Roman civilization. In middle and eastern France as far west as Lyons, Burgundian kings ruled. In southern France and Spain the Visigothic kings were supreme. In the Roman province of Africa, Vandal kings controlled the riches of the province and threatened the trade of the western Mediterranean. And finally, in Italy itself, in Dalmatia and northwards as far as the Danube, an Ostrogothic king was supreme.

---

[1] Gildas probably wrote about A.D. 550. His *Lament for Britain* is an attack upon five "kings or tyrants," whom he names, for destroying their country.

The King

All the supreme rulers of the barbarian military groups in control of what had been Roman provinces were called kings. The Latin word "rex," therefore, after the fifth century became the title of a supreme ruler in western Europe, and so remained until modern times. But the history of the word "rex" indicates that changes were occurring in the practice and theory of government, from the fifth to the ninth century. It is well known that the Romans had a traditional objection to the word "rex" because of the ancient legends of tyranny in the days before the Roman Republic was established. But the Latin word "rex" is closely allied to the Gothic "reiks," meaning a leader in war, which forms a part of such Gothic names as Alaric, Euric, Gaiseric, and Theodoric. The Gothic word means also "prince," as in the Gothic translation of the New Testament in such phrases as "the Prince of this world cometh"; and it has perhaps also some reference to hereditary right. In any case the word "rex" was evidently felt by the Romans to express the position of a barbarian ruler or leader; and it remained, in the Latin tongue at least, the title of a local or national chief as contrasted with the Emperor or Augustus. Even in the middle of the sixth century Procopius uses the word "rex," spelt in Greek letters; and explains that the barbarians used the term to describe their leader.[1] He clearly did not suppose that the word was Latin.

But the position of a king or "rex" was also affected in the fifth century by the fact that the Emperor himself was called "Basileus," of which the natural and obvious translation in Latin is the word "rex." The Greek word, however, had associations with Oriental magnificence, as in the phrase, "the great King," traditionally used to describe the Persian monarch; and it was also the title of the Hellenic rulers of eastern countries, who followed Alexander. The Greek word "basileus" indicates an hereditary monarch, as contrasted with a dictator whom the Greeks called a tyrant. But there was no suitable Greek word corresponding to the Latin "Imperator"

[1] *Hist.*, v, 1, 26. ῥὴξ . . οὕτω γὰρ σφῶν τοὺς ἡγεμόνας καλεῖν οἱ βάρβαροι νενομίκασι.

or "Augustus."[1] And therefore the "rex" of a barbarian people might acquire some of the prestige of the "Basileus" at Constantinople.

The contrast between a "basileus" or legitimate ruler and a "tyrant" is drawn by Procopius, in his account of the position of Theodoric the Ostrogoth, as will be explained later; and in that contrast the historian connects the word "rex" with tyranny rather than with lawful authority.

The account also given by Procopius, who was a contemporary, of the negotiations preceding the war in Africa contains an interesting indication of the position of a barbarian king. Justinian is said to have written to Gelimer, the king of the Vandals, who replied in these terms: "Basileus Gelimer to Basileus Justinian." The same title is used for both rulers, which Procopius clearly thinks is an insult in a letter from a barbarian "rex" to a Roman Emperor. The letter continues: "It is well for one to administer the kingly office which belongs to him and not to make the concerns of others his own. Hence, for you also who have a kingdom, meddling in the affairs of others is not just."[2] The status claimed by any barbarian king who felt himself to be independent of the Roman Empire was that of equality with the Roman Emperor. And it is also clear that in the sixth century the ridiculous conception of a State or system of government as a separate world of its own had already begun to throw its shadows upon the theory and practice of politics.

Again, the word "rex" had religious connections.[3] Jupiter was called "rex." And in the Latin translations of the Old and New Testament the word used for a ruler is "rex," and the word for his dominion is "regnum." There were no words in the biblical tradition for what would be now called a republic, a democracy or a president. The conception of government is monarchical

---

[1] Plutarch uses αὐτοκράτωρ (*Life of Galba*) for "Imperator." The word σεβαστὸς (revered) is used for "Augustus"; but it clearly has no such associations as the Latin word. [2] Procopius, *Hist.*, iii, 9, 20.

[3] The *rex sacrificulus* or *rex sacrorum*, a priest with primitive kingly functions, seems to have been appointed until the days of Theodosius I. The belief in the magical power of kings, discussed in Frazer's *Golden Bough*, probably survived from primitive times among the barbarians of the fifth century.

throughout the Bible; and the dominant phrase of the Gospels, "the Kingdom of Heaven," implies the position of a king as that of the supreme Authority most commonly understood by the subjects of any Government. It was therefore easier for the kings of the barbarians and their kingdoms to acquire a certain prestige from the tradition of Christianity; and in the centuries that divide the fifth from the ninth, the title "rex" was the more readily applied to Christ himself. Thus a title which, among the Romans of the second and third centuries, implied something barbaric or uncivilized in a ruler, became in the years which followed the Oriental monarchy of Constantine a word implying not only actual power but also moral or divine authority.

Barbarian Kingship

The foundations of barbarian kingship in western Europe are, no doubt, to be found in the position granted by the Roman Emperors to barbarian leaders as "allies" (federati). They might thus be regarded as agents of the civilization which they were supposed to maintain and defend; and their moral authority was enhanced by titles granted to them when they came into closer contact with the Empire. Thus Alaric, throughout his negotiations with the imperial Court at Ravenna, was much concerned to acquire for himself a Roman title which would give him, not only a definite status within the Roman system, but also prestige among his own followers who still held in awe the moral authority of Rome. Indeed, kingship in medieval and even modern Europe rests ultimately upon the prestige granted to barbarian leaders by the Roman Empire as well as upon the tribal loyalty of primitive peoples who chose their own kings.

Secondly, the barbarian kings and their armies were the only actual centres of armed force after the contests of Roman generals had destroyed the power and prestige of the imperial Authority, for which they contended. So long as the barbarian armed forces permitted themselves to be used by this or that ambitious Roman commander in his own interest against his superiors or his rivals, so long the barbarians merely added to the general confusion within the dissolving Empire. But when barbarian leaders used their forces for their own advantage, each successful leader could dominate a section of the old imperial territory without weakening his hold by attempting to subdue too vast a territory. For some time in the fifth century, the area and population which a barbarian king and his followers could hold in subjection was unknown. Adventures were undertaken and experiments made. Western Europe was passing from subjection under a single military dictatorship, resting upon slavery and the slave-trade, to government resting upon what would now be called a "national" basis defined by strategic or "natural" frontiers. But about four centuries passed before the main lines of modern European nation-states were clearly visible. In the fifth century the means of communication, the movements of armed forces, and therefore the area of control from any one centre had to be tested. Centralization on the Roman model had failed. But how "local" the new systems of government could afford to be, had to be discovered by trial and error. The barbarian kings and their followers were clearly quite unconscious of the process by which they were establishing a new governmental system in western Europe. And indeed, all the kingdoms founded among the ruins of the Roman Empire in the fifth century—except that of the Franks—were destroyed before the end of the sixth century. The barbarians had entered the Roman Empire first as settlers upon waste lands, and secondly as nomadic looters of portable wealth and slaves. But in the fifth century the barbarian armed forces found it more lucrative to settle in the wealthiest cities of the Empire, from which, under their kings, they could extract more booty than they could by continual raids.

As soon, however, as the kings had established themselves, not merely as conquerors, but as rulers, they and their followers were compelled to use the experience already acquired by the civilization they assisted to destroy. Thus, under the barbarian kings Roman methods of agriculture, building, manufacture and commerce were continued. The barbarians had nothing of their own to offer in these matters. For this reason also, Roman law and justice continued to operate in the barbarian kingdoms. And further, because the barbarian kings and their chiefs could neither read nor write, and because few of them had any ambitions more lofty than a good fight and a large feast afterwards, it was necessary for the barbarian kings to use as councillors and ambassadors such educated and able representatives of the old tradition as were willing to serve them. Thus Euric, the Visigothic king, had, as his chief minister, Leo, a Latin writer of distinction, trained in administration under the old regime. Similarly Theodoric the Ostrogoth used Cassiodorus as his chief minister. The survival of such educated laymen, connected with the service of the Empire and now advising barbarian kings, distinguishes the kingdoms of the fifth century from those which followed. In the sixth and later centuries, until the Renaissance, the only educated officials were clerics; and in those later ages, bishops acting either alone or in councils, were the advisers and ministers of kings. Thus they inherited from the civilian officials of the Roman Empire the civil functions which Diocletian had divided from those of the military. And the link between the civil service of the Empire and the clerical officials of the Middle Ages is to be found, under the first barbarian kings of the West, in such laymen as Leo and Cassiodorus.

Arianism

Finally, all the barbarian kings who established themselves within the old boundaries of the Empire in the fifth century were Christians of the Arian tradition. The conversion of the tribes who were later to overrun the western provinces of the Empire, had been due to bishops and priests who believed that in some sense Christ was not the equal of God the Father. The barbarians and their kings were not indeed likely to consider theological problems; but all the barbarian kingdoms had Arian bishops and priests attached to them, and these would naturally feel that the clergy of the old Roman world which they entered in Gaul, Spain, Africa and Italy, were their rivals.

This is not the place to discuss the theological doctrine of the Trinity or the difference between Arians and Catholics in their theories of deity. But in the study of social institutions it is important to notice the character of the religious differences which divide men into mutually hostile groups. In the case of Arianism in western Europe the difference between barbarian warriors and the Roman population subject to them was not a difference in abstract theorizing. The barbarians could neither read nor write, and even their bishops and priests do not appear to have been familiar with either Latin or Greek; and, on the other hand, the Latin Churches of the West were concerned with practice—that is to say, ritual and moral standards rather than with the subtleties of the Greeks.

But certain differences in practice, apart from the use of the Latin language and Roman fashions of dress, divided the Arian invaders from the Catholics. First, the worship of Christ as God was the accepted tradition of the Hellenic and Roman Christianity which could be distinguished from the Semitic or Oriental tradition for which God remained the sky-God of the Hebrews, aloof and unaffected by human suffering. The barbarians who had been converted to Arianism under this latter influence, were primitive warriors for whom the same kind of deity may have been acceptable, as was later to be accepted by the followers of Mohammed.

A certain theory in the history of the plastic arts connects the art of the Germanic tribes with Oriental forms. And whether this is true or not, the barbarian warriors of the North, in the fifth, and even in the ninth century seem to have been attracted by a sky-God rather than a God-Man. Again, the barbarians were victors and the invaded Roman people were victims. But Christ was a victim whose sufferings were shared by his people. Sympathy with the pain of Christ upon his Cross was a reflection of the feelings of a suffering people, as in the words of the hymn to the Cross: "Bend your boughs, tall tree: set the racked body free":[1] or, as a modern poet has written:—

> O sacred head, O desecrate,
> O labour-wounded feet and hands,
> O blood poured forth in pledge to fate
> Of nameless lives in divers lands.

[1] From the *Pange lingua* of Venantius Fortunatus.

O slain and spent and sacrificed
People, the grey-grown speechless Christ![1]

When the Arian kings required armed forces for raids or for defence, they had to rely partly upon local levies raised among the subject non-Arian population, which would hardly be an enthusiastic army, especially if their opponents were Catholic, as in the case of the armies of Justinian. Thus, the Arian kingdoms suffered from an internal division which prevented any of them becoming national in the modern sense of the word, not because of doctrinal differences, but because the rank and file of their subjects did not attend the same churches as their leaders, and were not served by the same clergy in public assistance or protection against injustice.

Finally, the Churches of the West already had their martyrologies and legends of saints who had suffered persecution. The barbarian warriors, their priests and bishops, had no such tradition behind them. They represented the victory of armed force. It is hardly strange, therefore, that fundamental differences of moral and religious attitude created difficulties when barbarian kings attempted to rule the more highly civilized populations of the West over whom the Catholic bishops already exercised a dominant influence. The contrast between armed force and moral authority was perhaps confused with the contrast between two forms of religious practice and belief.

Again, as the last chapter has shown, the Churches of the West used Latin; and the bishops who derived their right to the exercise of certain functions from the Emperors, naturally looked to the Roman Empire as the embodiment of public authority. The Churches sometimes acted as an "opposition" even within the imperial dictatorship; but they were even more inclined to be critical of the claims of barbarian kings who happened also to be Arian heretics. Thus, from the very beginning of the new systems of government in western Europe, the bishops stood in a peculiar relation to the kings. The kings were newcomers. They were ignorant and often violent. But the bishops, in the cities which the new kings took as capitals, belonged to an already established

[1] Swinburne, *Before a Crucifix*.

tradition of culture and the life in common. The State therefore, in its new form, was quite obviously subordinate to the Church, both as a centre of civilization and as an embodiment of moral authority.

The changed character of political and moral authority in this new situation may be best indicated by a short review of the new barbarian kingdoms in the West. All of them, except that of the Franks, were destined to disappear after about a century; but the experience gained from the relation of kings and bishops within them was carried on in the kingdoms of the seventh and eighth centuries which laid the foundations of the medieval system.

The Kingdom of the Visigoths

The first of the new kingdoms was that of the Visigoths, whose king established his capital at Toulouse, and at one time ruled most of Spain and southern France, west of the Rhone. These western Goths, after the marauding raids of Alaric and Adolf, had been permitted by the Roman Emperor to settle in south-western Gaul in A.D. 414. They had for many years been deeply influenced by Roman civilization; but although Christian, they followed the religion of the missionaries who had first converted them, and were therefore, from the point of view of the western Churches, Arian heretics. They had a translation of the Bible into Gothic, of which a few fragments have survived; but the majority of their kings and their warriors could neither read nor write; and they had bishops and priests of their own who adhered to the doctrines of the Arians.

The establishment of a settled Gothic domination in south-western Gaul committed the conquerors still more deeply to dependence upon the Roman system of law and administration. The kings, as well as the Gothic warriors, were without experience of the economic, political and administrative problems created by a more highly developed civilization. Inevitably, therefore, the Goths depended upon the old traditions and upon the experience of the Roman judges, administrators and other officials, over whom, theoretically, they held control. The Goths were a small minority in the Roman population—perhaps only five in every hundred in the Visigothic kingdom; and their desires in general did not go beyond fighting and feasting. The king was in practice the only official bond between the dominant military group and their conquered subjects. But intermarriage occurred; and within a century or two the language of the Goths was lost and the old Roman language, the mother-tongue of the majority, remained the language of the country. In the period of uncertainty when the Roman system seemed likely to be replaced either by complete chaos, or by some entirely new social structure, the bishops of the chief Churches were engaged in making their peace with the Gothic rulers. The bishops were not rival political authorities whom the Gothic kings would have been compelled to displace; but they were the only effectual representatives of the Christian communities, which now included most of the inhabitants of the cities. And all the bishops belonged to the old Roman tradition. They were "Catholic" and not Arian. The language of their religion was that of common life and trade in the Roman cities; and most of them had been selected as capable administrators of the increasing properties of the Churches and of the funds used for charitable purposes. Some bishops found it easier than others to be friendly with the new kings; but all, no doubt, were consciously or unconsciously critical of warriors whose ideas were simple and whose manners were, in general, coarse or even brutal.

The two attitudes towards Gothic kings in Gaul are very well expressed in the letters of Sidonius Apollinaris. He was a bishop of Clermont in Auvergne, who, in earlier life, had played a part in the politics of the crumbling Empire, and had even reached the goal of his ambitions as prefect of the city of Rome during a short residence there. He was a rich landowner who had married into an equally rich family; and his experience of public life, rather than any attachment to the Church, had led to his selection as bishop. He came into contact with two Gothic kings: one, Theodoric II, to whom he adopted a friendly attitude, and the other, Euric, to whom he found himself, as a bishop and a representative of the Roman tradition, violently opposed.

Sidonius Apollinaris gives a full account of the personal appearance and the daily occupations of Theodoric II. The letter in which this account is given was written about A.D. 454. The routine of his public life is described as follows[1]:—

Before daybreak he goes with a very small suite to attend the service of his priests. He prays with assiduity, but, if I may speak in confidence, one may suspect more of habit than of conviction in his piety. Administrative duties of the kingdom take up the rest of the morning. Armed nobles stand about the royal seat; the mass of guards in their garb of skins are admitted that they may be within call, but kept at the threshold for quiet's sake; only a murmur of them comes in from their post at the doors, between the curtain and the outer barrier. And now the foreign envoys are introduced. The king hears them out, and says little; if a thing needs more discussion he puts it off, and accelerates matters ripe for dispatch. The second hour arrives; he rises from the throne to inspect his treasure-chamber or stable. If the chase is the order of the day, he joins it. . . . On ordinary days his table resembles that of a private person. The board does not groan beneath the mass of dull and unpolished silver set on by panting servitors; the weight lies rather in the conversation than in the plate; there is either sensible talk or none. . . . The siesta after dinner is always slight, and sometimes intermitted. When inclined for a board-game, he is quick to gather up the dice, examines them with care, shakes the box with expert hand, throws rapidly, humorously apostrophizes them, and patiently waits the issue. . . . About the ninth hour, the burden of government begins again. Back come the importunate, back the ushers to remove them; on all sides buzz the voices of petitioners, a sound which lasts till evening, and does not diminish till interrupted by the royal request; even then they only disperse to attend their various patrons among the courtiers and are astir till bedtime. Sometimes, though this is rare, supper is enlivened by sallies of mimes, but no guest is ever exposed to the wound of a biting tongue. Withal there is no noise of hydraulic organ, or choir with its conductor intoning a set piece; you will hear no players of lyre or flute, no master of the music, no girls with cithera or tabor; the king cares for no strains but those which no less charm the mind with virtue than the ear with melody. When he rises to withdraw, the treasury watch begins its vigil; armed sentries stand on guard during the first hours of slumber.

This tells us nothing about the system of government; but it

[1] Trans. in *Letters of Sidonius*, by O. M. Dalton (1915), vol. i, p. 2.

implies that the Gothic king had become part of the established order in the administration of justice, and that his Court was regarded as, in some ways, a centre of social life. For the purpose here in view it is most interesting to observe that this local and half-civilized ruler absorbed most of the attention of his subjects, and that the figure of the Roman Emperor in eternal Rome had faded away beyond the horizon.

The other Gothic king of whom an account is given in the letters of Sidonius was Euric, who reigned from A.D. 466 to A.D. 485. His attempt to extend his kingdom in Gaul was evidently obstructed by the influence of the Catholic bishops who were opposed to an Arian king. As Sidonius writes:[1]

I must confess that, formidable as the mighty Goth may be, I dread him less as the assailant of our walls than as the subverter of our Christian laws. They say that the mere mention of the name of Catholic so embitters his countenance and heart that one might take him for the chief priest of the Arian sect rather than for the monarch of his nation. Omnipotent in arms, keen-witted, and in full vigour of life, he yet makes this single mistake—he attributes his success in his designs and enterprises to the orthodoxy of his belief, whereas the real cause lies in mere earthly fortune. For these reasons I would have you consider the secret malady of the Catholic Church, that you may hasten to apply an open remedy. Bordeaux, Perigueux, Rodez, Limoges, Jarols, Gauze, Bazas, Comminges, Auch, and many another city are all like bodies which have lost their heads through the deaths of their respective bishops. No successors have been appointed to fill their places and maintain the ministry in the lower orders of the Church; the boundaries of spiritual desolation are extended far and wide. Every day the ruin spreads by the deaths of more fathers in God; so pitiful is her state that the very heresiarchs of former times, to say nothing of contemporary heretics, might well have looked with pity on peoples orphaned of their pontiffs and oppressed by desperation at this catastrophe of their faith. Diocese and parish lie waste without ministers. You may see the rotten roofs of churches fallen in, the doors unhinged and blocked by growing brambles. More grievous still, you may see the cattle not only lying in the half-ruined porticoes, but grazing beside altars green with weeds. And this desolation is not found in country parishes alone; even the congregations

[1] Sid Apoll., Ep., vii, 6 (A.D 472–473), to Bishop Barilius on Euric's persecution. D alton's translation, ii, p. 107.

of urban churches begin to fall away. What comfort remains to the faithful, when not only the teaching of the clergy perishes, but their very memory is lost out of mind? When a priest departs this life, not merely the holder of the sacred office dies, but the office itself dies with him, unless with his failing breath he gives his blessing to a successor. What hope remains when the term of a man's life implies the end of religion in his parish? If you examine more closely the ills of the body spiritual, you will soon perceive that for every bishop snatched from our midst, the faith of a population is imperilled. I need not mention your colleagues Crocus and Simplicius, removed alike from their thrones and suffering a common exile, if different punishments. For one of them laments that he cannot see whither he is to return; the other that he sees only too clearly where he is to return no more. You for your part have about you the most holy bishops Faustus, Leontius, and Graecus, environed by the city, your order and their paternal love. To you these miserable treaties are submitted, the pacts and agreements of two king-doms pass through your hands. Do your best, as far as the royal con-descension suffers you, to obtain for our bishops the right of ordination in those parts of Gaul now included within the Gothic boundaries, that if we cannot keep them by treaty for the Roman State, we may at least hold them by religion for the Roman Church.

The capital of the Gothic kingdom, Toulouse, was thus for many years regarded as a centre of heresy. And when the king of the Franks had adopted the Roman form of Christianity, the influence of the Catholic bishops under the Gothic king tended to undermine his power in favour of that of the Franks.

Euric had begun a collection of laws for the western Goths; and under his successor, Alaric II, the famous *Breviarium* was issued, which was a summary of Roman Law, drawn largely from the Theodosian law-books, for use in cases affecting the Roman majority under his rule. Alaric himself was killed in battle with the Franks near Poitiers in A.D. 507; and the west Gothic kingdom after this was confined almost entirely to what is now called Spain. Alaric was a son-in-law of Theodoric the Ostrogoth, then reigning in Italy, and probably Theodoric's influence or military power pre-vented the entire destruction of the kingdom of the western Goths by the Franks. But the first experimental stage in the rule of an Arian and barbaric king in the most western parts of the Empire, was transformed in the later sixth century into a Catholic kingdom, by the conversion of king Reccared (A.D. 586–601).

The Vandal Kingdom

Another barbarian kingdom was that of the Vandals in Africa; but here the position of the king and his warriors and their relation to the old Roman civilization were somewhat different. The Vandals came, like other barbarians, as a marauding band with their camp-followers, seeking wealth and the sort of happiness they desired within the Roman Empire, first invading Gaul by crossing the Rhine at Mainz in A.D. 406; then, after a defeat by the Franks, crossing the Pyrenees in A.D. 409, and finally in A.D. 429 crossing into Africa. It is said that their leader in this last raid, Gaiseric or Genseric, counted eighty thousand males, including infants in arms, for his expedition into Africa. The ships were provided by Bonifacius, the Roman Governor of Africa, who invited the Vandals to assist him against the imperial Authority at Ravenna, and found in the end that he could not get rid of them.[1] By the end of the year A.D. 439 the Vandals had taken Carthage and established a kingdom in the Roman province of Africa which lasted for ninety-four years. From this position the Vandals controlled the islands and the trade routes of the western Mediterranean. Their fleets also undertook piratical expeditions, the most famous of which led to the sack of Rome itself in A.D. 455.

The Vandals seem to have been much less affected by the civilized people over whom they ruled, than were the Goths. Their kings acquired a reputation for violence and savagery, mainly because of their continued persecution of the Catholic bishops and priests of the province of Africa. Africa had already had experience of religious disunion in the quarrels between the Donatists and the Catholics; and now Arian bishops and priests, who appear to have used the Gothic language, displaced the Latin-speaking clergy. Thousands of bishops and priests of the Catholic Church in Africa were tortured or exiled, but perhaps rather for the purpose of extorting precious vessels and other wealth, than for any reason

[1] See above, Chapter III, p. 133.

that can be called religious. In A.D. 487 a description of the Vandal persecution was written by Victor Vitensis.[1] He says that preachers in the churches were spied upon lest any reference to tyranny in the Old Testament might be taken to apply to the Vandal kings;[2] and that after the sack of Rome a great number of slaves was brought back to Africa and divided between the Moors and the Vandals, husband being separated from wife and child from parent. In that situation the Catholic bishop, Deo Gratias, sold the church vessels in order to redeem captives and reunite families.[3] He is said to have accompanied doctors in their visits, and brought food supplies to the victims, whose health was broken by the voyage in slave-ships. Gaiseric died in A.D. 477; and his successor, Hunneric, at the request of the Emperor Zeno, permitted a Catholic bishop of Carthage to be elected. A great number of the Sees and Churches of Africa were without bishops and priests, and it was hoped that the persecution would cease; but according to Victor, the Arian bishops, fearing for their own position, influenced the king to undertake a new persecution.[4] Hunneric died in A.D. 484; and after an interval, during which older relatives were kings, Hilderic, the son of Hunneric and Eudocia, the Catholic daughter of Eudoxia, widow of the Emperor Valentinian, was acknowledged as king of the Vandals. Hilderic was a Catholic, but already aged and unacceptable to the Vandal warriors. He was, therefore, dethroned by his cousin Gelimer in A.D. 531; and this gave an opening for the Emperor Justinian to send expeditions from Constantinople against the Vandals, which eventually destroyed their power. The barbarian warriors, already deeply affected by the more luxurious habits of the rich Romans, whose wealth and property they had taken, gradually died out; their families were absorbed into the local populations and the province of Africa for a time passed under the authority of the Roman Emperor again. Neither in law nor in administration did the Vandals add anything to the traditions or

---

[1] Victor Vitensis, *De persec. Vandalica. Pat. Lat.*, vol. 58. *M.G.H.*, Auct. Aut. iii, part 1.

[2] *De persec. Vand.*, i, 7. References to Pharaoh or Holofernes were resented as reflecting "in personam regis."

[3] Ibid., i, 8. The names of the Latin bishops are significant: Deo Gratias, Habet-deus, Quid-vult-deus, etc.   [4] Ibid., ii, 1.

the West; but the fortunes of their kingdom at least served to prove that it was quite impossible to establish any authority in the western provinces of the Roman Empire in defiance of the Catholic Church.

Kingdom of the Burgundians

Another barbarian kingdom which covered a territory within the old Roman Empire was that of the Burgundians. By imperial Authority they were given territory in Savoy, after their defeat by the Huns in A.D. 435. Thus they entered within the Roman frontiers, to be soldiers and cultivators of land, as the result of the deliberate policy of the Roman Authorities. Amid the confusion in Gaul during the first half of the fifth century the kings of the Burgundians extended the territory over which they ruled and therefore increased the number of more civilized Latin-speaking communities under their domination. At the end of the fifth century the king of Burgundy ruled from his capital at Lyons the territory from the sources of the Rhone westward to the Loire and southward to Vienne. But the Burgundians were Arians; and the Catholic bishops, especially Avitus, bishop of Vienne, therefore made every effort to persuade the Burgundian king to forsake his Arian bishops and clergy. The strength of the Roman influence within his kingdom is indicated by the favourable position given in the Laws of Gundobad to the earlier residents in his territories. These Laws allow equal rights to "Romans" and Burgundians. They will be discussed in a later chapter. Also in the Burgundian kingdom the so-called "Roman Law of the Burgundians," or *Lex Papiana*, provided a summary of strictly Roman Law for the majority of the subjects of the Burgundian king.

The influence of the higher civilization of the Gallo-Roman population upon the barbarian warriors was evidently so strong that only one obstacle remained to prevent their complete absorption into the Latin tradition. This obstacle was the Arian clergy. But in A.D. 516 Sigismund succeeded his father Gundobad as king of the Burgundians; and Sigismund had already been converted to the Catholic Church by Avitus. In A.D. 517 the king held a Council of bishops and other clergy which confirmed the acceptance of Roman or Catholic Christianity in the Burgundian kingdom. Here then also it proved impossible to maintain an Arian kingdom within the territories which had been subject to Rome; and the Catholic Church succeeded in preserving the tradition of law and other forms of civilized life which the Empire had handed over to the barbarians.

The Early Frankish Kingdom

The Franks held the north-eastern part of Gaul in Belgium and beyond the Rhine, and made many raids into Roman territory during the fifth century. But it was not until Clovis became king of the Franks in A.D. 481 that the extension of Frankish territory began to promise a great future for this tribe. The other barbarian kingdoms were Arian in religion; but the Franks remained pagan at the time when Clovis defeated the representative of the old Roman authority, Syagrius, in A.D. 486. This Syagrius was the son of Aegidius, a "Roman general whom the Franks had unanimously chosen as king";[1] but after his father's death Syagrius was forced to flee from the new Frankish king Clovis, to seek refuge with Alaric II, king of the Visigoths. The latter, in fear of Clovis, gave up the refugee to him; and Clovis had the unfortunate Syagrius quietly killed.[2] Such was the heroism and loyalty of the Germanic kings. In A.D. 493 king Clovis married a niece of the king of Burgundy. She was a Catholic; and Clovis was baptized into the Catholic Church at Rheims by St. Remy in A.D. 496. The immediate result was that the king of the Franks was assured of support from the Catholic clergy, not only in his own kingdom but also in those of his neighbours. He was thus able to act as a crusader against heretics, when he found it convenient to conquer new territory. The Franks extended their power in the sixth century; and the development of closer relations between their kings and the Catholic bishops of the western Churches, including that of Rome itself, gave them an advantage over those other barbarian kings who were Arians, during the centuries that followed. In this kingdom

[1] Greg Tur., H.F., ii, 12. Pat. Lat., 71, col. 210.   [2] Ibid., ii, 27, col. 222.

at least there was no doubt of the usefulness to the military and political Authorities of the Catholic Church and its bishops. But the later development of this relationship between kings and bishops will be discussed in another chapter.

The Ostrogothic Kingdom in Italy

The most interesting of the first barbarian kings was Theodoric, the Ostrogoth, who ruled Italy and Dalmatia from A.D. 493 until his death in A.D. 526. The tribes of which he was the leader or king had been for nearly fifty years in close contact with Roman civilization. After the defeat of Attila they had settled in Roman lands near the Danube; and their relations with the Emperor at Constantinople were no more hostile than their relations with neighbouring tribes of their fellow-barbarians. Theodoric himself was sent as a hostage to the Court of Constantinople and spent ten years of adolescence and early manhood under the influence of Roman civilization there. But on his return to his own people in A.D. 471, his ambitions led eventually to conflict with the Empire; and in A.D. 488 he was induced, or himself decided, to invade Italy, where the political situation was confused.

Italy had been for thirteen years under the control of a barbarian king—Odovacar, who had destroyed the last traces of the Empire in the West. But Odovacar had used the surviving machinery of government and the officials of the Roman tradition. And thus, although a barbarian kingdom of Italy, extending eastwards as far as Belgrade and northwards as far as Vienna, had come into existence, the system of government remained much the same under a barbarian ruler and his armed forces as it had been under a Roman Emperor. It must be remembered also that the reigning Emperor at Constantinople was himself a barbarian of the Isaurian tribe, who had found it convenient to change his name from Tarasicodissa to Zeno; and for nearly twenty years men of his tribe controlled the Empire. It is not easy, therefore, to make a clear distinction in culture or status between an Emperor who was Roman in name only and a barbarian king of Italy who ruled through Roman officials. But the Emperor Zeno seems to have been willing enough to see Theodoric and his Ostrogoths marching upon Italy and thus removing from Constantinople the danger which their desire for loot might cause. In March A.D. 493, after victory in the field and treachery among the defeated, Theodoric established himself as king in Ravenna, having himself slain Odovacar treacherously at a banquet in the best barbarian manner. Theodoric and his Ostrogoths then controlled Italy until A.D. 526.

The succession of events has often been described. It is more important here to notice the character of the new kingdom in Italy. Theoretically the Ostrogoths held Italy by permission of the Emperor at Constantinople; but in practice their king was supreme within his dominions and ruled independently of the Emperor. As in all the barbarian kingdoms an indefinite attitude of respect for the Roman Empire survived among the new rulers. But Odovacar had broken the spell of moral authority in the name of Emperor by dethroning Romulus Augustulus; and Theodoric felt no need to seek authority for his administrative acts or his policy from any Emperor. In his negotiations with the barbarian kings of western Europe—Burgundians, Visigoths and Vandals—he took no account of the policy of the Emperor, whom he treated as a dangerous rival rather than a superior authority. According to Procopius the Berbers of Africa would not accept as a ruler anyone who lacked the insignia of imperial Rome. He describes such insignia as a silver staff with golden top, a silver cap, a white cloak and tunic and golden boots.[1] One may imagine, therefore, that the inhabitants of Italy would feel even more strongly than Africans the need for the external signs of authority. But of Theodoric himself Procopius says that "neither in name nor in dress did he think it right to be treated as basileus of the Romans; but he was called 'rex' all his life." "So far as the name went, Theodoric was a tyrant; but in fact he was a true basileus."[2]

Under Theodoric the Roman system of administration was continued, and officials of the Roman tradition held high office. The most important of these was Cassiodorus, whose father had already held office under Odovacar. The official letters, written by Cassio-

---

[1] Procopius, *Bell. Vand.*, iii, 25. [2] Ibid., *Bell. Goth.*, v, 1, 26–29.

dorus in the name of Theodoric, who himself could neither read nor write, indicate the extent to which the barbarian king was dependent upon the surviving Roman system of government.[1] Cassiodorus himself was Roman in the sense given to that word during his lifetime; that is to say, he was an educated member of a community which maintained an ancient traditional civilization. His family came from Syria and had settled in southern Italy where they held extensive property. But Rome was the source of his moral and intellectual standards, as it had been for Theodosius, the Emperor, and others who came from Spain; as it had been for the poets of the early fifth century, Claudian and Prudentius. The official career of Cassiodorus, however, depended entirely upon the barbarian kings of Italy; and as their adviser and secretary he has, no doubt, attributed to them sentiments and administrative decisions which were his own. Theodoric, the greatest of the kings whom he served, has excited the admiration of German scholars of the nineteenth century; but there is no evidence that he understood the policy which is expressed in the official letters, written for him by Cassiodorus. That Cassiodorus did not enjoy the duty he felt bound to perform in attempting to preserve the Roman tradition under a barbarian tyrant, is shown in his preface to his treatise on the Psalms. "At Ravenna," he writes, "I sometimes put aside official duties and forgot the evil smell of worldly cares in order to taste the soul's honey of the heavenly psalter. As happens to those who desire it, in my eagerness I lost myself in reading that I might drink in with delight the saving words after the bitterness of my daily work" (*post amarissimas actiones*).[2]

In the preface to the collection which he made of his official correspondence he indicated his hope that the work they represent will be useful for preserving the tradition he admired. In the first place these letters embody the decision of Theodoric to maintain the Roman administration. Letters addressed to the Senate from

[1] Theodoric used a stencil with the Latin word "legi" ("I have read") for signing documents. And exactly the same kind of stencil with the same letters is reported by Procopius to have been used by the contemporary Roman Emperor Justin who was an uneducated soldier, born in the district which is now Bulgaria.
[2] Cassiodorus, *In Psalterium Praef.*, *Pat. Lat.*, 70, col. 1.

the king express respect for senatorial authority and ask the Senate to accept or ratify some appointments made by the king. Again, the sixth book of the collection consists of "forms" (*formulae*) for the appointment to the traditional positions in the Roman system of government, such as the Consulate, the Prefecture of the City, the Quaestorships and the rulership of provinces. The "forms" composed by Cassiodorus are themselves proofs that the system he was attempting to preserve was already obsolete. The Rome he admired was dead; but he worshipped the dead body. It is all the more interesting to note that a hundred years later another book of "forms," by the monk Marculf, was produced in northern France to express a new system—the medieval.

The situation in the time of Cassiodorus is indicated by the way in which his "forms" address the persons who are appointed under them to different offices. For example, the form sent to a man appointed consul recounts the ancient custom of naming the year by its consuls, describes the dress (*palmatas vestes*) and notes the right to carry the fasces with the axe. All this is adduced to show what a great dignity a consul has. The comic element in archaism comes out in the sentence—"You have the apparatus of victory without the experience of war. . . . Your happy success as leaders is clear from your high honours, and yet you have not the annoyance of having to govern anybody."[1] The chronicle of Cassiodorus himself consists almost entirely of a mere list of the consuls, for the dating of the years by reference to the birth of Christ did not begin until the eighth century. In the time of Cassiodorus the consuls were still appointed, usually one in Constantinople and one in Rome. But they had no functions to perform. Even in the Theodosian law-books men of consular dignity are referred to only in a note on precedence.[2] But the forms of Cassiodorus are merely rhetorical descriptions of the ancient costumes and ceremonies associated with the different official posts. "Antiquity" is the final authority. The attitude is that of some half-educated inhabitant of a modern colony who thinks that being a Governor means wearing

[1] Cassiodorus, *Variae*, vi, 1.
[2] *Cod. Theod.*, vi, 19, 1. Rescript of September 29, A.D. 400.

a cocked hat. The symbols of power and authority in the fifth century survived what they had symbolized, and thus acquired a sort of magical efficacy. Institutions die from within, leaving the shell of ceremony erect, until it is discovered to be meaningless.

The official letters of Theodoric include orders for the repair and preservation of buildings, and the care for the aqueducts and drains of Rome. A letter to the prefect of the city orders him to assist a certain John to repair the drains of Rome "which so astound all who see them that they are greater than the wonders of other cities."[1] Other letters direct the sending of statues and pillars of marble from Rome to Ravenna, and the support of a water-expert for the finding of a new supply for Rome. This man had come to Rome from Africa, where water was difficult to find.[2] Again, Theodoric writes to the Praetorian Prefect to provide support for a certain Thomas, a famous charioteer, which gives Cassiodorus an opportunity to expatiate upon the excitement of the races in Rome;[3] and in another letter he admonishes the Senate to stop the rioting at the races. This gives him an opportunity to indulge in a little bad etymology concerning the derivation of the Latin words for riot and war.[4]

In matters of high policy the two chief difficulties seem to have been the friction between Goths and the "Romans" in Italy, and the attempts of Theodoric to prevent war between the neighbouring barbarian kings of Gaul, first by marrying them to his daughters; and next by a series of letters, dissuading the king of the Franks, Clovis, from war with Alaric, and to other kings urging them to assist in the prevention of war. Theodoric is made to say, in a letter to the king of the Burgundians, "It is our task to urge moderation upon kings who are youthful"; and to the king of the Franks, "We are astonished that you are so perturbed by quite unimportant issues that you want to undertake a disastrous war against our son king Alaric. . . . You are both kings of important peoples, both in the flower of youth. . . . Let not your valour be an unforeseen calamity to your country; because the ruin of their people for trivial ends does great injury to kings."[5] Whether these are the

[1] *Var.*, iii, 30.　[2] Ibid., iii, 53.　[3] Ibid., iii, 51.　[4] Ibid., i, 30　[5] Ibid., iii, 4.

sentiments of Theodoric or Cassiodorus, they indicate the beginning of the interminable wars for loot or prestige between the barbarian warriors who had displaced the Roman governors of the West.

The general effect of the rule of Theodoric in Italy, therefore, may be regarded as the introduction of a new form of political organization in the West. In the first place, the kings of western Europe and Africa formed a group of "sovereign governments," independent of the Roman Empire. The relationships between these kings formed, as it were, the roots of the medieval system. Secondly, Theodoric restored in his dominions the peace and prosperity which had been almost forgotten. He rebuilt aqueducts and baths and city walls and kept the peace so effectually that, as an anonymous chronicler says, "the merchants from various provinces came flocking to him, for so great was the order he maintained that, if anyone wished to leave gold or silver on his land, it was deemed as safe as if within a walled city. An indication of this was that throughout all Italy he never made gates for any cities and the gates that were in the cities were not closed. Anyone who had any business to transact did it at any hour of the night as securely as in the day."[1]

Theodoric was the subject of a panegyric by Ennodius, bishop of Pavia, the author of a Life of St. Epiphanius, his predecessor.[2] Ennodius addresses Theodoric as "greatest of kings" and "foundation of the State." The phrase "salve status reipublicae" addressed to Theodoric, is an interesting identification of the king with what was later called "the State," which makes good sense of the exclamation attributed to Louis XIV—"L'état c'est moi." Evidently the barbarian kingdoms of the fifth century were the sources from which the sovereignty of European States was derived. The turgid eloquence of Ennodius traces the life of Theodoric, whom "Greece brought up in the bosom of civilization," to his restoration of Roman rule. "It is a greater thing," he writes, "to prevent its downfall than to have established its foundations."

---

[1] *Anon. Vales.*, trans. in Hodgkin, *Italy*, vol. iii, p. 297.
[2] Ennodius, born at Arles in A.D. 473; died in A.D. 521. Educated at Milan. Married a rich and noble wife; later he gave up the marriage and became a deacon.

In another aspect also Theodoric's policy indicates the beginning of the Medieval and Renaissance State-System. He practised the policy of dynastic marriages. He himself had had a wife of inferior status (concubina) before he became king in Italy, and married later Audefleda, daughter of Childeric, king of the Salian Franks, and sister of Clovis, by whom he had a daughter, Amalasuntha. The two daughters of his earlier wife were married for purposes of policy, one to Sigismund, king of the Burgundians, and the other to Alaric II, king of the Visigoths. Theodoric's sister, Amalafrida, was married to Thrasamund, king of the Vandals;[1] and by another husband she had a daughter, Amalaberga, who was married to Hermanfrid, king of the Thuringians. The names are of no importance; but the policy implied in all these dynastic marriages evidently aimed at a form of peace between the new States which now covered the area of what had been the western parts of the Roman Empire from Belgium to northern Africa. As Hodgkin says, "this family compact binding together all the kingdoms of the West in a great confederacy, filling all the new barbarian thrones with the sons, the grandsons or nephews of Theodoric, was a matrimonial state-system surpassing anything that Hapsburg or Bourbon ever succeeded in accomplishing. . . . When it came to the tug-of-war between one barbarian chief and another, this family compact, like so many others in later days, snapped with the strain. Yet it was not at once a failure; for one generation at least the position of Theodoric as a kind of patriarch of the kingly clan . . . did undoubtedly promote the happiness of Europe."[2] The truth of the last sentence, however, is open to dispute. The hope that family relationships would prevent barbarians from fighting was certainly not based upon past experience. The slaughter of brothers by brothers was not unknown among the Goths and the Franks; but it is much more likely that the policy of dynastic marriages gave some kind of solidarity to the diverse barbarian groups, which were in a minority among the older populations of the fallen

[1] The letter from Theodoric, in the collection of Cassiodorus, which announces this marriage, makes the point that the sister of the Gothic king was of the Amal family and therefore of better blood than the king's own daughters! Also the lady was "litteris docta" (*Variae*, v, 43).   [2] Hodgkin, *Italy*, iii, p. 355.

Empire among whom they lived. The dynastic marriages of Theodoric's policy, therefore, if they did in any way promote peace, did so only by strengthening the hold of ignorant and incompetent rulers over their subjects. The happiness of the majority in Europe and Africa was perhaps reduced rather than increased by barbarian rule; and whatever strengthened that rule may actually have increased the difficulty of establishing a new form of civilization.

Again, the kingdom of Theodoric, like the other barbarian kingdoms in the West, was in essence the control of an armed band of barbarians over a subject Roman population. The two traditions were not assimilated either in administration or in law; although, no doubt, social intercourse and even intermarriage occurred. The language and customs of the Roman majority and its long-established traditions tended gradually to absorb the Gothic conquerors, as the conquered English gradually absorbed the Normans, in the eleventh and twelfth centuries. But the Gothic kingdom in Italy did not last long enough to unite barbarian with Roman traditions. In practice the Goths had their own customs and social status; and some of his warriors were deliberately stationed by Theodoric as representatives or even as spies on Roman estates, in order to preserve the king's control over his wealthier subjects. On the other hand, the Roman population continued to be governed by Roman law. The *Edictum Theodorici*, which will be discussed later, is nothing more than a summary statement of Roman law current at the time in Italy; and because the Goths had nothing of their own to contribute to the organization of a more highly developed city-civilization, the only possible policy for the barbarian king was the maintenance of the Roman system of personal property and trading relationships.

The most difficult problem for Theodoric was his relationship with the Catholic Church in Italy. As in other barbarian kingdoms, the king and his warriors were Arians; and among his followers were Arian priests and bishops. His great church in Ravenna, now "S. Apollinare nuovo," was built by him for Arians. But the Churches in Italy, when Theodoric conquered the country, were too strongly established upon the basis of the worship of Christ as

God for Arianism to spread. In any case, Theodoric showed no hostility to the established religion of the "Catholics" in Italy. The exceptional position, however, of the bishop of Rome made the situation much more difficult for an Arian king in Italy than it was, for example, in the Visigothic kingdom in Gaul. Theodoric had to deal with a Church which was not entirely local in its influence and prestige—with a Church of what might still be regarded as a capital. That Rome had not been the capital of an Empire for more than two centuries did not lessen—it may even have increased—the prestige of the bishop of a city which was rapidly becoming the capital of Latin Christendom. The policy of Theodoric, therefore, in dealing with the bishops of Rome was inevitably ambiguous. As the representative of the established order in law and government, he expected and was granted the support of the ecclesiastical Authorities. The bishop of Rome naturally deferred to the *de facto* ruler of Italy, especially because he was recognized, in some sense, by the Emperor, and also because he maintained the structure of the old imperial system. No doubt, also, the Church approved and supported the peace and the increase of prosperity which Italy enjoyed under the rule of Theodoric.

When, however, difficulties arose as to the succession in the Roman bishopric, Theodoric seems to have been used as the imperial Authority had been used in earlier years, to arbitrate between rivals. In A.D. 499 two rival bishops of Rome had been elected by opposed groups of clergy and people; and, as it has been noted above, an appeal was made to Theodoric to decide which bishop should be acknowledged. He gave his decision for Symmachus, who was less inclined than the other claimant to compromise with the policy of Constantinople on a doctrinal question then in dispute. The fundamental difficulty of the Gothic regime, however, could not be overcome. The bishop of Rome, however friendly he might be to the Arian king at Ravenna, had closer relationships with the Emperor at Constantinople. The Churches of Italy formed part of a Christian organization which spread far beyond the frontiers of Theodoric's kingdom; and the bishop of Rome was himself the only patriarch of the West of a status equal, or perhaps superior,

to that of the patriarchs within the jurisdiction of the Emperor at
Constantinople. Inevitably, therefore, the Roman Church had a
moral influence, drawn from its connections with eastern Christianity and the Empire, which might undermine the authority of
the king of Italy. Again, in A.D. 524 the Emperor Justin, at Constantinople began a persecution of the Arians in the East; and
Theodoric felt the contrast of this persecution with his own toleration of Catholics in Italy. He sent John I, bishop of Rome, to
Constantinople to negotiate a compromise and imprisoned him,
after his failure, when he returned to Ravenna. Theodoric's hostility
to the Emperor's persecution of Arians led him to suspect the
loyalty of his own Catholic subjects.

Worse still for the Gothic king, in Rome survived the Senate.
The Senators still preserved something of the prestige of an aristocracy which had once ruled the Roman world. They were
wealthy and cultured men. Some of them had literary and philosophical interests; others had had administrative experience. And
the Senate as a body was conscious of its own great past and of its
traditional relations with the successor of Augustus at Constantinople. Theodoric visited Rome in A.D. 500 and was received with
a suitable respect. He directed the repairs and restoration of ancient
buildings in Rome and elsewhere. But other barbarian kings had
dominated Rome from time to time during the past century; and
all had fallen from power, while the Roman Senate survived. It
can hardly be doubted, therefore, that there was a certain uneasiness
in the relations between the Senatorial aristocracy and the uneducated barbarian dictator. Dictators are sensitive not only to the
spoken words but also to the looks and manners of a wealthy and
educated class which might naturally be supposed to be critical.
Theodoric at Ravenna, therefore, could easily become suspicious of
the aristocracy in Rome; and in A.D. 526 rumours that the Senators
in Rome were in communication with the Emperor at Constantinople seem to have convinced the king that a plot was being
hatched against him. The Senators Boethius and Symmachus were
arrested and imprisoned at Pavia. Their Christianity, which was
perhaps that of philosophical men of the world, was in any case of

the Catholic tradition, which was hostile to Arian priests and kings.[1] It is by no means certain that any actual movement against Theodoric had taken place either in the Senate or in the Roman Church; but Boethius was executed and soon after Symmachus also.

The suspicions or the reports upon which Theodoric acted are clear indications that he realized the insecurity of his throne and foresaw the danger to the Gothic kingdom of Italy. For about thirty years he had ruled an alien population; and as he grew old, he must have felt that his successor would be in a difficult position. The situation was obviously changing; and when, a few months after the execution of Boethius, Theodoric himself died (August 30, A.D. 526), the continuance of the Gothic kingdom was rendered still more uncertain by disputes about the succession.

A Question of Policy

The new situation in Italy is indicated in the official letters which Cassiodorus continued to write as secretary to the Gothic rulers of Italy. There were two chief difficulties to be faced: first, securing the allegiance of the Gothic warriors for some successor to Theodoric, and secondly, forestalling the danger of an invasion of Italy for the restoration of the Roman Empire there under Justinian. The immediate successor of Theodoric was his grandson Athalaric, a child under the control of his mother Amalasuntha. There may have been distrust among the Goths either because the new queen and her son were educated in Roman traditions, or because a woman could not lead warriors. The letters of Cassiodorus in the eighth and ninth books of his collection are written in the name of Athalaric; and these are in the same tone as the official letters of Theodoric. But Athalaric died at the age of eighteen in A.D. 534,

---

[1] Boethius had great influence in medieval Europe because of his book on the *Consolation of Philosophy*. This book is supposed to have been written by Boethius during his imprisonment. The chief argument of the book is that Reason (Philosophy) and the universe revealed by Reason give consolation in times of trouble. There is no reference in it to Christ or Christian doctrine; but it is full of the teaching of Plato and of the Greek tradition in philosophy. Boethius was obviously a rationalist; and it was precisely his appeal to Reason which attracted readers in the medieval atmosphere of superstition and fear.

and Amalasuntha then called upon her cousin Theodad (Theodatus) to be joint ruler with her of the Gothic kingdom. In the letter announcing this decision to the Emperor Justinian, Amalasuntha is made to say: "We have appointed to the sceptre a man close to us in brotherly connection, in order to maintain the kingly dignity by strengthening us in sharing our councils." In the next letter Theodad is made to say to Justinian: "It is the custom of new kings among the different peoples to announce the joys of their succession in order that they may gain the respect of a foreign prince from the fact that both are rulers."[1] Theodad then had no further use for Amalasuntha, and so had her murdered; but Cassiodorus continued to write letters for him, both to persuade Justinian not to make wars upon the Goths and to persuade the Senate in Rome not to suspect or fear the advance of his armies. Evidently the hostility to the Goths in Italy had increased, especially among the inhabitants of Rome, and it was difficult for the new Gothic king to persuade the Senate that the Goths were defenders of their liberties against the Roman Emperor. To the people of Rome, Theodad, or rather Cassiodorus, writes: "Let no unsuitable suspicions and no shadow of fear disturb you. Your loyalty (*Fides vestra*) should be more clearly shown."[2] To the Senate he writes, in reference to the Gothic army outside Rome: "Let your armed defence stand outside your walls, and within them the quiet of civilized life."[3] The troops of Justinian had taken Sicily and were allowed by the son-in-law of the Gothic king, in A.D. 536, to cross the Straits to Reggio. At those same straits Alaric had been held up more than a hundred years before; and now a Roman army crossed them by the treachery of a Gothic prince to destroy the Gothic kingdom in Italy. The Goths, like other barbarians, were divided among themselves. Some of their warriors chose a certain Vitigis as king; and Theodad was murdered. Cassiodorus obediently writes in the name of the new king to all the Goths to announce that the Gothic people have found a "martial king."[4] Rome was captured and recaptured by

[1] Cassiodorus, *Var.*, x, 1 and 2. Theodad was the son of Amalafrida, sister to Theodoric. [2] Ibid., x, 14.
[3] Ibid., x, 17. "Foris sit armata defensio: intus vobis tranquilla civilitas."
[4] Ibid., x, 31. "Regem sibi martium geticus populus invenivit."

Belisarius, the general of Justinian's troops. A new Gothic king, Totila, was elected in A.D. 541, who emptied the city of Rome of all its inhabitants in A.D. 549 and was slain in a skirmish in A.D. 552. In that same year, for the fifth time, Rome was taken by the troops of Justinian; and the last remnants of Gothic control in Italy were destroyed after eighteen years of war in March A.D. 553. It is said that one-third of the population of Italy was destroyed as a result of the attempt of Justinian to annex to his empire the ancient seats of Roman authority.

The policy of Justinian was the crudest form of archaism. But in Italy those who maintained the Roman tradition had evidently conceived an alternative. Cassiodorus and the other officials who supported the same policy had hoped that Gothic rulers and warriors would restore and re-establish the Roman system of law and administration in the West. Cassiodorus himself had written a history of the Goths which was intended to be a political pamphlet in favour of this policy. He describes the purpose of this history in a letter written in the name of Athalaric to the Senate in Rome;[1] but the original is lost. It was read, however, probably at the residence of Cassiodorus himself, to which he had retired after the destruction of the Gothic kingdom, by Jordanes. Jordanes was a Goth who is believed to have become a Catholic bishop; and some years later he wrote, probably in Constantinople, a work on the history of the Goths which is almost entirely derived from the work of Cassiodorus.[2]

The history of the Goths by Jordanes is important as a source of information; but it is much more important for the present argument as an expression of policy. The policy may have been only that of a cultured few who faced the problem whether the Roman system could absorb and be invigorated by Gothic barbarism. But it was a policy which its supporters believed to be based upon the natural tendencies of their time; and it had at least somewhat less archaism than the ridiculous and wholly futile policy of Justinian. According to Jordanes the Goths have an important place in world

[1] *Var.*, ix, 25.
[2] Cassiodorus probably finished his history in A.D. 521, and in any case before the death of Athalaric in A.D. 534.

history. They are connected with the Amazons and even with the siege of Troy. The Emperor Maximinus was himself a Goth, and the Goths were allied to the Romans. Alaric, of course, sacked Rome long ago but did not, as barbarians do, set it on fire; nor did the Goths allow any injury to affect the sacred places. Later on the Visigoths assisted the Romans to destroy the Huns under Attila; and then the Emperor Zeno supported Theodoric in his conquest of Italy; but finally Belisarius destroyed the Gothic army there. And the history ends with the surrender of Vitigis. There is no mention of Totila or Narses. But the last words of the book refer to the marriage of Matasuentha, daughter of Amalasuntha, to Germanus, brother of the Emperor Justinian. The son of this marriage, according to Jordanes, united the hopes of both races. Evidently, therefore, it was to the Roman tradition that Jordanes was compelled to look; because all that was left of the Gothic kingdom of Italy was a small portion of the royal blood of Theodoric. There was no hope, in fact, for an assimilation of Roman civilization and Gothic barbarism upon equal terms.

General Conclusions

The general results of the creation of the first barbarian kingdoms in the West may be described in summary form as follows. Political, administrative and judicial authority as well as military force was decentralized. There were several independent and equal sources of governmental authority in place of dependent governorships under one military autocracy. The new kingdoms were the result of conquest by armed bands of ignorant, superstitious and treacherous barbarians, who subjected to their desire for wealth a more highly civilized population. The fact that different barbarians had succeeded in imposing their rule on different parts of the Roman Empire was generally regarded as the will of God. There was, no doubt, some disagreement in answering the question why God should have so willed; but no one at that date seems to have doubted that the greed and violence which were the real foundations of the barbarian kingdoms had results which should be accepted as decisions made by God. The bishops under the different barbarian kings usually accepted their authority so long as they did not actually persecute the Church. And although the Churches in all the different kingdoms retained the old Roman language and the sense of unity across the new frontiers, this did not seriously affect the division of political authority among many different kings. St. Augustine wrote that the division of the world into many different kingdoms was a result of sin, because he believed that the ideal form of government was that of a single Empire including all Christian peoples; and the same explanation of the existence of several States dominated the thought of the Middle Ages, as in the works of Aquinas and Dante. The existence, therefore, of several independent and equal kingdoms was regarded as a regrettable necessity and not as an improvement upon the imperial domination of a single dictator. But in practice the barbarian kingdoms were maintained, at least for some centuries, as the only possible form of government. The ruler in each kingdom was closer to his subjects than the Emperor had been; and his armed forces could operate more efficiently over a restricted area. The frontiers between the new kingdoms were not defined; and the balance of power between them was constantly changing, either because of internal disunion or as a result of warlike expeditions of one against the other. There was a centre of power and authority in each kingdom, but no clearly defined circumference to mark the limit of the efficacy of each Government. The very vagueness of the conception of a frontier in the new kingdoms has influenced political thought and practice ever since. The frontier of the Roman Empire had been clearly defined; but it was a military frontier, outside of which in the West was only barbarism. No one thought of the Roman Wall in Britain or of the *Limes* in Germany as anything but a system of exclusion. The frontiers in the Roman tradition, therefore, at least in the West, were not lines of contact between one State and another but divisions between civilization and barbarism. When, therefore, the new barbarian kingdoms came into existence as centres of authority and used, as far as their barbarism allowed, the Roman experience of law, government and public policy, they had neither a theory nor a practice of what would now be called international affairs, to rely upon. Each separate kingdom inherited the mistaken idea that a State was distinguished from what lay outside it, as civilization is distinguished from barbarism. There was no governmental system connecting the new States; and their relations, therefore, were what Hobbes called those of a "state of nature." Medieval and modern Europe inherited from these Dark Ages their intellectual and emotional darkness in what are now called international affairs.

Secondly, even to-day an obscure idea survives of distinction between the functions of Church and State, which is derived from the Middle Ages. The later medieval conception of two social organizations, one "spiritual," the other "temporal," one a "Church" and the other a "Kingdom" or "State," was not derived from any analysis of the nature of things or of human nature. Nor was it derived from texts of the Bible which were quoted in support of it. It arose out of the actual situation in western Europe after A.D. 400, when the bishops of the several Churches and the kings of the barbarian kingdoms had to find some way of living to-gether.[1] The organization of the Churches was in fact distinct from that of the old imperial regime. The Churches were in a very peculiar position of dependence upon the Emperor after Constantine had allowed Christianity its place as a recognized religion in Roman Law. Bishops did indeed rebuke Emperors; but they never wavered in their reverence for Roman Order. Roman civilization was obviously older than the Churches; and it embodied in law and administration a much fuller and more detailed system of organized social relations than the Churches. Also it was one system covering the whole known world; and the Churches until the fifth century were still separately organized and almost independent one of another. The Roman Empire had a kind of divinity of its own, as the kingdom of the Last Age, even if good Christians might find in it traces of the Devil. Thus at first the Church was inferior in prestige to the State.

But when the Roman Empire in western Europe disappeared,

[1] A similar situation occurred in Egypt between 300 and 200 B.C. when the Ptolemies, who were Greek "barbarian kings," had to reconcile the old Egyptian priesthood to the acceptance of their rule.

the barbarian kingdoms did not inherit directly the "divinity" of the old system of law and government. Such divine authority as could be acquired by the new kingdoms had to come, therefore, from the Church. It had been said that the Church lay within the Empire.[1] And when that was said, the Empire was obviously more inclusive than the Church. But when the barbarian kingdoms took the place of the Empire, each kingdom obviously lay within a Church whose prestige and authority extended far beyond the frontiers of any State. This new situation changed, both in practice and in theory, the relationship of the spiritual and temporal Powers.

It follows also that under the new system at the end of the fifth century there was a much clearer distinction than ever before between force as an instrument of government and moral authority as the justification for the use of such force. The Churches in the different kingdoms might indeed submit to conquest and subjection under barbarian kings, as men acquiesce in the results of a flood or earthquake. But such acquiescence does not imply an admission of moral authority in a destructive force. Even successful revolutionaries have sooner or later to discover some other ground than their success for their claim to be obeyed. The barbarian kings of the fifth century, therefore, were compelled to look to the Christian Churches, and primarily therefore to the bishops, for the maintenance of their moral authority over their subjects. And this situation continued for centuries into the Middle Ages. The dependence of the newly-established kingdoms upon the older Roman tradition of moral authority, now represented by the bishops, is one of the most important sources of the medieval difficulty about the relations of State and Church. The Church became in one sense superior to the State, because its prestige was greater in western Europe, from the fifth to the ninth century, than the prestige of any single king, however powerful.

Again, in all the early barbarian kingdoms from the fifth until perhaps the seventh century, there were two quite distinct groups of subjects under the king. The barbarian warriors and their families,

[1] Optatus Milev., *De Schismate Donat.* iii, 3. *Pat. Lat.*, 11.

PLATE 3.—SS. PETER AND PAUL (MOSAIC OF ABOUT A.D. 526 IN THE CHURCH OF SS. COSMAS AND DAMIAN IN ROME)

Referred to pages 116 and 513

N.B.—The central figure is that of a clerical saint (c. A.D. 800) which is inserted for comparison

who were encamped as conquerors in the old Roman lands, had laws and customs of their own. Their rights and duties were decided in accordance with their tribal conditions. On the other hand, the conquered Roman population continued to be governed in accordance with Roman Law. Therefore law and custom in western Europe for many centuries after the fifth were "personal" and not local. That is to say, a person had rights and duties and was judged in disputed cases as a member of a particular race or as a member of a social community distinct from another community within the same State or even the same city. In a famous passage of a treatise by Agobard, bishop of Lyons, in the ninth century, it is said that five men might be together, each of whom would have to be judged according to a different legal system.[1] This will be discussed later.

But besides the distinction between the barbarian conquerors and their Roman subjects, there was a distinction between the clergy of the Catholic Church and those who held political authority. From this point of view the great body of the Christian people was ruled by two distinct groups of men—the clergy, represented chiefly by bishops, and the warriors of the king's company. This is the origin in practice of the medieval contrast between the cleric (*clericus*) and the soldier (*miles*).[2] The distinction is not one of sacred and secular within the lives of all men, but a distinction between two types of authority, both claiming to be divinely appointed. Of the two the clergy were the more democratic, in the modern sense of the word, both because of the Christian tradition of equality among all Christians and because of the survival of some form of popular election as the basis of the authority of priests and bishops. The clergy had indeed, by the beginning of the fifth century, become a caste; and the original meaning of the word "caste" itself (*castus*—pure) indicates the reason for their separation from other Christians. But bishops and priests remained in closer touch than kings and warriors with the majority of the inhabitants of the new kingdoms,

[1] See below, p. 321.
[2] It has been noted already that "soldier" (*miles*) in the late Roman Empire is almost the equivalent of "barbarian" (*barbarus*): but in the Middle Ages the same word *miles* came to mean "knight."

H

partly because of a common language, Latin, and partly because they represented the tradition and customs of the old Roman civilization. The other authority, which in later times was called secular or temporal—the *miles* as contrasted with *clericus*—was alien, maintained by force of arms and suspicious of popular movements among its subjects. Here, then, is the origin of some aspects of the State in later times. When, for example, Ennodius called Theodoric "*status reipublicae*," he implied that "the State" was something external to the social system which the king controlled. The "State" was certainly not "the people." It was an external organization which cared for "the people" only as a good farmer cares for his cattle. The Germanic kings and their warriors were so ignorant and simple-minded, that they may have thought themselves superior to their subjects because they had a greater power to loot and to kill. But by all the standards of civilized life they were savages in control of a machine which they did not understand.

It follows from this contrast between the clergy and the political or military Authorities, combined perhaps with the conception of "personal" law, that the clergy could reasonably claim to be treated under a separate law of their own. In fact, synods and councils had for some centuries laid down canons which were rules, partly affecting all Christians, but mainly concerned with the organization and rights of the clergy. These canons will be discussed in a later chapter. For the purpose of the argument here it is necessary to note only that the canons of the different Churches were collected and enforced long before the barbarian kingdoms came into existence. Thus "Canon Law" in the new kingdoms had the prestige and authority of antiquity and of an older civilization, before the laws of the barbarian kingdoms were formulated. The rights of the clergy, which so disturbed kings in the Middle Ages, had their origin in this situation. The clergy of the Catholic Church, under barbarian kings who were at first all Arian heretics, claimed and were granted a distinct "personal" law, as the Roman population had a law which was distinct from that of the barbarians.

It is worth noting, finally, that in the new barbarian kingdoms, as contrasted with the later Roman Empire, the military forces upon which the rulers relied were not mercenaries. The barbarians had entered into the Roman Empire at first as instruments of imperial policy, paid for their services with loot or land. But now, in each barbarian kingdom, the barbarians fought and ruled for themselves under kings of their own choice. And the king, ruling in the midst of a subject population much more numerous than were his immediate barbarian followers, relied upon some form of personal loyalty to secure the support of his warriors. Some of these warriors were, in course of time, settled as holders of land within the barbarian kingdoms; but even before the new principle of service in payment for land-holding was established, a fundamental change had taken place in the organization of the military force under the control of a Government.

In the fifth and sixth centuries such thinking on social and political problems as remains, preserved in the documents of the time, was hampered by ideas and terminology drawn from the experience of the Roman Empire. The letters of bishops and kings in the sixth century, therefore, do not explicitly recognize the new situation. The actual relationship between kings and bishops, between political and ecclesiastical authority, had already begun to take the form which was familiar in the Middle Ages. But policy and the action of powerful personalities were far ahead of theory and doctrine. An experiment in social and political organization had begun in western Europe. An entirely new world was coming into existence. But those who thought at all on such matters still looked back and not forward for guidance.

It is clear from this description of the situation in western Europe at the beginning of the sixth century that two types of institution, the Church and the State, had developed in new forms since the disappearance of the Roman Empire in the West. The Churches in the West were not indeed yet united in one system so closely as they were in the Middle Ages; but already the tendency to unity was strong among them. And the tendency to division in law and administration was producing the many different States and systems of government of medieval and modern times. Again, the Churches maintained education and public services in support of the poor, as well as a traditional jurisdiction—functions which had hitherto been performed by the Roman Empire. The "State," on the other hand, in each barbarian kingdom, was hardly more than an instrument of armed force and a means of maintaining barbarian customs and traditions in a more civilized world.

CHAPTER VI

LATINS AND GREEKS

The western world of the First Europe was Latin. The eastern was Greek and Mohammedan. The division between the two began when the first barbarian kingdoms in Africa and Italy were destroyed by a restoration of the Roman Empire in the sixth century. But the Empire was then Roman only in name. Its capital was Constantinople. Greek and not Latin was the language of its Court, its educated class and its new laws; and the majority of the bishops in the Latin-speaking Churches of the West could speak no Greek. Commerce and intellectual intercourse between the countries of the western and those of the eastern Mediterranean had been interrupted by Vandal piracy and Gothic rule in Italy and Spain; and the restoration of unity in the sixth century, followed as it was by fifty years of disastrous plague, never reconciled the Latin-speaking West with the Greek-speaking Empire or its Churches. When, therefore, at the end of the seventh century a new and strange religion—"an armed doctrine"—almost suddenly overthrew the Roman provinces and the Catholic Churches of north Africa, and later the kings and bishops of Spain, the western world was already separate from that of the Greek-speaking Empire.

The first change in the situation in the western Mediterranean was largely due to the archaism of the Emperor Justinian, who revived military adventures in the old Roman manner. Expeditions of armed forces, calling themselves Roman, were sent to Africa, Italy and Spain. Belisarius won victories for the Emperor; and he and his generals destroyed the Vandal kingdom in Africa after many vicissitudes in A.D. 534. The Ostrogothic power in Italy was destroyed in the same manner in A.D. 536; and it seemed for a

229

time as if the Roman Emperor at Constantinople might once again look forward to governing an Empire in the West.

But the armies of Justinian were Roman only in name. Procopius, the secretary of Belisarius, who wrote in Greek a history of the Vandal and Gothic wars, often remarks upon the differences of language in the army and notes peculiarities of Latin or Roman terms.[1] The soldiers of Justinian were recruited among all the different nations of the East; and although at first welcomed by the people and the clergy of Africa and Italy as saviours from barbaric and heretical tyranny, they seem generally to have been treated in the West as "Greeks." The exactions and oppressions of the representatives of imperial power soon became even more hateful in Italy and Africa than the rule of Goths and Vandals. For more than a century, however, the province of Africa was united under the imperial system of government, with its capital at Constantinople; and the African Churches as well as the traditional Roman culture there survived so long, only to be destroyed entirely by the Mohammedan Conquest in the early eighth century. Elsewhere the destruction of Gothic kingdoms was followed, after a few years of imperial control, by new barbarian kingdoms under Catholic kings.

This destruction of kingdoms ruled by Arians and the establishment of kingdoms ruled by Catholics gave the bishops of the Western Churches new power and new responsibilities. The fundamental problem in the social situation, from the middle of the sixth to the end of the seventh century, was the place and nature of authority. The kings and their warriors maintained themselves in power by murder, treachery and war. And the use they made of their power was no less questionable than the means they took to obtain it. By most of the kings and warriors, power over other men was desired for the sake of wealth which could be expended upon feasting and the indulgence of the simplest sexual passions.

---

[1] Procopius, *Hist.*, iv, 13, 33; iv, 26, 17, κασοῦλον τῇ Λατίνων φωνῇ καλοῦσι Ρωμαῖοι. In v, 18, 40 and v, 25, 11, vii, 9, 22, vii, 21, 4, a Gothic warrior taunts the imperial army as "Greeks." And in vii, 26, 25, an Armenian soldier speaks no Greek, Latin or Gothic. At a later date Paul the Deacon in his history of the Lombards quite frankly calls the imperial armies "Greeks."

But the kings always claimed to administer justice; and although their justice was influenced by bribes, it may be supposed that some advantage fell to ordinary folk, if they could appeal from one oppressor to another. A king of sufficient military ability would also provide a certain amount of security for his subjects against the raids of rival kings or marauding warriors. But it can hardly be imagined that the early Frankish kings, for example, regarded themselves as "defenders of the peace" on behalf of common folk. Finally, the kings had a certain magic which accrued to them from the traditional reverence of their warriors, and may have been connected with the belief in a hereditary authority attached to persons of a certain family. One sign of authority at this date was long hair. As in many primitive communities, so among the Franks the hair seems to have been regarded as somewhat uncanny, or as containing some form of power. And many a Frankish prince suffered from the same treatment as Samson is said in the Old Testament to have suffered, when his rivals wished to degrade him. Here again, there may have been some value in the magic of king-ship for the common folk who paid by exactions for the privilege of being ruled. But not until the Churches, through bishops and monks, were able to dominate the minds of kings, did these kings learn to excuse their seizure of power on the plea that it was of advantage to their subjects. The conception of government, or even of armed force as a public service, is the basis of civilized life; but this conception was quite unintelligible to the ruffians who overran and ruled western Europe, until the influence of the Roman tradition was brought to bear upon them by the Roman Church. The Germanic kings and warriors—Franks in Gaul, Saxons in England and Lombards in Italy—in the sixth century contributed nothing to western civilization except their ability to learn its alphabet from Christian bishops.

The bishops, on the other hand, had to face a difficult problem. If they continued to act as opponents or critics, as they did under Arian kings, or if their acquiescence was unwilling, they might be unable to influence the kings and warriors who held control of the population. If, on the other hand, they supported the kings, they were committed to actions and policies of which the best bishops could hardly approve. In practice, the bishops supported the new kings; and in the course of the century the Church paid the price for thus attaining power. The bishops in general attempted to make the kings the instruments of Christianity, as they understood it. But the acceptance of Christianity by unlettered, violent and treacherous warriors changed the character of the religion which the bishops intended to promote. The Christianity of Augustine in the fifth century, in the midst of a Roman world, was very different from the Christianity of Gregory of Tours or Pope Gregory at the end of the sixth century. Christian religion, like government, acquired some of the characteristics of barbarism; but it survived.

Sources of the Power of Bishops

The influence of the bishops in the seventh century in Gaul, Italy, Spain and Britain, was due to two chief causes. In the first place, the great majority of the bishops, even at the worst period of moral degradation in the late seventh century, were morally and intellectually superior to the kings and their warriors. The best bishops did not aim at wealth. They controlled the properties of the Churches for the advantage of their people. They were still dependent upon clergy and people for the maintenance of their influence, even when, in the late seventh century, in Gaul, the kings had control of episcopal appointments. Again, the bishops never lost the conception of public service in the exercise of their functions. All the great bishops of this time claimed to be servants of the servants of God; and the moral prestige which flowed from this claim made the bishops powerful opponents of selfish and violent kings. Whatever may be said by those who call themselves "realists," the influence of a person who is obviously not working for his own advantage is greater, even in a savage society, than that of one who aims obviously at the satisfaction of his simplest appetites. It need not be supposed that the majority of bishops were men of outstanding virtue; and certainly in those days the conceptions of virtue were simple enough. But the bishops stood for a conception of human relationships and of justice far higher than was implied in the most bombastic claims of kings.

Not only in moral qualities, but also in intelligence and knowledge, the bishops in general were far superior to the kings and warriors; and in spite of the decay of learning and the general collapse of civilized life, the clergy alone among Christians preserved the remnants of the old literature and learning. The bishops were the patrons of such education as still existed. For example, Gregory of Tours describes how a bishop was deceived by a priest who claimed to be able to teach children, and eagerly appointed him to a school. Instruction and preaching were regarded as the chief tasks of bishops, as described in the *Pastoral Rule* of Gregory the Great. And, in a society in which few could read or write, and no king or warrior attempted to do so, acquaintance with letters carried a certain prestige. To the ignorant and the uneducated, the power derived from books seems almost magical. Knowledge, even when its nature is misunderstood, is impressive.

Indeed, the bishops lived intellectually in a world much larger than that of the kings and their warriors. For the bishops, the wide heaven extended over the whole known world. They were aware that the tradition they maintained had been growing for five or six hundred years. And the bishop of the most insignificant See in Gaul or Italy or Spain felt that he and his people formed part of a civilized world whose frontiers seemed to extend to the ends of the habitable earth. But the world in the mind of a Frankish, Visigothic or Lombard king was hardly more than a memory of his grandfather's prowess and of the extent of his own marauding. The military and political rulers of the time were therefore at a great disadvantage in dealing with the bishops, because of the limits of their intelligence and understanding; and it follows that, in the contest for influence in the new society, the advantage lay with the bishops.

The Monks

But the Christian Church had developed another instrument of moral authority, besides its clergy. The monks and nuns of western

Europe had been steadily increasing their influence from the fifth to the seventh century. Monasticism as a manner of living and the moral ideals it implied will be discussed later. Here it must be touched upon only as a force within the communities of western Europe, directing and controlling the development of law and order. At the beginning of the fifth century the work of Cassian established the eastern tradition of asceticism in southern Gaul; and at that date there were already in the cities of the western world religious enthusiasts, calling themselves monks, who annoyed St. Augustine in his more practical mood, as expressed in his treatise *On the Work of Monks*. In caves and other wild places were enthusiasts who also annoyed Rutilius because of their neglect of civic duty. But the ascetic movement which involved disregard of the collapse of civilized life was gradually organized under Caesarius of Arles, Columban, Cassiodorus and St. Benedict. The more enthusiastic Christians who retired from the world were induced to live together under some sort of regulation; and when, in the sixth century, St. Benedict used Roman common sense and the Roman tradition of order in the establishment of his Rule, the monastic movement was reunited with the general current of civilized life. From the middle of the sixth century monasteries under established authority were being founded all over western Europe. They became the centres of peaceful agricultural settlement and of such learning as still survived. And some of the greatest bishops and missionaries of the sixth and seventh centuries were trained within the monasteries. Nunneries were established within the same system; and both monks and nuns were brought into constitutional relations with the bishops and clergy.

These groups of men and women, removed from the contest for wealth and power and obviously superior in intelligence and character not only to the majority of common folk, but also to the barbarian kings and warriors, gained an immense influence over the whole social system. Their work in the civilizing of the First Europe during the sixth, seventh and eighth centuries can hardly be estimated too highly. They not only preserved what was left of the older tradition of civilized life, but also carried into the wilder parts of western Europe new methods of agriculture and other production.

Magic as a Source of Power

It would misrepresent, however, the climate of opinion in the sixth and seventh centuries to describe it only in terms of moral standards and intelligence. All men at that time were convinced of the existence of magical power which might be possessed by certain persons or made available for anyone if the right materials and rituals were used. The barbarians who ruled as kings and warriors were as frightened of unknown powers around them and as eager to know the trick for controlling them as any other savages. They brought from the forests and marshes of Germany into Gaul, Italy, Spain and Britain the simplest savage magic, such for example as was later developed in the ordeal. And it is clear from the accounts given at the time of the conversion of kings that the magical powers which were supposed to belong to Christian ritual were at least as powerful as any moral excellence in persuading the barbarians to accept Christianity. To the simple minds of savages, even the influence of an unselfish and high-minded bishop would seem to be magical. The awe inspired in Attila, for example, by Lupus and Leo was, no doubt, due less to a perception of superior moral stature than to fear of an uncanny power which he did not understand. Again, in the later sixth century and in the seventh century, the barbarians with whom the Churches had to deal, were not such men as the Goths and the Vandals of the fifth century, who had been already for some generations under the influence of Roman civilization. The new barbarians, the Franks in Gaul and the Saxons in Britain, were, in the simplest sense of the word, savages. They came from beyond the frontiers of the old Roman influence; and when they were converted to Catholic Christianity they passed over a chasm much deeper and wider than Theodoric faced when he conquered Italy, or Alaric II, king of the Visigoths, when he published his laws in south-western Gaul. The Franks were well known to the Romans as the most treacherous among barbarians; and the Saxons who eventually settled in Britain were pirates without any appreciation of the civilized life they destroyed. It was natural, therefore, for such men to seek in Christianity magical powers rather than moral excellence. Like all savages they believed in the efficacy of sacred formulas and taboos. And the Church provided both. The influence of the bishops, therefore, on the kings of the seventh century, depended partly, if not mainly, upon the supposed efficacy of the rituals they performed and upon the supposed power of the relics of saints whose guardians and agents they were. Clovis, for example, after his baptism, was evidently afraid of the power of the relics of St. Martin at Tours and commanded his army to be careful not to offend the saint on the expedition against Alaric, king of the Visigoths.[1] And when at a later date the Franks besieged Saragossa, they were terrified by a procession bearing the relics of St. Vincent and raised the siege.[2]

The belief in uncanny and dangerous powers, watching every man at every step, was shared generally by the whole world in the sixth and seventh centuries. And indeed, the bishops themselves, as is proved by Gregory's *History of the Franks*, shared the common belief in the power of relics to cure disease or ward off disaster. Gregory the Great, for example, writes in many of his letters that he is sending filings from the chains of St. Peter to his correspondents for the cure of sore eyes and other evils. As for the magical efficacy of ceremonies, a good example is to be found both in Gregory's *Dialogues* and in Bede's *History*, where the story is told of a captive who had Masses said for him at his home; and whenever the Masses were said, his chains fell off.[3]

The principle is the same as that implied in the use of ju-ju or obeah in West Africa and the West Indies. But it must not be imagined that the Christian clergy of the sixth century introduced or, at least at first, promoted magic. Both the barbarians and the Romanized populations of the sixth and later centuries believed in magic and magicians and in the presence of devils or demons everywhere. In fact, the Church actually reduced the number of magical practices, and organized them in some sort of connection

[1] Greg. Tur., *H.F.*, ii, 38.
[2] Ibid., iii, 29. *Pat. Lat.*, 71, col. 263, "timentes se ab ea civitate removerunt."
[3] Gregory, *Dial.*, iv, 57. Bede, *H.E.*, iv, 22.

with a simple standard of right and wrong. The power of the clergy and of the relics of saints was supposed to express the preference of God for justice and mercy. When, however, the magic of the clergy took the place of the traditional beliefs and practices common to the illiterate both in Roman civilization and in Germanic barbarism, it became more difficult for those who gained prestige or wealth from popular credulity to disregard their opportunities.

The magical power which gave the clergy such influence in the centuries between the fifth and the ninth, as well as later, had two sources. It came either from material objects regarded as sacred and taboo, or from persons who were believed to derive a special divine force from "ordination." The magical power of certain material objects is obviously believed in by all primitive peoples and by undeveloped minds, even in a civilized society. In the early Middle Ages, as in late Roman times, these material objects were the bones or clothes of saints, fragments of wood supposed to be parts of the "Cross," oil from lamps at saints' tombs, and even pieces of cloth which had touched a shrine.[1] Collecting relics and the "discovery" of saints' bodies were already highly developed in the fourth century; and relics were believed to be useful even for obtaining victory in battle from the sixth to the ninth century. All this will be discussed elsewhere in relation to the new moral standard. It is enough here to note that without the universal belief in the magical power of certain material objects the clergy could never have controlled the barbarian kings and their warriors.

But secondly, the clergy themselves claimed to have acquired by special rituals and formulas a magical force quite independent of their virtue or intelligence as individuals. Like the medicine-man in savage communities, the priest and bishop of the Christian Churches, after the fourth century, were regarded, not merely as sources of knowledge, but as holders of special magical powers derived directly from celestial Powers. This divides the clergy

---

[1] Gregory of Tours reports that a piece of cloth which had touched St. Peter's tomb "was so filled with divine virtue that it weighed much more than it had before" (De Gloria M., 28).

completely from monks and nuns, whose social influence was derived entirely from their own individual excellence as estimated according to the standards of that age. For a time it seemed as if the influence of the moral authority of such monks as St. Columban or St. Benedict might rival the power of bishops and priests. But the minds of the majority of men and women in those centuries were so completely saturated by the belief in magic that the clergy soon proved to have an influence far superior to that of any holy men; and even monks found that they acquired additional power when they became priests or bishops. The magical power of the clergy was expressed chiefly through the sacraments, of which they were the ministers. These sacraments, and the rituals connected with them, certainly impressed with a sense of uncanny power the simple kings and warriors upon whom the bishops conferred them. The Emperor Constantine, being baptized on his death-bed, and the Frankish king Clovis, being baptized before new military expeditions, would equally feel that something had happened to them, which lay outside their limited experience of natural events. Thus, bishops and priests were able to control and direct the whole of the primitive society of those days. Ritual acts performed by persons regarded as sacred leave an immense impression on the minds of believers.

Sources of Information

The written records of the period which happen to have survived are as follows. Procopius wrote a history of the Vandal war in Africa and the Gothic war in Italy. He was secretary to the commander-in-chief, Belisarius, and friendly to him; but clearly he had doubts of Justinian's wisdom in his policy of conquest. He was a non-Christian, who seems to have regarded the Christian Emperors of his time, Justin and his nephew Justinian, as uneducated or half-educated barbarians; and he also wrote, but never published, a book of scandalous stories, which has fortunately survived. In this he describes how the Emperor Justin, being unable to read or write—"which had never before occurred among the Romans"—used a stencil with the word "Legi" (I have read) for authorizing official documents.[1] Justinian, he says, was barbarian in dress and mentality, and spoke Greek with a bad accent.[2] His wife, Theodora, according to Procopius, had been a revue-actress with a reputation for immorality. But Procopius in his published work on the wars had acquired enough fame to be induced by the hope of further favours also to write a description of the buildings constructed under Justinian, which has survived and provides some evidence of Greek influences upon the Latin Churches of Africa.

Evagrius, a Syrian lawyer who acted on behalf of bishops, wrote a history of the Church from A.D. 431 (Council of Ephesus) to A.D. 594. He died soon after that year. He touches upon the situation in Africa and gives an interesting account of the great plague. Of the Latin documents which remain, the most important for the history of Africa is a tedious poem by Corippus, a schoolmaster. For Italy, the letters of Pope Gregory I provide the most important contemporary evidence. But Paul the Deacon, in the ninth century, adds some information in his *History of the Lombards*. The situation in Spain is explained in a short history of the Goths by Isidore, bishop of Seville; and there is a polemical pamphlet against the Franks by Julian, archbishop of Toledo. But the most important documents of the period are the records of the Councils of Toledo, which established the tradition of kingship in a recognizably medieval form.

The buildings and mosaics of the sixth and seventh centuries should not be forgotten. Some of those which remain, especially in Ravenna and Rome, contain evidence of the extinction of Arianism and of the influence of the Greek or Byzantine art of the Roman Empire. Under Theodoric, about A.D. 500, the church now known as St. Apollinare Nuovo was built, originally for the Arians, and dedicated to St. Martin. Some of its early mosaics belong to the Arian period; but there are two later mosaic decorations representing lines of male and female saints, which were added later, perhaps in order to replace less orthodox scenes. In Ravenna also is the originally Arian church of San Vitale, of about A.D. 520, in which are the elaborate Byzantine mosaics of the Emperor Justinian

---

[1] Procopius, *Anecdota*, vi, 11.　　　　[2] Ibid., xii, 2.

and his wife Theodora, of A.D. 547. The figures of the Emperor and Empress bear the nimbus.[1] The great church of St. Apollinare in Classe also belongs to this period. In Rome the church of St. Agatha was originally built for the Arian Goths; and Santa Maria in Aracoeli was first built under Gregory I. Many others of the older basilicas belong to the sixth and seventh centuries. But perhaps the most striking records of the period are the walls of Rome. As they now stand they follow the lines established by Aurelian (A.D. 271) and Probus (A.D. 280). Some of their work remains. According to Procopius, part of the walls was destroyed by the Goths.[2] They were repaired under Theodoric in A.D. 500, and by Belisarius in A.D. 560. The walls of cities of this date serve as a reminder of the marauding bands roaming the countryside, and of the unarmed city populations with no stable Governments in control.

New Forces in State and Church

During the sixth century new centres of social influence or power were formed by different forces in the five countries of the western world where the Roman Emperor had once ruled—in Africa, Italy, Spain, Gaul and Britain. In the first three the Roman Empire seemed likely in the sixth century to re-establish its authority; and there the old Roman names for the countries have survived until modern times, the province of Africa having later had its name extended to a vast continent then unknown. But in Gaul and Britain no attempt was made after the fifth century to re-establish Roman power; and in the seventh century the old names Gaul and Britain were changed, in the current Latin, to France (Francia) and England (Anglia). In these two non-Mediterranean countries the Franks and the Anglo-Saxons established the basis for a new social order; and they escaped the destruction and confusion which followed upon the Mohammedan conquests of the coasts of the Mediterranean. In all five countries, however, during the sixth and seventh centuries experiments were being made in law and government, both by the kings and the bishops.

[1] See reproduction, facing the title-page.   [2] Procopius, *Bell. Goth.*, iii, 22, 24.

In Africa, Italy and on the Mediterranean coast of Spain the authority of the Emperor at Constantinople was restored during the sixth century by the armies and fleets of Justinian. The peoples of Africa, Italy and southern Spain, who still retained the Roman tradition of civilized life in trade, manufacture and culture, were released from subjection to Germanic rulers. But the imperial forces which destroyed barbarian rule acted as conquerors in the old Roman territories; and most of the men in the fleets and armies were in no sense Roman. Not many years, therefore, after the re-establishment of the Empire, the common people of Africa, Italy and Spain suffered as much from the Empire as they had suffered under barbarian kings.

Again, the armed forces of Justinian destroyed the rule of Arian heretics and therefore the influence of the Arian clergy. The Empire stood for the Catholic Church; and its restoration in the West was at first welcomed by the Catholic bishops. At the same time, the increasing hostility of the people towards civil and military Authorities claiming to be Roman, who were, in fact, Greek or Asiatic, was soon reflected in the policy of the Churches. The bishop of Rome, in particular, was felt to have a special relation to the Roman Emperor; because, in fact, the Christian Empire had been deeply influenced by the authority of the Christian Rome of the Apostles and martyrs. It seemed for a time in the sixth century that the Roman Church would be committed by its connection with the Roman Empire to an ineradicable hostility against all barbarian rulers. But, as in the case of the common people, the bishops of Africa, Italy and southern Spain found that the restored Empire did more harm than good to the Latin Churches. And during the early seventh century the Churches of the West and, above all, the bishops of Rome, began to look to the kings in the West and not to the Emperor at Constantinople, for security and influence. While the Emperor still retained any power and authority in the western Mediterranean the bishops of the Catholic Church in that area felt themselves to be naturally allied with the Empire. They were in the same position as St. Augustine or Pope Leo I had been two centuries before. They were subjects of the Emperor. But as the Empire gradually lost its hold in Africa, Spain and Italy, the bishops were compelled to make terms with any kings or other authorities who could be regarded as Christian or as possible converts to the Catholic Church.

The situation, however, was changing continually throughout the seventh century, largely under the quite unforeseen pressure of a new religion, that of Mohammed. Conquests by the adherents of this new religion weakened the Empire in the East and eventually compelled the countries of the western Mediterranean to give up all hope of assistance from the Emperor at Constantinople. Even at the beginning of the seventh century the Popes expressed in their letters a sense of despair in their appeals to the Emperor. They looked for assistance and support either to kings in the West or to their own diplomatic powers. And by the end of the seventh century the whole southern coast of the Mediterranean had been conquered by Mohammedan warriors and the influence of the Churches in Africa was finally destroyed. A few years later the same conquerors destroyed the precarious system of ecclesiastical and civil government in Spain. The relation of bishops and kings, in that country, remained only as a memory in the recorded canons of councils. But the Catholic Church in Spain had long lost any real contact with the Empire. Even in Italy, where the bishop of Rome remained, in theory, a subject of the Emperor until at least the middle of the eighth century, the Churches were compelled to make their own compromises with barbarian kingdoms of the West. The old tradition of ecclesiastical and civil government, inherited from St. Augustine and still maintained at the end of the sixth century by Pope Gregory the Great, was breaking down. The changing situation made it impossible to maintain that there was one Christian Church in one Christian Empire, or that the moral authority of civil government was derived solely from the divinely appointed Emperor of a distant and alien people in Constantinople. At this time also the division of languages between the eastern and western Mediterranean began more deeply to affect the position of the Churches. As sea-borne trade decreased, Greek ceased to be useful in the trading centres. Pope Gregory the Great could speak no Greek, in spite of having resided as a Nuncio (Apocrisiarius) for many years at Constantinople; and the Latin Churches were often unaware of disputes and decisions in councils of bishops held in the East. In spite of the fact that a number of Syrians were bishops of Rome at the end of the seventh century, the language of the Roman Church and of all the Churches in the West was Latin. This alone would have divided the Churches in western Europe from the Empire, where Greek was being introduced even into the decrees of Roman law under Justinian.

The separation of the countries of the East from those of the West and North of Europe had, no doubt, many different causes. But that separation was already obvious in the early sixth century, at least a century before the Mohammedan invasions. The contrast between the *New Laws* (Novellae), of which the latest is dated A.D. 468, added to the law-books of Theodosius, in Latin, and the *New Laws* (Novellae) of Justinian, in Greek, proves that between about A.D. 470 and A.D. 550 the Latin world of western Europe was severed from the Greek world of Constantinople.[1] A difference of language is not merely a difference in the form of speech. It is a sign of difference in the climate of opinion. The Latin of the Roman Law and its derivatives united the countries of western Europe and divided them from the Greek-speaking world.

Both the Governments and the Churches of the West were distinguished as "Latin" from the Greek-speaking Empire and its Churches long before there was any final difference of doctrine or ritual. Each of the three countries on the coast of the western Mediterranean—Africa, Italy and Spain—had a direct and important influence upon the formation of medieval Christendom throughout the sixth century. But by the end of that century, in each of these countries, the structure of the Roman tradition was shaken or destroyed, in Africa and Spain by the Mohammedans, and in Italy by the Lombards. The situation, however, differed in certain important aspects in each of these countries; and it will, therefore, be necessary to consider them separately.

---

[1] A few of Justinian's *New Laws* are in Latin, addressed to officials in Illyricum and Italy; but the great majority are in Greek.

Africa and the Empire

The troops of Justinian, first under Belisarius, and later under Soloman, had destroyed the last remnants of the Vandal kingdom in Africa in A.D. 534. And from that time for more than a century the province of Africa and the northern coasts of the continent as far as the straits of Gibraltar, together with the islands of the western Mediterranean, were ruled by officials appointed by the Emperor at Constantinople. Soon after the defeat of the Vandals, the Governor of northern Africa took the title of Exarch. He was usually an alien supported by an army of occupation which was Roman only in name. But the new system of government represented the traditions of the Catholic Empire under Theodosius the Great; and Justinian clearly thought of his system of government in terms of ecclesiastical orthodoxy, as well as of imperial authority. The ruin and disorder in northern Africa, after a century of Vandal rule, and after the wars which extinguished it, seem to have been widespread. Cities were destroyed or deserted, fields uncultivated, and the population greatly reduced. Justinian's policy after re-conquest aimed at a restoration of the old conditions under Roman rule. Cities were rebuilt and water-supplies re-established. The Greek historian Evagrius, writing in A.D. 595, says: "Justinian is reported to have restored one hundred and fifty cities in Africa, some of which had been altogether, and others largely, ruined. This he did with extreme magnificence, in private and public works and adornments, in fortifications and other great structures by which cities are beautified and God is propitiated; also in aqueducts for use and ornament, the supply of water having been in some cases conveyed to the cities for the first time, in others restored to its former state."[1] The essay of Procopius on buildings gives details of the repair of walls and aqueducts, and the fortification of towns in Africa hitherto unwalled.[2]

Many churches were repaired or newly constructed. But the ecclesiastical organization was under the influence of Byzantine or

[1] Evagrius, *H.E.*, ch. xviii.
[2] Procopius, *Buildings*, vi, 2 sq. Procopius also reports that Justinian built a church of the Mother of God at a place eighty miles south of the Libyan coast, where, until his day (A.D. 535), Alexander was worshipped.

eastern religious fervour, as it is proved by the many dedications to eastern Saints and by the importation of relics from the East.[1] Again, there was a vigorous revival of synods and councils of bishops, after the long years of persecution under the Arian Vandals. The canons of these councils maintained the ancient tradition of the African Churches; and a famous summary of Canons (*Abbreviatio Canonum*) was made by Fulgentius Ferrandus (d. A.D. 546), at about this time in Africa. The Catholic Church had, therefore, revived after the restoration of the south-western coast of the Mediterranean to the Roman Empire. The gratitude of the Orthodox, who were restored to influence by the destruction of Arian power, might have confirmed the identity of interest between the Church and the Empire. The Churches in Africa did indeed support the imperial Authorities and extended their influence by missions to the heathen among the Moors of the interior. But in Africa and the islands the Churches remained Latin, in spite of the Greek influence of the Empire. Their language, ritual and customs bound them to old Rome rather than to the Emperor.

The restoration of prosperity, therefore, and of religious orthodoxy along the coast, did not solve the fundamental difficulty with which Justinian's policy had to contend. The "Roman" population of the cities spoke and thought in Latin. They had no traditional connection with Constantinople. On the other hand, the troops of Justinian's Roman Empire were commanded by Greek-speaking officers; they regarded themselves as an army of occupation; and they were used to make the province of Africa and the country to the west of it mainly a source of income for the Authorities at Constantinople. Commerce was directed towards Constantinople. Again, the Moors of the interior were unsubdued; and grievances against the imperial Authorities led to raids and revolts, of which the most serious seems to have been that of A.D. 548. This was

---

[1] An admirable summary will be found in *L'Afrique Chrétienne*, by Dom H. Leclercq, 2 vols., 1904, Paris. The relics of Saints, conveyed to new countries, were used to increase the influence of the places from which they came. In the eighth and ninth centuries, for example, Rome exported relics to England and Germany, to the great advantage of the Roman See.

suppressed by a general sent from Constantinople, whose victory forms the subject of some of the most painfully futile verses ever composed. The *Johannis*, written by an African schoolmaster, Corippus, about A.D. 550, describes the conflict with the various Moorish chieftains.[1] Corippus begins by remarking that Achilles had Homer, Aeneas had Virgil, and John had the author himself for a poet: to such a depth had the ancient tradition descended. The writer, however, carries on the history of the African wars for a few years later than those dealt with by Procopius; and, unlike that historian, he was a Christian. He therefore gives a very interesting account of the hymns sung and the Mass celebrated in the presence of the army of the Byzantines, in preparation for the final victory.

The suppression of Moorish revolts and the control of the discontent of the local population at an alien rule might have saved Justinian's Empire. But the ecclesiastical or theological policy of the Emperor was utterly fatal to it. Justinian, like Constantine and Theodosius before him, aimed at securing religious unity among all of his subjects; because he knew that controversies about ritual or doctrine easily led to riots and to disregard of the civil Authorities. But he made the same mistake as other Emperors before and after him, in supposing that he could impose unity of doctrine by his own imperial authority. In A.D. 544 he issued an Edict demanding the condemnation of three writers who were regarded as heretics. This opened the notorious controversy of the Three Chapters.[2] The bishop of Rome of that time, Vigilius, who had been appointed under imperial influence, was brought to Constantinople and made to sign an ambiguous document, the *Judicatum*. But the bishops of Africa were vigorously opposed to the policy of the Emperor; and Facundus, bishop of Hermiana, published, in A.D. 550, a pamphlet directed against the authority of the Emperor in matters of doctrine. He protested that the condemnation of dead bishops seemed to undermine the authority of the Council of Chalcedon which had

[1] Verses of Corippus in *M.G.H.*, *Auct. Ant.*, iii, part 2.
[2] The "Three Chapters" or three "headings" (*capitula*) contained the list of the writings to be condemned as unorthodox—a letter of Ibas, the writings of Theodoret against Cyril and of Theodore of Mopsuestia.

not condemned them. But he went further and attacked the use of the imperial Power in the attempt to enforce orthodoxy.[1]

The Churches of Italy, and especially the Church of the city of Rome, repudiating the concession made by Pope Vigilius, were united with the Churches of Africa in opposition to the Emperor's policy. But Justinian, who seems to have been determined to be master in theological doctrine, supported a persecution of the clergy in Africa who were opposed to him; and this was a further cause, both of disunion in Africa and of opposition to the imperial Government. Imperial authority, therefore, which had been regarded by the African Churches as a means of restoring Catholic unity, had become a source of opposition to the Latin tradition of the western Churches; but the death of Justinian (A.D. 565) and the succession of his nephew Justin II, who cared tor none of these things, brought peace to the Churches in Africa.

The one positive result of the doctrinal differences between Justinian and the Latin Churches, and of the restored contact with Constantinople in civil and military affairs, was the increased prestige of the bishops of Rome. The restoration of a Catholic Roman Empire with its Emperor at Constantinople naturally increased the importance of the bishop of "old" Rome. And the clergy of the Latin Churches were willing to use the bishop of Rome as their most powerful intermediary for protests to the Emperor. The increase in the influence of the Roman See was most obvious under Gregory the Great. His letters show that the Churches in Africa, Sicily and Sardinia, while the Emperor's agents and Exarchs ruled those countries, looked to the bishop of Rome for redress of grievances and protection against official oppression. Thus the bishop of Rome became a representative of the whole of the western world which was still part of the Roman Empire; but he acted in all his protests as a subject of the Emperor. Pope Gregory wrote to the Emperor Maurice (August, A.D. 596) to urge him to act on behalf on the Catholics in Africa:—

Bishops from the Province of Africa say that your commands have been disregarded by carelessness or connivance and that neither is the

[1] Facundus, *Defensio*, xii, 3. *Pat. Lat.*, 67.

judgement of God feared nor, so far, have the imperial decrees (against the Donatists) been put into effect. . . . I have thought it right to send these bishops to Your Piety that they may in person inform you of what, as they say, they have endured for the Christian faith.[1]

Again, the Pope attempted to correct the abuses of imperial administration in Sardinia, as a series of his letters shows.[2] He wrote to the Empress Constantina to ask her to bring to the Emperor's notice the abuses which were due to official action. These he describes as follows:[3]—

When I found that there were many heathens in the island of Sardinia, who, following the evil customs of heathenism offered sacrifices to idols, while the bishops of the island were not active in preaching the Redeemer to them, I sent thither one of the bishops of Italy, who, by God's help, has brought many heathens to the faith. He has, however, informed me of an impious custom in the island. He says that those who sacrifice to idols pay a sum of money to the governor for leave to do so. And when some of them were baptized and ceased to offer sacrifices to idols, the same governor, even after their baptism, compels them to pay the sum which they used to give for permission to sacrifice. And when the bishop reproved him, he said that he had promised so large a sum of money to procure his appointment to his office, that he could not possibly make it up without resorting to such expedients as this. The island of Corsica, too, is oppressed with such heavy exactions, levied besides with so much extortion, that the people can hardly meet them even by selling their children. Hence it comes to pass that those who own estates in the island forsake the Holy Empire, and are compelled to take refuge with the infamous Lombards. For what outrage can the barbarians inflict on them more cruel than to force them by oppression and extortion to sell their own children? In the island of Sicily we are informed that Stephen, the chartulary of the maritime district, is guilty of such injustice and oppression, in seizing the possessions of private individuals and claiming their lands and houses for the State, without any action at law, that a large volume would not suffice to record all his evil deeds.

Clearly, as a result of Justinian's policy, the bishop of Rome had increased prestige and power in Africa and the islands. The local Churches had been already weakened by schism and by the perse-

---

[1] Ep., vi, 61.   [2] Ibid., i, 47 etc. See Dudden, *Gregory the Great*, vol. ii, 241.
[3] Ibid., v, 38. Trans. Dudden.

cution of the Vandal kings. And when the Vandal kingdom was destroyed the African Church was no longer able to assert itself independently of the Roman Church, as in earlier days. Again, there were no local kings in Africa. The bishops had to deal only with an Emperor; and naturally, therefore, sought assistance from the only Patriarch in the West, the Pope, who could pass over the local officials and address himself directly to the Supreme Ruler in Constantinople.

Again, the Latin Churches were resolute in their support of the Council of Chalcedon, and therefore in opposition to the condemnation of the writers named in the three Chapters. Christianity in the West was more definitely Roman or Hellenic than it was in the eastern Mediterranean. The Latins who were determined, as against the Arians, to worship Christ as God, were equally determined, as against the Monophysites of the sixth century, to treat the Virgin Mary as the mother of a man. The Treatise (Tomus) of Leo I had become a gospel. The Latin Churches, therefore, were united in opposition to the Greek-speaking Roman Emperor. As Nicetius, bishop of Trier, wrote in a letter of protest to Justinian: "Be it known to you that all Italy, Africa, Spain and Gaul, weeping for your damnation, curse your name."[1] This clearly implies the existence of a sense of unity in the Latin West; and this sense of unity naturally reinforced the prestige of the bishop of Rome, who was both the successor of Leo I, and the only holder of an apostolic See among the Latin Churches.

But doctrinal discussion was less deadly to Roman civilization in Africa than the great plague which began in Egypt in A.D. 542 and spread with the renewed commerce along the coasts of north Africa, Spain and Italy. It was bubonic plague, like the so-called Black Death in the fourteenth century; and it continued throughout the imperial dominions for fifty years, with recurrent intensity every few years. It destroyed thousands on the north coast of Africa. It reached Italy in A.D. 543, and northern France in A.D. 546. In A.D. 565 it caused so much distress in Italy that no resistance could be offered to the invasion of the Lombards. Evidently the

[1] Nicetius Trev. *Ep. ad Justinianum*, Mansi, ix, 769.

infection came by sea, carried by rats or merchandise from the East. The effects of the plague are described by Evagrius.[1] He writes—"some cities were so severely afflicted as to be altogether depopulated, though in other places the visitation was less violent. . . . In my own case, at the beginning of this calamity I was afflicted with swellings (*buboes*) while still a schoolboy, and lost by its recurrence at different times several of my children, my wife, many relatives and many of my domestic and country servants. . . . Then, not quite two years before my writing this, being now fifty-eight years old, on the fourth attack of the plague, in Antioch, I lost a daughter and her son." Then follows the description of the symptoms and an account of the spread of the infection by the flight of people from the stricken cities.

Thus the whole Roman Empire was weakened at the end of the sixth century, both by religious dissensions and by plague. In A.D. 610 Heraclius, son of the Exarch of Africa, sailed with an armed force to Constantinople, and made himself Emperor. Nine years afterwards, as it is said,[2] he proposed to remove the capital of the Empire from Constantinople to Carthage, either because he was uncertain of his hold upon the Greek-speaking populations of the East, or because military disasters had followed upon invasion by the Persians. The Roman tradition of government and religion, however, in northern Africa was soon after threatened by an altogether unforeseen enemy—a new religion of the desert. The followers of Mohammed first conquered Syria; and a flood of Christian refugees, both monks and laymen, fled to Africa and Sicily. Some of these monks were Monophysites—that is to say, believers in the "one nature" of Christ, as opposed to the Catholic doctrine that Christ was equally both man and God. In the midst of the dangers of invasion, the Emperors continued to attempt to secure doctrinal unity; but the only result was that a strong anti-imperial party, chiefly among the monks and clergy, was organized in Egypt and Africa. In A.D. 640 the Mohammedans invaded Egypt and were welcomed by the Monophysites, because they destroyed all possibility of persecution by the imperialists (Melkites); and

---

[1] Evagrius, *Hist. of the Church*, ch. xxix.   [2] Nicephorus, *Chronicon.*, a. 617.

from that time the Copts, as Monophysites, have lived under Mohammedan rule.[1]

For nearly fifty years more the African Churches remained under imperial Authority, but greatly weakened by doctrinal dissensions and by the gradual advance of Mohammedan raiders.[2] In A.D. 647, after a revolt by the Exarch against the Emperor, the "Roman" army in Africa was defeated; and the imperial garrisons in the cities were greatly weakened. The Moors of the interior took the opportunity, once again, of raiding the Roman territories on the coast. The Mohammedans used the new situation; and in A.D. 698 Carthage fell into their hands. Northern Africa thus ceased to belong to the Roman and Christian tradition. The city of Septem (Ceuta) held out for another ten years; but the advance of the Mohammedans at the beginning of the eighth century was secured by its surrender and their entry into Spain. The conquest of north Africa by the Mohammedans was not the result of continuous successful policy. Efforts were made by the Emperors at Constantinople to resist them by sending fleets from the East. Sometimes the Christians of the coast were able to oppose the invaders. Often the Mohammedans themselves were divided and fought one another under rival chiefs. The Moors of the interior were sometimes able to destroy both Christians and Mohammedans. The gradual disappearance, therefore, of Christianity from northern Africa was like the extinction of a dying fire. There was no force left to oppose the establishment of a new and barbarous tyranny of desert warriors in a "holy war."

During the century that followed the first Mohammedan invasions, two important effects of their conquest were felt in the new Europe of the West. First, great numbers of Christians were enslaved in northern Africa after the capture of the cities. According to Theophanes, eighty thousand of the poorer "Romans" in Africa were taken as slaves.[3] Some Christians did indeed become Mohammedans. But throughout the early Middle Ages there were thousands of Christian slaves serving Mohammedan masters in northern

[1] The Copts were so called, from the Greek word "Aiguptos," an Egyptian.
[2] A good summary of events is in L. R. Holme, *The Extinction of the Christian Churches in North Africa*, 1898.   [3] Theophanes, *Chron.*, ad an. 661.

Africa; and the policy of the bishops of Rome, even in the thirteenth century, led to friendly communication with the Mohammedan rulers, with a view to the redemption of captive Christians.

A second, less enduring, effect of the Mohammedan conquest was a flow of refugees from northern Africa to Italy, Sicily, Germany and southern France. Clergy, monks, and the richer Christians of the cities, fled northwards from the invaders and brought to the people among whom they settled some of the traditions of the African Churches, in the same way as refugees from Spain, after the Mohammedan invasion there, brought the records of "Canon Law" into France. But the refugees were not all welcome, because Africa had been a fertile source of heresy. Thus Pope Gregory II, writing to Germany in the eighth century, warned the devout against the danger of the infiltration of heresy with the coming of the refugees from Africa.[1]

The first Mohammedan rulers of north Africa did not persecute Christians. They enslaved or taxed all non-Mohammedans; but the religion of Mohammed was believed by them to confer privileges, both in life and after death, which good Mohammedans were not eager to extend to their subjects by converting unbelievers. The Christians of north Africa, therefore, although reduced to slavery or subjection, still had their bishops and priests. But they were cut off from the rest of Christendom by the incessant wars and piratical raids of their masters. The Catholic Churches of Africa had always looked to the Roman Empire for support; and after surviving the Vandal persecution, they were reduced to insignificance under Mohammedan rule when the Empire finally lost control of the western Mediterranean.

Italy: the Empire and the Church

The situation in Italy was not so completely transformed by the destruction of Gothic power. The death of Theodoric had been followed by some few years of quarrelling about leadership and

---

[1] Gregory II, Ep., 4. *Pat. Lat.*, 89, col. 502. Afros passim ad ecclesiasticos ordines praetendentes nulla ratione suscipiat, quia aliqui eorum Manichaei, aliqui rebaptizati saepius sunt probati.

then by the military control of Totila, who was finally defeated by the forces of the Roman Empire in A.D. 536.

The Roman Emperor at Constantinople seemed to have established his authority again in Italy by the use of Greek-speaking and barbarian troops under Belisarius; and a new and more permanent situation seemed to have arisen when the Exarch, Narses, controlled sections of Italy, in the name of the Emperor, from his capital at Ravenna. For twelve years (A.D. 555–567) Narses attempted to repair the ravages of the war in Italy; and in A.D. 554 (August 13th) the "Pragmatic Sanction" of Justinian was issued, which attempted to establish a basis for Roman rule in Italy. This collection of decrees, "at the request of Vigilius, the venerable bishop of Old Rome," confirms laws made by Atalaric and other Gothic rulers, but not by Totila. It excludes civil cases from the military courts and puts them under civil judges who are to be chosen "by the bishops and chief persons of each region." The bishop and chief men (primates) of the district are to define conditions to be observed in the markets. The bishops are thus accepted as instruments of civil government by the imperial Authority.[1]

But although in name Roman, the imperial Authority in Italy was quite clearly alien. It was supported by an army of mercenaries, controlled by agents from Constantinople under the Exarchs at Ravenna. Even the Churches of Italy, which had looked to the Empire to save them from Arian rulers and barbarian soldiery, found little comfort in supporting a conquest which impoverished and enslaved them. But the Empire could not maintain its authority without the use of barbarian mercenaries; and when at last the Lombards were called into Italy to help, the final episode began in the gradual separation of the Churches of Italy, and above all the Church of Rome, from the Roman Empire. These new barbarians soon found that they could take for themselves the power which the Empire had hired them to protect.

Like other barbarians the Lombards were regarded at first as enemies both of the Catholic Church and of the Roman Empire whose officials had brought them to Italy to help in the conflict

[1] *Nov. Justinian.* clxiv, p. 354, vol. ii, in Teubner ed. (1881).

with the Goths. But by the end of the sixth century most of the bishops of Italy were compelled to acquiesce in the rule of Lombard kings and dukes. In A.D. 581 Pope Pelagius II appealed to the Emperor for help against Lombard oppression; and he also began the long effort to use the Frankish kings for the defence of the Roman Church. In a letter from the Pope to Aunarius, bishop of Auxerre, he says: "We believe that, not by chance nor without great consideration, Divine Providence has ordained that your kings be like the Roman Empire in the confession of the orthodox faith. Assuredly this was brought to pass in order that they might be neighbours and helpers of this city of Rome where that confession arose, and of the whole of Italy. We have sent the sacred relics which you and our glorious son asked for—therefore we urge that you should hasten to free from heathen pollution the temples of those whose strength you seek; and that you should persuade your kings quickly to cut themselves off by correct policy from all friendship and alliance with our most unspeakable enemies, the Lombards."[1]

The Exarchs at Ravenna proved to be entirely unable to resist the growth of Lombard power; and when Gregory the Great was elected Pope in A.D. 590, the bishops of the Churches in Italy still regarded the Roman Emperor at Constantinople as their protector against the barbarians. Meantime, however, a new figure, a woman, entered upon the stage. Theudelinda, daughter of the duke of the Bavarians, was married to the king of the Lombards; and at his death she remained queen and chose as her husband Agilulf, duke of Turin.[2] The marriage took place in November, A.D. 590. Theudelinda was an ardent Catholic, and under her influence the Lombard kingdom adopted a policy of friendship towards the Roman Church, then ruled by Gregory. As a result, in A.D. 599 the Pope himself concluded a peace with the Lombards, because the Emperor and his representatives in Italy did nothing to help. The anger of

---

[1] Pelagius II, Ep. 2, *Pat. Lat.*, 72, trans. partly in Hodgkin, *Italy*, v, p. 239. The letter is dated October 5, A.D. 581, *imperante domno Tiberio Constantinopoli Augusto, Anno VII*. Thus the bishop of Rome still acknowledges the Empire as the real basis of civilized life. *Virtus* is here used as the power of saints.

[2] Paulus Diac., *H.L.*, iii, 35; iv, 1.

the Pope at the inactivity of the Emperor was expressed when the Emperor himself was murdered and Gregory congratulated the murderer, the new Emperor, Phocas, in A.D. 603; but he himself died in the following year. Queen Theudelinda died in A.D. 628: and a succession of murders and murderous raids is all that is recorded of the immediately following years in the history of Italy.

The Roman Emperor, however, continued to hold such parts of Italy as could be controlled from the sea; and the Emperor Constans II actually visited the city of Rome in the year A.D. 663. He is said by one chronicler to have intended to make Rome the capital of the Empire once again; but in fact he spent the time of his visit in stripping the city of bronze and of works of art. He left Rome for Sicily and seems to have marked his journey from land to land by exactions from the people whom he had come ostensibly to rescue from the barbarians. As Hodgkin says, when Constans II entered Rome, "three hundred and seven years had elapsed since the awestricken Constantius, the son of Constantine the Great, had gazed on the glories of yet unruined Rome, and nearly two centuries since any person calling himself Emperor had stood upon the Palatine Hill."[1] When Constans II departed, the history of the subjection of the Roman Church to the Roman Empire came to an end. For although Pope Constantine went to Constantinople in A.D. 710, at the command of the Emperor, the Pope entered that city, not as a humble suppliant or prisoner but with a train of attendants of whom the future Pope, Gregory II, was the most important. And he returned to Italy with all the privileges of the Church renewed. He it was who introduced as the head-dress of a Pope, the tiara—a non-ecclesiastical but courtly decoration worn in the East.[2] The head-dress of an Oriental monarchy thus became a symbol of the monarchy which the bishop of Rome was to establish. It distinguishes the medieval from the earlier Papacy, as the anoint-

[1] Hodgkin, *Italy*, vii, 6, p. 276, ed. 1895. The description of the visit of Constantius is in Amm. Marcell., *Hist.*, xvi, 10.
[2] This tiara has no crown. The date at which the first crown or circlet was added is unknown. The second crown was added, with intention, by Boniface VIII. The third crown has not yet been satisfactorily explained. See below, p. 550.

ing of kings distinguishes the "divine right" from the warrior's sword in civil authority. The Pope after this time paid little reverence to the Emperor.

The concentrations of civil and ecclesiastical power in Italy were many and hostile, one to another. Part of Italy was under Lombard rulers; coast towns were governed by agents of the Emperor at Constantinople; and the Pope held a precarious position between the different forces. Italy was already becoming what it was during most of the Middle Ages, only a "geographical expression."

Spain: Kings and Bishops

In Spain the relation of bishops and kings proved to be important for the future of Europe. Between the defeat of Alaric, king of the Visigoths, in A.D. 507, and the first successful invasion by the Moslems in A.D. 711—for about two hundred years, therefore, a development can be traced in the efforts of the Churches to control and civilize the Germanic invaders of Spain and, on the other hand, in the struggle of Gothic kings and warriors to use the influence of the Church for their own ends. The play of forces in society was gradually bringing into opposition and co-operation the Church and the State, as they were for almost a thousand years afterwards in Europe.

The Visigothic kings of south-western Gaul and parts of Spain had been in difficulties (described in Chapter IV), because they were Arian heretics in the midst of a Catholic population. Sometimes they persecuted the Catholic clergy and sometimes tried to conciliate them. In the year before Alaric was defeated, he had apparently adopted a policy of conciliation, because he feared the friendship of the Catholic clergy in his dominions for the newly converted king of the Franks; and it is suggested that the issue of the *Breviarium*—a summary of Roman Law, for the use of his non-Gothic subjects, issued in A.D. 506—was intended to gain their friendship. But the king was defeated and slain by the Franks near Poitiers in A.D. 507; and the Visigothic Kingdom after that date was confined to Spain and, for a time, the country round Narbonne.

During these years there were two marriages of Catholic Frankish

PLATE 4.—CROWN OF VISIGOTHIC KING
RECCESWINTHE (A.D. 653–672)

(Musée de Cluny, Paris)—Referred to page 261

princesses to Arian kings of the Visigoths; but neither marriage resulted in the conversion of the kings, and the establishment of outposts of the Roman Empire under Justinian, centred round Carthagena, from the middle of the sixth century increased the pressure against Arian domination in Spain. A new political situation arose, however, after the conversion of Reccared, king of the Visigoths, to Catholicism in A.D. 587. At the third Council of Toledo in A.D. 589, at which sixty-two bishops, five metropolitans and some nobles were present, the king attempted to reconcile the Arian and Catholic clergy, but finally decided to adopt entirely the opinions and to support the organization of the Catholic bishops. A letter of Gregory the Great to king Reccared expresses his pleasure at the conversion of the king. "When I hear of this new miracle wrought in our own time, the conversion of the whole Gothic nation from the Arian heresy to the unity of the true faith, I gladly exclaim with the prophet, 'This is a change which the right hand of the Most High hath wrought.'" The Pope continues: "We have sent you a small key from the sacred body of St. Peter as a benediction from him. In this key is inserted some iron from his chains so that what bound his neck for martyrdom may deliver yours from all sins. I have also given to the bearer of this letter, as a present for you, a cross containing wood from Our Lord's cross and hairs of John the Baptist that you may always have the help of Our Saviour, through the intercession of his forerunner."[1]

In a later letter the Pope replies to a request that he should ask the Emperor for the copy of a treaty between Justinian and the reigning king of the Goths. The Pope says to Reccared: "You must look in your archives for documents which are unfavourable to you and not ask me to produce them."[2] Evidently the Pope, although a keen politician, was also a simple believer in the power of iron filings, wood and hair, somehow connected with celestial Powers. Pope Gregory often sent keys with iron filings to other friends, sometimes with the remark that they would be useful for physical health as well as salvation after death. The political, economic and social power of those who held such instruments of

[1] Ep., ix, 228.   [2] Ibid., ix, 229. See Dudden, *Gregory the Great*, i, p. 411.

I

security and happiness was dependent upon the general belief of most men at that time. And few doubted the efficacy of relics. They might give victory: they might protect from danger; they might, in the end, obtain entry to heaven for anyone lucky enough to possess them.

At the end of the sixth century Toledo became the capital of the Visigothic kingdom; and the frequent and very active Councils of Toledo mark the stages in the growth of ecclesiastical power. A struggle then began between the kings, generally supported by the bishops, and the more powerful landowners or warriors who are sometimes called "nobles." The policy of the bishops tended to support and exalt the king and also to unite the largest possible amount of territory under his rule. The "nobles," on the other hand, feared to lose wealth or power by submission to any superior authority and preferred to divide Spain in order that each part might be controlled by one of their number. The struggle is expressed in the canons of the fourth and fifth Councils of Toledo (A.D. 636 and A.D. 637). According to the canon 75 of the fourth Council, the king must be elected by bishops and nobles. Hereditary right, indeed, would destroy the power of the bishops and nobles over the kingship; and therefore the policy of both nobles and bishops favoured election.

The seventy-fifth canon follows a great number of rules dealing with ritual, the relations of clerics and women, the Jews and freedmen of the Church. The seventy-fifth canon, therefore, applies to a rather different subject matter—in fact, to politics. Its most important sentences run as follows: "Let no one among us presume to seize the kingdom. Let no one incite to civil war and no one plot the death of kings but, when a prince has died in peace, the chiefs of the whole race with the bishops must elect a successor in common council."[1]

This is part of a long exhortation phrased thus:—

After certain regulations of the ecclesiastical order or decrees which affect the discipline of some, all of us bishops have finally decided to

---

[1] Mansi, x, col. 611.

issue this final episcopal decree under God as Judge for the maintenance of our kings and the stability of the Gothic race. Such is the treachery of the souls of some people (as it is reported) that they disregard the fidelity promised under oath to their kings and pretend to swear with their mouths an oath, while in their minds they retain their impious treachery. Thus they swear to their kings and are false to the fealty which they promise, and do not fear that book of God's judgement in which the condemnation and punishment is written of those who swear falsely in the name of God (Jer. vii and xvii). What hope then can such people have when they struggle against their enemies? What trust can other peoples have in them in peace? What treaty would not be violated? What sworn agreement with enemies will stand, if they do not keep their sworn word to their own kings? Who then is so mad as to cut off his own head with his own hand? This is clear, that they forget the danger to their own salvation in killing themselves by their own hand, turning their own strength against themselves and their kings even though the Lord says "touch not my Anointed" (Christos) (Psalm 104), and David says—"Who will put out his hand against the Anointed (Christum) of the Lord and be innocent" (1 Kings 26).

These do not fear perjury nor the death of their kings. Trust in a treaty is given to enemies, not to be violated. But if in war trust holds, how much more should it hold among one's own people. It is sacrilege if the fealty promised by peoples to their own kings is violated, because not only does the breaking of the treaty affect these kings, but also God in whose name the promise is made. Hence it is that many of the kingdoms of the earth have been destroyed by the anger of heaven—that by the loss of faith and morals one might make amends for the other. Hence also we, too, should beware of the downfall of such peoples lest we may be struck by the same evil and punished cruelly. So also, God spared not the angels who revolted against Him, who lost by disobedience their heavenly home, as it is said in Isaiah, "my sword is drunken in heaven" (Isaiah xxxiv. 5), how much more should we fear the loss of our own salvation lest through our treachery we perish by the same sword of an angry God. But if we wish to avoid Divine anger and desire to change His severity to clemency we must preserve towards God the practice of religion with fear. We must guard the faith promised to our princes and let there not be, among us, as in certain peoples, an impious and subtle treachery, nor the perfidy of the mind, nor the sin of perjury, nor the accursed devising of plots. Let no one among us presume to seize the kingdom, no one incite to civil war, no one plot the death of kings, but when a prince has died in peace let the nobles of the whole nation, let the bishops elect a successor in a common council, so that while unity is preserved by us no quarrel in our Fatherland should arise by force or policy. But if this admonition does not correct our minds and lead our heart to the common safety, hear our decision. Whoever among us or the people of all Spain, by any plot shall weaken the oath of his fealty which he had given for the maintenance of his Fatherland and the Gothic race, or the safety of his king, or if anyone attempt to slay the king or destroy the power of his kingdom or usurp tyrannically the throne, let him be anathema in the eye of God the Father and His angels, and let him be expelled from the Catholic Church which he has profaned by perjury and separated from the Christian people with all the associates of his impiety; because the same punishment should fall on those who have committed the same sin.[1]

The seventh canon of the fifth Council of Toledo provides that this "decretum" shall be read at all Synods.

The numerous Councils of Toledo were dominated by the bishops; and through these Councils the bishops attempted both to civilize the barbarian warriors and to unite the country under one form of law and administration. In A.D. 642, however, one of the nobles became king and immediately killed or enslaved about seven hundred of his opponents. Others had apparently fled abroad and there was a danger that the Visigothic kingdom might be ruined by assistance given to such fugitives by foreign Governments. The Emperor at Constantinople still held some parts of the Spanish coast; and the Latin-speaking population as well as the Catholic clergy still looked to the Emperor as the source of moral authority in government. It is possible also that the Jews were regarded in Spain as aliens whose sympathies lay in the East; for the violent persecution of Jews in Spain began in A.D. 612 and was confirmed, although somewhat moderated, by the fourth Council of Toledo in A.D. 636. In any case, the seventh Council of Toledo, ten years later, decreed penalties against those who engage in plots outside the country; and urged non-intervention upon the rulers of neighbouring States. A further consolidation of the kingdom was marked by the abolition of Roman Law and the issue of one Book

[1] Mansi, x, col. 637, canon 75. The last of the Canons of the Council. It should be noted that the word for "anointed" in the text is "Christus"—"Nolite tangere Christos meos." Also "fides" meaning "fealty" or "trustworthiness" has no real equivalent in English.

of Law (*Liber Judiciorum* or *Forum Judicum*) for all the inhabitants of the king's territory.

This book was probably completed in its earliest form in A.D. 654. It is not only a collection of laws uniting the old Gothic and Roman laws in one system under the domination of Roman ideas; but it also contains statements of political theory and general social principles which are evidently due to the influence of the bishops. Thus, by the middle of the seventh century in Spain a single system of government dominated by the Roman tradition but under a Gothic kingship was established; and this was evidently due to the efforts of the bishops to establish and maintain order and justice.

A further step towards the establishment of a single civil and ecclesiastical system is marked by the introduction of the anointing of kings by bishops as a means of giving them moral authority. The use of anointment in the ceremony of coronation, as it will be shown later, was evidently due to the influence of the Old Testament, for the ceremony was perhaps used at about the same date in England and was certainly used at a later date in the case of Pippin, the king of the Franks.[1] In Spain, in A.D. 672, a new king, Wamba, already aged and unwilling, was elected by the bishops and nobles; and he appears to have been crowned and anointed on September 25, A.D. 672, in the Church of St. Peter and St. Paul at Toledo, by the bishop Quiricus. In A.D. 680 Wamba fell ill— according to one story, from poison administered in the interests of one of his nobles, named Erwig. Wamba recovered but resigned the kingship in favour of Erwig, who was elected and afterwards crowned and anointed at Toledo, by the new bishop, Julian. The twelfth Council of Toledo, held in January A.D. 681, confirmed the rights of king Erwig. The coronation and particularly the anointment of a king, with no hereditary right, who had been only one of many rival nobles, gave to kingship a divine or at least an ecclesiastical authority which successful usurpation could hardly supply. The consequences for both kings and bishops were important. Anointment was an ecclesiastical ceremony traditionally

---

[1] Crowns of a Visigothic royal family were found in the nineteenth century buried in Spain, and were preserved in the Musée de Cluny in Paris. (See Plate 4.)

used for the consecration of bishops. A king who became, therefore, by the action of bishops, "the Lord's anointed," might easily claim an ecclesiastical authority dangerous to the Church. On the other hand, the elevation of a king above the level of a merely elected leader evidently gave to the bishops a power and influence over the future of the kingdom which was far superior to that of any body of nobles.

The twelfth Council of Toledo also declared that the king's family is sacred; but plots against the king continued; and in some of these plots the bishops were involved as well as the nobles. The attempt to make the kingship dependent upon election and at the same time absolute by ecclesiastical anointment might have succeeded in establishing some new form of authority, combining the civil power with the ecclesiastical, in Spain. But the whole situation was radically altered by unforeseen external forces. In the year A.D. 711 Mohammedan warriors (Arabs and Berbers) crossed from Africa into Spain; and in the next half-century the Gothic and Roman traditions of Spain were entirely submerged under Mohammedan control. Spain, therefore, had nothing more to contribute to the development of methods of government in the First Europe; because the most highly civilized sections of its population, during most of the Middle Ages, looked to the East and not to the West.

Collapse of Mediterranean Civilization

In the three Mediterranean countries, therefore—Italy, Spain and Africa—the old Roman world of the Church as well as the State had come to an end in the eighth century. The civilization and at a later date the Christianity of the Roman Empire had depended upon the Mediterranean. The trade-routes across that sea had provided not only supplies but also ideas and emotions which could be shared by the whole Roman world. But by the middle of the eighth century Africa, Spain and Italy had been finally divided from both the old Rome and the new Rome—Constantinople. Two forces destroyed the old unity. The first was the disastrous policy of Justinian in his efforts to reconquer the West. The second, two centuries later, was the victorious advance of Mohammedanism.

Justinian's policy caused a greater disunion between the Christian peoples of the West and the East, whom his mercenaries were supposed to rescue from barbarian tyranny and to unite in the Roman Empire. And the disunion of the Christian peoples eventually made it possible for Mohammedan fleets and armies to cut off Latin Christianity from that of the Greeks.

Another effect of the new situation in the eighth century was the isolation of Rome. The city which had been for centuries, in theory if not in practice, the centre of the Roman world, became an outpost of an older world looking towards the new world of north-western Europe and the Middle Ages. And, on the other hand, Rome became no longer a centre of episcopal authority within the Empire but only a point of contact between the Latin Churches and the older Churches of Asia Minor and Constantinople. The bishop of Rome during the early years of the seventh century was in an ambiguous position. He was still, in theory, a subject of the Emperor at Constantinople. But, on the other hand, he negotiated with the new kingdoms of France and England as an independent Authority and certainly not as the Emperor's agent. In the eighth century the bishop of Rome must have seemed an Eastern to the peoples of the West and a Western to the peoples of the East. This, indeed, is one of the reasons why the Popes at the end of the eighth century, as it will be shown in a later chapter, were induced finally to turn to the West—not to Spain or Africa, but to France, England and Germany.

Again, the efforts of the bishops in Africa, Spain and Italy, failed to establish a new tradition of moral authority and political power, because first Justinian and afterwards the Mohammedans destroyed the Germanic kingdoms of those countries. The Catholic Churches in Africa and Spain collapsed when the civil Authorities, to which they were attached, were displaced. And even in Italy the Roman Church maintained with difficulty an independent existence when Lombard kings and dukes divided the peninsula and when first Byzantine, and afterwards Mohammedan, rulers established themselves in the coastal cities and in Sicily.

The ideas, however, which survived from the experience of

disaster in the Mediterranean, cannot be understood without reference to the new conceptions of civil and ecclesiastical authority which were at the same time being developed in France, Germany, Ireland and England. The medieval system of Church and State owed as much to the experiences of the new kingdoms in the North as it did to the traditions which survived from the ruins of Mediterranean civilization.

General Conclusions

In the study of the social institutions of the First Europe two important results of the failure of Justinian's policy and the advance of Mohammedanism may be noticed. The bishops of the countries bordering on the western Mediterranean learned by bitter experience to separate the fortunes of the Church from those of the Roman Empire; and secondly, the First Europe of the Latin Churches and the new barbarian kingdoms were forced into closer unity by the danger from the great enemy of medieval Christendom—the religion of Mohammed.

It has been shown above that the Catholics in northern Africa welcomed the armies of Justinian; and for about a century the bishops of Africa looked to Constantinople for support. But the Mohammedan invasions and the control of the western Mediterranean by Mohammedan fleets, cut off the western Churches of Africa from all civil and military assistance. Many of the laity and the clergy fled from Africa; and, although the Mohammedan rulers did not persecute, they enslaved Christians. The Christian bishops appear to have continued to exercise some of their functions for many centuries under Mohammedan rule. But clearly Christianity, reduced once more to a religion of scattered and helpless slaves and poor men, was unable to contribute anything comparable to the great work of the earlier African bishops, Cyprian and Augustine. And when the Turks, in the sixteenth century, conquered the earlier Mohammedan rulers, a violent persecution of Christians seems to have almost completely destroyed the remnants of Christianity in northern Africa. In this case the Church did not survive the Roman Empire.

In Spain the bishops learned to act independently of the Roman Empire because, first, the Empire itself had deserted its Catholic subjects, when it had submitted to the Visigothic settlement in south-western Gaul, and secondly, the Visigothic kings had always been willing to use Roman officials in their administration. The reconquest of part of the Mediterranean coast of Spain under Justinian seems to have made very little difference to the policy of the Spanish bishops. Since the Visigothic kings had become Catholic the bishops supported them and not the Roman Empire. The Councils of Toledo had indeed almost secured supreme authority for the bishops within the Visigothic kingdom. The Church, it seemed, could not only stand alone, but could actually support the State, when almost suddenly the rule of the Visigoths in Spain was destroyed by the Mohammedan invasion, and Christians reduced to subjection. But what the bishops had learnt in Spain had a great influence upon the development of the relations of the Church and State in later years in France, Germany and England.

In Italy the situation was more complicated. The bishops there were traditionally bound to the Roman Empire; and the bishop of Rome himself could hardly be indifferent to the policy of the Roman Emperor. Therefore, although Justinian's conquest of Italy very nearly destroyed all sympathy between the Latin Churches of Italy and the "Greeks" who called themselves the Roman army and Roman administrators, the Church of the city of Rome still regarded the Emperor at Constantinople as its only possible civil and military authority. When the Lombards came into Italy, the Latin Churches of Italy still looked to the Emperor for assistance and support; and even when the Lombard kings became Catholic, the bishops of Rome aimed at escaping from Lombard rule by retaining their connection with Constantinople. It was exceedingly difficult for the bishops of Italy to learn that the Catholic Church could exist independently of the support of the Roman Emperor. And even when, at last, in despair, the bishop of Rome in the eighth century turned to the king of the Franks for help, the Roman Church was unable to free itself from an obsolete assumption. The

Roman clergy could not bring themselves to believe that the Roman Empire had disappeared for ever in western Europe. They therefore produced a world of the imagination in the "Donation of Constantine," and a ghost from the graveyard of their hopes, the so-called "holy Roman Empire."

The Mohammedan conquests in northern Africa, Spain and the islands of the western Mediterranean, put the Latin Churches and the new kingdoms of north-western Europe on the defensive. Bishops and kings were compelled to unite, as far as local jealousies would permit, against a single great enemy. At the beginning of the eighth century, the conflict between Latin Christendom and the Mohammedans was hardly more than a series of frontier raids. But by the middle of the eighth century, as the letters of St. Boniface show, the fear of the "Saracens" had spread throughout north-western Europe. Christianity had hitherto had to contend with what is now called "Paganism," that is to say, the many different rites and beliefs of the pre-Christian world. It had succeeded in that struggle, partly at least because it was a single religion for all places and all peoples under the sky. Its unity and universality gave it strength against both local cults and esoteric mystery religions. But in the eighth century, for the first time, Christianity was faced by a rival religion of the same order as itself, which was derived in part from the same sources. Mohammedanism represented, as it were, the Judaic elements in Christianity, untouched by Hellenic influences. The God of Mohammed was the God of the Jews, aloof from the forms of man and animal; but the God of the Christians was the man Christ, whose manhood shared divinity as the heroes of the Greeks and Romans had done.

The God of the Mohammedans was a God of war, as the God of the Hebrews had been; and it was perhaps under the influence of the great rival creed that medieval Christendom was gradually persuaded to regard even Jesus as a God of war. It would be impolite, according to some historians, to say that as far back as the fourth century, the Emperors Constantine and Theodosius regarded the influence of Christ chiefly as an asset in securing victory. The use of the cross, in the legend of Constantine's vision—"In this sign shalt thou conquer"—evidently makes the cross a standard of armed forces. And the mosaic of the soldiers of Justinian, in St. Vitale at Ravenna, shows the monogram of Christ upon a shield. But whatever the connection between Christ and the military despotism of the Christian Empire, clearly the barbarian kings of the eighth and ninth centuries thought of war as a means of promoting religion, exactly as the Mohammedans did. Thus the rivalry between Latin Christendom and the Mohammedans who held the Holy Places, northern Africa and Spain, in the eighth century, was the source of that fantastic movement to promote the military unity of Christendom—the Crusades.

Christianity, therefore, in the First Europe became a military religion, largely because of the influence of Mohammedanism. Even in the fourth century the bishops had indeed accepted the necessity for the use of armed force by the civil Authorities in the defence against barbarism. But there had been no conception of a "holy war" for the extension of Christianity. In the eighth century, however, the "religious" war of Mohammedanism was countered by a religious war for Christianity. Probably the primitive Germanic warriors under Charles Martel and Charles the Great were devoted to war in any case as a manly exercise and were only too willing to accept an additional and, as it seemed, more exalted reason for slaughter, when the clergy suggested that war could be waged for the sake of Christianity. The first literary expression of this idea is in the *Chanson de Roland*. But it developed into monstrous proportions in the preaching of the Crusades, and in the two famous works of the early twelfth century, the *Gesta Francorum* and the *Gesta Dei per Francos* of Guibert of Nogent (d. 1124). In these the reconquest of the Holy Land from the Mohammedans had become a common purpose of united Latin Christendom; and if any proof were needed of the change which medievalism had wrought in Christianity, it may be found in the opening words of the *Gesta Francorum*, where the words of Jesus, "Let him take up his cross and follow me," are absurdly applied to the cross of the crusader and the expedition to Jerusalem. The Mohammedan conquests, therefore, of the seventh and eighth centuries were the direct causes of the military Christianity of the Middle Ages and of the transient attempts to unite Christendom in arms.

From the same source came the first form of a distinction between the East and the West, which has confused and confounded historians and politicians in succeeding generations. In making this distinction, "the West" is usually conceived to be north-western European civilization, and the "East" a combination of Mohammedanism and Greek Christianity. When the Mohammedans first invaded the Roman Empire, the Greek-speaking peoples of the eastern Mediterranean had been already separated from the Latin-speaking western Churches since the days of Justinian, that is to say, for about a century. The division between the two parts of the Mediterranean world was rendered more complete by the extension of the Latin Churches into Britain and Germany. The mutual attraction of the Roman See and new missionary countries of the North drew the whole Latin-speaking world away from the eastern Mediterranean. The plague and the wars against the Persians exhausted the powers of Roman Emperors at Constantinople. And when the Mohammedans assaulted the Empire in Syria and northern Africa, the division between eastern and western Christianity in sentiment, in customs and in relations with the State, was already complete.[1] The strangest effect upon the First Europe of the two quite distinct events, (a) the separation of the Greek-speaking and Latin-speaking Churches, and (b) the Mohammedan invasions, was that medieval Christendom treated as the "East" both the Roman Empire at Constantinople and the Mohammedan States. Thus, in the Gesta Dei per Francos the author points out that most heresies arose among "the Greeks";[2] and the hostility of the crusaders to the Emperor Alexius Comnenus was hardly less violent than their

[1] This is opposed to the view of Henri Pirenne in his Mahomet et Charlemagne (Eng. trans. 1939), where it is argued that Mohammedanism was the cause of the separation between East and West. But Pirenne's arguments do not allow sufficient weight to the evidence for the situation in Justinian's day.

[2] In the Gesta Dei per Francos, Guibert gives a supposed letter of the Emperor in which an inducement to a holy war is given as "the enjoyment of the most beautiful women"—which, as the good abbot remarks, implies that Greek women were prettier than "Gallic." This the abbot regards as an insult.

hostility to the Saracens. The climate of opinion in the early Middle Ages in Europe was so befogged with misunderstandings and illusions that later ages inherited entirely false conceptions of the nature of the opposition between Christendom and "the East."

CHAPTER VII

KINGS' BISHOPS

New barbarian kingdoms arose in the North, while the countries bordering upon the western Mediterranean were first re-united to the Roman Empire and the Catholic Church, and afterwards lost to both. In northern Gaul, in Ireland, in Britain, and later in Germany east of the Rhine, the roots of the First Europe struck deeper and spread wider than in the South. The new barbarian kingdoms had never been Arian. They passed directly from a primitive tribal paganism to Christianity which was Catholic and Roman. They had never been conquered or civilized by the Roman Empire. Rome, therefore, meant for their kings and peoples the Rome of St. Peter, not of Augustus; and the Roman tradition was represented in their eyes, not by generals and their legions, but by bishops and their clergy.

Among these barbarians, kings possessed a traditional authority; and when they became Christian, bishops supported their kings, and were in some cases chaplains to their queens. As on the chessboard, the move of the bishops was diagonal, because they had to compromise with the heroic ideals and simple desires of barbarism. To have opposed all the tribal traditions in the new barbarian kingdoms would have made it impossible to convert them to Christianity or to civilize them; but as advisers of the kings the bishops might hope to control them.

The relations between kings and bishops in north-western Europe differed from those in the Mediterranean area, partly, indeed, because of the disturbed situation in the South, but most obviously because entirely new concentrations of social power and authority, independent of the fortunes of the Roman Empire, were established in Gaul, Britain, Ireland and Germany. Church and State north of the Alps, after the fifth century, formed new relationships; and these new relationships, rather than the traditions of the South, were the origins of such typical medieval movements as Feudalism and the Crusades. Military Christianity was northern. So was Gothic architecture. Paris and London in the Middle Ages became the capitals of nations; while Rome, Venice, Genoa and Florence remained city-states of the old tradition. The sources, therefore, of the difference between northern European civilization and the Mediterranean system are important; and these sources can be traced most easily in the history of the sixth, seventh and eighth centuries.

The most important common characteristics of the communities north of the Alps were, first, that they were settlements of non-Christian tribes with local and traditional deities and kings, independent at first of all Roman influence. This is clearly true of the Anglo-Saxons in England, of the Irish and of the Germanic tribes outside the Roman Empire, all of whom were eventually converted to Christianity. But it is true also, though less obviously, of the Franks who had been in contact with the Roman Empire for many generations before they became Christians and conquered Gaul. The social and political situation, therefore, in the northern kingdoms was from the beginning quite different from that in the earlier barbarian kingdoms of the Goths, Burgundians and Vandals. Secondly, the Church, when it came into contact with the barbarians of the North, had already developed a strongly organized monasticism. This monasticism was strongest outside cities or towns or other settlements; but the Churches in the Mediterranean area were all at first dominated by clergy, not by monks. The Church in the Mediterranean area was essentially a city organization. Bishops were bishops of cities; and this had been so, long before monasticism had been organized. Indeed, the bishops of Rome when arranging for new bishoprics in the North, seem to have assumed that bishops in the newly converted countries would have their Sees in cities. But in the North, after the barbarian invasions, the cities in Britain were almost deserted, and there never had been any cities in Ireland or the non-Roman parts of Germany. Consequently monastic settlements which had no connection with city-life were centres as important for the spread of Christianity as bishoprics.

In the third place, most of the Christianity in the northern kingdoms was the result of the missionary activity of monks, as, for example, among the English and the Germans. In such cases the Church did not rely upon a basis of Roman civilization on which to build, as in southern Gaul. The Church itself, through her missionaries, had to introduce whatever elements of civilization were essential to the organization of Christianity. The Church had already also adopted the Latin language as its official medium for regulations, correspondence and rituals. Therefore the language of the Church in England and Germany during the Middle Ages remained alien to the local "climate of opinion" to a greater extent than it was in countries whose "vulgar tongue" was derived from a variety of Latin; and the Latin language carried with it all the implications of thought and emotion in the Roman tradition. But these were all strange to the barbarians converted during the sixth, seventh and eighth centuries. For them the Church was an alien institution representing a higher culture and wider interests; and not, as it had been in its earlier years in the Mediterranean area, an institution of the lower classes. Among the English, the Franks and the Germans east of the Rhine, Christianity was introduced as a religion of the kings and nobles. They were approached first by the missionaries; and their followers usually followed their lead. The tribesmen did not become Christian by a process of moral or intellectual decision concerning a new way of life, but mainly because of loyalty to a leader.

Apart from the common characteristics of the position of kings and bishops in north-western Europe, it is worth while to note a difference between the situation in Gaul and Britain or, as they should now be called, France and England. These two countries included, in later years, the chief centres of medieval thought and policy; but their traditions of ecclesiastical and civil authority differed greatly, even from the time when the Franks and the

Anglo-Saxons were first converted to Christianity. In France, even in the North but particularly in the South, the Church was firmly established and organized before the Frankish kings and warriors conquered the country. The organization and language of society in the whole of France was already Roman. Roman cities with their bishops, Roman villas and the Roman organization of agriculture and commerce, were like a fixed structure into which the newly-converted Franks had to insert their authority. These Franks were comparatively small bands of ignorant warriors with the very simplest outlook on life and the world and with primitive legal customs, later written down in Latin in the Salic and Ripuarian lands. The language of the Frankish kingdom, therefore, as well as its general structure gradually became a modified form of the Roman. French is not Frankish but Latin.

On the other hand, in England the Anglo-Saxons had established settlements and kingdoms for at least a century before they were converted to Christianity by missionaries from Ireland and Italy. The language, law and social customs of the English kingdoms formed, therefore, a structure into which the Church had to come from the outside. The bishops and other missionaries did, indeed, bring to the Anglo-Saxons immensely important elements of a higher civilization; but these had to be grafted upon a stock already firmly planted in a soil from which almost all Roman traditions had been uprooted. In England, therefore, the popular language remained different from the Latin of the Church; and although councils of bishops and canons of the Church had a great influence upon the development of civil government, this influence was always more external to the native tradition than it was in France.

These likenesses and differences will be observed more clearly in the history of the northern kingdoms, taken separately.

The Barbarians after the Fifth Century

As for the contribution made by the new barbarians to the future development of Europe, it seems necessary still to reject the mythology of the "noble savage." Some historians appear still to believe that vigour, or loyalty or purity of blood or manners, contrasted with a supposed decadence of the Roman tradition, were brought into European civilization by Franks, Saxons and other Germanic tribes. This is an illusion. Nothing of great value to civilized life was added to the Roman tradition by the barbarians. Their coming made life in Gaul and Britain and Italy more like the life of savages, "nasty, brutish and short." They brought from the forests and marshes of Germany nothing but simple minds and simple tastes. Their habits did include some very limited loyalty to a leader in war, as long as he was successful, and confidence in the supposed hereditary qualities of certain families, tempered by assassination of inconvenient members of them. Thus the entry of Franks, Lombards and Saxons into the European tradition of civilization involved a step backwards for the whole of the society in which they found themselves. The "decadence" of the old civilization, which was collapsing before they came, was perhaps due to social disintegration, as described in an earlier chapter. But the earlier believers in the "noble savage" treated as "decadence" a certain tendency to think, to wash and to taste food or choose suitable clothing. The new barbarians could not think; they did not wash; and they preferred to swallow large quantities of food and drink rather than to taste them. In fact not until the new-comers learned from the Roman tradition did they add anything to it. Their first entry took civilized life almost back to its beginnings.

That the step backwards did not, in fact, end in the desert of barbarism, as it had in earlier ages when Babylonian or Egyptian civilizations disappeared, was due entirely to the Christian Churches; and the Churches were able to introduce civilization among the barbarians because their bishops had learnt it from the Roman Empire. If the organization of the Churches had not survived the entry into the old Roman world of Saxons, Franks and Lombards, western Europe in the seventh century would have lost all traces of civilized life; and if the Churches of the sixth and seventh centuries had been as careless of the problems of government and production as the earlier Christians had been, they would not have been able to preserve law, justice or the applied arts. The barbarians who came into prominence during the second stage of Germanic rule in the West, had indeed their own simple social customs, for example, of marriage and property, and their own methods of administering justice. But their customs and laws were not written down and perhaps not anywhere clearly conceived before they came into contact with the Christian bishops. And even when Frankish, Anglo-Saxon and Lombardic laws were put into writing, they expressed only the very simple needs of a quarrelsome agricultural population. It must be remembered that the more normal manners and customs of the Germanic tribes in their forests as described, for example, by Tacitus, could not have survived among the bands of warriors and their camp-followers when they found themselves in the quite abnormal situation of nomadic raiders, looting the more civilized populations of Gaul, Britain and Italy.

It is not denied that the conquerors of the western world had a simple culture, art and social organization when they lived in communities of their own east of the Rhine and north of the Danube. Tribal organization, tribal custom, and the simpler forms of ornament were not derived by the Germanic invaders from the Romanized populations they destroyed or subdued. Probably, also, the Germanic tribes had a tradition of kingship distinct from that of the Mediterranean peoples. Their kings appear to have been supported by small groups of warriors, and perhaps also of priests acting as councillors and representatives of their tradition. But when the tribes, organized in settlements with their women and children, were disturbed by the exodus of their warriors and warleaders into the civilized countries of the West, the better parts of the simpler tradition obviously became less effectual. Where the invaders, as in England, could entirely displace or bring into subjection the earlier inhabitants, the Germanic tribes may have preserved more easily their own systems of social organization and custom. But where the invaders were never more than a small proportion of the older population, as in Gaul and Italy, their customs and traditions could survive only with the assistance of such intelligence and education as they could find among their new subjects. Language indicates the contrast between the two situations.

The earliest written English laws are in English; but the earliest laws of the Franks and the Lombards are in Latin.

The precise character, however, of the contribution made to the future civilization of Europe by the Saxons and the Franks need not be discussed in detail here. It can hardly be doubted that whatever contribution they did make, was of far less importance than that made by the Mediterranean tradition preserved in the Christian Church.

Gaul becomes France

In Gaul the situation was completely transformed by the baptism in A.D. 496 of Clovis, king of the Franks, into the Catholic Church. With Clovis "were baptized more than three thousand of his army"; although, according to Gregory of Tours, the king had been doubtful at first whether the people would support him in giving up paganism.[1] The king had married in A.D. 493 a Catholic, Clotilda, niece of the king of Burgundy. And doubtless her influence had been exerted on the side of the Catholic bishops. But Clovis was evidently not blind to the political advantage of a crusade against the Arian Goths. His acceptance of Catholic Christianity, as Dalton says, "placed at his disposal the whole body of the Gallo-Roman bishops, almost all of whom were drawn from distinguished provincial families. . . . No more valuable allies could have gathered to the Frankish standard. They brought, not only the strength of their virtues and accomplishments, but the influence which they were able to exert among the Gallo-Roman Catholics in Visigothic Aquitaine, who were both numerous and disaffected."[2] According to Gregory of Tours, when Alaric, king of the Goths, saw how king Clovis was steadily overcoming his neighbours in war, he sent envoys to him asking for a conference. At a conference on an island in the Loire near Amboise, the two kings swore mutual friendship and parted in peace. And Gregory continues: "Many people in Gaul at the time ardently desired to live under the dominion of the Franks. This was the reason why Quintianus,

[1] Greg. Tur., *H.F.*, ii (31). Gregory calls Clovis "a new Constantine," and St. Remy "a Silvester."   [2] Dalton, O. M., *History of the Franks*, Introd., vol. i.

bishop of Rodez, incurred hatred and was driven from the city. Men said to him: 'It is because thou desirest the Franks to become masters and possess the land.'[1] . . . Now king Clovis said to his men: 'It irketh me sore that these Arians hold a part of Gaul. Let us go forth then, and with God's aid bring the land under our own sway'." He then marched on Poitiers and defeated and killed Alaric ten miles outside the town; and "from this battle Amalaric, son of Alaric, fled into Spain and ruled with prudence his father's kingdom." Clovis, returning to Tours, received letters from the Emperor Anastasius, conferring the Consulate; and "in the church of the blessed Martin he was vested in the purple tunic and in a mantle and set the diadem upon his head. . . . From that day he was hailed as Consul or Augustus," and established the seat of his government at Paris.[2] Gregory is quite vague about the status of the king in the eyes of the rest of the world; but he is quite clear about the new capital. A new kingdom had been founded. The faint light from old Roman times might shine for a moment on the Frankish king; but he held his position by no treaty or grant of any Roman Emperor.

The extension of Frankish power throughout south-western and southern Gaul need not be described here. The invasion of Italy by Belisarius in A.D. 536 left the Ostrogothic control of southern Gaul so weakened that the Franks were able, for the first time, to establish a kingdom whose area covered what is now called France. With this supremacy of the Frankish king went the heightened prestige of the bishops of the Catholic Church in Gaul; but it also involved a much greater dependence of the bishops upon the king to whom they had given assistance. The bishops were still elected by the clergy and the people; but a new principle was introduced. The election of a candidate had to be announced to the king in a

[1] Greg. Tur., H.F., ii, 36 (Pat. Lat., 71). This bishop was from Africa. He was a nephew of one of the bishops exiled under the Vandal persecution. See Greg. Tur., Vitae Patrum, c. iv.

[2] Ibid., ii, 38. Pat. Lat., 71, col. 236. Dalton believes that Gregory is wrong about the title of "Augustus," which was adopted only at a later date by Frankish kings; but Gregory means nothing very definite by the title. Even Theodoric the Ostrogoth is called "Augustus" on an inscription erected in his reign.

document called a *consensus*, and he then granted a diploma (*praeceptio*), which was necessary before the new bishop could hold his See. The king of the Franks, in the middle of the sixth century, had the control of all appointments to bishoprics and frequently appointed laymen, not without receiving a high price from them for the honour and the power thus secured.[1] The result, under barbarian kings, was such as might well be expected. In some cases the bishops were good men struggling against the surrounding violence, rapacity and treachery of powerful kings and warriors. In other cases the bishops were men whose chief aim was the satisfaction of their own greed or lust.

As examples of good bishops we have, first, Avitus, bishop of Clermont or Auvergne (Averni), who died in A.D. 594. "After he had received the bishopric, he revealed the greatness of his character in all things; to the people he gave justice, to the poor succour, to the widow consolation, to the orphan the utmost help in his power. And to this day when a stranger comes to him, he receives so warm a welcome that he finds in him at once a father and a fatherland. May he prosper in the possession of his great virtues, keeping with his whole heart those things which are well pleasing in the sight of God; let him uproot wantonness in all hearts, and implant in them the chastity ordained of God."[2] And again, Nicetius, bishop of Lyons, "was a man excellent and holy in all his ways, and chaste in his life. The charity which the apostle bade men use towards all to the utmost of their power, he exercised in all things as far as in him lay; men saw that the Lord Himself, who is the true love, was manifest in his heart. For even if he were moved to anger against anyone for his negligence, the moment he amended his way he received him back to favour as if he had never taken offence. He chastised the transgressor but forgave the penitent; he was generous in almsgiving and strenuous in toil; he diligently gave his mind to the erection of churches, the building of houses, the sowing of fields, and the planting of vineyards; but these things did not distract him from prayer. After twenty-two years in the bishopric he passed to the Lord; to-day great miracles are wrought

[1] See Dalton, *op. cit.*, vol. i, p. 288.   [2] Greg. Tur., *H.F.*, iv, 35.

at his tomb for those who implore his aid. For by means of oil from the lamp which is daily lit at his tomb he has restored light to the eyes of the blind; he drives out evil spirits from the bodies of the possessed; he restores health to paralysed limbs; and in these present times is held a great protector by all the infirm."[1] Here, therefore, is sanctity turned into a magic power, by a development familiar throughout the Middle Ages.

There were many cases also of bishops who contrived to secure power and wealth for themselves and a life of unbridled desires. Gregory of Tours gives some examples of this type of bishop. He writes of two brothers, "both bishops, who armed themselves, not with the heavenly cross, but with the helm and mail-shirt of the world, and are said to have slain many of the foe with their own hands" in a battle near Embrun.[2] The same two bishops, Salonius, bishop of Embrun, and Sagittarius, bishop of Gap, as Gregory says, "were carried away by the joy of doing as they pleased and began abandoning themselves to a very fury of mad wickedness, robbing, wounding, slaying, committing adulteries and all manner of crimes to such a point that one day when Victor, bishop of St. Paul-Trois-Chateaux, was celebrating his anniversary, they fell upon him with a troop armed with swords and arrows. They came and rent his garments, beat his attendants, carried off all the vessels and furnishings of the feast, and left him thus grossly outraged."[3] King Gunthrum called a council of bishops at Lyons, which deprived the two villains of the "episcopal dignity." But they obtained permission from the king to appeal to the Pope, John III (A.D. 559–572), who sent them back with a letter to the king directing that they should be restored to their former rank. And this was done. The two bishops acted as before, beating certain inhabitants of their cities with clubs till the blood flowed; and the outcries of the common people were such that the king eventually ordered the two to be shut up in two monasteries far removed from each other. Another bishop, Badegisil of Lemans, was "a right savage man to his people, unjustly seizing and carrying off the goods of many.

---

[1] Greg. Tur., *H.F.*, iv, 36 (*Pat. Lat.*, 71), col. 299. [2] Ibid., iv, 29 (42).
[3] Ibid., v, 21. The *natalitium* which Victor was celebrating was not his "birthday," in our sense, but the anniversary of his consecration.

His wife, worse than himself, was ever urging him on to new crimes."[1]

Naturally the history of evil is more striking than the record of good deeds, most of them unnoticed at the time. But Gregory of Tours reports examples also of virtuous bishops whose difficulties were increased by the ambitions and avarice of the kings. The position of those in authority, therefore, in the Church and the State was gradually changing so that Catholic kings, no longer looking for support against heretics, felt themselves free to do as they liked in the appointment of bishops. They would reward their own warriors, counts or courtiers, by having them consecrated as bishops. And clearly such bishops valued their position for the wealth and licence it provided, rather than for any service they might perform for the unfortunate people or clergy whom they might rule. The Churches held considerable amounts of land and were able to collect money and other presents from nobles or from those who needed their protection. But as soon as the Churches had become wealthy and the bishops had secured riches with the support of the king, the power of the king could easily be extended. The bishops might soon have become simply dependents and agents of barbarian kings. The Council of Paris in A.D. 614 attempted to restrict the power of the Frankish king by a Resolution that the election of bishops should be carried out according to the early canons. But the king immediately rejected the implied limitation of his powers by a declaration that the royal diploma was indispensable to the holding of any See.

The later history of the kingship held by the Merovingians is partly a mere record of a succession of sordid struggles for power— at first between the rulers of Austrasia, or what is now called Belgium and western Germany, and Neustria, now northern France. This is the earliest sign in history of the long rivalry which has cursed Europe for more than a thousand years, between the Governments east and west of the Rhine. But another series of events at the end of the seventh century was more important for

---

[1] Greg. Tur., *H.F.*, viii, 39. The wife was a sadist: "nam saepius viris omnia pudenda cum ipsis ventris pellibus incidit: feminis secretiora corporis loca laminis conductibus perussit."

the immediate future. This was the struggle for the control of the government of the Franks by wealthy landowners who sought in the position of Major Domus, or Chief of the Palace, to control puppet kings. This struggle left the Major Domus, Pippin of Heristal, in complete control for twenty-seven years (A.D. 687 to A.D. 714). He was succeeded by his illegitimate son, Charles Martel, who led the Franks to victory over the Saracen invaders of Gaul near Poitiers in A.D. 732. For twenty-five years Charles Martel ruled over Neustria, Austrasia and Burgundy. The last of the Merovingian kings had died in A.D. 737; and the Chief of the Palace did not find it necessary to have another king. His victories on all sides, however, left him with a ravenous mob of warriors whom he had to satisfy for their services; and he used the estates of the Church for this purpose.[1] To some, as counts, he gave Church lands. Others he found it more convenient to appoint as abbots and bishops, who could thus use for their personal advantage the wealth of the monasteries and churches. One warrior was made bishop of both Trier and Rheims; and his nephew Hugo held at the same time the bishoprics of Paris, Rouen and Bayeux, as well as the abbacies of Fontenelle and Jumièges.[2] The result upon the fortunes of the Church is described by St. Boniface in a letter to Pope Zachary.[3] He asks advice from the Pope on such problems as these: "If I find among those called deacons men who from their childhood have always been whoring, in adultery and other filthiness, and with such a reputation become deacons, and as deacons have had four or five or more concubines at night in bed and yet are not ashamed to read the gospel and call themselves deacons and in such evil habits have come to the priesthood and continuing in the same sins, adding sin to sin, are then fulfilling the priestly office, so that they pray for the people and make the sacred offering—finally, what is worse, with such reputations they go through each of the orders and are ordained and nominated bishops: (if I

---

[1] Waitz, *Deutsche Verfassungsgeschichte* (2nd ed., 1883), vol. iii, p. 15, gives a long note, collecting all the different accounts of this use of Church lands. But Waitz's book is hardly more than a summary of extracts from chronicles.

[2] *Gesta Abbatum Font.*, section 8, p. 26, in Pertz, *Script. R.G.* (1886).

[3] Boniface, Ep. xlix (in *Pat. Lat.*); Ep. 50 (in *M.G.H.*).

find such, I ask) that I may have a written decision on such cases, and they may be pronounced and proved sinners by the apostolic answer. Also some of them are bishops, who although they say they do not commit fornication or adultery, are nevertheless drunken and unreliable, or go hunting or fight in the army, and with their own hand shed the blood of men, both Christian and pagan." This letter was written in April A.D. 742. In reply Pope Zachary writes in April A.D. 743 that if Boniface finds bishops, priests, or deacons acting against the canons: "that is, if they commit adultery or have many wives or shed the blood of Christians or pagans, apostolic authority by no means permits them to retain their office." And he quotes Leviticus xxi. 13, "Let my priests marry once only," and the Apostle (1 Tim. iii. 2), "the husband of one wife," and proceeds, "this is lawful before the priesthood (*sacerdotium*); for from that day they are prohibited from even that lawful marriage."

The whole situation was transformed by the final replacement of the line of Merovingian kings by Pippin, the son of Charles Martel, who became Major Domus in A.D. 741, and in A.D. 752 was anointed king of the Franks by St. Boniface himself at Soissons.[1] It is said by a chronicler that Pippin had sent in the year A.D. 750 to ask Pope Zachary whether "the man who held power in the kingdom should be called king and be king rather than he who bore the name."[2] The Pope is said to have recommended that Pippin should be made king. In any case the anointing of the new ruler was of immense importance.

In the first place, the bishops, in the person of St. Boniface and under the authority of the Roman See, had obtained a position of pre-eminent importance with regard to the kingship. Pippin was, in fact, a usurper. He had no hereditary right to the throne, and the Frankish nobles had in earlier time prevented an attempt, similar to Pippin's, of the Mayor of the Palace to displace the king.

[1] The Annals do not agree about the date. See Hodgkin, *Italy*, vii, p. 134 *n*.

[2] *Annales Laurissenses*, ann. 749. Acquiescence in an established order is sometimes difficult to distinguish from submission to a successful ruffian. The Pope comes very near to admitting the principle "might is right." In 1938 Cardinal Innitzer, in Vienna, issued a declaration ending with the words "Heil Hitler." "Victrix causa, diis placuit—et episcopis." The bishops are on the side of the big battalions.

But now, the authority of the Church displaced hereditary right, and a usurper was granted divine authority by the bishops. Secondly, the anointment of kings and the ceremony of ecclesiastical coronation were from that date established in the western kingdoms. The practice is based, not upon the Roman tradition of the Empire, nor upon the Germanic ritual for recognizing kingly authority, but upon the practice and theory recorded in the Old Testament. The monks and clergy in the West now began to use the position of prophets and priests in the Old Testament as one of the chief bases of their influence upon the civil and military authorities.[1] Anointment, in primitive custom, is a magical ceremony for turning an ordinary man into something better by smearing him with the fat of a sacrificial victim.[2] The use of oil is a later development. Anointment with oil was used by witches to turn themselves into non-human beings, as Apuleius says. Thus, the king became a divine being by the use of the oil of consecration, as the clergy also were anointed in the ritual of ordination.

The coronation of Pippin may have been influenced by the ceremony for the acknowledgment of an Emperor, organized by the clergy in Constantinople. This ceremony, from which, as Gibbon says, "the clergy have deduced the most formidable consequences," was performed for the first time when, in A.D. 457, the Emperor Leo I received the crown from the hands of the bishop.[3] But the first ceremony of the kind in a church occurred in A.D. 602 when Phocas, himself a usurper and murderer, was acknowledged as Emperor. In no case, however, was anointment used as part of the ceremony in Constantinople until the thirteenth century; and then in A.D. 1204 the Emperor Baldwin was anointed according to the Western rite.[4] On the other hand, in Spain in the seventh century, the anointment of a new king by bishops seems

---

[1] Thus in the coronation service of George VI, May 12, 1937, the choir sang the words from 1 Kings i, 39: "Zadok the priest and Nathan the prophet anointed Solomon king."
[2] See Robertson Smith, Religion of the Semites (ed. 1907, p. 384), "unction is primarily an application of the sacrificial fat, with its living virtues, to the persons of the worshippers."　　　　[3] Gibbon, Decline and Fall, chap. xxxvii, note.
[4] See the article on the Byzantine Imperial Coronation in Journal of Theological Studies, April 1901, by F. E. Brightman.

to have become an established custom, as it has been noted in an earlier chapter. It is probable, therefore, that if there was any influence other than that of the Old Testament, which confirmed the rite of consecration of kings, it came from Spain.

Britain becomes England

The story of the early influence of bishops in the conversion of kings and peoples in England is so well known and so admirably told by Bede that it is not necessary to do more than remind the reader of the situation in the seventh and eighth centuries. Augustine landed in Thanet in A.D. 597 with interpreters "from the nation of the Franks." Ethelbert, king of Kent, whose sovereignty extended as far as the Humber, "had heard before of the Christian religion, because he had a Christian wife of the royal family of the Franks, called Bertha, whom he had received from her parents upon condition that she should be permitted to practice her religion with the bishop Luidhard, who was sent with her to preserve her faith."[1] Thus, as in the case of Clotilda, wife of Clovis, and of Theudelinda, among the Lombards, the queen acted as a forerunner of the missionary. The queen's bishop was in the field before the king's. Queen Bertha used to pray in a church in Canterbury, dedicated in honour of St. Martin, built while the Romans were still in the island; and here Augustine and his companions also used to pray, until the king was converted and allowed them to build other churches. Augustine then travelled to Arles and was ordained archbishop of the English nation. He ordained two other bishops in A.D. 604, one to convert the East Saxons, Bishop Mellitus, for whom King Ethelbert built the church of St. Paul in London, and the other, Justus, to be bishop of Kent, with his See at Rochester. King Ethelbert added lands and possessions for the use of those who were with the bishops.[2] Similarly, Paulinus preached on the south side of the Humber and converted the governor of the city of Lincoln with his whole family. And within the domain of King Edwin, who was baptized at York in A.D. 627, Paulinus influenced the government "so that there was perfect peace in Britain where-

[1] Bede, H.E., i, 25.　　　　　　　　　　　　[2] Ibid., ii, 3.

soever the dominion of King Edwin extended." Pope Honorius wrote a letter to King Edwin, which is given by Bede, in which the king is praised because "his conduct as king is based upon the knowledge he had of God through the preaching of religion."[1]

It must not be imagined, however, that virtue and religion meant to Bede and his contemporaries what they mean now to anyone with a knowledge of history and science. Virtue did, indeed, include kindliness, self-sacrifice and the service of others; but it also included, as is clear in the letters of St. Boniface, asceticism and celibacy, as an ideal state, which were characteristic of the lives of monks and nuns. Religion then included a dread of demons in the world of nature; and it also promoted an extreme fear of celestial Powers which were prepared to burn and torture after death anyone displeasing to them. This fear is very strongly expressed in Bede's *History*, as in the story of the monk who was a carpenter, but a drunkard, and saw the hot place prepared for him in hell before his death. Religion also involved a general belief in the magical power of the clergy, as in the case of the captive, whose brother, a priest and abbot at Towcester, said Mass for him; and each time Mass was said, the chains of the captive fell off.[2] Or again, the cross erected by King Oswald on the field of battle is said to have proved useful, "for even to this day many cut off small chips from the wood of the cross which, being put into water, men or cattle drinking thereof are immediately restored to health."[3] Similarly a chip of the stake on which King Oswald's head was set up by the pagans, drunk with some blessed water, caused recovery from illness and a long life thereafter.[4] Relics therefore as well as ecclesiastical rituals contributed to the influence which the Church acquired over the barbarian kings and peoples of England. But everywhere in Europe at this date moral and religious teaching combined the most primitive magic with the first steps towards civilized life. It would be as foolish to underestimate the influence of magic among the ignorant as to despise

[1] Bede, *H.E.*, ii, 17.
[2] Ibid., iv, 22. Precisely the same story is in Gregory the Great's *Dialogues*, iv, 57; and, except for the Mass, in Ovid, *Fasti*, iii, 699.
[3] Ibid., iii, 2.   [4] Ibid., iii, 13.

the teaching of a finer morality, because the teacher was a man of his time, full of unreasonable fears and groundless beliefs.

All the bishops of the newly-converted English maintained the same theological beliefs and ritual practices, and thus united the peoples and kings of the many kingdoms into which England was then divided. But the older Christianity of the British who had been defeated and driven westwards, did not for many centuries lead to any friendship between the British and the Anglo-Saxons. Bede describes how Augustine failed to unite the bishops of the British people with his own work for the conversion of the English; and at a later date a Christian British king in alliance with the non-Christian Saxon king, Penda, defeated Christian Saxons in northern England, "as it is the custom to this day," in the words of Bede, "of the Britons to pay no respect to the faith and religion of the English."[1] The hatred of the British for those who had driven them from their country, was evidently not overcome by the conversion of these latter to Christianity. But no similar feeling stood in the way of the Christian Churches in Ireland and their converts in what is now called southern Scotland. Through these Christianity was introduced into northern England independently of the work of the missionaries from Rome.

Irish Christianity, however, had been organized on the basis of monastic settlements in which the bishops were subordinate to abbots; and missionary zeal led to adventurous expeditions of individual monks or hermits rather than to organized missions under bishops. The two types of Christianity, that of Ireland and that of Rome, met in northern England; and differences between them were at once perceived. The two differences which attracted most attention at the time were, first, the date of keeping Easter, and secondly, the style of the tonsure. These unimportant differences might have divided the Churches of England and made it impossible for the English bishops either to unite among themselves or to assist in uniting the English kingdom. But, fortunately, at a conference at Whitby in A.D. 664 King Oswy and the whole company present decided to follow the Roman customs and thus, without

[1] Bede, *H.E.*, ii, 20.

intending it, united all the future Churches of England and Scotland and made their connection with the Churches on the continent ultimately dependent upon Canterbury. From this time, in spite of many difficulties and the later destruction of the Churches in the north of England, the organization of Christianity in the whole of England was the same in practice as well as doctrine, under the control of bishops and kings, all of whom looked to Rome as a central authority.

The influence of the bishops in England is expressed in the text of the earliest English laws. The laws of Ethelbert are said by Bede to have been issued in accordance with the examples of the Romans.[1] They were written down some time before the death of Ethelbert in A.D. 616 or A.D. 617 "in the language of the English," and the first sentences, translated into modern English, run as follows: "These are the decrees which King Ethelbert established in the lifetime of Augustine. Theft of God's property and the Church's shall be compensated twelvefold; a bishop's property elevenfold, a priest's property ninefold. . . . If a freeman robs the king he shall pay in ninefold amount." It has been remarked that a bishop's property is treated as more important than a king's;[2] and even if the text of the laws, as we now have them, includes reference to some later customs than those of Augustine's day, the reference to the status of the clergy is probably original. Again, the Laws of Wihtred of about the year 695, begin as follows: "During the sovereignty of Wihtred, the most gracious king of Kent, in the fifth year of his reign, the ninth Indiction, the sixth day of Rugern, in the place which is called Barham, there was assembled a deliberative council of the notables. There were present Berhtwald, the chief bishop of Britain, and the above-mentioned king; the bishop of Rochester, who was called Gefinnud; and every order of the Church of the Province expressed itself in unanimity with the loyal laity (assembled there)."[3] And, finally, the Laws of Ine, of about the year A.D. 690, begin: "I, Ine, by the grace of God King

[1] Bede, *H.E.*, ii, 5.
[2] See F. L. Attenborough, *The Laws of the English Kings*, p. 175. The translations given here are from Attenborough.   [3] Attenborough, p. 25.

of Wessex, with the advice and instruction of Cenred, my father, of Hedde, my bishop, and of Erconwald, my bishop."[1]

Evidently the bishops in England were at first, in the simplest sense of the word, kings' bishops. Indeed, they seem to be attached to the kings recently converted almost as chaplains, or at least as advisers and guides among the kings' "wise men." But England was divided into many small kingdoms and the bishops never became so completely subordinated to their kings as to lose the sense of the unity of the Christian people in the different kingdoms. It was not, however, until Archbishop Theodore became archbishop of Canterbury, on the nomination of the Pope, that the English Church as a whole made a definite step forward to unity both for itself and the nation. To archbishop Theodore, and not to Augustine, its first missionary from Rome, the Church in England owed its organization, its unity, and its later influence in uniting the Germanic invaders in one English nation. Theodore was a Greek-speaking monk who had settled in Rome, probably among the refugees, if he was not himself a refugee, from Roman Asia after the Mohammedan invasion. Many such refugees from the East brought their learning and ability to the assistance of the Latin Churches. Thus, the Church in England was established upon a firm foundation, and the unity of the English nation made possible, not only by Anglo-Saxon institutions, but also by the civilizing influence of the Latin Churches and the administrative skill of a Greek.

Theodore arrived at Canterbury in A.D. 669, as Bede says: "the first archbishop whom all the English Church obeyed."[2] And in A.D. 673 a general synod of bishops of the Church in England was held at Hertford. The canons are given in Bede's *History*; and the evident purpose of the synod was to organize all the bishoprics of England in one system, while the different kingdoms remained continually at war. A second council of the bishops of England

[1] Attenborough, pp. 34–37.
[2] Bede, *H.E.*, iv, 2. In a letter of Pope Zachary to St. Boniface, Theodore is referred to as "Graeco-Latinus ante philosophus et Athenis eruditus, Romae ordinatus" (on March 26, 668). See Bonifacius, Ep. 80, in Pertz, *M.G.H.* (Berlin, 1916).

was held in A.D. 680 in order to confirm the adhesion of the Church in England to the condemnation of the Monophysite heresy; and this council further confirmed the unity of the English bishops. But a new difficulty arose about a hundred years later when Offa, king of the Mercians, planned to establish a Primate and archbishop at Lichfield, under his own immediate control, in opposition to the claims of Canterbury. The archbishop of Canterbury at the time seems to have been unacceptable to the king of Mercia, although Kent acknowledged his suzerainty. The Council of Chelsea in A.D. 789, at which two Papal Legates were present, consented to the policy of king Offa; but in A.D. 796, on the death of Offa, the See of Canterbury was again recognized as that of the Primate. Evidently the Church itself preserved its own organization and its unity by securing independence of any of the rival kingdoms; and when at last the greater part of England was unified politically for the first time under the kings of Wessex, Canterbury remained the ecclesiastical capital. The bishops of the Church in England were thus never identified with the fortunes of the State to such an extent as was the case in Spain.

Again, the bishops in England were continuously in contact with the bishops of other countries, and especially with the bishop of Rome. The Popes continued throughout the seventh and eighth centuries to exercise direct influence upon the Churches in England, which had indeed come into existence originally because of the energy and foresight of Pope Gregory the Great. And the influence of Rome, as a city of the Apostles and martyrs and not of emperors, made a deep impression upon the laity as well as the clergy of England. Thus many Saxon kings made the pilgrimage to Rome; and some resigned their crowns in order to spend the remainder of their days near the shrine of St. Peter. Thus, also, in the letters of St. Boniface mention is made of the many Englishwomen who undertook the pilgrimage to Rome, with some danger not only to their lives but also to their morals. In a letter of about the year 738, from Boniface to the Abbess Bugga, he advises her not to go to Rome until the confusion caused by the threat of the Saracens, who have lately set upon the Romans, shall have subsided.[1] In another letter, of the year 745 or 747, to archbishop Cuthbert of Canterbury, Boniface writes: "All the servants of God over here (on the Continent) think that it would be good, and the honour and purity of your Church would benefit in providing some relief from evil, if your synod and your nobles would prohibit laywomen and nuns to undertake the journey and join the concourse which goes and comes on the way to Rome, because the greater number of them perish and few remain untouched. There are few cities in Lombardy, in France (i.e. Germany) or in Gaul in which there is not an adultress or harlot of the English race, which is bad for the reputation of the whole of your Church."[2]

It is important also to notice in the correspondence of St. Boniface that he was able to criticize from his distant See in Germany the habits and customs of an English king. In the year 746 or 747 St. Boniface and about six other missionary bishops in Germany, all of them English, wrote to King Ethelbald of Mercia saying that the writers were rejoiced to hear that the king suppressed violence, established peace in his kingdom and was generous in almsgiving.[3] They have heard, however, that the king's sexual habits are the reverse of edifying. They ask him to reform, because even the pagans are opposed to adultery and fornication; "but if the English people (*Gens Anglorum*), as it is commonly said in these parts, and as we are jeered at in France and Italy on this account, lives an unclean life . . . they will be thought degenerate and finally neither strong in war nor stable in their faith, nor honoured among men nor loved by God—as it happened to the other peoples of Spain and Provence and to the Burgundians, who so departed from God in fornication until the Almighty Judge permitted the penalties of such crimes by ignorance of the law of God and by the invasion of the Saracens." Again, they protest that the king has suppressed the liberties of monasteries and that his counts do the same. They urge the king, therefore, with many quotations from the Book of Wisdom, to reform his life.

This letter was sent with another from Boniface himself to a

---

[1] Boniface, Ep. 27 (*M.G.H.*).
[2] Ibid., Ep. 78 (*M.G.H.*), in *Pat. Lat.*, 89, this letter is No. 63 and is dated A.D. 745 (col. 763).   [3] Ibid., Ep. 73 (*M.G.H.*).

priest, Herefrid, asking him to help in bringing the bishops' message
to the notice of the king; and a further letter from Boniface to
archbishop Egbert of York asks him to make what changes he
thinks fit in the letter to King Ethelbald and to support what he
thinks correct.[1] Evidently the kings of the different parts of England
were under continual criticism by bishops; and the Church thus
acted as a sort of opposition within these petty kingdoms. But in
most cases the bishops directed and advised kings in council with
other "wise men," while the kings were raised above their nobles
by the moral authority conferred upon them through ecclesiastical
rites and ceremonies.

An indication of the new position acquired by kings thus supported by bishops, is to be found in the ceremony for the anointing
of kings at their coronation. This ceremony must have been introduced into England at about the same date as it was into Spain,
and certainly before the anointing of the Frankish usurper Pippin
by Boniface in A.D. 752. The Pontifical of Egbert, archbishop of
York, the friend of Bede, contains the prayers and ritual for the
coronation of a king. Egbert became archbishop of York in
A.D. 732; but there is no clear evidence that the manuscripts at
present in existence contain rituals of that date. The manuscript
quoted below is of the tenth century.[2] This manuscript of the
Pontifical contains, among the other prayers and rituals to be found
in any Pontifical, a Mass for kings on the day of their coronation.
The ritual for "the Benediction of a king newly elected" directs:
"Here the bishop pours oil from a horn on the king's head with
the antiphon 'They anointed Solomon' and the psalm 'Lord in Thy
strength.' One of the bishops must say the prayer and the others
anoint." The prayer runs: "O God, who after the deluge by a
dove bearing the olive branch showed that peace was restored to
earth, and established as priest Aaron thy servant by anointing with
oil, and later by this same anointing made priests and kings and
prophets to rule the people of Israel . . . we pray that by this oil
you will bless this your servant and let him like the dove bring

[1] Boniface, Eps. 74 and 75 (*M.G.H.*).
[2] Printed for the Surtees Society, vol. xxvii (1853).

peace to the people subject to him, and keep his throne always in good counsel and just judgement." The ritual direction says here: "All the bishops with the nobles put a sceptre into the king's hand" and later a staff; and again: "All the bishops take the helmet and place it on the king's head."[1] Evidently the ceremony was sufficiently established in the English kingdoms; and it cannot have failed to give moral authority to the kings thus consecrated. They were thus made sacred persons, holding power by some "divine" authority, and so distinguished from the civil nobility and united with the clergy. Indeed, by anointing the king acquired some sacerdotal characteristics.

The Influence of Ireland

In Ireland, for a century after St. Patrick, the development of the Christian community can hardly be traced in any surviving documents. But by the seventh century Ireland had become the home not only of a vigorous monasticism, but also of learning and general culture much superior to that of the rest of western Europe. Monks from Ireland, like St. Columban, had acted as missionaries in Gaul, Germany and Italy. St. Columban himself had founded the monastery of Bobbio in northern Italy, which became a seat of learning. And the monastery founded near lake Constance by St. Gall, another Irishman, preserved the tradition of scholarship throughout the Middle Ages.[2] Irish Christianity was monastic rather than episcopal. It flourished in settlements controlled by abbots to whom bishops were subordinate. This was a result of the tribal organization in Ireland, where kings or leaders of the people were little more than local chieftains of pastoral or simple agricultural communities. Therefore Ireland did not contribute to the later organization of Church and State, except in so far as Irish missionaries converted the kings and people of southern Scotland and northern England. But one short treatise on social problems remains, which is now believed to have been written in Ireland,

[1] Sumant galeum et ponant super caput ipsius (p. 103). So in the Surtees Society's Text. But "galeum" may be only a misreading of the manuscript "galeam."

[2] The monastery was founded in A.D. 614. In A.D. 954 walls were built round it, for defence against the Saracens.

about the year 630. This is the book of the *Twelve Evils of the Age*.[1] It assumes, as all the teaching of that time assumed, that the fundamental problem was not the improvement of social institutions but the improvement of the morals of individuals. Thus, the evils of the Age in this book are the wise man who does nothing, the old man without religion, the young man without obedience, the rich man without charity, the woman without modesty, the lord without vigour, the Christian who is quarrelsome, the poor man who is proud, the unjust king, the negligent bishop, common folk without discipline, and a community without law. Of the local lords it is said that some are improved by their position and some made worse; and the duties of the king are declared to be the administration of justice, the defence of the Church and the protection of the fatherland. The conclusion of the whole treatise is a call to unity based upon the saying of St. Paul that all are one in Christ. This treatise, which became attached in some manuscripts to the works of St. Cyprian, is quoted as Cyprian's in Hincmar's book on the Organization of the Palace (*De Ordine Palatii*), which was written in the ninth century. It had, therefore, some influence on ideas of government and of social organization in the Middle Ages.

The development of ecclesiastical organization in Ireland, and the possibility of political unity there, as in England, under the influence of the Church, were prevented by the invasions of the Northmen in the ninth century. But probably the Christian communities in Ireland before that time, being organized upon a tribal and monastic basis, and not upon the Roman basis of city bishoprics, had for that reason less power to unite the different Irish tribes. In any case, the pagan invaders from the North sacked monasteries and other settlements, and thereby destroyed the great tradition of learning and piety in Ireland, which had for some centuries before illuminated western Europe. Northmen, now called Danes, raided Dublin Bay in A.D. 795. Other Northmen, now called Norwegians, came up the Shannon. Refugees from Ireland, such as Sedulius

---

[1] *De Duodecim Abusivis Saeculi*, pub. 1910 in *Altchr. Lit.*, vol. 34. *Texte und Untersuchungen*, Harnack und Schmidt.

Scottus and Johannes Scotus Erigena, took Irish learning to western Europe. But Ireland itself was no longer the home of learning or of the arts and sciences of civilized life.

Germany becomes Christian

In the parts of Germany which had been outside the influence of the Roman Empire, English missionaries in the seventh and eighth centuries extended the power of Christianity and the organization of the Church. But here also tribal society prevailed; and monasteries, which extended the cultivation of the soil in areas hitherto covered by forests and marshes, and also formed centres of learning and the arts, were at first more important than bishops and their clergy. The first missionary expedition which had some success among the peoples east of the Frankish dominions, was that of Willibrord, whose mission to the Frisians, in what is now called Holland, is described by Bede. Willibrord, a Yorkshireman who had studied for twelve years in Ireland, was ordained as a missionary bishop in Rome by Pope Sergius I in A.D. 695; and according to St. Boniface he preached for fifty years among the Frisians and converted most of them.[1] He died in A.D. 739. His great successor, St. Boniface, was the leader of many English missionaries who tried to convert the Germanic peoples to Christianity from the worship of the war-gods Woden and Thor.

The extension of Christianity into the tribal parts of what is now Germany, however, was largely dependent upon the influence and military power of the kings of the Franks. And it was in his efforts to use that influence, both for the spread of Christianity and for the reform of the clergy in the Frankish dominions, that St. Boniface eventually anointed the usurper Pippin as king. The kingship thereby secured, and afterwards supported by the Popes themselves, was one of the chief instruments for the increase of the power of the bishops in the newly-converted areas.

The connection between Rome and Germany, east of the Rhine,

[1] Boniface, Ep. 109 (*M.G.H.*). This letter is a complaint to Pope Stephen II (A.D. 753) that the bishop of Cologne had claimed jurisdiction over the old See of Willibrord (Tragectus=Utrecht) which Carloman had committed to Boniface himself.

was thus brought about by English missionaries; and throughout the Middle Ages, and perhaps even later, Germany was obsessed with the idea that a barbarian ruler could obtain prestige by using the title of a Roman Emperor and being crowned in Rome by the successor of St. Peter. In England, in the eighth century, Rome was looked upon as the original source of English Christianity; and English kings went to Rome as pilgrims, some even abdicating their kingship in order to live their last years near to the tomb of the gate-keeper of heaven. But the English missionaries among the Germanic tribes, in the eighth and ninth centuries, had special reasons for their dependence upon Rome and its bishops. Willibrord and Boniface, as well as the other monks and nuns who helped them in their missions, looked to Rome as a source from which to draw influence in their attempt to reform the Frankish clergy. The kings of the Franks who supported such reform, found in Rome an authority older than that of any Gallic bishopric. On the other hand, if the English missionaries in Germany had been too completely identified with the policy of the Frankish kings, political or tribal prejudice east of the Rhine would have obstructed their work. It was easier for Englishmen to convert the Germans than it would have been for the clergy and monks from the Latin-speaking districts west of the Rhine. Besides a similarity of language—and a portion of St. Boniface's catechism in a Germanic dialect has survived—there was an absence of traditional rivalries between England and Germany, such as had divided Roman Gaul from barbarian Germany.

The close association of the Frankish kings, however, with the English missionaries in Germany gave those kings an opportunity for extending their domains. As Clovis, in the sixth century, had found it very convenient to be a Catholic Christian when he saw an opportunity of invading the territory of an Arian king, so Charles Martel and Charles the Great, in the later eighth century, were not blind to the advantages of conquest in the name of Christ. The Germanic, and some Slavonic tribes in what is now Germany, were induced to become Christian by force of arms. This will be discussed in a later chapter. Here it is necessary only to note that, as a result of forcible conversion, the relation between kings and bishops in Germany was somewhat different from that in France and England. In France, or Gaul, under the Roman Empire Christianity had begun as a movement among the poor; and its extension was dependent upon preaching. Among the English, although Christianity had been accepted first by tribal kings, none of them was "converted" by force of arms. Persuasion and not force was the means of extending Christianity in France and England. In Germany, on the other hand, east of the Rhine, Christianity was introduced among the Saxons and the tribes in what is now Prussia, as a religion of warriors under a God of War. And the more civilized influence of the Englishmen Boniface and Alcuin was not strong enough to moderate the zeal of Germanic warriors for a holy war. Christianity, therefore, among the Germans of the Middle Ages and perhaps later, was closely associated with war. Support was found for this association in lessons from the Old Testament concerning Joshua, Gideon, Saul and David. Divine approval was implied in the text: "Saul hath slain his thousands, but David his tens of thousands."[1] Charles the Great, the ideal of medieval German rulers, was called David by his friends and admirers. His favourite bishops, indeed, were scholars; but by the middle of the ninth century many bishops and abbots bore arms and fought vigorously.

National Churches

In their relation to civil government, the bishops, after the disappearance of the Roman Empire in the West, had an important influence upon the formation of the "nations" of the First Europe and the connection between these nations. Under the Empire, ecclesiastical districts were in general similar to those of the civil administration.[2] A Roman province was an administrative unity, both for the imperial Authorities and the Churches. The bishops of a province met regularly in council; and, in later years, the bishop

[1] 1 Samuel xxix. 5. This text is used on the memorial to the machine-gun corps of the British army in the war of 1914–1918, which now stands at Hyde Park Corner in London. [2] See Duchesne, Christian Worship (Eng. trans. 1904).

of the chief city in a province, as "metropolitan," presided. The metropolitan acquired first prestige and then certain disciplinary powers. And when the Roman administration no longer existed in the West, the bishops continued to meet in council in the old districts until the new boundaries of barbarian kingdoms had been fixed by the fortunes of war. After that time it became impossible for the bishops of the districts under one king to meet in council with bishops under other kings because of the rivalry between them. Councils of bishops, therefore, which were not acting merely for a small district, became "national" almost in the modern sense of that word. Such councils were usually summoned by the king and often opened in his presence. Thus, the councils of Toledo acted for the kingdom of the Visigoths; and many councils of Orleans and Paris acted for the whole of the Frankish kingdom.[1] Such councils would naturally promote the unity of the populations ruled over by a king. In the case of England, as it has been noted in an earlier section of this chapter, councils of bishops from different small kingdoms actually preceded the unification of the English nation. In Italy there was no such "national" council of bishops, partly because of the early rivalry between the See of Milan and the See of Rome, when Milan was the capital from about A.D. 300 to about A.D. 400; and partly because the later bishops under Lombard kings were divided from the bishop of Rome so long as he remained a subject of the Roman Emperor.

The tendency towards the separation of one national Church from another, however, was counteracted by the use of the same Latin language in all councils of all kingdoms, and by the traditions of unity between all the Churches surviving from the Roman Empire. Again, the most definitely national councils—those of Toledo—ceased to meet when the Christian kingdom in southern Spain was destroyed by the Mohammedan invasions; and in the eighth century the Frankish Churches were reformed by reference to the canons and the ritual of the Roman Church. In the fifth, sixth and seventh centuries there were different rites and ceremonies in the Churches of Spain, Gaul, northern Italy and Rome; and

[1] See De Clercq, *Législation Religieuse Franque*, 1936.

K*

there were different collections of canons in these different districts. But in the eighth century the Roman Church, partly through the influence it exercised upon the Churches in Spain, Gaul and northern Italy, became the chief source of canons and of ritual for all the West.

General Conclusions: The Church and Civil Government

The results of the new relations between Church and State were similar in all the kingdoms of western Europe. Clearly, the bishops individually in each diocese and collectively in synods or councils were the real sources of civilization. With them were associated in the middle of the seventh century, the abbots of the great Benedictine monasteries. Councils of bishops and abbots, sometimes in association with the leading warriors of the kingdom, established under the king's authority the laws of his realm and directed or modified policy. It followed inevitably that the bishops and, to some extent, the abbots were drawn into the ordinary organization of government in each kingdom. Their functions in government became almost as important, if not more important, than their activities as preachers or teachers. But there was no other possible way of securing law, order and social progress in the new society. The bishops had a tradition, partly ecclesiastical and partly civil, derived from memories and records of the Roman Empire, which served as a guide in the art of government. They had also the Latin language to give them the means of expressing social relationships unfamiliar to the more primitive Franks and Saxons. This Latin language bound them to a world outside the frontiers of each kingdom, and was a means by which civilized habits and modes of thought could pass over the boundaries of barbaric dialects. Again, as it was pointed out above (Chapter VI), the bishops individually and councils of bishops stood for the common folk in each kingdom in a sense in which neither a king nor a local lord could be said to do so. In Gaul and Spain the language of the Church was the current popular language, at least among the majority. And even where, as in England, the official language of churchmen was different from that of the common people, the bishop was in closer contact, because of his ecclesiastical functions, with the dependants of lords and kings than any civil Authority could be. Even when the Feudal System was beginning, and the Christian community was being separated into distinct social classes, when most men and women were left in subjection, more or less complete, to the wealthy and the powerful, the Church continued to preach, even if it did not practise, the equality of all men, and to declare that manual labour and the service of others were divinely appointed and not in themselves either objectionable or degrading. In this aspect at least, as it will be argued more fully in a later chapter, the civilization of the Middle Ages had a wider and firmer basis than that of the Roman Empire. At the end of the eighth century Alcuin used exactly the same language about the equality of all men before God as had been used in the fifth century by Salvian;[1] and although after the conversion of kings, both civil and ecclesiastical Authorities forgot that Christianity had been established by working-men, the great Benedictine abbeys maintained throughout the Middle Ages the doctrine and the practice that all work is prayer (*Laborare est orare*). St. Boniface in his letter to Pope Zachary on the foundation of the monastery at Fulda, says of the monks that they were "satisfied by the labours of their own hands, without serfs."[2] This did not remain true of the greater monasteries in later years; but the tradition and the ideal implied had a widespread influence upon the status of manual work.

The kings and their warriors, on the other hand, provided armed force, with which the bishops had come to terms. The problem is the same in all forms of civilization; but it is most urgent in times of unsettlement and transition. If the bishops had relied only upon moral influence and the appeal to the example of the Saints, they might for a time have improved the way of life among a few enthusiasts in their immediate neighbourhood. But in practice moral influence is useless as a protection against the violence and treachery of those men and women who are determined to take as much as they can from anyone weaker than

---

[1] In the *De Virtutibus et Vitiis*.

[2] Boniface, Ep. 86 (A.D. 751), *M.G.H.*, "absque servis, proprio manuum suarum labore contentos."

themselves. The civilization of the great monasteries in northern England, so admirably apparent in the pages of Bede, was utterly destroyed soon after his death by Danish pirates and raiders. Bede himself, indeed, foresaw the danger to civilized life if a great number of Christians renounced or avoided their obligations in civil life. At the end of his *History* he writes: "Such is the prevailing peace of the times that many Northumbrian nobles and commoners lay aside their arms and dedicate themselves and their children rather to the tonsure and monastic vows than to the study of martial discipline. What will be the end of that the next age will show."[1] Similarly at the end of his life Bede wrote a letter of advice and exhortation to his friend Egbert, archbishop of York, in which he warned him against the establishment of large monastic settlements—hardly, in Bede's opinion, to be called true monasteries, in which landowners and workers on the land, in groups of families, lived together apart from the main current of life among their contemporaries, thus escaping some of the obligations of public service.[2] This was written in about A.D. 735; and forty years later the first Danish invasions began the destruction of civilized life in northern England. Similarly in Ireland the advancement of civilized life was interrupted by invasions of pagan Danes and Norsemen in the early ninth century, as described above. So, in earlier times, the civilization of Italy, Gaul and Spain would have been destroyed by kings and warriors, if some of them had not been induced by the bishops to protect, even for their own advantage, a part of the population against external attack. Even the change of barbarian raiders into rulers settled upon the land was due to the influence at first of the Roman Empire and afterwards of the Roman Church. It was easy enough for armed men to raid the cities and the countryside and to carry off captives and gold; but these same raiders soon found it necessary to learn the art of government, at least for the sake of retaining their ill-gotten gains.

[1] Bede, *H.E.*, v, 33, in fine.
[2] Ibid., Ep. Egbert, c. 11, "quod enim turpe est dicere, tot sub nomine monasteriorum loca hii qui monachicae vitae parum prorsus sunt expertes in suam dicionem acceperunt . . . ut omnino desit locus ubi filii nobilium aut emeritorum militum possessionem accipere possunt.

And of this art of government they brought with them from the forests and marshes of Germany or the coasts of Norway and Denmark little or nothing. They had, in fact, to learn the art at first from Roman civilians such as Leo and Cassiodorus; and later, when all those trained in the imperial service were dead, the barbarians were compelled to depend on the bishops. Indeed, it is difficult to see what the barbarian kings and warriors contributed to the later civilization of the Middle Ages, except as instruments of a policy not their own. Whenever the kings depended on the bishops, civilization advanced; and wherever the bishops depended on the kings civilization was cramped into a military system.

The Wealth of the Church

On the other hand, the maintenance of the tradition of civilized life by the Church in a barbarous age involved all moral authority in new difficulties. The kings and warriors had wealth and power. The bishops desired to use the kings and other lords for the good of their people; and the more persuasive the bishops became, the more generous their barbarian pupils showed themselves in bestowing wealth and power upon Churches and monasteries. Thus, by the middle of the eighth century the great monasteries and the holders of episcopal Sees owned or controlled large areas of land and considerable other wealth. The influence of the Church was certainly not only spiritual. It had a very present temporal power in all the kingdoms of western Europe from Italy to northern Britain and Ireland, and from Bavaria to Spain. The possession of wealth and power gave to the bishops and the abbots immense opportunities for "doing good." But here is the dilemma. As soon as any man or body of men obtains wealth and power, their policy tends to be dominated rather by the effort to keep what they have than to use it. Even a saintly man may easily persuade himself that it is better that he, rather than another, should control great wealth. Salvian himself in the fifth century, who inveighed against the wealthy, was concerned to secure wealth for the monasteries. So also in the eighth century bishops and abbots were not unwilling to accept more and more wealth from barbarian kings and warriors.

And under Charles Martel, as has been shown above, the Churches of Gaul were sufficiently wealthy to provide loot for a king with ravenous followers. The more saintly bishops of the eighth century were aware of the moral problem to which this situation gave rise. St. Boniface, for example, wrote to Daniel, bishop of Winchester, for advice on precisely this point of difficulty for all who desire to use wealth and power for the benefit of others. "Without the patronage," he says, "of the king of the Franks, I cannot control the members of the Church nor defend priests or clergy, monks or nuns. Nor can I without the king's authority and power suppress pagan rites and idolatry in Germany. But when for these reasons I seek such assistance, I cannot possibly escape communication with those whom, according to the canons, I ought to avoid. . . . I fear my preaching will suffer, if I do not approach the king of the Franks."[1] The bishop of Winchester replied, recognizing the danger; but, with many quotations from the Bible and the commentaries of St. Augustine and St. Jerome, he argued that the good man must not avoid the danger. He must use those in power so far as he can without destroying his own intention to do good; "and if you are accused by anyone of deceit or of some trickery because of this acquiescence in the established order, we read that sometimes pretence is useful and must be adopted."[2]

The effort to retain and increase wealth and power was natural enough among bishops and other churchmen; and the purpose they had in view—their hope of using such wealth—excused their absorption in the desire to retain it. But it was a dangerous situation; and in fact throughout the Middle Ages the Church was cursed by "great possessions."

There was another difficulty. As soon as bishoprics involved the control of great wealth, men of a new type strove to be bishops. Although wealth and power are in theory only means to be used for ends beyond themselves, in practice many men of great ability

[1] Boniface, Ep. 63, *M.G.H.* (A.D. 742–746).
[2] Ibid., Ep. 64, "legimus quod utilis simulatio adsumenda sit in tempore." It is amusing to note that this is the argument of Symmachus, in the fourth century, against the suppression of pagan rites. See Chapter II, p. 70, "dissimulatio proximorum."

in every age are more concerned with obtaining wealth and power than with using them. Again, to preserve control of wealth and power requires much energy and some ability; and every institution by which wealth is controlled produces men and women whose chief interest is the preservation and increase of that wealth. The bishops and the abbots of the sixth, seventh and eighth centuries in western Europe were, in practice, administrators of large estates, from which they did not hesitate to derive some advantage for themselves and for the clerical caste to which they belonged. It was easy for most of those in control of the wealth of the Churches to persuade themselves that the maintenance of their own prestige in the building of churches and monasteries was for the glory of God. "Christ's poor" in the greater monasteries soon became considerably richer than the majority of their neighbours. And the simple bishops' houses of early days, to which Gregory of Tours refers in his *History*, soon developed into mansions rivalling those of great landowners and kings. The Church had sought or accepted wealth and power as a means for directing the social forces of the time towards civilized life and Christianity, as it was then understood. But wealth and power, once obtained, quickly corrupted the institutions which had begun in protest against the desire to accumulate wealth and to seek power. Abbots and bishops were rich men, and most of them no better than other rich men of the time. Spiritual powers, relics and sacraments became sources of wealth—for the glory of God, no doubt, but also for the great advantage of the clergy. Jewelled shrines might excite the worshipper to some form of "devotion"; but they were also very useful financially to the keepers of the shrine. The Churches were no longer the simple groups of believers for whom the documents in the New Testament were originally composed.

Influence of the Old Testament

In the relations between Church and State in western Europe generally, one of the most important factors during the seventh and eighth centuries was the influence of the Old Testament. It has already been noted that in the case of Spain, England and

France, the anointment at the coronation of kings by bishops was based upon practices recorded in the Old Testament. From its earliest years the Christian Church had been deeply influenced by mystical or symbolic interpretation of the Old Testament. In the fifth century the clergy, already tending to separate themselves from the Christian laity, had used the authority of the Old Testament in its description of the position of the Levites. Thus clerics became a tribe or caste set apart. But the social and political systems of the Roman Empire, under which Christianity developed for four centuries, were obviously too unlike any such systems in the Old Testament for the Hebrew tradition to affect the relations of Church and State so long as the imperial system survived. The Roman Empire was a highly civilized widespread organization of law and administration based upon city-organization, utterly unlike the tribal kingships of the Old Testament. And even under the earlier barbarian kingdoms of the Goths, Burgundians and Vandals, the traditions of the Empire survived and were maintained by the Church. When, however, the new barbarians—Franks, Angles and Saxons—who were less influenced by the Roman tradition, established their kingdoms, the social situation was more primitive. Under the Franks and the Anglo-Saxons the relation between rulers and ecclesiastics was like that recorded in the books of *Samuel* and *Kings*. The climate of opinion was that of a tribal agricultural society, continually at war. And some of the established organizations and traditional policies in such a society would naturally receive confirmation and support from books believed to contain God's own directions and decisions. Thus barbarian kingship in Europe acquired additional prestige from the accident that Hebrew chieftains were called in the Latin text of the Old Testament "kings" (*reges*); and the distinction between priests and prophets in the Old Testament gave additional emphasis to the coincidence that in Europe the clergy were different from the monks. It will be remembered that the influence of the books of *Kings* had been feared by Ulfilas, the bishop who converted the Goths in the fourth century, who omitted from his translation of the Bible into Gothic these very books because they might incite to war a people already inclined to it. The moral standards of a man trained within the Roman Empire were higher than those of the primitive Hebrews. But later in north-western Europe and in Spain the anointing of kings was derived from the Old Testament largely because the custom met the needs of a simpler society in the seventh and eighth centuries. The kings needed moral authority; and they could most easily obtain it through the action of the bishops, while the bishops themselves might hope to restrain or direct the kings by the use of the power expressed in the oil of consecration.

Such passages as these provided the authority for the new system: "Then Samuel took a vial of oil and poured it upon Saul's head and kissed him and said: Is it not because the Lord has anointed thee to be captain over his inheritance?"[1] And again: "All the elders of Israel . . . anointed David king over Israel";[2] and again: Elisha sent one of the children of the prophets "with a box of oil to pour the oil on the head of Jehu and say: Thus saith the Lord: I have anointed thee king over Israel."[3] With such texts before them the monks and the clergy readily adopted the conception that their relation to public Authorities was like that of prophets and priests among the Hebrews. The difficulties of the seventh and eighth centuries in western Europe were not unlike those recorded in the Old Testament. Civil war often occurred in most countries; there was no generally accepted right of succession; there was no established means of recognizing the rightful ruler; and when anyone seized power, in order to hold it he was compelled to seek some means of acquiring also moral authority. The bishops were recognized by the population in Spain and Gaul to have moral authority as a divine gift; and when the Anglo-Saxon peoples became Christian, the bishops among them acquired a similar position. The bishops in Spain and Gaul accepted victorious kings as legitimate rulers; and in England the bishops looked to the kings for support. Divine authority for the connection between bishops and kings was found in the Old Testament; and the methods of expressing that connection were drawn from the same source. Thus kingship came to be the established form of civil authority

---

[1] I Samuel x. 1.   [2] 2 Samuel v. 3.   [3] 2 Kings ix. 3.

as well as of military leadership, through the use of the old Hebrew ceremonial by Christian bishops; and the power which the bishops thus acquired as the recognized sources of some at least of the king's prestige, considerably increased the influence of the Church among the people at large. It had also the effect of making kings and bishops in some way mutually dependent, as against the gatherings of warriors or nobles, who might otherwise treat the king as merely one of themselves. Thus, an anointed king might be more able both to resist his own powerful chieftains and to extend his domains wherever his authority might be regarded as divinely established. The dominant idea, thus almost accidentally arising out of the situation in the eighth century, became a political maxim later on, as in the phrase of king James I of England, "No bishop, no king," and in the devotion of the old Tory party to "Church and king." Obviously a form of absolute or autocratic government, such as monarchy, can survive most easily by appeal to ancient authority; and prestige attaches to all who preserve the ancient forms associated with the possession of power.

The bishops, on their part, derived from the new situation an increased protection which the properties of the Church might obtain from anointed kings. Thus, Pope Stephen wrote in A.D. 754 to Pippin and his two sons: "The Lord, by my humility and the assistance of Peter, anointed you as kings, in order that by your aid his holy Church should be exalted and the Prince of the Apostles receive his due."[1] This is, indeed, an indication of favours expected by the Church at large; for all bishops were aware of the debt owed to the Church by the barbarian kings. By grace of the bishops these ignorant and violent warriors had obtained the moral authority which attaches to civilized government; and it was both just and convenient that the Church should be rewarded.

Restriction of Political Development

The anointment of kings, however, is not the only example of

[1] *Cod. Car.*, vii, ap. Migne, *Pat. Lat.*, 98, col. 110. Ideo vos Dominus, per humilitatem meam, mediante Sancto Petro, unxit in reges, ut per vos sancta sua exaltetur Ecclesia et princeps apostolorum suam iustitiam suscipiat.

the influence of the Old Testament in changing the relation between bishops and kings. In the Old Testament, priests and prophets are given a divinely established power and influence in the choice and control of rulers. No such social or political theory is implied in the New Testament, where submission to established authority is the dominant idea; nor when Christianity was first accepted by the rulers of the Roman Empire was there any conception that imperial authority required confirmation or divine sanction from the action of bishops. But in the more primitive situation in the barbarian kingdoms of the North, the warriors and their kings who held power by force of arms, on becoming Christian, lost the prestige attached to them under their old deities, and could derive moral authority to support their military force only from monks and clergy. It was natural, therefore, for the bishops and the abbots, who acted as preachers and prophets, to find in the Old Testament the dominant ideas which established their own position. Thus, the text of the Old Testament became not merely symbolic or prophetic, but also a practical basis for the political and social ideas and customs of the seventh and eighth centuries.

One of the most important results was the restriction of political growth, or actual retrogression in the art of government, which always results from the study of ancient books. This is called "archaism." During the Middle Ages, and even later, it came to be regarded as natural that kingships and kingdoms should be the only legitimate form of government. There is no mention in the Old Testament, nor even in the New, of Republics or Presidents or popular legislative Assemblies. Therefore, all these more highly civilized institutions were regarded as somehow excluded from the divinely appointed systems of government. Thus, for about a thousand years European development in the art of government was hampered or obstructed by the use of biblical authority as the basis for political practice. The effect of the same primitive conceptions of government on the idea of heaven and the "king of heaven" will be discussed elsewhere.

Military Christianity

The use of the Old Testament as a source of political ideas also supported the military Christianity of the seventh and eighth and later centuries. The historical books of the Old Testament provided excuses for the appetite of barbarian kings for victory over their enemies. The slaughter of the enemies of the Hebrew people, as commanded by God in the books of *Deuteronomy* and *Joshua*, gave support to the wars of Christian kings against heretics and pagans. Even St. Ambrose, as it was pointed out in an earlier chapter, urged the Emperor Gratian to war as a Christian ruler; but the situation became much worse when every petty king of a barbarian kingdom could treat his particular armed gathering as the instrument of divine authority. Thus, also, Charles the Great was able with a good conscience to slaughter four thousand five hundred Saxon prisoners, as a method of converting the remainder of their tribes to "Christianity."

The Hebrew conception of divine authority for the use of war was also to be found in the New Testament. Even in heaven war had been waged; and the rebel angels had been defeated by the celestial Powers—thus showing that war was in the nature of things. It was written in the book of *Revelation* (xii. 7)—"There was war in heaven: Michael and his angels fought against the dragon: and the dragon fought and his angels, and prevailed not."[1] And St. Augustine in the *City of God* had discussed the position of the defeated angels before and after the battle.[2] Thus the statements of the Bible, taken in their obvious sense, supported the use of war by Christian kings.

The general passion for warlike adventures naturally affected even the clergy; and bishops and priests went out with armour and weapons to slaughter enemies. But the canons of the Church always forbade this. Great bishops, such as Boniface, resolutely opposed the bearing of arms by the clergy, and were able to per-

[1] So in *Jude*, 6: "the angels which kept not their first estate, he hath reserved in everlasting chains and darkness."
[2] Augustine, *De Civitate Dei*, xi, 13. Unfortunately the Middle Ages had not the advantage of Milton's description of the battle in heaven, with guns and other modern weapons. *Paradise Regained*, vi, 572 sq.

suade even the kings of the Franks to issue decrees forbidding the clergy to bear arms or to accompany armed forces, except as chaplains or for the saying of the Mass.[1] Thus, Carloman, then Chief of the Palace, who calls himself "dux et princeps Francorum," in the year 742 or 743 decreed: "We forbid the clergy to carry arms or to fight or to march against the enemy, except only those who are chosen for Divine Service, that is, to say Mass and carry the relics of the saints; thus, the general (*princeps*) may have one or two bishops with priests as chaplains, and each section-leader (*prefectus*) one priest who may hear confessions and assign the penance." In spite of the influence of the Old Testament, therefore, supporting the barbarian delight in warfare, the Church attempted to control, in the spirit of the New Testament, the majority of its clergy. It must not, however, be imagined that the clergy were believed to be useless in war. They were expected to assist in obtaining victory by specially effectual prayers, by rituals and the use of relics. As Clovis had been frightened at Saragossa by the tunic of St. Vincent—as the Ark of the Covenant had helped to destroy the walls of Jericho[2]—so the cloak (*cappa*) of St. Martin, carried into battle by the "chaplains" (*capellani*), was believed to bring the celestial Powers to the assistance of the Franks.

Old Testament Influence on Law

Again, probably the influence of the Old Testament in the un-critical reading of the Mosaic law, had an effect in establishing the idea that law could be announced from above by a king. As it will be shown in the next chapter, the earliest barbarian laws consist chiefly of statements of payments to be made in compensation for theft or violence. These are merely attempts to put upon record certain prevailing customs. But about the middle of the eighth century the kings of the Franks began to issue decrees (*capitularia*), which bear all the marks of a claim to absolute authority. The

[1] Boniface, Ep. 56, *M.G.H.* "Cum capellanis presbiteris." The capellani are those in charge of the capa or capella, the cloak of St. Martin, which the Frankish kings kept at their headquarters.
[2] *Joshua*, vi, 6 sq., "Take up the Ark of the Covenant and let seven priests bear seven trumpets before the Ark of the Lord."

conception of law as the expression, first, of a Divine Will and, secondly, of the will of a divinely appointed Authority, was evidently influenced by the Old Testament, although the Roman Dictatorship had also included the conception of law as the will of the ruler. In both traditions Oriental Monarchy is assumed to be the ideal government, established in heaven and copied on earth by true believers.

But the influence of the Old Testament upon the position of European kings extended even to the forms of speech. Thus the treatment of barbarian kings as the Lord's Anointed, as in the canons of the Council of Toledo, was in harmony with the habits of the courtiers of Charles the Great when they called him either David or Solomon. David was taken as the type of a warrior-king and Solomon of a wise judge. And perhaps their calling Charles by the names of two Hebrew kings, besides attributing to him victory and wisdom, may also have had some playful reference to the remarkable vigour of his sexual impulse.

Sabbatarianism

Another effect of the Old Testament was the Sabbatarianism expressed in some of the decrees of the Frankish kings. They apply the rules of ancient Hebrew custom to the life of the Christian people on Sundays. A prehistoric ritual avoidance of certain forms of labour was applied to conditions in north-western Europe in the eighth century—which shows how literally certain sections of the Old Testament were understood. At the very end of the sixth century, Gregory of Tours writes that because all "public work" was not stopped on Sundays, fire from heaven did damage at Limoges.[1] But the devout might go further. A nun repented of having washed her hair on a Saturday.[2] The danger, in any case, was great on Sunday night; for to procreate a child "on that night might produce a cripple or an epileptic or a leper."[3] The Sabbath was evidently protected by uncanny or magical influences. The fear

---

[1] Greg. Tur., *H.F.*, x, 30: "ne fiat in eo omne opus publicum."
[2] Ibid., *Gloria Conf.*, 5.
[3] Ibid., *Vita S. Martini*, ii, 24: "Qui in ea (die) coniuges simul convenerint, exinde aut contracti aut epileptici aut leprosi filii nascuntur."

of the anger of celestial Powers no doubt supported the prohibitions of the civil law, for example in the Capitularies and in the Lex Alamannorum (Tit. 38).[1]

Iconoclasm

Again, Charles the Great supported the opposition to the use of pictures and statues in the churches. This was an episode in the great Iconoclastic controversy, which will be discussed in a later chapter. The hostility of the Frankish king to the use of images may have been only a part of his general policy of opposition to the Roman Empire, whose reigning Empress at the time favoured images; or it may have been due to the influence of Mohammedanism. But in any case it was partly due to the condemnation of "graven images" in the Old Testament; and it led Charles the Great into implied criticism of the Pope and the Roman Church.[2]

Bishops and Kings in Theory

No general theory of Church and State had yet arisen at the end of the eighth century to excuse or justify the actual position. But one book of great influence set out the duties of bishops. This is the *Book of the Pastoral Rule*, by Pope Gregory the Great, written at the end of the sixth century for John, bishop of Ravenna. A copy was sent by the author to Leander, archbishop of Seville. It was circulated in Spain and, in a Greek translation, in the East. It was recognized as authoritative by councils held under Charles the Great in A.D. 813, and a copy seems to have been given to bishops at their consecration. King Alfred translated it under the title of "Shepherds' Book"; and throughout the Middle Ages it was regarded as a guide to the duties of a bishop. The moral standards expressed in it will be discussed elsewhere. Here it is necessary only to note that the chief function of a bishop is conceived to be the government of souls (*regimen animarum*), and that this consists largely in preaching or personal exhortation. Among the faithful to be directed to virtue by the bishop, are those holding public

[1] Provision for Sunday rest against "opera servilia."
[2] See below, Chapter XI, p. 597.

311

authority; but Gregory hesitates to recommend any criticism of rulers. He refers to the book of *Kings* and says: "The acts of rulers are not to be attacked with the sword of the mouth, even when they are righly considered worthy of blame, . . . for when we offend against those in authority, we oppose the ordering of him who put them over us. . . ."[1] This is the old doctrine of acquiescence expressed in the New Testament. But obviously the Pope and other bishops would not hesitate to threaten kings either by the use of relics or with the danger of hell. The material or "temporal" cares of a bishop are touched upon; but their nature and extent were sufficiently well known to need no description. The author, therefore, confines himself to saying that the mind of the bishop should not be altogether immersed in such cares. He warns the bishop, however, against the neglect of secular business (*secularia negotia*), saying that "those who neglect entirely the care of bodily needs, do not at all assist those whom they govern. Their preaching is naturally disregarded because, while they correct sinners, they do nothing to help them in the necessities of life."[2] Pope Gregory designed his book as a sermon or exhortation to bishops; and it cannot, therefore, be taken as expressing a general theory of their position in society. But it must have had a great effect in helping to maintain the fundamental idea of the bishop as representative of the teaching Church.

On kingship there is no treatise between that of Synesius and the book *On the Kingly Way*, by the Abbot Smaragdus, in the middle of the ninth century. But canons and official correspondence of the seventh and eighth centuries sufficiently indicate what were the generally accepted opinions concerning the duties and functions of a king; and as the great majority of kings and their non-clerical councillors could not read, it was hardly necessary to produce a treatise for them. It has been already noted that anointment and crowning by bishops gave the king not only moral authority, but also a sacerdotal character. This had both advantages and disadvantages for the clergy. It had effects upon the conception of Christ as a king and judge; and that conception again reacted upon the

---

[1] Greg. M., *Reg. Past.*, iii, 4.   [2] Ibid., ii, 7.

actual status of kings throughout the Middle Ages. Christ was a king; but no one ever called him a bishop or a pope. And the actual king in any kingdom, having acquired some sacredness, was easily conceived to unite in his person supreme authority both in civil and in ecclesiastical affairs. It is true that in earlier times it had been a commonplace of ecclesiastical authorities that Christ alone, following Melchizedek, was both king and priest.[1] And after the establishment of the "Temporal Power" in the ninth century, the Popes themselves claimed both civil and ecclesiastical authority. But in the time of transition for the kingship during the seventh and eighth centuries, kings in western Europe undoubtedly were given by anointment some ecclesiastical authority. Such authority was also implied in the position of the Christian Emperors, who had not been anointed but were accepted as presidents of ecclesiastical councils. The memory of the position of the Roman Emperor in the minds of the bishops of the seventh and eighth centuries, who had read Augustine and Gregory the Great, assisted their tendency to exalt barbarian kings. But medieval kingship was not due only to memories of Roman military dictatorships. It was also due, as it has been shown above, to the later historical books in the Old Testament.

Clearly, the form of government in the Roman Empire and in the new barbarian kingdoms, believed to be divinely established, and therefore having moral authority, was military despotism. In the old barbarian tradition the king was chiefly a leader in war. This remained as an element in Christian kingship. But the earlier barbarian kings had been leaders elected by a comradeship (*Comitatus*) of warriors or counts (*comites*); and these warriors, therefore, had some control over the king. Such control might lead to anarchy when the electors disagreed, as it had in Spain. But the "sacring" of a king by bishops made him, if not absolute, at least more independent of his warriors. Thus, the Church promoted autocracy or despotism, which was further supported in later ages by the theory of divine right.

---

[1] As it is argued in *Hebrews* (chapter vii) which, however (in verse II), seems to argue that the Levite's position was out of date.

One further aspect of the theory of kingship separates it from the more primitive form of barbarian leadership. The king, like Christ, is the supreme judge. He is regarded, first, as the person who formulates ancient custom, as in the collection and publication of the barbarian laws, and, secondly, in the eighth and later centuries, as the source of new laws and decrees. But his most important non-military function is that of deciding, according to some law, between disputants, or in cases of offence against his rule. All this, however, will become clearer from a consideration of the laws prevailing in western Europe after the fifth century. This will be discussed in the next chapter.

Separation of the Clergy

The effect of the new social situation upon the position of the bishops and the rest of the clergy, was the establishment of the distinct clerical caste which was peculiar to the First Europe. In the general decline of knowledge and skill during the seventh and eighth centuries, the beliefs and practices of Christianity were affected by the surrounding barbarism. Even among devout and intelligent men the standards of credibility in what might be believed and the moral standard directing conduct were reduced to lower levels. Quite apart from the vicious and self-seeking bishops and abbots, who can hardly be called Christian in any sense of that frequently misused word, the best men and women in the clergy and the laity retained a simplicity of mind which, if not barbaric, was childish. And as morals declined, magic increased its influence. Thus, the clergy who had been, in the early years of Christianity, only elected officials, acquired the status of magic-workers, or controllers of magical instruments for health or salvation. The kissing of a reliquary containing the bones or clothing of a saint or a piece of the "true cross" was used both for the cure of disease and in order to secure God's punishment for perjury. The clergy, among whom must be reckoned a great number of the monks, as controllers and directors of this system of belief, were more and more separated from other Christians not possessing such powers. The further segregation of a clerical caste by enforced

314

celibacy had not yet been completed by the ninth century; and it never occurred at all in the eastern Churches. But even in the seventh and eighth centuries in western Europe, the clergy were generally felt to form a distinct class of society, having specially intimate connections with God and the Saints. This segregation of the clergy was promoted by the almost accidental continuance of a special form of language and a special fashion of dress. Instead of translating ritual formulas and the Sacred Scriptures into the new dialects of the barbarian kingdoms, as they had been translated in earlier times from Greek into Latin, the Latin language was preserved as the sacred language of the Churches. This naturally supported the tendency to regard the clergy, who used Latin, as a separate caste. Again, what was later known as clerical costume, both in the streets and at the ceremonies of the Church, first began clearly to separate the clergy from the laity in the eighth century. As it has been noted in an earlier chapter, the Christian clergy of the fifth and sixth centuries, even in ritual ceremonies, used the ordinary fashions of dress in the Roman Empire. These fashions were continued when the establishment of the barbarian kingdoms led to the increasing use of such non-Roman garments as the short cloak and trousers. But they were at first the fashions of the upper classes among the Romanized population; and in the seventh century they had become the distinguishing marks of the "Roman" as contrasted with the barbarian. By the eighth century "sacred vestments" had begun to be used; that is to say, the old Roman fashions of the sixth century were preserved by the clergy for ritual or liturgical uses. The Roman white shirt (*tunica alba*) became the "alb"; the sixth-century cloak (*casula*) became the "chasuble," and the overcoat (*cappa*) became the "cope"; the scarf (*stola*) became a "stole"; and the handkerchief carried on the arm (*mappula*) became the "maniple." The priest in a religious ceremony was thus thoroughly separated from the vulgar throng; and writers in the Middle Ages invented the most fantastic significance for vestments which were merely the survival of obsolete fashions.

At the end of the eighth century collections of sacred vestments for Mass and other ceremonies were made in the greater churches of the cities and abbeys. Two interesting lists of such vestments, of many colours and materials, are to be found in the history of the abbey of St. Wandrille, which will be referred to in a later chapter. The delight in the simpler forms of drama in the early Middle Ages, which produced eventually the miracle-plays and mystery-plays, is to be observed in the processions and the elaborate cere-monies which gave the clergy opportunities for the use of vestments. And this tended more and more to separate the Christian com-munity within the walls of its church into a select body of clergy, later concealed behind a screen, and the laity who were excluded from the election or control of those who had Holy Orders or even the tonsure. The external signs of a sacred caste supported the exceptional position of the clergy in law, in what later became "benefit of clergy"; and medievalism thus injected the traditions of barbarism into Christendom.

Another great change which had occurred between the fifth and the ninth century was the separation within the clerical caste of the higher ranks from the lower. The Orders of the medieval Church were even more exactly divided than those of the old Roman "honours" in the *cursus honorum* through which a Roman gentleman used to increase his social status. And the sharpest dis-tinction of all was made between the bishops, who had complete control of the doctrine and discipline of Christendom, and the lower clergy. Costume assisted to express the distinction. The mitre and the pastoral staff were the signs of ecclesiastical power; and although the mitre was used in some instances by the abbots of the greater monasteries, it remained the symbol of control over ecclesiastical policy by the bishops.

CHAPTER VIII

LAWS AND CANONS

The concentrations of social power which were gradually established in western Europe from the fifth to the eighth century are expressed in the laws of those times. Two systems of law were developed. On the one hand the Civil Law, beginning with the single system of Roman Law, which covered the whole Roman Empire, ended with the development of the barbarian laws of the new kingdoms. On the other hand, synods or councils of bishops agreed upon canons or ecclesiastical laws, which began as local or regional regulations and were gradually assimilated so as to form one body of "canon law" for the whole Western Church.[1] In the histories of these two kinds of law, therefore, may be traced the beginnings of the medieval systems of jurisdiction. In civil government the "State" at the beginning of the fifth century was a single system covering the whole European world; but by the end of the seventh century civil government had been divided and localized, so that many separate "States," each with its own laws and customs, had been established.[2]

The history of ecclesiastical regulations in the West follows a contrary course. The canons of the Churches in the different districts were at first the results of local legislation by the bishops for meeting local difficulties, although from the earliest times one synod might adopt the statements of doctrine and custom already adopted by other synods. The canons of the General Councils of the fourth, fifth and sixth centuries were all eastern in origin; and

[1] The phrase "canon law" is presumably a translation of *"ius canonicum"* or "justice in the canons." "Canon law" would otherwise mean "law law" or "rule law," which is absurd.

[2] The use of the word "State," in its modern meaning, is somewhat misleading, if applied without qualification to the Roman *Respublica* or the medieval *Regnum*.

did not at first displace the canons of local or regional synods in the West. As time went on, however, the centralization of authority in the West under the bishop of Rome caused collections of canons to be made, which were regarded as binding upon all the Churches.

Another difference between the two kinds of law, civil and ecclesiastical, lay in the methods by which the law was established. At the beginning of the fifth century Roman Law was regarded as the expression of the will of the Emperor. He might refer to men learned in the traditional customs or to councillors who were able to give skilled advice. But new laws proceded, in fact, from the Emperor alone. This is the essence of military dictatorship. This is the source of that principle which has had such disastrous consequences—"Whatever the Prince wills has the force of law," usually quoted without the reason given in Roman Law, namely, that "the people gave the power to the Prince."[1] Law is thus conceived as the expression of an arbitrary, if also benevolent personal will. One effect of this conception of law is to be seen in the theory of the "divine" law, which dominated the Middle Ages, and even in the theory of "natural" law, as an expression of "will" or purpose, which was accepted by deists, such as Newton, in the seventeenth century. The conception of law as the basis of the moral life and of the "order of nature" clearly did not originate in the Roman Law. But Roman Law in the fifth century, especially as expressed in the Theodosian law-books, confirmed and made much more definite the conception of a celestial law-giver whose personal will was the source and only basis of the "commands" followed by good men and by the heavenly bodies. Thus the real dictator of an Empire whose inhabitants believed that it covered the whole habitable world, became the model for an ideal dictator in the skies. But the strange effects of the Roman Empire upon the conception of the universe will be discussed elsewhere.

In the Roman Law of the fifth century the Emperor was also regarded as the supreme judge. The final appeal in all cases was made to him; and his providence and clemency were assumed to

[1] In Justinian's *Institutes* (i, 2, 6), quod principi placuit, legis habet vigorem, cum . . . populus ei . . . potestatem concessit. And a similar reason in Gaius, *Instit.*, i, 5, cum ipse imperator per legem imperium accipiat.

extend to the least of his subjects. The kings of the barbarian king-doms which eventually took the place of the Roman Empire in the West, inherited from the Roman Law as well as from barbarian custom the conception of the king as the supreme judge. The king's Court of Law, therefore, became the ultimate Court of Appeal in the new kingdoms. And in the heavens also the law-giver became also the final judge. The climate of opinion favoured dictatorship as the only possible form of authority.

The decrees of the Emperor as lawgiver in the fifth century had a further effect in the eighth and ninth centuries, when the kings of the Franks issued their Capitularies. The barbarian tradition in most of the new kingdoms implied that the king collected and stated the law, drawn from traditional custom; and for evidence of this custom the king would normally depend upon the advice of his council. But for some years at the end of the eighth and begin-ning of the ninth centuries the Frankish monarchs issued decrees in the manner of the Roman Emperor. These decrees were, in fact, entirely different in character from the decrees of an Emperor; but they serve as an example of the way in which each of the early rulers of the Frankish kingdom attempted to play the part of an Augustus. They never understood the part they played; but they really believed that the will of the king made law.

Civil law in the same period, however, also included statements of custom among the different barbarian tribes, such as the laws of the Visigoths, the Salic Law, the Law of the Alamanni and of the Lombards, and the earlier Anglo-Saxon Laws. All these laws were definitely intended to refer only to persons of a particular race, living in a particular locality. They were local and tribal; and most of them did not survive the change in the social situation when the barbarians, for whom they were intended, became more civilized. But they stand in one class with the great body of Roman Law as expressions of the concentration of power and moral authority in what is now called the State.

From the fifth to the ninth century, however, in every country of western Europe, except England, Roman Law and the barbarian laws were the laws not of territories but of races. That is to say, in any one barbarian kingdom the earlier inhabitants would be judged in accordance with Roman Laws; and their barbarian conquerors, settled among them, would be judged in accordance with the laws of their own tribe. Thus, for some centuries after the disappearance of the Roman Empire in western Europe, two forms of social regulation existed in the same area; and in cities in which men of different races and tribes were living, several distinct systems of law might be applied. The conception that a person should be judged in accordance with the legal rules to which men of his language or race were accustomed, survived into modern times in the capitulations in Turkey and Egypt and in the extra-territorial rights of Europeans in China. Jurisdiction based upon race and not upon neighbourhood obviously weakens the power of a Government. But from the fifth to the ninth century in western Europe no other practice was possible. The barbarian kingdoms were not genuinely national. They were merely armed bands in control of alien populations; and therefore the conquerors, who were primitive warriors, kept their own primitive legal customs and were compelled to permit the more civilized population over whom they ruled to use their own more highly developed legal system. The barbarian laws did not contain adequate rules for application to the more complex disputes of a population accustomed to trade, property rights and rules of inheritance. It was necessary, therefore, for the two systems, Roman and barbarian, to amalgamate, or for one of them to disappear, before civil jurisdiction could be based upon neighbourhood or territory, as it is now.

In the formation of the new barbarian kingdoms the king might find under his authority not only persons accustomed to Roman Law but members of other barbarian tribes besides his own. And as one barbarian king extended his dominion over areas hitherto ruled by others, the number of personal laws in any city or district might increase. Thus Pippin, the Frankish leader, when he drove out the Mohammedans from Narbonne in A.D. 759, allowed the Visigoths of that area to continue living according to their own law.[1] And in the capitulary dealing with Aquitaine it is decreed

---

[1] *Chron. Moiss.*

that persons of that district shall live, each under his own law. Indeed, the process of dividing up communities according to race or tradition did not cease even when the Empire of Charles the Great was established. One of the effects of the new claims made by Charles the Great after A.D. 810 was that Roman Law ceased to be territorial anywhere. And it was many centuries before Roman Law came to be recognized as "Kaiserrecht."[1] Throughout these centuries the Church "lived Roman Law;" that is to say, this law covered not only the clergy, but also their dependants, at least in the areas where it had been the law of the majority of the population.[2]

The inconvenience, and indeed absurdity, of maintaining separate laws for neighbours in the same community, who belonged to different races, was recognized generally. But the clearest expression of the difficulty is in the words of Agobard, bishop of Lyons, where he says that five men might meet in a room, each of whom would be judged by a different law.[3] Agobard wrote as follows to the Emperor Louis the Pious: "If the Lord has suffered that we should be made one in Christ . . . I ask you if the unity of such a divine act is not obstructed by so great a diversity of laws, not only in single districts or cities, but even in many houses. For it often happens that five men come and sit together and not one of them has a law in common with the other in external and transitory things, although they are bound by the one law in Christ within them in eternal things. And although perhaps it happens that all are truly Christians, loving the truth of faith and trusting each other as brethren, and none of them despises the other's word when they are in good conversation—nevertheless, if it should suddenly happen that one of them has a dispute in the courts, none can have as witness any of his dearest friends with whom he keeps company, because the testimony of anyone is not acceptable under the law of Gundobad—and so on." Thus even in the ninth century

---

[1] Pollock and Maitland, *History of English Law*, p. 14.
[2] It seems probable that a cleric could claim to be judged as an individual, according to the law of his "nation" or race; but as a holder of Church property, he would be judged, as "the Church" lived, according to Roman Law.
[3] Agobard, *M.P.L.*, 104, col. 116. *Adversus Legem Gundobadi*, c. iv.

L

"personal" law survived within the Frankish dominions and was felt to be obstructive to the processes of justice.

On the other hand, the canons of the synods of bishops, in the different provinces of the kingdoms, derived their authority from the ecclesiastical power of the bishops, who remained, in theory at least, elected representatives of the whole body of Christians in the Churches. Thus the canons of the Church in the earlier years of Christianity were more nearly "democratic," in the modern sense of the word, than the civil law. Again, the canons were originally concerned with regulating the life of a voluntary association of those who professed Christianity in a world in which great numbers were still not Christian. The canons of any synod or council covered two subjects: first, the doctrines which should be professed by all members of the Church; and secondly, the rules of morality or custom which should govern all Christians and, in particular, the clergy. In both cases the canons were derived from the tradition of the Church, which was to be found by the bishops either in written texts of the Bible and the early Fathers or in the acknowledged practice of the Church in an earlier age. Thus the canons were neither decrees of a single dictator, nor were they, like the barbarian laws, merely statements of primitive custom. The earliest canons belong, indeed, to a time when the Christians in any one locality were still to be distinguished from a large surrounding population of non-Christians. They were, therefore, rules of belief and custom for a small, select community whose officials were of minor importance. But as the number of Christians increased, the canons of the Church obviously had to include reference to a much larger number of persons, much less strict in their understanding of what the profession of Christianity involved; and at the same time the officials of this larger community attained a greater importance. Thus the canons of the different Churches began to deal in greater detail with the rules for the clergy and to say less about the laity. As the Church became more and more identified with its officials, the clergy, so the canons came more and more to be regarded as principally regulations for the clergy.

Roman Law

This is not the place to discuss Roman Law in general; but some of its characteristics should be noted, which are of importance both in contrast with the characteristics of the barbarian laws and because of its effect in the Middle Ages. Roman Law in general, including both principles and regulations more extensive than those of the Theodosian law-books, covered most of the relations of a complex civilized society. In public law and in private law the Roman system implied an elaborate organization of government, trade and commerce, manufacture and production. Therefore jurisdiction under the Roman Law affected such social relations as those of marriage, inheritance, property, contract, personal dependence, either of slaves or workers or tenants, commerce and civil rights. But a system including all this could not fail to appear to belong to an entirely different world from that of the simple barbarian laws of compensation for personal injury or theft. The Roman Law, even when imperfectly recorded and hardly remembered, seemed to have that universality and eternity which the men of the early Middle Ages believed to be divine.

Again, Roman Law taken as a whole was an organized system of social customs, thought out through many generations and connected, in the work of the great jurists, with general principles. There is nothing comparable to this either in the barbarian laws or the capitularies of Frankish kings, or even in the collections of canons of the Church. Further, Roman Law assumes what would now be called territorial jurisdiction, that is to say, it applies to all the subjects of a single system of government; and although in the fourth and fifth centuries certain privileges were given, for example, to the clergy, the law is never conceived as having reference only to persons of a particular race, language or religion. After the establishment of the barbarian kingdoms in western Europe in the fifth century, Roman Law did indeed become the law of a distinct and separate section of the king's subjects. By its side in the same kingdom existed other laws applicable to persons of the invading barbarian races. The "Romans" to whom the Roman Law still applied, were members of the more civilized communities over which the barbarians ruled. But to reduce the range of Roman Law in this manner was to disregard the assumption on which the law itself was based.

Less important than these characteristics, but significant in the development of the First Europe, was the fact that the Latin of the Roman Law was the common language of the majority of the inhabitants in all the barbarian kingdoms of the West except those of England. The institutions, therefore, of the new barbarian kingdoms in Gaul, Spain, Italy and western Germany, grew up within communities which used some form of Latin in their daily intercourse, their commerce and their religious practices; and this explains the fact that the barbarian laws in western Europe were first written down in Latin. In England, on the other hand, the social institutions of the Anglo-Saxons developed for about a century before the influence of the Latin Churches began to be felt there. The earliest English laws, therefore, were written down in different forms of English. This fact alone would have made it possible for the law of England, arising out of tribal or local customs, to develop freely, without being encumbered by the Latin either of the canons of the Church or of the records of the barbarian laws in western Europe.

Finally, the Roman Law, especially after it had ceased to develop, appeared to the clergy and the rulers of the sixth, seventh and eighth centuries as something fixed and immutable, like the so-called "law" of the heavens, which was supposed to govern the stars. There was no historical knowledge at that time or even in the eleventh century, when the Roman Law was rediscovered, which would show that Roman, like any other law, was the product of particular times and places and social circumstances. The principles of Roman Law had, indeed, a more extensive application than those of any other system then known; but these principles were themselves derived from the experience of a particular community based upon slavery and extended by military conquest. The principles of Roman Law were not universally applicable, as the "whole world" (orbis) of the Roman Empire and of the Middle Ages was not in fact a world which included the Indians or the

Chinese. What was "catholic" or universal in the minds of St. Augustine, Gregory the Great and Charles the Great, was only a local system of beliefs and practices, which had grown up in the countries round the Mediterranean. But by contrast with the simpler and still more restricted local customs of the different Germanic tribes, the Roman Law appeared to be universal and eternal. Hence the illusion which has cursed the thinking of the Middle Ages and even of later times—the illusion of a single and unchanging law applicable to all peoples in all times and at all places. Just as the city of Rome was believed to be eternal in the fifth century, and even when it was destroyed continued to be eternal as a ghost in men's minds, so the Roman Law, when it was dead, continued to haunt the minds of scholars as if it contained the fundamental principles governing all human intercourse. The same illusion, that there is an eternal "divine" law, affected the understanding of the "Mosaic" Decalogue, which was a product of local difficulties in a Semitic tribal society. And about the end of the fourth century a document was produced—the *Collatio Legum Mosaicarum et Romanarum*—which attempts to show that the same principles are involved in the Decalogue, on the one hand, and on the other, in the opinions of Roman jurists and the rescripts of Roman Emperors. The historian, however, cannot admit that there is any law whose character is not determined by the social system in which it arose.

The Codex Theodosianus

The Roman Law which dominated western Europe in the fifth century is best represented to-day by the book of laws officially accepted and placed upon "the sacred shelves" in the imperial offices at Ravenna and Constantinople in February A.D. 438. This book of laws, the *Codex Theodosianus*, is in no sense a code. It is a compilation of extracts from the letters and decrees of Emperors from the days of Constantine to the year before that in which it was issued under Theodosius II. The compilation was begun in A.D. 425 and ended in A.D. 437. The oldest decree included belongs to the year A.D. 312 or A.D. 313. The latest decree issued in the

West is of the year A.D. 432; and among those issued in the East the latest is of the year A.D. 437. This compilation or book of laws remained the chief basis for imperial jurisdiction in the East until A.D. 529, under Justinian. But from that date Justinian's law-books, the *Codex*, *Digest* and *Institutes*, displaced the Theodosian law-books in the Roman Empire, which did not then include Britain, Gaul, Spain or the greater part of Italy. So great has been the later influence of the work done under Justinian, that the law-books of Theodosius have been completely eclipsed, in commentaries on Roman Law, by the later work; but until the eleventh century, when Justinian's law-books were introduced by scholars into the West, the influence of Roman Law outside the frontiers of the Byzantine Empire depended mainly upon the use made of the law-books of Theodosius. In this chapter, therefore, which is concerned only with the development of law in western Europe between the fifth and the ninth century, Roman Law is taken as best represented in the *Codex Theodosianus*.

The collection of laws made by the commission under Theodosius was intended to supplement earlier collections already in use. All such collections of imperial letters and decrees were kept in the chief administrative offices of the Empire and were used by lawyers and teachers in the schools of law. But the two chief collections of laws before that of Theodosius appear to have been made by scholars without governmental authority. The first was the Gregorianus of A.D. 295, and the second, the Hermogenianus of A.D. 314. Thus the Government under Theodosius II had only to collect documents issued under Constantine and after. These the Commissioners probably found in collections already used in the East in the Law School at Beyruth and in a western collection probably made at Carthage. All such collections, however, and the more inclusive Theodosian law-books themselves naturally contained only decisions and decrees of general importance. The normal function of the subordinate Roman law-courts must have been to apply a sort of Common Law much more extensive and detailed than anything to be found in the Emperor's edicts. It has been said that there was a "low" law, like "low" Latin—that is to say, vulgar and customary, not dependent upon texts. The evidence for this is in the land-books and in the few documents which now survive, affecting the ownership or transfer of land.[1]

The Theodosian law-books also imply the use in courts and schools of law of the opinion of Roman jurists and a generally accepted Roman view of the nature of law. Justinian's later collection of documents, indeed, included not only the *Codex*, which in the main is only a rearrangement of the Theodosian, but also the *Digest* containing extracts from the jurists and the *Institutes* or introduction to law. Both the *Digest* and the *Institutes* may be assumed to represent what was already in the minds of lawyers and administrators in the early fifth century. But whereas the Theodosian law-books, at the time they were issued, reflected an actual situation in the Empire in the West as well as in the East, Justinian's collections were out-of-date, in reference to the western world, before they were made. The Justinian law-books were, therefore, merely instances of what has been called "archaism"; and it has been remarked that Justinian himself, when he found it necessary to issue edicts, expressed them in Greek. The Theodosian law-books, on the other hand, used the Latin still dominant in official circles in the fifth century; and they provided the basis of the Roman Law which survived in the new kingdoms of western Europe from the fifth to the ninth centuries. Thus, Latin remained the actual language of law in western Europe, when Greek took its place in the so-called Roman Empire soon after the fourth century. Apart altogether, therefore, from the influence of the Latin used by the western Churches, the Governments in the new western kingdoms found it necessary, in law and administration, to use the different forms of Latin from which French, Italian and Spanish are derived. This is an indication of the different climate of opinion which divided the First Europe from the Greek-speaking population of the eastern Mediterranean, apart altogether from ecclesiastical or doctrinal disputes.

The Theodosian law-books remain the best evidence for the

---

[1] Brunner, *Rechtsgeschichte des römischen Reichs*, i, 187, referred to in Pollock and Maitland, *History of English Law*.

principles governing the Roman Empire in its last days in the West. The law-books are divided into sixteen sections, of which the first deals with the organization of the legal system of the Empire and the sixteenth (*de fide Catholica*) deals with Christian doctrine, the rights and duties of clergy and monks and the imperial opposition to pagans and heretics. It is worth noting, as a sign of the change in the relations of the Church and the Empire, that in Justinian's law-books, issued about a century later, the sixteenth section of the Theodosian law-books becomes the first section of Justinian's (*de summa Trinitate et de fide Catholica*).

The first book of the Theodosian collection deals with such matters as the validity of imperial decrees, only those dated being valid.[1] Ignorance of the law is not allowed as an excuse (i, 1, 2); a plaintiff may take his suit to the "Christian law" (i, 27, 1); and episcopal jurisdiction is valid for all (i, 27, 2). The fifth section deals with the very important problem of fugitive farmers, tenants and slaves. The imperial Authorities evidently found it difficult to control the desertion of agricultural estates by the cultivators; and the number of provisions against such fugitives is a proof that none of them was effectual. In the ninth section there are decrees which indicate the beginnings of later medieval practices. The Emperor forbids burials at the tombs of Apostles and martyrs, and commands that burials take place outside the city. This is a provision of A.D. 381.[2] Another rescript of A.D. 386 commands that "no one shall transfer a buried body to another place; . . . no one shall divide a martyr's bones and no one trade in them."[3] Then comes the section dealing with the right of sanctuary in churches. Regulations in the fifteenth section concern the water-supply—there must be no stealing for gardens; and other decrees concern actors and public performances. The sixteenth section first defines the Catholic faith, and then regulates the relations of the clergy to public duties and to their bishops. Of monks it is said that they must go into the deserts and not dwell in cities. And the imperial

---

[1] *Cod. Theod.*, i, 1, *a*, a rescript of Constantine, A.D. 322.   [2] Ibid., ix, 17, 6.
[3] Ibid., ix, 17, 7. Humatum corpus nemo ad alterum locum transferat: nemo martyrem distrahat: nemo mercetur.

decrees then deal with heretics, pagans, pagan sacrifices and temples. A decree of A.D. 423 refers to the "pagans who remain, although we believe that now there are none."[1]

For the purpose of the argument here it is enough to note that the Roman Empire in the Theodosian law-books is completely Christian and Catholic. The decrees suppress paganism and heresy and support the Christian bishops. They indicate a highly centralized system of government, in which public policy depends entirely upon the will of a dictator. The dictator-Emperor takes action and issues instructions to his officials directly, in all parts of his Empire; but his decrees and letters of instruction are based upon the long tradition of Roman Law and Roman administration.

When barbarian kings took control of the different parts of the Empire in the West, the great majority of the population continued to use Roman Law. The barbarian warriors settled within the old frontiers of the Empire were either military forces in control or, in theory, allies of the Emperor. In either case they had always been allowed by the imperial Authorities to live under their own customs and laws. Similarly the barbarian kings supported the use of Roman Law among their "Roman" subjects. Law courts and legal officials of the Roman tradition, therefore, continued to operate in Italy, Gaul and Spain, during the fifth, sixth and seventh centuries; and for the use of the "Roman" population summaries of the imperial law-books were made.

For the Gothic kingdom in Italy under Theodoric the so-called *Edict of Theodoric* was issued about A.D. 500. In that year the king spent six months in Rome; and it seems likely that the edict was prepared at that time. It is a collection of administrative orders or regulations applied both to "barbarians" and "Romans"; and throughout the document the Gothic followers of Theodoric are referred to as "barbarians." The sections are drawn directly from the "Opinions" of the jurist Paulus or from the Theodosian law-books. They begin with regulations about judges, and include regulations about inheritance, the making of wills, and property. The population of Italy is, therefore, treated as a more highly

[1] *Cod. Theod.*, xvi, 10, 22.

civilized community than is implied in the barbarian laws which will be discussed later.

A more important collection of Roman Laws for use in a barbarian kingdom is the *Roman Law of the Visigoths*, which is known as the *Breviarium Alarici*, issued in A.D. 506.[1] This is a summary and rearrangement of certain parts of the Theodosian law-books, together with sections on jurisprudence drawn from the works of Roman lawyers. The *Breviary* was intended for the use of the Roman subjects of the king of the Goths in southern Gaul and Spain; and it became the chief source of the influence of Roman Law in the West from the sixth to the eleventh century, because, as it has been already noted, during the early Middle Ages Justinian's law-books were not used.

Another summary of Roman Law for use in a barbarian kingdom is that known as the *Roman Law of the Burgundians*.[2] This collection was apparently issued about A.D. 503, that is to say, about forty years after the Burgundians had settled in Savoy. It applies only to "Romans" but makes continual reference to their relations with Burgundians. The laws collected are drawn, as in the case of the *Edict of Theodoric*, either from the "Opinions" of Paulus or from the Theodosian law-books. They refer to a settled and civilized agricultural community; for example, public paths are not to be ploughed up, and two years undisturbed use gives the right of property over water or tracks (Tit. xxi); and for light and air there must be ten feet between private dwellings and fifteen feet between public. In one section the Roman Law of divorce by the consent of both parties is recognized, as in the new laws of Theodosius II (*Novellae*, Tit. xii). It is worth noting that this Roman Law is not adopted in the Visigothic *Breviary* of Alaric, perhaps because of ecclesiastical influence. On the other hand, divorce was allowed by one of the new laws of Justinian, issued in A.D. 546, which declares that either a husband or wife has the right to dissolve marriage without the consent of the other party, if he or she desires to enter

[1] The text is in *M.G.H.*, *Leges*, tom. v. The preamble says that the following laws are those "quae barbari Romanique sequi debent."

[2] Text in *M.G.H.*, *Leges*, section i, tom. ii, part i (1882).

the monastic life.[1] Evidently the conception of marriage in the sixth century was being affected by both the Roman tradition of free choice and the Semitic or ecclesiastical conception of an indissoluble bond.

In general, therefore, Roman Law in principle and practice continued to supply the needs of the more civilized majority in the new barbarian kingdoms in the West in the fifth and sixth centuries. The subjects of the kings differed, not only in race and language, but also in the state of development of their social life. This was recognized by the barbarians, who did not desire and perhaps felt unable to replace the Roman tradition of law and administration by anything of their own.

Barbarian Laws

While the Roman Law of the whole Empire was gradually adapted to the needs of the Roman population under different barbarian kingdoms in the West, the barbarians themselves were learning the value of formulating their own traditional customs. Thus, under the influence of a settled society, and largely through the assistance of the Catholic clergy, collections of barbarian laws began to be made in the middle of the fifth century. These collections include the laws of the Visigoths, the two Frankish collections (the Salic Law and the Ripuarian), the laws of the Alamanni, of the Bavarians and of the Lombards. All these laws are in Latin, although they contain some words from the Germanic dialects. But the fact that barbarian customs should be first written down in the language of the Church and the subject population, shows how completely the barbarian kingdoms were dependent for their organization, law and government upon the earlier Roman civilization. That was the situation in all the kingdoms established in Italy, Gaul and Spain. It is all the more striking that the earliest formulations of barbarian custom in England in the seventh century were written in English and not in Latin, although in these earliest English Laws there is a clear statement of the dependence of the

---

[1] *Nov. Justin. Const.* clx, in the Teubner ed., 1881, vol. ii, p. 322. This expression of Justinian's devotion to monasticism was never accepted in the West.

kings upon the bishops. The laws in early English, however, have the same kind of content and imply the same structure of society as the Latin barbarian laws of the Continent.

In general, all the barbarian laws from the fifth to the eighth century express the customs and habits of mind of a very simple agricultural society. All the laws are concerned either with personal violence or with stealing and destruction of property, chiefly cattle. As compared with the older Roman Law, it is noticeable that the barbarian laws are not concerned with the more complex social relations of society, such as contracts, trade, marriage and taxation. Again, all the barbarian laws in their earlier clauses are merely lists of fines or compositions for particular offences. The law runs—"If a man does such an act, he shall pay so much." It is not the command of a superior, nor a prohibition; but merely a rule for compensating the injured party, who, no doubt, at an earlier stage of civilization would have obtained satisfaction for himself. It implies the existence of some form of court or judge. The purpose of the law is to guide the court in the assessment of damages; and the details given in some of the barbarian laws are ridiculously minute; as, for example, in the Salic Law where twenty sections deal only with the theft of pigs. In the sections of the barbarian laws which have been added at later dates provision is made for procedure or payments owing to public Authorities.

The difficulty in discussing all the barbarian laws is that the earliest manuscripts which now exist belong to the ninth century; and therefore it cannot be taken as certain that any provision in any collection is of the date which the text assigns to it. The students or copyists who collected earlier versions of laws, or wrote down what they believed to be primitive customs, certainly did not distinguish between the language or conceptions of different centuries. Again, among the barbarian laws whose text has survived, those which are earliest in date are certainly not the most primitive. For example, the sixth century laws of the Visigoths reflect the situation among a people which had for many years been in close contact with the higher civilization of the Roman Empire, whereas the laws of the Alamanni, apparently collected in the ninth century, reflect the much more primitive customs of a tribe almost untouched by Roman influence. In the form of their laws, therefore, the barbarian tribes were more or less civilized in proportion as their contact with the Roman tradition was more or less close. It is true that certain practices, such as the ordeal, were contributed to the European tradition by the barbarians; but these are precisely the practices which were eventually discarded as Europe became more civilized. Indeed, as soon as the new nations of western Europe had attained to a social development which made Roman Law intelligible to them, because it was applicable to their experience, the barbarian laws were discarded. Only in England, because of peculiar circumstances there, has the development of the law had its roots in the barbarian laws of the Anglo-Saxons. Elsewhere, as Latin was the basis of the French, Italian and Spanish languages, so the Roman Law became the basis of "national" laws on the Continent. This, however, was a much later development, after the Middle Ages. The first step from the collection of customs, called barbarian laws, was towards local customary laws of small districts.

Laws of the Visigoths

The earliest collection of barbarian laws was made under the Visigothic king Euric (A.D. 461–485). As Isidore says, "Under this king the Goths first had their laws written down, for hitherto they were ruled only by manners and customs."[1] A fragment of this first collection has survived; but other collections were made under succeeding kings and eventually an amalgamation of Gothic and Roman laws was made in a book named the Book of Judgements (Liber Judiciorum). The influence of the bishops, especially in the councils of Toledo, has already been discussed. Even the earliest laws of the Visigoths were written in Latin and, therefore, probably under the influence of the clergy; and the later use of Roman Laws to supply the deficiencies of the Gothic tradition was certainly due to the work of the bishops.

The earliest fragments of Visigothic Law that remain are state-

[1] Isidore, Hist. Goth., xxxv.

to fugitives and the sale of slaves. With regard to sales in general
the law says, "a sale made by writing shall hold good. Retainers of
a private person must return their arms when they transfer their
service." Clearly, such laws are merely collections of disconnected
statements about simple problems in a primitive society. A century
after Euric, King Leovigild (A.D. 568–586) is said to have added to
Euric's collection and corrected some of his laws. But the great
collection of laws intended to apply to all the subjects of the king,
including both the Goths and the Romanized population and the
Jews, is contained in the *Book of Judgements* mentioned above.

This book is an important example of an attempt not only to
codify traditional laws, Roman and Gothic, but also to provide a
kind of legal philosophy or jurisprudence. The first sections, dealing
with legal instruments, contain such statements as that law is "for
no private advantage but for the common utility of all citizens,"
and that "law is the soul of the whole body of the people."[1] The
second section deals with the legislature and says that God ordained
that there should be a head of the State, that no one should abuse
or criticize him, and that judges are appointed by the king's
authority. The third section deals with marriage, including a decree
that harlots are to be flogged with three hundred lashes, and that
if they do not change their habits, they must be given to a poor
man to remain in his service and not to enter a city. The same
section decrees that a man guilty of homosexual practices shall be
castrated. This is a provision parallel to that of the sixteenth Council
of Toledo, concerning bishops who are guilty of homosexual
practices: but offending clergy are condemned only to degradation
and exile.[2] Later sections deal with such crimes as torture, theft
and fraud, with fugitives and with the right of sanctuary. There
are the usual compensations set down for injury to trees and animals.
A decree decides on the division of the children of serfs, and between

[1] *Lib. Jud.*, i, 2, 3, "omnium civium utilitate communi. . . . Lex est anima totius
corporis popularis."
[2] *Mansi*, xii, col. 59 (Concil. Tolet., xvi, A.D. 693), qui . . . contra naturam
masculi in masculo hanc turpitudinem operaverint si quidem episcopus, presbyter
aut diaconus fuerit de proprii honoris gradu dejectus perpetui exilii manebit damna-
tione perculsus.

mother and father when separated by sales. The eleventh section deals with doctors, who are forbidden to bleed a free woman except in the presence of her father, brother, son or uncle. If a doctor cures cataract, he is to have five solidi. If he kills or weakens a person by bleeding, the doctor is to pay. The twelfth section contains decrees against oppression of the people by officials and the general decrees of King Ewrig (A.D. 683) confirming the canons of the thirteenth Council of Toledo against the Jews.

Laws of the Franks

The laws of the Franks include those of the Salian (Salic Law) and the Ripuarian tribes, which in their present form, in manuscripts of the eighth or ninth centuries, probably belong to the later years of the sixth century. These laws are much more primitive than the Visigothic. The Salic Law consists almost entirely of a list of payments in money for offences such as violence and theft; but it also includes a few regulations about the marriage of widows, debt, the robbing of tombs and the transfer of property. The simplicity of the law can be seen not only in the payments made for stealing pigs and bees or running away with women and girls, but also in the law which assigns the penalty of six hundred denarii or fifteen solidi if a free man squeezes the finger of a free woman, and double the amount if he squeezes her arm.[1] The mind of the time is also revealed in the sections which deal with putting witchcraft on a man or giving women drink to make them sterile.[2] Special provisions decree payments to be made if a Roman, attached to the king or possessing land, is killed. The famous section of the Salic Law which decrees that no Salic land shall be inherited by a woman is merely one unimportant section under the regulations dealing with inheritance of the property of free men.[3] Some provisions of the Salic Law include formulas for the statement of claims and a reference to the "Rachimburgi," about whom scholars have entered into lengthy discussions. But as a whole, the Salic Law is merely a collection of statements of penalties in the form

---

[1] *Lex Salica*, xxii.   [2] Ibid., xxi, 3, 4.   [3] Ibid., lxii, 6.

335

of payment for the more violent crimes of a simple society. Obviously, although the clergy must have collected and written in Latin this statement of traditional Frankish customs, they could never be applicable to the more elaborate relationships of the "Roman" populations under the kings of the Franks.

The law of the Ripuarian Franks, in its present form, is supposed to be a summary of customs among the Frankish tribes which were induced to acknowledge Clovis as their king in A.D. 510. The newly converted Christian and Catholic, Clovis, king of the Salian Franks, arranged for the assassination of Sigebert, king of the Ripuarians, and the removal of his son; and he was then raised on the shield and accepted as king.[1] But the Franks, called Ripuarian, because they lived higher up on the banks of the Rhine than the others, retained their own legal customs. The prologue to the laws says that Dagobert finally improved the laws by the advice of four councillors. The laws themselves contained the usual list of payments in money (solidi) for death, mutilation, theft and other such crimes of a simple society. The payments, as usual in the barbarian laws, indicate the different ranks, races or classes in society. To kill a sub-deacon costs four hundred solidi and to kill a bishop, nine hundred: to kill a Burgundian, a hundred and sixty solidi; a Roman, a hundred; and one of the Alamanni or Bavarians or Saxons, one hundred and sixty solidi. The "wergeld" in money can be commuted by giving a cow or bull, a mare, or a helmet or a lance and shield; and twelve denarii are to count as equal to one solidus. Evidently the intention is to make payment easier, either because of the lack of currency, or, more probably, because of the variation in value of the commodities.[2] A later section deals with the granting of liberty to serfs or slaves, which is to take place in churches; and the bishop is to order the archdeacon to inscribe the enfranchised person on a list "according to the Roman Law

[1] Greg. Tur., *H.F.*, ii, 40. *Pat. Lat.*, 71, col. 238. After giving this account, Gregory says that "God increased the kingdom of Clovis, because he did what was pleasing in God's eyes."

[2] *Lex Rip.*, Tit. xxxviii, art. 12. "Si quis weregeldum solvere debet bovem cornutum ... pro duobus solidis tribuat. Vaccam pro uno solido tribuat. ... Helmum cum directo pro sex solidis tribuat. ... Scutum cum lancea pro duobus solidis tribuat ... etc.

under which the Church lives."[1] The final section forbids judges or tax-officers to take the fee (*freda*) before payment has been made for the crime.

Laws of the Burgundians

The laws of the Burgundians are said to have been collected under King Gundobad, in A.D. 516. This collection contains the usual preface as well as the signs for the signatures of about thirty counts. The laws are somewhat more highly developed than those of the Franks and make provision for other punishments besides payments in money for crimes. The Burgundian laws refer definitely to a community divided into Burgundians and Romans; for they provide that a Roman, having a case against another Roman, shall not take a Burgundian as his assistant in defence.[2] The Burgundian laws allow the ordeal by battle which is discussed later in this chapter.

Another important collection of laws is that of the Alamanni, which is said to have been prepared under the king of the Franks, Clothar I (A.D. 537–563), but probably belongs to the second half of the eighth century. These laws, as well as the laws of the Bavarians (Lex Baiuvariorum), of about the same date, include reference to the ordeal by battle. The remaining laws of the barbarian tribes are of the same character. They include the so-called *Pactus Alamannorum* and the laws of the Frisians, of the Saxons and of the Angles and Werins.

Laws of the Lombards

The latest of the collections of barbarian laws is that of the Lombards.[3] These laws were written down in the Lombard kingdom of Italy; they begin with an edict of King Rotharic of A.D. 643, and are continued by new edicts of different dates until A.D. 755. The edict of Rotharic contains three hundred and eighty-eight sections (*capita*), the majority of which deal with compensation

---

[1] *Lex Rip.*, Tit. lx, art. 1. "Secundum legem Romanam qua ecclesia vivit."
[2] *Lex Burg.*, xxii and lv.
[3] Besides the text in *M.G.H.* there is a smaller edition in *Fontes Juris Germanici*, ed. Bluhme (1869).

for theft or personal violence. But there are some regulations as to the rule for gifts.[1] Under the laws of Grimwald (A.D. 668) thirty years' possession is decreed to bestow freehold. Under the laws of Liutprand, who is styled Christian and Catholic, leave is given for ordeal by battle on the ground that it was an ancient custom of the Lombards and, therefore, "we cannot forbid it." But the statement is made that "we are uncertain of the judgement of God and we have heard that many have unjustly lost their case through the ordeal by battle."[2] This shows clearly that the king of the Lombards or his advisers saw the absurdity of the ordeal as a test of justice.

Later sections of the laws (dated about A.D. 738), under Liutprand, contain interesting statements of actual cases in law used as a basis for decisions on principle. For example: "It is reported that a man found a woman bathing and ran off with her clothes. She could not remain in the water for ever and blushed to go home naked."[3] On this case the decision is made that she shall be paid her "wergeld" on the ground that, if her brother had found the thief, he would have been killed; and it is better that a feud should not grow out of the matter. Another case is that of a man who hired a mare, whose foal followed her. The foal kicked a child and killed it. The decision was that a fine should be paid by the man in charge of the mare.[4] These cases indicate the simplicity of the society ruled by the Lombard kings.

Judicial Procedure

Two interesting practices were introduced by the barbarians into the tradition of Latin Christendom—the taking of oaths and the ordeal by battle, water or iron, as a means of obtaining a decision from God in a doubtful case. The oath and the ordeal are closely connected, both in the history of their development and in the logical principle upon which their use depended. The ordeal by battle is actually stated, for example, in the laws of the Burgundians to be allowed because the use of the oath could not provide satis-

---

[1] Cap. 172. De thinx quod est donatio. Si quis res suas alii thingare voluerit.
[2] *Leges Liutprandi* (A.D. 731), 118, ii . . . propter consuetudinem gentis nostrae Langobardorum, legem ipsam vetare non possumus . . . incerti sumus de iudicio Dei.   [3] Ibid., 135, vi.   [4] Ibid., 137, viii.

factory evidence of guilt. In judicial procedure, both the ordeal and the oath are methods of appeal to divine judgement when human judges are unable to decide whether or not a lie has been told. The use of such methods indicates the close connection which was believed, in the Middle Ages, to exist between divine and human authority in the art of government. In primitive communities the spear, or the object upon which the oath is taken, is believed itself to have the power to injure the swearer if he lies; but by the sixth century in western Europe the result of perjury was believed to be injury or death caused by God or one of the saints on whose relics the oath had been sworn. Abundant evidence of this belief is to be found in the writings of Gregory of Tours. For example, a man accused of setting fire to his neighbour's house "raised both his hands and said, 'By almighty God and the power of St. Martin, his bishop, I did not cause the fire.' After the oath he seemed to be surrounded by fire and, immediately falling to the earth, he cried that he was being terribly burnt by the blessed bishop."[1] Again, "A certain man swore a false oath in a church and straight-way his tongue stiffened, and he was so dumb that he seemed to speak, not with human voice, but with the bleat of a sheep."[2] "A girl chose an article in the market, and took it from the seller. She then denied that she had received it, went to the tomb of St. Eugenius and, raising her hands to swear, they were immediately paralysed, her feet were fixed to the ground, her voice stuck in her throat, and not a word could come from her open mouth. The merchant then said, 'Much good may what you took from me do to you: the punishment inflicted by the martyr is enough for me.' "[3]

The fear of evil consequences following a lie told after an appeal to God or a saint, evidently did not restrain those who had com-mitted crimes. But the oath in all cases even in judicial procedure was not originally used as a test of truthfulness in a witness. It was used by the defendant when there is no certain evidence (*si probatio certa non fuit*).[4] In such a case the defendant had to find a certain

---

[1] Greg. Tur., *H.F.*, viii, 16. [2] Ibid., *Gloria Conf.*, 29. [3] Ibid., *Gloria Mart.*, 58,
[4] *Lex Salica*, xxxix, 2. A later section of the law. See Diamond, *Primitive Law*.
p. 374.

number of others to swear with him, who are called oath-helpers. Thus the oath was a means of calling to the assistance of the defendant certain persons whose presence might influence the decision. But the practice of calling great numbers of oath-helpers who did not pretend to be witnesses, and were simply asserting that they were friends of the defendant, naturally weakened the value of the system. An offender could escape penalties, if he had sufficient influence to secure support in his neighbourhood. In these circumstances the plaintiff, under the later barbarian laws which preserved a more primitive custom, could challenge the defendant to the ordeal by battle. The reason is given in the laws of the Burgundians in a section (Tit. 45) which is dated "under the consulate of Abienus," that is to say A.D. 502.[1] This section says "We recognize that many swear oaths about what is uncertain and do not hesitate to perjure themselves in matters in which they have full knowledge. We therefore decree that if the plaintiff does not wish to accept the witness against him and desires to refute his adversary in the risk of battle . . . then one of the witnesses offering to swear shall fight, submitting himself to the judgement of God. . . . If the oath-helper is beaten, all those who offered to swear with him shall pay a penalty of three hundred solidi. But if the plaintiff is killed in the combat, the victor shall be relieved of all charge and shall be paid out of the goods of the dead man nine times the value of his claims."

The ordeal by battle is allowed under the laws of the Alamanni, Saxons, Werins and other later collections; and in the laws of the Lombards, certain rules are given for ordeal by battle. But this barbarous custom did not reach England until the Norman conquest. It is said by Agobard, archbishop of Lyons, that Avitus, bishop of Vienne, protested in council to King Gundobad against the ordeal by battle; and Agobard himself petitioned Louis the Pious, three hundred years later, to abolish it. Agobard states quite clearly the fundamental principle that the distinction between the strong and the weak is not the same as the distinction between the just and the unjust. He writes: "If in this life the innocent were

---

[1] *Lex Burgund., M.G.G.*, vol. ii, part i, p. 75.

always victors and the guilty were vanquished . . . Herod would not have killed John, but John, Herod. Nor would that holy city, Jerusalem, in the times of grace illumined by great numbers of monks, clergy and other faithful, be subject to the Saracens even as other cities and districts. Nor would Rome be subject to the Goths, pagans and heretics together, nor Italy to the Lombards." Therefore, he appeals to Louis the Pious against the laws of Gundobad: "If it should please our lord, the Emperor, to transfer people to the Frankish Law, they would be made better, and this district would be relieved of its miseries; for, because of these laws, it often happens that not only strong men, but even the weak and old are bound to fight even for the slighest causes."[1]

Clearly the ordeal by battle forced itself into the legal system in the sixth century as a survival of the pre-judicial method of settling disputes; but it was supported by the general belief of the sixth and later centuries that God decided who was to be the victor in any conflict. Similar beliefs supported the ordeals by boiling water or red-hot iron, because God was supposed to intervene to protect the innocent against the natural effects of scalding or burning. The Church provided special prayers and ceremonies by which the clergy might invoke divine assistance for the barbarian custom of discovering guilt by magic. The ordeal by battle has not survived the advance of civilization; but the oath in judicial procedure continued to be used even after the decline of medievalism. The later substitution of a book for the relics of a saint does not affect the principle. A lie told after touching a sacred object is supposed to have worse effects upon the liar than a simple lie, unaccompanied by any ceremonial which may make it more emphatic.

The Capitularies

The last stage in the development of the barbarian laws is marked by the issue of "capitularies" to complete or amplify some of them. Under Charles the Great the imperial tradition of Rome was adapted to the needs of the Frankish kingdoms and in the name of Charles, as Emperor, *Capitula* or "headings" were issued,

---

[1] Agobard, *Adv. Leg. Gund.*, sections 9 and 7. *Pat. Lat.*

adding to the Salic Law in A.D. 803 and to the laws of the Bavarians in the same year. Similarly, capitularies were issued for the government of the Lombards in A.D. 806, A.D. 808, A.D. 809, A.D. 813 and A.D. 819. The king of the Franks, or the Frankish "king of the Lombards," had thus begun to adopt the methods of a dictator as law-giver. He issued his laws in Latin under the influence of the clergy; and the source of his authority as law-giver was presumably believed to be divine. But at this stage laws in western Europe had become part of the system now known as the medieval Empire; and the capitularies of Charles the Great, therefore, will be discussed in a later chapter in reference to the so-called Holy Roman Empire.

The most important capitularies, however, were not merely additions to existing collections of tribal laws; they were new laws or administrative orders issued by the Frankish kings from about the middle of the sixth century to the middle of the ninth. Both these legal provisions and administrative orders are divided into sections (*capitula*); and a collection of such sections was called a capitulary (*capitularium*). They represent the attempts of the kings of the Franks, and later of the kings who were called Emperors, to legislate for all their subjects and govern from one centre—the palace (*palatium*). They may have been the results partly of an attempt to imitate the edicts or rescripts of Roman Emperors, and partly of the effort of the clergy to increase the moral authority of the kings. They are all written in Latin; and a great number of them deal with the organization of the Church. But probably the majority of those which have survived are not in their original form. Collections of the capitularies were made in the ninth century without any regard to the date at which they were issued. And later editors of the texts have had to separate and analyse the traditional collections.[1]

There are three kinds of capitulary. First, those that deal with ecclesiastical organization; secondly, regulations to be observed by all subjects of the king; and thirdly, instructions issued to particular agents of the king. The capitularies which deal with ecclesiastical

---

[1] The most trustworthy edition so far produced is that in *M.G.H., Leges*, Hanover, 1883, edited by Boretius and Krause.

matters can hardly be called "laws" in the usual sense of that word. They are instructions about the duties of bishops, abbots, the subordinate clergy and monks, which probably were intended to reinforce the canons of the Church by the use of the king's authority. The kings of the Franks had, at any rate theoretically, a more extensive jurisdiction than any bishop or local synod; and the kings found it convenient to act as reformers of the Church, both because it added prestige to such "divine" authority as they obtained by anointing and coronation, and because the bishops could thus be used as agents of the king's authority. The organization of the Churches in the Frankish kingdom and the territories outside it, which were conquered by the kings of the Franks, was the only surviving remnant of the organization of the Roman Empire. If that had collapsed, the tradition of civilized life itself might have disappeared. The disorders and scandals among the clergy of the days of St. Boniface, which are referred to elsewhere, were in practice partly removed by the authority of kings. Thus, the capitularies dealing with ecclesiastical matters were attempts to improve social organization; but these methods did not continue in use after the ninth century. They may be compared with the attempts made by the Emperor Justinian in the sixth century to legislate in reference to the duties of monks, bishops and other clergy. But the attempt to concentrate both civil and ecclesiastical authority in the hands of the Emperor completely failed even in the East; and in the West the Frankish kings, even with the assistance of their bishops, never had either the intelligence or learning which might have made possible the king's control of the Church, such as occurred in some countries after the Reformation. In the ecclesiastical capitularies the hand is the king's but the voice is that of the bishops.

The capitularies which contain the regulations to be observed by all the king's subjects (*capitularia per se scribenda*) were generally issued after consultation with the king's council of nobles and bishops. They are not statements of crimes and penalties, but commands issued in the name of the king, and in later times merely pious exhortations. For example, Sundays are to be kept free of labour and tithes are to be paid for the maintenance of churches.

Such instructions are obviously interpretations of the Hebrew tradition in the Old Testament, which was accepted uncritically as a basis for social organization. The general rules for the conduct of the king's subjects are merely vague directions without the support of any power to enforce them. They are like the admonitions of an ineffectual parent, addressed to children who are not listening.

Capitularies of the third kind contain instructions sent from the *Palatium* to the royal agents (*missi dominici*), either in general or for the instruction of a particular official in a single district. Capitularies of this kind were put together uncritically at later times; and it seems probable that the famous capitulary *De Villis* is a collection of instructions issued at different times to controllers of the royal estates. The collection was perhaps intended to give a general view of the principles according to which all the royal estates should be managed. But such administrative orders, for example, about the storage of food and the growing of fruit, are clearly not laws in any sense. They are merely examples of an attempt to introduce a central administration, largely for purposes of supply, in a primitive agricultural society. Capitularies, therefore, of all kinds may be taken as indications of the vague and exceedingly confused ideas of the early Middle Ages, both about the nature of "law" and about the moral authority of any source of legislation. What is now called the "State" existed only in an embryonic form at that time. It was borne in the womb of the Church.

In the seventh, eighth and ninth centuries there was an abundant growth of charters (*diplomata*) which, although in no sense laws, greatly affected the legal system in the early Middle Ages, and perhaps even later. These documents were intended to establish immunities or privileges by which the recipient, person or institution, might be secure against local jurisdiction and, in some cases, even against the jurisdiction of the king's own agents. The justice administered by the courts of local lords was in many cases corrupt and tyrannical. Even in the Roman Empire, in its later days, it had been found almost impossible for the central Authority to control local judges and other officials. And those were days in which communication was still well organized. But by the seventh century

344

communication in western Europe was difficult and uncertain; and civil and ecclesiastical Authorities had very little control over those who, in theory, were their subordinates. The immunities granted by kings or other Authorities were intended to protect the dependants of certain persons or institutions from local tyranny. But this plan proved to be disastrous. It weakened the authority of the king's own agents and prevented the organization of large and inclusive communities, besides confusing the whole legal tradition by the introduction of so many exceptions that the rule appeared to be worthless. The Church itself contributed to the confusion. Many monasteries and other ecclesiastical bodies obtained immunities from kings or lords; and the Popes in the eighth century granted immunities even from the jurisdiction of bishops within their own dioceses.

The Canons

The Churches of the Roman Empire had developed a system of legislation and statements of law before anyone imagined that the imperial system might come to an end. The legislature of the Churches was a synod or council of bishops of a district, more or less extensive; and these bishops met from time to time at the principal city or metropolitan See, principally for the purpose of securing unity in doctrine and practice between their Churches. Naturally tradition made the basis of this unity both in doctrine and in practice; and as a result, the Churches with the oldest Christian tradition had most influence. But the bishops in synods and councils were also concerned with the regulation of current affairs in cases of mal-administration or charges brought against the clergy.

The councils of the Churches in different parts of the Empire were held independently of the councils in other parts; and their canons were written down for purely local or provincial use. This continued to be the case even after the age of oecumenical or "general" councils. For example, the councils of Carthage or Toledo, or, at a later date, of Hatfield, were quite independent legislative and judicial bodies. But the fact that the bishops of a district or province met in council from time to time and issued canons or rules, obviously tended to strengthen the power of the bishops as against both other clergy and monks. It made the bishops the instruments of unity between the Christian Churches, although in the earlier Christian ages such unity depended rather upon travelling apostles or preachers. Again, because the bishops were immune from effectual criticism outside the council, and because the majority in any council could always expel or degrade any individual bishop or small group of bishops for heresy or disagreement as to ritual, the councils of bishops took their decisions theoretically in unanimity. Thus the bishop's function in the Churches tended from early times towards a dictatorship. Discussion among the bishops in council was always possible and continued into the latest times; but it was never possible for other Christians or even clergy to dispute decisions when they had been made by a council of bishops. And since the basis of such decisions was always supposed to be the original Christian tradition, it was never possible for a later council to reverse what an earlier council had done, except by reinterpreting the same Christian tradition. Thus the development of Christian doctrine and practice was affected by "archaism." The past was supposed to contain rules and ideas which were the established models for action and thought in the future. Every reform had to be advocated as if it were a retrogression.

When the great change in the relation of the Christian Churches to the Roman Empire occurred under Constantine, its first effect was an attempt to carry further the unity of the Churches which had already been secured in different provinces by the councils. Thus, the Emperor himself called the first council of bishops of the whole Empire at Nicaea in A.D. 325. And for many centuries the Emperor at Constantinople strove to unite the Christian Churches in doctrine and in practice by means of such universal councils of bishops. Indeed, the possibility that all the different Churches of the world might be made parts of a single system by means of universal councils was always an alternative to the "imperial" system later introduced by the bishops of Rome. In the later Roman Empire the effort to unite the Churches through councils of bishops remained the policy of what is now called the Byzantine tradition; while the alternative policy of subordination of all other bishops to one—the bishop of Rome—was gradually established in the Churches of western Europe. Even after the Middle Ages, during the controversies concerning the Papacy in the fifteenth century, the "Conciliar" policy was regarded by some theologians as preferable to the Absolutism of medieval ecclesiastical policy.

During the period before Constantine the rules followed by any Christian Church or community were gradually committed to writing; and when the imperial Authorities gave their support for the first time under Constantine to the Christian Churches, the word "canon" (κανών, regula) had come to mean a rule of the Church, comparable to law but seldom referred to as law (νόμος, lex).[1] The canons of the Church, therefore, include both the "rule of faith," expressing authoritative or established beliefs, and also the "rule of the Church" which covered both the discipline regulating the personal life and conduct of Christians and the administration of the Church and discipline of the clergy. Decrees of councils or synods or bishops, later called canons, were conceived as particular applications or enforcements of "the canon."[2] In this chapter, however, the canons concerning the definition of Faith will be omitted from consideration and only the canons of discipline and administration will be discussed.

Collections of the canons of local Churches or synods were formed, partly under the influence of imperial edicts concerning the clergy, issued after the Edict of Milan in A.D. 313, and contained in the Theodosian law-books, partly by interpretations of Scripture and of the works of the Fathers. In the West the works of St. Augustine provided much material for later canons. The collection of canons in Latin made by Dionysius for Stephen, bishop of Salerno, deals chiefly with the regulation of Christian customs and rites. The first place is given to certain canons, treated as "apostolic," according to which a bishop must be consecrated by two other bishops. Again, in "the Sacrifice" (of the Mass) no honey, no

---

[1] *Concil. Nic.*, Can. 13, ὁ παλαιὸς καὶ κανονικὸς νόμος.

[2] Brightman, *Early History of the Church and Ministry*, ed. Swete, 1918, p. 358, note.

vegetables nor fowls must be offered. The fifteenth canon decrees that members of the clergy are not to wander from place to place. Canon 22 deals with the problem which seems to have caused much concern in all the early Churches, that of castration. The canon says that those who castrate themselves are not to be ordained. It is well known that the great Origen himself took the passage in St. Matthew's Gospel literally which says "some have made themselves eunuchs"[1] and, as a result, his ordination was objected to. It seems to have been the general rule that self-castration made ordination impossible, but not castration by doctors or by enemies. Canon 35 attempts to regulate the power of bishops, saying that the bishop must do nothing except with the consent of all. Canon 42 decrees that bishops who gamble or drink should be deprived of office or condemned. And Canon 49 says that baptism should be in the name of the Trinity and not of the Three Sons or Three Paracletes.

The canons of the Council of Nicaea emphasize again the opposition to self-castration; and later canons refer to other difficulties with regard to sex. The number of years of penance and exclusion from Communion is given in reference to different offences, as, for example, homosexuality and abortion; and Canon 38 of the Council of Ancyra touches upon an interesting problem when it says that "virgins are not to live as sisters."[2] Later canons again correct the Christian laity, as, for example, the canon which forbids a woman to wear men's clothes or forbids her to cut her hair. The danger of taking literally the phrase about "hating father and mother" is guarded against by the command that no one should despise parents or children because of the claims of Christianity.

The difficulties which a Christian community had to face in its

---

[1] *Matthew* xix. 12. The ancient practice of the priests and devotees of Attis must be remembered. St. Jerome feared that Christian priests might appear to be like the priests of Isis (see above, p. 161).

[2] The practice referred to was not unknown among modern "revivalists" in America and England. The sexual impulse is used to heighten religious enthusiasm by contact without sexual intercourse. See St. Paul's advice in 1 *Cor.* vii. 37, "He that will keep his virgin . . . doth well"; and St. John Chrysostom's *Treatise Against those who Keep Virgins* (Opera, Paris, 1839, vol. i, p. 279). Chrysostom protests that the care and tenderness bestowed on the virgin by the man with whom she lives causes scandal.

earliest days were largely due to the need for defining the conditions of membership in a Church. Therefore, the earliest canons are concerned with regulating the conduct of all Christians and assigning penalties or periods of "penance" for moral defects. Thus, there are canons which assign penalties either of excommunication or of fasting and other austerities for anyone injuring a slave or for sexual offences. But as the Churches came to include the greater part of the local population, the organization and discipline of the officials of the Church, the clergy, became more and more important. Thus, the canons had to prevent the transfer of bishops from place to place, to restrict the authority of bishops to particular dioceses, and to define the relation between the bishops and other members of the clergy.

As the Churches of the different districts within the Roman Empire came more closely into contact, differences in doctrine and practice needed to be removed. Therefore the canons of earlier times, or those which were believed to be connected with the primitive Church, became the bases of summaries which claimed to represent the beliefs and practices of Christianity as a whole. But the process by which all the canons recognized as authoritative were made to form parts of a single code, was a gradual development from the fifth to the ninth century. In this development three definite stages may be observed.[1] First, in the period from the publication of the Theodosian law-books to the destruction of the Arian kingdoms in the West (roughly from A.D. 438 to A.D. 523), collections of canons were formed in Rome. Secondly, from the issue of Justinian's law-books until the end of the sixth century (roughly from A.D. 523 to A.D. 700), collections were made in Gaul and Spain, and the Penitentials were composed, chiefly under the influence of Irish and English Christianity. Thirdly, from the establishment of the Frankish power in Gaul and Italy to the creation of the medieval Papacy (roughly A.D. 700 to A.D. 840), the Spanish and Roman collections came to dominate all authoritative ecclesiastical rules until, after the destruction of the

[1] For what follows see the admirable summary in P. Fournier and G. Le Bras, *Histoire des Collections Canoniques en Occident*, vol. i, Paris, 1931.

Church in Spain by the Mohammedan invasion, the Roman Church became undeniably the only source from which the canonical tradition in the West was derived.

In the first stages obviously the Churches in the West were in difficulties so long as the kings controlling the areas in which they worked were Arian heretics. For this reason it became necessary to ascertain the correct Christian tradition of doctrine and discipline; and this was done, partly by translation into Latin of the canons of the chief councils held in the East, partly by making summaries of doctrine and practice from among the documents preserved in the offices of the Roman Church. This Church was in many ways freer than other Churches in the West, even under the Arian king, Theodoric (A.D. 492–526), because of its connections with the Churches still under the Emperor's jurisdiction. Thus, from Gelasius, who became bishop of Rome in A.D. 492, to the death of Hormisdas, bishop of Rome in A.D. 523, Rome seemed likely to be a centre of unity for the western Churches. And the first collection of canons which was later regarded universally as authoritative, made by Dionysius the Little, was dedicated to Hormisdas.[1]

In the second stage of development the Roman Church was placed in an ambiguous and dangerous situation by the unfortunate activities of the Emperor Justinian. Not only did his ridiculous policy of conquest in the West disturb the relations between the Church in Rome and the Churches under the Frankish and Visigothic monarchs who had become Catholic, but his issue of regulations for the clergy in his law-books and "New Laws" obscured the distinction between the law of the "State" and the canons of the Church. The Churches of the Greek tradition at first added the laws of Justinian to their collections of canons and later treated them as part of the canonical tradition, calling them "Law Canons" (nomocanones). Meantime, in the West, Spain became the chief source of a consistent development of the canons, from the third Council of Toledo in A.D. 589 to the sixteenth and last Council of Toledo in A.D. 694. This was the direct result of the conversion of

---

[1] Dionysius the Little was a Syrian who, as Cassiodorus (de Div. Inst., 23) says, was "altogether a Roman in manners."

the Arian Visigoths to Catholicism. In Gaul there were thirty synods of bishops between A.D. 506 and A.D. 585 (Council of Mâcon), all of them adding or confirming regulations chiefly for the clergy. But after that date there were hardly any councils or synods of bishops until the end of the seventh century.

The Penitentials

A strange influence upon the growth of Church discipline came at this time from Ireland, England and northern Gaul. This is expressed in the Penitentials, which are lists of moral defects or sins to which particular penances or forms of "compensation" are attached. Innumerable manuscripts of various forms of Penitential exist; and some of these Penitentials are attached to the names of well-known saints, such as St. Columban. It has been pointed out above that Christianity in Ireland was dominated by monastic asceticism and not by episcopal organization. In Ireland, therefore, and in parts of England, the Christian tradition emphasized personal or individual spiritual excellence. The confession of sins and the practice of a stern asceticism naturally led to absorption in the moral problem of avoiding or curing the most obvious vices of the day. Among a barbarous and primitive people drunkenness, lust and robbery were only too frequent; and even those who took their Christianity seriously must have felt the difficulty of maintaining a high moral standard. The Penitentials are, therefore, plans for maintaining the moral standard by definite and detailed methods. As in the barbarian laws, each crime has a special compensation or "composition" attached to it—in the Salic Law, for example, there is a fine for squeezing a lady's finger, so in the Penitentials definite periods of fasting or some other penance are attached to particular sins. But none of these Penitentials had any official or episcopal authority. They were private and personal plans for the moral life. Some of the statements are called judgements (*judicia*) or, as it were, judicial opinions. But the different Penitentials do not agree either in their estimates of the comparative importance of different moral defects or in the amount of penance assigned for this or that sin. In some cases there is direct contradiction between the treatment of sins in different Penitentials.[1] The Penitentials, therefore, represent what may be called a primitive Protestantism or Puritanism. The individual Christian is assumed to be full of a "sense of sin" and eager to control "the flesh." But if any proof were needed that religious enthusiasm cannot survive without an organized institution—a Church—the history of the Penitentials would provide it. Enthusiasm may be destroyed in the effort to preserve an institution; but without an institution enthusiasm, however virtuous, will be wasted in personal eccentricities or unintelligent attempts to improve other people. The trouble was that extreme severity in the conduct of one individual might be in glaring contrast with the laxity of another; and the estimate made of the importance of any particular sin or virtue by any individual inevitably depended upon his personal constitution and circumstances.[2] The Christian tradition might, therefore, easily have been lost in a confusion of personal preferences or ascetic enthusiasms, if the Penitentials had not been definitely controlled and some of them suppressed by the authority of councils of bishops in the development of canons.

Revival of Canons

During the period in which the Penitentials are most prominent, however, collections of canons and of quotations from the Bible and the Fathers continued to be made. These were attempts to preserve an authoritative tradition. The collection known as the "Irish" (*Hibernensis*), for example, contains five hundred quotations from Scripture, of which about three hundred are from the Old Testament—another sign of the influence of the Old Testament in

[1] For example, two Penitentials, both claiming to be composed by St. Columban, have entirely different penalties attached to fornication and the shedding of blood by a monk.

[2] The Penitential connected with the name of Egbert, archbishop of York (A.D. 755–771), contains instructions that, if a mouse falls into a drink, the drink should be sprinkled with holy water; but if the mouse is dead, the drink should be thrown away. The following chapter (book ii, ch. vi) on smaller sins, deals with homo-sexuals. A bishop who is guilty must do fourteen years' penance, a priest twelve, a deacon ten, a sub-deacon eight, a cleric seven, and a layman five. If a man has intercourse with his wife during Lent he shall do one year's penance or pay twenty solidi to the Church.

this period. But an entirely new stage was reached in the history of the canons after about A.D. 700, when the influence of the Spanish councils and of the renewed vigour of the Roman Church became operative. The change coincides with the increase in the disagreement between the bishops of Rome and the Roman Emperors, which eventually led to the separation of the Greek from the Latin Churches. The council known as "In Trullo," which met in the imperial Palace at Constantinople in A.D. 692, issued one hundred and two canons. These are definitely opposed to the western traditions then established, in so far as they allow priests and deacons to continue in marriage and are less severe than the practices in the Latin Churches in regard to the celibacy of clergy. The thirty-sixth canon declares for equality between the See of Constantinople and that of Rome.

Among the Churches of the West the eighth century was a time of extreme difficulty, in which many older centres of Christianity were destroyed. The Mohammedan conquest of Spain brought to an end the development of the canons in the councils of Toledo; and refugee clergy brought Spanish collections of canons into the Frankish kingdom. The Lombard conquests in Italy divided the Church in Rome from other Churches in Italy. Danish invasions destroyed monastic settlements in Ireland and England, and in the Frankish kingdom many bishoprics and abbacies fell into the hands of unworthy men who divided and misused the properties of the Church.

About the year A.D. 740, however, reform began in the Frankish kingdom and was carried on with zeal and energy by St. Boniface and others like him. Councils in Gaul from A.D. 742 began again to issue canons for the regulation of the clergy and the security of ecclesiastical properties. Pippin, later ruler of the Franks, received letters on discipline from Pope Zachary; and a collection of canons regarded as authoritative by the Roman Church was eventually presented to Charles the Great in A.D. 774 by Pope Hadrian. This collection of canons was substantially the same as that made by Dionysius the Little; later Papal letters were added; and all these documents, together known as the Dionysio-Hadriana, formed the basis of ecclesiastical reforms under the dominant Frankish rule in western Europe, and established the Roman Church as the one authoritative source of canonical discipline. At the same time many councils condemned the use of the Penitentials; and although new Penitentials continued to be composed, by the middle of the ninth century these were all attempts to summarize the generally accepted rules of discipline in all the Churches, and not merely personal opinions about the proper penalties for sins. The Penitential connected with the name of Theodore, archbishop of Canterbury, was composed in the Frankish kingdom between A.D. 830 and A.D. 847; and there are two connected with the name of Hrabanus Maurus, bishop of Mainz, the first of A.D. 841 and the second of A.D. 853.

Collections of canons and other rules of discipline were multiplied, copied and re-copied during the early ninth century; and at one stage the bishops, imitating the legislative methods of the new Frankish Empire, issued Capitularies.[1] The attempt of individual bishops on their own authority to issue canonical rules was, however, doomed to failure. The weakness of the episcopate in general in face of the growing powers of a lay aristocracy, and the weakness of royal authority after the death of Charles the Great, led to the invention of imaginary canons and other documents. Falsification of ancient texts and the composition of documents which the authors and their supporters pretended to have been in existence in earlier centuries, were used both in the interests of reform and in the establishment of ecclesiastical authority. But it would be foolish to speak of all this as fraud. In the ninth century there was little or no sense of history, in the modern understanding of that phrase. Charters and canons and laws came out of the imagination of scribes or scholars in the monasteries or bishops' palaces. Such documents were felt to exist because they ought to exist; and without some appreciation of the attitude of mind of men who could compose or accept the "False Decretals" and other such documents, of which the most famous example is the "Donation of Constantine," it is impossible to understand the creation of the

---

[1] In de Clercq's *Législation religieuse*, etc., the text of the second Capitulary or Diocesan Statute of Theodulf, bishop of Orleans, is given. This deals with clerical discipline, celibacy and penance for sins.

medieval Papacy or the medieval Empire. Such institutions, as well as the documents which were used to establish them, were largely works of the creative imagination.

Dionysius included in his collection certain "decretals" of bishops of Rome from Siricius in A.D. 385 to Anastasius in A.D. 498; and in a prefatory letter he says that he collects these as precepts for guidance. Here, then, is the beginning of legislation or decrees issued by the Popes. The collections made by Dionysius were adopted officially by the Roman Church about A.D. 500; and the *Book of Canons* which Pope Hadrian I gave to Charles the Great in A.D. 774 was accepted as authoritative by the Frankish Churches in a council at Aachen in A.D. 802.

A short collection of canons of a general character was made by Fulgentius Ferrandus in A.D. 550. This represents the contribution of the African Churches, for which the collections of the canons of the councils of Carthage had formed the basis of ecclesiastical discipline. In Gaul collections of the canons of councils at Arles had most influence; and in Spain the canons of the councils of Toledo, which continued until A.D. 694, and were ended by the Mohammedan invasion.

The collections of canons, however, did not produce a single system of canonical jurisdiction until the canons were classified in reference to their subject-matter. The first collections, as it has been shown with regard to that of Dionysius, were based either upon a chronological order or upon geographical distinctions. But it is obviously of no importance to a judge or a court in deciding whether a rule has been broken, to know either the date or the place at which it was first issued. The second principle which was vaguely adopted in collections of canons led to the juxtaposition of canons dealing with the same subject, drawn from many sources, of different dates and places. But this principle only revealed differences and contradictions between the traditional canons. In the final stage, therefore, of their development the canons were classified according to subject-matter, excluding those which were contradictory, reconciling differences and modifying, sometimes recklessly, and perhaps inventing, canons or Papal decrees which were felt to express the real meaning of the ecclesiastical tradition. This stage in the history of canons had only just been reached in the ninth century; but it was not until the famous *Decretum* of Gratian was issued about A.D. 1150 that what is now known as medieval Canon Law was finally established.

General Conclusions

The laws which were operative in western Europe from the fifth to the ninth century indicate, in the first place, a society in transition from one form of civilization to another. Clearly, so far as law is concerned, there was no definite destruction of the Roman system and no definite substitution of another. The process of change was gradual; and many of the elements of the old Roman system were carried forward by the clergy into the new tribal or national systems of what eventually became medieval Europe. The barbarians did not destroy anything they could understand: they were only too willing to learn. And it must be remembered that after the middle of the fifth century an increasing number of the clergy and monks were themselves by race and tradition what the Romans would have called "barbarians." But the Roman Empire was never racial in its governing conception. Whoever adopted Roman culture and ideals was a "Roman"; and this tradition was continued by the Catholic Church. Thus, "Roman" continued to mean "civilized," as contrasted with "barbarian," long after the inhabitants of the western kingdoms were in "blood" or "race" the children of many intermarriages of the old Celtic tribes, the few "Italian" settlers and the invading Germanic peoples. And as the Church was the chief representative and agent of civilization, it was for that reason "Roman," quite apart from any connection a local Church might have with the Church of the city of Rome. On the other hand, after the fifth century, there were in western Europe two traditions of law and justice, operating side by side; first, the Roman, which provided for the needs of the original inhabitants before the barbarian invasions and was afterwards used by the Church and the dependants of ecclesiastical Authority; and secondly, barbarian legal customs which differed in different districts but all provided only for the simplest disputes. Clearly men living together in the same town or district could not, for many generations, continue to use entirely different systems of law and justice. Intermarriage and the transfer of property would naturally tend to unite in one system the different local customs. Indeed, it is surprising that they survived in separation so long. In the ninth century, as it has been shown from the opinion of Agobard of Lyons, it was felt to be absurd that any community should be divided by "personal" law. But even before then the difficulties created by the existence side by side of Roman and barbarian laws were obviously great. This is indicated by the attempts made in different barbarian laws to deal with disputes between persons who lived under laws of different origin.

The situation was obviously unstable; and it would have been impossible for anyone in the sixth and seventh centuries to foresee the very different courses taken by the development of law in England and the other countries of western Europe. The most important distinction which exists to-day between the system of English law and the European systems dominated by Roman Law can hardly be traced back to any laws earlier than the tenth or eleventh centuries. But a fundamental difference between the two systems is indicated by the fact that the earliest English laws were not written in Latin; and even the barbarian laws of the Germanic tribes in Spain, France, Italy and Germany, were all first recorded in that language. The Latin language prepared the way for the later domination of the Roman Law. And therefore also it supported the influence of the ancient Roman Empire in the development of kingship in western Europe. Kingship in England has always, even at the Renaissance, been freer from the defects of the Roman system of military dictatorship than kingship elsewhere.

Other contrasts between the English and other systems of law, even before the ninth century, may be noted. In the first place, there were no "Romans" in England who had a separate law or their own, or had to be allowed a separate place in local law. The law elsewhere in the early Middle Ages was greatly affected by the fact that the invading Germanic peoples in Gaul, Spain and

Italy, hardly amounted to more than about five in every hundred of the population. The remainder were "Romans." Secondly, in England the law of the locality either absorbed, or was absorbed by, the king's law. In France and Germany, on the other hand, the local customary law in the Middle Ages was contrasted with the king's law; and, after the eleventh century, when Roman Law was "rediscovered," its influence on the king's law led to an even sharper contrast between districts of written law, on the Roman basis, and districts in which local custom was accepted as the basis of law. This local custom (*costuma*, that is, *consuetudo*) was written down at a later date. In a locality in which it was accepted, the confusion of laws during the fifth and later centuries had been dissolved into one local tradition; but the traditions differed greatly in different districts, and therefore formed obstacles to the unification of the French nation. The State, therefore, in France, as a unifying force, at first a king's inheritance, has been traditionally separate in thought from the nation, whereas in England the State seems to have grown more directly out of the common life of the nation. Thus, the most difficult task of the French Revolution was the unification of the laws; because the territory called France was divided into so many jealous and exclusive units by the customary laws of the early Middle Ages and the laws of the local lords in later times. As Voltaire wrote in the *Dictionnaire Philosophique*, about France before A.D. 1789: "In one single province of Europe, between the Alps and the Pyrenees, there are more than one hundred and forty small peoples who call themselves compatriots, but who are really foreigners one to another." No such obstacle to national unity existed in England after the Norman Conquest.

A second characteristic of the legal systems between the fifth and ninth centuries is the recognition of numerous social classes or castes within a community. Roman Law and the canons provide for the clergy, free men and slaves; but the barbarian laws distinguish between many more different classes or ranks. Each person has the right to special compensation for injuries in accordance with his position in society. The "wergeld" is greatest for the king's men and nobles. Below them are free men and women;

and below these many different classes of half-free men and women, who might later be called villeins or serfs; and below these again were slaves, either of the Church or of lay owners. The Roman Law, for example, in the Theodosian law-books, recognizes different classes with different obligations; but it was not so crude as to set different prices on the limbs or lives of different castes. The conception that the State was opposed to any form of violence among those it governed, in its own right, and not because of the victim's grievance, was established in the Roman tradition. The functions of public Authority in protecting any *civis Romanus*, of whatever rank or order, were well understood. On the other hand, in the earlier barbarian laws the purpose of compensation for injury is not to redress any injury to the community in the "State." It is intended to prevent personal or family feuds. And public Authority is hardly more than an "outsider," receiving fees for its function as arbitrator.

The statements concerning fines for personal injury, in the barbarian laws, gave the amount due in terms of a person's wealth or status. This tended to divide the community. It kept men "in their place." It did, indeed, prevent a person falling lower in the scale of social value than his father; but it also prevented a person from approaching equality of rights with those above him. After the slave system in the Roman Empire, and the fluidity of society described in the second chapter above, the peoples of western Europe were being arranged in new ranks. A new order was arising. The Church continued to preach the equality of all men; but it could not maintain even the equality of Roman citizens which had been established under the Empire. The tradition embodied in the barbarian laws was too strong. The new society, therefore, was established upon the basis of many different ranks, one above the other; and this continued to affect the tradition of the nations of western Europe until they had developed a civilization more nearly approaching the Roman in its legal principles.

Again, in the barbarian laws, which represent a primitive agricultural society, the law is not concerned primarily with morals or religion, as those words are now understood. It is a mistake to suppose that primitive law is "religious" or is concerned with forms or rites.[1] All the earliest sections of the barbarian laws deal merely with personal compensation for personal injury. Justice is conceived merely as a sort of balance between the plaintiff and the defendant. The court, whether official or "popular," has to decide mainly how much the injury is worth—that is to say, how much the injured party will take to prevent his attempting revenge on his own account. The laws which have been preserved are "statutory," in the sense that they are provisions specially written down to confirm or improve one part of a complex system of customs. Their provisions as to compensation establish standards for what, no doubt, were variable estimates made by different courts or different judges. Again, the compensation referred to is calculated in terms of currency, which indicates that there was no general disappearance of the already established "money economy" of the Roman Empire. When the barbarian laws refer to payments in kind and their equivalent in money payments, the purpose, as indicated above, probably was to allow for variations in the money value of commodities in a district where famine in one year might be followed by glut in another. The conception of law, however, implied in all the barbarian systems, had hardly reached the stage of thought at which law is taken to be primarily a statement of the common or public interest. The clergy are given, for example, a high "wergeld" in the Anglo-Saxon laws, but merely as persons of a particular rank, similar to that of king's servants or nobles, and not because of any public function performed by them. No doubt, moral standards or ideals may have grown out of primitive laws; but all such law is much more like a statement of a business transaction than like expressions of disapproval or prohibition.

As for legislation, the barbarian laws generally have a preface declaring that the provisions which follow are the results of consultation between the king, his wise men or nobles and certain bishops. In the preface to the Frankish Laws the names of those who collected or wrote them down are given. It seems probable

---

[1] See A. S. Diamond, *Primitive Law* (1935), where Sir Henry Maine's conception of primitive law is completely refuted.

that the barbarian tradition in all the Germanic tribes implied that law was the result of an agreement, or at least a general consultation, concerning the provisions to be made either by general assembly or "moot," or by a less numerous king's council. In none of the traditional barbarian systems was the law conceived as the will of the king. In this matter the Roman dictatorship implied a different idea of legislation. But it was obviously the idea of law in the Roman dictatorship and not that in the barbarian traditions which caused the issue, at the end of the eighth century, of the capitularies of the Frankish kings. All the kings of the new barbarian kingdoms, under the influence of the clergy and the Roman tradition, tried to make themselves into little Emperors; and so it came to be thought at certain times in the later history of Europe that law was essentially an expression of the will of a single sovereign power—a monarch. But the tradition implied in the barbarian laws was entirely different; and support for it could be found by historians in later times even in the Roman tradition before the imperial dictatorship. Thus, legislation in the seventh and eighth centuries was probably conceived not as the issuing of a command from above but as a statement of general agreement by an assembly. The statement might be new. Its expression in writing certainly was. But the agreement itself rested upon what was supposed to be ancient custom. And even in Roman Law, memories of the Republic did not entirely disappear under the increasing centralization of the military dictators after Diocletian. Law, even in Rome, was believed to have been at one time a statement of ancient custom.

This "custom" may be misunderstood by students of history in the twentieth century, because custom in the eighteenth and nine- teenth centuries was used as an excuse for oppression or the restriction of enterprise. But the custom which was supposed to be the basis of barbarian laws, was, in part at least, a means of securing to the "small man" some measure of protection against the powerful and the wealthy. To establish a person in the status of his parents might prevent his rising; but it would also prevent his falling into a more complete dependence or slavery. As it will be shown in a later chapter, the half-free classes of the Middle Ages included some who had fallen from freedom into dependence, but also a far greater number who had risen from slavery without rights into a new, if limited, security. The classes or castes referred to in the barbarian laws, therefore, would have an interest of their own, quite apart from the convenience of any ruler or lord, in maintaining ancient custom and assisting its formulation. That small bodies of men might regard themselves as an assembly representing a whole people, was not unnatural in days before the more recent technique of the vote and the election of representatives was invented.

The clergy remained in the new communities a separate body. This is clearly implied in the "wergeld" and other special provisions for the clergy in the barbarian laws. The Church in the holding of property, and therefore the clergy and their dependants, "lived" by Roman Law; and all Christians, and especially the clergy, were governed by the canons. Even under the Roman Empire, after the Edict of Milan (A.D. 312), the clergy were granted special privileges by the imperial Authorities. One section of the Theodosian law-books, as it has been noted above, concerns the Church and its clergy. But the different Churches throughout the Christian world had gradually developed their own legal system in the canons; and throughout the Middle Ages these rules remained separate from the laws of the different kingdoms. The basis of distinction was never very clear in theory. The fantastic attempt of medieval theologians to distinguish between "spiritual" and "temporal" was never successful. The canons, for example, certainly dealt with marriage and other sexual relations; but it is impossible to say whether the sexual impulse belongs to the "body" or the "soul." In any case, the canons which were acknowledged in the western Churches between the fifth and ninth centuries, were more and more concerned, as time went on, with the clergy. And as the bishops were both the legislators in synods or councils and also the judicial authorities, supreme within the ranks of the clergy, canonical jurisdiction tended more and more to make of the whole body of the clergy a separate caste within all the European kingdoms.

It is generally agreed that law in any society performs two functions: first, it confirms and strengthens a traditional routine, thus giving men a certain security of expectation in their dealings with their fellows. Secondly, law should control and direct the formation of new social habits or a new routine. This second function of law has hardly been understood before modern times. But social situations change because of the development either of new moral standards and of new systems of production and exchange, or because of the growth or decline in the number of the members of a community. Therefore, if the art of government is to survive at all in a changing situation, law must look also to the future and not only to the past. It must establish new customs and not merely confirm the old. The recognition of this need was probably one of the reasons why the Frankish kings of the eighth and ninth centuries issued their Capitularies. These were attempts at legislation to extend control over situations not envisaged in the barbarian traditions. But these attempts were abandoned in the ninth century, because they were based upon archaism—a memory of Roman centralization which had no basis in the actual powers of the kings. Here it is necessary only to note that although assemblies or councils in the new barbarian kingdoms were used to confirm traditional or established customs in the laws of the barbarians, there was no instrument of legislation providing for the entirely new situation in the eighth century except the dictatorship of kings. In communities not yet far removed from barbarism, or in those which have relapsed into barbarism, dictatorship may be actually progressive.

It is worth while, finally, to note that the controversies of a much later date concerning "natural" law had one of their sources in the situation between the fifth and ninth century. It has been pointed out above that the two systems of jurisprudence now dominant in the western world are those of Roman Law and English Common Law. But this distinction is similar to the distinction between a so-called "natural" law expressing abstract rights of man in general, and, on the other hand, law arising out of the local custom of a particular community. In fact, what later writers called "natural" law, and in the Middle Ages "divine" law, in its civil uses is merely Roman Law. Roman Law is no more the law of men in the abstract, or of all men at all times, than any other kind of law. But in the centuries during which men believed that the past contained the fundamental rules of all possible human societies, it was easy for them to mistake the product of the Roman tradition for something different *in kind* from the laws of the new communities which arose when the Roman Empire no longer controlled the West. The obvious superiority of the Roman tradition of law was believed to be due to something universal, natural or divine. But, in fact, the contrast between the Roman and the barbarian tradition was simply the contrast between the particular form of civilization developed in one centre—Rome—and the undeveloped, primitive habits and customs of the new kingdoms of the West. The illusion of eternity clung to the name of Rome precisely because the civilization for which that name stood was already dead. After "life's fitful fever" it did not sleep, but rose again as a ghost, and seemed to be for ever established as a norm or model laid up in heaven. While France and England and the Italian cities of the Middle Ages were living and changing from day to day, the Latin language and the Roman Law remained, as it seemed, untouched by time. Even so, a ruin standing among the weeds of recent years may seem to be eternal; but the very fact that the ruin, however majestic, is a survival from a life which has vanished, makes it a dangerous model for the living form.

CHAPTER IX

MONKS AND NUNS

While the bishops secured power in social organization by co-operation with kings, the old tradition that Christianity had no concern with this world was continued and developed by hermits, monks and nuns. In the early fifth century monasticism was already established here and there in the West under the influence of the fame of eastern ascetics; but those who withdrew from the world into deserted places or lived as hermits near towns and cities, were at that time without any great influence. Their attitude and actions did not affect the tradition of civilized life in the West so much as it did in Syria, Egypt or even in the greater Greek cities, such as Alexandria and Constantinople.

This chapter is concerned with monasticism in the West only, and that only as a new system of social organization. It deals with the growth of monastic institutions from the days when a monastery or convent was a small group of men and women living apart from the rest of the world, to the days when monasteries and convents were the centres of widespread agricultural properties and schools of learning. This, therefore, is not a complete account of the monastic movement. It must exclude a full analysis and discussion of the moral and spiritual ideal expressed in the lives of monks and nuns. That ideal will be discussed elsewhere. For the purpose of this chapter, however, it is necessary to notice the intellectual and emotional needs which monasticism was intended to satisfy. Such needs were not, and are not, peculiar to the men and women of western Europe. Within the Christian tradition the Greek Churches were very much influenced by the development of monasticism; and it is well known that Buddhism has produced different forms of aceticism and monasticism in India, Burma,

Tibet, China and Japan. In every case hermits, monks and nuns have claimed to possess a deeper and more genuine understanding of true religion than other men and women.

In the medieval tradition which began in western Europe in the fifth century, the word "religio" is used to refer to the life of an ascetic. Thus, "to enter religion" meant to become a monk or nun; and when the monastic system in western Europe was reformed in the tenth and later centuries, the phrase "religious order" began to be used for the new foundations. Similarly, the decision of a person to enter the monastery is referred to by the word "conversion."[1] Christianity, in its earliest years, was for each Christian a "conversion" to a new way of life—to a "philosophy" rather than to a "religion" in the old sense of that word; but in the fifth century the majority were Christian, either because their parents were or because they followed the crowd under official patronage. Christianity, therefore, for the majority of Christians no longer meant the conscious acceptance of a new way of life. The ascetics, however, took Christianity to mean what they believed to be implied in such phrases of the Gospels as "Leave all and follow me" and "leaving father and mother."[2]

The ascetics in the West, like those in the East, did indeed claim to be in the truest sense Christians. It was not unreasonable to argue in the fifth century that, since the wealthy and the powerful were officially Christians, "real" Christianity had been forgotten. And in the sixth and seventh centuries, when everyone was nominally Christian in the Roman world and the barbarian kingdoms, it seemed not unlikely that nobody was "really" Christian. When St. Benedict composed his rule, the Roman Empire was governed by an imperial Court under the influence of the Empress, Theodora, who had begun her career as a "revue" actress. In the seventh and eighth centuries the treacherous and violent kings and queens of the Franks, and the rivals who contended for the Roman Empire

---

[1] Reg. St. Benedicti, c. 63. "Conversionis tempus"—translated in the edition of Dom Hunter Blair as "the time of his entering religion." So in Aquinas (Summa Theol., ii. iiae., q. 187, art. 1), "utrum sit tantum una religio." It is not a lapse into toleration when he decides that there can be many "religiones."

[2] So Cassian in his Conlationes makes his ascetics quote Matthew xix. 8.

by blinding and slitting the tongues of their opponents, all claimed to be Christians and Catholic. It was hardly strange, therefore, that those who took Christianity somewhat more seriously should flee from the world.

A Social Experiment

In the fifth century, however, the organization of the Churches under the clergy was already too strong to be controlled by enthusiasts. And yet, after four centuries, in the ninth century monasticism had become a powerful force affecting not only the organization of the Church but also the whole structure of society in the new kingdoms of western Europe. The history of the early growth of monasticism in the West, therefore, is the record of a social invention. A new type of institution was developed, which had been entirely unknown in the civilization of Greece and Rome.

No one in the early fifth century, still less anyone among the early Christians, could have foreseen the influence of the great abbots of the ninth century. Indeed, even the hermits of Lerins in the fifth century, who were the immediate predecessors of the monks of Fulda or St. Germain des Prés or Jarrow, would perhaps have been astonished to see the princely abbots of the First Europe, leading troops to battle, or providing armed retainers for war, in the name of Christianity. But the history of every great institution would astonish its founders. And those who in the twentieth century attempt to look back at the growth of monastic influence in European civilization, are in danger of forgetting that monasticism began as a social experiment. It is essential for understanding the history of such an experiment that it should not be supposed, even unconsciously, that what occurred in the ninth century was in any sense an inevitable result of what was attempted in the fifth. When the first hermits in western countries gathered in communities, the Roman Empire seemed to be still secure and eternal. But when St. Boniface founded the monastery at Fulda, the Empire was hardly remembered even by scholars. Again, the history of the early years of monasticism involves attention to the influence of great men, such as St. Benedict, whose character and intelligence cannot possibly be treated as an inevitable consequence of anything that had preceded him. But here is a paradox. Monasticism in the fifth century was a flight from Roman civilization. Those who fled into deserts or hermitages repudiated, not merely the social fashions of their time, but also the obligations of citizenship; and many cut themselves off, especially in the East, from the ceremonies and sacraments of the Church itself. But four centuries later, what had been a flight from civilized life had become an escape from barbarism; and the successors of those who had rejected Roman culture were the chief agents in preserving what was left of it. The monasteries of the ninth century in western Europe were the homes of such learning and such arts as could be retained or revived in the ashes of the Roman tradition. The evidence for this transformation will be found in a comparison of the most influential book of early monasticism, the *Conversations* of Cassian, with the work of the ninth century abbot, Walafridus Strabo *On Church Organization* and of Wandalbert of Prüm, whose poem *On the Signs of the Months* is a string of quotations from Ovid's *Fasti* and Virgil's *Georgics*. Two tendencies, no doubt, were always present in monasticism—the asceticism which seeks independence of all the external world and the absorption in the higher flights of the imagination and intelligence, which necessarily depends upon learning and the arts. Simple men and women, and those exhausted by the demands of normal life, seek refuge in mental inertia; but more subtle minds find relief from the minor cares of life in concentration upon objects and issues which are not obvious to the majority. Therefore the history of monasticism in all ages includes both the simpler and the more subtle forms of renunciation. But in general terms it is true that the monks and the hermits of the fifth century rejected learning and the arts, whereas those of the ninth and later centuries preserved them.

Asceticism in the West

Monasticism is based upon asceticism. The life of the ascetic had been admired in eastern countries long before the establishment of Christianity; and even in Greece the Cynics had reduced the doctrines of Stoicism to a form of the so-called "simple life." It was believed by some who claimed to be philosophers that the needs and still more the pleasures of what they called "the body" obstructed the life of what they chose to regard as "the spirit." As it has been well said, such ascetics "seek to make men free by breaking the ties that bind them to their fellow-men, to the objects of their desires, and to everything that is not themselves. But with every tie they break, with every relation they repudiate, their own life becomes poorer. . . . Refusing to weaken themselves by luxury, because it enslaves men to outward things, they end in counting everything a luxury which men can exist without, that is to say, everything except the satisfaction of the barest sensuous wants. And, after all, they find that man is bound to the world he would escape as firmly as ever, though now only by the vulgar tie of appetite."[1]

Indeed, the primitive attempt to explain human personality by supposing that it is a composite of two separable substances, body and spirit, underlies the whole theory and practice of traditional asceticism. But the theory of the "soul" must be discussed elsewhere. It is enough here to note that the traditional and popular philosophy was generally accepted in the fifth century by anyone who thought at all on such subjects, and that this theory had the strangest effects upon practical life and religious custom.

In accordance with the theory of the distinction between body and spirit, it was generally believed that fasting and the limitation of sensuous enjoyment released the "spirit" from "material" limitations. The old mistake of even the greatest philosophers, Plato and Aristotle, who supposed that thinking or contemplation did not involve the use of any bodily "instrument" or any "material" change in the organism, was perpetuated by the ascetics in their effort to escape from the objects of sight and hearing. An ancient and mistaken philosophy, still regarded by many as common sense, divides the objects of perception and thought into the "material" and "spiritual"; and perhaps, under the influence of certain Oriental creeds, Christianity in the fifth century had also accepted the false

---

[1] E. Caird, *Evolution of Theology in the Greek Philosophers* (1904), vol. ii, p. 64.

idea that what was "material" was somehow morally degrading. Thus, the ascetics could deny themselves, not only the use of water for washing, but also all food and drink except what was barely necessary, in the belief that such abstinence made the "soul" pure.

The most important form of abstinence preached by hermits, monks and nuns was perpetual celibacy. The fear of the sex impulse had led, from the earliest days of Christianity, to the attempt to restrict the marriage of the clergy. But the attempt was only partially successful in the early fifth century, when the introduction of monasticism in the West reinforced the same tendency. Those who cut themselves off from the world were specially concerned to avoid sexual intercourse and anything connected with it. Indeed, the violence of language of St. Jerome, in his attack on Vigilantius, who had proposed that the clergy should marry, is an indication that the fear of the sex impulse had become an obsession. St. Jerome declared that he himself had fled to the desert because he did not feel strong enough to resist the attractions of the other sex. And, according to the legend, St. Benedict had to fling himself naked into briers and nettles in order to escape from the memory of a woman he had seen.[1] In the history of monasticism from its earliest years, the fact that the communities in monasteries and convents were communities of celibates had an immense influence. Nature driven out, returned in the strangest forms. Repression, in the modern sense of that word, caused vision and terrors and often madness. In the earliest eastern Rule which had an influence upon the West, that of St. Pachomius, the dangers of homosexual practices are clearly implied in the regulation, for example, against washing and that concerning the distance between the beds of the monks. But apart from moral difficulties in the new form of asceticism, which will be discussed elsewhere, it should be recognized that the view of the universe and of man, of religion and of deity, developed in communities of celibates, was in many respects abnormal. Thus the philosophy and theology of a celibate caste are inevitably alien to the normal human experience upon which a wider and more exact knowledge is based. Celibates who fear

[1] Greg. M., *Dial.*, ii, 2.

the sexual impulse, often suffer from "visions" which are difficult to distinguish from reality. Again, the social effects of celibacy in monasteries and convents were also important, especially in a period of comparative barbarism. Monastic celibacy involved that many of the most intelligent and deeply religious men and women were without children, and, therefore, lacked the influence which as parents they might have had upon the future of society. Monastic asceticism, therefore, especially with respect to the sexual impulse, has had many unintended effects upon social institutions in general. It tended to perpetuate barbarism outside the circle of those who had no children and, therefore, could not transmit directly their own idealism. It obstructed progress by leaving the control of social power to the lower levels of human personality.

Religious Defeatism

The general theory and practice of asceticism, however, was reinforced in the fifth century in western Europe by the "failure of nerve," which led many to suppose that there was no hope of justice and peace in the world of their time; and this despair was reinforced by a sense, not altogether illusory, of the decay of ancient institutions. Men and women fled from a world which seemed to them to be falling in ruins. The belief that the Roman Empire was the last great system of government which would exist before the dissolution of all things, reinforced the sense of hopelessness which led such men as Paulinus of Nola to give up public office. Others, less intelligent and less earnest than he, might also feel that they were aliens in a world so largely controlled by those who desired nothing but wealth and power for themselves.

The depression which affects the finest minds in times of social ransition has many causes. New issues, not clearly understood, eave men and women exhausted, if their intelligence is not equal to their earnestness; and intelligence which is adequate for maintaining a tradition, may not be able to create new social institutions. Again, in the early fifth century the slave-system and continuous civil wars had reduced the number of children, leaving a larger proportion of the aged in most communities. But any community in which there is an increase in the number of the old and a decrease in the number of the young, suffers from "defeatism," or depression in the climate of opinion—the more so if its poets and preachers are childless men. The very fact that the Last Judgement was believed to be at hand led men and women to care little for a world which was soon to perish. St. Augustine wrote that it was useless for Christians to have many more children, because the seats vacated in heaven by the fallen angels were already almost full. Two centuries after Augustine, Gregory the Great was equally certain that the world was near its end; and in his *Book of Morals*, a commentary upon the Book of Job, which was intended for the use of monks, he indicates the sense of helplessness in the prevailing collapse of government, where he discusses the murder of a good man by brigands.[1] Both Augustine and Gregory agreed that God Himself designed the deaths of good men by violence, either to correct the sins of the world or to give them eternal happiness more speedily.

Finally, the flight from the world, with its pleasures and obligations, was partly due to an "infirmity of noble minds," not indeed ambition, but distrust of common folk and simple things. The ascetic, whether hermit, monk or nun, like many intellectuals to-day, was unable to see in common life anything but what was mean or trivial. And this blindness led to a desertion of the cities and the Churches on the part of those who might have saved their fellows. It is true that, as Paulinus of Nola said, their eyes were fixed upon the stars. And the confusion of the time, both in the fifth and in the seventh centuries, made it more difficult for the finer sort of man or woman to follow his highest inclination. But although the ascetics achieved something new, which is now to be described, they did so at a cost which has never been adequately recognized. There was no "necessity" in the collapse of Roman government or in the later collapse of ecclesiastical discipline. The seeping of barbarism through the dykes of social order was, indeed,

---

[1] Greg. Mag., *Moralia*, part iii, bk. ii. "Almighty God . . . suffers him either to be spoiled of his goods or even to be killed." The Book of Job had a great influence in promoting religious defeatism, and the exceedingly dubious virtue of "resignation."

partly due to the desertion of their fellows by those who sought first to save their own souls. The effort to preserve even the arts and sciences is no excuse for neglecting the defence and maintenance of the simpler bases of civilized life. And even heavenly visions are not legitimate substitutes for attending to the bare facts. The ascetics were in many ways mistaken. They took the wrong path in more than one crisis. But monasteries from the fifth to the ninth century nevertheless contrived to preserve at least some fragments of civilized life.

Two more points should be noted before considering the history of monasticism. First, the distinction between the clergy on the one hand and hermits, monks and nuns on the other; and secondly, the position of women. The clergy, from bishops to those in minor orders, were essentially officials of the Christian community. They were "ordained"; that is to say, they entered into "orders," like the "ordines" of the Roman tradition, by special rites and ceremonies. The duties of the clergy, and especially of the bishops, concerned directly the lives of all Christians. Their functions included the performance of public rites and ceremonies and the management of the properties of the Churches. But, as St. Jerome wrote, the position of monks and clergy was entirely different.[1] The clergy were at first regarded by ascetics as hardly more Christian than the unenthusiastic laity. Hermits, monks and nuns, on the other hand, were individuals who lived apart from the common life of the Christian community. They chose for themselves their manner of life and were not elected or set apart by any public act as were the clergy. In the early days of monasticism very few hermits or monks were priests and few became bishops. But as the monks developed a life in common among themselves, the need for the services and sacraments of the Church led to the ordination as priests of an increasing number of them. Thus, while monasticism affected the clergy by the spread of celibacy as an obligation of deacons, priests and bishops, the clergy affected monasticism by introducing into the monasteries those who were able to provide ceremonies and sacraments even for the laity who became in later

[1] Jerome, Ep. xiv, 8, "alia monachorum est causa, alia clericorum."

days neighbours and dependents of the greater monasteries. The monasteries, therefore, after the sixth century fulfilled certain new functions in the life of the Church as a whole and in the life of the communities around them.

As for the position of women, from the earliest days of Christianity women were excluded from the performance of the chief official functions of the Churches, and therefore from among the clergy. On the other hand, monasticism provided for complete equality of status between men and women. For example, Caesaria, the sister of Caesarius, bishop of Arles, governed a community of nuns in the sixth century. Later in that century, St. Radegunda established her convent at Poitiers and provided for the service of the aged and the sick. In the seventh century St. Hilda and St. Etheldreda governed communities of men as well as women; and in the eighth century the correspondence of St. Boniface and his friend, the Abbess Bugga, indicates the importance of the position acquired by women. This, however, will be discussed in greater detail in a later section of this chapter.

Early Monasticism in the West

In the last days of the Roman Empire in the West, hermits and solitaries lived both within the cities, aloof from public life, and in the wilder parts of the coasts and islands of Gaul and Italy. Rutilius complains in his poem of those who had deserted their civic duties to live in caves. He thinks of them as men who have returned to savagery, who are unclean and uneducated.[1] He could not have imagined that his poem would be preserved for later generations in a community of monks at Bobbio! But so far as he could see, ascetics left the civilized world without fulfilling their duties in it. On the other hand, as it was pointed out above, educated and wealthy men and women felt the need to retire into solitude. Some, like Paulinus of Nola, had held public office and wished to devote themselves to prayer, contemplation and charitable work. Others, like the Roman ladies who corresponded with St. Jerome, some of whom followed him to his hermitage in the Holy Land,

[1] Rutilius Namatianus, De Reditu, i, 440. Squallet lucifugis insula plena viris.

felt that the life of a true Christian could not be reconciled with
the customs of fashionable society. But among the many different
kinds of men and women who became hermits or monks, were
some who wandered from place to place, living upon the gifts of
devout Christians, and sometimes criticizing less enthusiastic members of the Churches. Thus, although the ascetic life for men and
women was everywhere praised and supported by the Christian
people and the authorities of the Church, the bishops might at
times feel some irritation, similar to that of the pagan poet, at the
eccentricities of "holy" men.

Such irritation is expressed in St. Augustine's treatise on *Monk's
Work*. He objects not only to the idleness of wandering "holy
men" but also to their sale of dubious relics.[1] But he is chiefly
annoyed by those among the ascetics who would, in modern
times, be called the *intelligentsia*, who claimed to possess a superior
education, and undertook the criticism of the Christian Church.
St. Augustine is doubtful of the superior value of the education of
such men;[2] and he remarks that it would be better for the Church
if they learnt to keep silence. As Augustine says, "Would that
those who don't want to work with their hands would refrain
from working with their tongues."[3] In every new movement there
are to be found a small number of men and women whose sense of
superior virtue or intelligence induces them to condemn simple
folk; and when a new moral ideal is being embodied in practice,
exaggeration and eccentricity may do more harm than quiet
persistence in ordinary life.

Nevertheless, the majority of men and women in the early fifth
century were very much impressed by examples of extreme asceticism. The effects of lack of food and clothing, and certain deficiencies
in cleanliness, were often mistaken by the simple-minded for
holiness; and besides, as in India to-day, abstinence from the
ordinary pleasures of life was supposed to give the ascetic excep-

---

[1] Augustine, *De opere monachorum* (*C.S.E.L.*), xxviii, 36, "alii membra martyrum,
si tamen martyrum, venditant; . . ."
[2] Ibid., xxi, 25, "non melius, sicut multi putant, sed, quod est verum, languidius
educati. . . ."
[3] Ibid., xxii, 26, "utinam isti, qui vacare volunt manibus, omnino vacarent et
linguis."

tional powers.[1] In the West examples of extreme wealth and luxury were fewer than in the East, and so were examples of extreme asceticism. But at the end of the fourth century there were already thousands of men and women in the West who freely adopted the physical conditions of life which were common among the slaves and impoverished workers of the time. The most famous of these ascetics was St. Martin of Tours, who had been a Roman soldier, had retired from civilization into the un-developed part of Gaul, and had attracted by his asceticism and spiritual enthusiasm many followers and imitators. His life by Sulpicius Severus, a contemporary, expresses both the growing appetite for miracles and the admiration for a new type of moral excellence, the saint of the Middle Ages.[2]

The variety of the self-tortures and the eccentricities of ascetics in the Latin Churches continued throughout the fifth and sixth centuries.[3] But, on the whole, the more extreme forms of asceticism, such as that of the Pillar Saints of the East, and the convulsions of unstable minds were gradually overcome by the influence of those more reasonable ascetics whose experience did not remove them entirely from contact with their fellows.[4] Such men and women gradually formed themselves into communities. Groups of hermits or solitaries lived as neighbours in desert places, in caves or on islands, and in such districts necessity drove them to clear the land and to cultivate what they required for food and clothing.

Of all the islands in the western Mediterranean to which hermits resorted, the most famous in the fifth century was Lerins. Thither Honoratus, a nobleman, had fled from the confusions which

---

[1] Buddha is said to have asked a fakir what he had gained by many years of self-torture; and when the fakir replied that he was now able to cross the river without wetting his feet, Buddha replied that the ferryman would have done it for him at the cost of a penny. "Fakir" is an Arabic word meaning "poor."

[2] St. Martin's cloak (*cappa*) became the magical relic of the Frankish kings in the eighth century, useful for securing victory in battle, and cared for by a priest, called *cappelanus* (chaplain).

[3] Greg. Tur., *Vitae Patr.*, 15 (A saint loaded with chains), and *Vitae Patr.*, 5 (A saint loaded with a large stone and refraining from all sleep).

[4] The one Pillar Saint of the West of whom there is any record had his pillar removed by the bishop of the diocese. Greg. Tur., *H.F.*, viii, 15.

accompanied the barbarian invasions of southern Gaul; and there he assembled round him a company of fellow-hermits and monks. These men had educated and vigorous minds, which soon made their settlement a centre of learning, although the school of thought which their chief writers represented was believed by the followers of St. Augustine to be tainted with the errors of Pelagius. At Lerins, Faustus wrote on the controversy concerning freewill and predestination; and Salvian wrote on the government of God. In Lerins also Vincent composed the *Commonitorium*, which contains the famous phrase concerning the Catholic faith, that it was what was believed always, everywhere and by all—"*quod semper, quod ubique, quod ab omnibus.*" Among the monks at Lerins some of the most famous bishops of Gaul had been trained: for example, Hilary, bishop of Arles, Lupus, bishop of Troyes, Germanus, bishop of Auxerre, and Caesarius, bishop of Arles. The tradition of monasticism at Lerins was that of the earlier solitaries or hermits, who lived indeed as neighbours although each pursued his own practices of asceticism.

It was not, however, until Cassian, an eastern monk, founded at Marseilles the monastery of St. Victor, that monasticism, as contrasted with the life of solitaries, can be said to have begun in western Europe. Cassian had visited the most famous ascetics in Egypt and Syria and had studied their manner of life. Coming to the West, he wrote in Latin two books which became the basis of monastic tradition and were used throughout the Middle Ages. The first work, *On the Customs of Those who Renounce the World*, was written about A.D. 420. This deals with the food and dress and daily habits of eastern ascetics, and therefore provides some guidance by which the eccentricities of enthusiasts may be corrected.[1] But even more important in its later influence was Cassian's second work, *Conversations of the Fathers of the Desert*,[2] which St. Benedict later assigned to be read by all his monks.[3] In the former book, although the customs followed by the eastern ascetics are described,

---

[1] *De Institutis Renuntiantium.*

[2] *Conlationes Patrum in Scittisco Eremo Commorantium.*

[3] A "collation" is a light meal, so called because it was taken while the *Collationes* of Cassian were being read.

no general rule is laid down and the old ascetic ideal of the solitary is accepted. Thus the groups of men and women who followed the old tradition could hardly yet be called monks and nuns. Similarly in Cassian's *Conversations* the emphasis lies upon the individual effort to preserve and develop the spiritual life. Cassian had visited many of the most noted or most holy ascetics of the desert; and the account he gives of the conversations with them deals with the motives for Christian asceticism, the methods of different hermits and the dangers or difficulties of the solitary life. But the moral ideals expressed in all this must be discussed elsewhere. So far as social organization is concerned, little more is implied in Cassian's teaching than a spiritual direction by some leading ascetic, who is called "abbas."

Half a century later Caesarius was consecrated bishop of Arles, at the age of thirty-three, in A.D. 502. He had been trained as a boy from the thirteenth year of his age among the hermits of Lerins, and had later lived the life of a solitary in Arles. He was bishop of Arles for forty years, and was at certain times in trouble with the Goths who controlled that part of Gaul, first under Alaric II and afterwards under Theodoric the Ostrogoth. He composed two lists of rules, one for monks and one for nuns, which were followed in the monastery he founded and the convent governed by his sister Caesaria, in Arles. These rules deal with submission to a superior; and they enter into great detail on some points of practice, as, for example, in the instructions that nuns should not take in certain washing from the laity. But the development of the monastic life was not carried very far in Gaul before the influence of St. Benedict had been felt.

Irish Monasticism

The same tradition of asceticism and life in solitude had a powerful development in Ireland, apparently soon after the death of St. Patrick. By the middle of the fifth century, therefore, the older form of monasticism—the practice of solitaries—seems to have dominated the Christian communities in Ireland. The social situation there was difficult and much more primitive than the situation in any of the countries which had been under the Roman dominion. The Irish, then known as Scots (Scotti), lived in small settlements of kinsfolk under patriarchal rulers. Christianity spread by the conversion of whole settlements; and within such settlements some of the more enthusiastic or earnest Christians lived apart as hermits or solitaries. Where the number of these ascetics was large, a ruler or abbot, in the earlier or eastern sense of the word, might govern not only the solitaries but also the whole community. Within such a community priests and bishops were subject to the rule of the abbot; and under one abbot there might be many bishops. But such bishops had no dioceses, as bishops had in the Roman tradition. Monasticism of this tradition in the sixth century dominated the organization of the Irish Churches. The clergy as officials and representatives of all Christians in a community, and especially the bishops who had the responsibility for the administration of sacraments and the performance of the most important ceremonies, were subordinate in influence and social prestige to the "holy men" whose position was secured by their personal virtue or ability. Thus, if the Irish tradition had survived, there might have been in part of Europe a monastic government similar to that of Tibet. The priests and the other officials of the Christian Churches would have become merely subordinate functionaries under the rule of a Grand Lama. Sacraments and ceremonies would have become merely popular "prayer-wheels" used by the unenlightened, under a select group of visionaries.

The Irish monks, however, combined with their desire for solitude a passion for missionary effort. Thus in A.D. 563 St. Columba, after having founded many monastic settlements in Ireland, established at Iona, an island on the coast of Mull, a monastery from which he and his fellow-monks went out to convert the peoples of what is now Scotland.[1] He seems to have travelled in many parts of Scotland and often revisited Ireland. He died in A.D. 597, that is, in the year when Augustine landed with his company of Benedictine monks from Rome in Kent. Under St. Columba

[1] His *Life* was written by the Benedictine abbot Adamnan (d. A.D. 704), *Pat. Lat.*, 88, col. 727 sq. Bede, *H.E.*, v, 16, reports how Adamnan adopted the "English" date for Easter. The *Life* of Columba is entirely a record of miracles, etc.

monasticism remained a life of ascetic solitaries, who studied and preached but had no definite life in common.

Fifty-four years before the death of Columba, in the year of the death of St. Benedict, A.D. 543, St. Columban was born in Ireland.[1] In A.D. 585 he left Ireland with twelve companions for France and established in Burgundy the great monastery of Luxeuil (Luxovium). The Rule, which is traditionally supposed to be his, deals mainly with the absolute obedience of the monks to their abbot and the effort at continuous self-discipline by each individual. Definite punishments or penances are laid down in the Rule for any offences against it, in the manner of the *Penitentials*, which had come into general use in Ireland and Great Britain. For twenty years St. Columban lived as far as possible in solitude in the Vosges mountains; but he went out at times to preach. His efforts to reform the clergy in the Burgundian kingdom, however, were seriously hampered by the fact that he brought with him the Irish method of fixing the date of Easter and the Irish style of the tonsure. Columban was attacked by the clergy at a synod in A.D. 602; and when he followed up his attempts at reforming them by public rebukes of queen Brunihault, who dominated her grandson king Theodoric (Thierry II), he was banished from the kingdom in A.D. 610.

Columban and his fellow-hermit, St. Gall, then retired to the hills near the Lake of Constance; but from there also St. Columban was compelled to flee when the Burgundians invaded those parts. Leaving St. Gall to establish the famous monastery which bears his name, where throughout the Middle Ages the collection and copying of manuscripts preserved the tradition of learning, Columban himself then went to Italy and was favourably received by Theudelinda, queen of the Lombards, a friend of Pope Gregory the Great. Near her capital Columban established a new monastery at Bobbio, where also the life of the solitaries was combined with the preservation of sacred and secular learning. Columban died in A.D. 615 in a cave to which he had retired, thus continuing throughout his life to maintain the old tradition of the ascetic solitary. For him

[1] Jonas, *Vita S. Columbani*, Pertz, *Script. R.G.*

and indeed for the whole of the early Irish tradition, the monastic ideal was that of hermits who happened to live in close proximity but without any organized labour in common. In its general effect upon the Church and society as a whole, this monastic tradition depended upon the preaching of individual ascetics and the influence of their personal abilities or virtues. Columban and other monks of his tradition laboured earnestly for the reform of the morals of the clergy and of the wealthy and powerful laity. They looked for support to the more virtuous bishops; but they had no definite connection with the organization of the Church. They were like the prophets of the Old Testament, who rebuked the kings. Columban communicated with the bishops of Rome in his efforts to reform the clergy. A letter of his to Gregory the Great asks advice for dealing with the bishops of Gaul and also argues a case for the Irish tradition in the dating of Easter; but it is not certain if this letter was ever despatched. Another letter of Columban to the later Pope, Boniface IV, argues the case against the official attitude of the bishops of Rome with regard to the controversy of the Three Chapters. The Saint writes in both letters with great respect for the See of St. Peter; but clearly he regards himself as competent to judge and rebuke any bishop however exalted. His efforts at reform, both in discipline and in doctrine, were those of an individual who believed himself to be under divine guidance. He established no new system of organization, and had very little influence outside the circle of his immediate acquaintance upon the course of ecclesiastical reform. The monasteries he founded became centres of piety and learning; but nothing could be more striking than the contrast between the influence of this earlier formless monastic tradition and the influence of the Rule of St. Benedict.

Monastic Learning: Cassiodorus

An entirely different tradition took the place of the old ideal of the solitaries. In the middle of the sixth century, while the Roman civilization in Italy was under the military control of Gothic kings, two men of good birth, educated in the old Roman tradition, established what was afterwards to become the dominant system of monasticism. Cassiodorus, the learned and wealthy Roman official, who served Theodoric and his immediate successors, retired at the age of seventy from public life, in A.D. 540, to his own estate at Vivarium in Bruttii. There he established a community of monks. A place was provided for those who desired to live in accordance with the customs of the hermits. But the most important members of the group were those under the guidance of Cassiodorus himself, who, besides practising a traditional asceticism, studied sacred and profane literature, copied manuscripts and otherwise maintained the earliest school of learning within the monastic system. Cassiodorus himself wrote his latest works for the use of his monks. He had hoped, as he explains, in earlier years to establish with the help of the bishop of Rome, in Rome itself, a school of Christian learning; but the continuous wars made it impossible to carry out this plan. It was, therefore, as a modification of an earlier plan that Cassiodorus founded the tradition of learning and literature in a monastic retreat. He was interested also in such science as was available, and is said to have spent some of his time in his monastery in the making of sundials and water-clocks. When he was ninety-three years old he composed a treatise on Grammar, which consists largely of extracts from the Classical Grammarians. Already, therefore, a monastery had become, not merely a refuge from the world, but a means of preserving a tradition of civilized life in the midst of surrounding barbarism. Here the life of a small community, removed from the dangers and difficulties of the wars which ruined Italy, was the basis not of the eccentricity of ascetics but of genuine study and thought.

The Monastic System: St. Benedict

The greatest step forward, however, at this time was made by the Roman, St. Benedict.[1] He is said to have been repelled by the licence of the youths of Rome, among whom he had been sent for his education. He left the city and lived as a hermit near what is now Subiaco. After failing to control the rebellious monks of a

---

[1] Most of the facts with regard to St. Benedict are known to us through Pope Gregory the Great, *Dialogues*, bk. ii.

settlement, whose members had asked him to be their abbot, he left and, returning to his old hermitage, was eventually surrounded by admiring disciples. From his experience in guiding these, no doubt, he derived the principles which he expressed in his Rule. He eventually established his chief monastery at Monte Cassino, where in A.D. 542 he is said to have been visited by the Gothic warrior king Totila. The story goes that he greeted the warrior with the words, "You have done evil: you have fought wars"; and the word "peace" became the motto of all Benedictine houses. St. Benedict's sister, Scholastica, had lived near the monastery, but whether as a hermit or as a member of a community of women is not clear. St. Benedict died in A.D. 543.

The Rule of St. Benedict was composed at the very time that the Emperor Justinian issued his law-books. The contrast between these two men and between the works which have preserved their influence into modern times may serve to indicate some of the problems of the transition from Roman civilization to that of the Middle Ages. This contrast between Benedict and Justinian must not be supposed to be that between good and evil; but it is a distinction between an absolute ruler concerned chiefly with wealth and power and the control over millions in far distant countries, and a man who cared for none of these things but sought through self-control to help a small number in intimate relationship with him to live in its finest form what is traditionally called the "inner life." But the characters of Justinian and Benedict need not be further discussed. It is more important for the present purpose to note that Justinian in his policy and in his law-books was an "archaist."[1] He attempted to revive the power of the Roman Empire in the West; and he authorized the collection of legal documents in Latin which were already obsolete under his own jurisdiction, as is shown by the fact that his own new laws were issued in Greek. Justinian, who was not Roman, strove to maintain the Roman Empire by preserving its past. St. Benedict, on the other hand, who was a Roman, trained in the Roman tradition,

[1] This word is used by Professor Toynbee in his *Study of History*, vol. vi, where he refers to Justinian's work.

established an entirely new social organization in a Rule derived from the immediate problems of a world in which civilized life was falling in ruin.

Again, the effect of Justinian's policy of conquest in the western Mediterranean was disastrous, and eventually caused the separation between the civilization of the West and the Roman Empire in the East. On the other hand, St. Benedict's influence increased immensely throughout western Christendom for about a thousand years after his death by the foundation of communities living under his Rule. The law-books of Justinian did, indeed, provide in the later Middle Ages for the study of law by a small intellectual caste; and they have had an effect upon all European systems of law which have been based upon the Roman. But the collections of decrees and opinions made by others under Justinian's authority, were merely the gleanings from a long-vanished past, even when these collections were made; and it is at least arguable that they have had a pernicious effect in tying legal principle and practice to the memory of an obsolete system of society. The Rule of St. Benedict, on the other hand, whatever its immediate sources, was an imaginative statement of a practical ideal of life in a community; and all the reforms of monasticism which were found necessary from the ninth to the thirteenth century were based upon efforts to return to the original simplicity and "discretion" of the Rule.[1]

The Rule of St. Benedict begins with instructions about the functions of the abbot. He is to have absolute authority; but he is chosen by the monks, and is directed to consult the whole community on all fundamental questions, and to allow the expression of opinion by each, even the youngest. On problems of smaller importance he is to consult a few of the older monks. It must be remembered that this was written in the middle of the sixth century, when slavery continued throughout the western world and personal

---

[1] The edition of the Rule by Dom Cuthbert Butler gives an indication of the sources used by St. Benedict. These include the works of St. Augustine, St. Jerome, Cassian, the Rules of St. Caesarius, St. Basil, St. Macarius, etc. The Rule as it now stands was not all written at the same time. The Introduction was probably the latest part composed.

violence was frequent. Even in monasteries such violence was not unknown. Cassian, for example, writes of an abbot who, during a visit of many other monks to his monastery, hit one of his own monks a blow which could be heard even by those sitting far off, because this monk had been a little slow in his service.[1] And Pope Gregory two centuries later writes in his *Dialogues* of an abbot who hit one of his monks first with his fists and then with a stool, bruising him badly in the face.[2] The writer in both cases does not blame the abbot but expresses admiration for the patience of the sufferers. The abbot of St. Benedict's Rule, however, is not merely to give due consideration to the opinions of his subjects; he is also directed to avoid oppressing the community by excessive discipline and austerities. It is laid down in the Rule, however, that whipping is to be the punishment for monks who do not reform their ways after milder correction, and for boys in the monasteries. St. Benedict also provided for other officials of the monastery and for the management of the common property. As for the daily life of the monks, the Rule advocates a moderate asceticism, but not great austerity. Indeed, the influence of St. Benedict was directed against both the extreme practices of self-torture, common among the eastern hermits, and against the competition in pain, dirt and starvation in which so many of the saints of the desert continually indulged. For such reasons as this Pope Gregory the Great remarks upon the "discretion" or moderation of the Rule.[3] The work of the day is to consist of "divine labour" (*opus divinum*), manual labour, implying mainly agricultural work, and reading or study. Divine labour meant the recitation of psalms and prayers at fixed hours. This is to take precedence of all other duties. Manual work in all the Benedictine monasteries from the sixth to the ninth century was necessarily in the main agricultural, especially in the monasteries which were founded in the wilder tracts of Europe in those days. Reading and study, as the duty of Benedictines, carried on the tradition established by Cassiodorus. It meant largely the study of the Scriptures and of the writings of the Christian Fathers, and was connected with the education of boys, which from the

[1] Cassian, *Col.*, xix, I.   [2] Greg. Mag., *Dial.*, i, 2.   [3] Ibid., ii, 36.

very beginning formed part of the work of all the great Benedictine monasteries.

The greater part of the Rule is concerned with spiritual direction concerning the individual life of the monks. But the moral ideal implied in all this will be discussed elsewhere. Much is taken for granted. Nothing, for example, is said about celibacy or the relation of the monastery as a whole to the world outside or even to the Church in general. Priests may be admitted as monks (c. 60); and if the abbot desires to have a priest or deacon ordained for himself (or the monastery), he must choose among his monks someone worthy of the priesthood (c. 62). Thus it was assumed that the majority of the monks were not members of the clergy. The seasonal manual labour (c. 48) is, no doubt, connected with the rule (c. 57) that, if there are any skilled workers (*artifices*) in the monastery, they should work at their crafts with the permission of the abbot. Also, ideally a monastery ought to be so organized that all things necessary are to be found within it—that is to say, water, a mill, a garden and various crafts, in order that it should not be necessary for the monks to go "outside" (c. 66). This rule is regarded as so important that it ends with the words—"this Rule we desire to be often read in the community lest any of the brethren have the excuse of ignorance of it."

The Benedictines

Monasteries under the Rule of St. Benedict were founded in many parts of Italy during the fifty years that separate the death of St. Benedict from the election of Gregory the Great as bishop of Rome. Gregory himself, who had had experience of administration in the civil service of the city, eventually decided to retire from worldly life and founded a monastery in his own house in Rome, in which he himself lived as one of the monks. His admiration for the Rule of St. Benedict is expressed in his *Dialogues*; and when he became bishop of Rome, he followed two policies: first, the foundation of many new monasteries and, secondly, the reformation of these monasteries and nunneries which had departed from the observance of the Benedictine Rule. Many of his letters support or encourage the foundation of monasteries by landowners on their estates. From his own personal property he endowed six new monasteries in Sicily besides that in Rome.[1] The estates of the Roman Church were also used by him to support various monasteries and nunneries. The reform of monasteries and nunneries was essential for the preservation of the monastic ideal, as can be seen both in the letters of Gregory the Great and in the *History of the Franks* by Gregory of Tours. The most obvious and most general difficulty arose from the abandonment of convents by nuns who desired to be married, the wandering of monks from place to place, and the accumulation of private property by individual monks. All these evils are recorded by the two Gregories at the end of the sixth century in Italy and Gaul; and they are referred to even in the Rule of St. Benedict, which condemns wandering monks and private ownership by monks.

Gregory the Great remained in spirit a monk when he became bishop of Rome; and the most important aspect of his influence upon later monasticism is the connection he established between the 'ergy, in particular the bishops, and the monks and nuns. Gregory looked to the bishops of the diocese to control the monks and nuns who had offended against the Rule. On the other hand, he prevented bishops from interfering too closely in the internal concerns of monasteries and nunneries. The councils of the Church, as it will be shown later, had from early times been concerned to prevent monks and monasteries being entirely exempt from the jurisdiction of the bishops. But owing to the influence of Gregory's general policy, both in preserving the observance of the Rule and in his use of monks as missionaries, the greater monasteries after the sixth century gained great independence of episcopal jurisdiction through closer relations with the Papacy. Indeed, a new stage in the history of monasticism was reached in the last decade of the sixth century when Gregory the Great sent out as missionaries from Rome to the peoples of England Augustine and about forty other monks from Gregory's own monastery on the Coelian hill. This small company of missionaries stopped on the way with the

[1] Dudden, *Gregory the Great*, ii, p. 174.

monks of Lerins; and at Aix, near Marseilles, they were so overcome by stories of the savagery of the Anglo-Saxons that Augustine
actually returned to Rome. But the Pope urged the missionaries
forward and arranged for support for them from the rulers of the
Franks and for interpreters to go with them from France to Britain.[1]

The eventual foundation of the first Benedictine monastery in
England at Canterbury, and the increase in the number and importance of these monasteries, are described in Bede's *History*. Bede
himself, in his character and works, was one of the most excellent
examples of the civilizing influence of the Benedictine Rule. He
says of his own life at the end of his *History* that he was "priest at
the monastery of the Blessed Apostles Peter and Paul, which is at
Wearmouth and Jarrow, born in the territory of that monastery,
and given at seven years of age to be educated by the most reverend
Abbot Benedict (Biscop) and afterwards by Ceolfrid. Spending all
the rest of my life in that monastery, I devoted myself wholly to
the study of Scripture and in the observance of regular discipline
and the daily care of singing in the church. I always took delight
in learning, teaching and writing. In the nineteenth year of my age
I was ordained deacon, and in the thirtieth ordained priest, in both
cases by the most reverend bishop John and by the order of the
Abbot Ceolfrid. From that time to the fifty-ninth year of my age
I have laboured for the use of myself and my fellows to compile
from the works of the Fathers and to interpret and explain the
following. . . ."[2] The list which follows is an indication of the
range of monastic learning in those days. As for the other arts,
Bede's life of his first abbot, Benedict, shows how the Roman
tradition was maintained. He writes that Benedict Biscop crossed
the sea to Gaul and "brought back with him masons to build a
church in the Roman style which he had always admired." This
church, dedicated to St. Peter, was completed within a year, "and
when it was nearing completion Benedict sent messengers to Gaul
to bring over glass-makers, who were at this time unknown in
Britain, that they might glaze the windows of his church and the

---

[1] An admirable summary of the account in Bede and in Gregory's letters is to
be found in Dudden, *Gregory the Great*, ii, p. 105 sq.　　[2] Bede, *H.E.*, in fine.

cloisters and dining-rooms. The glass-makers not only finished their work but taught the English their handicraft, which was useful for enclosing the lanterns of churches and for vessels for different purposes."[1] Sacred vessels and vestments the abbot bought and brought home from foreign parts because they could not be obtained in England. "Some decorations and muniments, which could not be procured even in Gaul, the pious founder determined to fetch from Rome, and he therefore made his fourth voyage to Rome and returned with more abundant merchandise than ever before—books, relics and pictures for the church. But above all he brought with him John, the Archchanter of the Church of S. Peter and Abbot of the Monastery of St. Martin, who taught personally and by many writings the Roman mode to the English."

The influences which led to the spread of monasticism in the West were very different in Italy, Spain and southern Gaul from what they were in the north of what is now France, in Ireland, England and Germany. Cassiodorus and St. Benedict retired from a world in which Roman civilization still survived. That civilization was indeed disappearing amid the confusions of the sixth century. But those who retired to monasteries at that time did not know this. They fled from a highly organized society to a simpler life in solitudes. In the North, on the other hand, the prevailing social system was that of barbarism. The men and women who adopted the monastic life in northern countries were ascetics; but intellectually and emotionally they lived a much less simple life than their contemporaries, the tribal kings and their people. The half-light of asceticism in the South came from the last rays of a setting sun. The half-light in the North was the dawn of the First Europe.

In the North forests and marshes were cleared and new lands cultivated by the monks and the villagers dependent upon them. Skill in the arts was extended among barbarian peoples. Thus, in the middle of the seventh century St. Wandrille founded the monastery of Fontanelle in the diocese of Rouen "in a fertile and pleasant place" by the river Seine.[2] This same place "where there

---

[1] Bede, *Lives of the Abbots*, i.

[2] Now called St. Wandrille (Wandregisilus), near Caudebec. The ruins were used by Maeterlinck in the early twentieth century for one of his plays.

are apple trees and green meadows" was once "thickly covered with thorn-bushes and useless glades and great swamps." Here, about A.D. 650, St. Wandrille laid the foundations of his monastery and built churches to St. Peter, St. Paul and St. Lawrence. He then sent to Rome for relics, which his messengers brought back as the gift of Pope Vitalianus (A.D. 657–672), together with "many volumes of the Holy Scriptures of the Old and the New Testament and the works of Pope Gregory the Great."[1] Large properties were acquired by the monastery under the abbot Benignus (d. A.D. 722); and much was lost when a later abbot, about the year A.D. 735, gave away one-third of them to his relatives and to the "king's men" under Charles Martel. But even in those evil days a beautiful chapel of St. Michael with a bell-tower was built by the Prior.[2]

The collection and copying of manuscripts became one of the most important tasks in the greater monasteries. Young boys at seven years of age or later (oblati) were sent to the monasteries by their parents for training; but clearly not many of them would be so well fitted as Bede for the limitations and opportunities of monastic discipline. Monasteries were also used to confine kings and other lords who had been deposed and forced to retire from public life, after having the long hair, which was a sign of royalty, cut. Thus, the decline of religious fervour and the corruption of morals followed upon the entry of unsuitable persons into monasteries and convents, while the wealth of the greater monasteries attracted ambitious men to become abbots. At St. Wandrille abbot Hugo (A.D. 723) was also abbot of Jumièges, archbishop of Rouen and bishop of Paris and Bayeux. And in A.D. 738 abbot Wido, who could neither read not write, always wore a sword and a military cloak; he was surrounded by hunting dogs and was exceptionally skilful in shooting birds, "giving his time," as the chronicle says, "rather to these than to ecclesiastical occupations." The

---

[1] *Gesta Abbatum Fontanellensium*, Pertz, *Script. R.G.*, p. 14. This history was written by an unknown monk of the monastery about A.D. 840, and is carried as far as the year A.D. 833.

[2] The skilled man who was engaged to cast the bell stole some of the metal, and afterwards every time the bell was rung he went mad, jumbled his words, and barked like a dog. (*Gesta Ab. Fontan.*, Pertz, p. 43.)

reform of monastic life and the return to a stricter observation of the Rule of St. Benedict was begun in the middle of the eighth century under the influence of such men as St. Boniface.

Women in Monasticism

The Christian Churches in the first century had excluded women from the ranks of the clergy; but, because they were "souls" to be saved, they could not be denied full membership in the Christian community. And from the earliest times devout women had been given special honour. Many women were honoured as martyrs in the lists kept by the Churches; and the influence of women is continually recognized in the Christian records, as in St. Augustine's account of his mother, Monica. The ascetic movement attracted women as well as men; and because the great majority of monks in the early fifth century were laymen and not members of the clergy, the status of anchoresses and nuns was equally high. During the sixth, seventh and eighth centuries, convents of women in all western countries became centres of religious life, culture and learning.

There were many instances in the Frankish kingdom of the foundation and government of convents in which women of strong character and wide sympathies could exercise influence; but the most striking figure in northern Gaul was Radegunda. She had been taken as booty and made the wife of the Frankish king; but she fled, entered the monastic life and founded a monastery at Poitiers, where she not only practised austerities but gave special care to the sick. In her *Life*, written by Venantius Fortunatus, she is said to have washed the heads of the diseased and to have provided baths for the women, thus continuing the earlier Christian tradition of hospital nursing in the Xenodochia.[1] The detailed description of Radegunda's treatment of the sick and the aged seems to indicate that it was based upon the personal observation of the author who was a close friend of the abbess and lived in the neighbourhood of her convent. When Radegunda died in A.D. 587,

[1] Venantius Fortunatus, *Vita S. Radegundae. Pat. Lat.*, 88, col. 497, and also in M.G.H.

however, a revolt of the nuns began against her successor. Many of the nuns came of noble families, and they were as difficult to control as their relatives outside the monastic life. Some left the convent and the quarrels of opposing groups caused great difficulties to the bishops in that part of the Frankish kingdom.[1] Evidently the personal ascendancy of a saintly woman was not a sufficient basis for maintaining an organization after her death.

The situation was less difficult in England a century later. Etheldreda, daughter of a king and wife to another, lived for twelve years with her husband and "yet preserved the glory of perfect virginity."[2] Eventually she persuaded her husband to allow her to enter as a nun the convent of the abbess who was the king's aunt; and a year after she herself became abbess in a convent built under her direction at Ely. At her death in A.D. 660 she was succeeded by her sister, Sexberga, who had been the wife of a king of Kent. The monastery continued to be a centre of civilizing influence for many generations; but it was destroyed by the Danes in A.D. 870. For a century the settlement at Ely lay desolate; and then in A.D. 970 a Benedictine monastery was founded there.

A still more famous abbess was Hilda, who ruled at Whitby both a convent of nuns and a monastery. Bede writes that "her prudence was so great that not only ordinary folk but even kings and princes asked and received her advice. . . . She made those under direction attend to the reading of Scriptures and the exercise of works of justice."[3] From among the monks under her rule five became bishops, "all of them men of singular merit and sanctity"; and among the brethren was Caedmon, who wrote, "with much sweetness and humility in English, which was his language," poems based upon stories from Scripture. The abbess Hilda died in A.D. 680; and her monasteries also continued to be centres of virtue and learning until the Danish invasions of the eighth and ninth centuries destroyed the homes of Bede and of those of whom he wrote in northern England. The tradition of great abbesses was continued in England throughout the Middle Ages.

These were exceptional women; but thousands of other women

[1] Greg. Tur., *H.F.*, ix, 42 sq.   [2] Bede, *H.E.*, iv, 19.   [3] Ibid., iv, 23.

of all social classes found in convents security and a more civilized life than was possible at the time outside them. Communities of women who had chosen to accept asceticism and the monastic rule were presented by kings, queens and other rich men and women with land and houses; and, as in the case of the great monasteries, communities of women became centres of agricultural and other production, as well as of the restricted culture of the day. Girls were committed by their parents to the care of these communities and became recruits for asceticism, in some cases with unhappy results. The violent quarrels of the nuns of St. Radegunda's convent at Poitiers have been referred to above. And the letters of St. Boniface, a century later, indicate the dangers to which devout women were exposed when they went on a pilgrimage. A pathetic little letter is preserved in the manuscripts of the letters of St. Boniface from an unknown nun to her brother, asking him why he never comes to see her, although she is far from home and has no one else left to her.[1] The later decline of monastic discipline in the ninth century, when the early enthusiasm for asceticism had somewhat diminished, affected very seriously some convents of women. In a canon of the Council of Aachen in A.D. 836, it is said that "the convents of women in certain places seem to be brothels rather than convents."[2]

English Monks in Germany

The missionary work of Benedictine monks by which the English had been first converted to Christianity and brought into close connection with the Roman Church, was carried another step forward when English Benedictines went as missionaries to what is now Holland and south-western Germany. The two most famous leaders of the missionary bands of monks and of nuns were St. Willibrord and St. Boniface. As Augustine, at first prior and abbot, was ordained bishop after the success of his mission to Kent, thus founding the ecclesiastical organization of all England, so Willibrord became bishop of Utrecht and Boniface bishop of Mainz. St.

[1] Bonifacius, *Ep. Selectae*, Pertz, *Script. R.G.*, No. 143.
[2] *Concil. Aquisgran. Ann.* 836, can. xii.

Willibrord came from northern England and had spent about eleven years with monks in Ireland. His missionary work in Holland had the support of the Frankish ruler, Pippin, whose territories bordered on those of the pagan Frisians. But Willibrord sought also and received the special attention of the bishop of Rome. Pope Sergius ordained him bishop, under the name of Clemens, in A.D. 696. He established many Churches in distant parts, as far north as Denmark; and founded the famous monastery of Echternach near Trier.[1]

The labours of St. Boniface for the reform of the Frankish Churches and for the establishment of bishoprics among the newly converted Germans, are parts of the history of episcopal organization rather than of monasticism. But he also founded the great monastery of Fulda, about which he wrote to Pope Zachary in A.D. 751: "There is a wooded region in a desert of immense solitude in the midst of the tribes to whom we have preached; and there we have established monks to build a monastery, who live under the Rule of the holy father, Benedict—men of strict abstinences without meat and wine, without strong drinks and serfs, satisfied with the labour of their own hands. This place I acquired by my best efforts through religious and God-fearing men, principally Carloman, sometime lord of the Franks, and dedicated in honour of the Holy Saviour. In this place, with the consent of Your Reverence, I propose a little or for a few days to rest and recuperate my body already tired in old age, and after death to lie there; for four of the tribes to whom, by the grace of God, we have spoken Christ's word, are known to live around this place, to whom with your prayers I may be useful as long as I live and have energy enough."[2] Pope Zachary replied to this letter, giving to the new monastery the special protection of the Apostolic See;[3] and the

---

[1] At the time when this was written (in 1939) the Dutch Goverment was issuing stamps decorated with the head of St. Willibrord as a commemoration of his death in A.D. 739 at eighty-one years of age. See Bede, *H.E.*; and Alcuin, *Vita Willibrordi.*
[2] Boniface, Ep. 86, *M.G.H.*
[3] Ibid., Ep. 87, *M.G.H.* (November 4, 751). It is worth noting that the Pope adds that no jackdaws, crows or storks are to be eaten by Christians, nor beavers, hares or wild horses: "but you are well aware of all that is written in the Scriptures." Here is a strange influence of the Mosaic law. It seems possible that the avoidance of horse-flesh was meant to exclude pagan horse-sacrifice.

manuscripts of the letters of St. Boniface contain versions of the Papal decree which established the direct control of the Roman Church over the monastery of Fulda, removing it from the jurisdiction of any other Church. This is an early example of a practice which became commoner and still more important in later centuries. It involved the direct influence of the bishop of Rome within the dioceses of other bishops, and made of the greater monasteries powerful centres of influence tending to the centralization of ecclesiastical authority.

Reforms in Monasticism

The Rule of St. Benedict, which was the basis of monastic reform and of the extension of monasticism in the seventh and eighth centuries, was not in practice always enough to prevent abuses within convents and monasteries or the demoralization of whole communities of monks and nuns.[1] Therefore, in the succeeding centuries many efforts were made to reform the monastic life, either by a return to original Rule or by the establishment of settlements on the basis of the old practice of hermits or solitaries. But the later development of monasticism by the Cistercians, Carthusians and the monks of Camaldoli, belongs to the history of the Middle Ages. The problems which arose before the ninth century were not solved by any great movement affecting monasticism as a whole. Reforms of particular monasteries or convents were undertaken either by bishops or by the more vigorous monks and nuns. And the Rule of St. Benedict remained the only basis of reform. The most important of the reformers of the early ninth century was Benedict of Aniane, who died in A.D. 821. At one time he had twelve monasteries under his direction; and he recalled them to the original simplicity of the Rule of St. Benedict. He made a collection of many traditional Rules, both eastern and western, but did not attempt to compose a new one.[2]

[1] It is possible that the daily reading of parts of the Rule still continued in Benedictine houses, had become an unintelligible ritual, in an unknown Latin tongue. Thus, Alcuin in a letter to the monks of Wearmouth in A.D. 793 advises that the Rule be "explained in English that it may be understood by all." Ep. 19, M.G.H., Scriptores Ep., vol. iv.   [2] Life of Benedict and his *Codex Regularum*. Pat. Lat., 103.

It is important, however, to note that the later reforms of the eleventh century introduced a new principle of organization, now known as a "Religious Order," that is to say, a single centralized system by which all the monks, following the same Rule in all districts and countries, are governed by one "General," having under him "Provincials" of the different countries or nations. This was not the original Benedictine system. Indeed, it is not correct to speak of a Benedictine Order. The monasteries and convents of the original Benedictine tradition were, each of them, separate, self-governing institutions. The abbots and abbesses were of equal status and had no superiors within the monastic system. This made it easier for the great Benedictine houses to look directly to the Papacy as their supreme authority; and also made it possible for the Popes to act directly in the different countries through the heads of the Benedictine houses. The Benedictine houses themselves did not form a separate system. Thus, the centralization of ecclesiastical authority at the end of the eighth century was achieved by the Papacy, partly through its new relations to the bishops of the "missionary" countries, but partly also through papal grants of *privilegia* or exemptions from the control of diocesan bishops, to the separate Benedictine houses in different countries.

Monasticism and the State

The relation of the monks and nuns to the State and to the Authorities of the Church went through many changes between the fifth and the ninth century. So far as the State was concerned the Theodosian law-books contain the evidence for the Roman Empire in the fifth century. The difficulties created by the monastic movement seem to have been two: first, there were monks or other ascetics who went from place to place and caused disorder because they were under no superior; and although they claimed to be holy men, like the fakirs in India, many of them were untrustworthy. The civil Authorities were, therefore, concerned to compel wandering ascetics to keep out of the cities or to stay in some monastic foundation. Thus an edict of September 2, 390, declares that "those who are found to be monks must be ordered to go and live in deserted places, or in the great solitudes."[1] In the second place, the civil Authorities were concerned with the possibility that some of those who became hermits or monks might escape their civil obligations. Thus a decree of the Emperors Valentinian and Valens reads: "Certain adherents of cowardice, deserting their duties as citizens, go to deserts, and under the pretence of religion, associate with the crowds of monks. Such men, taken in Egypt, we order to be dragged from their hiding-places by the count of the East and recalled to their civic duties, or deprived of their property—which is to be taken over by those who fulfil such duties."[2]

But the practical difficulties for the civil Authorities were even greater under the ecclesiastical imperialism of the Greek Church than they were in the West. Indeed, it was fortunate for the development of western monasticism on the lines laid down by St. Benedict that the influence of eastern ascetics in the West was ended, first, by the severance of the Greek and Latin Churches, and afterwards by the Mohammedan invasions, as described in an earlier chapter.[3] The monks of the Greek Churches were often in revolt against the imperial Authorities, whereas in the West there was no such conflict. Again, in the West there was no racial or class distinction between the monks and the civil or ecclesiastical Authorities. But in the countries of the eastern Mediterranean asceticism and monasticism, at any rate in part, were reactions of subject Oriental peoples against the domination of a Greek tradition in Church and State. For this reason the Monophysite monks of Egypt in the seventh century assisted in undermining imperial Authority there, which was eventually destroyed by Mohammedan invaders. Eastern monasticism in the Greek Churches, whatever its "spiritual" qualities, was dangerous to the civil Authorities.

Such difficulties seem to have troubled the civil Authorities even at the end of the sixth century. Thus, Gregory the Great wrote to protest in A.D. 593 to the Emperor Maurice against a decree which forbade any public official to enter a monastery or any soldier to become a monk until his term of service had expired.[4] The point of

---

[1] Cod. Theod., xvi, 3, 1.   [2] Ibid., xii, 1, 63.
[3] Chapter V, p. 264 sq.   [4] See Dudden, Gregory the Great, ii, p. 181.

view of a bishop of Rome, who had been trained as a monk and lived in the midst of a dissolution of all civil Authority in Italy, could hardly be reconciled with the interests of the imperial Authority in Constantinople. The "other" world was plainly in conflict with this world, when officials and soldiers could escape from the labour of maintaining civil government in order to save their own souls.

In the West, after the disappearance of the Roman Empire and the setting up of barbarian kingdoms, the civil Authorities were not greatly concerned with monasticism until the days of Pippin and Charles the Great. The barbarian laws allow for the clergy with whose assistance they were written down; but all forms of civil and military authority in the Frankish and Anglo-Saxon kingdoms were so primitive until the end of the eighth century that no special provision was made concerning the status of monks. This does not mean, however, that monasteries were unimportant. Kings and other lords gave lands for the foundation and support of monasteries; but the regulation of their relations to the Church as a whole and to society was left to the bishops. Monks and nuns were among the laity. They claimed no such special status under the civil law as the clergy did.

When the law-making of Roman rulers was imitated by Frankish kings, in the issue of Capitularies in the eighth century, civil legislation again referred to monks and nuns. The civil Authorities and the bishops combined to issue regulations, as, for example, in the Frankfurt Capitulary of A.D. 794.[1] This begins by saying that a synod of bishops, among whom king Charles himself sat, issues "the statute of the Lord King and Sacred Synod." "If any one of the abbots, priests, deacons or other clerics does not obey his bishop, he must appeal to the metropolitan and he must decide with the suffragans." Rules follow with regard to monks and hermits. For example, "the abbot shall sleep with his monks according to the Rule of St. Benedict." . . . "As cellarers in monasteries money-makers (*avari*) shall not be chosen but such men selected as the Rule of St. Benedict teaches." Again, "We have

---

[1] Migne, *P.L.*, 97, col. 191.

heard that certain abbots, led by greed, demand payment for those entering the monastery. We and the Holy Synod therefore decide that no money shall be required for receiving brethren into the holy order, but they shall be received according to the Rule of St. Benedict."

Monasticism and the Church

Ecclesiastical regulation of monks and monasteries began as soon as the monastic system became powerful in the East. The difficulties which the bishops had to face were obvious. Ascetics, hermits or monks, claiming to be more truly Christian than other members of the Church, sometimes forsook ceremonies and sacraments and, whether living isolated in cities or in deserted places, often did not forbear from criticizing the clergy and laity. Some of them claimed privileges and refused to submit to the obligations of the Christian community. The irritation of the bishops at the habits of some "holy men" has been already mentioned in reference to St. Augustine's treatise on *Monks' Work*. The situation in the Greek Churches in the eastern Mediterranean was made still more difficult when large bodies of monks led riots in the great cities against some bishop or some doctrine which they opposed. This, however, did not occur in the West within the Latin Churches.

A permanent difficulty remained, because the abbot and his monks naturally desired to live in accordance with their own Rules; and the bishop of the diocese, on the other hand, could hardly allow Christians within his jurisdiction to disregard his authority. The General Councils and local synods of bishops, therefore, issued canons regulating the relations of bishops and monks, especially heads of monasteries or abbots. The bishops were recognized to have legislative authority; and almost all monks, until the ninth century, were laymen. Similarly nuns belonged to the laity. Therefore the relations of bishops to monks and nuns, as defined by the councils and synods, naturally expressed the point of view of the bishops. Thus, the Council of Chalcedon (Canons 4 and 8) declares that all monks and monasteries are subject to the jurisdiction of the bishop of the diocese.

In the West the most important canons concerning monasteries were those of the councils of bishops in Gaul. For example, the Council of Agde (A.D. 506) decides that no new monasteries are to be founded except with the permission of the bishop of the diocese (Canon 58). The Council of Orleans (A.D. 511) decrees that abbots should be subject to bishops (Canon 19), and that no one should be allowed to become a hermit without the bishop's permission (Canon 22). The Council of Arles (A.D. 554) decrees that monks should be under the supervision of bishops (Canons 2 and 5).

The increase in the number of abbots and monks who were also ordained priests, naturally led to an extension of the power of bishops over monasteries. In St. Benedict's day both the abbot and his monks were laymen, although they might have a chaplain among them; but by the ninth century the difference between the monks and the clergy was very much smaller. The increasing importance of the ceremonies and sacraments of the Church gave the clergy greater influence in monasticism; and, on the other hand, the ideals and customs of monasticism increasingly affected the clergy. Thus, as celibacy had been introduced among the clergy under the influence of asceticism, so in the sixth and seventh centuries the tonsure, originally used only by hermits and monks, was gradually adopted as a sign of clerical status.[1] Again, the custom of life in common and the recitation or singing of the canonical hours was followed, in imitation of the monks, by the clergy of large churches. This is the origin of the Canons of Cathedrals, who followed such quasi-monastic rules as those established by Chrodegang, bishop of Metz (A.D. 743-766).[2] After the eighth century, therefore, monasticism had been firmly welded into the ecclesiastical system under the authority of the bishops.

On the other hand, it was recognized that the following of the Rule within the monastery or convent was a matter for the abbot

---

[1] At the end of the sixth century the shaven crown and smooth chin of the priests of Attis had become the signs of the clerical caste. Gregory of Tours believed that this "tonsure" had been established by St. Peter (de Gloria M., 28) and that Nicetius, bishop of Trier, had been born with a clerical tonsure (coronam clerici). Vitae Pat., 17. See also Bede, H.E., v, 22.   [2] Regula canonicorum, Pat. Lat., 89.

or abbess to deal with. The Rule of St. Benedict itself provides for various punishments which may be used by the abbot or abbess; and the abbot or abbess had a right, not indeed strictly defined, to require from the bishop of the diocese either the service of a priest to say Mass within the monastery or convent, or, in the case of monasteries, the choice of one of the monks for ordination as a priest by the bishop. It remained, however, the function of the bishop to investigate and correct any scandals or indiscipline in all monastic foundations within his diocese.

The exercise of episcopal authority was not always to the advantage either of the monastic life or of the Church in general. Bishops were not all prudent; and some of them used their own authority, under the canons, to obstruct the monks and nuns and to enrich their own churches or themselves. In the letters of Gregory the Great there are many rebukes addressed to bishops of Italy for opposing the foundation of new monasteries, for taking the property of the monks, or for refusing to support the abbot against his rebellious monks.[1]

On the whole, however, the jurisdiction of the bishops over monks and their abbots, and over nuns and abbesses, was maintained according to the tradition of the canons. From about the middle of the sixth century kings and local lords who founded monasteries and gave them property, also protected them from possible infringement of their rights by the bishops. A royal foundation, especially one governed by an abbot or abbess of royal or noble blood, could resist any excessive control by the bishop of the diocese. But this was obviously a mere conflict of different authorities without any definite legal sanction. The greater security of monastic foundations from undue interference on the part of a bishop was provided after the sixth century by a new method—a form of exemption from local jurisdiction by the placing of a monastery directly under the authority of the Pope. As it has been pointed out in an earlier chapter, the Popes from the days of Gregory the Great supported by their influence the missionary activities in England and Germany which were carried on by

[1] Dudden, *Gregory the Great*, ii, p. 186.

monks and nuns. Quite obviously it was the bishop of Rome and no other bishop of the West who directed and supported, in the old Roman tradition, the extension of the empire of the Church; and this gave to the monastic establishments in the missionary countries a special connection overriding from the very beginning their connection with the bishops of the neighbouring dioceses. When new Sees were founded, as by Augustine at Canterbury, Paulinus at York, Willibrord at Utrecht, Boniface at Mainz, the new areas thus won by the monastic missionaries became part of the ordinary territorial divisions of the Church. But all the great missionary monks also founded new monasteries and sought for these foundations a special connection with the Roman See. Thus, certain great monastic foundations were granted by the Popes a kind of extra-territorial position connecting them directly with the See of Rome and thereby increasing the difference in prestige and authority between that See and all others among the Latin Churches.

General Conclusions

Monasticism as a social institution made at least three important contributions to the new civilization of Europe in the Middle Ages, upon which modern civilization is based. The later developments of the monastic orders after the ninth century, and of the Friars, are not within the scope of this chapter. But the foundations of all such medieval movements were laid in the years between the fourth and the tenth centuries. In what are called the Dark Ages, monasticism produced (1) a new system of centres of culture and education, quite unknown to the Greek and Roman civilization; (2) a new force tending to establish civilized life upon the country-side when the cities were ruined; and (3) a new system of corporate ownership, lasting through many generations.

Centres of Culture

Monasteries and convents from the beginning of the fifth century in the West included men and women of the best education of that time. Many of these belonged to wealthy and powerful families; but at that time few even of the wealthy and powerful could read or write; and obviously the great majority of the population were even more ignorant. In the days of Ausonius, Paulinus of Nola and Sidonius Apollinaris, learning and culture were to be found among the rich on their estates or in the cities. It was a bloodless culture, living on phrases culled from dead writers, and out of touch with the political and social life of the time; and it was preserved by the correspondence of individuals and some contact between educated men and women in the cities. But by the beginning of the ninth century all that shadowy world had disappeared. The monasteries and convents were the only centres of study, of the arts and of such theoretical and applied science as existed.

The intellectual and emotional connections between the two worlds, the dead world of the Roman Empire and the new world of the Middle Ages, are to be found in the hymns of Prudentius and the sermons of Augustine and Gregory the Great. But this development must be discussed elsewhere. For the present argument it is enough to note that the monasteries and convents after the age of St. Benedict were communities of men or women of many different social classes, who were all united in their several centres in the preservation of the tradition of culture. The cloister had become a school of letters. Its language in all the countries of the West was Latin; and this language bound together all the different centres of culture in the First Europe, thus forming a learned caste, later identified with the clergy or clerks (*clerici*), whose members recognized their common interests in the arts and learning. The monasteries and convents, therefore, of the so-called Dark Ages laid the foundation for that common Latin culture of the medieval universities and of the later learned societies whose members continued to write and speak in Latin until the eighteenth century.

The cloister was the centre for the development of illumination and painting and of the new music of the medieval tradition; and it is hardly necessary to remark that architecture was most highly developed from its beginnings in the cloisters of the ninth century. Again, the education of boys in monasteries and of girls in convents was carried on under a new system, unknown in ancient Greece and Rome, which was developed further in medieval and modern schools. All this foretold a new form of civilization. The dependence of the arts and sciences upon the wealthy leisured class, under the slave civilization of imperial Rome, gave place to a tradition, inspired by religious fervour, in which all men of any rank or race could find opportunities to develop their own abilities. After the seventh century and throughout the Middle Ages, learning and the arts were independent of the wealthy and powerful, except in so far as gifts were bestowed by the rich upon the cloisters and later upon the colleges of students. Modern European civilization is separated from that world by the revival, after the Renaissance, of the patronage of learning by princes. The *clericus* of the Middle Ages then became merely the clerk in a private business or the humble tutor in a wealthy house. But in spite of that reaction towards Roman patronage, the traditions of the cloister are in some ways preserved in modern universities and colleges.

The limitations and defects of monastic learning before and during the Middle Ages are obvious. In some ways it was a loss to mental vigour that Latin was the only language of culture; because the learned were cut off by what became a mere jargon from the wider experience of common folk speaking living languages. Again, learning was then almost entirely the repetition of old knowledge and old phrases. Commentary had not yet grown into criticism. But in a world dominated by barbarian warriors it was a great step forward to secure anywhere a corner for the cultivation of the arts. And works such as Bede's *Historia Ecclesiastica*, and the treatises of the great abbots of the ninth century, are certainly as original and as valuable as any of the Latin literature of the late Roman Empire.[1] It is also worthy of note that learning and the arts under the monastic system were the work of communities of men or women in co-operation and not of isolated scholars. The studies in the cloister were governed by the most important require-ment of the Rule that the *opus divinum*, the recitation of Divine

[1] The treatises referred to are such as the *De Ecclesiasticis Rebus* of Walafridus Strabo, the *De Via Regia* of Smaragdus and the work of Hrabanus Maurus.

Office, should be the chief duty. This involved not merely the reading or singing of the psalms and prayers at the seven canonical hours but also caused attention to be paid to the astronomical basis for fixing the dates of the festivals of the Church. Thus Bede worked on the problems of chronology. And further, in the monasteries were developed the methods of marking time which led to the construction of clocks. Cassiodorus, as it has been noted above, spent some of his time in his monastic retreat in devising new forms of apparatus for measuring the hours.

A Rural Civilization

Medieval civilization, as contrasted with that of Greece and Rome, depended upon the country-side and not upon the cities. The monasteries and convents of the Dark Ages assisted in building up this new Europe. Almost all monastic settlements were outside the towns and some were in the wilderness. They were thus independent of such city life as remained—even in Italy. But they were not merely agricultural estates; they were also centres of manufacture, of some trading and of the arts. Again, the greater monasteries under capable abbots developed agriculture much more thoroughly than the secular lords. Thus, the monasteries spread through large areas of Europe, hitherto uncultivated, the system of production known as medieval. The extensive trade in corn and wine, familiar to students of the Roman Empire, had disappeared; and production for local needs had taken the place of production for export. The monasteries were among the most important centres of the new economic system. Under the influence of the Rule of St. Benedict, however, a new conception of manual work began to take the place of the assumptions implied in slave-labour. The Rule provides that monks should work with their hands and, if skilled, practise the crafts. The organization of work in common, in agriculture and handicrafts, for the common good of a community, established the fact that all labour might be ennobling. The greatest philosophers who lived under the slave system of Greece and Rome, had never known this; but it is a principle which leads inevitably to the humanization of the manual worker and to the obsolescence of slavery. Thus, monasticism in its earliest form in the West, began a revaluation of human labour which is not yet complete in practice. It still remains an assumption among men and women, educated upon the basis of Greek and Roman culture, that manual workers are merely instruments of a civilization which they do not share; but it is beginning to be perceived that such an assumption is an obsolete survival of a slave system.

Where the monastery or convent held land already under cultivation and controlled labour for agriculture or manufacture, the abbot, abbess or agent acted in the same way as any other landowners or their agents. And monastic property might thus become the envy of neighbouring lords or of kings or even of local bishops. It was not impossible for property which had been given to monks or nuns to be taken away again; and besides, disorders or warfare in the neighbourhood might destroy monastic settlements which had no defences of their own or did not contribute to the common defence of the locality. Thus, the Danes destroyed monasteries and convents in England in the eighth and ninth centuries; and St. Benedict's monastery at Monte Cassino itself was destroyed by the Lombards about A.D. 585, rebuilt in A.D. 720, and sacked by the Saracens in A.D. 884.

As for settlements in the wilderness, these involved at first the clearance and bringing into cultivation of new land. But if the settlement was well organized, it soon became a valuable part of the area of civilization. Thus, the monastic system acted as a method by which "the desert" was driven back from "the sown," and new areas used for the production of goods under the control of some form of government. In many cases the monks were the pioneers of Europe in the seventh and eighth centuries, whose achievements for the advance of civilization were more valuable and more permanent than the conquests of ambitious kings or crusading warriors.

The growth of monastic properties naturally increased the prestige and power of the abbots in their relations to the outer world. They were referred to as "prelates" (*prelati*); and the abbots of the greater monasteries became the equals of bishops in the councils of kings and in the performance of some public duties. Abbots, and in some cases the more learned among the monks, were used as diplomats by kings and Popes, both for conveying messages and negotiating agreements.

Again, the abbots of greater monasteries had some power as administrators apart from their functions as controllers of the monastic property. From the beginning of the eighth century, in the Frankish kingdom at least, the owners of landed estates were obliged to supply men for the armed forces of the king; and the monastic estates also, therefore, formed part of the military machine. Ecclesiastical law and custom forbade abbots and, indeed, also bishops from themselves taking up arms. Thus, Pope Zachary wrote[1] in A.D. 748 to Pippin as Chief of the Palace (*Major Domus*), saying that prelates and priests should give counsel and prayer and not join in warlike action. Inevitably, however, abbots in control of the lands from which armed men were drawn, tended to go out at the head of their forces as non-ecclesiastical lords usually did. That certain abbots were involved in battles, even if unarmed, is to be seen in the "Lament for Abbot Hugo," killed in battle in A.D. 844, and wept for by king Pippin:—

> Hug dulce nomen, Hug propage nobilis,
> Insons sub armis tam repente soncius
> occubuisti.[2]

Again, the monasteries were centres of a population dependent upon the monks—men, women and children, working at agriculture, the manufacture of clothing and the crafts of a simple society. The monastic agents controlling agriculture and other production, kept accounts and prepared lists of the labourers and others dependent upon the estate. The most striking example of such a list is the *Polypticum* of the abbot Irminon of the monastery of St. Germain des Prés, composed about A.D. 811. This will be referred to in greater detail in the discussion of social conditions in general.

[1] *Codex Carolinus*, Ep. iii.
[2] *M.G.H.*, *Poetae Aev. Car.*, vol. ii.
> "Hug, sweet name! Hug, son of nobles!
> Unwounding in battle, suddenly wounded
> You died."

Clearly, although the methods of agriculture and the uses of labour on monastic estates were the same as those on other great estates at the same date, the monasteries in general controlled what may be called "model" estates, in so far as the ownership remained the same through many generations and there was greater stability of tenure for workers upon them. At the beginning of the ninth century the abbey of St. Germain des Prés had about one hundred and twenty monks and about forty thousand men, women and children dependent upon the rule of the abbot; and at about the same date the abbey of St. Wandrille near Caudebec had about twenty-five thousand persons on its estates.

It is well known that all monasteries and convents also served as centres for the support of the sick, the aged and the poor. All the great Churches, such as those of Rome or Tours, supported with their funds many dependants whose names were kept upon lists (*matriculae*). Similar dependants were cared for by the monks and nuns.

Corporate Ownership

Finally, a monastic foundation is an instance of corporate ownership, not hereditary, continuing through many generations. The lands and other properties of monasteries were not added to by war or theft or marriage—the usual methods of improving the position of noble families. But the greater monasteries had already become wealthy by the ninth century and their abbots controlled large territories. The increase of monastic wealth was due partly to gifts but partly also to the ability of great administrators. No doubt, increasing wealth had some evil consequences both for the monastic tradition and for the outside world. But it was a new feature of the civilization which was taking the place of the Roman that bodies of men and women, not primarily concerned with wealth and power, should continue from generation to generation to administer and use land and labour in their control. The monastic system, which in some of its features and in its official language was an extension of Roman culture among the barbarians, was nevertheless in its essence a new experiment in moral idealism and social organization.

CHAPTER X

WORKERS AND PILGRIMS

While the new concentrations of social power were being organized by bishops and kings in place of the Roman Empire, new relationships between ordinary folk were also arising. The desire of a few able or energetic men and women to extend their own influence over others, is more obvious in every age than is the willingness of the great majority to accept whatever little livelihood and liberty for themselves may be available without too great effort. The records of the past, therefore, always contain a clearer account of the struggle for power than of the labour for bread and peace. But those changes which occur in a social system during times of transition are most important and enduring, which affect the lives of the great majority who leave no record—except in the fields, tilled for generations, and the stones and timber of buildings on which they have worked. If power or authority forms, as it were, the nucleus in any social system, the protoplasm of that system is the established custom followed by the majority of men and women. And when the Roman organization in western Europe gave place to the medieval, the change in the protoplasm was as important as the change in the nucleus. The habits and customs of the great majority of manual workers were changed fundamentally in the four centuries between A.D. 400 and A.D. 800.[1] As in all ages, these men and women had to grow the food and the material for clothing on which the rich and the powerful depended for their existence. The labour of these common folk therefore was the basis of all the culture, the learning, the law and the military force of their own and later ages.

[1] This chapter was written before the publication of *The Cambridge Economic History of Europe from the Decline of the Roman Empire*, vol. i (1941). *The Agrarian Life of the Middle Ages*.

In the most general terms, a slave system which dominated all social relationships in A.D. 400 was replaced before A.D. 800 by a system of serfs or villeins in permanent relationship with particular lords on particular estates. In this change, the slave-trade and the treatment of great numbers of men and women as cattle for the service of others, gradually disappeared; and instead, the lives of the majority were affected by new conceptions of mutual service, which gave, at least in theory, some rights of protection and security of expectation to the lower as against the higher ranks of society. Slavery and the slave-trade were not abolished. They continued to be fairly extensive in western Europe even at the beginning of the seventh century. But by the beginning of the ninth century the medieval system was already dominant. As compared with the Roman system, this was an extension of liberty; although in the eyes of later generations it seemed to be mainly a continuance of the relationship of slavery by enforced dependence of the majority upon the few.

What happened in the centuries between A.D. 400 and A.D. 800 may be illustrated by certain aspects of social transition in our own day. The earliest stages of the Russian Revolution in 1917 were marked by the division of the land of large estates among the peasants, who were accustomed to the traditional obligations of serfs, although serfdom had been abolished by law some time before. In the same way, in the fifth century, amid the confusion caused by civil war and barbarian invasion, the poorer classes were able to settle upon the land or to find a better livelihood and greater security in work upon the estates of great landowners; and in the century following, when the traditional power of the great land-owners was weakened, small men, no doubt, were able to extend their own independence. But, as in Russia in 1918 and the following years, the new Authority—the Soviet Government—took control of the sporadic and unorganized efforts of the peasantry, so in the seventh and eighth centuries in western Europe the new lordships of the Churches and civil Authorities organized production upon the basis of a personal dependence not very different from that of the clients of a Roman patron. Thus serfdom in the medieval system was, in one aspect, a reorganization of society to replace a slave-system in dissolution.

Another example of a similar change, not yet complete, is to be found in the results of the abolition of slavery and the slave-trade in the West Indies. A century ago the great majority of workers on the estates in the West Indies were negro slaves. Then, quite suddenly, by the action of a distant Parliament, the slaves were freed from their masters; and presumably it was believed that the wages-system, which after about a thousand years had gradually developed in England, would take the place of slavery in the West Indies. But the actual result has been that, a century after the abolition of slavery, the descendants of slaves continue to live on the land of the estate-owners in entire dependence upon them for their livelihood but without any legal right to claim anything from the local lord. There is little waste land on the smaller islands on which masterless men can settle; and the need of the estate-owner for labour, of which there is an increasing surplus, is much less than was the need of the governing few in Europe before the Middle Ages began. To-day, therefore, in the West Indies there is an example of the difficulties of the transition from slavery to free labour where legal and customary serfdom has not been attempted. Indentured labour from India was introduced into some parts of the West Indies to form a class of hired workers instead of slaves. But this system did not endure. The transition from slavery is not yet completed.

Again, in South America the situation described by a traveller in 1937 is strangely similar to that prevailing in western Europe during the last years of the Roman social system and the earlier years of the Middle Ages: "It is the custom in most countries in South America to allow the Indian farm labourers and their families to have a small piece of land, if possible an acre or so, to till for themselves: this in return for so many days a week on which the peon will work on the land of his master. The condition of servitude varies from the new freedom of the squatter-sovereign in Colombia, to countries like Ecuador, Peru and Bolivia, where the Indians are very often nothing less than slaves, and are sold like cattle with the land when a farm changes hands."[1] Thus some of the Indian farm-labourers in South America in the twentieth century are in the position of Roman *coloni*; and others are in the position of medieval serfs or *manicipia*. And similar social conditions, no doubt, are to be found in many other countries outside the European tradition.

Such rapid changes from slavery or serfdom as occurred in Russia and the West Indies are like the changes which occurred very gradually during the centuries which followed the disappearance of the Roman Empire in western Europe. There was no revolution against the old system. There was no "class war." Certain groups, such as the *bagaudae*, might take up arms and ravage the estates of the rich, as they did in the fourth and fifth centuries in Gaul. But there was no clear idea of any alternative to slavery; and the slaves themselves in western Europe differed too much in language, race and custom to form any united opposition to their masters. The influences which operated to dissolve the slave-system were mainly unconscious—depopulation, the failure of the supply of slaves, and the need for concessions to workers on the land in order to maintain the supply of the necessaries of life. And in so far as there were conscious influences at work, the slave-system was dissolved by a radical change in the moral and religious climate of opinion rather than by any "economic" causes.

Slavery changed into serfdom, not because men planned a new system of production, but because they learnt to treat their fellow-men as human beings. The consciousness of men, apart from the natural or physical changes of four hundred years, controlled the direction in which the new civilization moved; and their consciousness was mainly a new awareness of certain moral and religious factors in human life. The Church converted the kings and their warriors to an understanding that armed force was useless without moral authority. The Church converted also whole communities to the conception that all their members were "children of God." There may have been "material" or "economic" causes at work in support of the new ideals of the Christian communities;

[1] N. Farson, *Transgressor in the Tropics* (1937), p. 185.

but these ideals were themselves the chief causes of still more important "economic" changes than had occurred before the ideals became effectual. It is impossible, for example, to deny that the monastic ideal of life had important "economic" or "material" effects in the extension of the cultivated areas in the eighth and ninth centuries. Slavery under the Roman Republic had involved cruelty. Even Cicero implied in his treatise on *Morals* that masters may have "to be cruel to their slaves, if they cannot hold them in subjection otherwise."[1] And under the Empire, Tacitus describes how, in the year A.D. 61, four hundred slaves of the Prefect of the City were killed, because the murderer of their master could not be discovered. In the discussion on the murder in the Senate it was said: "This scum cannot be controlled except by terror."[2] Meantime, largely under the influence of Greek thought, humanitarian feeling increased, as rationalism weakened the prejudices associated with traditional religious beliefs and practices. The Stoics maintained that slavery was not based upon natural differences between human beings, as Aristotle had absurdly attempted to prove, but that it was only a custom which the peoples had found it convenient to enforce. In the *Institutes* of Gaius it is written: "The power of masters over slaves is derived from a conception of right common to the peoples (*juris gentium est*). . . . But at this time it is not lawful either for Roman citizens, or for any others under Roman jurisdiction, to use extreme measures without cause against their slaves; for under the law of the most sacred Emperor Antoninus, whoever kills his slave without cause is commanded to be treated as no less guilty than if he killed the slave of another; and too great severity of masters is repressed by a law of the same prince . . . because we ought not to misuse what is within our power; and this is the reason for which the spendthrift is forbidden to administer his own property."[3] The same principle is expressed in the *Institutes* of Justinian.

The influence of Christianity, however, went somewhat further. In the Epistles of St. Paul the writer explains that the master should

---

[1] Cicero, *De Off.*, ii, 7.　　　　[2] Tacitus, *Ann.*, xiv, 42–45.
[3] Gaius, *Instit.*, i, 52. It will be noticed that the reason is not the slave's nature, but the spoiling of an instrument.

treat his slaves kindly and without the methods of terror (Eph. vi. 9); and that slaves should obey with a good will (Eph. vi. 5; Col. iii. 22). The principle that Christianity disregarded difference of social class, expressed in St. Paul's phrase "neither slave nor free, but you are one in Christ" (Gal. iii. 28), was repeated by St. Ambrose and later writers.[1] St. John Chrysostom in a sermon asks "whence comes slavery and how has it been established?"—and answers: "Avarice, jealousy and insatiable greed have brought slavery into existence."[2] An added dignity in the Christian Church was acquired by slaves who had been martyrs, as in the case of the slave-girl Blandina, reported in the letter of the Church of Lyons.[3] "She had so little bodily strength," says the letter, "that all the Christians, among whom was her mistress, feared that she would give way under the torture." . . . "In the end she was executed, and the pagans confessed that they had never seen a woman who had endured such great tortures." Christianity did not base its appeal to slaves upon their grievances or their sufferings, but upon the possibility of humanizing and even ennobling their service. They were told that they could contribute in that service to the life of the community. The Church, however, always used its influence, after the Emperors had become Christian, to increase the number of slaves who were given their freedom. Under Constantine, a law of A.D. 316 gave permission for the enfranchisement of slaves in churches in presence of the congregation. And a later law of A.D. 321 declared that the ceremony in a church should be the equivalent to the traditional form of enfranchisement.[4]

Also slaves and other dependants were allowed by the law to become priests and monks, in general with the consent of their masters or patrons. The civil Authorities, even after the general acceptance of Christianity, opposed the marriage of free women with slaves who had been given freedom; and the contrast between "cohabitation" (*contubernium*) for slaves and real marriage (*coniugium*) was maintained by law. But the marriage of slaves was recognized by the Churches as valid; and in the process of time

---

[1] Ambrose, *Exhortatio Virg.*, i, 3.
[2] John Chrysos., *Hom.*, xxii, 2, in Ep. ad Ephes.
[3] Eusebius, *Hist. Eccl.*, v, 1, gives the text of the letter.   [4] *Cod. Theod.*, iv, 7, 1.

the personality of each man and woman became the accepted basis of rights in the law of marriage, as it had been in Christian practice. The slave was no longer merely an animal or an instrument. As St. Augustine wrote: "A Christian ought not to possess a slave in the same way as he may possess a horse or money, although the price of a slave may be less than that of a horse. But if this slave is better treated by you, and better trained in the service of God than he would be by anyone who wants to buy him, I do not believe that you can say that you can part with him as with a coat, because a man ought to love his neighbour as himself."[1]

But perhaps the most powerful influence tending towards the abolition of slavery was the Christian tradition of the dignity of service of all kinds, and in particular of personal labour. Preachers reminded their congregations that Christianity had been founded by manual workers. Hermits and monks accepted work with their hands as consonant with the "spiritual" life. And Christian writers in the fourth and fifth centuries continually referred to the life of the poorer manual workers as preferable to that of the idle rich. This teaching naturally caused a widespread raising of the level of human intercourse, affecting all the relationships of human beings in society, and therefore reducing the difference of status between the free worker and the slave.

Before discussing, however, the different stages in the change from slavery to serfdom, the meaning of these two words must be made quite clear. A slave is a human being who is treated in law and in practice as an animal. Men and women who are slaves may be the instruments of the civilization of others, as cattle may be. The slave-owner may be kind to his slaves; and if he is wise, he will give them food and shelter enough, at least, to maintain their productive power. But the essential fact in the relation between slaves and others in a slave civilization is that slaves have no rights, no voice in the formation of civilized society and no contribution to make to it as slaves, except such as may be made by beasts of burden. In a slave civilization the slave-owners and those who share their privileges pay no more attention to slaves in their history and

---

[1] Augustine, *De Sermone Dom.*, i, 19.

literature than they do to their domestic animals. A civilization, therefore, such as that of Greece and Rome, can present itself as admirable by its very silence concerning the cost of its achievements. Serfdom, on the other hand, is a condition of dependence indeed, but of dependence limited by acknowledged rights of the serf and duties of his lord. The serf is not an animal either in law or in practice. His dependence on his lord may be almost complete; but he is bound to the soil even more than to his lord. He was, in later years, protected against anyone but his lord by the king's justice. And probably from the earliest times he had some protection even against his lord by the traditional customary law of his community. Thus, whereas in slavery men and women can be taken from place to place, sold to new masters for new uses and discarded without compunction by the whole of society when useless, under serfdom there is no transfer of men and women from the homes in which they have lived. Therefore in the First Europe under serfdom there was a greater probability that children would be born and trained by their parents, even in the lowest class of the community. And, therefore also, serfdom provided one means of escape from the depopulation caused by a slave-system.

Again, under serfdom, at least in western Europe, the Christian Churches found a place among their members for those with the least livelihood or liberty. It was not merely that serfs or their children could become monks or priests. Even those who did not escape from subjection to their local lord had a place in their local Church, as "souls to be saved," at least theoretically equal to that of kings and lords. The serfs, villeins or other dependants of those in power received the same sacraments, attended the same ceremonies and heard the same Gospel as their lords. The local community, which had been divided into rulers and outcasts under the Roman Empire, was again united in the local Church. The Church, indeed, did not oppose slavery, although it attempted to lighten the burden of slaves and to ransom some of those who had been sold into slavery; nor did the Church create the new principles of serfdom. Its influence upon both systems was indirect; but the transition from the one to the other was certainly due to the estab-

lishment in practice of the belief that each human being had a soul
to be saved.

The Transition

The transition from the Roman to the medieval system of production took place gradually, during more than four hundred years.
The Roman system was in dissolution even before the fifth century.
The medieval system was hardly established outside France and
England before the ninth century; and clearly social conditions
differed very much in different parts of western Europe during all
the centuries between the fifth and ninth. But the change which
occurred is most clearly revealed by the different treatment of the
system of production in the documents of three different centuries,
the fifth, the seventh and the ninth. It must be remembered that
almost all these documents were produced by those in power or
for the maintenance of power by those who shared in it. The great
majority who were manual workers could neither read nor write.
But their position and their feelings can be discovered under the
surface of the written records. In the fifth century there are the
official Theodosian law-books; the poor man's point of view is
expressed by Orosius and Salvian; and the rich man's by Sidonius
Apollinaris. It will be noticed that all these belong to the Mediterranean countries. The Roman system of production was most
highly developed in the South. Probably in the North the cultivated
areas were smaller and the population sparser; and there also older
pre-Roman social systems survived. It is, however, possible to speak
of a single slave-system of production throughout the Roman
Empire, interlocked with its administration, and a single system of
trade with distant parts, organized in the cities. The production of
necessities was carried out by slave-labour—that is to say, by men
and women brought from distant parts, who had no roots in the
place where they worked and no home of their own. Most of
them died without having reared children; and when the wars of
the Roman system no longer produced new captives to take the
place of the old, the supply of "man-power" diminished.

The second stage in the transition can be seen best in the letters of Gregory the Great, in the *History* of Gregory of Tours, and in some of the barbarian laws, which were, however, written down in later years. The material upon which the historian must rely for evidence concerning this second stage, therefore, includes some evidence for northern France and Britain. The slave-trade survived; but slaves were fewer. The estates of very wealthy landowners no longer existed in such numbers as under the Roman system; and the estates of the Church were widespread. The "upper" class was a warrior class with little or no education; and the descendants of slaves or land-labourers were all, at least nominally, Christian.

During the third stage of the transition, at the beginning of the ninth century, the evidence is more abundant. There are the official Capitularies, especially the Capitulary *De Villis*, the *Polyptychum* of abbot Irminon, Charters and Formularies. Such evidence concerns mainly north-western Europe, within which the typical medieval social system—including the Manor and Feudalism—was developed. The Mediterranean countries, except northern Italy, had disappeared out of the picture. Cities which had been the centres of Roman were on frontiers of medieval civilization. A new world had come into existence. Slavery had practically disappeared; and serfdom was the foundation above which were built the different ranks and functions of medievalism. Production of necessities was local and for subsistence, not trade. The towns were merely local markets. A few merchants and pilgrims still travelled far; but there was no security for anyone who left his native locality. The peoples of the new Europe struck roots in different centres separated by a sort of no-man's-land, not a "frontier," where the effectual control of any one lord ended.

The Fifth Century

Concerning the Roman system which was in dissolution at the beginning of the fifth century, little need be added here to what has been said in the second chapter. The most important fact about that system, from the present point of view, is that it was based upon slavery, and that the consequences of slavery were corroding it. The supply of slaves was decreasing; the wealthy slave-owners were more and more careless of public duty and independent of the imperial Authorities. Impoverishment, starvation and insecurity, as Salvian said, were leading great numbers of poor men to seek refuge on the estates of those who still seemed powerful enough to protect them, but used such power to enslave them by debt and forced labour. Some sought refuge and bare livelihood where the barbarians had control of the situation. No doubt, poor men would be left to labour in the fields or at the crafts so long as barbarian warriors could find nothing to take from them. It was liberty of a sort, as Salvian said, but liberty unorganized, unprotected, precarious and transitory.

The system of production and use maintained under the Roman Empire may be briefly described as follows. Food, clothing, and materials for shelter were produced on country estates. In the fifth century these were chiefly of two kinds, the estates of private landowners (*fundi rei privatae*) and imperial estates (*fundi et saltus domus divinae*).[1] On both kinds of estates the labour was provided partly by slaves, who lived in huts near the owner's country house or farmhouse (*villa rustica*), and partly by tenant farmers (*coloni*), who had to give some days labour as part of the rent. The management of an estate was in the hands of a bailiff (*villicus*); and the workers on the estate were very early called "people of the villa" (*villani or villeins*). The wealthier landowners had so many estates, and spent so much time in cities or at holiday resorts, that the management of slaves and farmers fell into the hands of their agents. On the imperial estates the manager was a public official; and the *coloni* had greater security of tenure than on private estates, as "Caesar's men" or "men of the Augustan house."[2] Some of these imperial estates were taken over by the barbarian kings in the fifth century and some presented to the Churches in different districts.

A wealthy landowner might possess estates as well as country houses in Gaul, Spain, Italy, Africa and Greece; and some of these landowners had incomes, valued in modern currency, of about a quarter of a million pounds. But after the civil wars and the bar-

---

[1] *Cod. Theod.*, v, 13. De fundis rei privatae et saltibus divinae domus.

[2] Ibid., x, 26. De conductoribus et hominibus domus Augustae. See Pelham, H.F., *Essays* (1911), p. 275, on the Imperial Domains.

barian invasions of the fifth century in the West many landowners fled or lost their property, while the workers on their estates remained to cultivate for themselves and their fellows what was necessary. The pressure of the imperial bureaucracy, however, and the general unsettlement of society in the early fifth century drove many of the tenant farmers, and perhaps also slaves, to flee from the estates on which they worked.

The difficulty of the Roman Authorities was that the population would not stay upon the land. Decrees and official action provided for penalties against the escape of *coloni* and slaves, and against sheltering fugitives. But from the point of view of these fugitives clearly the purpose of the imperial Authorities was to tax them or otherwise extract labour and goods from them. They fled to escape intolerable burdens; and it was not until the new medieval system of serfdom or villeinage was established that the labouring population became fixed in one place at work. This obviously implies an advantage, from the point of view of the worker, to be found in the medieval as against the Roman system. The flight from the towns in the fifth century had similar causes. The Roman Government could not resist the escape of men and women from cities in which they could find nothing to do and in which the Government could no longer supply gratuitous food.

As for the barbarians, those who were settled within the Roman Empire were either ex-soldiers working land distributed among them in compact settlements, or they were a few warriors attempting to take the place of Roman officials and landowners, and therefore dependent upon whatever labouring population could be induced to remain at work. But as these barbarians, even when they called themselves kings, extracted less than the Roman officials from the common folk, the transfer of power to them led to a greater willingness on the part of the people to continue at work on the land or in towns. In some ways, indeed, the very ignorance and the limitations of the wants of the barbarian rulers saved the remnants of a productive system which was being ruined by the extortion of Roman officials and the absorption of wealth by an imperial Court. It is certain that the landed estates and the towns, maintained under the Roman system, continued to be the basis of production and exchange under the new barbarian kingdoms.[1] The transition was gradual, not catastrophic. The essential force which carried on the lives of the majority of men and women from the Roman to the medieval system was the desire of common folk for settled conditions in one place; and these settled conditions were much more easily obtained by the poor and illiterate when the barbarians took the place of the Roman officials. The transition was in some cases made easier by the Roman practice of *precarium* or land allowed, at the will of the owner, to be farmed by dependants on payment of a portion of the produce.

The desire for settlement in one place was accompanied by the desire of any ordinary couple, man and woman, to remain together and to rear children. But both these natural desires are frustrated in a system of slavery. The imperial Authorities, therefore, while attempting to prevent *coloni* or slaves from leaving the land, were forced to support some measures for giving these helpless people security against the landowners and the rich. Some of the disabilities of slaves were removed by the Christian Emperors, no doubt, partly under the influence of Christianity; but partly, also, because the maintenance of the economic system required the satisfaction of some of the slaves' desires. In all periods of history the manual workers are more kindly treated when the need for their work becomes obvious even to the rich. As for the *coloni*, or small farmer tenants, they found some security in the old Roman tradition or patronage (*patrocinium*). This was mainly a system of protection for dependants in the interest of the protector. But it implied at least an economic interest of the rich man in the maintenance or the farmer's productive power, and this, no doubt, was one of the sources out of which the medieval system, implying the rights of serfs or villeins against their lords, may have developed. But clearly patronage is a form of despotism, even when it is benevolent; and

---

[1] This is the main argument of Fustel de Coulanges in *Les Institutions politiques* etc., and it is applied to Germany east of the Rhine by Dopsch, *Economic and Social Foundations of European Civilization*, 1937, a condensed translation from the German (Vienna, 1924), *Wirtschaftliche und Soziale Grundlagen der Europäischen Kulturentwicklung aus der Zeit von Caesar bis auf Karl den Grossen*.

common folk would never have won even the moderate amount of liberty and livelihood which they enjoyed, as a right, in the Middle Ages, unless the upper classes of the Roman world had died out or been replaced by barbarian warriors.

The position of the rich in the fifth century is very well expressed in the letters of Sidonius Apollinaris. The rich were both blind to the defects of the system from which they derived benefit, and irresponsible in the use of their power, as it has been shown in the second chapter of this book. But this is true of all periods in which great private wealth of a few is maintained by the subjection and impoverishment of the majority. The situation was not very different in eighteenth-century France; and it is the same in some parts of the world to-day. But the barbarian warriors who looted the Roman Empire in the fifth century, even where they attempted, as in Africa, to take the place of the great Roman landowners, weakened the hold of the rich upon the poor. Sidonius Apollinaris, both before and after he became a Christian bishop, and many other rich men like him, came to terms with the barbarians. On their part the barbarian warriors appreciated the services of educated Roman officials. But the Roman system had really depended upon the rich men of the Empire "hanging together"; and when the landowner of any province found it convenient to make terms individually with barbarian warriors, the old system was evidently at an end. Such private wealth and personal power as then came into existence were local and insecure. The barbarian warrior who had taken part of the land and its inhabitants from Roman individuals or from public Authorities had no established system to support him, even if his property had been bestowed upon him by a king. Thus, from the very beginnings of the social transition to the Middle Ages the new holders of power and wealth had to find some method of securing their own position. The efforts to reach such security in any locality were among the first sources of what later became the Feudal System. But throughout the fifth and sixth centuries quite obviously the production of necessities was decreasing; and the insecurity of life became greater both for the poor and the rich. Not only barbarian pressure undermined the power of rich landowners. The Christian conscience was also at work. As it has been noted above, Paulinus of Nola and his wife gave up their riches to the poor; and the same ideas are expressed in the will of Perpetuus, bishop of Tours from A.D. 461, a very rich man and successor as bishop to one of his own family. The text is as follows: "In the first place, I, Perpetuus, will that all the men and women that I have in the Villa Saponaria whom I bought with my own money shall be free; and so also the servants whom I have not freed in the church on the day of my death, but so that they shall serve freely my Church as long as they live and without servitude transferable to heirs and attached to the soil." After leaving to his Church a field and woods, he leaves his small gold cross to his sister—"remember me, my dearest. Amen." To his successor he leaves "whatever he wishes to select for episcopal use from my chamber and my office." At the end of the will are the words: "But you, my beloved dear brothers, my crown and joy, my lords and my children—Christ's poor, the destitute, the dependent, the sick, widows and orphans—you I write down as my heirs." There is no such example of the change of attitude among rich men except under the influence of Christianity, although Stoic philosophers and their pupils often freed their slaves at their deaths.[1] It will be noted that the bishop in his lifetime had bought some and had freed some of his servants "in the Church"; and that he regards the Church of Tours as the chief heir of his private wealth, especially in so far as it could be used for the support of the poor and the weak.

Enter the Barbarians

The new masters of western Europe, whom the Romans called the barbarians, were not themselves united. It is an illusion to think of a single Germanic or Teutonic invasion The Roman world formed a unity, although the dominant Latin-speaking social classes

[1] Perpetuus, in *Pat. Lat.*, 58. Testamentum: In primis ego Perpetuus volo liberos esse liberasque homines et feminas quotquot habeo in Villa Saponaria quos emi de mea pecunia, ut et pueros quos in die discessus mei non manumisero in ecclesia, ita tamen ut libere servant quamdiu vixerint Ecclesiae meae, sed absque servitute ad heredes transmissibili et glebatica.

in the West belonged to many different races. The system was one, not merely because of a single language and a centralized administration, but also because it expressed one particular type of civilized life and culture. Theatres, amphitheatres, baths, well-decorated villas in the country and well-paved streets in cities, including rich men's houses, all these were to be found throughout the Roman world in almost the same form in Italy, Africa, Spain, Gaul and far-distant Britain. The system of agricultural production, where the subject tribes did not continue their traditional methods in outlying regions, was the same. Supplies of necessities were taken great distances to the cities; and as the city populations increased, greater numbers were idle, without any master or patron and unable to purchase what they needed. Therefore, in the first place, the civil Authorities and the Churches had to distribute food gratuitously; and, secondly, the market for necessities was so diminished that production itself declined.

Into this world came groups of warriors of different tribes, speaking different dialects, each group much more willing to fight the others than to destroy the Roman system. Indeed, the wars of the fifth and sixth centuries between Goths and Burgundians and Franks, and the later wars in England of one Saxon tribe against another, were more destructive of civilized life than any attack of barbarians upon Romans. The treachery and violence of one German against another were much more disastrous for common folk than was the change of masters from rich Roman landowners to ignorant and gluttonous barbarian warriors. Thus the Burgundian king came down into Liguria and took off into slavery for sale at Lyons the subjects of Theodoric, the Ostrogoth, some of whom were restored to their homes by the efforts of St. Ephiphanius.[1] It is true that the barbarian kings, raiding for slaves and gold, were merely imitating the earlier Roman conquerors. But in the fifth and sixth centuries western Europe was already divided between groups of barbarian warriors, the forerunners of medieval lords; and no one group was strong enough to destroy the other. Besides, each group of barbarians—Goth, Vandal, Frank or Saxon—

[1] See Chapter V, p. 179.

424

was a loosely connected band of jealous and treacherous individuals each willing to play for his own hand. In such a world the lives of ordinary men and women who tilled the fields and tended the flocks and herds, were indeed insecure; but they were the only elements of stability. These unknown and unrecorded common folk carried on the basic tradition of civilized life, which does not consist of letters or luxury but of well-tried methods of production and manufacture. The Roman landowners disappeared. The barbarian warriors ruined and ravaged the cities. But the same fields were tilled and sown and reaped year after year by the children and the grand-children of the unknown manual workers. Their hands built the churches and brought into use the food and clothing of their day. They were the founders of the new civilization of Europe which replaced the Roman.

The Seventh Century

The next stage in the development may be marked by a description of the situation two hundred years later, in the year A.D. 600 and shortly after. Two hundred years separate the year 1940 from 1740, and in that time clearly the transformation of society has been very rapid, owing to the growth of the industrial system and applied scientific knowledge. No such forces were at work between A.D. 400 and A.D. 600; but the social changes caused by the disappearance of the Roman Empire in the West and the establishment of the Catholic barbarian kingdoms were no less fundamental. In A.D. 600 medieval Europe was already visible. The Frankish kingdom dominated north-western Europe. The Anglo-Saxons were dividing the spoil in Britain. Church buildings of great magnificence had risen in Italy and Gaul. Monasteries had acquired great properties. The Latin West was already separated from the Greek East. All this implies social invention and discovery, which is probably as important as the scientific invention of mechanisms or the discovery of the facts of the physical world. The relationship between human beings was radically altered in practice and in principle. A universal military despotism no longer supported or was supported by the Mediterranean type of civilization. There were no longer large slave-markets, supplying "labour" derived from wars; and the great monastic movement was attracting the best men and women into communities which spread a civilization of a new order.

The clearest evidence for the social position of common folk in the early seventh century is to be found in the letters of Gregory the Great, which deal with the administration of the estates of the Roman Church—*patrimonium Sancti Petri*. These estates about A.D. 600 were in Sicily, Campania, Calabria, Dalmatia, Gaul, Corsica and Sardinia, and in some other parts of Italy, besides the outskirts of Rome. The bishop of Rome had evidently become a great landowner, like the great Roman landowners of the fifth and sixth centuries. The estates of the Church were scattered, but were under a central administration at Rome, like that of the earlier imperial estates. Gregory the Great exercised a close supervision over the archdeacons and other officials whom he appointed as his agents on the different estates. The most striking of his letters on this subject are those to Peter the sub-deacon, his agent in Sicily. .n one letter he directs Peter to see that the work-people on the estates are legally dependent on the Church and not fugitives from other estates.[1] Again, Peter is told not to overcharge the country-folk (*rusticos ecclesiae*) who apparently suffered, as in the days when Cicero attacked Verres, from the fluctuation of the price of corn in good and bad seasons.[2] Peter is to see to the shipments to Rome, to take regular payments and to prevent overcharging on debts or excessive fees for marriages. He is to be careful not to injure the heirs of any property which may be left to the Church. Contractors are not to overcharge the country-folk, and, if they do, repayment must be made even if the Church loses by it: "We do not wish to soil the purse of the Church by unworthy gain."[3] Peter, of whose energies Gregory was decidedly critical, is told in a later letter that cows on the estates which are too old to have calves must be sold, and the mares handed over to contractors, "for

[1] Greg. M., Ep. i, 36 (*Pat. Lat.*).
[2] Gregory writes: Volumus ut justa pretia publica omni tempore, sive minus sive amplius frumenta nascuntur, in eis comparationis mensura teneatur.
[3] Nos sacculum ecclesiae in lucris turpibus nolumus inquinare. Ep. i, 44.

it is very hard to be paying sixty *solidi* to herdsmen and not getting sixty pence for the herds." Peter is further directed to come at once to Rome and bring the payments of the ninth and tenth indictions and all the accounts. The Pope complains: "Besides, you sent me one wretched horse and five good asses. The horse I cannot ride because it is such a wretched beast, and the good beasts I cannot ride because they are asses." To his agent on the estates in Gaul, Gregory writes: "Gregory to Candidus the priest, going to the property in Gaul. As you are going with the help of Our Lord God, Jesus Christ, to manage the property which is in Gaul, we wish that you, my dear friend (*dilectio tua*), should buy with the money which you obtain, some clothing for the poor or some English boys, who are about seventeen or eighteen years old, that they may be educated in the monasteries—that is, in so far as the Gallic money, which cannot be spent in our country, can be usefully spent on the spot. But if there is any surplus of the money which is called 'contributions' (*ablatae*) that you receive, with this also we want you to buy clothing for the poor or, as we have said above, boys who can progress in the service of Almighty God. But, because those who can be found there are pagans, I wish that a priest may be sent with them, lest there should be any illness on the journey—that he may baptize any of them whom he thinks worthy of it. So then you, my dear friend, must take care to fulfil this order quickly."[1] This letter may be compared with one written about fifty years before, in the days of Justinian's invasion of Italy. Pelagius I, bishop of Rome (A.D. 555–560), wrote on December 14, 556, to Sapaudus, bishop of Arles, requesting him to send the sums collected for rents on the estate of the Roman Church in Gaul. He writes that "the Italian farms are so ruined that no one is able to repair or restore them." The bishop of Arles is, therefore, asked to buy in Gaul, with the money owing to the Roman Church, thick woollen-padded coats, white tunics, cowls and jackets without sleeves. These are to be sent by a suitable ship.[2] It is well known that the *solidus* minted in Gaul was of a lighter weight than that of

[1] Greg. M., Ep. vi, 7 (*Pat. Lat.*).
[2] *M.G.H.*, Epistolae iii. Ep. Merov. et Karol. Aevi, i.

427

Italy and other parts of the Empire; and this, no doubt, is the reason why both Pelagius and Gregory directed that the monies owing to the Roman Church in Gaul should be spent there on commodities needed for the poor and other dependants of the Church in Rome.

The income of the Roman Church and probably of all the Churches included, first, coin (*solidi*) derived from payments for land, or from sales of goods and the so-called contributions or levies (*ablatae*). Secondly, the income included corn and other food-stuffs shipped, if necessary, for the use of the owner. Thirdly, there was cloth or made-up clothing, referred to in Gregory's letters as "clothing for the poor."[1] As for the expenditure of the Church in Rome, apart from the maintenance of the estates, first came the support of the poor in Rome. The Roman Church in this service evidently took the place of the imperial Authorities from the fifth century onwards. Secondly, both money and commodities were used for Church ceremonies and the maintenance of the clergy. Thirdly, the Roman Church had to pay for Embassies to Constantinople and to the kings of western Europe. And finally, from the days of Gregory onwards, the Church paid tribute to the Lombard kings or dukes. Thus, Gregory wrote to the Empress Constantina: "It is now seven and twenty years that we have been living in this city, beset by the swords of the Lombards. How much we have to pay them daily from the Church's treasury in order to live among them at all, it is impossible to compute. I will merely say that, as at Ravenna the Emperor has a paymaster for the first army of Italy who defrays the daily expenses as need arises, so at Rome for such purposes I am the paymaster." He says, too, that "this Church at one and the same time is incessantly spending so much money on the clergy, on the monasteries, on the poor, on the people, and, moreover, on the Lombards."[2]

The reference to the purchase of Saxon boy slaves in Gaul, in Gregory's letter quoted above, indicates both the continuance of the slave-trade and the change in its character under the influence

---

[1] The income of the Roman Church in A.D. 600 is calculated to have been £300,000 a year. See Dudden, *Gregory the Great*, vol. i.   [2] Ep. v, 39.

of the Church; for Gregory evidently intended to use the boys as future missionaries. Saxon slaves at the beginning of the seventh century were sold in great numbers in the slave-markets of Gaul. They were probably captives taken by one side or the other in the interminable wars between different marauding bands who formed what are called the kingdoms of that time in England. Thus, in the *Life* of St. Eligius (St. Eloi), who was a rich goldsmith and master of the mint to the king of the Franks, in the early seventh century in northern Gaul, it is said that "he used his money for redeeming captives in batches of twenty, thirty or even a hundred—Romans, Britons, Moors, but especially those of the Saxon race who in great numbers at that time, like herds torn from their own homes, were scattered in all directions."[1] St. Eligius is said to have sold even his clothing in order to free the slaves, and then to have given them the choice either of returning to their native land (for which he gave them money), or to live and work with him, or to become monks or nuns. After the expenditure of all his wealth, gained in his official position, Eligius entered a monastery and was made bishop of Noyon in A.D. 640.

Among the Saxon slaves of a later date was a little girl, a captive from England, who was sold at a low price to a Frankish nobleman.[2] Her name was Balthildis. She is said to have been, even as a child, lovely, bright and silent. Her owner placed her in a convent to be educated; but when, later on, he desired to marry her, she fled and hid from him. Eventually she married Clovis II, king of the Franks, and founded many monasteries and convents and gave support to many of the poor. The admiration for her beauty, her grace of movement and her high intelligence, shines through the clumsy words of the writer of her *Life*. At the death of her husband she controlled the kingdom for some time; and her three sons eventually all became kings of the Franks. She herself died in the year A.D. 680, after having entered one of the convents which she had founded. Like Radegunda, also a captive, and Theudelinda, an

---

[1] *S. Eligii Vita*, i, 10, *Pat. Lat.*, 87 (A.D. 588–659). Treasurer to Dagobert, son of Clothaire. He also went as missionary to the Frisians and Belgians. His *Life* was written by Audoenus (Ouen).

[2] *S. Balthildis Vita, Pat. Lat.*, 87. Cf. also *Cont. Fred., Pat. Lat.*, 71, col. 665.

exile, Balthildis stands for something which Greek and Roman civilization had not known. But she is long since dead and forgotten:

> A lost lady of old years
> With her beauteous vain endeavour
> And her goodness unrepaid as ever.

The sale of slaves in the early seventh century in France is indicated in the formulas of Marculf by a model receipt which runs as follows: "N. to M. To my lord brother. This is to certify that I have sold you a slave of my property or servant maid, named N.—not a thief, not a fugitive, nor decrepit (*cadivum = chétif*) but of good mind and body. For whom I accepted from you as price, of my own will, so many *solidi* of gold, good and paid over, and the slave I handed over to you at the same time to possess, so that from this day you have the right of holding and doing what you will. But if anyone—which we do not believe will happen—or if I myself or any of my heirs or any person shall try to upset the sale or break its terms, he shall pay you so much gold under the compulsion of the law, or as much as the slave himself shall have increased in value at that time, and this sale must remain fixed for all time with the added arrangement. Done at such a place at such a time."[1]

In the *History of the Franks* by Gregory of Tours there are few references to the lives of common folk, except when they suffer from famine, plague, oppression or slaughter. He writes of a riot of the lower classes (*minor populus*) against Egidius, bishop of Rheims, and the king's nobles. The rioters called out: "Let those who sell the kingdom and put his cities under another's rule be driven from the king's side." When morning came, they took up arms and rushed to the king's camp to capture the bishop and the lords and beat or slay them. The bishop fled, while the people flung stones at him, cursing him; and as they had no horses, he escaped, but in such a fright that he left one of his shoes behind.[2] Again, Gregory writes that the people of Limoges were engaged in "common work" on a Sunday, although it is not clear whether the *opus*

---

[1] Marculf, *Form.*, ii, 22.　　　　　　[2] Greg. Tur., *H.F.*, vi, 31.

publicum was work in common or simply work in the fields. Of private traders (*negotiatores*) Gregory writes that they took advantage of famine conditions throughout most of Gaul to despoil the people by charging high prices, and that the poor gave themselves up as slaves in order to get a little food. At that time a merchant, hearing that there was a large supply of wine in Orleans, went there and was bringing back wine when he was set upon and killed by his two Saxon slaves who hated him.[1] Again, another merchant, who was a Syrian, paid large sums and managed to become bishop of Paris, putting into the bishop's household other Syrians and dismissing his predecessor's staff and clergy.[2]

Some further light on the conditions of the time may be derived from the "model documents" collected or composed by the monk Marculf, for a bishop, probably about A.D. 650. As Marculf says in his preface that he was seventy years old or more, with a trembling hand, bad eyesight and a tired mind, it may be assumed that his formulas represent the conditions of the early seventh century. In one model letter for a king, announcing to his counts the birth of an heir, it is written that three men and three women who are serfs in each villa are to be set free;[3] and in a later letter it is directed that "all Romans, Franks or other nations"—presumably under the count's jurisdiction—"are to meet the king's agent (*missus*) and swear allegiance to the king's son."[4] Forms are also given for the receipt of debt paid and for the freeing of slaves after the death of the owner. There is also a hint of some functions of the Church in the Form which reads: "As I have taken you to wife without your parents' consent, and have escaped punishment by the intercession of priests and good men, therefore I now bestow upon you so much land, so many cows, pigs, etc."[5] There are also forms for the sale of property in cities or of fields.

Several collections of Formulas, or model documents, were made in the seventh century in Gaul. These collections correspond to the legal Forms which were in use in the later Roman Empire as Titles to land or as Contracts. But by the seventh century the official

---

[1] Greg. Tur., *H.F.*, vii, 45–46.   [2] Ibid., x, 26.
[3] Marculf, *Form.*, i, 39.   [4] Ibid., i, 39.   [5] Ibid., ii, 16.

written documents of administrative orders or of private contracts, like the charters (*diplomata*), were already medieval in tone and substance. The position of ordinary folk in the community thus came more and more to depend upon written documents modelled upon fixed forms. But obviously, as the great majority could neither read nor write, these documents were, in the original sense of the word, hieroglyphs. For ignorant kings, as well as for the majority of ordinary men and women, the written document, produced by the clergy, had an almost magical efficacy.

The general features of the social and economic system at the beginning of the seventh century may be briefly described as follows. The chief contrast which strikes the reader of contemporary documents between the new situation and that of two centuries before, is that the organization and control of labour and production was under local landowners, lords secular or ecclesiastical, who were more or less equals in authority, with no effectual superior over them. Two centuries earlier, the Roman imperial Authorities could exact taxation and, at least in theory, administer justice according to one system covering the whole of western Asia, Europe (except Germany) and northern Africa. The dissolution of imperial authority had left the bishops and abbots in practice supreme in the administration of Church estates; and it had left the Germanic warriors and the survivors of Roman landowning families either supreme on their estates or under a very loose allegiance to a barbarian king. Some of these warriors held land as personal followers of the king (*optimates regis*), others as nobles of their race. But the barbarian kings had no official organization for the control of either. Similarly, ecclesiastical properties, although affected by the common Christian conception of the duty of the lord to his servants, were independent units. A good bishop would increase the wealth and happiness on his estates; a bad bishop would exploit them for his own personal advantage. But each estate or group of estates was under the complete control of its owner or administrator. Roman imperial taxation had ceased and was partially replaced by tribute, paid largely to "lords," in commodities and not in coin. The administration of justice was local, and dependent upon local customs, which differed for men of different races.

For the great majority, who were unknown, illiterate and long-suffering men and women, life in the fields, marked by the changes of the seasons for ploughing and sowing and reaping, was the whole of experience. It was not unhappy, except when the quarrels or oppressions of their superiors destroyed their meagre supplies of food or shelter. Their lives were made more endurable by the festivals and ceremonies of the local Churches, which had now spread outside the cities of the Roman system into the countryside and taken the place of the old local rituals of the gods of streams and trees. In the South, no doubt, the Roman methods of agriculture continued, as is implied in the letters of Gregory the Great. But in northern Gaul and in Britain, perhaps, pre-Roman systems of co-operation between equals in work on the fields revived; or perhaps invaders, such as the Saxons in England, established small communities of free men working the land. In either case production was no longer dependent upon large concentrations of slave-labour; and the slaves who still existed seem to have been few, dependent upon small "masters," working side by side with free men.[1]

In general, agricultural production in the early seventh century was for local consumption. The life of the countryside dominated the minds of men of that time, and not the life of cities.[2] The greater cities of the Roman world, such as Trier, Arles, Milan, Rome and Carthage, were partly ruined and much reduced in population. Above all, taxation and the administration of justice in the countryside no longer depended upon the administration in the cities. The agricultural areas, plough-land, meadows and forests, were organized under local lords; and the maintenance of such lords, both ecclesiastical and secular, required little more than local supplies. The tastes of the new controllers of common life were

[1] The "northern" methods of organization, whether survivals of Celtic or introductions of Teutonic usage, are deduced by such scholars as Vinogradoff (*The Growth of the Manor*, etc.) from later documents. There is no direct evidence comparable to that in the letters of Gregory the Great.

[2] The most striking statement of this contrast is in Guizot's *Civilization of France.*

simple, if not barbaric; and it was obviously in their interest to give security to their dependants in order to maintain continuous production by local labour; because there was no longer any source, either in great wars or in foreign trade, for a large supply of slaves.

In the South—in Italy, Africa and Spain—the Roman system of cultivating large estates by the labour of *servi* and *coloni* seems to have continued. But these *servi* and *coloni* were no longer merely the slaves and farmers of the old imperial system. Perhaps the two classes were already included in the new medieval conception of a *serf*. They were not free or independent; but, as can be seen in the letters of Gregory the Great, they were not treated merely as chattels. The Mediterranean countries, however, were ruined in the seventh and early eighth centuries, first by the Lombard wars in Italy, and secondly by Mohammedan invasion. Whatever ordinary production in agriculture and trade still continued was, therefore, only a remnant. All the sources of supply in the fields or in the workshops were blocked or destroyed by raiding warriors or by quarrels among the conquerors about the division of the spoil. The life of common folk in the South, in Mediterranean lands, after Gregory the Great, became less and less secure. Whatever was left of order and settled custom was a mere survival of an earlier system.

In the North, that is, in northern Gaul and in Britain, a new system of production seems to have begun, or perhaps revived, where Roman rule had been forgotten. This is the system of production by labour in common on fields divided among the workers and by crafts directly dependent upon agricultural life. The methods of production and manufacture were, no doubt, similar in the whole of north-western Europe and in Britain. But they were not "racial"—Celtic or Teutonic. They were simply the natural systems of a society passing through its earliest agricultural stages. The men and women who grew the food or made the clothing necessary for themselves and for any lord who might demand a share, seem to have belonged to communities less subject to superiors in the early seventh century than either before or after. A period of masterless co-operation between small groups of ordinary men and women

434

seems to have intervened between the slave-system of the Roman Empire and the manorial system of lords and villeins, which was already in existence in the ninth century. But local liberty to work and to eat in a small group of equals was insecure. Armed men might raid the district. Scarcity, famine or disease might fall upon a small community lacking connections with its neighbours. The area of cultivated land was small in proportion to the surrounding forests or marshes; and the more energetic of the younger generation, in a community with limited resources, had to seek their fortunes elsewhere. In these small communities a practical equality of conditions did not imply an equality of status. Some men and women were still slaves. But the slaves seem to have been comparatively free; and they formed parts of small households and worked at the side of their masters.

The administration of justice, like the methods of production, was locally organized. The custom of the district was the basis of the rules more or less enforced by the community. Such rules, as expressed in the barbarian laws, have been described above. Evidently in the simple agricultural or pastoral societies of north-western Europe and Britain, personal violence and the theft or destruction of animals were regarded as the chief crimes. Against these the best men of the locality provided a system of compensation for wrongs. But underlying all the difficulties of these early efforts to develop a legal system was the common life of poor men dependent for their food and clothing upon the pigs and sheep and restricted corn-lands of the district. The life of the herdsman, the wood-cutter, the gang at the ploughing and reaping, the women spinning and weaving, and all men, women and children gathered together in the local festivities—this was the life of a new world in which the Roman system was gradually forgotten and the medieval system established.

It must not be imagined that, in the early seventh century, cities and towns did not exist. Although the population in the country-side was now settled upon the land, either as small farmers paying rent in goods and services or as serfs in complete dependence upon a great lord, a bishop or an abbot, the towns continued to supply the products of certain crafts. Thus, Gregory of Tours describes a man walking through the streets of Tours and admiring the shops. There is evidence of the manufacture by craftsmen in the towns of the finer kinds of clothing, of pottery, glass and candles. Jewellery also was greatly admired both in the churches and at the courts of kings; and the jewellers were obviously town-craftsmen. The greater towns also contained districts in which Jews and Syrians resided.

The cities survived from Roman times at least in Italy, France and western Germany, although they were partly in ruins and greatly reduced in population. The public buildings were gradually falling into decay.[1] Such cities were centres of ecclesiastical organization, of military control under the barbarian counts (*comites*) who took the place of the counts of the later Roman Empire, and in the cities taxes were collected and travelling merchants carried on trade. Thus, although the barbarian warriors preferred the life of the country, with its hunting and feasting upon crude food and drink, and although the agricultural population was much more numerous than that of the towns and cities, the whole "economic" life of the seventh century was not agricultural. The transition from Roman city life to the life of medieval castles and country villages involved no sudden break with the practice of handicraft and trade in towns.

The Ninth Century

The third stage in the change from the Roman to the medieval system is expressed most clearly in the documents of the early ninth century. Of these the most important are the Capitulary *De Villis* of A.D. 812, the *Polyptychum* of the abbot Irminon of St. Germain-des-Prés, of about the year A.D. 811, and the poems of Theodulf, bishop of Orleans, written about the year A.D. 800.

The situation described in the Capitulary *De Villis* is an organization of labour and production which is supposed to be applied to all the royal estates in the widespread domains of Charles the Great.

---

[1] It seems probable from archaeological evidence that the cities of Roman Britain were deserted and not destroyed. See Collingwood and Myres, *Roman Britain*, *etc.*

The organization is placed in the hands of officials, called *judices*, who may be regarded as bailiffs or agents with some judicial power, directly subordinate to the central authority or palace (*palatium*) or court of the king. The agents are directed not to seek their own advantage in using the products of the estates: they are to pay regular visits to the palace; to hold courts (*audientias*), to arrest robbers, to keep regular accounts and to send a full statement of properties and provisions on the estates, annually at Christmas, to the palace. Subordinates of the agents are also to keep accounts. Among the people on the estate a "mayor" (*major*) is to be selected, "not from the richer men, but from those of moderate means who are trustworthy."[1] He is to speak for the common folk of the district and is, in some particulars, responsible to the lord's agent.[2]

The workers on the royal estates are referred to as *familia nostra*, the old terms for household slaves, but now evidently used to mean only "our people." They are not to be reduced to poverty, and, although little is said about them in the Capitulary, their work is implied in the provisions of most of the sections. The agent is to organize available labour, both in the fields and in the women's workrooms. But clearly, it is assumed that the work-people are not unwilling instruments. The agent has only to see that each estate is properly provided with the required amount of different kinds of labour or craftwork, of agricultural and other tools and of supplies. On each estate houses are to be provided and buildings kept in repair. All tools, such as axes and chains, are to be kept in store; and, at the women's workrooms, there should be wool, oil, combs, soap and whatever else is required for spinning and weaving. The women's workrooms must have good doors and be properly protected. Each estate also has flocks and beasts of burden; bees and chickens near the mills, as well as fish-ponds and herds of pigs. The fields and meadows and surrounding woods must be properly cared for. Swans, pheasants and other fowl are to be kept, and fat bacon properly prepared. Wine is not to be made by pressing the grapes with the feet, but by clean wine-presses. In addition to the

[1] *De Villis*, 60. Not from "potentes" but only from "mediocres qui fideles sunt."
[2] The "men of the divine house," resident on imperial estates in the fifth century, also had representatives.

agricultural labour and the women working on woollen garments, each estate should have good craftsmen or skilled workers such as carpenters, falconers, fishermen, soap-makers and skilled makers of strong drink—beer, cider and perry, "or any other liquor suitable for drinking." Here is a new life on country estates. The majority are not slaves, as under the Roman system; but they are dependent upon the lord's agent. "The characteristic of the Middle Ages, so far as the lower classes are concerned, was not oppression but subjection," as Fustel de Coulanges has admirably said.[1] The work of common folk is now organized upon a basis of reciprocal duties and rights. The happiness of common folk, no doubt, depended too much upon the individual character of their lord or his agents; but they had some rights against oppression even if the lord were the oppressor. A tenth of the produce of the estate is to go to the support of the Churches, but "only clergy from among our own people or from our chapel" are to hold livings. A proportion of produce is to be regularly sent to the king's court; and for Lent especially vegetables, butter, mustard, vinegar and honey. And in the last section of the Capitulary a long list is given of the herbs, flowers and fruit which should be grown in the gardens. Any surplus produce must be either stored or sold. Fowls and fish are to be sold; but goat-skins and horns are to be put down in the annual account, and wolves' skins are to be sent to the palace. Every year in May wolves are to be hunted and the young destroyed by poison, if necessary.

The estates are also to provide stores and other necessaries for war. Waggons for use against the enemy are to be well made and able to cross water. Each is to carry some corn, a shield, and spear and bow. Barrels, also to be provided, are not to be made of hides. The wars of kings and other lords now depend, not upon mercenaries, but upon a levy made from the workers in the fields. They had to defend their district from raiders, and they had to assemble when called upon, in the early summer, and march with their lords. But, as they had also to work in the fields, the "armies" of the kings, from the seventh to the ninth century, melted away at

[1] Fustel de C., *Institutions*, vol. iv, p. 424.

the close of each summer. Common folk returned homewards if
they could.

It is implied in the royal documents of the early ninth century
in north-western Europe that the majority of the population in the
countryside live and work on the estates of the king, the Churches
or great lords. The workers must have depended for their own
food and clothing upon such land as they could use for themselves,
and upon the rights of pasture or of feeding their pigs (*pastio*) in
parts of the forest. Workers and their families on any estate had to
supply a fixed amount of goods and services to the lord; and it
was clearly an advantage in the worker's household, and perhaps
also for the lord, that each household should contain growing
children. Children could help in the work of their father and
mother. The new system, therefore, tended to increase the population again, after the disastrous effects of a decaying slave-system.
Also, as the amount of uncultivated land in western Europe was
still very great, a larger population could be maintained by the
extension of agriculture or pastoral land into the area of forest or
marsh. The great majority of ordinary workers, being no longer
captives brought from distant parts, or men and women without
rights or interests in their families—as under a slave-system—it was
now possible for common folk to have a vital interest in their own
homes. Also, as more of the labourers and craftsmen secured a
livelihood, "markets" would extend, consumption increase and the
prices of commodities, in terms of money, fall. The obstacles in
the way of trade and the difficulties of transport after the fifth
century, naturally had an opposite effect; that is to say, they raised
prices in terms of coin. But, on the whole, there is no doubt that
the majority of men and women were better fed and clothed in
the ninth century than in the seventh. Wars and famines and
diseases still took their toll. But local famines or droughts did not
prevent a general advance; and, whereas in the early fifth century
the system of production and trade tended towards depopulation
and impoverishment, in spite of the survival of some very wealthy
families, at the beginning of the ninth century economic tendencies
promoted an improvement in the lot of the majority of men and

women. Even the invasions of Northmen and Saracens in the later ninth century, although they caused death and destruction, could not undermine the strong forces released by the disappearance of the Roman slave-system. Common folk, although dependent upon their lords, were free enough to build the foundations of medieval civilization.

The position of the workers on the great estates is more clearly expressed in the fragments of estate accounts which happen to have survived. There is a short section of such an account concerning the estates of the bishop of Augsburg, the monastery of Weissenberg and some of the royal domains.[1] In this fragment it is stated, for example, that "in the same place we found a farm and house of the manor with other buildings belonging to the same church. On this farm there is ploughland of seven hundred and forty days' work; meadows from which six hundred and ten loads of hay can be taken . . . one horse, twenty-six cattle, twenty cows, one bull, sixty-one smaller animals . . . forty pigs . . . fifty fowls, seventeen bee-hives. . . ." Other sections of the same document give the names of holders of farms and the extent of their holdings. This fragment represents the kind of account rendered by agents to landowners. The position of the dependent population on great estates is still more clearly expressed in the Register (*Polyptychum*) of Abbot Irminon. The monastery of which he was the abbot, in A.D. 811 contained two hundred and twelve monks, whose names are given in a list found at Reichenau and now preserved at Zürich.[2] The fragment of the manuscript of Abbot Irminon, which now exists, amounts probably to only a quarter of the whole. It was originally a list of all the properties of the Abbey of St. Germain, including both those worked by the Abbey authorities and those granted as *beneficia*.

A rendering of some sections of the record will give an indication of the kind of information it contains. For example, the summary for Cella Equalina begins: "It has in Cella Equalina[3] a farm with

[1] *Capitularia* (A.D. 812), *Pat. Lat.*, 97, col. 341.
[2] *M.G.H.*, Libri Confraternitatum, etc. (1881).
[3] Celle-les-Bordes (S. et O.) near Rambouillet. The text and Introduction here used is that published in 1895 by Auguste Longnon, which is based upon the original

a house and out-buildings enough. It has there eight ploughlands which contain sixty-five *bunuaria* (fifteen-acre sections) and can be sown for three hundred *modii* of corn. It has a vineyard of one and a half *aripenni* (one and a half acres each); of new land thirteen *aripenni*; of meadow thirty-eight *aripenni*. It has there of woodland five leagues in circuit where a thousand pigs can be fed. It has there two mills: from them in tax twenty-seven *modii* of corn, in money one *solidus*. It has there two churches with all furnishings, carefully constructed. Belonging to them ten *bunuaria* of ploughland, half an *aripennus* of vineyard, two *aripenni* of meadow. Besides, it has there two free farms, having ten *bunuaria* of ploughland, one and a quarter *aripenni* of vineyard, two *aripenni* of meadow.

"Arnulfus, a *colonus*, and his wife, a *colona*, named Farberta, men of St. Germain, have with them six children named Guntbertus, Farbertus, Elianta, Gerburc, Alboelt, Gerlaus. Gausbertus, a *colonus* of St. Germain, has with him four children named Gunsoinus, Ernoldus, Guntfredus, Gunsoildis. These two hold one free farm containing eleven *bunuaria* of ploughland; they have an *aripennus* of vineyard, two *aripenni* of meadow. They pay in war tax two *solidi* of silver and every second year one *solidus*. They pay for pig-feeding four *denarii*; they plough in the winter four perches and in spring, two perches; at Christmas one hoe, three fowls, fifteen eggs, land work, carting, labour, tree-cutting—as much as is demanded of them."[1] So the list continues of the men of St. Germain with their wives and children, and the size of their holdings; and the note at the end of most of the entries runs—"the payment is the same." In other parts of the *Polyptychum* we have the names of men entered as serfs (*servi*), some of whom are married to wives of the higher rank of the *colonus*. There is a third kind of dependent who is called a *lidus*. And the farms differ in status in the same way, some being free (*ingenuiles*), some servile (*serviles*), some of *lidus* standing. Some of the wives are put down as strangers (*extraneae*), that is to say, originally dependent upon

text and studies of Guérard. The measurements in their modern equivalents are explained in the Introduction (vol. i, in the 1895 edition). Text (1886 edition), p. 29.
[1] For an imaginative realization of the position of one of these families, see Eileen Power's *Mediaeval People*, ch. i.

some other lord. And at certain parts of the account a mere list of names is given under the heading: "These pay poll tax" (which is followed by thirty-eight names), and another list: "These pay one fowl, eggs, and three days."

For the purpose of the argument here the important point is that the Abbey takes account of each man, woman and child on its estates as an individual. In very many cases two households share the same farm. The personal status of the holders and their wives differs greatly; but the majority on the larger farms appear to have been ranked as *coloni*. The *lidi* are evidently of similar status, but less closely attached to the land and more clearly dependent upon their lord. The *servi* are already what the medieval writers would recognize as serfs; for they too hold farms and are not treated as in the possession of their lords. But the estates evidently had also a certain number of labourers, craftsmen and other dependants who did not hold land. They too are known by name and their payments or services are definite—not those of slaves. The whole number of the dependants of the Abbey, if allowance is made for the fact that only a quarter of the manuscript remains, must have amounted to about forty thousand. The number of the swine given in the manuscript is about seven thousand, so that the whole number on the monastic estates must have been about twenty-eight thousand. There must have been, in the seventh century, at least five or six such large monastic establishments in what is now called France; a similar number in Germany and in Italy, and, before the Danish invasions, in England. And besides these there were hundreds of smaller foundations, with fewer dependants. The effect, therefore, of monastic estates upon the lives of common folk in the new Europe was considerable and widespread. And throughout all western Europe on the country estates the old Roman methods of agriculture, of craftwork and of spinning and weaving were developed in a comparatively "free" society. Nothing of that kind existed under the Roman Empire in western Europe.

Another aspect of common life in the ninth century is reflected in the verses of Theodulf, bishop of Orleans, *Against Officials*

(*Contra Judices*).[1] In this very long composition of elegiac verses, with fragments of Ovid, Virgil, Prudentius and the Psalms interwoven, Theodulf first describes his journey to Arles. He had been sent with Laidrad, as a Legate of Charles the Great (*missus dominicus*). His verses describe how, at his approach, he was met by a crowd of petitioners, all offering gifts or bribes, if he would give them what they wanted.[2] One man whispers to the servant of Theodulf that he has a very valuable and highly decorated ancient cup, which he will give, if Theodulf accepts his plea. Some want other people's property; others dispute about what their father left. But all offer bribes. This, says the writer, could not happen unless it were a common defect of officials to take bribes.[3] But he himself does not want to appear "superior"; and therefore he accepts small gifts, such as eggs or bread or fowls. He then proceeds to address the officials, and urges them to keep the balance of justice equal, to care nothing for bribes, to come to court in good time and stay until the cases are finished, above all not to sit on the official dais after eating and drinking too much, to let the poor man have his chance of a hearing, to remember the justice of heaven, and to have mercy on those who have done evil. The verses indicate the difficulties of a system of law and administration in the hands of local officials, without the control of superiors. These local officials had, no doubt, to make their own living by such fees as they could obtain. But the difference between a fee and a bribe is always difficult to discover; and the absence of an established legal system obviously gave too much power to those who were sufficiently rich or sufficiently reckless to injure their neighbours by personal influence with the judge or other official. The king's agents (*missi dominici*) might give some protection to the poor and might maintain justice; but, as it appears from the verses of Theodulf, they were not themselves immune from bribery. In such a situation the rich would become richer and the poor poorer.

---

[1] *M.G.H., Poetae Latini*, vol. i, p. 493 (1881).

[2] *Contra Judices*, line 253. "Fidebant munere cuncti: Nec se quis quiddam, ni det, habere putant."

[3] Ibid., line 259. Flectere sic properant me, nec tamen esse putarent Talem ni talis ante fuisset ibi.

Travel and Trade

The lives of labourers and craftsmen were affected also at this date by the new kinds of travellers—pilgrims, ambassadors and small traders. The changes between A.D. 400 and A.D. 800 may be traced in the surviving records of travel. The journey described by Sidonius Apollinaris in the fifth century, when he went on an official mission from Gaul to Rome, following the imperial route and admiring, as a literary man, the scenery reflected in Virgil,[1] may be compared with the journey of Venantius Fortunatus from Italy to northern Gaul at the end of the sixth century,[2] and with the journey of Willibald to Rome and Palestine.[3] Of these three the two latter were pilgrims. And the three journeys show how the situation had changed in this connection between cities, between the fifth and the ninth century. Sidonius went South to Rome as a centre of Empire. Fortunatus went North, to follow in the steps of St. Martin, and stayed at his shrine at Tours. Willibald, his father, brother and friends left England in 721 A.D. for Rome; and he himself was on pilgrimage for ten years.

Pilgrimage, the most significant new form of travel, had hardly existed under the Roman system. In the second and third centuries Christian pilgrims used to go to Jerusalem; and in the fourth century, when Christianity was reconciled with the Empire, many monks and nuns, as well as other devout Christians, used to visit the Holy Land. At the end of that century, or at the beginning of the fifth, large settlements of hermits, monks and nuns were established near Bethlehem and Jerusalem, and provided a welcome for pilgrims from the West and the far North. Guide books (*itineraria*) to the Holy Places were written;[4] and the flow of pilgrims from the Latin Churches of the West was not interrupted entirely even after the Mohammedan conquest of Jerusalem. But other centres had arisen to which pilgrims went. The greatest of these was

[1] Sid. Apoll., Ep. i, 4 (A.D. 467), quos fluvios poetarum carminibus illustres.
[2] Venant. Fort. in *M.G.H.*, *A.A.*, iv, 368. Introductory verses in *Pat. Lat.* 88.
[3] *Hodœporicon* and *Itinerarium Willibaldi*.
[4] The so-called Itinerary of Sylvia (about A.D. 380) and that of the Pilgrim from Bordeaux (about A.D. 330) were followed by that of Theodosius (about A.D. 530) and of Adamnan who reports the journey of Arculfus (about A.D. 670) and is copied by Bede, *De locis sanctis. Itinera Hierosolymitana*, *C.S.E.L.*, vol. 38 (1888).

Rome—not as the capital of a Government, nor even as the See of St. Peter, but as the city of martyrs. At the beginning of the fifth century the chief other centres of pilgrimage were Nola, the shrine of St. Felix, to which Paulinus and his wife went, and Tours, the shrine of St. Martin. In the eighth or ninth century the shrine of St. James at Compostella in Galicia became a famous pilgrimage centre.

The Christian Churches never laid such emphasis upon pilgrimage as did the Mohammedan religion, which prescribes the pilgrimage to Mecca for the devout Mohammedan. But in the sixth and seventh centuries official arrangements were made to facilitate the pilgrim's journey. Letters were given to him by his bishop, which would assist him to obtain food and shelter at monasteries and ecclesiastical houses on his journey. The majority of pilgrims were still clergy, monks or nuns; but laymen, especially kings and nobles, came from all parts of the North to Rome. The export of relics from Rome to the northern countries was already considerable in the seventh century; and these relics were used in the establishment of local centres of pilgrimage. The pilgrims travelled for edification—seeing where Christ or the martyrs had suffered, for the cure of disease, and also, no doubt, for the sake of the interest in seeing famous places. Thus a unity was formed among the classes and races of the First Europe. But that unity must not be "sentimentalized" or idealized. In one aspect, indeed, it was a common admiration for certain restricted types of virtue—usually that of ascetics, or of preachers and martyrs—irrespective of country, race or local language. This set one moral standard for Europe. But in another aspect the unity was merely a common belief in primitive magic. The great majority believed that there was a magical efficacy for salvation or health in certain places, or in the bones or other relics of dead men and women—and this in spite of protests which continued from Jerome[1] to Theodulf.[2] It must be

---

[1] Jerome, Ep. 58, 3, "the gates of heaven are open even in Britain," and Ep. 47, 2.
[2] Theodulph, *M.G.H., Poetae Aev. Kar.*, i, 67.
    Quod deus non loco querendus sit, sed pietate colendus;
  Non tantum isse juvat Romam bene vivere quantum,
    Vel Romae, vel ubi vita agitur hominis.
  Non via, credo, pedum, sed morum ducit ad astra:
    Quis quid ubique gerit, spectat ab arce deus.

recognized that a good man such as Gregory of Tours, and one with a wide view of human character and public policy, could nevertheless believe that the dust from a saint's tomb, taken in water, would cure disease, and that a piece of cloth touching a saint's tomb would acquire "virtue" (*virtus*) which actually made it weigh more! Kings and bishops as well as common folk shared this strange mixture of moral idealism and primitive magic. And the result was the binding together of the peoples of the new Europe in the Christianity of the medieval Latin Church. Pilgrimage to Rome and the many northern shrines did more than the marching of Roman legions in earlier times to make a unity of the First Europe, independent of eastern influence.

The division of north-western Europe into different kingdoms and different centres of ecclesiastical authority led, in the centuries between the fifth and the ninth, to frequent journeys of ambassadors, legates and bearers of letters. In the eighth century the most important of the ambassadors were the abbots of the greater monasteries, such as Monte Cassino and St. Denis near Paris. These men kept the connection between the different parts of the new Europe intact in spite of frequent war and the devastation of large areas. They influenced the policy of Popes and kings; and their frequent journeys, accompanied by servants and officials, prevented the complete isolation of the new kingdoms and the scattered Churches of north-western Europe. They were the forerunners of the diplomatists of later days.

The travel of merchants more directly affected the lives of common folk. Even in northern Gaul, or the new France, a great number of the merchants were Syrians or Jews; but for commodities such as corn and wine, wool and hides, local merchants, not travelling far, supplied the markets. They had to pay various forms of tax or toll but were under the protection of local lords, laymen or ecclesiastics, who found it lucrative to have markets held on their estates.

The slave-trade continued into the eighth and ninth centuries. Pope Zachary (A.D. 750) redeemed slaves who had been bought in the slave-market in Rome by Venetian merchants for sale to the

Saracens in Africa; and he forbad any further such trade in Rome.[1] But about twenty years later Hadrian I wrote to Charles the Great to explain that the slave-trade was beyond his control. "It is true," the Pope writes, "that the unspeakable Greeks have traded along the Lombard shore and bought families from there and formed an alliance for slave-trading purposes with the Lombards. We ordered Duke Allo to prepare many ships that he might capture the Greeks and burn their fleet; but he refused to obey our commands. As for us, we have neither ships nor sailors to catch them with. But God is our witness that we have done all we could to suppress this mischief, for we ordered the ships of the Greeks that were in our harbour at Civita Vecchia to be burned, and we detained the crews in prison for a long time. But the Lombards themselves, as we have been told, constrained by hunger, have sold many families into slavery. And others of the Lombards have of their own accord gone on board the slave-ships of the Greeks because they have no other hope of livelihood."[2] In the North, at the end of the eighth century, Jewish merchants bought Slavs in the Rhine cities, who had been captured by German warriors, and sold these prisoners to Mohammedan lords in Spain. These slaves acted as body-guards of local Mohammedan kings. The slave-markets, however, were no longer of such importance as they had been under the Roman system; and the supply of slaves decreased when the local population was settled upon the estates of the lords of the land.

For the use of markets, local mints were set up by ecclesiastical authority (*racio ecclesiae*) or by kings (*racio fisci*). The existence of trade depended upon coinage. The mints of the Roman Empire were taken over by the barbarian kings in the fifth century; and until the middle of the sixth century the coins produced under the authority of these kings still bore the insignia of the reigning Roman Emperor. Then came a period in which the barbarian kings set up their own models of coinage; and independent mints were established by great lords and bishops. The supply of gold and silver in bars seems to have been adequate for the comparatively restricted

---

[1] *Lib. Pont.*, *Vita Zach.*
[2] *Cod. Carol.*, Ep. 64. Trans. in Hodgkin, *Italy*, viii, p. 45.

trade of the seventh century. There were reforms of the currency under the Frankish king, Charibert II (A.D. 628–630), and again under Charles the Great.[1] The production of coinage was organized by any powerful local lord, who gave gold and silver to a trustworthy goldsmith, as in the case of St. Eligius. An amusing result of the general confusion of the day with regard to coinage was the production in England of the first "Peter's Pence." King Offa of Mercia, at the end of the eighth century, agreed to make to the Pope an annual payment, for which a gold coin was produced, called a *mancus*, on which the inscription was in Arabic, copied from the coins of the Saracens.[2] Thus the influence of Mohammed affected the payment of tribute by an English king to a bishop of Rome. In the four centuries from A.D. 400 to A.D. 800 the evidence shows that there was enough coinage of gold, silver and other metals for common folk to use in trade and in payment of taxes or fines. At no time in these years was trading reduced entirely to barter even in places distant from the old centres of Roman civilization. Great lords and Churchmen might have hoards of gold and silver coins such as are found in their graves.[3] Many councils of the Church forbade the clergy to lend money at interest; and it has been shown above, from the letters of Gregory the Great, that debt created difficulties for the poorer country folk. That great numbers of comparatively poor people used coinage is proved by the number of local mints which existed in Spain in the sixth century and in France in the seventh, eighth and ninth centuries. The same conclusion follows from the naming of money-payments in the barbarian laws, both as compensations for injury and for sales, marriage dowries and other purposes.

Refugees

Among travellers must be classed the refugees. They were im-

[1] A similar reform of the coinage occurred at Constantinople under the Emperor Heraclius (A.D. 610–641).

[2] The word *mancus* is Arabic and means "stamped." See Chadwick, *Studies in Anglo-Saxon Institutions*, chap. i (1905). See Plate 2.

[3] The recent (1939) discovery of the grave of a minor king in East Anglia showed that he had not only coin but also ornamental cups from Byzantium in the seventh century.

portant during the years between A.D. 400 and A.D. 800, because they brought from one land to another ideas and ideals, ability and intelligence. They were not manual workers nor among the very poor, although some of these may have fled from their homes to avoid slavery or death. On the other hand, the very rich who fled from one of their estates to another, were of no importance in the history of civilized life. The refugees who affected western Europe, were men and women of what would now be called an educated "middle" class—scholars, monks, religious women and clergy. The invasions and disturbances of the four centuries caused the flight of such men and women from one part of western Europe to another and from the East to the Latin West.

In the early fifth century, during the Gothic invasions of Italy and Gaul, refugees went from those countries to Africa, thereby reinforcing the connection of the Catholics in that country with the Churches of the northern Mediterranean area. A few went to Palestine, as reported in the letters of St. Jerome. From Britain, some years later, the Saxon invasions drove refugees into what is now Brittany; and many of the saints to whom churches are dedicated in Brittany are said to have been Christian priests who had accompanied their fellow-Christians across the Channel. In the sixth century the persecution of Catholic clergy under the Vandal kings in Africa led to the flight of refugees to Italy and Gaul. Some may have gone to the eastern Mediterranean and there reinforced the desire of the imperial Authorities to reconquer Africa from the Arian Vandals. At the beginning of the seventh century the Mohammedan invasions in the countries of the eastern Mediterranean led to a flow of refugees from Syria and other Greek-speaking countries—chiefly to Sicily and Italy. In Sicily many Syrian monks extended the influence of the Greek-speaking Churches. Eastern monks and priests came also to Rome; and, either for this reason, or because of the connections of the Roman Church with Sicily, there was, during the seventh and eighth centuries, a succession of Syrians and Greeks selected as bishops of Rome. The *Liber Pontificalis* notes as "of Syrian race" (*natione Syrus*) the following bishops of Rome: John V (A.D. 685), Sergius (A.D. 687), Sisinnius

(A.D. 708), Constantine (A.D. 708–715), and Gregory III (A.D. 731–741); and as "Greek" in the same period: John VI (A.D. 701), John VII (A.D. 705), and Zachary (A.D. 741–752). After Zachary there was a line of "Romans" as bishops. In the eighth century Mohammedan invasions had spread along the north coast of Africa and into Spain. Refugees from both of these countries fled into France and Germany. Spanish clergy brought with them the collections of canons which had been adopted by the councils of Toledo; and it was, no doubt, because of the influence of refugees from Spain that the fame of Isidore of Seville spread to the Rhine country and caused the use of his name as a cover for the invention of ecclesiastical documents. The invasions of the Saracens and the Northmen during the early ninth century probably caused scholars to flee from one land to another; but the First Europe was already becoming settled in its new centres, and the history of refugees, therefore, ceases until after the Middle Ages in the second great transition, which is known as the Renaissance and Reformation.

The influence of refugees in the formation of the First Europe had two aspects. On the one hand, the refugees brought from the outside into the countries of north-western Europe new experience and learning, which were of great assistance. For example, Theodore of Tarsus, the Greek who came from Rome to be archbishop of Canterbury, not only established a centre of scholarship at Canterbury, but also laid the foundations, as it has been noted in an earlier chapter, of the unity of the English Church. Again, the Syrian Pope Zachary, in his letters to St. Boniface in Germany, shows in an exceptional degree, both religious feeling and political common sense. Refugees were in some cases feared by the conservative, lest they might introduce heresy, as appears in the warning issued by Pope Gregory II against the "Africans" in Germany, which has been referred to in an earlier chapter. On the other hand, the influence of refugees tended to unite the Churches of the First Europe by contributing the ideas and experience of one area to all the Latin-speaking countries. Thus, their influence tended to support the unification of the canons of different Churches, and the assimilation of rituals. Thus also the African and Spanish Churches were able to contribute something to the common store of medieval Christendom, even in their decay and death.

General Conclusions

One of the most important characteristics of the four centuries A.D. 400 to 800 was the transformation of social classes. A social class, in this sense, is a group of persons with common customs of dress, food and dwellings, sharing a common outlook upon ordinary life, which is distinct from others in other groups of the same community. It is assumed that persons in the same community use the same speech and have the same religious and moral traditions; and that the social classes differ from one another in less fundamental matters. Thus the local communities of the ninth century, especially in agricultural areas, were more homogeneous than those under the Roman Empire in custom, race, religion and speech; and they were divided into social classes which were less completely divided than slaves are from their masters under a slave-system.

At the beginning of the fifth century the most obvious social classes were, first, a small group of very wealthy landowners and slave-owners with great influence in local affairs and a common literary culture, based upon the poets and rhetoricians who had used the Greek and Latin languages. Secondly, there was a class of less wealthy, but rich, members of the local councils, the *curiales*. These men bore the chief burden of public services, and performed most of the duties of local government. The richer among them were climbing out of their responsibilities into the ranks of Senators of the Empire, among the wealthy landowners. The poorer *curiales* were falling into the lower class of local farmers dependent upon great men. The imperial rescripts which attempted to prevent *curiales* from escaping their obligations were evidently quite ineffectual.

A lower class was formed by the *coloni*, who were in the main farmers of small areas of land, most of them paying a kind of rent or in some way dependent upon the great man of the neighbourhood. These men paid a poll-tax to the imperial Authorities, which was collected through local tax-gatherers. It was probably difficult

451

to distinguish them clearly from freedmen or ex-slaves, who, although in some sense free, were still dependent upon a patron. And as the poll-tax was levied on all members of the family, it did not "pay" the poorer classes to have children. This was one great cause of depopulation. In the towns and villages the craftsmen and small traders may perhaps be reckoned as belonging to the same social class. But, as in all civilized communities, some rich craftsmen, such as goldsmiths, and some rich ship-owning traders, might be regarded as belonging to a social "upper" class, so far at least as their habits of life were concerned. It will be remembered that Salvian complained that the *nobiles* in his day were simply the rich.

During the rapid decline of the Roman system in the fifth century, the rank and file of the soldiery were in an ambiguous social position. Traditionally the officer class in the higher commands was senatorial, or at least equestrian in rank; and the lower ranks were levied from among the *coloni*. But before the beginning of the fifth century the highest commands were held by barbarians such as Stilicho under Honorius; and an increasing number in the armies were mercenaries who were also barbarians. These barbarians could neither read nor write, and preserved their own social standards both in dress and food. They may, however, be counted as in some way closer to the social class of farmers and traders than to any other. When the Roman Government could persuade its mercenaries to settle down to a life of production rather than exploitation, the majority of them became free farmers holding small amounts of land, as did many of the Burgundians. But even in these cases they preserved their own "laws" or customs in their own communities.

The lowest social class consisted of slaves. In the early fifth century the slaves in the western provinces of the Roman Empire were of many different races, speaking different languages and perhaps preserving the remnants of different traditional religions. But, in general, it seems likely that a change had occurred in the slave population during the two centuries immediately preceding the fifth. The wars in the East had originally supplied the Roman slave-owners with men and women to work at agriculture and the crafts, who were already accustomed to a society in which slavery was extensive. But, when Julius Caesar began the enslavement of northern nations in Gaul, slaves of a new kind were introduced into the Roman system. These new slaves, Gauls, Germans, and later Britons, were what would now be called "savages." They made decorative, if not skilful house-servants; but, as it has been noted in the second chapter of this book, they were not accustomed to the life of a slave-society. At the beginning of the fifth century slaves who were Germans, Goths or Scythians, evidently were numerous in all the great cities. They were probably useless for the old Roman system of agriculture by slave labour; and clearly they did not include, as the slaves of an earlier generation did, men who could teach or practise the arts. Again, the northern slaves were more closely united among themselves than slaves from the East had been. Their features and colouring set them apart, and they may have felt some common interest as opposed to those of their masters, precisely because of those resemblances which the Romans had always feared as a source of trouble among slaves, when it was proposed to clothe them all in the same uniform dress. Worse still, these northern slaves belonged to the same races from which the soldiers of the Roman Empire were increasingly recruited. The social class, therefore, of slaves was restless, and was obviously feared by the Roman Authorities. Nevertheless, at the beginning of the fifth century civilization depended upon a slave-system, which could be continued only by successful wars. The so-called *Pax Romana* was based upon war against all neighbours who could be used as slaves when captured.

Two hundred years later great changes had taken place, both in the characteristics of the social classes and in the relations between them. In A.D. 600 the highest class of very wealthy landowners had almost disappeared; and the lowest class of slaves had acquired some rights as human beings, at least as members of the Christian Churches. The leading men of the day no longer possessed the traditional literary culture of Greece and Rome. Gregory of Tours, for example, who belonged to an old and wealthy family, acknowledges that his Latin was not what it might have been; and Gregory the Great was suspicious of secular learning. A new culture had arisen and was preserved by the clergy; but the great landowners, whether of barbarian or Roman descent, were no longer concerned with reading and writing. The disappearance of the imperial system in the West had freed the small landowners and farmers from exploitation and released the traders from control by officials. But the general confusion caused by struggles between different barbarian chieftains reduced the livelihood of most men and women. For the majority, the bare necessities of food and clothing were all that was available. The social classes were in confusion; and in the midst of them a new order—the clergy and the monks—had acquired great social influence.

Two centuries again passed, and at the beginning of the ninth century the social situation had been completely transformed from what it was under the Roman Empire. The social classes of the ninth century in western Europe were already like those of the Middle Ages; and although they were, as before, what may be called upper, middle and lower classes, the relations between them were in general closer or more intimate than they had been under the Roman system. Also, the divisions of the different parts of Europe, which are now called "nations," were beginning to appear. The language of the majority in each district was beginning to develop a literature; and the old official and ecclesiastical Latin language had already become that of a learned caste. The social classes were slightly different in different parts of the western Europe. In Italy, for example, merchants and traders in the cities were more important than in the North; while in England and northern France the warrior class was more powerful than elsewhere.

In general the new social classes were—first, the king's men and the leading churchmen, bishops and abbots; secondly, local lords, counts or dukes; thirdly, free craftsmen or merchants in the cities; and fourthly, serfs or villeins in different forms of dependence upon the local lords. This lowest class had been recruited mainly from the slaves of earlier times, who had risen in status, and partly from the *coloni*, who had fallen in status. The old words *servi, mancipia* and *coloni*, still continued to be used; but the word *villanus* had become more common. The most important characteristic, however, of all this lowest class was that they were somebody's "men" (*homines*). Their position may have developed out of the Roman system of patronage. The lord and his men, like the patron and his clients, had mutual obligations. But Christianity had made much more difference to their relationship than any economic or political change. Not only did the Christian theory of the equality of all men before God affect the situation—although theory had little influence upon practice—but also in practice the members of the lowest social class attended the same churches and received the same sacraments as their superiors. Again, although the lower ranks of the clergy were very far divided from the great bishops and abbots, these lower ranks of the clergy who lived among the serfs, some of whom might be themselves the sons of serfs, were regarded generally as belonging to a sacred company, outside the control of the wealthy and powerful. There is no parallel to this situation under the Roman system.

The second general characteristic of the new society, therefore, was its unity—a unity of all classes in any one locality and of all the different localities in the Christendom of western Europe. It has been shown in the second chapter that in the last days of the Roman Empire society was deeply divided, both in economic and political matters and in religion. But the new society which was formed between the fifth and ninth centuries had a unity such as had never existed under the Roman Empire. Each man and woman had a place in a society which was conceived to be universal, and which did in fact include all those western countries in which the First Europe arose. The medieval system, which developed from the institutions of the Dark Ages, was the basis of what is now known as European civilization, contrasted with the half-Oriental civilization of the Mediterranean basin, which culminated in the Roman Empire. Thus, the unity of Europe, such as it was in the Middle Ages and the Renaissance, was based not upon the Roman Empire, which included parts of Asia and Africa, but upon the Latin Churches and the new kingdoms of the ninth century.

Another general conclusion is that, during the centuries from the fifth to the ninth, political power as well as intellectual and artistic vigour, passed from the southern lands bordering the western Mediterranean to north-western Europe. In this change the cities of northern Italy were the link between the old world and the new. But clearly, from the days of Charles the Great in northern France and Germany, and of Offa in England, the new Europe had its greatest vitality in the north-west. There it was that the first national kingdoms arose and the first great ecclesiastical schools which were the origins of the medieval universities. Similarly, it was in the North that what is called Romanesque architecture developed into Gothic. And in the North the manorial system, typical of the Middle Ages, was most strongly developed. The characteristics of the life of labourers and craftsmen in the Middle Ages were to be found most obviously in the France, the England and the Germany which established the First Europe.

Finally, the organization of supply and the use of labour and commodities was much more local in the ninth century than it was under the Roman Empire. This is indicated by the description of estates given above. The Roman trade-routes across the Mediterranean had been destroyed by piracy and war. Roman roads were not repaired, and the traffic on them was not protected against robbery and violence. The population of the great cities decreased, and the slave-trade died down. Labour, therefore, had to be organized locally among people born and bred in the district; and the manual workers, therefore, struck roots on the estates of the early Middle Ages and there produced what was needed locally. Pilgrims, indeed, went from one country to another, and a few traders brought rare or costly goods from afar. But the "bulk" commodities of Roman commerce, such as wheat and wool, were produced and used locally. Thus, in the First Europe, the majority of people were more closely united in religious belief and practice than they had been under the Roman Empire. But they were less united physically by the interchange of goods and services. It remained to be discovered whether, or under what conditions, the local organization of supply and use could survive.

CHAPTER XI

LORDS OF THE LAND

In the new Europe which arose among the ruins of the Roman
Empire the division of one district from another was even more
significant for the art of government than the similarity of customs
and beliefs. In place of the Emperor and his subordinates, the lords
of the land in different districts controlled the First Europe. Centralization in the Roman Empire had involved not only the accumulation of supreme power over the whole Mediterranean area in
the hands of the most successful soldier or politician. It also involved
the centralization of commerce in a few great cities, all of them
dominated by Rome, the one city which weighed in the balance as
much as the rest of the world. It involved further a centralization
of intellectual and artistic interests which brought writers and other
artists to Rome. The ghost of this ancient centralization survived in
the medieval belief that all roads led to Rome, and in the instructions
of medieval Popes "to the city and the world" (urbi et orbi).[1] In
the fifth and sixth centuries this centralization of government, trade
and intellectual standards, gave place to a localization of human
activities which was the first sign of the medieval structure of
civilization. One Province was divided from another; and each
district within each Province was thrown upon its own resources.
This localization of government, trade and thought was the direct
result of the weakness of the central Authority. It was an obvious
sign, in the eyes of the majority in each district, of that dissolution
of the social system which has been described in the second chapter

[1] Urbem fecisti quod prius orbis erat. In the address to Rome by Rutilius Namatianus, de Reditu, i, 66.

of this book.[1] The weakening of the central Authority was followed
by the barbarian invasions, and by the collapse of the means of
communication by land and sea. From this point of view localization was the effect of a disease. On the other hand, the very fact
that the people of any district had no help from outside compelled
them to take the initiative. They had to look to themselves for the
supply of their needs, and for their own defences. They learnt in
each district, from the bitter experience of marauding bands and
diminishing supplies, to find local leaders and to defend themselves.
From this point of view, therefore, the localization of defence and
supply in western Europe which followed the collapse of the
centralized system of the Roman Empire, was a step forward in
the tradition of civilized life. Local responsibility and local initiative
were called upon to meet local needs; and therefore emotional and
intellectual abilities in great numbers of men and women were
brought into play, which had been left unused under the Roman
Empire.

In the fourth and fifth centuries of the Christian era, as in modern
times, the distaste for war led idealists to dream of a golden age
of peace when armed forces would be no longer necessary. The
Christian tradition, as it has been shown in earlier chapters, contained within itself a doctrine and practice of aloofness from the
problems of government. And before the Roman Empire became
Christian this aspect of the Christian tradition was naturally more
prominent. But it survived even the official association of the
Empire with Christianity. A small group of enthusiasts, protected
from difficulties which they found it distasteful to face, by the
structure of society in which they lived, were able to dream of a
world in which all men would be like them, safe without trouble.
But even outside the Christian Church, the distaste for war had
produced hopes of a peace in which there would be no armed
forces. Thus, in the *Historia Augusta*, in the *Life* of the Emperor
Probus, probably written in the early fourth century, his saying is
recorded that when the Roman Empire is secure "in a short time

[1] Fustel de Coulanges, *Institutions Politiques de la France*, ii, p. 206: "C'est un
énervement général de l'autorité. Cette maladie a fait périr plus d'Etats que les
insurrections n'en ont renversé."

458

we shall need no more soldiers."[1] And the writer continues: "What great bliss would then have shone forth, if under his rule there had ceased to be soldiers! No rations would have to be provided by any provincial, no pay for the troops taken out of the public largesses, the commonwealth of Rome would keep its treasures for ever, no payments would be made by the Prince, no tax required of the holder of land; it was in very truth a golden age that he promised. There would be no camps, nowhere should we have to hear the blast of the trumpet, nowhere fashion arms. That throng of fighting-men which now harries the commonwealth with civil wars, would be at the plough, would be busy with study, or learning the arts, or sailing the seas. Add to this, that none would be slain in war."[2]

The civilized peoples of the Roman Empire were weary of continuous wars and barbarian raids. But they meant by peace only the absence of war, not a new system of social organization. The strain upon men who had both to carry on production and also to stand to arms, had been expressed many centuries before by Ovid, writing of the settler on the frontiers: "Unhappy man! With one hand he ploughs and with the other grasps his weapons."[3] Relief was found in the fourth and fifth centuries by a separation of functions between the civilian and the military. The civil population was to carry on with the labours of peace, while war and the preparation for war were to be left to troops on the frontier, largely recruited from the barbarians, and to barbarian mercenaries.

The frontiers of the Roman Empire on the Rhine and the Danube were defended in the fourth century by fortified posts and well-trained soldiers. There, as from Hadrian's wall in northern England, Rome looked out upon the barbarians from behind her watch-towers and garrisons. But within the frontier there was no system of local defence. The governing idea seemed to be, as Cassiodorus wrote in the sixth century, that "the quiet of civilized life could

---

[1] *Hist. Aug. Vita Probi*, xx, 5. The *Historia Augusta* is a patchwork of biographies of Emperors, some of which are believed by some scholars to have been compiled as late as the fifth century. The *Life* of Probus, however, was probably written under Diocletian.   [2] Ibid, chap. xxiii, i, trans. in Loeb ed.
[3] Ovid, *Tristia*, V. x, 24—"Hac arat infelix, hac tenet arma manu."

be sheltered behind the defence of armed forces." Behind the "Maginot line" there was nothing! And when the line was broken in the early fifth century, there was no "home guard" to meet the invaders. From this point of view, the chief problem of the early Middle Ages was the organization of the home guard.[1]

The reason why there was no "home guard" is even more important than the fact that there was none. The imperial Authorities feared that armed forces organized locally would not support a system of centralization which drained the Provinces for the support of an Oriental Court, and exhausted agricultural districts to supply the great cities. Even in the days of Constantine the Great, it was said, the imperial Authorities preferred to use the barbarians for the support of their power rather than to run the risk of arming their own subjects. Again, civil war was always occurring and was perhaps inevitable under the Roman system of military dictatorship. It was therefore dangerous for any Emperor to permit the local organization of armed forces which might be used against him by rivals. In the fourth and fifth centuries, therefore, the Roman administration discouraged military service among its more civilized subjects, and increasingly relied upon the use of barbarians recruited on the frontier for the defence of the frontier.[2] With this policy, no doubt, went the unwillingness of the more civilized upper classes in the Empire to adopt a military career in which their commanders or their comrades would be barbarians who could neither read nor write; and the distaste for war in the early fifth century was widely shared by poor men who lived in the safety and among the more civilized interests of the Roman cities or Roman estates, who were called to serve in the ranks.[3] The

[1] The Roman *Limes* in Germany, like the Maginot line, did not run as far as the coast. It ended at Rheinbrohl, on the Rhine just below Coblenz. Southward it turned at Lorsch to a point near Ratisbon on the Danube.

[2] The imperial Authorities were willing to accept money instead of recruits from among their own subjects. Thus, a decree of A.D. 397 says: "Our clemency accepts the petition of the Senate that money should be offered instead of recruits" (*Cod. Theod.*, vii, 13, 13).

[3] Many sought to evade military service by cutting off their fingers. A decree of A.D. 367 declares that "those who avoid military service by cutting off their fingers (*castra fugiunt*), according to the decree of the Divine Constantine your sincerity must not allow them to escape if they can be used in any public service" (*Cod. Theod.*, vii, 13, 4). And again, a decree which may be as late as A.D. 353,

Roman Empire which had been established and maintained by the virtues of the soldier proved unable to adjust itself to the more subtle necessities of peace.

When Honorius wrote to the inhabitants of Britain, who had asked for the support of Roman legions, that they must look to their own defences, the imperial Authorities themselves confessed to the failure of their system. And in the Theodosian law-books there is an edict, quoted elsewhere, urging the inhabitants of any locality, and even the slaves, to assist in military defence.[1] But such "home guards" could not be organized effectively in a crisis. Resistance to marauding bands was offered where the ability and valour of a leader happened to be found, as in the case of Ecdicius, reported by Sidonius Apollinaris. And when the Huns advanced into Gaul in A.D. 451 Anianus, bishop of Orleans, organized the defence of the city. But in most cases, from the days of Alaric to those of the Lombards in the seventh century, when the barbarians had passed the frontier, little or no resistance was offered to them.

The local forces which defended any district from marauding bands during the sixth, seventh and eighth centuries were organized under the lords of the land, who were the predecessors of the later feudal nobility and landed gentry. They had to provide, not merely a local command in times of danger, but also some organization of local production, supply and transport. Their influence in later times proved to be an obstacle to the unification of law, government and supply over the larger areas which eventually formed the nations of the later Middle Ages. Their power has been taken by some historians as an example of feudal anarchy. But in the centuries from the sixth to the ninth their position and influence promoted the transition from the centralized Roman system to the system of Nation-States which has lasted from the fifteenth to the twentieth century. These lords of the land, therefore, are important both in the study of the localization of responsibility for defence

addressed to the Praetorian Prefect of Gaul, says: "If anyone in order to avoid military service (*sacramenta militiae*) has cut off his fingers, he must be branded and his master punished" (*Cod. Theod.*, vii, 13, 5).

[1] *Cod. Theod.*, vii, 13, 16 (April 17, 406). Issued at Ravenna by Arcadius and Theodosius to the Provincials.

and supply, and in the study of the transition from the villa of the late Roman Empire to the castle of the Middle Ages.

The contrast between what may be called the aristocracy of the Roman Empire and that of the Middle Ages was not completely developed in most countries of western Europe before about the thirteenth century. But the control of local defence and production by lords, counts, or dukes, almost independent of any superior authority, was already evident before the ninth century. The roots of the First Europe had already struck deeply into the soil; and although feudalism can hardly be supposed to have begun before the ninth or tenth centuries, traces can be found, three or four centuries earlier, of the localization of power in the hands of the landowners, which eventually led to an almost imaginary, but historically important "feudal system."

In the fifth century, under the Roman Empire, the rich aristocracy or governing class, "the powerful" (*potentes*), were formed by a city life, a literary education, and a generally accepted taste for the refinements of civilized life. They enjoyed baths and well-warmed apartments in their country houses. They were able to read and write; their wives and daughters were their equals in everything but the attainment of public office; and their estates were managed for them by freedmen in control of slaves or tenant farmers. In the Middle Ages, on the other hand, the governing class was country-bred; and most of its members were illiterate, skilful only in hunting and fighting, voracious and vigorous, and often violent. Their residences were dark, cold and damp fortresses where baths and good cooking or fine wines were unknown. The higher clergy, chiefly bishops and abbots, generally belonged to the same class; but they had acquired some education and a greater refinement of manners. The medieval lord, however, was less completely separated from his dependants, whether retainers in his castle or villeins on his estates, than the Roman magnate had been from his slaves. As mountains may be worn down by the storms of centuries and valleys filled up, so the heights of civilization had been reduced in the confusion of four or five hundred years; but the general level of intercourse between men was higher. The Fine

Arts were less appreciated by the ruling classes; but the general standard of taste in craftsmanship was shared by the poorest men and women. When the First Europe had been firmly established in the eleventh century, the great cathedrals and abbey churches had at least an equal value in terms of beauty with the temples of pre-Christian Mediterranean civilization. But there is nothing in that ancient world to compare with the churches of the common people in the towns and small villages; and there is more vitality in medieval sculpture than in that of the Roman Empire. In music it is impossible to estimate the value of the Greek and Roman tradition, because so little is known of it. But the earliest melodies of the Middle Ages are certainly of the first rank. In the fifth century Sidonius Apollinaris mentions entertainment by musical instruments; and in the sixth century Boethius wrote on music. But in the Roman tradition the making of music was left to slaves or social inferiors, whereas in the Middle Ages minstrels were highly honoured and Froissart's model knight, Gaston de Foix, "had great joy in the use of instruments of music of all kinds; and he could do it right well himself." The civilization, therefore, of the countryside and of the small town dependent upon the neighbouring castle, was at a lower level than the civilization of the Roman villa with its city-bred upper class; but the basis of the civilization of the First Europe was broader and stronger. In both "patterns of culture" a ruling class played an important part; but their importance in either case must be estimated by reference to the whole texture of civilized life in the two ages.

The change from Roman civilization to that of the First Europe is most easily described by making an arbitrary distinction between the social situations in the three centuries following the collapse of the Roman system. It will be understood that no abrupt change actually took place. But if it is assumed that the Roman system existed in most of western Europe during the whole fifth century, then the three stages of development are as follows:—

(a) The settlement of barbarian warriors on the land between A.D. 500 and 600 led to a gradual replacement of the landowners who had looked to the centralized government of the

Roman Empire. The change was not racial; for there was inter-marriage, and the barbarian warriors were few. It was the intellectual outlook or climate of opinion which had changed.

(b) Between A.D. 600 and 750 there was a conflict of the new "nobles" for power over the king, or for complete independence for themselves in the districts which they could control by expeditions on horseback.

(c) A final attempt was made between A.D. 750 and 850 by the Frankish kings to centralize their control over large areas, which led to the complete collapse of the whole system of the so-called Holy Roman Empire in the ninth century, and a hundred years of new barbarian invasions from the North, and the East.

But the First Europe still survived. And it survived, not because of the kings and bishops, but because the localization of supply and defence had been so firmly established that the lords of the land could organize the people of each district for the protection of what they could save. The "troubles" of Europe from A.D. 800 to 1000 were the forcing ground for the development of feudalism.[1] But this subject is beyond the scope of the present argument. It is enough to note that the so-called feudal system which was hardly a system at any date, was an attempt to reconcile local defence and production with central government and trade over a large area. The result was the development of what are now called Nation-States. In the formation of these States, or kingdoms, kingship stood for centralization. The king in effect claimed that all men, even the lords' men, were in some sense his men; and secondly, that all lords held power and land in some sense by the king's leave. On the other hand, localism, which was perhaps merely tribalism, implied in the eyes of the lord, that the men who lived near him were his men, and that he was established in authority before the king was recognized. But it also implied, no doubt, in the eyes of a local population, that they or their ancestors had been

---

[1] According to Marc Bloch, *La Société Féodale* (1939), the terms "feudalism" and "feudal system" were not used before the eighteenth century to indicate what is now meant by them. "All lordships were not fiefs, nor were all fiefs lordships." But the National Assembly of 1789 declared that it destroyed "the feudal system."

established on the land before the lord.[1] It was, therefore, by reconciling such opposite tendencies that feudalism led the way to the Nation-State.

The Roman Villa

To return to the consideration of the landed aristocracy under the Roman system, the most important characteristics for the purpose of the argument here are these. The great landowners of any district were influential or powerful (*potentes*) because of their control of production and employment. But imperial Authorities controlled public affairs. Although the term *res publica* ceased to be intelligible after the sixth century,[2] in the fifth century civilian officials of the central Government administered law and justice, city services, roads and bridges; and the imperial armed forces were trained and maintained under military officers of the Empire. The great landowners could, and did, exert influence upon these officials, as it has been already shown in the second chapter. The situation was not unlike that in British colonies in the twentieth century, where there are local estate-owners or planters, and also officials sent out by the imperial central Government. Such officials have no family connections in the colony, and are likely to leave it on retirement. They have no roots in the districts they administer, and are naturally under the influence of those whose families for generations have lived there, just as the *judices* came under the influence of the *potentes* under the Roman system. Modern colonial officials, moreover, look for their status and income to a central Authority, even if they undoubtedly desire to promote the interests of the subject peoples. In the Roman system, during the fifth century, the officials of the Empire acted, or seemed to act, chiefly as tax-collectors for a distant imperial Court; and even in colonies of the twentieth century officials are in many cases more often

[1] In the memoirs of Lord Saye and Sele the author says that he boasted to one of his tenants that his ancestors had come over with William the Conqueror, to which the tenant replied, "And my ancestors were here to receive them!"

[2] It was used again in the ninth century, under the influence of a revived study of Latin literature, as in the treatise of Sedulius Scotus, *De Rectoribus Christianis* (*Pat. Lat.*, 103). But the sense had changed. It now meant "public interest" rather than "public organization."

concerned with the need of the central Government for the supply of raw materials to industry than with a "subsistence economy" in the colonies themselves. In the disorders of the fifth century the problem of organizing a subsistence economy and promoting local interests, which the Roman Empire had been unable to solve, was forced by unforeseen circumstances upon western Europe. But the local lords of the land under the Empire had neither the moral authority nor the power to exercise all the functions of government. Their dependants were either their own slaves in the house or on the estate, or ex-slaves holding land by ambiguous and oppressive grants (*precaria*); or they were small farmers (*coloni*), theoretically free and independent, but bound to the great men by their need for a protector. The relation of the *patronus* and the *cliens*, so well known in city life under the Roman system, was almost the same as that of the great landowner and the small farmer who lived in the neighbourhood of his estate. Most of the cultivated land and its inhabitants were under the jurisdiction of the city-units (*civitates*) of the Roman Empire. But the whole of this world of city and countryside within the Roman Empire assumed the continuance of peace and security. The defences of the system were on the frontiers. Civil wars and barbarian invasions and armed bands of hungry, poor men (*bagaudae*) during the fifth century compelled those who lived out of the reach of the cities to devise some protection for themselves. Walls were erected round some of the great houses or farmsteads; and probably the local residents were prepared to defend themselves. The difference between the sword and the ploughshare in those days was not very great. The swords and spears of raiders were not much more effectual than the sickles and scythes and pitchforks of the farm-worker. But as disorder increased, the imperial Authorities inevitably lost authority and power, which naturally passed to the local great man, if he was not incompetent, and did not desert his estates.

Under the Roman system, even the great landowners, like the rich men and women of the twentieth century, were without roots in the soil. A rich man might have estates, both in Gaul and Italy, and in Africa, and Greece and Syria. He might, therefore, flee from one country to another; and still live well on an estate in Africa when the barbarians had looted his estate in Gaul. Other landowners, like Paulinus of Nola and Sidonius Apollinaris, might transfer their lands to the Church and become bishops. The social position, therefore, of the lords of the land at the end of the fifth century was unstable.

The Christian Churches, however, which by the middle of the fifth century had extended their influence outside the cities, began to affect the conception of moral authority even among officials who were in theory subordinate. The individual official, governor or judge, who was a good Christian, was made aware of a responsibility to God which was in some way independent of his responsibility to the central Authority. So also the rich and powerful in the countryside were reminded of the obligations of Christian charity. And without this change in the climate of opinion the localization of authority in the early Middle Ages could hardly have led to an improvement in social relationships. The idea that the service of others is honourable, which made it easy for some great landowners to become bishops, affected also the military and civil control of a local population exercised by a count or a duke.

An example of the moral standards applied to the functions of a subordinate ruler, is to be found in a letter of Fulgentius Ferrandus, who died about A.D. 547 in Africa, to Count Reginus.[1] The writer lays down seven principles covering the duties of a count. The ruler of a district who is a true Christian, ought not to take credit for his actions, but give the credit to God. He should govern by influence (*imitatio*) not force (*potestas*). He should aim at service not mastery (*non praeesse sed prodesse*). He should love the common good as himself; because, says the author, the Gospel tells us to love our neighbour, and the neighbour of a ruler (*dux*) is the common good (*res publica*). In this connection the count is urged to avoid the use of informers (*delatores*). Next, the good ruler prays and reads and obeys the clergy. Again, the good governor

[1] Fulgentius Ferrandus, Ep. vii.

467

should not be too strict; he must allow for human weakness; for "although strict justice makes a ruler feared, kindliness makes him loved," and "the governor who is loved, is the defence of his country."[1] Finally, "when you have to draw the sword remember that you are a Christian and must not be angry with your brother without a cause: punish the crime and not the criminal." Thus the Christian writers and preachers in the sixth century strove to apply the conception of service by those in power, not to the maintenance of a system, but to the care for the needs and interests of the common people.

This, however, was a moral ideal which promoted and perhaps excused an important economic and political relationship—the connection between the ownership of land and jurisdiction over the people who lived on it. The connection between ownership and government already existed under the Roman system, partly because the owner of goods and land was also an owner of slaves, who provided the labour essential for the use of goods and land, and partly because Roman Law held the landowner responsible for providing men for military service and for payments of the poll-tax on his dependants. Besides, the wealthy who held public offices were of the same social class as the rich landowners. Thus it was natural to confuse the possession of wealth with the exercise of the art of government over men. And after the collapse of the Roman imperial system in western Europe, the power to govern fell inevitably into the hands of those who had property in land. The result in the centuries immediately following affected the formation of the so-called feudal system. The lords of the land became the acknowledged lords of the people. The change from slavery to serfdom did indeed prevent the uprooting of the families of the poor from the land they cultivated. Serfs and villeins formed part of an estate. But, on the other hand, they paid for a certain security of tenure by a greater dependence upon the jurisdiction, and therefore upon the arbitrary will of the lord of the estate.

[1] Licet justitia facit ducem terribilem, pietas facit amabilem . . . dux amabilis murus patriae. See the medallion of Fausta, the wife of Constantine the Great, with the inscription "Pietas Augusti," facing p. 128.

(a) Settlement of Barbarians: A.D. 500–600

When the barbarian raiders of the fifth century had begun to settle upon the lands they had invaded, their kings and warriors at first merely displaced the military Authorities of the Empire and its armed forces. In many districts, as it has been shown in the third chapter, the policy of the imperial Authorities actually supported the establishment of the barbarians within the Empire. The king of the Visigoths in Gaul, for example, and his warriors, like the king of the Ostrogoths in Italy, could claim imperial authority for his exercise of power. But when the whole country was clearly controlled by barbarian armed forces under their own king, the warriors sought their reward, not in sporadic looting, but in taking possession of portions of the available land. The king might quarter some of his warriors as "Guests" on the estate of a Roman land-owner; or he might distribute land to those whom he did not desire to keep at his Court, by taking a portion of the land of individual owners or by distributing parts of the land hitherto held by the Emperor. Thus, in the sixth century, the settlement of barbarian warriors created a new type of landowner, more like the knights of the Middle Ages than like the Roman Senators. Neither the king nor his warriors could read or write; and therefore the records of this change are scanty. Bishops who wrote letters and monks who wrote chronicles were more concerned with the king than with the warriors who seemed to be dependent upon his will; and therefore mention the new governing class incidentally and only seldom. But clearly the new situation involved the gradual disappearance of educated laymen as great landowners and the increase in the number of simple-minded and ignorant local chief-tains. By the end of the sixth century, in most parts of western Europe, the military chieftain, settled on an estate far out of reach of the king or other superior, had begun to regard his land and the people on it as a family possession to be inherited by his sons at his death. The old forms of Roman tenure may have been preserved partly because the language of the majority in western Europe, except for those in Germany and the British Isles, was some form

469

of Latin, and partly because the only records ever made were written down by monks or clergy in their own official Latin. All living language is a "mother" tongue; but although language is for this reason essential to tradition and continuity of customs, it may also act as an obstacle to progress. New institutions and new kinds of social relationship are sometimes disguised, sometimes emasculated by the attempt to express them in the language of the past.

The barbarian king who had led the invaders into Roman territory usually kept in personal contact with himself a comrade-ship (*comitatus*) of young warriors, who served partly as members of what would be called in later ages a general staff, and partly as courtiers. This primitive system had already been adopted by the military despots, who called themselves Roman Emperors, in the fourth and fifth centuries. The *consistorium*, or privy council of high officials, was a civilized version of the officers of a king's body-guard, which was maintained by the later Emperors, and by their imitator in Italy, Theodoric the Ostrogoth. Each member of such company was a comrade or companion (*comes*), or what was later called a "count." And the counts also received gifts of land from the king, and soon began, like other warriors, to regard the gift as a possession to be inherited by their sons. At the same time any powerful military leader, whether claiming complete independence or admitting the superiority of a king, was given the title of "leader" or duke (*dux*) or, as army leader, the German herzog.[1] Among the Anglo-Saxons the earl corresponded to the count in France, Italy and Spain. Thus in the sixth century the functions of a primitive military society gave rise to titles which progressively lost significance as they gained social prestige. In the organization of local control the counts and the dukes of the seventh century had acquired some moral authority by their association with the royal power, and by taking over some of the functions which had hitherto been those of imperial officials. Thus, the land-owner no longer, as under the Roman system, merely sits with the

---

[1] The so-called "Führer-prinzip" is therefore a retrogression to barbarian military organization; and the "Duce" of twentieth-century Italy is the ghost of a Roman "Dux" in the decadence of the Empire.

judges, but himself becomes a judge. And in later ages the seignorial courts and the lords' justice were rivals of those of the king.

(b) Nobles against Kings: A.D. 600–750

During the seventh century, from about A.D. 600 to 750, the position of the great landowners, or of military chieftains in control of some estates, at least north of the Alps, had become recognizably medieval. Each great landowner, now an illiterate warrior, had his own body of armed retainers, to whom could be added for warlike purposes the able-bodied men on his estates (*rustici*). Also, all the great landowners fought and intrigued to control such moral authority as the king might retain. Strangely enough the bishops never attempted to anoint or crown dukes or counts. No such persons appeared either in the Bible or in the old Roman tradition. Moral authority, therefore, still remained to some degree centralized in kingdoms, even when actual power in any locality was entirely in the hands of a magnate less exalted than a king.

The most famous struggle of the lords to control the king was that which occurred in western and eastern France—Neustria and Austrasia—when the Chief of the Palace first dominated, and later displaced the kings of the Merovingian line. The great lords formed themselves into rival parties. But no principle of public policy divided them. Both parties were merely collections of landowners and their retainers, each of whom aimed at increasing his possessions or his power.

It was essential for the contending warriors to follow some leader on either side, and by the beginning of the eighth century, as explained in an earlier chapter, the rivalry of the two parties in the Frankish kingdom divided the warriors of western France from those of eastern France. It is possible that the Franks of what is now called France were more deeply affected by Roman civilization, and by the Christian Churches which had grown up under the Roman Empire, than were the Franks in the less Romanized regions of what is now Belgium and the Rhineland. There may, therefore, have been some difference of outlook and policy dividing the warriors of the West and the East in the First Europe. But the final success of the less Romanized eastern Franks under Charles Martel concluded the struggle for power over the Frankish kingship. And when the great landowner, Pippin, the son of Charles Martel, himself usurped the Frankish throne, and was crowned by St. Boniface as king of the Franks, a new stage in the development of local lordships had begun. There was then no longer a Chief of the Palace who, as a great noble, controlled the king. But the king himself had been one among many great landowners; and the prestige which he had secured for his family, the Carolingian dynasty, seemed likely to establish a central power which might control the lords of all the lands whose people acknowledged his authority.

The records concerning Eudo, Duke of Aquitaine, may serve as an example of the position of the great magnate who was not king. Eudo, according to the chronicler who continued the annals of Fredegarius, was opposed to Charles Martel in A.D. 718, in the interests of Chilperic, whom the Neustrian lords had made king of the Franks. The chronicler was an Austrasian, a supporter of Charles. He writes that Eudo "received gifts and royal authority,"[1] and raised an army of Basques, but was driven into flight by Charles, who later sent a legation to him. Whereupon Eudo made peace with Charles, and gave up to him king Chilperic. Charles then departed on an expedition against the Saxons and advanced as far as the Danube; and Eudo seized the opportunity to break his pact; and, either before or after meeting Charles in battle, he entered into an alliance with the Saracens. The Saracens, under one of their leaders, crossed the Garonne, sacked Bordeaux, burnt the basilica of St. Hilary at Poitiers, and advanced to destroy the shrine of St. Martin. Eudo thereupon changed sides again, and according to Paul the Lombard, joined Charles in the great battle which destroyed the Saracen invaders of France.[2] According to the *Liber Pontificalis*, Eudo sent a message to the reigning Pope, Gregory II, explaining

---

[1] Fred. Schol., *Chron. Cont.*, ii, 107, "regnum et munera tradunt." *Regnum* is here taken to mean "royal authority" and not "the crown" (*Pat. Lat.*, 71, col. 674). Cf. Thomas Aq., *Summa Theol.*, where "regnum" means "potestas regnativa."
[2] Paul Diac, *H.L.*, vi, 46.

that his victory was due to the fact that he had divided a sponge, which had been used for the Pope's table, into many small portions and given the bits to his warriors to swallow.[1] The great duke's frequent treachery, his self-seeking, his desire for collecting loot with the assistance of any who would help him, and his primitive belief in magic, are all typical of the mentality of the lords of the land in the early Middle Ages.

Evidently the cultured aristocracy of the fifth century had disappeared; and in their place the great landowners were simpleminded warriors. This does not imply, however, a contrast between virtue and vice. It was rather a contrast between the civilized taste and pursuits of men interested in literature and the other arts, and the barbarism of counts and dukes, most of whom could neither read nor write. Control of the country population in the eighth century was exercised by men who were engaged chiefly in war as a method of increasing their own wealth and power, and spent their leisure chiefly in hunting and feasting. Thus, the lords of the land were confirmed in their barbarism by the ease with which they could loot or exploit the common people, and by the continual struggle of each lord against neighbouring rulers. The Church which might have refined the manners and illuminated the intelligence of these barbarians, was committed to an ascetic ideal of morality, which implied a refusal to attach any importance to manners or taste. The preachers and writers, therefore, who taught that the best men and women should avoid natural human emotions and thought about common things, must bear part of the responsibility for the long continuance of barbarism among the lords of the First Europe.

(c) Attempts at Centralization

In the following century, from about A.D. 750 to A.D. 850, the historical records and other documents are largely concerned with the conquests of the king of the Franks, and the establishment of

---

[1] *Liber Pont. Vita Greg.* II. It is not clear whether this was a sponge used for the altar, as in the ceremony of washing the altar at Easter, which is still continued in the Roman Church.

what was called the Holy Roman Empire. This Empire of the Franks existed chiefly in the imagination, as it will be explained in a later chapter. But for the purpose of the argument here, its importance lay in the reinforcement which the name of Emperor gave to the attempts at centralizing authority over large areas in north-western Europe. Whoever claimed to rule over an extensive territory was continually moving on expeditions to the boundaries against invaders or within his realm to suppress rebellion. Thus Charles Martel had to lead his armed forces from the middle of Germany to the borders of Spain. Pippin, his successor, was induced to make an expedition into Italy; but in this case it is recorded that some of his lords and their retainers refused to follow him.[1] And Charles the Great spent most of his energy in collecting armed forces to fight, at one time against the Saracens in Spain, at another against the Saxons in Germany, and at another against the Lombards in Italy. These kings would summon their lords to bring their retainers to some appointed centre for each summer campaign; and the policy of Charles the Great, even after he had accepted the title of Emperor, was exactly the same as that of his predecessors. He led armies on expeditions; but these armies were simply the armed retainers of the lords, spiritual and temporal, and a levy of agricultural workers with the very simplest arms and no military training. Neither the lords nor their men had any enthusiasm for such a system. Local production was reduced by the removal of labour; and supplies which might have raised the standard of living in a district, were commandeered for the king's expeditions. This centralization of the use of armed forces was perhaps due, partly to the traditional Germanic organization of raids for loot, and partly to the misunderstanding of the Roman tradition of strategy directed by an Emperor. During the lifetime of Charles the Great his restless vigour and tireless endurance obscured the real facts of the situation. But the system which he inherited and maintained was obviously futile. Some years before he died invasions of the Northmen (*Nordmanni*) from Scandinavia, and of Saracens from the South, were proving that his method of defence by expedition

---

[1] This was in A.D. 754.

was useless. The Northmen came across the sea and up the rivers, and sacked towns and monasteries, while Saracen raiders drove those Christians who had escaped capture and enslavement from the coasts of Italy and southern France. Such raids could not possibly be prevented by a summer campaign of hastily collected armed forces under a single commander.

At the beginning of the ninth century, therefore, two new social tendencies appeared. First, a widespread unwillingness of the workers in any district, and of their lords, to sally forth upon distant expeditions; and secondly, a consolidation of local defence, either in small towns or round the castle of some lord. It was this consolidation of local defence which eventually preserved Europe from the assaults of pagans from the north and east, and of Mohammedans from the south. This is what may be called the organization of the "home guard." If it appears, on the one hand, to have been a disadvantage that the countries of the First Europe were divided into many independent local units under lords or other leaders, on the other hand, it was a great step forward for the people of each district to discover that the supply and protection which they needed must depend upon their own energies and abilities.

In England the local militia, the fyrd, appears to have been superseded or reorganized during the ninth century. In the first place, the earls had acquired, in their hus-carles or personal retainers, a more efficient military force than the old militia; and in the further organization of large areas for defence, the king's sheriffs appear to have organized the military power of the county (*posse comitatus*). But at this point, clearly, the organization of government was developing upon a larger scale than that of the organization of production, which still remained local.

In France the attempt to combine local defence with a system of government covering large areas is to be found in the history of the methods by which the Norman invasions were resisted. In A.D. 865, Charles the Bald is reported to have "consulted about the bridges at Anvers-sur-Oise and Charentes-le-Pont, because the inhabitants of the district who had from old time kept the bridge in repair, were no longer able to do so owing to Norman invasions.

Therefore those who came from farther parts to repair the bank of the Seine were set to repair these bridges in the urgent need of the time, lest in the future those who had formerly repaired them would be exhausted in the effort."[1] In the same year Charles is reported to have gone to Rouy (Dept. Aisne) and removed from their positions three counts to whom he had given the duty of defence against the Normans, "because they had been quite useless; and he conferred the 'honours' upon others."[2] This is an early example of the use of the word "honour" to mean a position of dignity conferred or allowed by a king. But the actual power exercised by a local lord was in practice dependent upon his own ability; and the acceptance of the hereditary principle eventually made it impossible for any king to remove from his seat of authority a lord who had succeeded to his father's position.

Methods of Warfare

Two changes in the methods of warfare had an important influence in the formation of medieval lordships.[3] First, the use of cavalry with body-armour, and secondly, the fortification of local strong-points, which later became medieval castles. At the beginning of the fifth century the Roman legions of the Republican tradition no longer formed the chief striking-force of the imperial armies. Cavalry had become more important, both because they were more useful in overtaking scattered raids of barbarians, and because the larger bodies of barbarian invaders relied chiefly upon the weight of a charge by horsemen. At the end of the century the walls of Roman cities had either decayed or been destroyed. As Procopius says: the Vandals in Africa "reasoned that they would be better off if all the towns of the region should be without walls. . . . So they immediately tore down all the walls to the ground."[4] The barbarians had no skill in assaulting fortifications or in defending them. In the sixth century the efforts of Justinian to restore the

---

[1] *Annales Bertiniani*, ann. 865.
[2] Ibid., quia nihil utilitatis contra Nordmannos egerant, conlatos honores tollit et per diversos eosdem honores disponit.
[3] See Oman, *History of the Art of War: The Middle Ages* (1898).
[4] Procopius, *Buildings*, vi, 5.

power of the Roman Empire led to the building, not only of city-walls, but also of fortified strong-points. Thus, Procopius reports that after completing fortifications on the frontiers of the Balkan countries, Justinian "reflected that if it should ever be possible for the enemy to break through somehow, they would then fall upon fields entirely unguarded, and enslave the whole population and plunder their property." He therefore built "defences so continuous on the estates that each farm is either a stronghold, or is near to one that is fortified."[1] At about the same date Nicetius, bishop of Trier, built "a fortress where there had been a wood," as described by Venantius Fortunatus. Such fortresses, used as places of refuge, and manned by a garrison, developed into medieval castles.

Meantime the use of cavalry led to a change in the tactics of archers. The charge of horsemen was weakened by missiles before they could close with the enemy. The unprotected bodies of the cavalry of the Goths and the Huns in the fifth and sixth centuries were, therefore, later protected as far as possible by armour gradually improved and made available for greater numbers. By the eighth century the kings in western Europe and their chief retainers went to war as horsemen with body-armour and spears. But obviously the cost of such equipment was too great for the majority of those who formed the rank and file of the levies in such armies as those of Charles the Great and his immediate successors. The lord of the land and his retainers, who had by that time become professional soldiers, therefore secured an immense advantage over the badly armed labourers who were called upon to serve on foot during summer campaigns. The invasions of Northmen and Saracens in the tenth century led to more skilful and widespread use of fortified strong-points and of cavalry with body-armour. The local fortress, garrisoned by a professional soldiery under a lord, and the improvement in body-armour which still remained too expensive for the rank and file, produced the medieval knight and his lord. Medieval lordship thus formed a system of local defence by men trained for war.

[1] Procopius, *Buildings*, iv, 1.

Grants of land and other sources of wealth conferred by kings or great lords upon their followers were supposed to be both rewards for service and securities for future fidelity. These benefices (*beneficia*), which later became fiefs, were supposed to bind the scattered defenders of a large district into one system. In some cases the holder of the benefice required a renewal of the grant periodically, or at the death of his former patron. But each important benefice inevitably became a private possession held by inheritance; and, therefore, the system, in so far as it was a system, gave more independence to the local lord and less control to his superior than was necessary for government over a large area. The institution of lords' agents (*missi dominici*) under Charles the Great, who were travelling inspectors of the efficiency of local courts, proved to be a failure, and was abandoned in the early ninth century. And the ultimate effect, therefore, of the system of defence by local lordships was a division of the districts, one from another, without any adequate superior control.

Social Position of the Lords of the Land

The position of the lords of the land in the ninth century naturally differed in the "Latin" countries from that among Germanic peoples, because in France, Italy and northern Spain these lords still represented a foreign conquest of barbarians over a Latin-speaking population, whereas in England and western Germany the lords were of the same race and spoke the same language as their subjects. In the Latin-speaking countries, therefore, there was a sharper division between the landed aristocracy and the villeins and serfs than was the case elsewhere. But even in Germany the local inhabitants were by no means always friendly to their lords. For example, one chronicler says that in A.D. 841 "throughout the whole of Saxony the power of their serfs greatly increased over their lords, and they took to themselves the name of Stellingae, and they committed many irrational acts. And the nobles of that country were greatly afflicted and humiliated by their serfs." But in the next year, he writes, "Louis went into Saxony and nobly striking down the Saxon serfs who had been exalted by pride, restored them to their proper place" (*ad propriam naturam*).[1] Another chronicle, written by Prudentius, bishop of Troyes, reports in reference to the same revolt that when Louis had offered the Saxons the choice of any law or of their old customs, they being "always inclined to evil, chose rather to follow pagan rites than to hold to the sacred worship (*sacramenta*) of the Christian faith."[2]

In all the countries of the First Europe the accumulation of wealth and power in the hands of local lords led to a social *malaise* in the relations between the dependent population and their rulers. Serfdom was less oppressive than slavery; but even serfdom generated that fear and suspicion which always trouble the irresponsible master and his helpless dependants. Thus, the feeling that the lower classes threatened to overturn the social structure, seems to have been common even among Churchmen—among those at least who were conscious of their connections with kings and nobles. In the life of Louis the Pious, written by Theganus, the bishops, who joined the sons of Louis in their rebellion against their father, are said to have been of "the lowest class of serfs." Ebo, archbishop of Reims, "who was descended from serfs," is said to have been the worst of these; and the writer adds a caution, by way of conclusion to the episode, that the king shall take care "not to exalt men of the status of serfs, for they desire only to oppress the nobles and to lift up their own relatives of the lowest class."[3] The writer was a *chorepiscopus* or assistant bishop in the diocese of Trier. Christianity had indeed changed since the days in which it was the religion of the *humiles*—the poor and helpless. And now in the ninth century a bishop repudiates almost in so many words the declaration of the *Magnificat* that God "hath put down the mighty from their seats and exalted them of low degree." The king is advised against any such action.

The efforts of the Church to soften the rigours of local lordships are well indicated in the letters of Einhard. For example: "To our

[1] *Ann. Xantenses, M.G.H.*, ad ann. 841, 842. Nithard, *Hist.*, iv, 2, 4, 6.
[2] *Ann. Bertin.*, ad ann. 841.
[3] Theganus, *Vita Lud. Pii.* (*Pat. Lat.*, 106). "Praecavendum est, ne amplius fiet, ut servi sint consiliarii sui (i.e. Imperatoris); quia si possunt hoc maxime construunt, ut nobiles opprimant et eos cum vilissima propinquitate eorum exaltare studeant." Compare the Vulgate—"Deposuit potentes de sede et exaltavit humiles."

dearest friend, the glorious count Hatto, eternal greeting in the Lord. A certain man of yours, named Hunno, has come to the shrine of SS. Peter and Marcellinus, seeking pardon because he has married without your leave a fellow serf, your servant. Therefore we pray your kindness that he may deserve to receive pardon for what he has done, if the crime can be rightly forgiven." Again, in another letter of Einhard: "To the magnificent, honourable, illustrious and gracious count Poppo, greeting in the Lord. Two poor men have fled to the shrine of Christ's blessed martyrs, Marcellinus and Peter, confessing their guilt. They were convicted in your presence of theft—that is to say, stealing game in the lord's forest. They have already paid part of the fine and owe more; but, as they say, they cannot pay because of their poverty. Therefore we pray your kindness that you will deign to spare them in so far as it is possible, for the love of the blessed martyrs of Christ to whom they have fled, lest they should utterly perish for their guilt. May they rather feel that they have gained your favour by their approach to the tombs of the martyrs."[1] These letters indicate the use of "sanctuary" and the effect of ecclesiastical influence upon the operation of lordship. Such influence of the clergy and monks as guardians of shrines was due partly to the widespread fear of the uncanny power in the bones or other relics of saints, and partly, in a smaller degree, to reverence for the virtues of saints.

A treatise by Paulinus, the archbishop or patriarch of Aquileia, written in A.D. 795, may serve as an example of the attempt by the Church to influence subordinate rulers. This is a *Book of Exhortation* addressed to Henry, Count of Friuli.[2] In contrast with the letter of Fulgentius Ferrandus, referred to above, the exhortations of Paulinus are typical of the change in the climate of opinion which distinguishes the medieval from the Roman social system. The bishop quotes John Pomerius on the contemplative life, and tells the count that he must pursue virtue "although he is a layman" (*etsi laicus*). He points out that Christ gave his promises and shed his blood "not only for us clergy," but also for the laity, and that

---

[1] Einhard, Ep. 46 and 47, in M.G.H., *Epistolae*, v, Ep. *Karolini Aevi*, iii, p. 133. The offence in the second case is "furando feramina in dominica foraste."

[2] Paulinus Aq., *Liber Exhortationis*, Pat. Lat., 99.

PLATE 5.—WALLED TOWN AND WARRIORS, *c.* 800 (TWO SCENES)

(Utrecht Psalter)

"the palace in the skies is open, not only for the clergy" (caeleste palatium patet non solum clericis). The medieval assumption is here evident, that the clergy are a caste specially cared for by Christ. The count is told to make all his subjects (*subiecti*) mindful of virtue—to keep them from fornication, anger and drunkenness; because he is responsible to God for their salvation. He is to control his own flesh; because "the soul does not sin, except through the flesh" (non peccat anima nisi per carnem). He is to think of heaven and hell, of the howling and gnashing of teeth, of tears and pain unending, which those would suffer who are condemned at the Last Judgement, at which the devil acts as an accuser and Christ as a judge "whose palace no bishop nor abbot nor count can corrupt by gold and silver" (cuius palatium auro argentoque nullus episcopus, nec abbas, nec comes corrumpere poterit). The treatise ends with a prayer for the use of the count, against lust, gluttony and other sins. There could be no clearer indication of the medieval blindness to the problems of social institutions and social justice. By the ninth century the tradition was established which survived throughout the Middle Ages, that the moral or spiritual influence of Christianity and of the Church should reform the characters of rulers and their subjects without regard to the good or evil in the system of social relationships. Medieval writers assumed that the institutions familiar to them were either inevitable or ideal. But the limitations of the medieval mind are also evident in the treatise of Paulinus, in so far as he conceives the virtues of a ruler without reference to the functions of government in the administration of justice and the organization of supply and defence. Evidently, for the patriarch of Aquileia, virtue meant chiefly the sort of life which a celibate clergy could most easily lead.

The collapse of the Carolingian Empire and dynasty in the later ninth century, naturally led to a strengthening of local lordships. Invasions by Normans, Magyars and Saracens could be resisted only by armed force organized in the localities which the invaders attempted to loot. From this situation, therefore, developed the local stronghold or castle, with its lord and his armed horsemen or knights, and in Italy and southern France the walled town of the

Middle Ages. The history, however, of the later development of local defence and its co-ordination in great dukedoms or kingdoms lies beyond the scope of the present chapter.

In the fifth century, while the Roman system of government and commerce was decaying, villas distant from the cities were fortified. In later centuries the home-farm of the landowner was defended by palisades and ditches, and finally, in the ninth century local defence began to depend upon the first primitive castles. The life of the inhabitants of these strongholds and of the villages dependent upon them was isolated and monotonous. As roads and bridges fell into ruin, as brigands or foreign raiders roamed the forest or ascended the rivers, famine increased and disease followed upon famine. Thus, death and destruction became more familiar than the normal pleasures of life. The dominant fears of the time made it easy to think of life as trivial, while fear and hope together built up in the imagination the pains of hell and the joys of heaven.

Medieval Lordship

Medieval lordship (*dominium, seigneurie, herrschaft*) was not an institution which can be accepted or dismissed merely as a fact. It involved certain estimates of moral value on which depended the moral authority of the lords, both spiritual and temporal. It was, indeed, partly the effect of unconscious tendencies during the many centuries between the fourth and the ninth; but it was also partly the result of the moral teaching of the clergy. The accepted view implied, first, that the lord should have unquestioned authority over his subordinates, and secondly, that those who were dependent upon him should render obedience, limited only by some ancient customs, and by the general duty of benevolence on the part of those who held power. Again, this lordship involved responsibility to an over-lord, and finally to God, but not responsibility to those who were governed. The power and authority of God was conceived to be absolute, and kings and lords, both spiritual and temporal, were assumed, not merely to have received their status from God, but also to exercise their functions as God did.

The medieval lord was responsible primarily, as all his teachers

482

told him, for the "salvation" of his people; that is to say for their establishment in heaven after death. He was responsible for the security of their lives and property, but not for the removal of the evils of famine and disease, partly because it was not known that disease could be prevented, and it was therefore accepted as "the will of God," and partly because the Church and not the lords and kings had inherited social services from the Roman Empire. Therefore, the conception of the art of government developed in the First Europe, disregarded all the organization of social services. In the Middle Ages there was no current discussion such as existed under the Roman system, of water-supply or roads, of methods of taxation, or of public buildings and services.[1] The concentration upon the idea of personal salvation implied that each man and woman could be and should be virtuous in any circumstances; and that, therefore, social conditions and social relationships were of little importance. But this is precisely the mistake of all primitive ideas of morality. The distinction between personal virtue and social responsibility was not clearly perceived. And for this reason, the medieval conception of lordship disregarded the problem whether the position of a lord with absolute authority, and a serf in complete dependence upon him, is consonant with social justice.

The historian is not, indeed, concerned to apply the standards of a later age to the actions of men long since dead. But he is concerned to say how far their knowledge of facts and estimates of moral value were defective, in the light of what is known of man and the universe at the time when the historian writes. Thus, medieval rulers cannot be blamed for their ignorance of the action of bacteria in epidemic disease; but it would be foolish to omit to observe that they were ignorant of it. Similarly, those who wrote on lordship and the art of government, between the fourth and the ninth centuries, were ignorant of the fact that social institutions can be consciously changed in response to a demand for social justice. And they also thought that moral standards and the principles of government were stated finally and for all circumstances in certain sacred writings. They were as defective in their estimates of

---

[1] As, for example, in the works of Frontinus.

moral value and political principles as in their knowledge of facts.

Influential bishops and monks, however, reminded the lords of the land to be merciful and benevolent. They softened the rigours of serfdom as earlier Christian teachers had improved the treatment of slaves. The teaching of the Churches, indeed, assumed the necessity of absolute authority and uncritical obedience. But there were always critics of the actual use of power by those who held it; and revolts of peasants and towns-folk sometimes received sympathy from the lesser clergy, even when the more powerful abbots and bishops made common cause with the lords of the land.[1] The Christian tradition expressed in the New Testament and in the earliest Christian records contained an explosive force which has always threatened an established order. In that tradition someone might, at any time, remember that Christianity was founded by manual workers, or that there was a time "when Adam delved and Eve span."

The principle of government generally accepted was authoritarian. What would now be called democratic government was clearly condemned by the most influential teachers. Thus, Alcuin wrote: "The people according to divine decisions is to be led and not to be followed. And for witness reliable persons are preferably chosen. We must not listen to those who say that 'the voice of the people is the voice of God,' because the restlessness of the crowd is always near to madness."[2] Authoritarian government, however, in the early Middle Ages by no means involved the unlimited absolutism which was later advocated and practised in Renaissance Europe. No king or lord was ever conceived in western Europe, after the fall of the Roman Empire, to be free from all restraint of law. And in practice the promulgation of laws and the exercise of executive authority were always subject to the advice of coun-

---

[1] At a slightly later date there is a most striking example of the hostility of a great abbot to popular movements in the story of the commune of Laon, given by Guibert de Nogent in his autobiography.

[2] Alcuin, Ep. 253 in Jaffé, *Bibl. Rer. German.* vi, *Alcuiniana*, ix. Populus juxta sanctiones divinas ducendus est, non sequendus; et ad testimonium personae magis eliguntur honestae. Nec audiendi qui solent dicere: *Vox populi, vox Dei.* Cum tumultuositas vulgi semper insaniae proxima sit. (The title is: Alcuinus Caroli regis ad interrogationes quasdam respondet.)

cillors or "witnesses" who could say what the traditional custom was which the law was supposed to express. This appears to be the meaning of Alcuin's phrase, in the letter quoted above, which indicates that reliable evidence is required from selected persons in the art of government. Thus, as the king was advised by his council of bishops and nobles, so the local lord, even in the early Middle Ages, was in some way controlled by meetings of reliable persons who bore witness to the established customs of the locality; and therefore lordship, although in practice often tyrannical, never in theory involved absolute and unlimited power. Quite apart from the influence of the Church in the preaching of benevolence and of the duty of service, the earliest tradition of lordship in the First Europe implied the supremacy of law which limited the rights and restricted the powers of all rulers. The limitation of the power of rulers by reference to customary law was not due to any abstract theory, nor to the application of any principle of government. It was only the recognition of certain facts in the situation. The majority of lordships among peoples who had hitherto lived under the Roman Empire were the results of invasion by ignorant barbarians without experience of government. In these cases, therefore, representative opinion on the estate, or in the district ruled by the lord, might be useful to him for guidance, or too ancient for him to neglect. In other cases, as in England, and on estates granted as benefices by kings, the local population had probably been organized for production and the protection of property before the new lordship was established. In these cases also, therefore, local custom was too strong and too useful to be disregarded.

General Conclusions

The increase in the power and moral authority of the great landowners in the early Middle Ages proved that it was impossible to centralize government in the First Europe upon the Roman plan. Indeed, the medieval conception of what the Roman Empire had been, was an obstacle to the formation of a public policy which was based upon the actual situation. Archaism afflicted both the Roman Church, in its attempt at securing an imperial centralization of ecclesiastical authority, and the unfortunate German kings who claimed to be Roman Emperors. The old system could not possibly be revived, either in Church or State; but it haunted the minds of men throughout the Middle Ages. Meantime the only possible basis for a centralized government was found in the common language of a district, which divided it from all others. Out of these divisions and the unstable unities of changing languages and dialects came the Nation-States of the Second Europe, after the Renaissance.

The political structure of the First Europe had its roots in the local lordships by which the new barbarian invasions of the ninth and tenth centuries were resisted. These invasions did not destroy the roots of the First Europe as the invasions of the fifth century had destroyed the Roman Empire in the West; and one reason for this was the organization of the "home guard" under the local lordship. By the amalgamation of some of these lordships and the subordination of some to others, the kingdoms of the Middle Ages were eventually established. But between the barbarian kingdoms of the fifth and sixth centuries and the medieval kingdoms, such as those of France and England, lay many centuries of trial and error in the establishment of central and local government. It never proved to be possible to unite the kingdoms of Europe under a central Empire or any other single Authority.

The reasons why it was impossible to revive the Roman centralization of government in western Europe are probably these. First, the new civilization was based upon the organization of the Churches; and despite all the centralizing efforts of the bishops, the local community or Church was the chief source of religious and social experience for the majority of Christians. Sacraments, ceremonies and festivals united the members of any one community in any locality, although there were differences of class or rank or wealth among its members. The village church or town church was a source and symbol of local patriotism; and great landowners, as early as the fifth century, built and maintained churches of their own for the people on their estates.

Christianity had been organized in the cities long before the peasants were Christian. For example, St. Martin of Tours, in the late fourth century, seeing a procession of peasants, assumed, quite wrongly as it turned out, that it was part of a pagan ceremony. In these circumstances Christian preachers advocated the building of churches by landowners on their estates. St. John Chrysostom argued that it would "pay" both spiritually and materially. In a sermon he says: "Many will build markets and baths, but not churches. Anything rather than that! ... Therefore I advise and pray, indeed command that no one should have an estate without a church. . . . This is useful for peace among the peasants. . . . Baths make them weaker and taverns greedier, and yet you build these for show. Markets and meeting-places make them quarrel-some; but churches quite otherwise. How wonderful to see the priest, like Abraham, going out, white-headed, dressed for labour, digging and working. An estate which has a church is like God's garden. No shouting there, nor tumult, nor enemies, nor heresies. All are friends, sharing the same opinion."[1]

The imperial Authorities ordered that churches on private estates should have clergy taken from the same estate, and a number sufficient, in the judgement of the bishop, for their service.[2] In the West, as in the East, the building of churches by landowners on their estates promoted the spread of Christianity. But by the begin-ning of the sixth century difficulties arose with respect to the control of the funds and the clergy of these "private" churches. In A.D. 511, for example, the Council of Orleans (canon 15) declared that the bishops should have control of whatever land and other property had been given to country churches, and that a third of the income of the church should be paid over to the bishop.[3] Again, the fourth Council of Orleans, in A.D. 541, declared (canon 33): "If anyone has on his property, or desires to have, a parish church (diocesim), first, he must assign to it sufficient land and clergy for its service, that suitable respect should be paid to sacred places."[4]

When the richer classes, following imperial guidance, adhered to Christianity, the great landowners naturally assumed the respon-

---

John Chrysostom, *Hom.*, xviii. In Acts vii. 54. (*Opera*, vol. ix, Paris, 1837.)
Co d .*Theod.*, xvi, 2, 33.   [3] Mansi, *Concil.* viii.   [4] Ibid., ix.

sibility of providing, not merely for the economic organization of their estates, but also for the religious needs of the people. Therefore, the landowner paid for the building of the church and appointed its priest, thus becoming the chief influence in the local organization of the Church. The bishops, on the other hand, whose power rested upon the Christian organization in the cities, naturally feared that their jurisdiction would be restricted in country districts, if the great landowners had control of the country churches and their clergy. The controversy about appointment to "livings" by local lords continued throughout the Middle Ages and even later. Eventually the bishops secured control of the clergy, perhaps mainly through the archdeacons, who were known as the "eyes of the bishop." But in any case, for the purpose of the present argument, local communities of Christians outside the cities were maintained and strengthened by the use of the principle of local lordship, which was derived from the Roman tradition.[1]

Local saints express the connection between the Christian community of a locality and the community as a unit of production and government. The local saint was sometimes a person who had lived in the neighbourhood—as St. Martin became the patron of Tours—and sometimes a legendary figure, whose supposed relics brought power and influence, as in the case of St. Vitus at the Abbey of New Corbey in Germany. Even the greatest figures of the Christian Olympus were in some cases associated with particular places, as St. Peter was with Rome, not only adding influence to its bishops, but even, as Procopius writes, defending its walls. The local patron saint of the early Middle Ages was in some ways similar to the local hero or deity of pre-Christian times; and there may have been some cases in which the pre-Christian hero actually developed into a Christian saint. But clearly the growth of the worship of local patron saints was a natural development of the common life and tradition of the Christian community in any district. Each community preserved the memory of its martyrs, its hermits, or its saintly bishops. And even when, in the ninth century,

[1] See A. Dopsch, *Economic and Social Foundations* (Eng. trans., p. 244 sq.), where it is shown that private churches on estates were not due to Germanic influences.

the bishop of Rome attained a kind of imperial authority among ecclesiastics, the local saint still retained the devotion of those who lived near to his tomb.

A second obstacle to centralization was the growth of independent local communities for production and defence or local peace. These gave rise to the establishment of local customs as the basis of law and justice. No doubt, the breakdown of the communications by land and sea which had existed under the Roman system, was the primary cause of the development of production for local needs and the independent organization of the township or the village under the protection of a local lord, secular or ecclesiastical. No doubt, also, the lack of communications led to local famines. But the civilization of the First Europe struck deeper roots than those of the Roman imperial system, precisely because it arose out of a sort of federation of local communities, each with its own established customs, and not out of the conquest by one community of Roman farmer-soldiers which had extended its sway over all others. The general level of civilized life was lower between the fifth and ninth centuries than it had been before; but there was no longer any dominance of the great city over its provinces. Local communities, therefore, were more nearly equal in such resources of material, intellectual and emotional life, as are necessary for any type of civilization. A monastic settlement, for example, in the "wilderness," might contain as much literature and learning, as much agricultural and architectural skill as might be found in a town or at the Court of a king or other lord. Culture, although superficial, was not dependent upon a few centres, and for that reason it survived even when invasions destroyed such seats of learning as the monastery at which Bede lived and worked. The looting and burning of towns and monasteries, the loss of manuscripts and works of art during the invasions of the ninth century, might have done more harm to the tradition of civilized life than the invasions of the fifth century, but for the fact that the centres of civilization were more numerous and independent than in Roman times.

A third reason for the growth of local, as contrasted with central government, was the influence of personal loyalty. The lord of the land attracted a following, not merely of armed retainers, but of smaller men living in the shadow of his protection. Some historians have attempted to trace personal loyalty to the habits and customs of Germanic warriors. But apart from the fact that examples of desertion and treachery are frequently to be found in the history of all the barbarian kingdoms, there is no reason to suppose that loyalty to a patron, or a lord and master, was unknown in Roman civilization. The rich man or the great landowner, even in the midst of the slave-system, as in the fifth century, must have been regarded in many places as a protector and leader. How otherwise can it be explained that so many rich landowners were chosen by the people of their own districts to be their bishops? But even if the local lord exacted labour and tribute which it was hard to bear, his control might well be accepted as an alternative to unknown dangers from marauders or passing armed bands. The principle that one should stick to the devil one knows is not unreasonable. But the Roman tradition of the fatherly care (*patrocinium*) of the great man concerned with his dependants, was never lost. The Church, as it has been shown above, always reminded the rich and powerful of their duties to the poor and weak,

The need for local organization of supply and defence, however, led in the early Middle Ages to an excess of localism, which reduced the units of government to a chaos of segregate atoms, often in conflict. Public policy was, therefore, reduced to the level of village squabbles and hole-and-corner tyranny; and the development of law was restricted by reference back to the customs of the ignorant ancestors of the local community. In Germany, which had never had experience of large-scale government, the castles of minor lords divided authority; and in Italy, where the traditions of central government had been destroyed by invasions from all quarters of the compass, walled cities began their endless medieval rivalries. But even among peoples more fortunate, in their efforts to subordinate local lordships to national unity, the extremes of localism drove the best minds to an equally impracticable dream of uniting the whole of medieval Christendom under one supreme Authority.

CHAPTER XII

THE MAKING OF THE PAPACY

The two efforts, first, to preserve the traditions of civilized life, and secondly, to maintain the unity of the Christian Church, had one outstanding result—the medieval Papacy. The only civilized tradition known in western Europe from the fifth to the ninth century was the Roman. And the only unity which the men of that day could imagine was that of the Roman Empire. Therefore the Latin Churches of the fifth century became, in the ninth, the imperial Church of Rome. The bishops of Rome, in the fifth century, had equals in the apostolic tradition—the patriarchs of Antioch, Alexandria and Jerusalem. And at that time their rivals in political influence were the patriarchs of Constantinople, who were in close touch with the imperial Court. But by the ninth century the Mohammedans had destroyed the influence of the three apostolic patriarchates in the East; and the Emperor at Constantinople, and therefore his patriarch in "New Rome," had no power at all in the West. Thus, the influence of Rome as the only known source of civilization and the only centre of unity among the barbarian kingdoms of the ninth century, together with the decline in the prestige of the most important eastern patriarchates, left the bishop of Rome the sole heir to supreme authority in the Latin Churches. But conscious policy also played its part. Not only the bishops contending with kings, but also reformers among the clergy and monks, after the disorders of the seventh century, looked to Rome in order to protect the local Churches against robber warriors, and to maintain the standard of morals and organization expressed in the canons of the Church. The bishops in barbarian kingdoms, who might easily have become merely chaplains of the Court, were not likely to be able unaided to protect ecclesiastical property against kings, or even to prevent the appointment of unworthy men to ecclesiastical offices. Those bishops, therefore, who sought to resist the royal influence, or the secularization of the episcopate, finding even episcopal councils ineffectual, turned to Rome. That name had an authority which in the eighth century was derived both from the prestige of Roman culture and from the tradition of the early martyrs. On the other hand, reformers in the kingdoms of the Franks and the Anglo-Saxons could appeal to the standard of Christian conduct and ecclesiastical discipline associated with the collection of canons and the letters of the bishops of Rome, without any too exact knowledge of the actual situation in the Roman Church of their day. Indeed, in later centuries, even when the Papacy itself was the centre of corrupt intrigue, the Pope, as head of the Christian Church, remained in the imagination of the Middle Ages an ideal legislator and guide.

The Medieval Papacy

By the middle of the ninth century the medieval Papacy was already a reality. But as an institution it was the result of gradual development and diverse experiments in ecclesiastical organization, which had been going on for at least five centuries before. It is difficult, indeed, for the student who knows the character of the Papacy in the Middle Ages and later times, to recognize how gradual was the change from the position of the bishop of Rome in the early fifth century to that of the Pope in the ninth. In the first place, the medieval controversies about the authority of the Pope and the Emperor tend to obscure the history of earlier centuries, during which there was no clearly expressed theory of ecclesiastical or civil authority. It is dangerous, therefore, to refer back to the earlier centuries distinctions and differences which arose only after the medieval system of government in States and Churches was established. As the men of the Middle Ages made the Simon Peter of the Gospels, not only into a bishop but also into a pope, wearing a tiara, so, even to-day, some historians read into the phrases used in early Christian times the interpretations placed upon them by medieval theologians. In opposition to this misreading of history, it must be quite clearly understood that the bishop of Rome in the fifth century was in no sense a Pope of the ninth century; and what follows here is mainly intended to show how the transformation took place.

Again, even language is misleading. The word Pope (Papa) was used even in the Latin Churches as late as the sixth century to refer to any bishop whose See or whose personal virtues gave him exceptional prestige. Thus, towards the end of the sixth century, it is recorded by Gregory of Tours as a royal joke when a king pretended to be astonished that the "Papa" to whom an appellant referred was not the Pope of Rome;[1] and the Formulas of Marculf collected about A.D. 650, are dedicated to a "Papa" who was a subordinate bishop. But the word "Pope" became so clearly a name for the bishop of Rome alone during the Middle Ages, that historians still tend to use the word in reference to the earliest Roman bishops. It is important, therefore, to recognize that there is no higher rank in the ecclesiastical hierarchy than that of bishop. Gregory the Great, writing to the bishop of Alexandria in A.D. 598, says that all bishops are equal,[2] and Pope Zachary, writing to St. Boniface in A.D. 751, refers to himself as a "co-episcopus." The election of a bishop of Rome, even later than the ninth century, was still a matter for the local Church in the city of Rome and did not concern bishops of far-distant Sees. Even to-day, the fact that members of the conclave of Cardinals may come from America or Asia, should not be allowed to obscure the fact that these men hold their right of election only as clergy of the *tituli* or parish-churches of the city of Rome and bishops of the suburban bishoprics. In any case, the word "Pope," as a distinctive title for the bishop of Rome, is entirely out of place with reference to the situation before the fifth century.

Again, the medieval Papacy was a dictatorship; but it must not be assumed that the principle of dictatorship, as a method of obtaining unity in the Church, was inevitable before the ninth century. So long as all the Christian Churches in the eastern Mediterranean,

---

[1] Greg. Tur., *H.F.* iv, 26.   [2] Greg. M., Ep. viii, 29.

as well as in Africa, Spain, Italy and Gaul were united, their unity was expressed and maintained by General Councils of bishops. In the earlier Councils, all of which took place in countries of the eastern Mediterranean, the bishop of Rome and other western bishops played no very important part. As the Churches in the West were weakened during the fifth and sixth centuries by the control of Arian kings, the bishop of Rome came to be regarded in the East as a representative of the whole of western Christendom, both because his See was the only Patriarchate in the West, and because it was the only See continuously in contact with the imperial Authorities at Constantinople. But the tendency of eastern Christianity to seek for unity among the Churches by a kind of federation of bishoprics, acting through Councils, might easily have established the principle that the Churches were united by General Councils and not by subordination of all other bishops to one. Even among the Latin Churches, the first attempts at securing and extending the unity of Christendom were made in councils of bishops. But as it has been indicated in an earlier chapter, the division of western Europe into separate and rival kingdoms, led to the establishment of a tradition of councils of bishops upon a "national" basis. The Councils of Toledo included only bishops of the Visigothic kingdom; and the councils of different cities in Gaul included only bishops of the Frankish kingdom. In practice it was impossible for any council of bishops from all the western kingdoms to be organized. Thus, the alternative method of securing unity was adopted—the dictatorship of the Pope in an imperial Church. But by the time that system was established, half of the Christian Churches were already separated from communion with the See of Rome. The eastern Churches continued the earlier Christian tradition of the equality of all bishops. The principle of dictatorship as a means of securing unity was so easily taken for granted in the Middle Ages that, until the revival of the conciliar theory in the fifteenth century, it was generally believed that the western bishops had always been subject to the supreme authority of a Pope. But the papal dictatorship itself was an experiment. In some of its aspects it was forced upon the bishops of Rome and not sought by them. But, in discussing its early development, it must not be forgotten that the centuries from the fifth to the ninth do not contain anything more than the roots from which the great ecclesiastical system of the Middle Ages grew.

The medieval Papacy, which in no sense existed in the fifth century, but can be perceived in its earliest form in the ninth, had peculiar characteristics, which must not be confused with those of the bishopric of Rome, either before the ninth century or after the Protestant Reformation of the sixteenth century. By the medieval Papacy is here meant the generally acknowledged position and authority in all the Christian Churches of the West, of the bishops of Rome, between about A.D. 800 and 1500. Before A.D. 800 the Latin Churches did not form an imperial system under a dictatorship; and after the Protestant Reformation most of those who claimed to be Christians in north-western Europe no longer acknowledged the authority of the bishop of Rome either in doctrine or in discipline. The medieval Papacy has, therefore, disappeared as completely as the Holy Roman Empire.

But in order that the system of which it formed a part may be kept in mind, the final result of the development before the ninth century may be summarily described as follows. The medieval Papacy was a highly centralized dictatorship of the bishop of Rome and his Court over all the bishops, other clergy and laity of the Latin Churches of the West. In this system the bishop of Rome, who was in the Middle Ages known exclusively as "Pope," acted first as a supreme court of appeal. Abbots, bishops and other clergy could appeal to Rome, and the decision there obtained would generally be regarded as final in matters of discipline or ecclesiastical rights. Secondly, the Pope became the supreme exponent of doctrine and the supreme legislator. Thus, he took the place of the Universal Councils of Bishops, such as those of Nicaea and Chalcedon. The Pope decided the correct interpretation of the Christian tradition, and issued statements of doctrine to be held by all Christians, and Decretals, or additions to the canons. He was also assumed, until perhaps the fifteenth century, to be the only bishop who could summon a general council. But clearly, by the time this power was claimed for the Papacy, the summons could no longer be addressed to the whole Christian Church; because the Greek Churches would have disregarded it. Thirdly, the medieval Papacy exercised the administrative powers of a dictatorship. As Charles the Great and his successors tried to exercise administrative control through their *missi*, so the medieval Pope sent out Legates and, at a later date, Nuncios. He was the only Christian bishop who had direct representatives of his own within the dioceses of other bishops. And it also happened that he was the only bishop who, after the establishment of the Papal State in the ninth century, was the subject of no king or local lord. Obviously such characteristics of the institution were developed gradually. The position of Boniface VIII, Innocent III or Gregory VII was by no means the same as that of Hadrian I; and his position, again, even in the Church, and certainly with regard to the civil Authorities, was entirely different from that of Leo I. The transition from prestige to actual power was not continuous. There were many interruptions and accidents in the growth of papal authority. And if, in modern times, the transition is obvious in the reverse direction—from authority which will be obeyed, to prestige which may be respected or ignored at will—that fact may be taken as an example of the general truth that primitive institutions have short lives in their actual operation, and longer lives as ghosts. The Papacy of to-day is only a ghost of that once supreme authority of the Middle Ages. But here the history of the institution in its earliest form must be discussed, on the assumption that its maturity and greatest strength are to be found between the ninth and sixteenth century.

Finally, the medieval Papacy implied what was later known as the Temporal Power of the Pope. After the middle of the eighth century the bishop of Rome was not merely the ecclesiastical head of a diocese, not merely the administrator of Church properties, but the ruler of a population in central Italy. That is to say, he was, like the Prince-Bishops of Germany and Austria, a dictator who exercised the functions of civil government and military control, by the methods familiar to any medieval duke or prince. Not until after the Middle Ages was the Pope definitely called "King,"[1] because he was in fact always dependent upon alien armed forces for the maintenance of his power in Italy at least until the sixteenth century. But the medieval Papacy certainly implied supreme civil and military authority over the population of the papal estates, even when for about seventy years (A.D. 1305-1377) the bishop of Rome held his Court at Avignon. His position as what the Renaissance called a "sovereign," having "Temporal Power," made it all the more difficult to believe that, as the Spiritual Power, he could decide what king should have moral authority in any country, or whether the subjects of any king should obey him. But the origin of all the strange policies which the later Papacy was compelled to adopt in defence of the Temporal Power is to be found in the situation in Rome in the eighth and ninth centuries.

The most obvious formative influences, apart from conscious policy, which tended to produce the medieval Papacy were, first, the prestige of the city of Rome; secondly, the unity of the Latin Churches in language and customs, both originally derived from Rome; and thirdly, the Legend of St. Peter.

The Prestige of Rome

The prestige of the city of Rome was strongly expressed by the Christian poet Prudentius at the end of the fourth century. Prudentius was a Spaniard; but he wrote his verses *Against Symmachus* to prove that Rome owed its power to its own virtues and not to its Gods. "It is an insult to our legions," he says, "to take from Rome what belongs to her, and to honour Venus for the effects of our own valour."[2] And as a result of the virtues of Rome "all men now live as citizens of the same city or relatives in the same house. . . . The blood of all races mingles, and of many nations is formed one people."[3] For Prudentius, in his hymn to St. Lawrence, heaven

[1] As late as the early twentieth century the cry "Viva il Papa Ré" was used by good Catholics in Rome, as a form of protest against the kingdom of Italy.

[2] Prudentius, *Contra Sym.*, ii, 553. See above p. 73n. Admiration for pre-Christian Rome is expressed by SS. Ambrose and Augustine, and as late as A.D. 550 by Cosmas Indicopleustes (Topog. xi).

[3] Ibid., ii, 610 . . . sub legibus iisdem Romanos omnes fieri . . . ius fecit commune pares et nomine eodem nexuit et domitos fraterna in vincla redegit.

itself is "Roma caelestis," which elects the Saint as consul for all eternity.[1] But when he wrote the centre of the Empire had been, for almost a century, established at Constantinople, and Rome had become identified with Christianity. According to Prudentius, God had given success to Rome, uniting the world under the sway of that city, to prepare it for unity under Christ.[2] In the middle of the fifth century Pope Leo I declares, in one of his sermons, that at the coming of the Holy Ghost, as recorded in the Acts, St. Peter had been assigned the task of going to Rome as the centre of authority in the world. God, he says, favoured the conquests of Rome in order to prepare for Christianity.[3] And throughout the Middle Ages the prestige of Rome continued to depend, at least partly, upon the power and authority of the pre-Christian Republic and Empire. Thus, the influence of Rome upon the future history of the Latin Churches was partly due to the prestige of its conquests and its government, which had been acquired long before the Christian era.

On the other hand, in the hymns of Prudentius Rome is the city, not of Emperors, but of apostles and martyrs. The poet describes with enthusiasm the shrines and basilicas of Rome. Pope Leo I says that SS. Peter and Paul made Rome "a holy people, a priestly city," whose religious authority was more widespread than its Empire had been.[4] The catacombs outside Rome contained great numbers of tombs of Christians, buried there during the three centuries before Constantine. By an accident of geology, which turned out to be fortunate for the Church of Rome, the dry tufa rock preserved the bones and garments, and so provided a great store of relics which was drawn upon in the seventh and eighth centuries in order to connect the new Churches of northern Europe with the ancient Christian tradition. The lists of Saints commemorated in the churches of Rome and of the festivals of the Roman Church were carefully preserved in the central office of the bishopric.

---

[1] Prudentius, *Peri.*, ii, 258, quem Roma caelestis sibi legit perennem consulem.
[2] Prudentius, *Peristephanon*, ii, 429. (*Contra Sym.*, ii, 632.) En omne sub regnum Remi mortale concessit genus . . . hoc destinatum, quo magis ius christiani nominis . . . quodque terrarum iacet uno inligaret vinculo.
[3] Leo, *Sermo*, 83, 2. *Pat. Lat.*, 54.   [4] Ibid., 83, 1.

The readings (*legenda*) commemorating the sufferings of martyrs were soon adorned by the imagination, which aimed at edifying rather than at historical instruction. And Rome became a centre of pilgrimage. After the fifth century it was the chief rival of Jerusalem as an attraction both for pilgrims and for those who wished to spend their last years in places sacred to the Christian tradition. Thus, during the Middle Ages, quite apart from the power and authority of its bishops, Christian Rome had a great influence upon the mind of the First Europe, as it is expressed in the verses, "At the threshold of the Apostles," which were written early in the ninth century:

> O Rome illustrious, of the world Empress,
> Over all cities, thou Queen in thy goodliness. . . .[1]

A similar but more pedestrian enthusiasm is expressed in the guide-book to Rome written at the beginning of the twelfth century, the *Mirabilia Romae*, of which many manuscript versions remain. This contains lists of the famous ruins and relics in Rome which claimed the attention of the Middle Ages. Rome, besides exporting relics to the North, collected more of them throughout the Middle Ages; and thus Rome, especially after the conquest of the Holy Land by the Mohammedans, became for the First Europe above all others a sacred city.[2]

It has been shown in an earlier chapter than the word "sanctus," meaning "revered," "of moral authority" rather than "holy" in the modern sense, was attached from the earliest times to officials in the city of Rome, and especially to Emperors and their subordinates. For this reason it was natural that the throne of the bishop of Rome should be called *sancta sedes* and the bishop of Rome

---

[1] Trans. by J. A. Symonds. The original is most easily found in Gaselee's *Oxford Book of Medieval Latin Verse*, p. 39:

> O Roma nobilis, orbis et domina
> cunctarum urbium excellentissima,
> roseo martyrum sanguine rubea,
> albis et virginum liliis candida;
> salutem dicimus tibi per omnia,
> te benedicimus—salve per saecula!

[2] The relics noted in the *Mirabilia* include such things as the "praeputium Christ et eius umbilicus" (in edition of G. Parthey, Berlin, 1869, p. 52).

Sanctissimus Papa; though neither the See nor the "Father" were originally conceived to be "holy" in the modern sense of the word. The "holiness" of the See of Rome is directly derived, indeed, not from its Christianity, but from its inheritance of pre-Christian imperial prestige. Again, in Rome were the chief offices of the imperial civil service during the first three centuries of our era. And even after the Emperors established their Courts at Constantinople, Milan, or Ravenna, the offices and civil services of the Empire continued to preserve records and issue decrees in Rome. The experience thus gained was naturally taken up and used by the Roman Church, which seems to have had from its earliest years its central office (*scrinium*) and its collection of documents, as a basis of continuous policy and claims of ancient rights. The bishops of Rome issued letters of instruction, as the Emperors had issued "rescripts." The letters of Trajan and Pliny were earlier essays in that same practice by which Gregory the Great wrote advice to bishops or secular rulers in Spain, Gaul and England. And in the central office of the Roman Church at the Lateran Palace, after the fourth century, were preserved the records of the past, which in the sixth century became the basis for the *Liber Pontificalis*. Similarly the Roman Church preserved the first Latin version of the collected canons of the eastern Councils. And the *Liber Diurnus* of the Roman Church, a collection of models for official letters, made in the seventh or eighth century, shows how carefully the Roman imperial tradition was preserved by the central office of the bishops of Rome.

The language of Roman imperial administration was preserved by the bishops of Rome. The *decreta* of Emperors became the *decreta* of the Pope in the Middle Ages; the medieval "interdict" which forbids the use of ecclesiastical ceremonies, is the *interdictum* of the Roman praetor "when he forbids something to be done," as Gaius says.[1] The word *curia*, meaning a city council, has been kept for the college of cardinals who are recognized as "princes of the Church," as senators were referred to as "princes of the world" (*mundi principes*).[2]

---

[1] Gaius, *Institutes*, iv, 140.   [2] In the *Vita Probi*, xi, in the *Historia Augusta*.

The Latin Language and Liturgy

The second influence which went to the formation of the medieval Papacy was the unity of the Latin Churches as against their common difference from the Churches of the eastern Mediterranean. During its early years Christianity was dominated by the Greek language and Greek methods of thought, even when it continued certain Hebrew traditions. The New Testament and the works of the most influential early Fathers were written in Greek; and Greek words have remained the source in all western languages of ecclesiastical terms: for the sacraments, baptism and eucharist; for official ranks, bishop and deacon; for ecclesiastical areas, diocese and parish—all these are forms of Greek words. Even as late as the end of the fourth century, in St. Augustine's day, as he himself indicates, Latin translations of the Bible were by no means reliable; and, as is well known, St. Jerome's most important work was his collection and improvement of the old Latin versions, to form what is now called the Vulgate.[1] The early Christian missions, even in the West, had been formed among Syrian and Jewish traders, who spoke Greek; and, indeed, not Christianity only was dependent upon Greek. It was the general language of trade and perhaps of culture even in the West, as French was the language of culture in Germany in the eighteenth century. The Emperor Marcus Aurelius wrote down his private meditations in Greek; and when Constantine the Great established his capital on the Bosphorus, the Greek language inevitably dominated the Court and the administration.

But Latin remained the common language of the peoples of western Europe. And the Churches of the West, in Africa, Italy, Spain and Gaul, produced a literature of sermons and hymns in Latin. Translations of the fundamental creeds and canons of Greek councils, which claimed to represent the Universal Church, had hardly begun, when, as noted above, Dionysius the Little made the

---

[1] In St. Jerome's letter to Pope Damasus, introducing his version of the New Testament, he writes that the Latin versions differ among themselves so much that there are as many different meanings as there are copies of the text. St. Augustine writes to St. Jerome, objecting to one of his translations.

first collection of canons, which was intended to represent the mind of all the Churches. At the end of the sixth century Pope Gregory the Great could speak no Greek, in spite of some years of residence in Constantinople before he became Pope. The missionaries he sent to England brought with them Latin as the language of the Church. And the English missionaries of the eighth century in Germany took with them Latin, again, as the language of the Church, although they preached and catechized in Germanic dialects. In the eighth century a succession of Syrians, elected as bishops of Rome, perhaps because of the strong Syrian colony in Sicily, kept the connection at Rome between the Latin and the Greek Churches. But ever since the days of Justinian in the early sixth century, the two worlds were drifting apart—the Empire with its Greek Churches, and western Europe in which the language of all the Churches was Latin. A difference of language cuts deeply into social organization, as we know to our cost in contemporary Europe. A different language is not merely another way of saying the same thing. It is a different form of thought, emotion, or even experience as a whole. Thus, the ambiguity involved in translating Christian creeds, elaborated in Greek, into appropriate Latin terms, was one of the chief difficulties of the Latin Churches. Greek thought on the Trinity, for example, expressed itself in the terms "being" (οὐσία) and "growth" (φύσις); but they have only the most ambiguous connections with the Latin terms "substance" (substantia) and "nature" (natura). Herein lay the source of trouble when the West began to think, in the Middle Ages. But all this must be discussed elsewhere.

It is even more important that not only doctrine but also ritual and ecclesiastical literature in all the western Churches was expressed in the language of Rome. The fact that Latin was the language of all the western Churches gave great prestige to the bishop of the city whose official language had always been Latin. And even the development of new languages out of Latin—French, Italian and Spanish—did not divide the peoples who are still referred to as "Latin," from a Church which spoke and still speaks the Latin of the fifth century. The situation has always been different in missionary countries, such as England and Germany, where the majority of ordinary men and women have never spoken Latin. But it was precisely in those countries in which the language of the Church was quite different from the mother tongue that the connection with the bishop of Rome was strongest from the days of their conversion until the end of the ninth century. Indeed because Latin was the common speech of Italy and Gaul, the Latin of Gregory of Tours or of Pope Hadrian I was more "corrupt" than the Latin of Bede or Alcuin. The Englishmen wrote "better" Latin, precisely because they studied it as a foreign language which was already almost dead. And the prestige of Rome and its bishops was all the more exalted by the use of its own language in days when ecclesiastical ritual savoured of magic. In proportion as Latin died out in ordinary intercourse, its ghostly survival in ritual more deeply impressed the minds of the majority as the magic tongue of another world; and what at first had been a language of interpretation to the western world of a Greek-speaking religion, gradually became to the minds of the majority a collection of sacred formulas, unintelligible except to the caste of clergy. But the caste began more and more to regard itself as essentially "the Church," and to look for the preservation of its privileges to its connection with the bishop of Rome.

The Latin Churches were not merely divided from the Greek in language and thought before they differed in doctrine. They were also more united among themselves by the very fact that the Churches of the nations never subjected to the Roman Empire, began to dominate western Europe before the beginning of the Middle Ages. The Churches of Ireland, of the English and the Saxons, of the Franks and other German tribes, were not successors in their customs or language to the local city organizations of the Roman Empire, as the Churches of Italy, Africa, Spain and southern Gaul had been. The northern Churches were infiltrations of Latin culture among peoples who had never spoken Latin. But their influence over the whole of western Christianity after the sixth century was due to the accident that the older Churches of Africa, Spain and southern Gaul were destroyed or diminished in authority by the Mohammedan invasions. The increased influence of the newer Churches of the North in the ninth century might have led to a loss of influence over them by the Church in Rome and its bishop. In the eighth century, as it will be shown later, Rome might have become eastern—an outpost of the Greek-speaking Empire. But, in fact, Rome became an outpost of the West, and therefore dependent upon the Latin Churches. The supremacy, therefore, which the bishop of Rome eventually secured over the Latin Churches was, from another point of view, an admission of his dependence upon the Churches of the new Europe, after the quarrel of the Pope with the Emperors at Constantinople concerning the worship of images.

This result was due to two causes. First, the preservation of the Latin tradition and its essential documents in canons and episcopal letters in the offices of the bishop of Rome; and, secondly, the policy of the Frankish monarchy. Latin had become by the end of the seventh century the only common language uniting the peoples of western Europe. It was the language of the only educated class— the clergy, monks and nuns. And it became the official language of the Frankish kingdom and its dependencies under the Carolingians. The so-called revival of learning at the end of the eighth century under Charles the Great was mainly a study of the Latin Bible, the Latin Fathers and Latin authors, such as Virgil, Ovid and Suetonius. The Latin language was preserved and used for new purposes in the First Europe; and thus naturally confirmed and increased the prestige of the city of Rome.

In dress also, the influence of Roman fashions supported the prestige of the bishop of Rome. During the centuries before the eighth, when there were no "sacred vestments," the clergy wore the ordinary Roman costume of the middle and upper classes; and later, when this costume was transformed into liturgical vestments, the fact that these were originally Roman made it natural for the Latin Churches to look to the city of Rome for guidance in ritual. In the seventh century the bishops of Rome sent a special decoration, called by the old Roman name *pallium*, to bishops who had a special importance for the Roman See. This was a scarf, probably derived from the Roman toga, which had been used by imperial Authorities to indicate a special civil dignity. It seems to have been conferred on bishops by Emperors. But by the end of the fifth century, the *pallium* had become a sign of special favour conferred by the bishops of Rome upon certain metropolitans; and its new use therefore assisted to centralize authority in the Pope.[1]

The Legend of St. Peter

Another influence which went to the making of the medieval Papacy was the legend of St. Peter. It was commonly believed by Christians, at any rate in the West, as early as the third century, that the Simon Peter who was mentioned in the Gospels had come to Rome and had been executed there. The text of the Gospel of St. Matthew, "to thee I will give the keys," was generally taken as the expression of Christ's decision that Peter of the Gospels should be in some way the chief of the Apostles, and therefore head of the Christian community on earth.[2] But clearly the text says nothing about successors to this primacy; and it certainly does not refer to Rome. However, there were two early Christian letters in Greek which were eventually accepted as Peter's. The tradition of his mission on earth added that he had been for seven years bishop of Antioch; and the Latin Churches still keep the feast of the Chair of St. Peter at Antioch on February 22nd. After that he went to Rome, where he was bishop for a little more than twenty-five years. Tradition is rather confused, because in some versions he came to Rome under Nero and was executed by him; but Nero reigned only fourteen years! In Rome Peter refuted Simon Magus in an argument; and when fleeing from persecution, was met by Christ himself outside the city and eventually went back. He was imprisoned on the Capitol Hill, where no prison existed till the fifth century, near a temple of Janus. The chains which were put

[1] See Duchesne, *Christian Worship* (Eng. trans., 1904, p. 384).
[2] The earlier text of St. Mark's Gospel seems to imply that the nickname "Peter" referred, not to a rock upon which a man might build a home, but to the personal characteristic of Simon as an impulsive man, a "Thunder-stone," as the twin apostles were nicknamed "Boanerges"—that is to say, "Sons of Thunder"—Gregory the Great derives the name Peter "from the firmness of his mind" (Ep. vii, 37).

on him in Jerusalem, were discovered by a Jew in the fifth century, who sold them to the Empress Eudoxia; and soon after, other chains which Peter had borne in Rome were also discovered, and both sets placed in the new basilica (*Sancti Petri ad Vincula*) on the Esquiline, built by the Empress. Tradition also related that Peter was crucified in the Circus of Nero in the Vatican, on the same day as St. Paul was executed on the Via Ostia. In the fifth century the tomb of St. Peter was believed to be where the great basilica was built (St. Peter's in the Vatican), which stood from the middle of the fourth century until it was replaced by the present St. Peter's in the middle of the sixteenth century.[1] The tomb or *confessio*, which is the central point of both basilicas, the old and the new, was the source of the influence which attracted innumerable pilgrims, and eventually gave supreme ecclesiastical power to the bishops of Rome. It should be added, however, that the tomb and its basilica lie outside the city; and that the cathedral of the bishop of Rome is within the city, attached to the Lateran Palace. This is the basilica dedicated to the Saviour and rededicated by Sergius III (A.D. 904–911) to St. John the Baptist. It was known later as "mother and head of all the Churches in the city and the world." During the Middle Ages, the basilica was believed to include among its relics the heads of St. Peter and St. Paul.

So far the legend of St. Peter deals with his position on earth; but the tradition which describes his position in heaven was equally important for the medieval Papacy. By the beginning of the fifth century it was generally believed that Peter, who had been given the keys as the sign of authority on earth, had after his death become key-bearer (*claviger*) or the keeper (janitor) of the gates of heaven in the sky. This conception of St. Peter at the gates in the sky was taken quite literally in the fifth century and throughout the Middle Ages. For example, in Bede's account of the settlement of a dispute about the date of Easter, King Oswy is said to have

---

[1] Hodgkin has remarked that the first St. Peter's had already stood for five hundred years when Charles the Great was crowned in it; and that it lasted altogether about twelve hundred years; whereas the present St. Peter's has been in existence for only four hundred years. The medieval Papacy may be regarded as having existed for the seven hundred years of the old St. Peter's from A.D. 800 to A.D. 1500. For legends, see Acta Apost. Apoc., I (ed. Lipsius).

accepted the Roman tradition concerning the date, on the ground that St. Peter "is the door-keeper, whom I will not contradict . . . lest when I come to the gates of the kingdom of heaven, there should be none to open them, he being my adversary who is proved to have the keys."[1] The Peter of the Gospels was thus conceived to be still living in the sky and to have control of entry to it.

St. Peter had become primarily *claviger*, the key-bearer, by the beginning of the fifth century. He was known to earlier Christian poets as the bearer of a key; but the earliest use of the actual word *claviger* for St. Peter appears to be in a letter of Felix II, bishop of Rome, A.D. 355–358, who writes of "the authority of this holy See and of our teacher Peter, the key-bearer."[2] Again, Anastasius II, bishop of Rome (A.D. 496–498), describes St. Peter as "the blessed key-bearer of the heavenly Jerusalem";[3] and in Arator's poem of the sixth century there is the sentence: "The ethereal key-bearer sees heaven open."[4] In later centuries and throughout the Middle Ages the title *claviger* for St. Peter was commonly used.

His position as key-bearer gave exceptional prestige to the bishop of the city of Rome, who claimed to be his successor. The keys, generally two in number, became the sign of the Roman bishop and symbols of an authority, at first moral or spiritual, derived from the interpretation then accepted of the meaning of the words in St. Matthew's Gospel: "To thee (Peter) I will give the keys of the kingdom of heaven." What the words originally meant in the Greek to the man who first wrote them down, it is impossible to discuss here; but clearly they were intended to refer to the words of the prophet Isaiah (Isaiah xxii. 22)—"the key of the house of David will I lay upon his shoulders; so he shall open and no one shall shut; and he shall shut and no one shall open."[5]

[1] Bede, *H.E.*, iii, 25.

[2] "Illi qui ab eis perperam excommunicati aut damnati fuerunt, auctoritate huius sanctae sedis et beati praeceptoris nostri clavigeri Petri potestate solvuntur atque restituantur." *Pat. Lat.*, vol. 13, col. 22.

[3] Ep. 2: ad Clodaveum Francorum regem (A.D. 497). "Coelestis Jerusalem beatus claviger."

[4] "Claviger aetherius coelum conspexit apertum." *Pat. Lat.*, vol. 68, col. 166.

[5] Compare Rev. iii. 7. Again a reference to a person of authority, not a gate-keeper, although the reference is to an open door. The best study of the scriptural sources is still G. E. Steitz, *Der Neutest. Begriff der Schlüsselgewart*, S. und K., 1866.

These words of the prophet definitely refer to a person called in the Authorized Version a "Treasurer." The key is the symbol of the authority of the majordomo, or chief of the palace of an Oriental king. His authority is described in St. Matthew's Gospel and in Isaiah as that of "binding" and "loosing," or, in modern language, shutting and opening. But the keys of a chief official in a palace are not the keys of doors or gates of a kingdom, but of treasure-chambers and treasure-chests. A city may have gates and keys, but not a kingdom. The authority of the chief of the palace is shown, not in the function of porter or door-keeper, but in his function of treasurer and archivist. A porter or door-keeper is a minor official. Thus, even if the keys of St. Matthew's Gospel do indicate authority of some kind, they are by no means necessarily connected with doors or gates. If the kingdom of heaven has keys, it does not follow that it has doors. In the book of *Revelation* however, we read of the "keys" of hell and death (Rev. i. 18) and also of the "door of heaven" (Rev. iv. 1). The problem of chief interest here is how the holder of the "keys" of authority in the Church came to be regarded as a gate-keeper or porter in the skies—certainly not a position of great authority, either in Oriental Courts or in the Christian ecclesiastical tradition. How did an apostle come to be regarded merely as an *ostiarius* or janitor in the skies? The answer is that the Christian *claviger*, St. Peter, took over the functions in Rome of the pre-Christian *claviger* and janitor of heaven, the god Janus. Probably, owing to the transference of the god's keys to the Saint, the Saint came to be believed to have his tomb in the field under the hill sacred to Janus "in the temple of Apollo," that is to say, in the sanctuary of Janus, as the sun-god, who opened the gates of the sky at sunrise and sunset.

The identification of the god and the apostle probably took place at some time between the middle of the third and the beginning of the fifth century. It is one example of the frequent transference of functions from non-Christian gods or heroes to Christian saints. A similar transference occurs in the history of religion whenever there is a transition from one form of doctrine or ritual to another. In Rome itself there is an example of transference when the gods of the Greek Olympus came to be identified with old Roman divinities about two centuries before the Christian era. Thus, Mars or Mavors, an old vegetation god, who guarded cattle, was confused with the Greek Ares, a youthful adventurer; Venus, a sex-impulse in cattle, was improved by connection with Aphrodite, the love born of the foam of the sea at dawn; and Minerva, the Roman cunning in war, was furbished up to look like Athena, the Greek builder and keeper of cities. In the transference, therefore, of functions and character from gods and heroes to saints in the early years of Christianity in the West, a similar process was at work.

The authority of the Roman See, which is derived from the "power of the keys," had its source not only in a certain interpretation of a gospel text, but also in the growth in the city of Rome itself of the legend of St. Peter. First, it is important to note that, according to the *Liber Pontificalis*, Peter was buried in "the temple of Apollo." The *Liber Pontificalis*, however, does not say that St. Peter was so buried immediately after his death. Indeed it is quite clear from the same book (under Cornelius, A.D. 251–253) that in the middle of the third century the bodies of St. Peter and St. Paul were in the catacombs; and, as the book says, "the blessed bishop Cornelius took the body of blessed Peter the apostle and placed it near the spot where he was crucified, among the bodies of the saints in the Temple of Apollo in Golden Mountain in the Vatican palace of Nero, 29th of June."[1] The traditional belief identifies the place in an area near the Vatican hill, outside the city of Rome, by the road which ran beside the circus of Nero. There, under the canopy of the high altar of the present St. Peter's, are early Christian tombs. But it has seemed strange, even to Roman Catholic scholars, that St. Peter should have been buried in a temple or in the temple precincts. Excavations, however, have shown that in this district there was a temple of the Mother of the Gods, whose worship was closely connected with that of the Sun or Apollo.[2] The spot

---

[1] Duchesne in his edition of the *Liber Pontificalis* assumes that the entry under "Cornelius" refers to a *return* of the body to the Vatican tomb. But there is no indication in the text that it had been originally buried there.

[2] Inscriptions in *C.I.L.*, vi, 497–504. See Frazer, *Adonis, Attis and Osiris*, p. 230. The Emperor Heliogabalus destroyed tombs in this district in order to drive his chariot there.

traditionally believed to be the burial-place of St. Peter was certainly connected for many centuries, even after the beginning of the fifth century, with sun-worship. Indeed, there are two definite complaints from Christian bishops that Christians visiting the tomb of St. Peter, continued to practice the rituals or festivities connected with sun-worship. In the minds of the populace, confused perhaps by the transition from Paganism to Christianity, from Apollo to Christ, it was not very clear which was which. Thus, Pope Leo I, in his sermon for Christmas Day, writes: "Even certain Christians think that they are acting religiously when, before they enter the basilica of St. Peter, which is dedicated to the one living and true God, having mounted the steps which go up to the platform of the upper square, turning their bodies to the rising sun, with bowed heads they bend forward in honour of the splendid sun. We regret greatly that this should occur, partly through ignorance, partly in the spirit of paganism; because, although perhaps they pay reverence to the creator of the glorious sun rather than to the sun, which is created, nevertheless this kind of ritual must be avoided, which, when found among us Christians, will make the man who has left the worship of the gods, keep part of his old opinion as probably true, since it is common to both the Christian and the impious."[1]

It should be noticed that the basilica of St. Peter is dedicated primarily not to St. Peter but to Christ as Saviour, the successor of the Sun-God who gave his name to the Lord's Day, Sunday; and that the tomb of St. Peter was evidently connected in the earlier part of the fifth century with the worship of the sun. More than three hundred years passed; and the same kind of sun-worship was connected with the tomb of St. Peter in the Vatican when St. Boniface wrote his letter in A.D. 742 to complain to Pope Zachary about it. He wrote: "Certain private persons, Alamanni, Bavarians or Franks, if they see something done in Rome which we forbid, think that it is allowed by the bishops, and dispute our condemnation. For example, they say they have seen every year in Rome, at the church of St. Peter, by day or night, at the beginning of the

---

[1] See the text in Appendix to this chapter.

Kalends of January, according to pagan custom, dances in the squares, pagan cries and songs, and tables laden with food day or night, while no one will provide from his own house fire or food, or any other help to his neighbour. They say they have seen there women, with head-dresses or bows on the arms and legs, in the pagan manner, offering themselves for sale to others. All this, which is seen there by unspiritual and foolish men, hampers our work here in preaching and doctrine. Of such things the apostle complains: 'You mark the days and the seasons; I fear that I have laboured among you in vain.' And St. Augustine said: 'For whoever believes in head-bands and other charms, even if he fasts, prays, or gives alms—it will be useless for him, so long as he does not give up this sacrilege.' But if your Fatherhood had forbidden in the city of Rome these pagan rites, it would be a great advantage to you and to us in the teaching of the Church."[1]

Pope Zachary replied in a letter dated April 1, 743, not denying that these festivities did take place, but saying that they had been condemned. He writes: "As for the Kalends of January and the other charms, head-dresses and incantations, or the ceremonies which you say have been carried on in the pagan manner at St. Peter's or in Rome, these we think hateful to us and to all Christians, as God has said (Levit. xix. 26): 'Ye shall not eat anything with the blood: neither shall ye use enchantments, nor practise augury'; and again, Scripture says (Num. xxiii. 23): 'Surely there is no enchantment with Jacob, neither is there any divination with Israel . . .' and because by the suggestion of the devil these things flourished again, we have forbidden them from the day on which the divine clemency appointed us to take the place of the apostle."[2] Clearly the basilica in the Vatican, dedicated to Christ, was connected with ceremonies of sun-worship as lately as the eighth century.

It may be assumed, as it is agreed by all scholars, that the date of the birth of Christ was adopted from that of "the lord," the "unconquered sun" (Mithras) and with the opening of the new

---

[1] Boniface, Ep. 50, *M.G.H.*; see extract at the end of this chapter.
[2] Ibid., Ep. 51, *M.G.H.*

year in the month sacred to Janus, the ancient sun-god. Apollo, in whose temple St. Peter was buried, was recognized in the early fifth century as Janus. Thus in the *Saturnalia* Macrobius writes: "Some think that Janus is the same as Apollo and Diana, and that both Powers are expressed in this one. As Nigidius says: 'Apollo is worshipped among the Greeks under the name of Gate-Keeper, and his altars are placed at doors to show his power over exit and entry . . . but among us the name of Janus shows that he presides over all doors (*Janua*) which is like the Greek θυραῖος, for he is depicted with a key and a rod, as the guard of all gates, and the ruler of streets. . . . Janus some believe to be the sun, and therefore the genuine power over both the gates of heaven, who in the morning opens for the day, and in the evening closes. . . . As if he brought to the Gods the prayers of suppliants through his gates, and was Janitor of heaven and hell.' "[1]

Thus, the keys of Janus are the keys of the gates of the sky, out of which the sun comes in the morning, and into which he goes in the evening. Janus is the sun-god in the Vatican temple of "Apollo"; and St. Peter, believed to be buried there, has inherited not only his keys but also his rod; for in the basilica, even to-day, one may see the rod of Janus beside the confessional of the Canon Penitentiary. This rod, or whip, is still used to touch the penitent on the shoulder or head, thus conferring an indulgence.[2] At the Vatican basilica also is a sacred door (*Porta Sancta*) like that of Janus, which is kept bricked-up, except in years of jubilee. Janus, as Frazer has shown, was not originally the god of doors in general, but only of the doors in the sky.[3] He is the great sun-god "Dianus," as the moon is Diana. He is the oldest of the gods, first to be mentioned in prayer.[4] Ovid says that "he holds the rod in his right hand and the key in his left";[5] that "he presides over the gates of

---

[1] Macrobius, *Saturnalia*, i, 5. See the text in the Appendix to this chapter.
[2] Cardinal Lepicier (*Indulgences*, Eng. ed., 1928, p. 187) says that the rod is derived from the *ferula*, by which the lictor freed the slave. No evidence is given for this belief.
[3] See Frazer's edition of the *Fasti*, vol. ii, p. 91. Frazer notes that St. Augustine (*De civ. Dei*, vi. 7) does not mention Janus among the gods of the house-door.
[4] Ovid, *Fasti*, i. 171.
[5] Ibid., i, 99: "ille tenens baculum dextra clavemque sinistra."

PLATE 6.—ADORATION OF MAGI

Virgin and Child (Mosaic in Church of S. Maria Maggiore in Rome, *c.* A.D. 435)—
Referred to page 529

heaven," and that approach is made to all the other gods through him "who guards their thresholds" (*limina*).[1] The phrase *ad limina* was used, at least from the fifth century and throughout the Middle Ages, to indicate a visit to St. Peter's in the Vatican. And the Vatican hill itself was known as the Janiculum, the valley beneath it being also sacred to Janus.[2] His is the first of the twelve months, whose first day was celebrated at St. Peter's. It is also worth noting that in the earliest Christian representations of St. Peter, as, for example, in the mosaic of SS. Cosmas and Damian in Rome, St. Peter does not carry a key or keys.[3] Not until about the eighth century are the keys in his hand the invariable sign in representations of St. Peter. In some cases he carries one large key, but usually two, which are no doubt intended to represent the two doors, one of heaven, the other of hell—which take the place in Christianity of the two doors of the sky, at dawn and evening. Gregory the Great, as bishop of Rome, often sent with his letters a key made from filings of what he believed to be the chains of St. Peter; and great play was made throughout the Middle Ages, not only by Popes, with "keys" as signs of authority. The "keys" of Jerusalem were sent by the Patriarch of that See to Charles the Great in A.D. 801; and the "keys" of cities were presented to conquerors. But in the sky the keys have only one meaning. They indicate from the fourth to the fifteenth century the authority of a Porter, St. Peter, still living up above, to allow souls to enter. Janus, according to Macrobius, is the janitor of the world above the sky and that below the earth; and at the beginning of the ninth century, Paulinus, patriarch of Aquileia, in his hymn on the chair of St. Peter, calls St. Peter "the janitor of heaven." The "janitor" of a Roman house being a slave, was sometimes chained to his post, as St. Peter was chained in Rome. In the general confusion of rituals and beliefs which occurred during the centuries at the beginning of the Christian era, the legend of St. Peter as the gate-keeper of heaven gradually developed.

---

[1] Ovid, *Fasti*, i, 173: "ut possis aditum per me qui limina servo Ad quoscunque voles" inquit "habere deos."

[2] Horace, *Odes*, i, 20, 7. "Mons Vaticanus." Ovid, *Fasti*, i, 245. "Collis … quem vulgus nomine nostro nuncupat."   [3] See the reproduction facing page 224.

But other Roman traditions assisted, besides that of sun-worship. The feast of SS. Peter and Paul (June 29th) unites the two apostles, one as key-bearer, and the other as teacher. But the day is obviously felt to belong to St. Peter primarily, as the chief ceremony takes place in his basilica at the Vatican; and the day after, amends are made to St. Paul, as it is the feast of the "commemoration" of St. Paul. St. Peter himself is regarded as the special power protecting Rome, as Procopius informs us in the sixth century.[1] The two apostles together, however, are regarded in the Roman tradition as similar to the two consuls, the two praetors, the two tribunes, and, finally, the two Augusti. St. Jerome calls SS. Peter and Paul "generals of the army of Christ";[2] and in the hymn for their feast, they are referred to as Princes (Principes).[3] It will be remembered that twin-worship is implied in the earliest legends of Rome in the story of Romulus and Remus, and of the twin brethren who fought for the Romans at the battle of Lake Regillus. The "twins" of Christian Rome are Peter and Paul; and there is a hint of difficulties arising from the old legends in the condemnation at the end of the fourth century of the belief that one of the apostles suffered martyrdom a year after the other, although on the same day. In twin-worship one twin is usually regarded as divine, the other as mortal; and in the legend of Castor and Pollux, each takes a turn of life every alternate year.[4] It was more seemly for the Roman Church to believe that both the apostles were martyred at exactly the same moment. Again, the feast of St. Peter in the Roman Church on June 29th, is the same as the feast of Romulus as Quirinus, the founder of the city. Pope Leo I, in his sermon for that day, contrasts Peter and Paul with Romulus and Remus, Peter being founder of the new Rome to which, according to Leo, he was sent on the day of Pentecost, as to the chief city of the world.[5] But in the earliest calendar of the Roman Church now sur-

---

[1] Procopius, Bell. Goth., v, 235. [2] Jerome, Ep. 46.
[3] The words are: O Roma felix, quae duorum principum
                     Es consecrata glorioso sanguine, . . .

[4] It may be assumed that the Roman institution of "doubles" for officials (consuls, etc.) is a relic of twin-worship, and not a political idea, as Mommsen supposed.
[5] Leo I, Sermo 82, In Natali Apost. P. et P. See text at end of this chapter.

viving, the feast of St. Peter (June 29th) is held in the catacombs, under the date A.D. 258. And the place of his burial there is the shrine of an unknown Christian martyr, named Quirinus. St. Peter has, therefore, also inherited something from Romulus.

The legends connecting St. Peter with Rome seem to have been fully developed by the beginning of the fifth century. But such legends continued to grow in the centuries between the fifth and the ninth. They had the effect of separating Christian Rome—the Rome of the martyrs and the pilgrims, whose chief citizens are now living in the sky—from pagan Rome—the Rome of the Caesars and the persecutors of Christianity who are now in hell.[1] The influence emanating from the tomb of St. Peter gave to the bishops of Rome, who claimed to be his successors, not only the power of the keys or authority on earth, but also a direct connection with the key-bearer at the gate of heaven. Thus, in the collection of Papal letters, known as the *Codex Carolinus,* Pope Stephen III's letter to the king of the Franks is written in the name of St. Peter.

The power of the See of Rome was greatly increased by the belief that other great bishoprics had been founded by preachers sent to them from Rome by St. Peter himself. The belief of the fourth century, recorded by Eusebius, expressed a tradition that St. Mark, who was supposed to be closely connected with St. Peter, had been sent by him to be bishop of Alexandria.[2] And the See of Alexandria was from early times recognized as a patriarchate equal in status to those of Antioch and Rome. Among the Latin Churches the predominance of St. Peter was supported by the tradition that the first bishop of Arles, St. Trophimus, had been

[1] All the Emperors before Constantine were in hell, except Trajan who was granted a special relief by God at the request of Gregory I, on the understanding that no further such request should be made. This appears to be a later medieval story. For legends, see Graf, *Roma nella memoria del medio evo.*

[2] Another Mark, that is to say, Mark Antony, had a temple built to him as a god, in Alexandria. This was finished as a temple of Augustus, when Antony fell. Four hundred years later, Eudocia, wife of Theodosius II, noticed that the people of Alexandria still celebrated the death of Mark Antony on August 1st. She therefore commanded that they should celebrate on that day the delivery of St. Peter from prison.

sent there from Rome by St. Peter.[1] St. Apollinaris, traditionally believed to have been the first bishop of Ravenna, was also said to have been sent there from Rome by St. Peter. The prestige of the See of Peter continued to grow throughout the Middle Ages owing to the embellishments added by the medieval imagination to the traditions of early Christianity.

The Prestige of Christian Rome

The process by which the bishop of Rome became the medieval Pope was long and gradual. It had begun, no doubt, before the beginning of the fifth century, because the bishop of Rome was the only bishop among the western Churches who claimed to be the direct successor of an apostle as founder of his See; and the bishop of Rome was also the only patriarch of the Churches in the western world, while in the East there were patriarchs of Antioch, Alexandria and Jerusalem, tracing their authority back to the earliest days of Christianity. Again, the removal of the capital of the Empire from Rome to Constantinople by Constantine, the first Christian Emperor, undoubtedly made the bishop of old Rome the most important figure in the city. Even when there was an Emperor reigning in the West, he did not use Rome as his capital; and the name of Rome, although officially adapted to the uses of imperial authority in the new capitals, either at Constantinople or at Ravenna, came to be associated much more realistically with the episcopal authority which actually had its seat in Rome. Indeed, the policy of the bishops of Rome before the fifth century, although it was by no means clearly aimed at securing the authority over all the Latin Churches which was attained in the ninth century, was certainly affected by the feeling that a bishop of so great a city was exceptional among bishops. The growth of the legend of St. Peter itself may have been partly due to the conscious policy of bishops of Rome, who sought quite reasonably to increase their own prestige.

Before the days of Constantine the bishops of Rome had made

---

[1] Zosimus, bishop of Rome, in a letter of A.D. 417 (*Pat. Lat.*, 20, Ep. i), and the bishops of the Province of Arles in a letter to Leo I (*Pat. Lat.*, 54), express this tradition.

two important advances towards the achievement of the authority later embodied in the medieval Papacy. In the first place, the See of Rome had a generally acknowledged moral prestige among all the Christian Churches. Even in the East the status of a See, which was believed, after about the second century, to have been founded by St. Peter, was acknowledged to be of outstanding importance. But it must be remembered that the See of Antioch was also supposed to have been founded by St. Peter, and the See of Alexandria by Peter's disciple, Mark. All these, therefore—Rome, Antioch and Alexandria—were equally the Sees of Peter, as Gregory the Great asserted.[1] The See of Rome, in addition, had the prestige of a long line of martyrs, which was believed to begin with the Princes of the Apostles, Peter and Paul. At the end of the second century the moral prestige of the See of Rome allowed the Roman bishops to claim recognition for the practice, rituals and beliefs of their Church. Thus Victor, bishop of Rome (A.D. 188–198), condemned an early version of the theory that Christ was an adopted son of God, and attempted to enforce elsewhere the practice of the Church of Rome with regard to the date of Easter. The moral prestige of the Roman See was, no doubt, great enough to secure the acceptance of the views of its bishops in most cases, even among the eastern Churches, and certainly among the Churches of the West, which made no claim to apostolic foundation. But moral prestige is not administrative power, still less the power to legislate or to define doctrine for the whole Church.

In matters of doctrine, however, the See of Rome had acquired, even before the days of Constantine, some exceptional consideration among the Churches—derived, no doubt, from the interpretation at that date placed upon the words of Christ to St. Peter: "I have prayed for thee that thy faith fail not: and when thou art converted strengthen thy brethren."[2] But when, under Constantine, the Christian Churches were given a new position in the Roman Empire, the See of Rome appears to have acquired even more moral authority. It is well known that Constantine and his immediate successors made many efforts to reconcile the differences

[1] Gregory, Ep. vii, 37. *M.G.H.*   [2] *Gospel of St. Luke* xxii. 32.

of practice and belief among Christians. The Donatists in the West, and the Arians in the East, were at first the chief obstacles to unity. Constantine attempted to use a synod in Rome for solving the Donatist difficulty (A.D. 313); but the attempt failed. He attempted, more successfully, at the Council of Nicaea in the East, and without special regard to Rome, to deal with the Arian difficulty. But towards the end of the century, the Church of the city of Rome was declared by imperial Authority to be the model of doctrinal purity. In a Rescript of A.D. 370 of the Emperors Valens, Valentinian and Gratian, addressed to Damasus, bishop of Rome, and in another Rescript, of A.D. 380, of the Emperors Gratian, Valentinian II and Theodosius, the true religion is declared to be that of the See of Rome, of Peter and his successor, Damasus.[1] Whether an imperial decree has theological efficacy in matters of doctrine, may be regarded as doubtful; but evidently, just before the fifth century, the imperial Authorities, searching in all directions for some means of making Christians agree among themselves, accepted the See of Rome as an authority on doctrine. Here again, however, it must be observed that no such power is implied as the medieval Papacy acquired. The bishop of Rome and the Church of the imperial city may have preserved the purest form of the Christian tradition; but it had, at that date, no power to enforce its teaching, its ritual or its discipline upon other Churches.

Unity of Doctrine

The authority of the See of Rome in matters of doctrine, as expressed in the imperial Rescripts, must not be misunderstood. The Emperors were not concerned with what philosophers call "truth," but with unity. Neither officials nor clergy in the West were philosophers. They were practical men whose aim was to prevent the dissensions and riots which were caused by disagreements among Christians. It is somewhat unfair to them to state the contrast too clearly; but it is one thing that everyone should believe or at least repeat the same creed, and quite another that the creed should be a statement of truth. In the Greek Churches theological

[1] *Cod. Theod.*, xvi, v. 2. See above, Chapter IV, p. 166.

discussions were vigorous and concerned mainly with the meaning of certain texts. In the West, and especially in the Church of Rome, the chief interest of the more vigorous clergy was not the correctness or truth of an interpretation of texts, but the adherence of as many as possible to the same formula. Rome stood for unity; and adherence to what was said by the Roman Church was the best possible test, in the eyes of the civil Authorities, for the avoidance of heresy or schism. For practical politics, it did not matter whether all were wrong, so long as all said the same thing.

From the point of view of the western clergy, also, it was the unity of the Christian Churches, not the correctness of their beliefs, which mattered most; although clearly the belief that each section favoured was assumed by it to be correct. Thus, the two famous phrases of St. Augustine, "Outside the Church is no salvation," and "the whole world is safe in its judgement,"[1] are expressions, not of a test of "truth," in the language of philosophers, but of a single allegiance. In the eyes of St. Augustine, the chief offence of the Donatists was that they disagreed with the greater number of the Christian Churches about practice or discipline with regard to baptism. Obviously, indeed, the idea that the whole world, or even the majority, are safe in their judgement, makes no sense at all, if it is a test of truth. A proposition is not proved to be true by counting the heads of those who believe it; and although so confused a thinker as St. Augustine may have thought a popular belief necessarily true, that was not what concerned him most. The other typical writer of the West in the early fifth century, Vincent of Lerins, expresses the same attitude towards correctness of belief. In his famous phrase—"the Catholic Faith is what is held always, everywhere and by all"[2]—obviously Vincent did not imply that what he believed had been believed "always," in the sense including the centuries before the Christian era, nor "everywhere" in the sense that there were no human beings outside the Roman

---

[1] Extra ecclesiam nulla salus, is in Cyprian, Ep. 73; and in another version (*Extra ecclesiam catholicam Totum potest praeter salutem*) in Augustine, *Sermo ad Caesar. Eccl. Pleb.*, securus judicat orbis terrarum. Augustine, *Contra epist. Parmen.*, lib. iii, p. 24.

[2] "Quod semper, quod ubique, quod ab omnibus." Vincentius Lerin. *Commonitorium*, ii, 3.

world, nor "by all" in the sense that every Christian agreed with all others. He meant that the "Catholic faith" was what held together those who agreed with him in his corner of southern Gaul and such other places as he knew. The "whole world," in the minds of St. Augustine and of Vincent of Lerins, was the population of the countries round the Mediterranean, with the possible addition of those in Britain. And what held them together was "fides," or "trustworthiness." Indeed, the word "fides" had hardly yet, in the fifth century, changed its meaning from the original Roman idea of "faithfulness" to the later medieval idea of "faith." The "*catholica*" *fides* was therefore the faithfulness or allegiance of men, scattered throughout the only part of the earth that counted, to one system of ecclesiastical teaching and discipline. It was not so much the correctness of their views as their reliability, which made the members of the Catholic Church, in the eyes of Augustine and of Vincent, one body of the "faithful." The "fideles" were not necessarily those who believed a creed, but those who were trustworthy in a single allegiance. In the same sense, in the eighth century, Charles the Great used the word "fideles," meaning all who were loyal to him. "Infidels" were those who did not belong to that community. The "faith," therefore, which was established as doctrine by the Roman Church, was as much a rule of allegiance as a statement of belief.

Clearly, it cannot be denied that the principle upon which the test of loyalty rested was the assumption that morality or religious experience depended upon the acceptance of a certain form of cosmology. And this acceptance might be called belief in the sense in which the word "believe" (*credo*) is used in the creeds. This ancient Roman tradition was expressed by the non-Christian Cicero, in the words: "If we reject devotion to the gods, good faith (*fides*) and all the associations of human life, and the best of virtues, justice, may also disappear."[1] Thus *fides*, in the sense of trustworthiness, is thought to be dependent upon a creed. But even a creed is not necessarily a statement of "truths." It is mainly an expression of reliance or confidence. Thus the phrase "credo in

Cicero, *Nat. Deor.*, i, 2.

unum deum" meant "I place confidence in one god as opposed to many," and not "I believe it to be true that there is one god."[1]

Another aspect of the unity for which the Church of Rome was conceived to stand is perhaps even less intelligible in modern times. It depends upon the close connection between creed and ritual, in the centuries from the fifth to the ninth. Here again the Greek Churches, or at any rate their chief scholars, differed from the Churches of the West. The Latin creeds and the theological language of the West were translations from the Greek—in most cases inexact, and always misleading. But the recitation of the creeds in Latin had become parts of the ritual in early Christian Churches; and it was of the essence of a ritual, especially in the Roman tradition, that the formulas recited should be always the same. In a well-established ritual, the meaning of the formula is of minor importance; and the truth of the statements contained in it of no importance at all. The magical efficacy of the formula, like that of the acts performed, was generally believed to be the chief reason for adhering to it. But even the more subtle minds of the fifth and later centuries were not concerned with abstract "truth." They felt the unity of the congregation expressed in the whole of a ritual or ceremony and in the creed as part of that ceremony.

The Apostles' Creed in its earliest version was probably a formula of the Roman Church, used in the ceremony of baptism. The Nicene Creed, originally a formula for baptism, probably in the Church of Jerusalem, adopted by the Council of Nicaea (A.D. 325) and often amended in Greek by later councils, was inserted in a Latin version in the Canon of the Mass, with the much later addition of the phrase "Filioque." This insertion has nothing corresponding to it in the Greek creeds of the council, but was forced upon the Roman Church at the end of the eighth century by the Frankish king, Charles the Great, and his bishops. The "Athanasian" Creed, written in southern Gaul, probably at Lerins, in the fifth century, and intended for chanting or for instruction in a "catechism," was used as part of a ritual, at latest at the beginning of

[1] Credit is not credulity. "Credo" means primarily "I rely upon." It is a translation of the original Christian πίστις, which meant "trust" in God.

the eighth century. All these creeds, therefore, are not primarily expressions of a philosophy or theory, but of the unity of worshippers in a Church. That is the doctrinal unity for which the Church of the city of Rome and its bishops came to stand. Belief was dependent upon ritual or practice; or as the bishop of Rome, Celestine I (A.D. 422–432), wrote to the bishops of Gaul: "The law of prayer should establish the law of belief."[1]

Again, it may be noticed that the heresies of the western world were quite different in their subject-matter from those of the East. In the East there was disagreement about the nature of Deity. Arianism, Nestorianism and Monophysitism were all concerned with the relation between Christ and the Father. But in the West heresies, which hardly existed before the fifth century, were concerned mainly with questions of Christian practice or morals. The Donatists argued about the second baptism of those Christians who had lapsed from the faith. Priscillian, at the end of the fourth century, and his followers appear to have favoured a rigid asceticism, and avoidance of all that seemed to them "material," such as marriage. Pelagius, at the beginning of the fifth century, was concerned mainly with the idea that a good life and not a divine decision was the basis for salvation; but such a doctrine would obviously tend to undermine the belief in the efficacy of the powers of the clergy. These heresies which concerned practice and not theory, were opposed by men chiefly concerned with preserving among all Christians the same rules of life and traditional rituals. The most obvious danger was a division of the Churches, destroying the unity of Christians as the unity of the Empire had been destroyed by the barbarian kingdoms. In the West, therefore, and especially under the influence of the Roman bishops, unity of doctrine meant the suppression of sectional organizations under independent leadership within the Christian Churches.

A Summary

The tendencies which went to form the medieval Papacy were

[1] Celestine I, *Epist.* 21, *ad Episcopos Gall.*, *Pat. Lat.*, 50, col. 535, "ut legem credendi lex statuat supplicandi."

in full flood at the beginning of the fifth century. The streams of pre-Christian and Christian tradition which met in Rome had by then become one united force. All that remained was to canalize it in a conscious policy. But before describing the growth of that policy it may be useful to state in a summary form what has been so far concluded. The prestige of pre-Christian republican and imperial Rome still remained in the early fifth century strong enough to fill the barbarians with awe, and to cause a thrill of admiration in all who saw the shining temples and palaces of that older world. Four centuries after Augustus, the buildings he had begun, and other monuments of marble and bronze, still glittered under that sun which saw nothing in all its journeys that was not Roman.[1] The legends of the older gods and of the great Romans of the past were still in the minds of men; and these gave power to the name of Rome. Pre-Christian Rome survived in the memory of medieval Europe. The elements of comedy in the medieval attempt to perpetuate pre-Christian Roman titles and customs should not be allowed to obscure the solemn earnestness of those who called themselves consuls or tribunes. Pope Leo IV in A.D. 853 appointed Alfred, afterwards king of Wessex, a "consul," and dressed him in what was then believed to be a consular costume, when he was visiting Rome at the age of five years. The little boy was girded with a sword and covered with a purple cloak.[2] In later ages leaders of rebellion against the temporal power of the Popes, such as Cola di Rienzi, called themselves tribunes. The muse of history introduced more comedy when the successor of St. Peter adopted the title of "Pontifex Maximus," which had been rejected by the Emperor Gratian as too obviously pagan. And comic relief has been afforded in modern tragedy by the more recent revival of the "Fasces" of republican Rome.

To this old store of legend and custom Christian Rome added the legend of St. Peter and the records of early Christian martyrs buried in the outskirts of the city. Christian Rome thus became

[1] Rutilius Nam., *De Reditu*, i, 57, addressing Rome:—
Volvitur ipse tibi, qui continet omnia Phoebus,
Eque tuis ortos in tua condit equos.
[2] See the note in Stevenson's ed. of Asser's *Life of Alfred*.

both the goal of pilgrimage and the source from which relics, more or less authentic, were brought to all parts of the First Europe. The Mohammedan invasions of the seventh century, which made pilgrimage to the Holy Land more difficult, therefore by accident increased the influence of the city of Rome. English kings laid down their crowns and came to spend their last years near the shrine of St. Peter. Hospices of the northern nations were established near that shrine for the comfort of the thousands of pilgrims, many of whom died, not unhappily, of the malaria and other diseases of medieval Rome. And in the ninth century, as Einhard candidly confesses, a lucrative trade and abundant fraud provided the northern nations with a large supply of Roman relics.[1]

Finally, the Roman spirit of order and unity and law survived the change from Republic to Empire and from Empire to Church, and made Rome appear, even in the Middle Ages, to be the natural source of authority in discipline and doctrine. Thus the unity of the First Europe, so deeply desired by the best men and women amid the conflicts and confusions of their time, seemed to depend upon the supremacy of Rome. It was of no importance that the actual city was in ruins and its people a remnant of quarrelsome ruffians. The Rome of the idealists in the First Europe was "the shadow of a great name,"[2] ghostly, as a shadow would be that lay across the road when the body that cast it had gone.

APPENDIX TO CHAPTER XII

TEXTS RELATING TO THE LEGEND OF ST. PETER

1. Macrobius, *Saturnalia* (Teubner, 1868).

(i, 5, page 40.) Sunt qui Janum eundem esse atque Apollinem et Dianam dicant et in hoc uno utriumque exprimi numen adfirment. Et enim sicut Nigidius quoque refert, apud Graecos Apollo colitur qui θυραῖος vocatur, eiusque aras ante foras suas celebrant, ipsum exitus et introitus demonstrantes potentem . . . sed apud nos Janum omnibus praeesse ianuis nomen ostendit; quod est simile θυραίῳ, nam et cum

[1] As in Einhard's story of his purchase of the relics of SS. Peter and Marcellinus.
[2] Lucan, *Pharsalia*, i, 135, magni nominis umbra.

clavi ac virga figuratur quasi omnium et portarum custos et rector viarum. . . . Janum quidam solem demonstrari volunt et ideo geminum quasi utriusque januae coelestis potentem qui exoriens aperiat diem, occidens claudat . . . quasi preces supplicium per portas suas ad deos ipse transmittat . . . quasi superum atque inferum janitorem.

2. Leo I, *Sermo*, 27, 4 (*Pat. Lat.*, 54).

Nonnulli etiam Christiani adeo se religiose facere putant ut priusquam ad B. Petri Basilicam quae uni Deo vivo et vero est dedicata perveniant, superatis gradibus quibus ad suggestum areae superioris ascenditur, converso corpore ad nascentem se solem reflectant et curvatis cervicibus, in honorem se splendidi orbis inclinent. Quod fieri partim ignorantiae vitio partim paganitatis spiritu, multum tabescimus et dolemus; quia etsi quidam forte creatorem potius pulchri luminis quam ipsum lumen quod est creatura venerantur abstinendum tamen est ab ipsa specie huius officii, quam cum in nostris invenit qui deorum cultum reliquit, nonne hanc secum partem opinionis vetustae tanquam probabilem retentabit quam Christianis et impiis viderit esse communem?

3. Boniface, Ep. 50.

Et quia carnales homines idiote, Alamanni vel Baivarii si iuxta Romanam urbem aliquid facere viderint ex his peccatis, quae nos prohibemus, licitum et concessum a sacerdotibus esse putant et nobis inproperium deputant, sibi scandalum vitae accipiunt. Sicut adfirmant se vidisse annis singulis in Romana urbe et iuxta ecclesiam sancti Petri in die vel nocte, quando Kalende Januarii intrant, paganorum consuetudine chorus ducere per plateas et adclamationes ritu gentilium et cantationes sacrilegas celebrare et mensas illa die vel nocte dapibus onerare et nullum de domo sua vel ignem vel ferramentum vel aliquid commodi vicino suo prestare velle. Dicunt quoque se vidisse ibi mulieres pagano ritu filacteria et ligaturas et in brachiis et cruris ligatus habere et publice ad vendendum venales ad comparandum aliis offerre. Quae omnia si quod ibi a carnalibus et insipientibus videntur, nobis hic inproperium et impedimentum predicationis et doctrine perficiunt. De talibus ait apostolus increpans: Dies observatis et tempora: timeo ne sine causa laboraverim in vobis. Et sanctus Augustinus dixit: Nam qui filacteriis et aliis quibuslibet auguriis crediderit, etsi ieiunet, etsi oret, etsi iugiter ad ecclesiam currat, etsi largas elymosinas faciat, etsi corpusculum suum in omni adflictione cruciaverit, nihil ei proderit, quamdiu sacrilegia illa non relinquerit. Nam si istas paganias ibi paternitas vestra in Romana urbe prohibuerit, et sibi mercedem et nobis maximum profectum in doctrina ecclesiastica proficerit.

CHAPTER XIII

THE IMPERIAL CHURCH

Conscious policy during the centuries from the fifth to the ninth eventually used the tendencies in the Roman tradition for the establishment of the medieval Papacy and the imperial Church. But it must not be imagined that such policy was designed by scheming priests who were anxious to increase their own wealth and power. Nor must it be supposed that there was one consistent policy of succeeding bishops of Rome, which was directed to a single clearly conceived end. The policy which eventually established the medieval Papacy was in fact a succession of steps, each of which was intended to overcome a different obstacle. Thus, in the fifth century the bishops of Rome had to face the situation which was the result of the collapse of the Roman Empire in western Europe. In the sixth century their successors had to find a way for their own and other Latin Churches by which barbarian kings could be induced to leave their Catholic subjects in peace. In the seventh and eighth centuries the bishops of Rome directed the missionary efforts for the conversion of pagans in the North; and in the ninth century, when the medieval Papacy was first clearly to be seen, the Roman Church was compelled to seek defence from the Saracens and the northern barbarians by appeals to the kings of the Franks. Thus, policy at every step was intended to solve particular problems; and not until the ninth century did it clearly point to the establishment of an imperial Church under the dictatorship of the bishop of Rome.

The medieval Papacy first clearly appears in the letters of Pope Leo I (A.D. 440–461).[1] A Roman of the Romans in birth and spirit,

---

[1] The most recent history covering the period is Caspar's *Geschichte des Papsttums.* vol. i, to the death of Leo I (A.D. 461); vol. ii, to the death of Zachary, about A.D. 730.

entirely ignorant of Greek, trained as an official in the Roman clergy, his hard and narrow intelligence was combined with vigour in policy and forceful influence upon the civil Authorities. In the making of the Papacy his work was important, first, in his definite exposition of doctrine; secondly, in the assertion of the supremacy of the See of Rome in prestige and in its authority for the settlement of disputes among Latin bishops; and thirdly, in his relations with the Emperor. His exposition of doctrine must be considered first, and the other aspects of his work in later sections of this chapter.

After a century and a half of officially recognized Christianity, he was the last bishop of Rome in an imperial Church, in the old sense of that phrase—that is to say, a religious organization of the Roman Empire. In his day the fundamental assumption of St. Augustine in his *City of God* still corresponded to reality. The Empire was Christian. The bishops were officials within a single Christian State, superior in moral authority and yet subject to a single civil power. Thus, Leo I as bishop of Rome went out with a senatorial embassy to placate Attila, and again, later, attempted to persuade the Vandals to spare Rome. He was protecting the Empire as well as the Church. But fifteen years after the death of Leo, the Empire had lost all its western provinces. Arian kings or barbarian tribes ruled Italy, Gaul, Spain and Africa, and in the Latin West the old form of an imperial Church had ceased to exist. Leo could not foresee that collapse. His mind was still that of a Roman in the universal Empire.

Doctrine and the Papacy

In securing for the See of Rome authority in matters of doctrine, Leo touches upon three heresies which belonged chiefly to the western or Latin Churches. Against Priscillian, he writes that the civil Authorities were correct in executing the heretic—"for they saw that all care for honour, all bonds of marriage, would be destroyed, and divine as well as human law undermined, if they allowed men of that sort to live with such a doctrine."[1] The same

[1] Leo M., Ep. xv, *Pat. Lat.*, vol. 54, col. 679.

letter, to Turribius, bishop of Astorga in northern Spain, makes a summary of all Priscillian's doctrines, on the Trinity, on astrology and on asceticism. The chief offence of Priscillian was that he had established a sect or following of his own. Of Pelagius, he wrote that the theory of salvation being dependent upon moral excellence, would imply that God was compelled by human acts to grant future happiness.[1] This obviously would be inconsistent with the supreme dictatorship of the Deity; and although Pelagius founded no sect, the spread of his doctrine would have weakened the power of the clergy and the sacraments as instruments of salvation. But Leo was most angry with the Manichaeans, many of whom seem to have fled to Rome after the Vandal invasion of Africa. He writes with extreme horror of the practices of these heretics, and especially of their use of ceremonial sexual intercourse. But he is not concerned with abstract theory. It is the practice of a secret society which horrifies him. In his sermon on "the Fast," he describes the trial of some girl and boy and their supporters and bishops; and shows that all these lack modesty.[2]

The most striking controversy, however, of the period during which Leo was Pope, concerned the person of Christ. The question was whether the Jesus of the Gospels was really and entirely both a man and a God. In the eastern Churches, in which Semitic or non-Hellenic tendencies survived under the surface of the Greek tradition, there had always been a tendency to exalt the Godhead by separating all earthly and human elements from it. This tendency has already been touched upon in reference to the Arian kings.[3] The Nicene Council had decided that Christ was really God; but in the fifth century the problem whether he could be at the same time really a man, seems to have come into prominence in reference chiefly to his relationship with his mother. The theological or philosophical issues need not be discussed here; but it must be remembered that these issues did not concern merely the meaning of words, nor even the correctness of a theory, but also problems of ritual or worship. In so far as it was a question how Christ should

[1] Leo M., Ep. i, in *Pat. Lat.*, vol. 54, col. 595.
[2] Ibid., *Sermo*, xvi, 5, "adulescentulus vitiator puellae."
[3] See Chapter IV, p. 197.

be worshipped, it also affected the position and prestige of the clergy.

The issue eventually turned on the use of the word θεοτόκος (God-bearer), or "Mother of God," for the Virgin Mary. The Council of Ephesus in A.D. 431, nine years before Leo became Pope, had decided in favour of the title, thus establishing canonically the doctrine that Christ was really a man and the practice of the worship of his mother. In that year women were in control of the Roman Empire, both in the East and in the West. In the East, Pulcheria, a virgin, the sister of the Emperor Theodosius II, and in the West, Galla Placidia, the mother of the Emperor Valentinian III, were the dominant personalities in civil and religious policy. The exaltation, therefore, of the Virgin Mother of God was not altogether without its political aspects; and it is interesting to compare a medallion showing Galla Placidia wearing a nimbus, with a mosaic of the same date in St. Mary the Greater in Rome, showing the Mother of God, without a nimbus, holding Christ, wearing a nimbus. This mosaic is part of the decoration of the existing basilica erected by Sixtus III (A.D. 432–440) a few years after the Council of Ephesus, and then dedicated to Sancta Maria Mater Dei. It may also be remarked that the Council which acknowledged officially for the Virgin Mary the title "Mother of God" met at Ephesus, the city in which nearly four centuries before, Christianity was opposed by the cry—"Great is Diana of the Ephesians." This Diana was the Greek virgin Artemis, or the Roman Diana, in her connections with the moon, and also the Great Mother of the Gods.[1] Again, at the time of the Council, the tomb and the body of the Virgin were believed to be in Ephesus; and the meeting of the Fathers was held in her church.

---

[1] In later Christian art the Mother of God is connected with the moon. August 13th was the Roman feast of Diana at the full moon, a festival of slaves and the lower classes. The feast of the Assumption is on August 15th, and in the office for the feast in the Roman Breviary, the phrase is used "pulchra ut luna" (Ad Laudes). The legend of the earlier basilica (basilica Liberiana), on the site of S. Maria Maggiore, says that it was founded where snow appeared on August 5th. August 13th in the Roman Calendar was the feast of St. Hippolytus, who is said, in the Roman Breviary, to have been killed by being dragged behind horses. An earlier Hippolytus was one of the many youths loved by Diana of Nemi; and he also was killed by runaway horses.

The controversy continued, however, after Leo had become Pope. In A.D. 449 another Council met at Ephesus, which partially reversed the former decision; but this Council, in no way remarkably different from that which had preceded it, was later repudiated as unorthodox. And in A.D. 451 a new Council, at Chalcedon, returned to the doctrine of the former Council at Ephesus. At this Council of Chalcedon, a Treatise (*Tomus*) in the form of a letter from the bishop of Rome was read and accepted with acclamation by the assembled bishops as a correct statement of doctrine. The *Tomus*, indeed, became an authoritative document which gave prestige to the Roman Church, and was afterwards accepted as a correct statement of faith by the Churches of Italy, Gaul and Spain. The fourth Canon of the Council of Chalcedon decreed that "whoever does not accept the letter of the most holy bishop Leo, is anathema." And, at the end of the sixth century, Gregory the Great repeated the words in one of his letters—"if anyone presumes to say anything against the *Tomus* and the decision of Pope Leo of holy memory, let him be anathema."[1] The *Tomus* was also appointed to be read in Advent in later years in the "books of readings" (*lectionaria*) of the Vatican basilica and of some churches in Italy and Gaul.

This is not the place to discuss the theology of Pope Leo. It is enough to note that the *Tomus* is a letter, written on June 13, 449, to Flavianus, bishop of Constantinople.[2] It contains many phrases identical with those of Pope Leo's sermon (*Sermo* 23) on the nativity. The chief point of the letter is in the statement that Christ was really a man; and as in Pope Leo's sermons, the idea of procreation in birth is somewhat crude, if compared with modern physiological knowledge. The Virgin Mother is said to have "supplied the material flesh."[3] Christ is proved to be a man because he was hungry, thirsty and tired, and "whoever believes in his death, recognizes his flesh." Eutyches, against whom the letter is directed, is quoted as saying that he believed in two "natures" before their

---

[1] Greg. M., Ep. vi, 2, 8. "Leonis Papae tomum atque definitionem."
[2] Leo, Ep. 38, *Pat. Lat.*, vol. 54, col. 755.
[3] Ibid., Ep. 38, cap. iv, "inviolata virginitas . . . carnis materiam ministravit."

"junction" and one only afterwards.[1] But the treatment of the difficulties by the bishop of Rome is more important for the present purpose than the character of the explanation he offered. Doctrine, for Pope Leo, was not the result of subtle philosophical reasoning, but the plainest possible statement, in the established Latin words, of the contemporary meaning given to traditional phrases. Clearly, a Church whose bishop does not argue, but lays down the law about doctrine, has a great advantage over the Greek Churches which had inherited the dangerous habit of reasoning from ancient Athens.

The doctrinal difficulties which seem to have been satisfactorily settled by the statement of Leo I, at least so far as the Latin Churches were concerned—if indeed they had ever had any intellectual difficulties—were by no means settled in the East. The Monophysites continued in the eastern Churches to declare that Christ had only one nature; and, worse still, their refusal of friendly intercourse with those who disagreed with them caused political difficulties. The Emperor Zeno, therefore, in A.D. 482, in agreement with the patriarch of Constantinople, Acacius, issued his *Henoticon*, which was an attempt to reconcile the extremists. The bishops of Rome, adhering to the statements of Pope Leo, therefore refused communion with Acacius, and struck off his name from the list of those for whom special prayers were offered. In A.D. 496, however, a less intransigent bishop was elected to the See of St. Peter—Anastasius II—who, according to the *Liber Pontificalis*, "wished to restore the name of Acacius." Nothing of importance seems to have happened, and the Roman See soon returned to its more rigid attitude; but owing to an unfortunate misunderstanding of history, Dante placed Pope Anastasius in hell for his leniency.[2]

During the following century political troubles and the ambiguous relation of the bishop of Rome to the Roman Emperor so occupied the minds of men that theological disputes did not receive much attention. The line of Emperors in the West had come to an end; and Italy was ruled by kings of the Ostrogoths.

---

[1] The difficulty of squaring the Latin words *natura* and *adunatio* with the Greek words φύσις and ἕνωσις, obviously makes the solution of a Greek difficulty by the Latins almost unintelligible. [2] Dante, *Inferno*, xi, 8.

The bishops of Rome had to adjust their policy to the needs of the Latin Churches in the new barbarian kingdoms; and the barbarians, although Arian heretics, do not appear to have been at all inclined to discuss doctrine. Thus, during more than fifty years, at this stage of the transition from Roman civilization to the Middle Ages, the Roman Church was not concerned with doctrine. The chief efforts of the Latin Churches were absorbed in preserving as much as they could of the ancient tradition, under a flood of barbarism, and with extending, into new tribes or nations, the teaching of the Catholic Churches which had secured imperial support. The See of Rome was naturally the most powerful representative of this policy.

The Roman tradition at the end of the sixth century with regard to doctrine, was stated most clearly by Gregory the Great. He writes in the *Moralia* that the Church does not teach by authority, but reasonably argues "that when it says what is incomprehensible, human reason ought not to inquire into what is hidden."[1] Again, he says that "divine mysteries always should be studied, but never discussed by the intellect; for often when the human mind does not discover the reason of certain things, it plunges into the whirlpool of doubt. . . . What is strange must be believed by faith, and must not be examined by the reason; because, if such things were revealed to our eyes by reason, they would not be strange."[2] The philosophical difficulty does not concern the present argument. Clearly it is impossible to "believe" a proposition which has no meaning. One may repeat it; and that only is required in practice. The *gleichshaltung* of modern dictatorship is based upon the same principle. Doctrinal orthodoxy based upon acceptance of statements without understanding them, does indeed secure that all should appear to think alike on a subject about which nobody thinks at all.

The situation had greatly changed in the century between Leo I

[1] Greg. M., *Mor.*, viii, 3. "Quae etsi quando dicit quod ratione comprehendi non valet, ne de occultis humana ratio quaeri debeat, rationabiliter suadet."
[2] Ibid., *Mor.*, vi, 19. "Divina miracula et semper debent considerari per studium, et nunquam discuti per intellectum. Saepe namque humanus sensus dum quarundum rerum rationem quaerens non invenit in dubitationis se voraginem mergit. . . . Mira igitur ex fide credenda sunt, perscrutanda per rationem non sunt; quia, si haec nostris oculis ratio expanderet, mira non essent."

and Gregory the Great. The standard of learning and of civilization in general had been lowered, and contact with the more highly educated clergy of the Greek Churches had been almost entirely lost among the Latin Churches in barbarian kingdoms. The beliefs and practices of the uneducated majority in the West had begun to affect the Authorities in the ecclesiastical system more than the intellectual discussions of the eastern Mediterranean. Thus, when Gregory the Great advocated the acceptance of the mysterious or unintelligible without criticism or reasoning about it, he was expressing the mind of his time in most of the Latin Churches. His writings indicate the growing belief in the efficacy of relics and in the widespread activities of devils which are typical of later medieval religion. By contrast, neither the letters nor the sermons of his predecessor Leo pay any attention to relics or to devils.

Without actually announcing a new doctrine Gregory's writings indicated the growth of picturesque imagery which eventually, in practice, modified the way in which Christians envisaged the world. Thus, he first gave definite expression to the idea of purgatory. This was an attempt to meet the objection that God would be unjust if he tortured the dead for ever in hell on account of trivial sins. The idea of purgatory had also the additional advantage of increasing the prestige of the clergy and the ceremonies of the Church; because they could provide means of diminishing the time of imprisonment for the dead who were eventually to enter heaven. And among all those who could expedite the entry into heaven, obviously none was more powerful than the key-bearer, St. Peter, and his representative on earth, the bishop of Rome. Similarly, Gregory taught the western world to accept the ancient imagery of heaven and hell which was eventually made the basis of Dante's vision. According to Gregory, hell is at the same distance under the surface of the earth, as heaven is above it. In his day and throughout the Middle Ages, obviously the blue sky was taken to be the floor of heaven at a fixed distance from the earth. Again, on the earth devils were numerous, widely distributed and powerful. Thus Gregory reports that the Devil and his assistant devils were seen holding a meeting in an ancient temple of Apollo.[1] And he says that a certain nun ate lettuce on which a devil was sitting, who flung her down in a faint until expelled by prayer.[2] Finally, Gregory's letters contain many references to the models of keys containing fragments of the chains of St. Peter which are to be used for curing sore eyes and other physical or spiritual evils. The magical use of relics was evidently established. In such a world the miraculous or the strange (*miracula, mira*) could obviously not be subjected to critical reasoning. These things must be left to the Church; because, as Gregory says, it is written of the Church "Thy nose is as the tower which is in Lebanon"—using, in the traditional manner, the Hebrew love-song, about the large nose of the beloved, in reference to the "spouse of Christ." "Thus," says Gregory, "by the nose is expressed discernment, for holy Church perceives by discernment what temptations arise from various causes."[3] Doctrine, in the eyes of the Roman Church, had therefore become a certain number of traditional statements to be accepted by the faithful without discussion, and the expression of a picturesque and primitive cosmology concerning the life after death. No difficulty was felt with regard to the exact meaning of different statements or with regard to the connections between them. And the imaginations of writers and preachers in the Latin Churches, as can be perceived in the visions reported by Bede, were open to all kinds of suggestions from popular custom and belief.

Under Honorius, bishop of Rome (A.D. 625–638), the Roman Church was again faced by doctrinal problems which arose, as before, in the East. The trouble once more concerned the question whether Christ was really God. Another attempt was made to reconcile the Monophysites with those who accepted the decisions of the Council of Chalcedon. That Council, like Pope Leo I, had decided that there were two distinct natures in Christ. But as the two were also stated to have been completely united, it might be

---

[1] Gregory, *Dial.*, iii, 7. A bishop of Funda had been tempted to pat a nun on her back as a joke. [2] Ibid., *Dial.*, i, 4.
[3] Ibid., *Reg. Pastor.*, i, 11. Referring to the Song of Solomon vii. 4. Thus Cassiodorus in his commentary on the Song says that the breasts of the beloved (iv. 5) are the Old and New Testament.

supposed that Christ had only one "will." If that were the will of the reason or "word" of God, the logos, the Monophysites would be satisfied. A new doctrine, therefore, was put forward, maintaining the "one will." Honorius wrote a letter to the patriarch of Constantinople which included the phrase "we confess one will of our Lord Jesus Christ," thus making himself a Monothelite.[1] But the effort to reach agreement on this compromise in the eastern Churches entirely failed.

The Roman Emperors were still obstructed in their administration and policy by divisions among their Christian subjects in these matters of doctrine, and therefore the Emperor Heraclius issued in A.D. 638 his "*Ecthesis*," or setting forth of doctrine, and his successor Constans II issued in A.D. 648 the so-called "*Typus*." This document was a pathetic attempt to stop doctrinal controversies. It includes the sentences—"We declare to our subjects that from the present moment they no longer have permission in any way to contend or to quarrel with one another about 'one will' and 'one energy' or 'two energies or two wills.' . . . Whoever ventures to transgress this command is subject above all to the judgement of God, but he will also be liable to the punishment of those who despise imperial commands."[2] Unfortunately for the civil Government theological controversy did not cease; and the Roman Church, with which alone this chapter is concerned, in its desire to retain the tradition of Leo I, was eventually constrained to condemn Pope Honorius as a Monothelite heretic. The correct doctrine was asserted to be that Christ had two wills. In A.D. 649 a synod at the Lateran condemned the eastern supporters of the doctrine of one will; and in A.D. 680 a General Council at Constantinople included Pope Honorius by name among the heretics condemned. Pope Leo II (A.D. 682), who knew Greek, and translated the canons of the Council, admitted the heresy of Honorius; and in later years an

---

[1] The Latin original of this letter no longer exists, but the Greek original read at the sixth General Council at Constantinople, A.D. 680, was acknowledged as correct, and later translated into Latin; see Mansi, *Conc.* xi, pp. 195, 736, 738, 922, and Hefele, *History of Councils*, Eng. trans., vol. v, p. 28 sq. The Latin words are "unam voluntatem fatemur."

[2] Mansi, *Conc.*, x, p. 1029, trans. in Hefele, *Hist. of Councils*. English trans., vol. v, p. 96.

early version of the Roman Breviary itself included the name of Pope Honorius among the heretics referred to in the lessons for the festival of Leo II. The unfortunate attempt of a Pope to accept a compromise in a quarrel between Greek theologians was later forgotten.

Once again, for nearly a century, questions of doctrine did not create difficulties for the bishops of Rome. The confusions in Italy under Lombard rule were sufficient to cause increasing concentration of the Roman Church upon the preservation of its properties. But in the early eighth century an Isaurian soldier became Roman Emperor; and he had little sympathy with the doctrines and practices of the more strictly Greek Churches. He represented, in fact, the non-Hellenic common people, whose Christianity was closer to Semitic than to Hellenic traditions. His suppression of the worship of images in the Greek Churches, led to conflicts with the bishops of Rome, which will be described in a later section; for these conflicts, although superficially doctrinal, were in fact more important in their political effects. They were primary causes of the final separation between the See of Rome and the Roman Empire.

Discipline

The dominant position of the Roman Church with regard to discipline, which had been attained in the ninth century in the West, was the result of a gradual development after about the beginning of the fifth century. The changes in the situation were similar to those which took place with regard to doctrine. It has been already explained that doctrine itself, during these centuries, had been treated mainly as a matter of discipline. But, discipline in the sense in which the word is here used, refers not to the forms of creed which members of the Church were expected to accept, but to the *system of organization* established and maintained. In this sense of the word, discipline includes the treatment of two distinct issues: first, the right of the Churches to govern themselves, with due regard to the needs of civil Authorities but without subjection to them; secondly, the rules to be followed by clergy, monks and laity—that is the canons.

The Roman Church had special advantages over all others in the treatment of these issues, especially after the fourth century. It was the only one of the Latin Churches which claimed apostolic foundation and had behind it the prestige of an ancient centre of legislation and administration. It had also the advantage over the Greek Churches in being far removed from the more powerful Emperors at Constantinople. Since Constantine the Great had, in the words of Dante, "made himself a Greek," no vigorous Emperor had held power in the West for more than a few years at a time; and by the end of the fifth century no Roman Emperor at all was reigning in the West. The Roman Church, therefore, whatever the policy it might choose to adopt, was inevitably much less influenced than the patriarchates of Antioch, Alexandria, Jerusalem and Constantinople by the policies of reigning Emperors. Again, in the more definitely ecclesiastical sphere, the Roman Church was fortunately free from the influence of the crowds of monks, which often disturbed the peace of the Church in Alexandria and Constantinople. Monasticism was eastern in origin and had developed to enormous proportions among Christians in the East, before the beginning of the fifth century. It had been introduced, as described in an earlier chapter, into the Latin Churches at about that time; and by the middle of the sixth century it had been organized in the Roman spirit in the West by St. Benedict. From the earliest times, however, and throughout later centuries, the monasteries in Rome and its surroundings were small. There were many foundations; but each had few members, as compared with the great numbers in eastern bishoprics. In Rome no such riotous violence was ever caused by religious fanatics as ended in the murder of Hypatia in Alexandria in March, 415.[1] And in the West no hordes of monks attempted to influence the doctrine of councils as often happened in the East. In the Roman Church the clergy and ecclesiastical officials formed parts of a strong organization before the days of monasticism in the West; and, although there were sometimes violent riots, in which the clergy took part, for and against candidates for the Papacy, there was no large

[1] The account is given in Socrates, *H.E.*, vii, 15.

body of monks in Rome, beyond the control of episcopal authority.

On the other hand, in the Roman Church and some of the other Latin Churches celibacy, which in the East was the characteristic of monks and not of priests, gradually became the established rule for the higher clergy. The earlier discussions of sacerdotal celibacy have been referred to in a former chapter. Ascetics found it difficult to suppress the earlier Christian tradition of a married clergy. But throughout the centuries from the fifth to the ninth, the enforcement of sacerdotal celibacy was more and more extended in the Latin Churches; and this practice became eventually one of the chief distinctions between the Greek and Latin Churches. Thus, in the canons of the so-called Trullan Council of A.D. 692, canon xiii reads: "In the Roman Church those who wish to receive the diaconate or priesthood must promise to have no further intercourse with their wives. We, however [that is, the Greek bishops], in accordance with the apostolic canons allow them to continue in matrimony. If anyone seeks to dissolve such marriages he shall be deposed and the cleric who, under pretence of religion, sends away his wife shall be excommunicated."[1] The practice of the Roman Church gave additional power to its bishops, both because it prevented the tendency to make ecclesiastical offices hereditary and also because it made the clergy a separate caste without family interests, more easily controlled by the bishops.

The policy of the bishops of Rome with regard to discipline was concerned, first, with independence from the control of the civil Authorities. The problem naturally arose after the acceptance of Christianity by Constantine. Before that time the Christian Churches had organized their own system of government. They owed neither their foundation nor their maintenance to imperial authority; and when the Empire found it convenient to support them, it could not be allowed to substitute a new form of ecclesiastical government for the traditional authority of the bishops, selected by the several Churches. The bishops of all the Christian Churches were glad to have the support of the Roman Emperor and his officials;

[1] Trans. in Hefele, *History of Councils*, vol. v, p. 226.

but there was no "head of the Church" to speak for all of them or to exercise authority from any centre. The unity of the Churches was represented by the General Councils, all of which, between the fourth and ninth centuries, met in the East. Indeed, the chief efforts of the bishops of Rome during these centuries were directed to preserving their equality of status with the patriarchs of the East and to guarding against the dangerous implications of the fact that the General Councils were called, and sometimes presided over, by the Emperor. The danger which the bishops of Rome, before the fifth century, most clearly foresaw was that either the Emperor himself might become the acknowledged head of the Christian Churches or that some bishop, closer to the imperial Court than the bishop of Rome, might attain to supreme authority in ecclesiastical affairs with the aid of the Emperor.

The principle, therefore, of the separation between ecclesiastical and civil authority was expressed in the earliest days, for example, in the words of Pope Leo I in his letter to Pulcheria, the Augusta, at Constantinople—"Human affairs cannot be secure unless both the kingly and the priestly authority defend what concerns the Faith."[1] It should be remembered that at this time the Empress, Galla Placidia, and her son, the Emperor Valentian III, were in Rome under the direct influence of Pope Leo, who persuaded them, as their letters say, to write to the Emperor Theodosius II, and his sister, the Empress Pulcheria, to urge the pre-eminence of the Roman See. The letter of Valentinian III (February 450) to his brother Emperor, whom he addresses as "holy father" and "venerable Emperor," speaks of "the blessed bishop of the city of Rome on whom antiquity conferred the princedom of the priesthood above all."[2] The relation, therefore, of the Roman bishop to the Roman Emperor was that of the chief representative of a different system of social organization.

The principle is more clearly stated by Pope Gelasius (A.D. 492–

---

[1] Leo I, Ep. 60 (March 17, 450), Pat. Lat., vol. 54, col. 873, "res humanae aliter tutae esse non possunt, nisi quae ad divinam confessionem pertinent, et regia et sacerdotalis defendat auctoritas."

[2] The letters are among those of Leo (Pat. Lat., vol. 54, Ep. 55–58. The replies from Constantinople are given in the same vol., Ep. 62–64).

496) in a letter to the Emperor Anastasius, in which he says: "As a Roman born I love, serve and acknowledge you, the Roman Emperor. . . . Revered Emperor, there are two (forces) by which chiefly the world is governed—the sacred authority of the bishops and the power of royalty."[1] He goes on to tell the Emperor that in matters of religion he must submit to the authority of the clergy. Another statement by Gelasius asserts that, although Melchizedek had been both priest and king, since the establishment of Christianity the two powers were separate, the Emperors dependent on the bishops for salvation and the bishops on the Emperors for mundane administration.[2] In ecclesiastical affairs the only appeal is to the See of Rome.[3] The close connection, therefore, between the Emperor and the bishop of Rome survived the disappearance of imperial Authority in Italy and the West. But the disciplinary authority of the Roman See over other bishoprics in the Latin Churches had already been asserted by Leo I and supported by an imperial Rescript issued in July 445 under the direct influence of Leo himself. Leo's letter of that year to the bishops of the province of Vienne is an attack on Hilary, bishop of Arles, based upon the authority of St. Peter "that the building of the eternal temple should be established upon the solidity of Peter."[4] In support of Leo's letter the imperial Rescript sent with the letter, in the names of the two Emperors but obviously composed in Rome, is addressed to Aetius, Count and master of the soldiery. In it the Emperors are made to say: "Since the dignity of the city of Rome and the authority of the sacred Council has established the Primacy of the Apostolic See of St. Peter, who is chief of the circle of bishops, that nothing should be attempted without the authority of this See, the peace of the Churches will be everywhere preserved if all acknowledge their ruler."[5] The Emperor himself is thus made to say that the Roman

---

[1] Gelasius, Ep. 8 (*Pat. Lat.*, 59). Duo quippe sunt, imperator Auguste, quibus principaliter mundus hic regitur: auctoritas sacra pontificum et regalis potestas.

[2] Ibid., *De Anath. Vinculo, Pat. Lat.*, 59, col. 102.

[3] Ibid., col. 107. Totum in sedis apostolicae positum est potestate.

[4] Leo, Ep. 10. Ut aeterni templi aedificatio . . . in Petri soliditate consisteret.

[5] Rescript in *Pat. Lat.*, vol. 54; among Leo's letters, Ep. xi. "Petri . . . qui princeps est episcopalis coronae . . . si rectorem suum agnoscat universitas." The "corona" is obviously the "circle" of bishops as in Paulinus of Aquileia who wrote of a council sitting "in modum coronae." "Corona," in Cicero, means a "crowd" as an audience.

See should have an authority over the Churches similar to that of the Roman Emperor.

A good example of the way in which the bishop of Rome took the place of the imperial Authorities is to be found in the comparison between a Rescript of Honorius and Theodosius II in A.D. 418, and the letter of Vigilius, bishop of Rome, to all the bishops in Gaul under the rule of Childebert, in A.D. 546.[1] The imperial Rescript issued at Constantinople on April 17, 418, was received at Arles on May 23rd. It is directed to Agraecola, prefect of the Gauls. And it instructs him to hold a council of the chief officials in all the provinces of Gaul at Arles, between the middle of August and middle of September in every year. If any of the officials cannot attend, he may send a representative (*legatus*). If any of the officials (*judices*) can come and does not come, he is to be fined five pounds of gold; and if any person of dignity (*honoratus*) or member of a city council (*curialis*), he is to be fined three pounds of gold.

In a similar letter of Pope Vigilius (August 23, 546) the text runs: "In so far as Christ, our Lord God and Saviour, has given us the position of the first of the Apostles, it becomes us to care for the peace of all the Churches which, although in many different parts, is one, spread throughout the whole world. And as Moses appointed Aaron and Ur (Exodus xxiv. 14), so peace may be kept by someone who takes our place in Gaul. We appoint the bishop of Arles as our representative, and decide that there shall be a council of bishops at the established times. If anyone cannot come to the council (*synodum*), he can send a priest or deacon."

It should be noted that the council of bishops at Arles is composed of the bishops of a single kingdom, that representatives may be used by the bishops as under the imperial Rescript by the officials; that the purpose of the bishop's council is chiefly to preserve the unity of the Churches in Gaul; and that the Pope assigned no penalty for non-attendance, although the Emperors did. Further, in the imperial Rescript, one hundred and twenty-eight years earlier, reasons are given why Arles should be the meeting-place for the

[1] Both documents in *M.G.H.*, Ep. iii. *Ep. merow. et karol. aevi*, i, pp. 13 and 63.

541

annual council. The Rescript says that at Arles "all the riches of the East, of Africa and of Spain come together." And the ships come up the Rhone. That is in the early fifth century. By the middle of the sixth century, Arles still remains the natural centre for councils of bishops throughout the Frankish kingdom. The Empire and its officials had long since disappeared. A barbarian king ruled the old Roman cities from his Court at Paris; but Rome, in the person of her bishop, still directed the only organization which then preserved the remnants of Roman civilization. The bishops of Rome perhaps intended only to imitate the civil organization of the Empire; but in fact they were laying the foundations of an entirely new order which was to be dependent on the Churches and, in the West, upon the See of St. Peter. The imperial Church, as an organization of the Roman Empire, was gradually becoming an imperial Church in a new sense—that is to say, a Church which was itself an Empire.

The change was already made in the early seventh century, when Gregory the Great had won for the Roman Church the English people, outside the frontiers of the Empire, and was able to write to the Emperor at Constantinople on behalf of all the Latin Churches. This has been discussed in an earlier chapter. But Gregory himself was not aware of the revolution which had occurred. He wrote to the Emperor Maurice, and his successor, the usurper, Phocas, with the same reverence that Leo had shown to Theodosius II.

The second aspect of ecclesiastical discipline is the promulgation of rules for the Christian clergy and laity. As it has been explained before (Chapter VIII, Laws and Canons), in the earliest days of Christianity the authorities in each Church made its rules. Later, councils of bishops from the Churches of a province, district or kingdom established rules for all their Churches. And, finally, in the fourth century, after Constantine, General Councils, consisting chiefly of eastern bishops but with a few representatives of the Latin Churches, published canons which were intended to apply to all the Christian Churches. At the beginning of the fifth century, however, no single and complete collection of canons was accepted, as authoritative, at any rate in the Latin Churches. The most important collections of canons were those of the Churches of Africa and of the Churches of Spain. There were also important collections made by councils in Gaul. The Roman Church, like other great Churches, held its synods of subordinate or neighbouring bishops in Italy; but the proceedings of these synods had no greater prestige outside the jurisdiction of the bishops of Italy than had the proceedings at Carthage or Toledo. In the sixth century, however, the translation or re-translation of Greek canons was made into Latin by Dionysius the Little; and this, together with the letters of bishops of Rome (Decretals) from A.D. 384 to 496, became the authoritative basis of canonical jurisdiction in the Roman Church. By this time the only Roman Emperor resided at Constantinople; and the prestige of Rome as a source of legislation gradually disappeared. Again, Justinian, who had become Emperor in A.D. 527, seemed likely to become the supreme legislator for the Church as well as the State. The dangerous conception implied in the use of the word "*nomocanones*," that is to say, rules of the Church which are at the same time laws of the State, clearly threatened to engulf the Christian Churches in the policies of the Roman Empire. But, as it has been explained already, the Churches of Ireland in their Penitentials and councils of bishops in the western kingdoms, in Spain and Gaul, continued independently to develop the rules of Christian life and organization.

The bishop of Rome was in a difficult position. He and his subordinate bishops in Italy were subjects of the Roman Emperor in the East; but he had influence and authority in the West among peoples in Gaul and Spain far outside the reach of the Emperor. After Gregory the Great, the Roman Church had the additional authority acquired by its successful missionary work in England; and later its influence was extended in Germany under Popes Gregory II and Zachary. Meantime, two entirely unforeseen events occurred, which gave supreme authority in the West, in matters of discipline, to the bishop of Rome. First, Mohammedan conquests destroyed the great Churches of Africa and Spain, and therefore stopped the development of the canons there; and, secondly, the Churches of Gaul, in the later years of the seventh century, fell into complete disorder and moral confusion. There were few councils in Gaul in the last half of the seventh century, and none at all from A.D. 695 to A.D. 742. After about A.D. 675 there were no bishops in many of the most important Sees in Gaul.[1] This situation in the Latin Churches left the Church of Rome and its bishop the only exponents of continuous development in the rules of the Church. The preservation, therefore, of the early canons of General Councils and of Decretals of earlier Popes, became of supreme importance. The Roman Church, as it has been shown in an earlier chapter, became the source of reform in Gaul and the chief support of missionary efforts in Germany. The position of the bishop of Rome as the supreme authority, in matters of discipline, became evident when, on the first visit of Charles the Great to the shrine of St. Peter in A.D. 787, Pope Hadrian I presented him with a copy of the Dionysian collection of canons with later additions. This then became the basis for the future development of canons affecting all the Latin Churches in the Middle Ages.

Pope Hadrian at the same time gave to the Frankish king the Roman Sacramentary which thus became a means of reforming and unifying the Mass-books of the northern Churches. And according to the story of an early chronicle, the method of singing at ceremonies in the Roman Church was chosen by Charles the Great, as the best, after an argument had arisen between some who sang in the Gallic tradition and others who sang in the Roman.[2] The king asked the Pope to send Roman singers back to the North with him. Thus the Roman Church became, not merely the model of doctrine and discipline, but also of ceremonies and ecclesiastical music.

Separation from the Empire

The policy which finally made the medieval Papacy inevitable was the release of the bishop of Rome from the civil authority of the Roman Emperor. This policy can hardly be said to have been

---

[1] The details are in Duchesne, *Fastes épiscopaux de l'ancienne Gaule.*

[2] *Ann. R.F.,* ann. 787, *Pat. Lat.,* vol. 104, col. 427. The Franks could not manage the tremolos or the smooth connections "in their natural barbarian tone, breaking the words in the throat rather than bringing them out."

PLATE 7.—PRESENTATION IN TEMPLE

Virgin and Child (Mosaic in Church of S. Maria Maggiore in Rome,
c. A.D. 435)—Referred to page 529

at first deliberate; but it certainly was a conscious reaction of the Roman Church to the changes in the relations between western Europe and the Empire, in the years between the end of the fifth century and the beginning of the ninth. In the days of Leo I and in those of Gelasius (A.D. 440–496) the bishop of Rome was still quite clearly a subject of the Roman Emperor. Among other bishops he held an exceptional position with respect to the Emperor, as the bishop of the Eternal City. But he was, nevertheless, dependent upon the Emperor for military protection and subordinate to him in all civil matters. But in the days of Hadrian I (A.D. 772–795), the bishop of Rome, then clearly "the Pope" in the medieval sense of the word, no longer depended upon the armed forces of the Empire; nor did he render to the Emperor more than a distant and shadowy reverence. The changes which brought about this transformation must now be shortly described.

There were three stages in the development of papal policy. First, there was a period of estrangement, from the days of Symmachus under Theodoric the Ostrogoth, to the exile and death of Pope Martin I. Secondly, there was a short period of reconciliation, before Iconoclasm was adopted as a policy by the Emperors. And, finally, there was a third period of open opposition, passing into complete divergence of interests, between the Empire and the Latin Churches.

The rule of Theodoric the Ostrogoth in Italy included one strange episode in the history of the Papacy. Theodoric was illiterate and an Arian heretic. But he was friendly to the Catholic Church in Italy; and he showed great favour in the presents which he bestowed on St. Peter's basilica during his visit to Rome in A.D. 500. He used Roman officials, such as Cassiodorus; and he held his kingdom, at least in theory, by agreement with the Roman Emperor at Constantinople. While he reigned at Ravenna, however, the dispute arose in Rome which has been referred to above, concerning the recognition of the patriarch Acacius. On the death of Pope Anastasius II, who had worked for compromise with the eastern Churches, two parties in Rome selected each a candidate for the Papacy. The clergy seem to have favoured a stricter attitude towards Constantinople. The laity, or at any rate the richer classes, desired closer connections with the Empire. For some reason it seems to have been agreed that the decision as to which candidate should be bishop of Rome should be left to the Arian king of the Goths in Italy. Theodoric decided in favour of Symmachus. He may have been influenced by the fear, which he certainly showed in the later years of his life, lest the richer laity in Rome might undermine his authority by a closer connection with the Roman Emperor. But in any case the change in the position of the bishop of Rome was striking enough. Then came the attempt of the Emperor Justinian (A.D. 527–565) to reconquer Italy, and the capture of Rome from the Goths by his general, Belisarius. The bishop of Rome again became, quite clearly, a subject in imperial territory. But Justinian, like many other Emperors, was obstructed in his administration by theological quarrels among eastern bishops and monks. The chief theological issue was still the problem whether or in what sense Christ was God. The Monophysites continued to refuse to accept the decisions of the Council of Chalcedon; and it is said that the Empress Theodora supported their views.

Justinian issued, about A.D. 544, an edict condemning the writings of three Greek theologians—the three "headings" (capitula) are known as the "Three Chapters"—which were thought to favour the Monophysite view; and he required Vigilius, bishop of Rome, to accept the edict. Vigilius had been ordained bishop of Rome in A.D. 537 under the influence of Belisarius, the Emperor's general in Rome, and with the support of the Empress Theodora, although another bishop, Silverius, had been elected to the See in A.D. 536 and was still living later than June 538. Vigilius was, therefore, regarded as an instrument of the imperial policy; but he refused to accept the Emperor's edict and was summoned to Constantinople, where he arrived in A.D. 547. For seven years he remained in the East, either under guard or in flight; and only after submitting to a compromise with the Emperor's policy, was he allowed to depart. This, then, was an example of conflict between a powerful Emperor and his subject, the bishop of Rome, in which the Emperor seemed strong enough to have his way, even in a matter of doctrine. This matter of doctrine, however, was clearly causing danger to the civil Authorities in Egypt and Syria; and in A.D. 567, under the Emperor Justin II, hostilities between the two parties in Alexandria went so far that two patriarchs were established for the Churches there—one for the Greeks and the other for the majority of the inhabitants, who favoured the Monophysite view.[1] Hostility to the Emperors at Constantinople eventually became so strong that the Monophysites in A.D. 639 welcomed the Mohammedan invaders; and Egypt was lost to the Empire.

Meantime in Italy the bishops of Rome were chiefly concerned with political problems of their own. The Lombard invasions have been already referred to; and their final result will be discussed below. But their most important effect for the argument here was the vain attempt of the bishops of Rome to obtain protection or support from the Emperor. The Emperor's representative in Italy, the Exarch at Ravenna, and his armed forces, were either unable or unwilling to stop the extension of Lombard power; and even after the Lombard chiefs became Catholic, the bishops of Rome seemed to have feared both a possible loss of their estates and a degradation of Rome itself by subjection to a Lombard king, in his capital at Pavia. The letters of Gregory the Great to the Emperor and his officials contain the clearest evidence of the appeals made by the See of Rome, representing the Emperor's subjects there, and the failure of those appeals. In this period, therefore, in the earliest years of the seventh century, the bishop of Rome was made to feel the helplessness of the civil and military Authorities of the Roman Empire to which in theory he owed allegiance. The Church of Rome was thus compelled by circumstances to look to the barbarian kings in the West on whom the other Latin Churches already depended.

Increasing pressure on the Empire from the Mohammedan in-

---

[1] The patriarch of the Greeks was appointed by the Emperor, and his followers were called "Melkites" or "Imperialists." The Coptic language, with various dialects, was derived from the ancient Egyptian; and, although in the liturgy of the Coptic Church it was supplanted by Arabic, the Gospels are still read in an early Coptic dialect.

vaders led the Emperors to make desperate efforts to bring to an end the new controversy which had arisen among their eastern subjects with regard to the two wills of Christ. These efforts have been described above. In A.D. 649 they led to complete estrangement between the Roman Emperor and the newly elected Pope, Martin I (elected July 6, 649). The Pope refused to accept the Emperor's *Typus*; presided at the Lateran Synod, which rejected the Emperor's policy, and was arrested in the Lateran Palace by the Exarch's soldiers in A.D. 653. He was taken as a prisoner to Constantinople and given a form of trial, apparently on the charge of being concerned with treasonable opposition to the Emperor. The real offence was obviously Pope Martin's refusal to accept the Emperor's policy of compromise with the Monophysites and Monothelites; and he was exiled to the Crimea, where he died after great suffering in A.D. 655 (September 16th); the Roman clergy having meantime elected a new bishop on September 8, 654. A Pope, therefore, who dared to resist an Emperor was in danger of arrest, exile and death.

The next act in the drama has something of the character of retribution. The Emperor, Constans II, left his capital in fear of a public commotion and reached Rome on July 5, 663. He was received by the Pope then reigning, Vitalianus, with all the honours due from the bishop of Rome to the supreme ruler of the Empire. It was said, in later times, that the Emperor intended to make Rome itself his capital and to abandon Constantinople. But, in fact, he stayed only twelve days in Rome directing the collection of valuables from the Churches for his own use. He left for Sicily and was there murdered, because of some private grievance, by one of his slaves. Such was the end of the last visit ever paid to Rome by a Roman Emperor.

The Emperors who followed, Constantine IV and Justinian II, held two councils which have been already referred to. They continued to be pressed by the advance of the Mohammedan conquerors in the East, and became more and more helpless in the West. Justinian II ordered the arrest of Pope Sergius in A.D. 687; but the armed forces in the city of Rome itself resisted the Emperor's agents; and a later Pope, John VI, actually used his influence to save the life of the Exarch during a mutiny of his soldiers. The position of the Papacy during this period is indicated by a succession of Syrian Popes. The *Liber Pontificalis* adds the phrase "of Syrian nationality" (*natione Syrus*) after the names of five Popes from John V (A.D. 685) to Gregory III (A.D. 731). Of the others in those years one is called "Phrygian" and two "Greek" with Zachary (Pope from A.D. 741–752) also a Greek, before the long line of Roman Popes begins. That is to say, for more than half a century (A.D. 685–752) only one Pope, Gregory II (A.D.715–731), was a Roman; and he it was who broke with the Roman Emperor on the question of images, as it will be explained below. The Syrian and Greek Popes of this period may have come from Sicily, where the Roman Church had important dependencies; but there were evidently many Greek monks in Rome itself; and it seems probable that some of these at least were refugees driven out of Palestine and Egypt by the Mohammedan invasions. Their learning, their knowledge of Greek and their contact with the non-Latin Churches proved valuable to the Roman See. Refugees from oppression have always increased the power of resistance and developed the culture of the peoples which welcomed them. Thus, at a later date, in the eighth century refugees from among the Spanish clergy increased the knowledge of the canons of the Church in France. Indeed, even before the line of eastern Popes began, thirty-seven Greek monks had attended the Lateran Council of A.D. 649 and presented a statement in Greek, which was translated into Latin for the Council, condemning the policy of the Emperor. During this period, therefore, the Roman Church might have become an outpost of the East, facing the Latin world, and not, as it actually became, an outpost of the West. The policy of reconciliation between the bishop of Rome and the Greek Emperor is marked most strikingly by the visit of Pope Constantine, himself a Syrian, to Constantinople in A.D. 711. He was the last Pope to make the journey from Rome at the command of the Emperor, as Martin I had done fifty years before. But Pope Constantine was received with exceptional honours and returned to Rome, after reaching some agreement with the Emperor Justinian II, the nature of which is not known. The long controversy seemed to be ended. The Greek Churches which still remained within the Emperor's dominions—the patriarchates of Alexandria, Jerusalem and Antioch having been lost—were in unity with the Roman See and the Latin Churches. It may be remarked as significant that Pope Constantine had introduced into Rome the Court head-dress or Phrygian cap, which later became the tiara.[1] But, when the efforts of generations seemed at last to have succeeded in restoring the unity of the Churches, the final break suddenly came between the Latins and the Greeks.

The final separation of the Roman Church from the Roman Emperors at Constantinople was the result of controversy about the worship of images. Open opposition between the bishop of Rome and the Emperor followed immediately after the publication in Italy in A.D. 731 of the decree of the Emperor Leo III, which was issued in A.D. 726, forbidding the use of images or pictures in churches. Against this decree the Roman Church maintained the opinion which had become traditional both in the Greek and Latin Churches since the days of Constantine the Great.

While idolatry in paganism was still regarded by the Christian Churches as a danger, the use of pictures was sometimes opposed. The Council of Elvira in A.D. 306 had forbidden their use in churches. And while the influence of Jewish converts to Christianity was still strong in the Christian Churches, the Jewish tradition, no doubt, limited the use of images. But, as can be seen in the Roman catacombs, symbolical figures were used in the very earliest years of the Roman Church; and at the end of the sixth century Gregory the Great stated the principle upon which the Roman Church afterwards relied. In a letter to Serenus, bishop of Marseilles, who had removed pictures from churches, Gregory argues that such pictures are useful for teaching those who cannot read.[2] The bishop of Rome did not fear to adapt to Christian uses even obviously pagan religious customs, as is evident from his message to Augustine

---

[1] See *Liber Pontificalis: Vita Constantini*; and the notes in *Pat. Lat.*, 89, on "Caumelaunicum," the Greek name of the cap which Constantine "used to wear in Rome" (ut solitus est Romae procedere).   [2] Greg. M., Ep. ix, 9.

at Canterbury, quoted by Bede, advising him not to destroy pagan temples but to use them and to allow the continuance of feasting under the boughs of trees.[1] The Roman Church was even more confirmed in that policy at the beginning of the eighth century. When, therefore, the edict of Leo III against images was published in Italy, Pope Gregory II protested against it; and a popular movement in Italy expressed the resistance of the West to the Oriental or Semitic tradition which would abolish images.[2] The Emperor took measures to have the Pope arrested. The attempt failed; and the succeeding Pope, Gregory III, a Syrian, repeated the protest.

The immediate result in A.D. 731 was the confiscation by imperial Authority of the estates of the Roman Church in Sicily and Calabria and the transfer of the bishoprics of Illyria and others on the eastern side of the Adriatic from the jurisdiction of the Roman patriarch to that of the patriarch in Constantinople. The Emperor who succeeded Leo III as Constantine V (*Copronymus*) persecuted the supporters of religious pictures, relics and the worship of saints, and held a council at Constantinople in A.D. 754. The three hundred and thirty-eight bishops present condemned the use of religious pictures; and from their decrees it is clear that the chief objection lay in the representation of Christ or the Logos, on the ground that it cast doubt upon the doctrine that he was God. Thus, Canon vi reads: "If anyone represents the flesh made Divine by its union with the Word in a picture, and thus separates it from the Godhead, let him be anathema." And Canon viii reads: "If anyone represents the forms of the saints in lifeless pictures . . . and does not rather represent their virtues as living images in himself, let him be anathema.' [3]

Meantime the disagreement in Italy between the imperial Authorities and the Roman Church had led to the occupation of Ravenna by the Lombards and the expulsion of the imperial Ex-

---

[1] Bede, *H.E.*, i, 30. (The advice to Augustine is sent in a letter to the abbot Mellitus, then going to England, A.D. 601.)

[2] The letters of Gregory II, quoted by Gibbon, ch. xlix (A.D. 728), are now believed to be late forgeries. See Hodgkin, *Italy*, vi, p. 501, and Bury, Appendix 14, in vol. v of the 1898 ed. of Gibbon. The popular movement is recorded in the *Liber Pontificalis*.

[3] See Hefele, *History of the Councils*, Eng. trans., vol. v, p. 314.

arch. The Lombard king was believed by the Pope, Stephen II, to intend to occupy Rome; and the Pope, in spite of the quarrel about the worship of images, appealed to the Emperor for assistance. It was the last attempt of the Papacy to obtain protection from the Roman Empire. No help came and the Pope appealed to Pippin, king of the Franks, who invaded Italy, captured Ravenna and handed it over, not to the Emperor, but to the Pope.[1] This was regarded as a "restitution"; and therefore it was perhaps supposed that the Pope represented the Roman Empire. In any case, this, and not the possession of estates, the *Patrimonium Petri*, is the origin of the temporal power or sovereignty of the Pope. The loss of the estates of the Church in Sicily was strangely compensated by the establishment of the Pope's authority in rivalry with that of the Emperor over the Exarchate.

The Emperor in A.D. 757 attempted to influence the king of the Franks by an embassy which brought, among other presents, an organ—the first, according to the chroniclers, that ever reached France. But the Latin Churches remained opposed to the ecclesiastical policy of the Emperor. Ten years later in A.D. 767 at a synod, held at Gentilly under King Pippin, there was an argument, according to the earliest chronicle, "between the Romans and the Greeks about images and the Holy Trinity."[2] This was followed in A.D. 769 by a synod held in the Lateran basilica at which several Frankish bishops were present. The synod was mainly concerned with the deposition of the preceding Pope, Constantine, who had been blinded by his opponents and was now put on trial by his successor, and with the rules for the election of the Pope, excluding all laymen from the right to elect. The new Pope, Stephen III, and the other bishops confessed themselves sinners for having hitherto supported Pope Constantine—"and had hypocritical litanies sung over them, which must have made the angels smile, if angels smile."[3]

---

[1] Two letters of Pope Stephen to Pippin are in the *Cod. Carol.*, one of A.D. 754 and the other, written in the name of St. Peter himself, of A.D. 755.

[2] *Ann. Laurissen.*, ann. A.D. 767. Some historians have been puzzled by the reference to the Trinity but, as the extract from the Council of Constantinople above quoted has shown, the issue was really about the Divinity of Christ.

[3] "qui durent provoquer le sourire des anges, si les anges sourient." Duchesne, *Les Premiers Temps de l'état Pontifical*, 3rd ed., 1911, p. 125.

But the synod also condemned the canons of the Council of Constantinople (A.D. 754) on the use of images.

In A.D. 780 the Emperor, Leo IV, who had continued the Iconoclast policy, was succeeded by his nine-year-old son, Constantine VI, under the control of his mother, Irene.[1] This lady was an Athenian who held strongly the Greek and Roman view of the use of religious pictures; and under her influence in A.D. 787 the second Council of Nicaea restored in the Greek Churches the traditional usage. As it will be recounted in the next chapter, the Pope, Hadrian I, made friendly overtures to the Empress Irene. But it was too late for the imperial Authorities at Constantinople to restore their power and authority over Rome, for by this time the king of the Franks was the protector of the Roman Church.

The Temporal Power

The last step in the formation of the characteristics of the medieval Papacy was the establishment of the bishop of Rome as an independent ruler over what was eventually called the "Papal State." This step was made towards the end of the eighth century, but it was not entirely the result of deliberate policy. It was largely the inevitable consequence of the withdrawal of all the power and authority of the Roman Emperor from his territories in central Italy. Iconoclasm, which had compelled the Popes to oppose the policy of the Roman Emperors, led also to the confiscation by imperial authority of the properties of the Roman Church in Sicily and Calabria. Meantime, the increase of the power of the Lombards in Italy had destroyed the Exarchate at Ravenna, and therefore left the Duke of Rome (*Dux Romae*), who had been his subordinate, in an ambiguous position. Feeling in Rome prevented the appointment of a Duke by the Emperor at Constantinople, and the military forces in Rome thus became an independent army under local leaders (*Duces*), who in later days became the dukes and "princes" of Rome and its surroundings. In this situation the clergy of Rome and the bishops of the suburban Sees, with the bishop of Rome at

[1] Constantine VI had been crowned when he was six years old by the patriarch of Constantinople and proclaimed partner in his father's title.

their head, naturally became the civil authority of the Duchy and of those lands in central Italy, from Rome as far as the Adriatic, which had been held in the seventh century by the Roman Empire, and which in the eighth century the Emperor could no longer protect.

Again, in those days the distinction between the owner of land and the governor of those who dwelt upon it, was not clearly understood. The so-called "manorial system" had begun. The lord of the land was the governor of the people. But the Roman Church held large properties in Rome and near it, and in the areas eastward and northward of the city, lying between the territories controlled by the king of the Lombards and those held by the Lombard dukes of Spoleto and Benevento. These properties of the Roman Church, the *Patrimonium Sancti Petri*, in the days of Gregory the Great had been administered by the bishop of Rome and his agents, who were subjects of the Roman Emperor. Imperial law and military control, therefore, protected all the dwellers on ecclesiastical estates, in the same way as the laws and military force of barbarian kings protected the dwellers on the properties of other Churches. When, therefore, in the middle of the eighth century the Roman Church was in conflict with the Emperor about the worship of images and had had its estates confiscated in imperial territory, the other estates in central Italy might have fallen under the civil and military juris-diction of Lombard kings or dukes. But if this had occurred, the bishop of Rome and his clergy would have become subjects of the Lombard rulers. Apart from the danger that such rulers would confiscate the estates, it was evidently felt by the clergy and soldiery of Rome that it would be a degradation for them to be subjects in a kingdom of minor importance, which was still regarded as bar-barian. Again, in the middle of the eighth century, the bishops of Rome already had the prestige of medieval Popes as reformers of the Church and supporters of missionary effort in the North. But they could hardly have maintained this prestige, if they had become as dependent upon a Lombard king as a bishop might be dependent upon some local ruler in England. The prestige of Rome itself was too great to allow of its absorption into a Lombard kingdom with its capital at Pavia. It follows that the bishop of Rome was driven to become himself the sovereign ruler of the territories in central Italy, where the properties of the Church then chiefly lay.

The Duke of Rome, unlike the Doge of Venice, had not sufficient status to take the place of imperial Authority, precisely because the prestige of Rome itself had already passed to its bishop.[1] Therefore, in Rome and its dependent territories two forces struggled for the remnant of civil authority which had been left derelict by the Roman Empire. On the one hand, the Duke of Rome and other so-called dukes or leaders of the army (optimates militiae), controlled such military force as was available in the disorganized population. On the other hand, the clergy of the Roman Church, strongly organized in the central office of the bishopric at the Lateran, with the bishops of the suburban Sees and the Pope at their head, claimed the final control over government and policy. The early years of the "temporal power," therefore, were filled with continual struggles between the army and the clergy, chiefly for the power to control the election of the Pope.

The establishment of the "temporal power," in its medieval form, may be taken as complete before A.D. 826 under Eugenius II, after the Constitution of Louis the Pious and the decrees of the Roman synod of that year. The steps by which the new position was reached may be briefly described as follows. The appeals of Pope Gregory III to Charles Martel and of Stephen II to Pippin, eventually brought the Papacy into dependence on the armed forces of the kings of the Franks. By that time, the Emperor at Constantinople no longer had any power in Italy. Ravenna had fallen into the hands of the Lombard king, and the imperial Exarchate ceased to exist. Pippin, at the request of the Pope, attacked the Lombard king, and, having deprived him of Ravenna and neighbouring imperial territory, seems to have presented them, in some form, to the Pope (A.D. 754). The "patrimony of St. Peter," therefore, besides including the ownership of certain landed property recovered from the Lombards, was extended by a vaguely con-

[1] The *Dux Romae* is not named after A.D. 754. See Duchesne, *L'État Pont.*, p. 65.

ceived and ill-defined governmental authority over some areas hitherto subject to the Roman Emperor at Constantinople.

The next Pope, Hadrian I, found himself again in difficulties with the Lombards, and persuaded the new king of the Franks, Charles the Great, not only to attack the Lombards, but also to visit Rome and form the closest possible relation between his family and the Papacy. From this situation the Pope appears to have derived, in the last years of the eighth century, authority as an independent, if "protected" ruler, over the central part of Italy, stretching from Ravenna and the Adriatic coast to Rome and its coast towns on the other side.[1] Charles the Great, however, established himself and his heirs in Italy as kings of the Lombards. The Papacy, therefore, in its opposition to the Lombards since the days of Gregory the Great had finally succeeded in replacing them by the Franks, leaving for a time the independent Lombard dukes, south of the papal territories, to be conquered later by Frankish expeditions.

Either under Hadrian I, or at about his time, was composed the so-called *Donation of Constantine*. This document asserts that when the Emperor Constantine the Great decided to make his capital in the East, Rome and the western provinces were left by him under the jurisdiction of Pope Silvester. The document is now known to have been composed in the Lateran palace or by some papal officials towards the end of the eighth century, that is to say, almost five hundred years after Constantine. But it was used throughout the Middle Ages to reinforce the claims of the Papacy, not merely to jurisdiction over central Italy, but also to authority in all the western kingdoms. It was first proved to be entirely unhistorical by the Renaissance scholar, Lorenzo Valla, in A.D. 1440. But to call the *Donation of Constantine* a forgery would imply a misunderstanding of the climate of opinion in the eighth century. It may perhaps be called a work of imagination; for its chief importance

[1] The question whether Pope Hadrian really claimed or received governmental authority, not only in the parts of Italy mentioned above but also in Corsica, is discussed by Hodgkin, *Italy and her Invaders*, vol. viii. He disputes Duchesne's theory in his notes on the *Liber Pontificalis*. But it seems probable that the ideas of the writer of the relevant passage in the *Liber Pontificalis* were considerably more confused than either Duchesne or Hodgkin seems to suppose.

is that it indicates the nature of the policy which affected certain circles of the clergy in Rome when it had become clear to them that the severance of Rome and the West from the Roman Emperor at Constantinople was final. It may even have been intended to contrast the faith and works of the first Christian Emperor with the hostility to image-worship, and therefore to the Roman Church, of Constantine V at the end of the eighth century. But above all it was useful in supporting the claim of the bishop of Rome to take over the Exarchate and other imperial territories in Italy.

The *Donation of Constantine* runs as follows. After an elaborate confession of faith, based on the Nicene Creed,[1] and a short summary of the fall of Adam and the birth of Christ, Constantine is made to say that he was suffering from leprosy, had tried many doctors without effect and had then been approached by "the priests of the Capitol." They proposed that he should slaughter several infants and be washed in their blood, and thus be cleansed. The infants were brought, but Constantine, seeing their mothers' tears, restored their children to them. That night the apostles Peter and Paul appeared to him and told him that Silvester, bishop of Rome, was hiding in a cave at Mount Soracte. The bishop would cure him. On waking he went to Silvester, the "universal pope" *(universalis papa)*, who told him that Peter and Paul were not Gods but apostles; and showed him a picture by which he recognized the figures he had seen in his dream and admitted it in front of all his satraps *(coram omnibus satrapis meis)*. Then Silvester assigned him a period of penance in a hair-shirt; and after confessing his belief in Almighty God, he was baptized with a triple immersion; and while in the font he saw with his own eyes a hand from heaven touching him. He was thus cured of his leprosy and gave up worshipping idols. He then quotes *Matthew* xvi—"Thou art Peter." Then, "with all his satraps, the Senate, his nobles and the whole Roman people, he thought it good to grant supreme power to the See of Peter," and superiority over the four other chief Sees,

---

[1] *Tres formae, sed una potestas* is a peculiar version of the traditional phrase here inserted.

Antioch, Alexandria, Jerusalem and Constantinople. He then built a church in his Palace of the Lateran, which was to be the head of all the Churches in the whole world, and he also built the churches of St. Peter and St. Paul. On the universal Pope, Silvester, he then conferred his crown, the tiara (*phrygium id est, mitram*) and other imperial garments. The Roman Church was to have secretaries, porters and guards, like the Emperors. The Roman clergy was to have the right to ride with white horse-cloths, and to use white laced shoes, like the Senators. He himself, Constantine, placed the white tiara on the Pope's head and held the reins of his horse as a groom (*stratoris officium*). And he left to "Silvester and his successors Rome and all the provinces, districts and cities of Italy and the West to be subject to the Roman Church for ever" (*Juri Sanctae Romanae ecclesiae concedimus*), while he removed his Empire and kingly power to the East, where he had decided to build a city in his own home and to establish his Empire—"because where the princedom of bishops (*principatus sacerdotum*) and the head of the Christian religion has been established by the heavenly Emperor it is not just that an earthly Emperor should have power." He placed the document, signed by his own hand, on the body of St. Peter, to be kept inviolable by the Emperors that should succeed him. "Given at Rome on the third day before the Kalends of April, our lord Flavius Constantine, Augustus, for the fourth time, and Gallicanus consuls."[1]

It is hardly necessary to point out the many absurdities of this document. There is conclusive evidence that Constantine was baptized on his death-bed by an Arian bishop at his palace near Nicomedia. It is not known where the story of his leprosy came from. It is obviously absurd to make Constantine speak of his "satraps," or of Silvester as "Universal Pope"—the title which horrified Gregory the Great; and the tiara was not introduced into the Roman Church before the days of Pope Constantine in about A.D. 710. The Roman clergy's desire for the dress and trappings of the imperial officials was expressed in the late sixth century in a

---

[1] The text has been often printed. It is found in Migne, *Pat. Lat.*, vol. 8, col. 567. It is known as *Edictum Constantini* or *Constitutum Constantini*.

protest of Gregory the Great to the clergy of Ravenna. But the most important section of the document throughout all the Middle Ages was the short and insignificant statement of the transfer of imperial authority to the Pope. This was used by supporters of papal power against the medieval German "Emperors"; but unfortunately for their argument, if that power rests on the gift of an Emperor, an Emperor is superior to the Pope! It is also interesting to note that the Roman clergy desired to have no Emperor at all in the West, about twenty or thirty years before Pope Leo III crowned Charles the Great as Emperor. The *Donation of Constantine*, however, remained throughout the Middle Ages the legal basis for the "temporal power."[1] It fixed in the minds of that time the conception of the Pope as a ruler or "temporal" sovereign over certain territories. The flight of Pope Leo III from Rome and his return there under the protection of the armed forces of Charles the Great in A.D. 800 established in fact, if not in theory, what the Greek historian Theophanes perceived to be the first complete control of Rome by the Frankish king.[2] The ambiguous relations between that king and the Pope, which were the results of the coronation of Charles as "Emperor," will be discussed in the next chapter. But so far as the temporal power of the Papacy is concerned, its dependence upon alien armed forces was not believed in the ninth century or later to destroy the supremacy of the Pope as ruler of the territories of the Roman Church. From the beginning of the ninth century, when the Pope was in some sense a king, the struggles of rival parties in Rome and its neighbourhood, at the election of each new Pope, became more riotous and bloody. Clearly the rivalry was partly due to an attempt by the armed warriors of Rome or sections of the clergy to take advantage of the magical powers which were believed to belong to the successor of St. Peter. But it was also a struggle for wealth and the control of ecclesiastical property. A division of the spoils generally followed

---

[1] It was the basis for the forged grant by the English Pope Hadrian IV to the king of England, Henry II, of the right to conquer Ireland, to convert its inhabitants, and to make them pay tribute to the Papacy: "Hiberniam et omnes insulas . . . ad ius beati Petri et S.R.E. non est dubium pertinere." Text in Dollinger, *Fables of the Popes*, Appendix D.   [2] See below, page 601.

the success of one party or the other in securing the Papacy for its candidate.

When Leo III died in A.D. 816 (June 12th) many attempts at rebellion against his rule in Rome had already been suppressed since the death of Charles the Great in A.D. 814. The new Pope, Stephen IV, first commanded the Romans to swear fidelity to the new Emperor, Louis, who had been crowned by his father at Aachen, and not by a Pope in Rome. Stephen IV then journeyed to Rheims; and there in October 816 Louis and his wife were crowned by the Pope, who had brought with him a golden crown. The succeeding Pope, Paschal, sent a papal official to ask for a renewal of the Frankish king's grant to the Papacy; and the grant was renewed in a "Constitutum" containing the earliest surviving statement of the extent of the "Temporal Power" of the Papacy in A.D. 817.[1] It establishes a guarantee, by the controller of the Frankish armed forces, of papal rule over Rome, its neighbourhood, the Exarchate and parts of Tuscany, besides some properties in southern Italy. Conditions are attached: first, that there should be no unjust oppression; and secondly, that each Pope after his consecration should send an embassy to the king of the Franks, renewing the treaty with him. The result of the establishment of papal rule was a series of still more violent conflicts in Rome; and a later Constitution lays it down that the Emperor's power protects the inhabitants as well as the Pope, who rules the territories of St. Peter; that the officials in Rome should be known to the Emperor; and that two "missi," one of the Pope and one of the Emperor, should reside permanently in Rome.[2] This arrangement was accepted by the new Pope, Eugenius II, who had been elected under the influence of the "nobles," or military leaders of Rome. And in A.D. 826 a council of sixty-two bishops was held in Rome, which decreed

[1] See Duchesne, L'État Pontifical, p. 189.
[2] The text is in Pat. Lat., vol. 97, col. 459. Article 3 decrees that the election of a Pope should be made only by those inhabitants of Rome who have traditionally the right. Article 4 says that the two missi (of the Pope and the Emperor) shall report annually how the military and civil Authorities behave (duces et judices). Article 5, that the whole Roman people shall be asked under what law they desire to be judged. Article 8, that all civil officials of Rome should appear before the Emperor. This Constitutum is followed by a form of oath taken by the Romans promising a loyalty to the Emperors and obedience to the rules of papal election.

rules covering the regulations imposed by the Emperor, and accepting his decision as to the method of electing a Pope by the clergy, the nobles and the laity of the Roman Church. Thus, the Temporal Power was finally established as a result indeed of the policy of the earlier Popes, but under the direct control of the king of the Franks, who was then treated as "Emperor of the Romans."

Effect of the Temporal Power

The character of the medieval Papacy was deeply affected by the Temporal Power. The Church of Rome had had large estates since the beginning of the fifth century; and even when it lost its estates in Sicily during its quarrel with the iconoclast Emperors, it still retained much land and other wealth in Italy and elsewhere. The defence and civil administration of its estates had always been in the hands of an emperor or king; and the Church used its wealth for the maintenance of its clergy, its ceremonies, and the poor of Rome and other cities. But at the end of the eighth century the bishop of Rome became the supreme ruler of the population of the city, of the estates of the Church, and of the territories then known as the Patrimony of St. Peter. The wealth of the Church had, therefore, to be devoted partly to the maintenance of military force and civil administration. The Peter's Pence which came from distant countries were used partly to support the armed forces of the papal Government; and the controllers of such Government could hardly be believed, by those who knew the facts, to be purely "spiritual" in their interests. Again, with the attainment of Temporal Power, the Papacy became a kingdom among other kingdoms. It could not, therefore, be believed to be above or outside the struggle for power among competing rulers. It was not "international" in the sense in which modern science or music is international. The Pope as a king, during the Middle Ages, was never strong enough to be independent of the influence of more powerful rulers; and the existence of the Temporal Power, therefore, made it always possible for critics of the Papacy to regard it as an instrument or plaything of some king or emperor. The inevitable result upon the spiritual authority of the Papacy was evident in the type of person who was elected bishop of Rome during the ninth and tenth centuries and even later. Indeed, it was only because of the widespread ignorance of the actual situation in Rome which prevailed in northern Europe, that the myth of a wholly spiritual power embodied in the Papacy was able to survive.

Four centuries after the establishment of the Temporal Power, Dante in his great poem lamented the *Donation of Constantine*, by which the Emperor "made himself a Greek,"[1] and cursed the pursuit of wealth to which the attainment of the Temporal Power had led the Pope.[2]

The effects of the Temporal Power on the moral authority of the Papacy were clearly disastrous. But even more disastrous for Italy as a whole was the insertion into the very centre of the peninsula of a half-independent State, ruled by a bishop. This State divided the Lombard territories in the north from those in the south of Italy. And throughout the Middle Ages its ruler could call upon alien armies to support his policy against his neighbours. Thus, the Temporal Power of the Papacy was the chief obstacle to the unity and progress of Italy, until it was destroyed in 1870.[3] This same rule of the Pope, based upon the prestige of an obsolete system of city government, also supported the restoration of city government in medieval Italy, which caused the interminable wars, like the wars of ancient Greek cities, between Florence, Pisa and the rest. And these wars again prevented the unification of Italy.

The opposition between the Papacy and the Lombards for the two hundred years, A.D. 600 to 800, has not been treated by historians from the Lombard point of view. All the documents express the papal policy. But ever since the days when Gregory the Great complained against the Lombards, the Popes acted as aliens, in the eyes of the rulers of the rest of Italy. Sometimes the Pope of the day would pay tribute to the Lombard king or seek

---

[1] Dante, *Par.*, xx, 57.   [2] Ibid., *Inf.*, xix, 115.

[3] The establishment of a fictitious sovereignty of the Pope under the Lateran Treaty of 1929 is historically an absurdity. The Pope's kingdom is now called "the Vatican City"—a city wholly unknown to history, entirely outside the area of historical Rome, and having no connection with the Cathedral of the bishop of Rome, in the Lateran Palace. The so-called "Vatican city" is part of the "Leonine city"—the defensive works of which were built in A.D. 851.

support from a Lombard duke in southern Italy. But always the Papacy refused to become subject to the civil and military authority which controlled the greater part of Italy. The result during the eighth and ninth centuries was that the papal State formed a barrier between the north and the south of Italy. The Lombard king, from his capital at Pavia, naturally resented the obstacle which prevented the reduction of the great dukes of Benevento and Spoleto to subordination in a single kingdom. In the early seventh century the Popes represented the power of the Emperor at Constantinople. And the Emperor, clinging to the remnants of territory left by Justinian's ridiculous policy in Italy, was naturally regarded as an enemy by the Lombard king. In the eighth century the Popes lost all hope of support from Constantinople; but instead of permitting the unity of Italy under the Lombards, appealed, as the Emperors had sometimes done before them, to another German tribe, the Franks, to destroy Lombard power. In A.D. 800 Lombard rule had disappeared in northern Italy; but it was merely replaced by Frankish control. The same difficulty, however, faced the Frankish king. The Pope's attempt to retain an independent civil and military control of central Italy stood always in the way of any unification of the government of the peninsula. Even in the year A.D. 890, when Pope Stephen V in theory admitted the status of Guy, king of Italy, whom he crowned as Emperor in St. Peter's, the Pope was nevertheless at the same time appealing to Arnulf the king of the eastern Franks. Thus, every effort of the rulers of different parts of Italy, during the early Middle Ages, to bring the country into such unity as it had enjoyed under the Roman Empire and the kings of the Ostrogoths, was frustrated by the maintenance of the Temporal Power of the Papacy.

General Conclusion

The characteristics of the medieval Papacy, which are to be most clearly seen in the early ninth century, may be summarized under the headings used above—in doctrine, discipline and independence of civil authority. As for doctrine, clearly the character of the Papacy was much more affected by Rome and its traditions than by the writings or teachings of early Christianity. That is to say, Rome made St. Peter supreme, and not St. Peter, Rome. Nobody has ever argued that the Church at Antioch, for example, was supreme over other Christian Churches when St. Peter, according to tradition, was its bishop for seven years. His supremacy over the Universal Church, as conceived in the Middle Ages, appears to have begun only when he reached Rome. But even more interesting is the effect of the Roman tradition upon doctrine, as understood in the Latin Churches. Rome was long believed to be the supreme source of law; and Roman law in the fifth century in practice, and in later centuries in theory, had a universality which made it appear to be the law of all human beings. The Roman Church, in its view of doctrine, was greatly influenced by the Roman attitude towards law. Statements of doctrine came to be regarded as if they were promulgations of a law. This legalistic view of doctrine, whatever its defects, was useful in the period of transition, not only because it increased the power and prestige of the Roman See, but also because it preserved, among the uncritical barbarians of the North, a moderate and reasonable expression of Christian ideas and practices. From the fifth to the ninth century, as perhaps in other ages, there were two dangers to which religion was exposed. One was too much theology; the other was too much revivalism. The legalistic view of doctrine was an attempt to escape from both these dangers. The "intellectuals" of the Greek tradition argued interminably and probably seemed to the simpler mentality of the Latin West to end by arguing only about the meaning of words, without reference to the religious experience which those words were intended to preserve. The Roman Church, therefore, as Gregory the Great plainly said, was not inclined to do too much thinking—a reasonable precaution among men and women unaccustomed to that exercise. On the other hand, the revivalism of enthusiasts who claimed to be better Christians than their fellows, had undoubtedly led mainly in the Greek, but also in some of the Latin Churches, to a reckless asceticism and a disregard for the ceremonies and sacraments which met the needs of simpler folk. The sense of virtue had often been confused with virtue itself. Not without reason, therefore, did the Latin Churches accept from the Roman Church direction in doctrine and practice, which might be limited in its outlook, but was at any rate definite.

For the maintenance and development of religious experience, the legalistic treatment of doctrine and discipline, under the influence of the Roman tradition, played its part in the establishment of Christianity in the First Europe. Christianity was indeed changed in character while it was spread and established in north-western Europe. But it remains doubtful whether, without this change of character, Christianity would have survived at all. Certainly Christendom would never have come into existence; and Christendom, not Christianity, is the peculiar characteristic of the First Europe.

With regard to discipline, the most important general effect of the development between the fifth and the ninth century was the increase in the social influence of the clergy as a separate caste whose members had powers not available to other men and women. The general tendency throughout western Europe to rely upon the efficacy of relics, sacraments and ceremonies, was expressed in its extremist form in the status and power of the Pope. St. Peter, or St. Peter and St. Paul together, the Roman Saints, became the greatest figures in the heavenly Court; and the bishop of Rome, who was most closely associated with their tombs and relics on earth, naturally seemed to stand at the very gateway of heaven. The belief that he could shut the gate by such measures as the Interdict, was characteristic of the Middle Ages, both in their religious practice and in their politics. Again, any bishop might call down the anger of heaven; but the medieval Pope was exceptionally powerful. Thus, when the Emperor Louis II, in A.D. 861, entered Rome, in hostility to Pope Nicholas, and his troops attacked a religious procession going to St. Peter's, the Pope went secretly to the Apostle's tomb. His prayers there were believed to have resulted first, in the sudden death of one of the Emperor's soldiers, and secondly, in the serious illness of the Emperor. The Emperor's wife, Engelberga, overcome with terror at the Pope's power, persuaded him to forgive her husband. This is but one instance of the terror inspired by the uncanny power which the Popes were

supposed to possess; and more sceptical opponents found it necessary in the ninth century to engage Mohammedan soldiers, who
were unaffected by the current Christian beliefs.

Again, in reference to the position of the Popes as against other
bishops and all secular authorities, the desire for unity increased
with the increasing dissensions and disorders of the First Europe.
But unity was conceived in the ninth century in very simple terms.
The first principle of unity which was generally accepted, was that
it meant preserving a connection with the past, by contrast with
the disorderly society of the day. The past, in which Rome was
the centre of unity, seemed to be almost a golden age. This had its
effect, as will be shown in the next chapter, upon the crowning
of Charles the Great as Emperor of the Romans. But it had also
an effect upon the Papacy. The Roman Church preserved always
its connection with the earliest Christian times. The unity of the
Church, therefore, seemed to mean that all roads of doctrine or
discipline led back to the Rome of St. Peter. No other bishop in
the West had so long and so impressive a line of predecessors as
the bishop of Rome.

In his relations with kings or emperors, the Pope could also
claim that he stood for the unity which all men desired. That
unity, however, was conceived, in the terms of the Roman imperial
tradition, as a form of cosmopolitanism. That is to say, the unity
of all men was conceived to be independent of their differences in
race, language and custom. The unity of the Church, expressed in
subordination to the Pope, was not international. It was a unity of
individuals, not of nations or their Governments. It disregarded
altogether the fundamental differences between nations. The Church
Triumphant in heaven had no national or racial divisions; and
therefore such divisions on earth could be regarded as unimportant.
Such a unity seemed reasonable so long as nations, in the modern
sense of that word, did not yet exist. So long as the various barbarian tribes—*nationes* in the Roman sense—were without literary
languages of their own, or while each was not conscious of a distinguishable community of feeling, the unity of the First Europe
could be reasonably conceived in the terms of cosmopolitanism.

Local loyalties seemed irrelevant or trivial to a cultured or religious person in the First Europe. As Christians, men seemed to belong to a single community, conceived to be spiritual, without vital connection in the body of daily habits and customs. It is true that the ceremonies, sacraments and festivals of the Church entered deeply into the common life of all the peoples of Christendom; but the language of religion was Latin, already a language of the dead. That language did not belong to any people or place. It was without roots in the life of the Middle Ages, and served not to unite the peoples but rather to separate the learned class and the unity for which it stood from the increasing vitality of the several nations which were already developing their own literatures.

The unity of the Christian Churches had been, for a century after Constantine, dependent on the unity of the Roman Empire. Both Prudentius and Leo I had written that the world was united under Roman rule as a preparation for Christianity. But the Roman Empire in the Latin West was dissolved into separate barbarian kingdoms; and the unity of the Catholic Church survived. It was inevitable, therefore, that the unity of the Latin Churches should preserve many of the features of the imperial unity on which it had been originally based. But now the Church itself had become the only basis of unity in a world divided by barbarian kings. And in order to make that unity visible the Church itself became an Empire. It was centralized at the end of the eighth century under a monarchy like that of the Caesars when the head of the Church of the city of Rome took over the power and authority of the Emperor in that city. In Rome "Saint Caesar in the Palace" had a feast-day and procession to his church on the Palatine.[1] In this church, which was attached to the official residence and central office of the Emperor, of the Exarch and the Duke of Rome, the portraits (*imagines*) of the Emperors were kept. But the Pope, as the *Donation of Constantine* shows, had already acquired at the end of the eighth century, in the eyes of the Roman clergy, the status of an Emperor of the western world. And in the ninth century Walafridus Strabo (Cock-eyed Wilfred), the pupil of Alcuin and

[1] On *Sanctus Caesar in Palatio* see Duchesne, *L'État Pontifical*, ed. 1911, p. 96.

abbot of Reichenau, in A.D. 842 wrote: "As the race of the Romans is said to have held the monarchy of the whole world, so the Supreme Pontiff, holding the place of St. Peter in the Roman See, is raised to the highest position in the Church . . . the Roman Pope, therefore, is compared with the Augusti and the Caesars; and the Patriarchs with the Patricii who came first after the Caesars in the Empire."[1] Thus by the middle of the ninth century the Pope as the head of the Roman Church had become the supreme ruler of all Latin Christendom in the imperial Church. The loosely organized Christianity of the fifth century had become the highly centralized Christendom of the Middle Ages. The unity of the First Europe was achieved, in the peculiar form which was to last for seven centuries, until the Reformation.

[1] Walafridus Strabo, *De Rebus Eccl.*, cap. 31. *Pat. Lat.*, vol. 114.

CHAPTER XIV

THE PLAY EMPEROR

On Christmas Day, A.D. 800, Charles the Great, the king of the Franks, was crowned as Emperor and Augustus in the basilica of St. Peter in the Vatican by Pope Leo III.[1] Each of the chief actors in this episode was playing a part. And in view of the later history of the Holy Roman Empire, which was supposed by some historians to have then come into existence, the parts make the play almost a comedy. But that is from the point of view of a much later age. At the time and throughout the Middle Ages, the majority of men who thought at all on such subjects, no doubt, seriously believed that Charles was a successor of the Emperor Augustus, and that the successor of St. Peter had the power to make him so.

It may be difficult in modern times to recognize the power of make-believe in the ninth century and the Middle Ages. The historical imagination was entirely lacking. The habits and customs of the ninth century could easily be confused with what was then supposed to have occurred in the first century, just as the Hebrew records of kings and prophets could be confused with the actions and policies of Germanic warriors and their bishops. Eight hundred years divided the first Augustus from Charles the Great, and Peter the Apostle from Pope Leo III; but perhaps both the Frankish king and the Pope were thinking chiefly of the last claimant to the title of Augustus at Constantinople, Constantine VI, who had been blinded by order of his devout Christian mother and deposed three years before, on August 18, 797. Charles the Great may have thought that he was a successor of that Augustus; but it is by no means certain that he himself took his new titles as seriously as did some

---

[1] Charles the Great and not Charlemagne will be the name used here, because "Charlemagne" means the mythical figure of the romances.

of his followers. He may have known that the pageant in which the part of Emperor had been assigned to him, had very little connection with real life.

In a play by Pirandello, called *Henry IV*, the plot turns upon the position of a man who had played the part of the Emperor, Henry IV, in a pageant; and having fallen from his horse, was for some time unable to distinguish himself from the Emperor. The gradual return of sanity leaves the friends, who had supported the illusion by accepting him as Emperor, in some difficulty. The force of the play depends upon the recognition by the audience that the play-Emperor has recovered from his illusion, while the other characters in the piece are still uncertain how to treat him.

Charles the Great was a play-Emperor. The "Holy Roman Empire" in the West, throughout the Middle Ages, was an historical pageant, without any relation to the realities of the time. No doubt it was believed by some to be a continuation of that Empire which had disappeared in western Europe four centuries before Charles the Great. But that same Empire continued to exist in the East with its capital at Constantinople, as in the days of the first Christian Emperor; and both Charles and the Pope knew that the Roman Empire was actually in existence, with its central government and its military forces, at the time when the episode in the basilica of St. Peter's in Rome was being performed. It is impossible to believe that either the barbarian king or the Pope who had been lately rehabilitated by him, thought that the coronation in St Peter's, either in right or in fact, transferred the central government of the Roman Empire from Constantinople to Rome. And neither their words nor acts, as recorded, give any ground for believing that they thought that they were establishing a new system of government.

The phrase "Holy Roman Empire" has misled some scholars and most popular historians. The Roman Empire, from its earliest days, continued to use the word "holy" (*sanctus*) in the sense familiar long before Christianity began. That Empire and its Emperors, as well as its chief officials, had always been called "holy," but not in the modern sense of that word. The word "*sanctus*," as explained above in Chapter III, meant "revered," or "possessed of uncanny power"; and the ghostly "Roman Empire" of the Middle Ages merely continued the phraseology of the real Empire. In the same sense, the See of the bishop of Rome was called the "Holy See" (*sancta sedes*) without exclusive reference to any moral quality. But the later development of the meaning of the word "*sanctus*" or "saint" led to the quite illegitimate distinction between an earlier "Roman Empire" and a later "Holy Roman Empire." No such distinction would have been intelligible to Charles the Great or Pope Leo III. Both of them were thinking of the only Emperor or Augustus who had ever existed, in an Empire which had always been called "holy."

It may be assumed as obvious that there never had been two Roman Empires—one of the East and one of the West. In practice, as well as in theory, the whole Empire had, at certain times, been administered by two Emperors of equal authority, just as under the Roman Republic two consuls of equal authority had administered different parts of the Roman Dominions. Thus when the rule of the Roman Emperor ceased to exist in western Europe in A.D. 479, the Roman Empire continued unchanged, except for its lost territory. It is therefore quite misleading to speak of a western Roman Empire; and thus, when Justinian restored Italy and Africa to the Empire again, no "western" Empire came into existence. Charles the Great and Pope Leo III knew quite well that there was only one Roman Empire; but they may have imagined that two Emperors of equal authority could exist in the ninth century as in the fifth. Even if, however, that was their belief, they cannot have supposed that the people of Rome or the bishops of that city had any right or power to give to Charles, as Emperor and Augustus, control of the imperial system centred in Constantinople.

At the time of the coronation of Charles as Emperor, indeed, an Empress and not an Emperor reigned in Constantinople. The Empress Irene had dethroned her son, the Emperor, in A.D. 797; and then ruled alone. It is possible that there was a general feeling, especially in the West, that the imperial authority could not be rightly claimed by a woman in her own name. The negotiations of Charles the Great, with the view to his marriage with Irene, may also indicate that he intended to succeed Constantine as Emperor; but these negotiations came to nothing and, in any case, Charles the Great cannot have supposed that the bishop of Rome had the power to make him Emperor at Constantinople.

That no new institution was founded and no old one revived in A.D. 800 is proved by the action of those who bore the title of Emperor. Rome was never made the seat of imperial authority by Charles the Great or his successors. No "palace" (*palatium*) or central office was established in Rome. But the newly crowned "Emperor" returned immediately to his old seat of government at Aachen; and almost all the Frankish and other barbarian successors of the new Emperor resided and exerted what authority they had, north of the Alps. The conception of a Roman Empire, therefore, in western Europe during the Middle Ages, was entirely fantastic; and the ceremony which was supposed to found that Empire in A.D. 800 was as fantastic as any of the documents to which the ninth century gave birth—the false Decretals and the rest.

What then made it possible to impose upon western Europe a play-Emperor? The steps made in conscious policy by the kings of the Franks and the Popes of the eighth century were, no doubt, the chief causes of the coronation of Charles the Great as "Emperor." Conscious policy on the part of the Popes, as described in the last chapter, had led to their centralization of control over the Latin Churches. And conscious policy, especially on the part of the usurper, Pippin the Frank, led to an extension of the Dominions of his descendants. But before discussing the character and purpose of any such conscious policy, it is useful to notice, as in the case of the Papacy, the more indefinite forces which tended to support the idea of a new kind of Emperor.

Prestige of Imperial Rome

In the first place, the prestige of imperial Rome had never entirely faded from the minds of the kings of the Franks. It is said by Gregory of Tours that in A.D. 508 Clovis, when he returned from his victory over the Visigoths, assumed the title of "Augustus";

and although such an act may seem to have been ridiculous, there is no reason to doubt that either Clovis actually adopted the title or was generally believed, in Gregory's day, to have done so.[1] When Hincmar, archbishop of Reims in the ninth century, wrote the life of his predecessor, St. Remy, he compared Clovis to Constantine the Great and St. Remy to Pope Silvester, baptizing the Emperor.[2] Thus the prestige of imperial Rome was used for many generations by the Frankish kings as an instrument of their policy.

The interest in imperial Rome, however, as contrasted with ecclesiastical Rome, revived in northern Europe most vigorously under Charles the Great. Charles collected at his Court scholars from different countries, whose one common interest was the revival of Latin literature and learning. The king and his closest friends among these scholars shared a very simple form of humorous intercourse, in which each person was given a nickname. Thus Charles himself was referred to as "David" or "Solomon," and sometimes, in verses, as "Augustus"—meaning "revered majesty" or as "Caesar." This family name thus began its career as the title of a monarch, to be transformed later into "Kaiser" and "Tsar."[3] Adalhard, Abbot of Corbie, was called "Antonius"; Alcuin was called "Flaccus"; and Angilbert was called "Homer." Again, in Angilbert's poem, "Charles the Great and Pope Leo," written just before the coronation of A.D. 800, Charles is said to have established a "second Rome," with a "forum and sacred senate" and marble halls and aqueducts all of which is taken word for word from the first book of Virgil's *Aeneid*.[4] The verses of Alcuin and Angilbert and Theodulf of Orleans are full of phrases taken from Virgil and Ovid. And the *Life of Charles the Great* by Einhard, also a member of his Court, is a patchwork of quotations from Suetonius's *Lives of the Caesars*. Evidently the Court of Charles the Great enjoyed "make-believe," as children do. They knew they were pretending; and yet, like children, they were not very certain where pretence

---

[1] Greg. Tur., *H.F.*, i, 38. Chlodovectus ab Anastasio imperatore codicillos de consulatu suscepit . . . et ab ea die tanquam consul aut Augustus vocitatur.

[2] Hincmar, *Vita Sancti Remigii*, ch. 39. (*Pat. Lat.*, vol. 125.)

[3] The only Caesar now left is the king of England, who is Kaisar-i-Hind.

[4] Angilbert, Poems in *M.G.H.*, *Poetae Aevi Kar.*, i, pp. 366 sq.

ended and reality began. But in the minds of them all the life and literature of early imperial Rome had a profound significance.

Christian Rome

Christian Rome—the Rome of the martyrs and successors of St. Peter—had also an influence upon the kings of the Franks. When Charles Martel was in conflict with the older Churches of Gaul or western France (*Francia occidentalis*) his support of the missionary bishops in Germany or eastern France (*Francia orientalis*) brought him into direct contact with the Roman See, because these bishops looked to Rome to direct their policy of reform and missionary work. Again when Pippin, the son of Charles Martel, decided to usurp the throne, he is said to have appealed to the bishop of Rome for a judgement upon his rights. But Christian Rome exerted an even greater influence in north-western Europe, as a source from which the relics of martyrs could be brought. Thus both Gregory of Tours and Bede report travels of envoys from the North seeking relics in Rome. As early as the fifth century Prudentius wrote: "It is hardly known how full Rome is of buried saints—how richly the city's soil blossoms with sacred tombs."[1]

In the sixth and seventh centuries, one of the complaints made against the Lombards was that they rifled the Christian tombs in the catacombs in their search for relics. The tufa rock in which the graves were cut, preserved the bones and memorials of early Christians in Rome, while those buried in earth elsewhere had long since vanished. In the eighth century again Rome was the source from which relics were brought to the new churches of the recently converted Germans; and this practice continued into the ninth century as, for example, when the relics of SS. Peter and Marcellinus were taken by Einhard to Seligenstadt, the relics of St. Alexander to Wildeshausen in Westphalia, and the relics of St. Vitus, in A.D. 836, to the new monastery at Corvey (*Corbeia nova*) on

[1] Prudentius, *Peristephanon*, ii, 541.

"Vix fama nota est, abditis
quam plena sanctis Roma sit,
quam diues urbanum solum
sacris sepulcris floreat."

the far north-eastern frontiers of the Frankish Kingdom.[1] Thus the influence of Christian and ecclesiastical Rome, both in policy and religious practice, greatly affected the Franks.

The Roman Church

The unconscious tendencies which drove the Roman Church towards the establishment of a new Emperor were probably these. First, an increasing need for an alternative to the Emperor at Constantinople as protector and defender. This need, as it will be shown later, was hardly conscious in the Roman See before the middle of the eighth century; and it cannot be said that, at any stage, the Popes deliberately substituted any other civil authority for that of the Roman Emperor. Nevertheless the conquests of the Mohammedans and the weakness of the Government at Constantinople in defence of its Italian dependencies undermined the respect which the Popes continued to show for the Roman Emperor. Pope Stephen had appealed to the Emperor at Constantinople before he sent his first appeal to Pippin, king of the Franks. But the Emperor failed him. Secondly, the desire to promote unity among the Latin Churches, which led to the establishment of the medieval Papacy, also created a tendency in the Roman Church to support any movement which might lead to a unity of the civil and military authorities in western Europe. Obviously it would obstruct the unity of the Churches if the bishops in the different kingdoms or dukedoms found their kings or dukes at war one with another. It is a difficulty which the Christian Churches have not yet solved. Although war between Christian nations may not theoretically affect the Christianity of either side, clearly the bishops of one area could not practically oppose the military policy of the king on whom they depended. And because bishops and abbots as landowners had to supply military forces, even when they did not lead

[1] Here St. Vitus became the saint to whom prayer was specially made for the cure of chorea or St. Vitus' dance. It may be noted that a religious dance for the cure of disease has survived to our own day on Whit-Tuesday at Echternach, near Trier, where St. Willibrord was buried. The monastery at Corvey was so called because its first members at its foundation in A.D. 820 were Benedictines from Corbie in Picardy (Corbeia vetus). A letter of A.D. 831 or 833 from a monk of Corbie to the Abbot of Corvey shows the connection between the two houses, M.G.H., Ep. vi, Ep. K.A., 1, p. 132.

them to battle—as some did in defiance of the canons—the Churches were so closely associated with the military lordships of the day that continuous war naturally tended to divide the Churches of one area from those of another. It was natural, therefore, for the Church in Rome, representing the unity of the Christian Churches, to desire to unite all Christian kings. But unity in the eighth century and throughout the Middle Ages was assumed to involve subordination to the authority of one person. This assumption was partly due to the tradition of imperial Rome and partly due to the primitive conception that the ideal unity of men was like that of a war-band under its leader. This primitive conception in the ninth century was naturally stronger among peoples east of the Rhine than it was in the older civilization further west. The conception that an Empire, including many kingdoms or superior to them, is desirable, is not explicitly stated before the coronation of Charles the Great. But there was clearly an unconscious tendency in this direction, which affected the Popes in the second half of the eighth century, because of their desire to use any means for preserving and increasing the unity of the Churches. This same tendency to seek unity for the Christian Churches by means of political unity under one ruler certainly affected Alcuin and his friends at the Court of Charles the Great. The letters of Alcuin show that, as a good churchman and as abbot and teacher in the monastery of St. Martin at Tours, his chief interest was the unity and reform of the Church. There is no proof that he ever imagined that a revived Roman Empire would assist the Church; but undoubtedly, as will be shown later, he believed that the extension of the power and prestige of his friend, the king of the Franks, would promote peace in the Church. All the bishops and abbots of the ninth century, in Rome and north-western Europe, who desired the reform of the Church, were affected by the same tendencies, which eventually produced the medieval Empire.

The New North

A third unconscious tendency leading towards the medieval conception of an Empire was due to the influence of what may be

PLATE 8.—LEO III AND CHARLES THE GREAT WITH
ST. PETER

(Copy made in A.D. 1738 of Mosaic, A.D. 800, at the Lateran)

Note the pallium given to the Pope and the banner of Rome
given to Charles

called "the new North." As late as the middle of the sixth century, writers in most of western Europe still seem to have thought of Roman civilization as dependent upon the connection between the East and the West or the Greeks and the Latins, embodied most clearly in the connection between old Rome and new Rome. Even when in the seventh century the bishop of Rome had come to be known, among bishops in the West, as above all others, "Apostolicus" and "Pope," the connection between Pope and Emperor, between supreme power in the spiritual and supreme power in the temporal sphere, meant the relationship between the Latin Churches and the Roman Emperor then reigning at Constantinople. But while the conscious policy of the Churches in Italy and Spain was still affected by the traditional respect for the Emperor in the East, unconsciously the influence of writers, missionaries, bishops and abbots in northern Gaul (or Francia), in England and in Ireland had made a deep impression on all the Latin Churches and particularly the Church of Rome. Before the eighth century the chief influences affecting the thought and policy of the Roman Church had come either from Africa or from Syria and Alexandria. By the middle of the eighth century, however, the chief influences were coming from northern France and England.[1] Augustine of Canterbury and Theodore had brought the influence of Rome into England; and Willibrord and Boniface had extended that same influence in the districts east of the Rhine. But the result was that these countries, newly conquered for the Roman See and now producing their own literature, brought their influence to bear upon all the Latin Churches, including that of Rome. Therefore, by the middle of the eighth century, an unconscious tendency had begun to operate which made men look from Rome, not eastwards, but northwards, in their conceptions of Catholic Christianity. At the end of the eighth century, Paris, Tours, Reims, Canterbury, York, and afterwards Mainz and Cologne, had become centres of Christian life, replacing, at any rate for the Latin Churches, the African and Asiatic cities which had been reduced to subjection by Moham-

---

[1] On the influence of Syrians in the West from the fifth to the eighth century. See Bréhier, *Colonies d'Orientaux en Occident* (*Byzant. Zeitschr. 1903*).

medan invaders. In that atmosphere—the new currents of doctrine and practice flowing from the North—conscious policy was devised and carried out.

Sources of Information

Before discussing the policy which led to the crowning of Charles the Great as "Emperor," the sources may be briefly indicated, upon which all historians must depend. First, there are numerous versions of annals covering the years from Charles Martel to Charles the Great. They are generally monastic chronicles of the "Kingdom of the Franks." But as most of the surviving manuscripts of different chronicles are copies, emendations or additions, made in the ninth and later centuries, to a few bald sentences of earlier records, the many different annals are not separate sources of information. Some are definitely misleading, because they add to earlier records of an event, results which followed twenty or thirty years later, which are then given as reasons for the original event. But everyone knows that what actually happened, after a victory or defeat or the promulgation of a law, is very seldom the conscious purpose in the minds of the actors in the original drama. Also all the annals suffer from what would now be called "war-propaganda." Thus the annals often report a complete victory of the Franks, which is followed immediately after by a hurried mustering of Frankish armies to go to the help of the victors! Again the annals, like all other written documents of the time, are ecclesiastical or clerical; that is to say, they are written by monks and priests; and they are bare chronicles of events, not histories. For this period (A.D. 750–850) and in reference to Charles the Great, there is nothing comparable to the work of Procopius in the sixth century or of Gregory of Tours in the seventh or of Bede in the early eighth century. It is a period of great forgeries, such as the canons of the pseudo-Isidore and the *Donation of Constantine*, although "forgery" is not quite the correct name for works of the imagination, written by men entirely ignorant of history. It is also the period of the earliest romances or picturesque stories of great warriors and paladins (*palatini*). The *palatium* or Court officials of the Carolingian Frankish kings soon became, in the imagination of courtly poets, loyal and valiant heroes. Imagination, therefore, is a strong ingredient in the chronicles of the period.

The other sources are collections of letters, of which the chief are those of St. Boniface, of Alcuin and his friends, and of the Popes whose letters to the Frankish kings, from Charles Martel to Charles the Great, are collected in the *Codex Carolinus*. This collection was originally written out on parchment under the direction of Charles the Great in A.D. 791; but unfortunately it contains only the letters *from* Rome, and not those sent by the Frankish kings to the Popes. It may be noted that all these letters were written by churchmen who were closely concerned with the policy and public affairs of their day. On the other hand, the chief interest of St. Boniface and of Alcuin, both of them Englishmen and admirers of Bede, was the reform and extension of Christianity. They advised and supported the Frankish kings, but cared nothing for the extension of their military power or wealth. Their letters often indicate the difficulties of intelligent men, working for the common good, in a society dominated by illiterate, violent and passionate kings and warriors.

The third source of information is to be found in the lives of the great men of the period, chiefly the *Life of Charles the Great* by Einhard. This is a vigorous but not very trustworthy account of an idealized king, written by one who had been an unimportant member of his Court. It was written about twenty years after the famous crowning in St. Peter's of A.D. 800 and about ten years after the death of Charles. The author was then an old man evidently affected by the disappointments and distresses of the reign of Louis the Pious, the son and successor of the writer's hero. It is a patch-work of phrases from Suetonius's *Lives of the Caesars*, in which Charles's corpulence, his appetite, and even the scandals about his daughters, are described or hinted at in phrases long since used about the Caesars. The new "Caesar," as contemporary verses call him, is worked up by Einhard out of Suetonius into a sort of model for medieval chivalry.

The later lives of Charles the Great, such as that of the monk of

St. Gall, are frankly affected by popular legends. But there are some historical facts to be discovered in certain monastic documents about the translation of the relics of saints in the later eighth or earlier ninth century. The foundation of new bishoprics and new monasteries in the areas east of the Rhine, conquered by the Carolingian kings of the Franks, led to a transfer of the relics of early Christian saints to the cathedrals and abbey-churches of Germany. These transfers are described in contemporary documents such as the *Translations of SS. Peter and Marcellinus* by Einhard. From all these sources may be derived not only a record of events, but also an indication of the climate of opinion in which a mysterious past, connected with the earliest history of Christian Rome, affected the imagination and the ideals of the leading men of the time.

The Policy of the Carolingians

The steps taken by those in control of social power, which led eventually to the crowning of Charles the Great, may be shortly described as follows. They are all connected with the three names—Charles Martel, Pippin his son, and Charles the Great his grandson. It is the story of the conquest of supreme power by a Frankish family, of its entanglement in Italian rivalries and of the final acceptance of a theocratic authority, as a method of preserving and extending military conquests. Conscious policy was that of barbarian warriors who could extend their power by armed force but found, as all barbarians are surprised to find, that they could not hold their conquests except by acquiring some moral authority.

Charles Martel, the illegitimate son of Pippin of Heristal, made his first bid for power at the age of twenty-five, on the death of his father (A.D. 714). His father had secured, at the end of interminable and confused struggles and treacheries, the power to control, as chief of the Palace, the king of the Franks. Charles Martel had to fight battles and employ the traditional treachery, in order to secure his power. But, with the assistance of the Frankish warriors who held land in Austrasia, and of those from Neustria who were discontented with the recent efforts to restore power to the king's Court (*palatium*), he contrived eventually to secure the greatest military power in the kingdom for himself. His control of Neustria or northern France compelled him to take account of the advance of the Saracens northwards from Spain; and in A.D. 732 he defeated the Saracen raiders in a great battle near Poitiers. This battle has been given by some historians an exaggerated importance. It is even said to have saved western Europe from becoming Mohammedan. But it seems likely, in fact, that the Saracen raiders defeated by Charles Martel were only seeking for loot and not for permanent conquest; and besides, the Saracen leaders were already divided among themselves before meeting the Frankish forces. Their dissensions may have largely contributed to their defeat.

For the future policy of the Frankish leaders, however, what was generally believed was more important than what actually occurred. It was believed that Charles Martel had defended the whole of western Christendom and defeated its chief enemies. Thus he became the instrument of God's will and the protector of the Faith against "infidels." It has been noted in an earlier chapter that Charles Martel used the lands of the Churches in Neustria to reward his military followers; and from this point of view he may be regarded as an enemy of the Church. But the complaints against him came from the western part of his domains; and whatever hostility there was to his power and policy on the part of some ecclesiastics, the Churches in his eastern or Austrasian domains, as well as the Church of Rome, evidently regarded him as a protector of Christendom.

Two years after the defeat of the Saracens, Charles Martel attacked and conquered the pagans of Frisia, thereby extending the fields for missionary effort. St. Willibrord, who has been referred to in an earlier chapter, had been working in Frisia since about A.D. 690 and had had the support of Pippin, the father of Charles Martel. After the conquest of Frisia by the latter, Willibrord continued his work until his death in A.D. 738; and as he had always maintained the closest relations with Rome, Charles Martel may be regarded as promoting the missionary efforts of the bishops of Rome.

In A.D. 738 Charles Martel led an expedition against the pagan Saxons, and in that same year St. Boniface paid his third visit to

Rome, returning thence with authority for organizing the Church in Bavaria. He had already in A.D. 723 been commissioned by the Pope, in a letter to Charles Martel, not only to extend the missions of Christianity eastward but also to reform the Frankish Churches. A certain number of English clergy, monks and nuns came from England to help in the work of St. Boniface in Germany; and, as it is clear from the letter of Boniface to the bishop of Winchester, quoted above, the work of missionaries and reformers, carried out under the direct supervision of the Popes of the day, was largely dependent upon assistance given to it by Charles Martel. Here again, therefore, the Frankish ruler was an instrument for the reform and progress of Christianity.

Finally in A.D. 739 and 740 two letters, the first two in the collection known as the *Codex Carolinus*, were addressed by Pope Gregory III to Charles Martel, asking him to assist the Roman See against the Lombards. In both these letters Charles is addressed as *Subregulus* or "under-king." The last king of the Merovingian line (Thierry II), under whom in theory Charles Martel had exercised authority, had died in A.D. 727; and Charles had not troubled to select another. He himself, however, died in A.D. 741, before there was time for him to act as the Pope desired.

The appeal of the Pope was regarded as significant by the chronicler of the Carolingians who wrote, under the year A.D. 741: "At that time twice the blessed Pope Gregory III from Rome, the See of St. Peter the Apostle, sent to the renowned Prince keys of the revered tomb with the chains of St. Peter and infinitely great gifts—a delegation which had never at any time before this been heard of or seen. On the understanding that he should depart from the regions under the Emperor and he would confer the Roman consulate on the aforesaid Prince, Charles." The chronicler wrote obscurely; but he evidently felt that the appeal to Charles marked an advance in the status of his hero.[1] If the chronicler is to be

---

[1] *Fred. Scholast. Chron.*, part iii, *Pat. Lat.*, 71, col. 680. The chronicler continues by naming the delegation sent in return by Charles—the Abbot of Corbie, a monastery established by St. Balthildis, and Sigibert, a hermit of the basilica of St. Denis. The English version in the text above is intentionally confused in order to represent the Latin version.

believed, the Pope proposed to confer on the Frankish "under-king" the Roman title of "Consul." In any case, clearly tradition connected the policy of the Popes with the offer of imperial titles. Already the new ideas are evident, which were later to be expressed in the *Donation of Constantine* and the coronation of Charles the Great.

Mohammedan Invasions

A new tradition had been established; the leader of the Frankish war-bands had become the defender of Christendom against the Saracens of the South and the pagans of the North-East. It is worth while to consider, therefore, at this point what the opposition to Christianity meant, in the minds of men in the early eighth century.

The Mohammedan warriors, who are referred to in most of the literature of the time as "Saracens," were the successors of a wholly unexpected irruption, into the old domains of the Roman Empire, of barbarians from the deserts of Arabia. But these barbarians, unlike those of the forests in the North, had a new religion of their own. Six hundred years after Christianity had begun to make its way in the West, Mohammed had made for himself and a few followers a new religion, out of the half-understood Hebrew tradi-tions embodied in the Old Testament and in the legends connected with them. With this he combined some fragmentary knowledge of Christian beliefs. But his aim seems to have been to replace the fetishism and local superstitions of Arab tribes by the worship of one divine Being in the over-arching skies of the desert, and to confirm this worship by detailed provisions with regard to customs in his new society. He allowed polygamy, as in the Old Testament, but forbade the use of wine in accordance with his admiration for the Christian ascetics, of whom he seems to have heard. The earliest military successes of the followers of Mohammed against the sup-porters of the old order in Arabia seem to have passed quite un-noticed in the Roman Empire, whose rulers indeed were accustomed to the recurrence of bloodthirsty struggles between Arabs and Jews or other Semitic tribes on their borders. Soon after Mohammed's death, however, his religion and the political and military system which supported it, proved to be an explosive force.

In A.D. 636 the Mohammedans completed their conquest of Syria. In A.D. 642 they had conquered Egypt. In A.D. 650 they were attacking Sicily; and in A.D. 698 they took Carthage. In A.D. 711 the Mohammedans or "Saracens" landed in Spain and soon reduced to subjection its southern provinces. In about one century, therefore, or about three generations, the Saracens had destroyed the domination of Christianity in Syria, Egypt, Africa and Spain. They did not seek to convert the populations to their creed. Indeed, Mohammedanism was regarded by its conquering warriors as a privilege of their own—a revelation for their own guidance on earth and a promise of special provision for their enjoyment after death. The Mohammedan heaven is not the ideal of ascetics, monks or priests, but of warriors resting after battle and enjoying both sexual pleasures and feasting. The subject populations in the lands they conquered were more easily taxed if they were not converted; and they were therefore permitted to keep their own forms of religion.

The complete subjugation of the great Christian Churches, however, from Syria to Spain cannot be explained by a merely military conquest. In all the lands which the Saracens conquered there was, even before their coming, a serious division of opinion and feeling in the populations which were superficially united as Christian. In Syria the Christian Churches, which seem to modern Europe to have been "Eastern," were probably regarded by the majority of the Syrian population as Western. That is to say, they carried on the tradition of Hellenic conquest under Alexander and Hellenic rule under his successors. They were alien to the feelings of the native populations over which Greek culture and Greek theology had spread a thin veneer. In Egypt the success of the Saracens was even more obviously due to the hatred felt by the local population for the Greek Emperor at Constantinople. The Monophysites of Egypt were not unwilling to transfer their allegiance from an Emperor whom they hated as a heretic and persecutor to a Mohammedan conqueror who cared for none of these things. Similarly in the Roman province of Africa the Berber and Moorish tribes had always stood outside the influence of the culture and the Christianity of the Roman cities. In Spain civil war was endemic; and the hatred and persecution of the Jews, expressed in the Councils of Toledo and in various decrees of the Visigothic kings, indicate the fear of an alien influence looking to the East, which troubled the minds of Christians. Thus the Mohammedan conquests in the eastern and southern Mediterranean revealed fundamental differences of outlook within the populations which the writers of that time assumed to be all Christian.

Christianity itself from its earliest years was the result of compromise between the Judaic and Hellenic points of view, in theology and in ritual. And for at least four centuries the compromise was unstable. But when in the seventh century the new Semitic religion from the deserts of Arabia challenged the control of Christian rulers and bishops, the Semitic elements in Christianity rose into prominence again. There were two obvious differences between official Christianity and the religion of Mohammed. One was the objection to image-worship or the use of the images of men and animals in Islam, as contrasted with the use of images in the Greek and Roman tradition of Christianity. The objection to the use of images in religious practice was to be found in the Old Testament and in the Jewish tradition. Iconoclasm, which began about A.D. 726, was an attempt in the eastern or Greek Churches to meet the charge of idolatry, for which charge Islam could find support in the Old Testament. But the philosophical attitude underlying Iconoclasm will be discussed elsewhere. The other great difference between Semitic and Greek religion was the conception of deity expressed in each. The religions of the desert expressed the unity and aloofness of God in the over-arching sky. The religion of the Greeks and Romans conceived of God in human form. The attempt to reconcile the two traditions is expressed in the doctrine of the Trinity. But that doctrine seemed to Mohammed and his followers, as well as to the Jews, to be a form of polytheism. Islam was, therefore, conceived by its followers to be a genuine belief in one God, as contrasted with the Christian belief in three. And in this case also the "heresies" of the eastern Churches, from that of the Arians to that of the Monophysites, were attempts to compromise with the Semitic conception of the unity of God. Another attempt at compromise was the theory that Christ was the adopted Son of God (Adoptianism), which was maintained in Spain about the year A.D. 780 and after by the archbishop of Toledo and the bishop of Urgel. This revival of an ancient heresy condemned by Pope Victor in A.D. 195 took place after the establishment of Mohammedan power in Spain, and was obviously an attempt to rebut the charge that Christians did not believe in one God only. The conquests of the Mohammedans in the seventh and eighth centuries, therefore, implied a challenge to western Christianity that was far more fundamental than a mere conflict of military forces. The fear and hatred of the Saracens felt in medieval Europe was obviously an expression of a sense of weakness in some of the elements of the Christian tradition. Therefore when later ages conceived the idea that Charles Martel was a foremost defender of Christianity against the Mohammedans, they were not thinking only of military success. His opponents were "infidels" (*infideles*), not merely because they did not believe the Christian creed, but also because they were not loyal members (*fideles*) of the Christian community. The first Europe, which organized its opposition to invasion from the South, remained conscious of itself throughout the Middle Ages as a community of the faithful united against the infidels.

Northern Paganism

On the other side of the new Europe, based upon the organization of Latin Christendom, lay the pagan tribes of the North-East, in what is now called central and northern Germany, which had never been subject to the Roman Empire. The policy of Charles Martel, of his son Pippin and his grandson, Charles the Great, with regard to these tribes, was at first one of defence against raids combined with the support of the missionary efforts of monks and priests. The Frisians, in what is now northern Holland, and the Saxon tribes, which inhabited the lands from the mouth of the Elbe through Westphalia as far as Thuringia, were dangerous to the peace of the Frankish kingdom. They raided Frankish territory, as the ancestors of the Franks had raided Roman territory. And they were pagans who looted churches and monasteries, because portable treasure was to be found there. Unlike the Mohammedans in the South, they had neither a new religion nor a new rule of life to oppose to Christianity. The Carolingians, therefore, adopted the policy of punitive expeditions. It was the policy of the "open frontier"—in some ways similar to the policy of the British Government in India with regard to the north-west frontier. This policy of "butcher and bolt," as it was called in the case of India, "added to the scarcity which was the main incentive to raiding and taught the tribes the art of fighting."[1]

But the influence of the great English missionaries, St. Willibrord and St. Boniface, gave another purpose to the policy. The raiding tribes could be converted to Christianity by preachers and teachers. And for some time the policy of punitive expeditions was combined with a policy of support for missionary efforts, outside the areas which were under Frankish control. Both policies had failed in the early years of the ninth century under Charles the Great; and a new policy of permanent conquest and established ecclesiastical centres eventually extended the Frankish kingdom as far as the Elbe. But even in the days of Charles Martel, the leader of the Franks was looked upon as the defender and protagonist of Christendom against the pagans north and east of the Rhine. The victories of the Franks were generally regarded as proof of divine favour; and the extension of Frankish rule was believed to be in accordance with the will of God. Indeed, God Himself had merely used the Franks as the instrument of his own policy—*Gesta Dei per Francos!*

The Franks in Italy

The next step in the formation of the imperial idea was taken by Pippin, the son of Charles Martel. The expedition against the Lombards in Italy, which Gregory III had asked Charles to undertake, was eventually led into Italy by Pippin in A.D. 754; but not before the Pope, Stephen II, had travelled North to make intercession

---

[1] Thompson and Garratt, *British Rule in India* (1934), p. 502.

himself with Pippin. By this time Pippin had been already crowned and anointed by St. Boniface as king of the Franks (see above, Chapter VII, p. 282); and the Pope himself again anointed Pippin and his two sons at the monastery of St. Denis on January 6, 754. In the early summer after an assembly of the Franks, at which the policy was opposed by Frankish nobles, Pippin advanced into Italy and laid siege to Pavia, the Lombard capital. The Pope returned to Rome in October of that year; and from this time the king of the Franks was addressed in papal letters as *Patricius Romanorum*. The Lombard king had agreed to yield some territories over which the Pope claimed authority; but two years later, in A.D. 756, he laid siege to Rome itself.

The title *Patricius* or "patrician" was apparently conferred on the Frankish king by the Pope, on his own authority. In theory it was a title of an imperial official of high standing, like the exarch at Ravenna, directly subordinate to the Emperor at Constantinople. There was, for example, a Patrician of Sicily; but, in theory, the highest civil and military authority in the Roman duchy was the Duke of Rome (*Dux Romae*). Once more, as in the chronicler's tradition about Charles Martel, a Pope offered an imperial title to a Frankish leader, as a reward for armed assistance. But Pippin himself seems never to have accepted or used the title *Patricius* officially. Evidently there was some difference between the policy of the king and that of the Pope with regard to the Roman Emperor. Pippin was moving carefully. In A.D. 756 he had taken Ravenna, the seat of imperial authority in Italy, from the Lombards; and he had left in control of it, not the Emperor but the Pope. In A.D. 762, however, he sent a friendly embassy to Constantinople and received in return, a few years later, an embassy from the Emperor, raising the question of the marriage of Pippin's daughter to the Emperor's son. Finally in A.D. 767 a council or synod was held at Gentilly, at which discussions arose, according to the earliest Chronicle, "between the Romans and the Greeks about the Holy Trinity and about images."[1] The king of the Franks, besides negotiating an imperial connection for his family, was evidently becoming involved

[1] *Annales. R.F. (Laurissenses) Ann.* A.D. 767.

in the controversies about images, in which the Emperor at Constantinople led the opposition to the use of images.

The position of the Frankish king was therefore ambiguous, when Pippin died in A.D. 768 and was succeeded by his two sons Carloman and Charles, later called the Great. Meantime the violent struggles of rival Popes in Rome had ended with the election of Pope Stephen III, in whose name a letter and embassy had been sent to the Frankish king, explaining the situation. The two young kings who then divided the Frankish kingdom were in some way concerned with the mission of bishops from their kingdom who met the Italian bishops at the Council of the Lateran in A.D. 769. But Frankish policy was not advanced to a new stage until a new and more vigorous Pope, Hadrian I (A.D. 772–795), appealed to Charles the Great for help against the Lombards.

Charles the Great

Carloman had died; and the intricate policies of the Lombard king, as protector of his sons, cannot be discussed here. Charles, in fact, was the recognized king of all the Frankish territories. At the request of Pope Hadrian he led his armies into northern Italy—this time not as a punitive expedition, but for the conquest of the Lombard kingdom. Charles, already holding the title of Patrician of the Romans, left his armies besieging the Lombard king in his capital, Pavia, and unlike his father, Pippin, he entered Rome himself at Easter A.D. 774. At some distance from the city he was received by Pope Hadrian and citizens of Rome with the ceremony traditionally used for the welcome of an Exarch—not an Emperor. Before he left Rome the Pope presented him with a copy of the collection of canons, based upon the translation made by Dionysius the Little.[1] This collection had great influence in confirming the authority of the Roman Church as a source of reform among the Frankish Churches. Finally Charles confirmed the donation of his father, Pippin; but, after victory against the Lombards, himself adopted the title of king of the Lombards.

An entirely new situation had arisen. The Frankish defender of

[1] See above, Chapter VIII, p. 355.

the Papacy was now in control of large areas in northern Italy; and his armed forces were within easy reach of Rome. Hitherto all papal letters, even those addressed to the king of the Franks, were dated by the years of the reign of the Roman Emperor; but the last papal letter still existing, which was so dated, is Hadrian's letter of A.D. 772. The Papacy no longer looked to "the Greeks." During the next twenty years Charles the Great moved with his armies from one frontier of his kingdoms to another, in recurrent warfare with the Saracens in the South and the pagans of the North-East; but he always held military control of northern and central Italy.

For explaining the policy which led to the medieval Empire, it is not necessary to describe in detail the campaigns of Charles the Great. It is enough to say that he extended the areas over which Charles Martel had ruled to the south of the Pyrenees—against the Saracens, and north-east, to the Elbe, against the Saxons, besides securing some control over the Slav tribes who lived beyond the Germanic peoples in the East of what we now call Germany. He was believed later and may have believed himself to have been "the defender of the Faith" against the Mohammedans who could not be converted, and the pagans of the North who could at least be baptized. The famous defeat of the Franks at Roncesvalles, in an early retirement from Spain, was followed many years after by an extension of the frontiers controlled by Louis, the son of Charles, as far as the Ebro. Even that, however, was due to disputes between Mohammedan chieftains rather than to the prowess of the Franks; and Charles was willing enough to receive embassies of peace both from the Mohammedan rulers of southern Spain and from Haroun-al-Raschid, the Caliph of Baghdad (A.D. 763–809).

The "defender of the Faith" had more trouble with the pagans in the North. Whenever he was away from his northern territories bands of Saxons would raid Frankish settlements; and for many years Charles led punitive expeditions into the forests and marshes inhabited by the Saxon tribes. In the early summers he would gather his hosts at Paderborn, or some other eastern meeting-place, and lead them out or send detachments against the Saxons. In A.D. 780 he thought he had pacified the "open frontier." Many

Saxons were baptized; and missionaries were sent into their settlements.

But the next expedition of Charles into Italy (A.D. 780–782), which will be discussed later, provided an opportunity for the Saxons again to attack the Franks. Charles led his army against them in A.D. 782; and, having taken four thousand five hundred hostages, had them slaughtered in cold blood. But terrorism was no more successful than penal laws; and the fighting went on until, in A.D. 785, Charles thought that he had won a complete victory, when the chief leader of the Saxons, Widukind, accepted baptism. A letter of Pope Hadrian, written in A.D. 786, contains a reply to Charles's announcement of his victory. The Pope wrote that services of thanksgiving for victory, safety and prosperity would be held, from the eve of the feast of St. John to the eve of St. Peter's feast, "in all those parts which are under the jurisdiction of your spiritual Mother, the Holy Roman Church." The letter continues in the same way: "Your royal power must direct in all the territories or lands across the sea where the Christian people dwells."[1]

A vigorous, not to say ferocious, capitulary for controlling the Saxons was issued by Charles in A.D. 785 or 787, prescribing the death penalty for all kinds of offences against the Church or its priests.[2] Section VIII decrees that any Saxon refusing to be baptized shall be executed. Section XIX decrees that anyone who does not have his child baptized in the course of the year shall pay a fine of a hundred and twenty *solidi* if he is a noble, sixty *solidi* if he is a freeman and thirty if he is a *lidus*. Articles XVI and XVII decree the payment of tithes to the clergy by all Saxons. The principle is evidently "Christianity or death."[3] And it must be remembered also that death for those who refused baptism was believed by the authors and agents of this policy to be followed by the burning of its victims in hell for all eternity.

The best men in the Church were altogether opposed to the policy of compulsory Christianity which the barbarian king had

---

[1] *Codex Carolinus*, Ep. 67, *M.G.H.*, Ep. Merov. et Kar. A., i.

[2] *M.G.H.*, Capitularia I, No. 26. This Capitulary is given by Halphen (*Études Critiques*, 1920, p. 171) the date A.D. 785, but by C. de Clercq (*Législation*, etc., 1936, p. 167) the date A.D. 787.   [3] Halphen, op. cit., p. 175.

adopted. It was not unlike the policy of some Mohammedan warriors in the South at the same date; but, to do them justice, the Mohammedans usually preferred that their conquered subjects should not become Mohammedan, and therefore should pay a larger tribute. The clearest criticism of Charles's barbarism was expressed by his old friend, Alcuin. Alcuin wrote, some time after August 796, to Charles's treasurer, Manfred, asking him to remind his "beloved David" that "faith, as St. Augustine says, is something voluntary, not compulsory. A man may be drawn to faith but cannot be forced into it. He can be forced to baptism but he makes no progress in faith. . . . An adult must answer for himself what he believes or what he desires; and if he professes the faith dishonestly, truly he will not have salvation."[1] Again, "if the preaching to the Saxons were as constant as the demand for tithes, perhaps they would not hate the Sacrament of Baptism." In A.D. 796 Alcuin wrote to his old friend Arno, bishop of Salzburg, who was going with the army against the Avars, telling him "not to exact tithes— for tithes, it is reported, have undermined the faith of the Saxons."[2] And later in the same year he wrote again to Arno, warning him against baptizing people who did not understand Christianity. "The miserable race of the Saxons has so often lost the Sacrament of Baptism, because it never had in its heart the foundation of faith. But this must be remembered that faith comes by willing assent, not by compulsion, as St. Augustine says. How can a man be forced to believe what he does not believe? He can be forced to baptism but not to faith. A man who has reason and intelligence must be taught and attracted by teaching."[3]

Alcuin was an Englishman and when he wrote these letters was abbot of the monastery of St. Martin at Tours which had been founded long before the Franks were Christians. He knew that the Christianity of Gaul and of England had been established without armed force and, indeed, largely in defiance of those who held power. He may well have doubted the sincerity and permanence

[1] *M.G.H.*, Ep. iv, Kar. Aevi. ii, p. 160.
[2] Alcuin, Ep. 107. *M.G.H.*, Ep. iv, Kar. Aevi. ii, p. 153. "Et esto predicator pietatis non decimarum exactor."
[3] Ibid., Ep. 113. *M.G.H.*, Ep. iv, Kar. Aevi. ii, p. 163.

of Christian beliefs and practices among the Germanic and neighbouring Slav tribes, which had been forced upon them by defeat
in battle. The victories of Charles the Great evidently did not
satisfy even his admirers.

The Saxons rose against the Franks and burnt churches and
monasteries again in A.D. 793–795; and in A.D. 797 Charles appears
to have adopted a new policy in the effort to conciliate the peoples
whose "conversion" by force lasted only so long as his armies were
in their neighbourhood. He issued a Capitulary at Aachen in
A.D. 797, after some consultation with Saxon leaders, which was
much less violent and oppressive than the Capitulary of A.D. 787.[1]
Frankish lords, bishops and monasteries had been placed in control
of territories inhabited by the Saxons. This was a new policy—the
policy of the "closed" frontier. The domination of Frankish warriors
and churchmen was to keep the Saxons in subjection to Charles's
form of Christianity. But even this proved ineffectual. The final
policy adopted therefore by Charles was the removal of the Saxon
population from their own lands. They were scattered in the territories already fully controlled by the Franks; and their lands were
given to the Obotrites, a non-Germanic people. The frontier of the
Frankish kingdom was thus finally advanced in A.D. 809 to the
Elbe. What is now called north-western Prussia was made a part
of East France (*Francia orientalis*) or Germany, by the settlement
of Slavs in territories hitherto inhabited by Germanic tribes. And
this was done by a Germanic king.

The efforts of Charles the Great to subdue the Saxons and other
non-Christian tribes in Germany continued until the very end of
his life and left the Frankish kingdom, east of the Rhine, with an
unsolved problem. The frontier was not secure; and those living
within it had racial and linguistic connections with non-Christian
tribes living outside it. In the South-West, on the other hand, that
is to say in Spain, the frontier was more securely guarded; and the
Frankish rulers and their subjects were clearly divided from the
population ruled by adherents of a new and militant religion. On
the whole, therefore, the king of the Franks could be reasonably

[1] Cap. Saxonicum, A.D. 797, in *Pat. Lat.*, vol. 97, col. 199.

regarded as the leader and defender of Christendom in that First Europe of the North-West in which the foundations of medieval custom and belief were established.

Charles in Italy

With such prestige as a leader Charles the Great supported his policy in Italy, which led directly to his adoption of the title of Emperor. It has been shown above that his first visit to Rome in A.D. 774 established a close connection between himself and the Pope. It is now necessary to discuss the three later visits which Charles the Great made to Rome in A.D. 781, A.D. 786 and A.D. 800. While the difficulties with the Saxons still embarrassed the Frankish king, an embassy of Mohammedan chiefs from Spain had come to Charles at Paderborn and induced him to undertake an expedition into Spain, which ended in a retreat and the disastrous defeat of a rearguard at Roncesvalles (August 15, 778). But in addition to raiding expeditions in the South-West and North-East, Charles as king of the Lombards found it necessary to lead his forces into Italy in A.D. 780; and in that year he issued the Capitulary in which an attempt was made to organize the Churches of northern Italy. The Easter of A.D. 781 was kept by Charles at Rome; and the presence of an ambitious and powerful Frankish king in Italy, no doubt, attracted the attention of the imperial Court at Constantinople, which still controlled Venice, Sicily and some parts of southern Italy. Irene, the mother of the Emperor, was then in control of imperial policy; and in A.D. 781 negotiations were begun for the marriage of Charles's daughter, Rotruda, to the young Emperor Constantine VI. According to Theophanes, the Greek historian, a secretary, who was a eunuch from the imperial Court, was sent "to teach the young lady Greek literature and speech and to educate her in the manners and customs of the Roman Empire."[1] It will be noticed that the language of the Court was Greek and the title of the Court was Roman. But similar contrasts have occurred in later history. There is an Empire which is called "British," whose

---

[1] Theophanes, *Chron. A.M.*, 6274 (*Pat. Gr.*, 108, col. 917) πρὸς τὸ διδάξαι αὐτὴν τά τε τῶν Γραικῶν γράμματα καὶ τὴν γλῶσσαν καὶ παιδεῦσαι αὐτὴν τὰ ἤθη τῆς Ῥωμαίων Βασιλείας.

language and customs are those of Saxons. The ancestors of the English destroyed the Britons or reduced them to slavery; but modern Saxons called themselves Britons. Similarly in the ninth century, when there were no more Romans, the Greeks in Constantinople called their Empire "Roman" and their ruler a Roman Emperor.

The plan of marrying his daughter to the Emperor shows that Charles was at this date inclined to forestall any suspicions of his policy in Italy, which the imperial Authorities might entertain. On the other hand, Irene, the mother of the Emperor, seems to have been inclined to maintain peace with the most powerful king in the West. The marriage of their daughters by ambitious kings was an element of policy, which has already been noticed in the case of Theodoric the Ostrogoth; and Charles himself, who had nine more or less legitimate daughters, had at an earlier date negotiated for the marriage of one of them with the son of Offa, king of the Mercians, when that king seemed to hold the *imperium* of most of England. But neither marriage ever took place. Policy was obstructed by affection. Charles the Great could not bear to part with any of his daughters or to allow them to marry, in spite of the scandals which connected their names with those of his courtiers.

In A.D. 781, in Rome, Pope Hadrian at St. Peter's in the Vatican crowned two of Charles's seven legitimate sons—Pippin, then three years old, as king of the Lombards, and Louis, who was two years old, as king of the Franks. In this same year the letters of the papal Chancellery began to be dated, not in reference to the Emperor's reign, but by the year succeeding the Pope's accession. The Papacy had become anti-imperial, since the controversy about the worship of images; but Charles the Great was evidently not pursuing the same policy. So far as the situation in A.D. 781 was concerned, the Papacy might have become an entirely independent power with a policy of its own.

For the third time in A.D. 786 Charles the Great led an expedition into Italy, this time against the duke of Benevento—thus extending his rule into southern Italy, in spite of military and naval support of the duke, sent by the imperial Authorities from Constantinople.

During this expedition also, Charles entered Rome, but departed again northwards without making any important change in his relations with the Papacy. In A.D. 787, however, the controversy about the worship of images reached a new stage in the East. The second Council of Nicaea met in that year and restored in the Greek Churches the worship of images, thus reversing the policy of the Emperors, which had been initiated in A.D. 726. For more than thirty years most of the Greek Churches had been without images or pictures of devotion. But the policy of Iconoclasm was evidently due, at least in part, to the direct influence of Emperors who came from Asia Minor and were soldiers rather than theologians. Its purpose seems to have been, first, to establish some sort of compromise with Mohammedan and Jewish influences which were affecting the Emperors' subjects in Asia Minor and, secondly, to express the submerged tradition of non-Hellenic Christian Churches in the East. As it has been noted above, in reference to Mohammedan conquest, the Christianity of the Greek-speaking Churches was regarded as oriental by the Roman and other Latin Churches of the West; but from the point of view of Syrian, Armenian and other non-Hellenic Churches, the Greek-speaking Churches were "Western." The hostility to the use of images in churches may, therefore, have been not only a concession to the followers of Mohammed but also the expression of hostility to the Greek tradition, established long before the Christian era, which accepted the representation of the divine in human form. But at last in A.D. 787, largely under the influence of the Empress Irene, herself a Greek, images and pictures were restored in the churches of the eastern Mediterranean by the canons of the second Council of Nicaea. The decrees of this Council were approved by Pope Hadrian; and forwarded by him to Charles the Great.

The king of the Franks, however, at first adopted a policy of opposition to that expressed in the decrees of the second Council of Nicaea. The so-called "Caroline Books" (Libri Carolini), issued under Charles's authority, contained not merely an attack on the worship of images but also a criticism of the claims of imperial Authority in Constantinople with respect to Christian doctrine and practice. The argument against images in the "Caroline Books" rests largely upon interpretations of certain passages from the Old Testament, and is evidently intended to support the compromise with Mohammedan and Jewish prejudices which the Emperors had followed before Irene took control into her own hands. It is also possible that the northern scholars and clergy at Charles's Court were conscious of the dangers of idolatry among the recently converted Germanic tribes, and therefore did not feel at ease with the growing attention to sacred images in the Latin Churches. Charles himself sent the "Caroline Books" to Pope Hadrian, which implies a rebuke to the Roman Church for its maintenance of the ecclesiastical use of images. The king of the Franks was evidently beginning to hold a more extensive view of the rights and duties of a defender of the Faith. But the Pope replied in a long and conclusive letter, rejecting the arguments of the "Caroline Books."[1] The Roman Church had decided to maintain a compromise between the extreme interpretations of the Nicene canons and the fear of image-worship in the northern Churches.[2]

The situation in Constantinople changed again in A.D. 790, when Irene discovered a plot against her authority and had her son, the Emperor Constantine VI, then twenty years of age, beaten like a naughty child, for his suspected connection with it. Two years later, under Irene's direction, the Emperor's uncle was blinded and his four brothers had their tongues cut out. The news evidently strengthened, in the West, the distaste for Irene's policy, in spite of the fact that she was regarded by the Authorities in the Latin Churches as orthodox on the question of images.

The next step in the development of the policy of Charles the Great was the calling of the Council of Frankfurt in A.D. 794. This Council included bishops or representatives from all the Latin Churches, two legates from the Pope and some scholars from the English Church, but none from the Churches in the East. As Paulinus, patriarch of Aquileia, writes in his report to the Council

[1] *M.G.H.*, Ep. Kar. Aevi. iii, Ep. 2.
[2] The controversy continued in later years. In A.D. 825 the Synod of Paris declared that Pope Hadrian had gone too far in approving of the Greek Council—and Agobard, bishop of Lyons (A.D. 840), wrote a book against image-worship.

on the question at issue—the Spanish heresy of Adoptianism[1]—"a multitude of bishops obeying the sacred precepts met with the least possible delay in one Convention under the guidance of the Holy Spirit and from zeal of the Catholic Faith, which moved the glorious king Charles, lord of the earth, by decree of his authority[2] in the many provinces of the kingdom which are subject to him. On a certain day when all were seated in the Council chamber of the palace priests, deacons and all the clergy being present in the circle,[3] in the presence also of the above-mentioned prince, a letter was read from Elipandus . . . and the venerable prince rising at once from the throne, stood on the dais and delivered a long address on the Faith."

The report by Paulinus ends with a prayer for Charles the Great—"May he be lord and father, king and priest, the reconciling ruler of all Christians."[4] The king of the Franks had therefore become, six years before his coronation in Rome, the holder of a sacred office and the ruler of "all Christians"; but obviously his subjects did not include the Christians of England, Ireland, or of the eastern Churches. After receiving other reports on the heresy under discussion, the Council of Frankfurt condemned Adoptianism, accepted the decision on images of the second Council of Nicaea and enacted various disciplinary canons. Examples of these are canon IV on the fixed price of corn, canon V that the new *denarii* must be accepted by everyone everywhere, canon XVII that an abbot should not be elected without consent of the bishop, canon XXI how Sunday should be kept, canon XXII that bishops are not to be consecrated in country estates or villages,[5] canon XLIII on the destruction of trees and groves, and canon LII that God is not to be prayed to in three languages only. The many different subjects dealt with in the canons indicate the various problems with which this council of bishops was concerned, under the supervision of Charles the Great.

[1] Paulinus Aquil., *Libellus*, *Pat. Lat.*, vol. 99, col. 151.
[2] —"imperii eius decreto."   [3] —"in modum coronae."
[4] Paulinus Aquil., *P.L.*, vol. 99, col. 166, "sit dominus aut pater, sit rex et sacerdos, sit omnium Christianorum moderantissimus gubernator."
[5] Ne in villis aut vicis ordinentur episcopi.

The Roman Empire

In the year following the Council of Frankfurt, Pope Hadrian died and was succeeded by Leo III (A.D. 795–816). The new Pope at once sent an embassy to Charles the Great to announce his election and to present to him the keys of the "Confession" of St. Peter and the banner of the city of Rome. Leo evidently intended to carry on the policy of Hadrian. But events in Constantinople drastically altered the situation, at any rate in the minds of Charles and his advisers. In A.D. 797 the Emperor, Constantine VI, was blinded by order of his mother, who thrust him from the imperial throne and assumed supreme authority herself.[1] Irene favoured the worship of images and was supported by the monks and most of the clergy in the East. She might, therefore, have expected support for her policy in the West. But evidently the violent deposition of an Emperor by his own mother and the assumption by a woman, for the first time in history, of supreme authority in the Roman Empire, caused consternation among those who followed public policy.

Two years later a still greater shock to sentiment in the North affected the situation. Pope Leo III, going in procession at the Greater Litanies, April 25, 799, was set upon by officials of the Roman Church, relatives of the late Pope, who beat him to the ground and attempted to tear out his eyes and tongue. They left him for dead. But his own friends rescued him; and he fled as a suppliant to Charles the Great at Paderborn. Charles received him with honour; and an elaborate poem by Angilbert, abbot of St. Riquier, describes the procession of Charles and his beautiful daughters and the splendid feast prepared for the Pope. The impression made by these events, in so far as it affected policy, is well expressed in a letter from Alcuin to Charles the Great, containing the following passage.

"There have been until now three persons who were highest in the world. That is, the Apostolic Sublimity which rules as Vicar the seat of St. Peter, Prince of the Apostles. And what has happened to him who was the holder of that seat, your respected kindness

---

[1] Constantine was then twenty-seven years old and lived on for about twenty-three years after.

has informed me. Another is the Imperial Dignity, the secular power of the second Rome (Constantinople). How impiously the governor of that Empire has been deposed, not by foreigners but by those of his own household and city, is everywhere increasingly narrated. The third is the Kingly Dignity in which the dispensation of Our Lord Jesus Christ has placed you as ruler of the Christian people—a ruler superior in power to the other above-mentioned dignities, more noble in wisdom and higher in the dignity of rule. Lo, now on you alone rests the whole safety of the Churches of Christ—you are the avenger of crime; you are the ruler of the sinful; you are the comforter of those who weep and the exaltation of the virtuous."[1]

It will be noticed that Alcuin does not suggest any change in the status or function of the king of the Franks. Indeed, he definitely makes a distinction between the imperial and the regal power, and treats the second as the instrument for the assistance of the Church and the Christian people. The use of the word *imperium* in an earlier letter of Alcuin to Charles indicates only the same sort of indefinite, superior authority as was intended by Bede when he wrote that the king of Kent had an *imperium* over eastern England. For Alcuin, Charles is always "King David" and not the Emperor Augustus. Thus, in a letter of A.D. 789 to Charles the Great, Alcuin writes: "May God grant eternal salvation and the glory of empire (*decus imperii*) to you, beloved David."[2] Clearly "imperium," in this use, has no definite reference to the Roman Empire.

The same vague use of titles drawn from the ancient tradition before the actual coronation of Charles by Pope Leo, is to be found in the poem of Angilbert, referred to above, which describes the meeting of Charles the Great and the fugitive Pope Leo. In that poem Charles is referred to as "king, ruler, revered chief, augustus"; and some lines farther down as "head of the world, chief of Europe, hero and augustus."[3] When, in the poet's imagination, the Pope

[1] *Pat. Lat.*, vol. 100, Ep. 95.
[2] Alcuin, Ep. 86, *Pat. Lat.*, vol. 100. The letter concerns the phases of the moon.
[3] Angilbert, *Karolus Magnus et Leo Papa* (*M.G.H.*, Poetae Aevi Kar. i).
    line 64. Rex, rector, venerandus apex, augustus, opimus
    line 92. Rex Karolus, caput orbis, amor populique decusque
        Europae venerandus apex, pater optimus, heros
        Augustus.

appears to Charles in a dream, the phrase from Lucan's *Pharsalia* is used—"cold fear held the limbs of the Augustus."[1] Clearly "augustus" was not intended to imply in any exact sense the traditional imperial authority. It was to Charles, as the great *king*, that his followers turned.

A Pope suppliant at the Court of a Frankish king, asking to be restored to his authority over his rebellious subjects, created a new situation, of which Charles was evidently not unwilling to take advantage. He sent the Pope back to Rome under the protection of Frankish armed forces and himself followed with his Court and retainers, reaching Rome on November 24, 800. For some weeks consultations or discussions of policy were carried on in Rome. The opponents of the Pope had charged him with perjury, adultery and other crimes; and had excused their violence as a legitimate rebellion against tyranny. The king of the Franks, who had restored the Pope and was now in control of the city of Rome, evidently could not altogether disregard the charges brought against Leo. But there was no attempt to set up any public court or council for a decision of the case; and on December 23, 800, in St. Peter's, in the presence of Charles and his warriors, the Pope swore a solemn oath rebutting all the charges against him. The Greek historian, Theophanes, was in no doubt about the political situation thus established. He writes that then "for the first time the city of Rome came under the power of the Franks."[2] And according to Einhard, on the same day on which the Pope's oath was sworn, Charles received an embassy from the patriarch of Jerusalem which brought to him the keys of the Sepulchre, as well as the keys and the banner of the city itself, then in control of the Mohammedans.

The Coronation

The play at this point reaches the scene in St. Peter's when Charles was crowned by the Pope; but so many different interpre-

---

[1] Angilbert, op. cit.
>   *line* 331. Solicitos gelidus pavor occupat artus
>   Augusti.
>   Compare Lucan, *Phars.*, i, 246.

[2] Theophanes, *Chron.*, *Pat. Graec.*, vol. 108, col. 952.

tations have been placed upon what occurred, that it may be well to state explicitly what explanation will be given below. In the view here maintained the coronation was arranged beforehand between the Pope and Charles, and was probably the outcome of the policy, not of the Pope but of Charles himself. Secondly, the ceremony was intended by Charles to indicate the assumption of a *title*, and not the establishment of an *institution*—still less the claim to control an ancient institution already in existence, the Roman Empire. Thirdly, the title was intended to add prestige to the king of the Franks in all his territories indeed but primarily to express his new position in relation to the Pope. It implied the recognition of a higher status than that of Patrician; and from the Pope's point of view, it expressed the assumption that the king of the Franks was the official protector of the papal territories.

What actually occurred in St. Peter's on Christmas Day A.D. 800 is described in four different documents, of which two at least contain accounts amended in view of the political effects of the coronation in later years. These two accounts are in the *Annales Laureshamenses* of about A.D. 803 and in the *Life of Charles* by Einhard, composed about twenty-five years after the event. But even the two more reliable accounts, one in the *Liber Pontificalis* the other in the *Annals of the Kingdom of the Franks* (*Annales Laurissenses*), are affected by two different points of view—the former that of the Roman clergy, the latter that of the Frankish Court. Allowance must, therefore, be made for the elements of what would now be called "propaganda" in all the documents now available. Each writer of these documents was affected by the policy current in his circle and by the atmosphere of his time. It is childish to treat any record, however contemporary, as a colourless scientific formula.

The record in the *Liber Pontificalis*, which was probably written at the death of Leo III in A.D. 816, runs as follows: "After this [that is, after the ceremony of Leo's oath] on Christmas Day in the same basilica of St. Peter all were again gathered. And then the venerable and kindly bishop with his own hands crowned him with a precious crown. Then all the Roman faithful, seeing the great protection and love which he had for the Holy Roman Church and its Vicar, unanimously with a loud voice, at a sign from God and St. Peter the key-bearer of the Kingdom of Heaven, cried out—'To Charles, the devout, Augustus, crowned by God, great and pacific Emperor, life and victory!' Before the holy Confession of St. Peter, the Apostle, invoking many saints, it was three times said; and by all he was constituted Emperor of the Romans."[1]

The account in the Frankish *Annals* runs as follows: "On the holy day of Christmas when the king, at Mass before the Confession of St. Peter, rose from prayer, Pope Leo placed a crown on his head and the cry was raised by the whole Roman people—'To Charles, Augustus, crowned by God, great and pacific Emperor of the Romans, life and victory!' And after acclamations, he was adored by the Pope in the manner of the ancient princes; and, dropping the title Patrician, he was called Emperor and Augustus."[2]

It seems clear from these straightforward accounts, first, that Charles was quite well aware of what the Pope was going to do; secondly, that the crowd in the basilica, euphemistically called "the whole Roman people," knew beforehand what to call out; and thirdly, that the ceremony indicated the adoption of a title, not the assertion of new powers. It is extremely doubtful whether anyone in St. Peter's on that day was thinking of the Roman Empire which had its capital at Constantinople; and indeed the Greek historian, Theophanes, mentions the event in the short phrase—"In this year Charles, the king of the Franks, was crowned by Pope Leo"[3]—as if crowning were a habit in the West, of not much importance.

After the coronation Charles returned to his favourite residence at Aachen, in the early months of the year A.D. 801. There he received an embassy bringing gifts from Haroun-al-Raschid, the Caliph of Baghdad, with whom Charles evidently intended to be on good terms. In the same year negotiations were begun for the marriage of Charles with the Empress Irene—which certainly indi-

---

[1] *Liber Pontificalis, Vita Leonis III.* In both accounts the word *augustus* is ambiguous. It may be the official title of an Emperor, like "Your Majesty," or it may mean only "august" or "revered."   [2] *Ann. R.F. ann.* A.D. 801.

[3] Theophanes, *Chron. A.M.,* 6293, *Pat Gr.,* col. 956. τούτῳ τῷ ἔτει . . . Κάρουλος ὁ τῶν φράγγων ῥῆξ ἐστέφθη ὑπὸ Λέοντος τοῦ πάπα.

cates a desire on both sides to compromise over possible rivalries implied in the titles each had adopted. The Court at Constantinople had feared that Charles might attempt to extend his conquests into Sicily and both Charles and Irene might strengthen their claim to the imperial title, if the first Germanic king who claimed to be Roman Emperor were married to the first woman who claimed to rule the Romans in her own right. But the negotiations for marriage came to nothing; and in October 802 Irene was deposed when a new Roman Emperor, Nicephorus, ascended the throne. The position of Charles, with his new titles of Augustus and Emperor, was certainly difficult.

Either in A.D. 803 or shortly after, therefore, a new account was concocted to explain what had happened in Rome on Christmas Day A.D. 800. The *Annales Laureshamenses* and *Moissacenses* say that "because the name of Emperor no longer existed among the Greeks and they had a woman to rule them, then it seemed good to Pope Leo and all the holy fathers who were in the Council or the remaining Christian people that Charles, king of the Franks, ought to be named Emperor, because he held Rome itself (which had always been the seat of the Caesars), or the other seats which he held in Italy, Gaul and Germany. Because Almighty God granted him power over all these places, therefore it seemed to them right that he should have the name, by the petition of the whole Christian people. Their petition king Charles himself was unwilling to reject; but with all humility, submitting to God and to the petition of the bishops and the whole Christian people, he accepted the name of Emperor with the consecration of Pope Leo."[1] This account evidently has in view the difficulties which had arisen with the real Roman Emperor in Constantinople; but it is an attempt to excuse Charles for a policy which he seems never to have adopted, the policy of succeeding the Emperor Constantine VI in the Roman Empire. Difficulties continued. The new Emperor at Constantinople was uncertain whether Charles meant to claim his throne; but negotiations for a peaceful settlement began; and in A.D. 811 a new Frankish Chronicle actually uses the words "that Pope Leo placed

[1] *Ann. Lauresham. M.G.H.*, i, p. 38.

the crown on his head when the lord Charles did not know what was happening."[1] So Charles really was an Emperor without knowing it! The legend grows.

The next stage is reached by the imaginative Einhard in his *Life of Charles the Great,* written about twenty-five years after the event. Einhard says: "At this time he received the name of Emperor and Augustus. But at first he was so opposed to it that he used to say that he would not have gone into the church that day, although it was an important feast, if he had known beforehand the Pope's intention."[2] So now Charles is not merely innocent, but unwilling; and the real difficulty is to be found quite easily in Einhard's later statement that the Roman Emperors in Constantinople did not like Charles's assumption of the title, but that Charles "bore their irritation with the greatest meekness."[3] It is indeed probably quite true that he was astonished by the suspicion his coronation had aroused in Constantinople. He had intended only to adopt a title.

The Title and its Meaning

But what actual title had Charles been given in the West? The earliest accounts say that "the *Roman* faithful" or "the whole *Roman* people" cried out—"Long live the Emperor." That is to say, the title referred only to his relation with the clergy and people of the city of Rome, and expressed only a change from the title of "patricius." It did not refer to the whole western world. Charles remained king of the Franks and Lombards; and in addition he was Emperor in the city of Rome. But in the later accounts "the whole *Christian* people" ask him to be their Emperor—a wholly fantastic idea.

The title of Emperor and Augustus, adopted by Charles, although it had little or no reference to the Roman Empire, undoubtedly added and was intended to add dignity or prestige to the barbarian king of the Franks. Like his predecessors, Alaric and Theodoric, Charles was willing enough to dress himself in the Roman fashion,

---

[1] *Ann. Maximin. M.G.H.,* xiii, p. 23 (nesciente domino Carolo).
[2] Einhard, *Vita Karoli,* 28.
[3] Ibid., 28. "Invidiam tamen suscepti nominis, Romanis imperatoribus super hoc indignantibus, magna tulit pacientia."

at any rate on the Roman stage.[1] But besides prestige, the new title, no doubt, expressed the king's new position in relation to the Pope. As *Patricius* he could not claim so definite a status as an Augustus. But the title of Emperor gave Charles at least the conventional right of being informed at each election of a Pope; and it gave the Pope a right to regard him as protector of the Church of the city of Rome. Again, the new title expressed no additional power, but a new relationship between the king of the Franks and all Christians in the West. From this time the ruler of the Franks, whether in western France or eastern France (*Francia orientalis*)— Germany, was regarded as protector of Christians in the Holy Land and other Mohammedan territories. The "whole Christian people," to which the documents of the early ninth century refer as the "faithful" (*fideles*) of Charles the Great, are now confined to the Latin Churches which from this date called themselves—using a Greek word—"Catholic." And this word, in the Middle Ages, continued to be used to distinguish the Churches of the West from the Christian Churches of the East—Latin from the Greek Christianity. Nobody after the ninth century would have dreamt of including among the "faithful" of Charles in the "Catholic" Church the subjects of the Roman Emperor who were members of the Greek Churches.

The attitude and policy of Charles the Great, after his assumption of the new title, are indicated by his actions during the thirteen years of his life, remaining after the year A.D. 800. He never returned to Rome; nor did he treat it as a capital in any sense, although he left his agents (*missi*) there. He governed his dominions chiefly from his residence at Aachen, holding his councils there, and issuing from the *palatium* there his general Capitulary and his orders to his officials. The Frankish kingdom, indeed, and its subordinate kingdoms of Lombardy and Aquitaine had no capitals in the civilized sense of the word. The king of the Franks remained the leader of war-bands and their attendant clergy, whose central office

---

[1] Einhard, *Vita K.M.*, 25. "He used the Frankish dress, trousers, shirt and belt: . . . foreign garments however beautiful he despised and never condescended to use them except that at Rome, when Pope Hadrian asked him and again Leo, he put on Roman dress."

(*palatium*) moved with him on his expeditions or in his changes from one royal residence to another.

In A.D. 802 Charles issued his general Capitulary from Aachen, which prescribed that an oath should be taken of fidelity to him personally by all the inhabitants of his kingdoms. This oath, in the first place, was, no doubt, intended to counteract the tendency towards what was later called feudalism; that is to say, loyalty to a local lord through whom alone the dependent population was supposed to be related to the higher authority of a king. The attempt of Charles to concentrate all loyalty upon himself and his successors, may be connected with the similar tendency in ecclesiastical jurisdiction whereby the members of the Latin Churches were connected directly with the Pope and not merely through their several bishops. The same oath exacted by Charles bound each of his faithful to fulfil the duties of his station in life and obey all the laws. Under the same Capitulary the king revised the old practice (organized in A.D. 789) of sending out legates or agents. These are now to be of higher rank and to go in pairs, one a bishop and one a count, to examine into the administration of justice and the collection of taxes and the fulfilment of public duties in all the districts of the kingdom.

The second significant act of policy was the "division of the kingdom"[1] made by Charles the Great in A.D. 806. This division followed the traditional Frankish custom of treating a kingdom as property to be equally divided between the sons of the king. It is not the act of an Emperor transferring an Empire to his successor, but of a barbarian king following his tradition. The division proved useless; for two of Charles's sons died—the younger, Charles, in A.D. 810 and Pippin in A.D. 811.

Policy with regard to the Roman Emperors was evidently based upon a desire for peace. At the beginning of the year A.D. 811, Charles wrote to the new Emperor Nicephorus at Constantinople a polite letter saying that he was glad to receive an embassy which had been sent to his son Pippin who had died. In this letter Charles expresses his desire for peace with "your fraternity" (*fraternitatis*

___
[1] *Divisio regni*, not *divisio imperii*, in the Chronicles.

tue).[1] Two years afterwards another letter was sent by Charles to the new Emperor Michael, at the beginning of A.D. 813. The heading reads: "Charles by the Divine Grace, Emperor and Augustus, and also king of the Franks and Lombards, to his beloved and honourable brother Michael, the glorious Emperor and Augustus." The letter says: "We praise God that in our time peace has been established between the Eastern and Western Empire as well as the unity and peace of His holy and immaculate Catholic Church which is spread throughout the world." Charles asks that a treaty should be prepared by the Emperor, written in Greek, and sent back by the embassy which bears the letter.[2] It will be noticed that the word "Roman" is avoided in the titles used in the heading of the letter. But Charles the Great evidently claimed an *imperium* equal in status with that of the Roman Emperor, although in no sense a substitute for it. He certainly never claimed to be the ruler of the Roman Empire which still continued to exist in an unbroken line from Constantine the Great, at Constantinople.

The death of Charles's two younger sons, leaving one only surviving, led to his final act of policy. This was the coronation of Louis the Pious, the eldest surviving son of Charles the Great, at Aachen on September 11, 813. The annals report the event in the following words: "After a general Congress had been held, his son, Louis, king of Aquitaine, was summoned to his presence at Aachen; and he (Charles) placed a crown upon him and made him partner with himself in the title of Emperor.[3]" Thus the new "Emperor" was crowned by his father. No Pope or bishop was concerned with it; and what was transferred to him was a share in a title.

In A.D. 814 Charles the Great died; and Louis the Pious succeeded to his throne as king of the Franks. But in A.D. 816 Louis was again

---

[1] *M.G.H.*, Ep. iv, K.A. ii, No. 32.

[2] Ibid., Ep. iv, K.A. ii, No. 37. The use of "eastern and western Empire" and of "Catholic" may seem to cast doubt upon the date usually assigned to the letter. But the words are diplomatically indefinite.

[3] *Ann. R.F.*, A.D. 813. "Ac deinde, habito generali conventu, evocatum ad se apud Aquisgrani filium suum Hludowicum, Aquitaniae regem, coronam illi inposuit et imperialis nominis sibi consortem fecit." Another account says that Louis placed the crown on his own head.

CHRIST ENTHRONED

OTTO II EMPEROR (A.D. 950) ENTHRONED AND
SURROUNDED BY THE FOUR NATIONS OF EMPIRE

(Miniature in the Museum at Chantilly)

PLATE 9.

crowned, this time by Pope Stephen IV—and at Reims, not at Rome. Louis, however, continued the practice of his father; and in A.D. 817 after a general Congress, held at Aachen, he crowned his own eldest son, making him a "partner of his own title and Empire." He also named his two other sons "kings"—one of Aquitaine and the other of Bavaria. Coronation, therefore, had not yet become an act of papal authority and was still considered as the transference of a title. As late as A.D. 823, when Pope Paschal crowned Lothair in Rome, the chronicler says that "he received the crown of the kingdom and the title of Emperor and Augustus." Clearly neither Charles nor his immediate successors thought of an Empire in the modern sense of the word, nor even in the old Roman sense. Political authority implied the existence of a kingdom whose ruler might or might not be given the title of Emperor or Augustus, just as he might be called "Caesar," without any clear reference either to the original holders of that name or to its later meaning under Diocletian.

If anything more were needed to show that Charles the Great did not establish an Empire, and was not in anything but name an Emperor, a brief review of the actual situation in which he left Europe would be conclusive. There was no capital or permanent centre of administration and law. The old barbarian custom continued of moving the king's officials and retinue from villa to villa. It made no difference in practice that a villa or country residence of a king might be called a "palace" (palatium). Indeed, this use of the word is merely another sign of make-believe by which the central offices of ancient Rome on the Palatine Hill gave their name to any of the scattered houses of a barbarian chieftain. Again there was no central administration. The king's agents (missi dominici) were quite unable to control the counts or other local landowners who had established themselves in almost independent power over different districts. Worse still, there was no permanent armed force, either for internal order or for defence against foreign enemies. Charles the Great followed the old practice of summoning for an expedition as many armed men as he could collect in the early summer, and of allowing them to return to their scattered homes in the autumn. He did, indeed, attempt to establish small permanent outposts on his north-eastern frontier, manned by counts and their armed retainers; but that there was no single defensive system is proved by the number of expeditions the king had to make, to help these outposts. Finally, in the system established or rather continued under Charles the Great, there was none of that "providence" (*providentia*) with which the Emperor was credited under the old Roman system. He made no roads. His system of government did not require them. He conceived a plan of a canal between the Main and Danube; but when the work was begun, it was abandoned because the sides fell in, owing to the lack of competent workers. He repaired the old Roman harbour at Boulogne, but seems never to have grasped the need for new harbours, as a protection against the raids of the Northmen. He did, indeed, give money and land for the building and maintenance of churches and monasteries—which may be taken to correspond to the building of temples and public baths by the Roman Emperors; but the administration of what would now be called "social services" was in the hands of the clergy and not of the king or his counts.

In short, Charles the Great, stripped of the romances which adorned "Charlemagne," was simply a barbarian warrior of great energy, limited intelligence, no education and great simplicity of mind. Like Clovis, three hundred years before him, he believed that he could promote Christianity in the form familiar to him by killing some of those who had never heard of it and compelling the others to be baptized. He was intelligent enough to appreciate the services of scholars and to support their efforts for the promotion of learning and music among the clergy. His ambitions and ideals were those of a barbarian chieftain; and his leisure was spent in hunting and swimming. He was frugal in food and drink and clothing, but somewhat expansive in his affections. The number of his concubines and illegitimate children is not known; and he enjoyed having about him all his daughters. But in an age in which savage cruelty and reckless treachery were not uncommon, even at the Court of the Roman Emperor, which claimed to be the centre of civilized life, Charles the Great was exceptional in attracting faithful supporters and in exciting admiration for the power of his personality.

He was a sincere Christian, in one of the many different meanings of that word.[1] His correspondence shows that he was interested in the peculiar habits of the moon, in the status of the Holy Ghost, in the restriction of the use of religious pictures and in the correct method of administering Baptism. He was not interested in the more subtle moral issues which perhaps would have seemed important to Paulinus of Nola or to St. Boniface. He is said by Einhard to have listened with attention to the reading of St. Augustine's *City of God* and to have kept a writing tablet under his pillow at night, in order to practise writing the alphabet, which he never succeeded in doing. He spoke usually his own Germanic dialect but could speak Latin also fluently; and he understood Greek, although he could not speak it. He extended the dominions which Frankish warriors and churchmen controlled; but he left them so badly organized that soon after his death they were continually troubled by civil war and so badly defended that they were raided year after year by the Northmen and by the Saracens.

General Conclusions

In order to explain the effect upon the Middle Ages and upon later times of the establishment of the so-called "Holy Roman Empire," it is best to summarize first the essential facts which have been so far reviewed and then to draw a general conclusion.

The essential facts are these. The Carolingian Kingdom had its source and centre east of the Rhine. It arose, at least partly, because of the rivalry between Austrasia and Neustria, in which, at first,

---

[1] Of China in 1940 it is reported: "The commander who opened the offensive on this front . . . is a Christian who carries a big black book of hymns with him. He is fat, hearty and cheerful and has a voice that belongs to the battlefield. One evening, while machine-guns pounded not far away, we had supper together, and afterwards he took his hymn-book and sang. When modulated in singing his voice is a rich, deep bass. 'Al-la-luh-ya!' he sang, and the thatch roof on our poor peasant hut nearly trembled. He is a broadminded Christian also, and will worship in any kind of church. Once while passing a French Catholic church he turned to enter. Someone reminded him that he was a Protestant, but with a scornful wave of his hand at their narrow-mindedness he said with a voice of finality, 'It's all the same!' And in he went."—Agnes Smedley in *Manchester Guardian*, March 28, 1940.

the rulers of Neustria had the advantage of an older culture and more extensive organization. Secondly, the centre of the kingdom lay in "missionary lands" where Christianity had been recently introduced by English monks in close connection with the See of St. Peter. Thus Rome, as a symbol of civilization, to those who dwelt east of the Rhine, meant the Rome of St. Peter. Thirdly, the Carolingians supported reform of the ancient Churches of Gaul and, under the guidance of St. Boniface, looked to the Roman See as an instrument of this reform. Fourthly, the kingdom was "German" in the laws of its peoples and its popular and military ballads, which Charles the Great loved and ordered to be collected. Fifthly, the kingdom soon after Charles the Great was divided into east and west Francia; and, except under Charles the Bald, the kingdom east and not west of the Rhine had the closer connection with Italy. The "axis" existed even in the ninth century; but it was weak even in those days, because "Italia" included Rome; and the See of St. Peter could never be committed to a separation from France and England.

Finally the date at which the Carolingian kingdom was most extensive, is important. Charles the Great was crowned about a hundred years after Islam had dominated the western Mediterranean and driven back the Roman Empire to a small territory which could be still defended from Constantinople. The influence of Islam, as a social system, closely combining military prowess with religious enthusiasm, had its effect upon Charles the Great and his successors, as "Caliphs" of Christendom. Again, the title of Emperor was adopted by Charles nearly seventy years after Iconoclasm arose in the Greek Churches. Whether this was due to an attempt to counteract Moslem propaganda against idolatry in the East or to a revived interpretation of the Old Testament—in either case, it induced Charles for some years to oppose the traditional use of images in the Churches of the West. And further, the date of the crowning of Charles the Great marks the conclusion of the long process of separation of the See of Rome from the Greek Churches. Such are the facts.

The conclusions to be drawn are as follows. The Carolingian

"Empire," or at least the adoption of the titles "Augustus" and "Emperor," was an attempt to use the prestige of Rome for the support of a military system. The Frankish kings took advantage of the work of the Christian missionaries in Germany and of the Roman Church in Italy. The coronation of an "Emperor" was a kind of consecration, giving moral authority to military power by connecting it with Christian Rome—the Rome of the martyrs and apostles. Charles the Great, no doubt, was a sincere Christian, in his understanding of Christianity. He honestly believed, as many medieval warriors and kings did after him, that his wars were waged in the interests of Christianity, even when he attacked a Christian and Catholic king of the Lombards or duke of Benevento. The Christian Churches of Germany and France did indeed derive some advantage from the support given by Charles the Great to missionaries and reformers. And it is difficult to disentangle the motives of any man who has great power over his fellows. Charles may have thought of himself sometimes as the instrument of Christian Rome. But clearly he was never a passive instrument controlled by the policy of others. He expressed definite ideas of his own on ecclesiastical and even theological matters. It is, therefore, probable that he, like his father and grandfather, was not unaware of the use to which Christianity could be put in extending his conquests. The Christianity, for example, imposed by Charles the Great upon the Saxons was not "a way of life" supported by reasoning on evidence, but submission to a military leader and his ecclesiastical and lay officials.

But the titles "Augustus" and "Emperor" were not Christian in origin; and the second was definitely military. The prestige attached to them therefore came, not from Christian, but from pre-Christian imperial Rome. Indeed, difficulties arose in later times from the doubt whether the successor of St. Peter could have any power to confer a title which had existed before Christianity was accepted by the Emperors. In the ninth century Frankish poets described the transfer of power from the Romans to the Franks, as if the Franks had inherited a universal dominion which the Romans had transferred to them. Again Hincmar, in his life of St. Remy, says that the Franks came from Troy, as the Romans did, and that the Emperor Valentinian named them "Franks," "using the Greek word which means fierce."[1] The Franks were, therefore, associated with the Romans as warriors and conquerors, not as makers of laws or of roads.

But the prestige of imperial Rome, in the ninth century and indeed in later times, perhaps even until modern times, had two very different meanings. The Roman Empire, to which medieval Europe looked back, was in fact both a military system of conquest and a civilian system of law and of administration. The Rome to which Charles the Great looked back was *military*, even if the sword was now in the service of St. Peter and not of the Caesars. But the Rome which remained the traditional source of the civilization of Gaul, surviving in Neustria or western France, was *civilian*—the Rome of law, administration and trade. The contrast between these two aspects of the Roman system in the minds of men of the ninth century must not be exaggerated. No doubt, Charles the Great was influenced by Roman Emperors as law-givers when he issued his Capitularies. But he was, above all, a soldier— a leader of expeditions against the Saracens and against the Saxons— a successor therefore of Alaric and Theodoric, as well as of Roman Emperors who had extended the Empire.

West of the Rhine, in the lands to which the name "Francia" was later confined, the prestige of Rome depended upon an ancient tradition of law and administration, largely civilian in its atmosphere, which was preserved in the Christian Churches, but was quite plainly, in law and in literature, an inheritance from the Rome of the great pre-Christian administrators. West of the Rhine, the dominions of Charles the Great were the results of a settlement of the Franks, Burgundians and Visigoths, within a social organization already firmly established for many centuries in Roman Gaul. The dominant language was a form of Latin; and the Christian Churches with their bishops had taken over or initiated many social functions, long before the kings of the Franks had become Christian and Catholic. The barbarian tradition of military adventure

[1] Hincmar, *Vita St. Rem.*, chap. 29. *Pat. Lat.*, vol. 125, col. 1155.

was, therefore, fitted into a social system much stronger, more civilized and more enduring than that of the newcomers.

As early as the fifth century the civilization of Europe west of the Rhine was the result of a continuous tradition, which had indeed been disturbed by invasion and social upheavals, but retained many of the characteristics of the old Roman system. That system was in dissolution in the fifth century; but many of its best features were preserved in the Christian Churches which traced their history back to the days of the martyrs of Lyons and of the persecutions of Christianity. Christianity in Gaul had begun in defiance of the power of the Roman Empire. The Roman tradition, even in the Christian Churches, was indeed almost forgotten in the seventh and early eighth centuries. But throughout the Middle Ages the Churches of "Francia" preserved the memory of their great bishops and other saints who had lived long before Charles the Great and his Franks had ever been heard of. Many of their great bishops in the past had been officials of the Roman Empire or had belonged to senatorial families. And there was nothing in learning or literature, as late as the eighth century, east of the Rhine, to compare with the work of Ausonius, Sidonius Apollinaris, Caesarius of Arles, Venantius Fortunatus and Gregory of Tours.

East of the Rhine, on the other hand, what was "Roman," in the minds of Charles the Great and his successors, was a system of belief and ritual, imposed by scholars, priests and kings, upon a barbarian and loosely organized population of local lordships and customs, speaking Germanic dialects. The "Roman Empire," among such peoples, was something mysterious, ghostly, fallen from heaven. It was something which had been given by heaven to the Germans and could thus, many centuries later, become the "Roman" Empire "of the German Folk." It was this mythical or legendary Roman Empire which affected the peoples of what was later called Germania, throughout the Middle Ages. East of the Rhine, the civilization dependent upon the memory of Rome—the only form of civilization possible at that time and place—was an adaptation of social ideas and customs, entirely alien, by peoples who had never been conquered by the armies of ancient Rome, peoples who had had no experience of Roman roads or of Roman law. This does not imply that civilization east of the Rhine valley was defective. Indeed, even in the ninth century it may have had more vitality than the ancient civilization of Gaul. It was the result partly indeed of military conquest by Charles the Great and his predecessors, but partly also of the missionary activities of English monks. But Christianity east of the valleys of the Rhine and the Main was imposed by force of arms upon recalcitrant German tribes. It was the religion of victors in war, and Christ himself thus became a God of war in the minds of Germanic warriors. The Christian Churches of what was later called "Germania," were superimposed upon a variety of pagan tribes, seven hundred years after the beginning of the Christian era and about five hundred years after the Christian Churches of Gaul had been established. But whereas the tradition of Roman civilization in Gaul was older than Christianity there, imperial and pre-Christian Rome became known to the peoples of Germany chiefly as a shadowy figure in a mythical past brought to their knowledge by the Christian Church long after the Roman Empire had ceased to exist in the West. The Rome of the Carolingian "Emperors," east of the Rhine, therefore, was the Rome of the ninth century imagination, which produced both the original *Chansons des Gestes* and the not less imaginative *False Decretals*. It was the Rome of the Middle Ages— the Rome of the *Mirabilia Romae*, in which the ghosts of Nero and others walked abroad.

The contrast between the influence of the Roman tradition east and west of the Rhine is, indeed, one of the most important characteristics in the history of the First Europe. It is a contrast between civilized life and culture as a natural growth of the soil and both as foreign importations. Long before the days of Charles the Great, the peoples inhabiting what is now called France were deeply affected by the traditions of Roman civilization, to which indeed they had made notable contributions. East of the Rhine, on the other hand, at any rate beyond the Roman cities, Trier and Köln, as late as the ninth century there were barbarian tribes, with the virtues and defects of barbarism. In the earliest years of the Christian era, a comparison had been made by Tacitus, in his *Germania*, between barbarian virtue and civilized decadence, in which the Germans are made to play the part of models for Romans. But Tacitus was writing a political pamphlet on behalf of "the good old times," which has been taken too seriously by later historians. The Christian Fathers also expressed horror at the luxuries of civilized life; and a tradition grew up concerning the virtues of barbarians, which has more than once misled those who desire to return to "nature" or the "simple life." But the barbarians of the fifth and sixth centuries, as it has been shown above, never intended to destroy Roman civilization. Indeed, they admired it so much that they desired to appropriate its advantages and to imitate its manners and customs.

Unfortunately barbarians do not always understand what they desire to imitate; nor is the principle correct according to which they distinguish what is good and what is bad in civilized life. In the eighth and ninth centuries, therefore, the Carolingian warriors and kings were attracted by imperial Rome, chiefly because of the history of its conquests. And Charles the Great himself reinforced the barbarian admiration for military exploits by extending his territories into Germany far beyond the limits of the rule of Roman Emperors. Therefore throughout the Middle Ages, and perhaps even in later times, civilization has been believed by the peoples east of the Rhine to be, in its essence, military. As early as the ninth century there was a fundamental distinction between the characteristics of civilization and culture in France and Germany.

But the division between the peoples east and west of the Rhine proved to be less important for medieval Christendom than the fact that the Roman Empire, which Charles the Great was believed to have restored, became the source of a disastrous archaism. The localization of government, referred to in an earlier chapter, and the later absorption of subordinate rulers in rival national kingdoms, were felt to be obstacles to peace. It was reasonably argued that the unity of all Christians should be expressed and confirmed by the political or governmental unity of Christendom. But the only form in which this unity was conceived was the form it had taken under the Roman Empire. That is to say, political unity was believed to imply the subordination of many peoples to one supreme Authority. Therefore, some of the most active minds in the First Europe aimed at establishing peace on the model of the *pax Romana*, that is to say, by conquest and centralization. The very success of the Roman Church in the establishment of the Papacy misled political idealists. But in the art of government the failure of an archaistic ideal of unity was obvious soon after the death of Charles the Great. His "empire" dissolved; his kingdoms were divided. His grandsons fought his son, and later fought among themselves. But, unfortunately, the very disasters caused by the futile and indeed ridiculous attempt to establish a Germanic "Roman Empire" led to a romantic idealization of the barbarian warrior who had held together a ramshackle structure of primitive kingdoms for the last few years of his life.

CHAPTER XV

THEORY AND PRACTICE

The actors have all appeared on the stage. The play begins. It is traditionally called the Middle Ages; but it would be better called the First Europe. The play lasted for about five hundred years— from about A.D. 1000 to about 1500. The characters, in the order of their appearance, but not perhaps in the order of their interest for most historians, were these. First come the serfs and the villeins, successors to the slaves, the farmers and labourers on the estates of the Roman villa: these appear in the fifth century in a general dispersal of population, some fleeing from raiders or joining them, others as captives of one marauding band or another; but by the ninth century they are settled on agricultural land, providing for the basic needs of medieval society. Next come pilgrims and other travellers of the Church. Next the merchants and tradesmen of the towns; and after them warriors of barbarian stock, who later became the knights and nobles of the Middle Ages. Then come kings, anointed and crowned by bishops, in the confused scene of the play, in which the Old Testament and the Roman tradition are united by a strange fantasy. These are the figures which attract the attention of the chroniclers. The chroniclers themselves had already entered as prompters and scene-shifters. These are clergy, monks and nuns, whose organizations and ideals dominated the Middle Ages. They are a strange company of celibates, much affected by the repressions which gave rise to dreams and visions. As chroniclers in the play they are of supreme importance, because these embody both the excellences and defects of medieval Europe. High above them, with his entry well prepared, comes a leading figure on the medieval stage, the imperial Pope; and, in a series of vanishing tricks, like the ghost of Hamlet's father, appears the final character of medievalism, the Emperor of the Holy Roman Empire.

The first scene of the play, in which all the characters appear, occurred during the ninth and tenth centuries, which, if the traditional classification is used, may be treated as belonging either to the Dark Ages or to the Middle Ages. The social institutions of these centuries were the results of two different forces, one destructive, the other confirming the social discoveries and inventions made after the fall of the Roman Empire in the West. The destructive forces were invasions from the North, East and South. From the North came the Normans (*Nordmanni*) or Danes. These pirates destroyed the centres of learning in Ireland, and put back the clock in the development of Irish civilization. In England they destroyed monasteries, churches and peaceful settlements in the North and East. And they would perhaps have destroyed English learning and English civil government, if the descendants of the earlier Saxon invaders had not had such leaders as Alfred the Great. In what are now the Low Countries and in France, the raids of Norman pirates were equally destructive; but in the tenth century in France these pirates made settlements of their own and were gradually absorbed into Christendom. By one of the strangest transformations in history the successors of the Norman pirates in northern Europe became the champions of Christendom against the Saracens in the Mediterranean.

Secondly, on the eastern borders of Christendom, in what is now Germany, invasions by the Hungarians (Magyars) carried destruction into Bavaria (A.D. 910) and Burgundy (A.D. 955). But the Magyars were defeated by Otto I (at Lechfeld in A.D. 955); and the German Pope Silvester II (Gerbert) sent a royal crown to the Magyar chieftain, Stephen I, in A.D. 1001.

The "crown of St. Stephen" became the symbol of the entry of the Magyars into the structure of Latin Christendom. That entry was secured only two centuries after the establishment of the First Europe with which we are concerned; but it may serve to show the power of expansion which had been acquired in earlier centuries by the new form of civilization in western Europe.[1] After their first contact with European peoples, the Magyars seem to have been uncertain whether to look for the advantages of civilization to the Latin tradition of the West, or to the Greek tradition of Constantinople. To accept the Latin tradition, represented by German kings, might have involved too complete a subordination; and therefore the policy of Magyar chieftains looked sometimes to Germany and sometimes to Italy, until a German Pope connected them definitely with Rome. Again, the Magyars had thrust themselves into the plains hitherto occupied by Huns and Avars, between the Slavs of the North, later called Czechs and Poles, and the Southern Slavs, who were under the influence of the Greek-speaking Churches of the Roman Empire; and this separation of the Slav peoples by Magyar invasion eventually caused the Slavs of the North to enter the structure of Latin Christendom, while the Southern Slavs retained the tradition and customs of the Greek Churches.

The third destructive force was the piracy of Saracen raiders on the coasts of Italy and southern France. The Mohammedan rulers of northern Africa and southern Spain were not unwilling to profit by expeditions against the Christians for slaves and other loot. In a few places in Italy and southern France Mohammedan settlements were established; but they were hardly more than pirate lairs. Sicily was controlled by the Saracens until the Normans reconquered it for Christendom. But no policy, either of religious hostility or political ambition, seems to have been involved in the looting of such places as the Benedictine monastery at Monte Cassino and the shrine of St. Peter in the Vatican. Christendom was not able to absorb these raiders, as it absorbed Northmen and Hungarians. Christian kings and bishops, however, including the Popes, were able to enter into peaceful negotiations with Mohammedan rulers; and Christendom, even in the tenth century, owed some of its learning and its arts to the Mohammedans. Thus Gerbert, afterwards Pope Silvester II, is said to have acquired some learning among the Mohammedans in Spain.

[1] It may be noted that Latin Christendom and not the Christianity of the Greek Churches has expanded into new continents unknown to the Middle Ages.

Between the Mohammedans and Christians of the First Europe, the Jews acted both as a link and an irritant. There were Jewish merchants and money-lenders in many of the cities of Christendom; and in Spain, as it was explained in an earlier chapter, the Jews suffered .persecution before the Mohammedan conquest of that country, apparently because of the belief that they were enemy aliens, not unwilling to negotiate with invaders hostile to Christianity. Such feelings, surviving in the ninth and tenth centuries, are expressed in the story of a certain German deacon named Bodo, who had been brought up in the Christian religion and educated at the Court of the king of the Franks in divine and human letters, and who went to Rome in A.D. 838.[1] In the course of negotiations with the Jews for the sale of some slaves to the "Pagans," as the chronicler called the Saracens, he was induced to accept Judaism. He was circumcised; grew his hair and beard; took the name of Eleazar; put on a sword; married a Jewess; forced his nephew also to accept Judaism and went to Saragossa with the Jews. There, in A.D. 847, he persuaded the "king of the Saracens" to threaten with death any Christians who would not accept either Judaism or Mohammedanism. The Jews throughout the Middle Ages continued to be regarded with suspicion, largely because of their supposed connection with the Mohammedan enemies of Christendom.

While piracy on all sides and the struggle of different kings and dukes destroyed some of the resources of the ninth century, the progress of civilized life was maintained. The traditions of the Germanic tribes were preserved and expanded in ballads and romances. In the dark days of the ninth century the imagination played about remembered names. Theodoric the Ostrogoth, became Diedrich von Bern (Verona); and the rough old warrior Charles the Great, became the great Christian Emperor Charlemagne, who "had left all Europe filled with all happiness."[2] The monk of St. Gall and Latin versifiers began the establishment of a mythical

---

[1] *Ann. Bertiniani*, ann. A.D. 839.
[2] Nithard, *Hist.*, i. See above p. 23. The "malkerg" glosses on the Salic Law indicate Germanic survivals in law courts.

Charlemagne, who appears to have survived in the imagination of the Germans even into the twentieth century.[1] The Paladins (*Paladini*), Roland and Oliver and the rest, began their long career in Romance. The Germanic invaders of the fifth to the ninth century may be regarded as the originators of medieval Romance in all its forms. But the tradition of Latin grace and serenity was preserved in the same dark days of the ninth century by the growing volume of religious literature, especially in hymns and sequences.[2] There was a light in the darkness.

To the ninth century later ages owed the new form of writing established by Alcuin, and the manuscript copies which preserved the remnants of Latin literature. In that century also the work and influence of Alfred the Great in the translation of Orosius and Boethius preserved the continuity of thought. And the name of John Scotus Erigena may serve as an indication of the survival, even in those days, of the ancient tradition of neo-Platonic philosophy, which was to become one of the sources of medieval scholasticism.

In medieval Europe the imagination was stronger than the perception of facts. So it is in the childhood of individuals; and indeed, the child's conception of the world, as studied by Piaget, is not unlike the dominant conception of it in the Middle Ages. In simple or primitive communities also, the imagination plays a great part and the sense of evidence is not acute. Travellers' tales are readily believed; and such records as survive from the past are uncritically accepted at their face value. In some ages the imagination is defective, even for the purposes of science and history, not to speak of the Fine Arts. But in the First Europe the imagination was dominated by fear and hope rather than by the facts of the situation. In those days it was difficult for most men to distinguish between their dreams and what they could see when they were awake.

In a time of social confusion men surrounded by unknown dangers and the prospect of sudden death, had their natural fears increased by the terrors of the imagination. But the best men and

---

[1] Adolf Hitler is reported to have had the crown and sword of Charles the Great removed to the interior of Germany from Aachen, where the Emperor waits, according to the medieval legend, for his second coming.

[2] The great hymn *Veni, creator Spiritus* belongs to the end of the ninth century.

women of that time were aware of their own limitations and of the difficulties which bred credulity out of fear. The best churchmen neither supported nor increased the general belief in magic and demons, but endeavoured to control and, with their limited resources, to reduce the terrors of ignorance. Thus, Agobard, bishop of Lyons, wrote in the early ninth century: "Such foolishness now burdens the poor world that Christians of our time believe greater absurdities than anyone could ever, before this, have persuaded pagans to believe, who knew nothing of the creator."[1]

In the ninth and tenth centuries when the play begins, which is recognizably medieval and no longer Roman, there is a world of confused movements. But in spite of incessant local conflicts within the First Europe, and recurrent barbarian invasions from the North, the East and the South, the new civilization was not fundamentally altered. Its roots were strengthened by the winds which stripped its first leaves and broke some of its branches. And the new civilization which emerged was one of violent contrasts. It has been well said that the Middle Ages knew every virtue except moderation, and every vice but vulgarity. It is more important, however, to notice that after the ninth century until the sixteenth, so far at least as social institutions are concerned, there was a violent contrast between theory and practice. What men seriously believed about the Church and State, and about the world they lived in, had only the slightest relation to what was actually happening. They believed they were imitating the past; and they were really creating the future. They looked back to the Roman Empire, the Fathers, the New Testament and the Old. And in their almost complete ignorance of the history of civilization they misread or misunderstood the evidence. That was why they made Alexander the Great into a medieval knight, changed Simon Peter, the Galilean fisherman, into a medieval Pope, and gave armorial bearings to Adam and Eve.

The dominant theories of the First Europe with regard to social institutions were these. First, it was believed that there was a distinction between the spiritual and the temporal, embodied in the

[1] Agobard, *Contra insulsam vulgi opinionem. Pat. Lat.*, 104.

Church, on the one hand, and on the other, in many kingdoms, the two forms of dominant social organization having moral authority. This distinction is obviously connected with the distinction between the soul and the body of the human person. Secondly, in the First Europe men believed that the whole of humanity either was, or ought to be, united in one universal religion organized by centralization in Rome; and in one form of government—kingship—with an association of local kings vaguely inferior in status to a shadowy Emperor. Thirdly, in the First Europe it was believed that there were two entirely different forms of existence called "this world" and another; and that in the other the obvious defects of their own experience were removed in a permanent state of things in which justice, as the men of their time conceived it, already prevailed. This last belief explained and justified the endurance of defective institutions and evil acts in a world which would soon come to an end.

The Two Powers

The contrast between the spiritual and the temporal Powers engaged the attention and excited the emotions of the best minds in medieval Europe. This contrast was already perceived almost in its medieval form as early as the fifth century. But, as it has been explained above, writers in later years used selected phrases from the Fathers or the letters of bishops in such a way as to make medieval ideas appear to have been accepted much earlier than they really were. When a bishop of Rome, or any other bishop, wrote in the sixth or seventh centuries about the contrast between his authority and that of emperors or kings, he was usually attempting to solve a particular difficulty. His theory, such as it was, arose out of the actual position of bishops in his own time and place; and when a writer selected from the Old Testament passages about Melchizedek, he was merely seeking support for a position which he had already adopted. Whatever the theory of St. Augustine or of Gregory the Great or of Hadrian I may have been about the spiritual and temporal Powers, each theory was derived from the actual social situation in which the writer found himself, and not from the study of the Scriptures. The selection of disconnected texts from the Scriptures was governed by the needs of each writer. Theory is an attempt, never quite successful, to see what one is doing, instead of doing it blindly. But what each person sees is partly dependent upon what he expects or hopes to see, especially as defined by inherited language and custom. It is difficult to see clearly what there is no language to describe.

The medieval theory of the two Powers and the medieval ideal of social organization did not develop fully until the thirteenth century. But the sources of both the theory and ideal are to be found in the social condition of western Europe between the fifth and ninth centuries. This is not the place to discuss the fully developed medieval conceptions; but because the early traces of them can be more easily understood by some reference to the monstrous growth of utopianism in medieval controversies, a short statement must be attempted of the latest form taken by the theory of the two Powers. In the thirteenth and fourteenth centuries it was assumed that there were two organizations of Christendom, controlled by two Authorities, one temporal, the other spiritual. They were either co-ordinate, as some writers maintained, each holding its place by direct appointment from God, or as other writers held, one was superior to the other. The functions of the two Authorities were distinguished. The civil Authority—kings and emperors and their agents—were to provide defence against domestic brawls and foreign invasion, chiefly by the administration of law-courts and the use of armed force. The ecclesiastical Authority existed chiefly for the sake of salvation after death in another world. For this, it was provided with special means of its own—sacraments, ceremonies and prayer. But in this world it had to support and maintain the civil Authorities, and could use them as instruments for the maintenance of "the Church Militant."

The general statement of the medieval theory of the Powers somewhat obscured the fact that the real problem in the minds of most writers, was the nature of the influence of the clergy. But behind this problem lay the still more fundamental question of moral authority in the life of a community. What was the real basis for the moral authority of civil government? Was it to be found in the essential functions of government, or was it derived from some other system of organization? Again, with regard to the Church, or the social organization of religion and culture, what was the basis of the moral authority of teachers and preachers? Was this basis their knowledge of the subject or some magical power? And finally, what was the place of force, and particularly of armed force, in a civilized community? From the fifth to the ninth century, and throughout the Middle Ages, the attempt was made to solve these problems in the terms which had been inherited from the past. But no solution of such problems was possible on the assumption of the existence of two separate and independent temporal and spiritual Powers. The use of these terms led to endless and futile controversy, and eventually to the collapse of medieval Christendom. But the theory and the ideals of the Middle Ages were inevitable in the First Europe. The solution could not be found because the problem was badly stated. So true it is that, as the philosophical bishop Berkeley has said, "We raise the dust and then complain that we cannot see."

The medieval contrast between spiritual and temporal was due to the fact that the bishops and their Churches between the fifth and ninth centuries took over many of the functions hitherto performed by the civilian Authorities of the Roman Empire, while the barbarian kings and their warriors inherited the prestige and power of the Roman military organization. Thus, the medieval contrast between the two Powers was the result of an accident of history in western Europe. It was not the result of anything that can be called the nature or essential quality of the Church or the State.

But writers and other teachers, as early as the fifth century, and throughout the Middle Ages, seriously believed that the situation in which they found themselves, in the conflict between bishop and king, was the result of some fundamental or essential distinction of functions between two kinds of social institutions. They knew little of the history of ideas and events which had led to the establishment of the Papacy and of the ghostly Empire at the end of the eighth century; and they were dominated by an uncritical belief in fixed eternal principles which could be applied to all social situations. Therefore they believed that all human society was naturally or divinely organized as that of the early Middle Ages in western Europe happened to be.

Their imagination played so freely about the facts of their own times that they saw in bishops and kings, Popes and Emperors, independent Authorities with clearly distinguished functions, whereas in practice, as it will be explained later, it was entirely uncertain in any country, at any time, where the authority of the Church ended and that of the civil Government began. But the misreading of facts was less important than the attempt which continued throughout the Middle Ages, to make an imaginary situation into an ideal of public policy. Some men strenuously worked for an organization of Europe in which the spiritual and temporal Powers would be co-ordinate, equal and independent; while others strove to make one or other of the two Powers supreme. These great controversies of the Middle Ages had not yet developed in the ninth century; but their nature and methods were already to be seen in the treatises and letters of that and even earlier centuries. The most fantastic interpretations of arbitrarily selected scriptural texts were used to justify either the division of social Authorities into temporal or spiritual, or the supremacy of one over the other. It must be assumed here that the words of the New Testament: "Give unto Caesar . . ." or "There are two swords . . ." have nothing whatever to do with Pope or Emperor or with the organization of society. Obviously also the mention of Melchizedek in *Genesis* has no bearing whatever upon the position of bishops and kings in the early Middle Ages. But it must be remembered that in those days the quoting of texts from Scripture, which it was said the Devil himself could do, was somewhat uncritical; and it is difficult in the twentieth century to appreciate fully the climate of opinion in which scriptural texts can be used in support of current ecclesiastical or other policy. It will be remembered that Maximus, bishop of Turin, said that Christ was the stone with which David killed Goliath; that Cassiodorus said that the breasts of the girl in the Hebrew love-song, the "Song of Solomon," were the Old and New Testament, and that Gregory the Great wrote that the large nose of the beloved stood for the ability of the Church to smell out heresy. When such interpretations were possible, it was not difficult to find the medieval system indicated in the relation between prophets and kings as recorded in Hebrew history. And thus a misinterpretation of contemporary facts and past history produced an ideal in men's minds which they strove vainly for five hundred years to embody in real life.

The Theory of Two Powers

A typical statement of the medieval theory of the two Powers is in the treatise of Jonas, bishop of Orleans (A.D. 821–843), on Kingship.[1] This was written probably in A.D. 828 for Pippin, king of France, just before he entered into plots and rebellion against his father, Louis the Pious. It is an exhortation to live a moral life and not a statement of political theory; and the later chapters repeat sections of another work of the same author on the layman's duties (de institutione laicali). The moral teaching of the latter work includes an exhortation to go to church and pray, which is repeated among the lists of duties of kings; and it expresses the traditional medieval obsession of the clergy with sexual intercourse, supported by quotations from St. Augustine and St. Jerome.[2] The letter to King Pippin, which serves as a preface to the treatise on kingship, tells him that temporal joys are transitory and that he should concentrate his thoughts upon death and judgement. This was the established moral teaching of medieval Europe. It rests upon arguments as weak as those which might induce a man to avoid the enjoyment of sunshine because, some hours after, the sun will set. Of kingship, bishop Jonas writes with his eye upon the Old Testament. He begins by quoting the traditionally selected sentence of Pope Gelasius to the Emperor Anastasius (Epist. VIII)—"There are two

[1] Jonas Aurel., de Institutione regia. Pat. Lat., 106, col. 279 sq.
[2] There is in book ii, ch. vi, the clearest statement of the traditional morality that sexual intercourse should take place only for the sake of procreation, and not for pleasure (voluptas). This doctrine was stated fully in St. Augustine's de Nuptiis et Concupiscentia.

(powers), august Emperor, by which this world is chiefly governed, the sacred authority of bishops and the royal power (*regalis potestas*). Of these the weight of the bishops is the greater, in so far as they have to give an account at the divine judgement also for the kings of men themselves." Naturally a Frankish bishop of the ninth century had no idea whatever of the political situation implied in the letter of a fifth-century bishop of Rome to a Roman Emperor in Constantinople. But the purpose of the bishop of Orleans was sufficiently served, if he could adduce authority for his teaching that kings must obey bishops. The further duties of kings are drawn from disconnected sentences of the books of Deuteronomy and Proverbs, and from sections of the works of Fulgentius, Isidore and Gregory the Great. Indeed, the author belongs to that great company of preachers who select quotations which happen to include the same word—in this case the word "king"—without any regard for the different meanings which that word may bear in different contexts and in different works by different authors. The king, says bishop Jonas, does not hold his power by heredity, nor by the choice of men, but only by gift from God. Bad kings are allowed by God, and good kings supported by Him. The king is to labour at his own personal virtue and to assist others to be virtuous; because, as St. Augustine says (*De civ. Dei*, v. 24), good Emperors are not those who have conquered foreign enemies or domestic rebels, since these things have reference only to this life, but those only who fear, love and worship God. The whole book, indeed, is an example of the emphasis placed in the ninth century upon personal virtue and of the complete blindness of the teachers of that time to the problems of social justice. Thus, the whole of the Middle Ages in its theory of government was dominated by an unconscious acceptance of the existing relationship between bishops and kings, as if it were eternal or ideal; and the duty of a ruler seemed, therefore, to be concerned only with being as benevolent as possible in a given situation, without any suspicion that the situation itself might be morally defective. This was the effect of the Christian tradition which told the slave-owner, for example, to be kind to his slaves, and did not suggest that slavery itself was morally wrong.

The conception, therefore, of the two Powers, which underlies the treatise of Jonas of Orleans, and the many other later works which repeated his quotations and his simple-minded moral teaching, was hardly more than an uncritical assumption that the institutions of the ninth century were of permanent value.

A good example of the confusion of defective historical knowledge and simple ideals of public policy is to be found in the last chapter of the book *On Ecclesiastical Matters* by Walafridus Strabo already quoted in part (p. 568), in reference to the Papacy. He writes, in the chapter on "A Comparison of the Ecclesiastical and Secular Orders": "As the race of the Romans is said to have held the monarchy of the whole world, so the supreme pontiff, holding the place of St. Peter in the Roman See, is raised to the summit of the whole Church. . . . Therefore the Roman Pope is the equivalent of the Augusti and the Caesars. The patriarchs are equivalent to the patricians, who, it seems, came first in imperial authority after the Caesars; so also, those, who are rather few, are ranked first after the bishops of the three Sees (Antioch, Alexandria, Rome).[1] Again we count archbishops, who are above the metropolitans, equivalent to kings; and metropolitans equivalent to dukes. What counts or prefects are in secular matters that other bishops are in the Church. . . . Advisers at Court or counts of the Court who discuss secular matters, are like those whom the Franks call the chief chaplains. . . . Hundred-men (*centenarii*) are equivalent to priests; . . . From the unity of the two orders, the one house of God is built, the one body of Christ is made: the eye in wise men, the mouth in teachers . . . the stomach in those who are submissive."[2] The two powers, or rather the ecclesiastical and secular Orders, were thus conceived to be exactly equivalent in all their ranks. But the author of this statement, like other men of his time, had only the vaguest ideas of Roman organization. He did not know the history of the title "patrician" nor understand the status of a town-councillor (*decurio*). He did not know that the Church had adapted her Holy Orders to

---

[1] This seems to refer to such patriarchates as that of Aquileia.

[2] Walafridus Strabo, *De eccl. rerum exordiis et incrementis*, cap. 31. Migne, *Pat. Lat.*, 114, col. 919. The book deals with the origin of altars, etc., and (in chap. viii) with images and pictures.

the "orders" (*ordines*) of the Roman world, and afterwards introduced a similar organization among the servants of kings in so-
called "palaces." He writes vaguely of the Emperor having
authority similar to that of the Pope. Although he wrote some
fifty years after the crowning of Charles the Great, he does not
assume the existence of one universal Empire. But his description
of the parallel between the ecclesiastical and civil organization
shows that they were conceived to be contrasted with one another
in all their ranks, and not merely by opposition between the
supreme Authorities on either side. The theory involved a complete diarchy in social institutions; but it had very little bearing
upon facts.

Another document which implies a similar theory is a letter of
Agobard, bishop of Lyons from A.D. 814 to 840, to the Emperor
Louis the Pious, concerning the comparison between ecclesiastical
and civil power.[1] This, however, is frankly a political pamphlet,
which aimed at justifying the opposition of the Emperor to Pope
Gregory IV, who had taken the side of the Emperor's rebellious
sons. The letter begins with the assertion that there are two Powers,
one ecclesiastical, the other "military" (*militarem*). This is at least
an indication that the Temporal Power was conceived in the early
ninth century as the power of the sword; and it is, therefore, clearly
believed to be the successor to the military organization of the
Roman Empire.

About forty years later, in A.D. 882, Hincmar, archbishop of
Reims, wrote his treatise on the *Organization of the Palace*.[2] This
book was intended for the use of "good and wise men" under
Charles the Bald, king of the Franks. It is partly copied from a
book by Adalbald, abbot of Corbey, and it refers to the Irish
treatise "On the Abuses of the Age," as if it were by St. Cyprian.
Hincmar repeats the statement of Pope Gelasius that "there are two
things by which chiefly this world is ruled, the sacred authority of
bishops and the kingly power."[3] This he proves by reference to the

---

[1] Agobard, *De Comparatione Reg.*, *Pat. Lat.*, 104.
[2] Hincmar, *De ordine Palatii*. Fontes Juris Germ. (1894).
[3] Ibid., op. cit., cap. ii. Duo sunt quibus principaliter mundus hic regitur:
autoritas sacra pontificum et regalis potestas.

section of the *Book of Chronicles* which says: "Then they brought out the king's son, and put upon him the crown, and gave him the testimony, and made him king. And Jehoiada and his sons anointed him, and said, 'God save the King'."[1] It is by no means clear that Hincmar used the words "authority" and "power" in reference to bishops and kings in order to indicate a contrast between the character of the influence of the Church and that of the State, as he conceived them; but he certainly identifies the bishops with the prophets of the Old Testament in their relation to kings. The book, however, is not concerned with abstract theory. It is a description of the organization of central government at the Court of Charles the Great, and only by implication describes the rival Authorities.

Bishops and abbots were concerned to explain to kings both the practical policy they should adopt and the virtues with which they should be adorned. Thus, the abbot Smaragdus, who went to Rome in A.D. 810 as a delegate of Charles the Great, wrote a book on *The Royal Way*,[2] which instructs the king in the virtues which lead to the kingdoms of the heavens. The way is shown by David, Solomon and Ozias. The king is anointed with the "sacred chrism" and wears the crown. His virtues are the fear of God, justice and other moral qualities, as well as some definite action, such as defending the poor, paying tithes to the Church, preventing judges from receiving bribes, opposing the use of false measures, and making the capture of slaves impossible within his realm. It is worth noting that almost all the scriptural quotations which support the abbot's teaching are drawn from the Old Testament; but it is still more important that the theory implied in this teaching is the right and duty of ecclesiastics to keep the Temporal Power aware of its true function.

Another exhortation to kingly virtue is the treatise of Sedulius Scotus *On Christian Rulers*, addressed to Louis the Pious about A.D. 818. It contains nothing new or original; but the writer makes use of examples from the history of Roman Emperors, especially Antoninus, Constantine and Theodosius. He remarks also that "no art is more difficult than government," and that "there is nothing

---

[1] *II Chronicles* xxiii. 11.   [2] Smaragdus Abbas, *De via Regia, Pat. Lat.*, 102.

which makes a good ruler more acceptable to his subjects than clemency and peace."[1]

The Facts of Politics

The actual events of the ninth and tenth centuries proved that the theory of the spiritual and the temporal Powers was fantastic. In practice kings and emperors were the chief agents, at any rate in northern Europe, for the reform of the morals of the clergy and the maintenance of ecclesiastical discipline. The Capitularies of Louis the Pious especially are concerned mainly with ecclesiastical matters. In these documents bishops, abbots, clergy and monks are informed of their duty by the Emperor. It is true that in such matters the king or emperor was the instrument of reforming bishops; but, in the first place, bishops who desired to reform the Church found it impossible to do so without using the prestige of the Temporal Power; and secondly, the anointment of a king made him a sacred person. There was, therefore, a complete confusion between the functions of temporal and spiritual Authorities. Again, the highest spiritual Authority, the bishop of Rome, was from time to time subjected to control by kings claiming to be emperors, sometimes indeed for merely political reasons, but sometimes also for the enforcement of some moral standard in the choice of Popes and in the policy of this or that Pope. Indeed, the Papacy would hardly have maintained its moral authority during the Middle Ages, if German kings had not compelled the turbulent clergy and people of Rome from time to time to select and support a Pope who was neither a brigand nor a murderer.

Books of moral instruction written by bishops or monks for the use of kings who could hardly themselves read or write, and probably understood very little Latin, should not be taken as proof that the Church as an organization was in practice morally superior to the civil Authorities. The events of the ninth and tenth centuries proved clearly enough that kings and emperors reformed the Papacy and the Church more frequently than the Spiritual Power reformed the Temporal. Charles the Great restored Pope Leo III

[1] Sedulius Scotus, De Rect. Christ. (Pat. Lat., 103), ch. vi and ch. ix.

by force of arms to power over the clergy and people of Rome, after they had rebelled and almost killed the Pope, whom they accused of serious crimes. That was at the end of the eighth century. And almost a century later, in A.D. 891, Formosus, bishop of Porto, was elected bishop of Rome in violation of the ancient canon which forbade the removal of a bishop of one See to another, when the German faction among the bishops under the last Carolingian Emperor, Charles the Fat, took control of the Papacy. Formosus had already been excommunicated for plots against Pope John VIII; but John's successor, Marinus (A.D. 882–884), had absolved him from the sentence. As Pope, Formosus first sent the imperial crown to the son of Guido, an Italian duke, and later crowned the German Arnulf as Emperor in Rome in A.D. 896. The successor of Formosus, Boniface VII, died fifteen days after his election, of the results of a life so scandalous that he had been at one time actually degraded from the priesthood. The anti-German party in Rome then established Stephen VI as Pope; and the dead body of Formosus was taken from its tomb and tried before a council under the presidency of the new Pope, Stephen, for disobedience to the canons. Stephen, however, was soon strangled by his opponents; and when his successor, John IX, was obliged to sever the connection with Germany, the Papacy fell for almost a hundred years into the hands of any armed gang in Rome or its neighbourhood that desired to control the wealth and prestige of the Roman Church. It was during this time that Theodora, mistress of Pope John IX, and Marozia, her daughter, were able to control the policy of the Papacy and the election of Popes. The son of Marozia was made Pope, as John XI, in A.D. 931;[1] and her grandson Octavian, who had inherited from his grandfather and father the military control of Rome, made himself Pope as John XII in A.D. 955. In the confused struggles of the time this Pope was driven to seek the support of a new German king, the Saxon Otto the Great, who entered Rome with his army and was crowned as Emperor in St. Peter's in A.D. 962. By this action the Empire of Charles the Great was

---

[1] John XI is said to have been the son of Pope Sergius (A.D. 904–911). Liutprand, *Antapodosis*, ii, 48.

supposed to have been refounded, although Otto controlled only parts of Germany, or as it was then called "Eastern France." Pope John XII deserted his protector as soon as the new Emperor had retired again to Germany; but Otto brought his army back to Rome in the year following and held a council of bishops, which dethroned the Pope and selected as his successor Leo VIII.[1] He died; and after some trouble with the armed bands in Rome, who had set up a new Pope, Benedict V, Otto once again entered Rome with armed forces, and established John XIII as Pope, after a slaughter and devastation in the city, which is said to have horrified even the Roman Emperor then reigning at Constantinople. It is sufficient for the purpose of the argument here to note that Otto III, the grandson of Otto the Great, in a further attempt to control the unseemly wrangling for the Papacy, held a council of German bishops at Ratisbon for the reform of the Church, in A.D. 996, and afterwards marched on Rome. There he established his own relative and chaplain as Pope Gregory V, and was "anointed Emperor" by him.[2] Otto went north again; and immediately an anti-Pope, John XVI, replaced the German Gregory. But the new Emperor returned to Rome and had the anti-Pope blinded, his nose cut off, his tongue cut out, ejected him from the Papacy and thus restored his relative to power.[3] On Gregory's death in A.D. 999, Otto III established Gerbert in Rome as Pope Silvester II. Gerbert was one of the most learned and virtuous ecclesiastics of his day, who had taught in the cathedral schools of Reims; had been elected archbishop there, and then dethroned; had become archbishop of Ravenna; and had probably inspired the new Emperor with the fantastic idea of reviving Rome itself as the capital of his Empire.

Clearly the Emperor and the different kings or dukes who controlled the Papacy from time to time were not regarded in practice as morally inferior to the so-called spiritual Power. The few bishops

---

[1] Liutprand, *Hist. Ottonis*, 10 sq. The charges against the Pope were that he turned the Lateran palace into a brothel; castrated a sub-deacon; invoked Venus while playing dice, and bore arms.

[2] Thietmar, *Chron.*, iv, 27, "unctionem imperialem percepit." Otto was then fifteen years old.

[3] Ibid., *Chron.*, iv, 30, ". . . a fidelibus Christi et Caesaris captus linguam cum oculis ac naribus amisit."

and abbots who wrote treatises or letters might adopt the superior morality of prophets of the Old Testament; but the majority of the rulers of the Church were not treated by the leaders of armed bands as models of probity. The so-called Temporal Power was not in practice "temporal" when it reformed the Church; but worse still for the theory, it was not a power. In practice no large area of Europe in the ninth and tenth centuries was controlled by a single central Authority. Any person with enough energy and ability to collect an armed band could overcome his neighbours; and if he subdued a sufficient number, might be called a king. The influence of the armed forces of any one of these lords or kings reached only so far as he and his men could travel in a summer campaign. Especially in the case of the strange succession of leaders of armed bands who called themselves Roman Emperors, it is clear that their influence disappeared from any district as soon as their armies departed.

As for the spiritual Power, the term is misleading if it is taken to mean that the bishops of the Latin Churches, and in particular the bishop of Rome, exerted only what in later times would have been called moral authority. The words "spirit" and "spiritual" in the Middle Ages had very simple meanings. What was regarded as "spiritual" in those times was the uncanny, magical or mysterious. It had no necessary connection with moral excellence, although the influence of a virtuous person might also be regarded as "spiritual," because to simple minds such influence appears to be mysterious. As an example of the climate of opinion in which disputes about the spiritual Power arose, a story may be quoted from the *Annals* of Hincmar, archbishop of Reims—an exceptionally able and intelligent scholar of the later ninth century. It runs as follows: "At that time a miracle happened at Therouanne. The servant of a certain citizen of that place, on the morning of the Assumption (August 15th), began to press a linen garment which is called a shirt, for his master to wear when going to Mass; and as soon as he pressed it, the garment became all bloody. And so, whenever he pressed it, blood flowed, until the whole garment was saturated with it. This garment Hunfrid, the bishop of the city, had brought to him and kept in his church as a proof; and because that festival was not kept by the people of his diocese, he ordered that it should be solemnly observed by all."[1] The strangest element in this story is the implication that the blood on the shirt was a sign from heaven in favour of keeping a feast. But such stories and such interpretations fill the pages of the dialogues of Gregory the Great, and of the book on the *Glory of the Saints* by Gregory of Tours, both of whom lived at the end of the sixth century. The prevailing opinion since those days and throughout the Middle Ages accepted as "spiritual" any uncanny or unusual experience; and the spiritual Power, therefore, meant the ability to make such events occur, or to interpret them. The medieval Pope, bishop or priest, was much more like a magician than a moral teacher. The tradition of Christian virtues, however, also survived; and it was always possible for reformers to appeal to the generally accepted moral standards. This was done at times by Popes, as when Nicholas I rebuked king Lothair for repudiating his first wife and taking another as his wife. At another time the cardinals appealed to moral standards when they accused the reigning Pope, John XII, of sexual promiscuity. In practice, therefore, the spiritual Power of the Middle Ages was partly but not usually concerned with moral standards.

Worse still for the theory, the spiritual Power of the Popes and of the greatest bishops was "temporal" enough to use its own armed force. The situation in Rome and southern Italy in the ninth and tenth centuries was so difficult that the Popes can hardly be blamed for organizing the defence of their territories. Thus, in A.D. 851 Leo IV, "from fear of the Saracens, surrounded St. Peter's in the Vatican with a wall, and brought the wall to the edge of the city of Rome."[2]

The so-called "Temporal Power" of the Popes, which has been discussed in an earlier chapter, violated the medieval theory of the

[1] *Ann. Bertiniani*, ann. 862. The Greeks are said to have thought in 1940 that the Italians would be defeated because they had torpedoed a cruiser on the feast of the Assumption.

[2] Ibid., ann. 851. This is the so-called "Leonine City," part of which has become the so-called Vatican City. It would have astonished Leo IV to know that his successor was confined to part of the Leonine City as "sovereign."

separation of the two Powers. The bishop of Rome, as the "temporal" ruler of the people in a small section of Italy, was merely a prince or duke among other princes; and the policy of his government was inevitably affected by the wealth and power of other princes. He could not, therefore, reasonably claim to be "above the battle." His power as a ruler depended either upon his own armed forces, or upon a skilful policy (similar to that of any small State) making use of the rivalry of powerful neighbours, so that one or other might become his protector. The Temporal Power of the Papacy may have been conceived by some of its supporters in the Middle Ages as the only means of securing the independence of the Pope's judgement on moral or spiritual issues. But even so, it provided clear evidence of the impossibility of separating in practice the "temporal Power" from the "spiritual Power." After Leo IV, Pope Nicholas I may be regarded as having relied chiefly upon the spiritual Power, as understood in the Middle Ages. As it has been noted above, he appealed to moral standards, in order to correct the erratic matrimonial habits of Lothair II, in spite of the support given to him by some bishops. But he was also able to make use of the current belief in magical powers. When Louis, the brother of Lothair, who was accepted as Emperor, descended upon Rome with an army, the Pope turned to prayers and processions. The Emperor's soldiers dispersed a procession on the way to St. Peter's; but one of them, who had broken the processional cross, fell dead, and Louis was taken ill with a sudden fever. These two events were accepted as the results of the Pope's prayers; and the Emperor's wife was thus frightened into negotiating a reconciliation with Pope Nicholas. The bishops of Cologne and Trier, who had come to Rome on behalf of Lothair, were excommunicated; and their reply is given in Hincmar's *Annals*: "This Lord Nicholas, who is called Pope, and counts himself an apostle among the apostles, and makes himself Emperor of the whole world, who wants to send us to damnation, finds opponents to his madness; and its results will bring trouble on him later."[1] This is hardly reverence for papal

---

[1] *Ann. Bertiniani*, ann. 864. *Scriptores R.G.*, p. 68. The words are: "totius mundi imperatorem se facit"—a clear charge of "temporal" supremacy.

authority; but the Pope, using his influence with kings, succeeded in establishing his authority over the greatest metropolitans, including Hincmar, the archbishop of Reims.

The supremacy of the bishop of Rome over all other clergy was at the same time supported by the general acceptance of the so-called "False Decretals." These are letters and other documents, some genuinely ancient, and others composed about the year A.D. 850 in western Germany by an imaginative and pious author, who assigned some of them to the most ancient Popes and to councils which never existed. The purpose of the collection was the reinforcement of the authority of the bishop of Rome; and these documents were accepted throughout the Middle Ages as authentic. But these were the ages in which it was generally believed that the column of the Flagellation was brought to Rome by a cardinal of the Colonna (Column) family, and that a fourth-century painting was the kerchief of St. Veronica (*verum icon*, true image), imprinted miraculously by the face of Christ. The False Decretals were used by Nicholas I and his successors in order to complete the centralization of the spiritual Power. Clearly, however, the spiritual Power in this sense means not the moral influence of the virtuous or learned in society, but the power of the clergy, and in particular of the bishops, with the bishop of Rome in control of them. Pope Nicholas was also concerned with the eastern or Greek-speaking Churches, over which he claimed the same supreme authority. In Constantinople a rivalry of political groups led to the dethronement of one patriarch and the appointment of another. At first the two parties among the Greek-speaking clergy at Constantinople appear to have been willing to accept the decision of the Pope; but when this decision went against Photius, the patriarch backed by the local Emperor, a council of bishops in Constantinople (A.D. 867) condemned not only the Pope but all the Latin Churches. According to Hincmar, Pope Nicholas wrote a letter to inform the bishops of western Europe that "the Emperors of the Greeks and the eastern bishops had abused the whole Church which uses the Latin language, because we fast on Saturdays, because we say that the Holy Ghost proceeds from the Father and the Son, and because we forbid priests to have wives; . . . because at Easter, in the manner of Jews, we bless and offer a lamb, together with the Lord's body; because clerics among us shave their beards, and because among us a deacon is ordained bishop without having been ordained priest."[1] The Pope excommunicated the Patriarch, and the Patriarch the Pope; and from this date the Latin and Greek-speaking Churches were finally estranged—to the great advantage of the bishop of Rome, who thereby excluded possible rivals in his claim to be supreme over the whole "Catholic" Church. From this date, therefore, "Catholic" refers only to the Latin Churches and excludes more than half of the Christian world. But within this obviously non-universal system, the bishop of Rome had secured a predominance which was partly due to his connection with the apostle St. Peter and partly to his position as a "temporal" Power.[2]

The spiritual Power was even more completely confused with the control of "temporal" armed force under Pope John VIII (A.D. 872–882). This Pope claims in his letters actually to have appointed the Emperor; and he regards those who oppose the person of his choice, Charles the Bald, as the enemies of God.[3] This was politics, however disguised as Christian teaching. And the Pope also issued letters of excommunication throughout his reign to assist one political group against the other. Excommunication was disregarded by the opponents of those princes favoured by the Pope; but it became a recognized weapon to be used by Popes and other bishops during the Middle Ages. Finally, Pope John VIII was driven, by danger from the Saracens and the untrustworthiness of Christian rulers in southern Italy, to lead an army and prepare a fleet of his own. But the confusion of temporal and spiritual was clearly not confined to the See of Rome. The bishop of Naples, Athanasius, brother of the duke of that city, seized the dukedom,

---

[1] *Ann. Bertiniani*, ann. 867. The point about the use of the Latin language (omnem ecclesiam quae Latina utitur lingua) led to bitter controversy. The Pope replied: "The Emperor should either cease to call himself Emperor of the Romans or avoid abuse of the Roman language."

[2] At about this date also the word "Apostolicus" is used as an ordinary name for the bishop of Rome.

[3] John VIII, Ep. 23 (A.D. 876). *Pat. Lat.*, 126. In the Papal letter excommunication is based on Jeremiah xv and Matthew ix, "cast out the offending eye."

X

killed his brother's supporters by the direction of the Pope, and
had his brother's eyes put out.[1] He then ruled Naples both as bishop
and duke (A.D. 876). Other bishops in the North were princes and
military leaders in their own districts. It would, therefore, be
difficult to distinguish in practice the spiritual from the temporal
Power except in so far as all bishops, and in particular the bishop
of Rome, could use the current belief in their magical powers to
reinforce their control of the situation.

The theory that Christendom was in fact organized in two co-
ordinate systems, although at variance with the facts, remained an
ideal throughout the Middle Ages. But it was even more misleading
as an ideal than as a theory for explaining the actual situation; and
it was as an ideal that it misled Thomas Aquinas and Dante, and
obstructed progress in the art of government. It is not true that any
civilized community *ought* to be so organized that the clergy have
either equal or superior moral authority as compared with the
officials and agents of civil government. It is true that any person,
man or woman, with moral insight and influence ought to criticize
and correct those who hold power; but such men and women have
never been all included within the clergy, and have often been
excluded from organizations claiming to represent the spiritual
Power. From the fifth to the ninth century the conception of what
was later called the "State" was confused. Personal duties were
more generally understood than social institutions. The clergy, and
particularly the bishops, drifted into a relationship with the kings
of the new barbarian kingdoms which was largely due to the disappearance of an educated aristocracy of laymen by the middle of
the sixth century; and therefore, almost by accident, the control
of education during the Middle Ages fell into the hands of the
clergy. Boethius and Cassiodorus had no successors among lay
scholars until the Renaissance. It is absurd, therefore, to suppose
that a social ideal for public policy with regard to the relations of
Church and State, can be derived from the almost accidental circumstances prevailing in a primitive community.

Again, it proved impossible, even in the Middle Ages, to dis-

[1] The facts are reported in Erchempert's *History of the Lombard Dukes*, ch. 39.

tinguish clearly in practice between the functions of the temporal and spiritual Powers. And it was impossible because the analysis of the functions required to be performed in a community, was mistaken. It was as misleading as the equally faulty analysis of a human person into a body and soul. But this will be discussed elsewhere. So far as the social ideal is concerned, the attempt to separate the temporal from the spiritual, which must inevitably fail in any living community, could end only in the death of that community. But the experience of the centuries between the fifth and the ninth unfortunately set idealists upon the wrong road. During that time, and throughout the Middle Ages, the best writers and teachers devoted their efforts to making men live up to a social ideal; and the ideal itself was an illusion.

Again, the social ideal of the ninth and later centuries was a natural result of inexperience in the art of government, and ignorance of the subtleties of social organization. The medieval ideal implied an absolute Authority, immune from criticism or opposition, whether this Authority was temporal or spiritual. In periods of social confusion, such as continued for centuries after the fifth century in western Europe, men naturally over-estimate the importance of authority, on the one hand, and of obedience, on the other. It was difficult enough in the sixth century to keep even monks in order. But the conceptions of authority and obedience end in illusion, if either of them is believed to be best when it is unlimited. Social authority without criticism or opposition causes a rigidity in government, which can end only in the collapse of the system. That is the lesson of the Roman dictatorship, which the men of the Middle Ages never learnt. On the other hand, unlimited obedience or uncritical trust in rulers either of Church or State, leads inevitably to the exhaustion of all initiative in the community. Thus, the social ideal of the two Powers, each highly centralized, was one of the chief causes of the final collapse of the medieval system in the sixteenth century.

The Catholic Church

The second dominant idea of the Middle Ages was that the

beliefs and practices of north-western Europe either were or ought to be those of the whole world. This is the meaning of the Greek phrase which became the word "Catholic." That word began to be used in reference to the Roman system of civilization at about the time when the first Christian Emperors were under the influence of the Greek tradition in Constantinople. There are two aspects of the medieval conception of catholicity: first, the whole world was supposed to be included in the same system of government, ecclesiastical organization, and religious practice and belief; secondly, this whole world was supposed to have preserved the same beliefs and customs for many generations. As for the first point, every great civilization which has arisen out of the amalgamation of many local practices and beliefs, has been felt to include the whole world. The over-arching sky becomes the symbol of unity in contrast with the local hills and rivers with their separate gods and distinguishing customs. Thus, the Emperor of China was called the "Son of Heaven." The Roman Empire also, before it was Christian, was believed to include the whole world. Thus Ovid wrote that "whatever Jupiter beholds in the whole world is Roman."[1] The same conception was preserved in the Christian Roman Empire, and gradually transferred from the Roman system of government to the Christianity which it maintained. It will be remembered that in earlier chapters attention was called to the saying of Orosius that he was "among fellow-Romans in the whole world"; of St. Augustine, that "the whole world (orbis terrarum) judged correctly"; and of Vincent of Lerins that the Christian faith was held "everywhere and by everybody." Again, Pope Celestine I (A.D. 422–432) refers to the whole world (totus mundus) as using Roman ritual.[2] All these belong to the fifth century, when the Roman Empire still united all the lands of the Mediterranean basin. But the word "catholic" and the conception of a "whole world" was retained by the Latin Churches even in the ninth century and throughout the Middle Ages. In theory also, the whole world of north-western Europe was united; and the unity was identified by

[1] Ovid, Fasti, i, 85. Jupiter arce sua totum cum spectat in orbem,
Nil nisi Romanum quod tueretur, habet.
[2] Celestine I, Ad Episc. Galliarum. Pat. Lat., 50, col. 535.

tradition with peace.[1] It was supposed that the peoples living within the Catholic Church, in the ninth-century meaning of that term, were not naturally inclined to wage war between themselves. On that assumption was based the promotion of the Crusades by the Popes, as well as efforts to secure occasional peace, connected with the "Truce of God."

Unity seems also to have meant in the Middle Ages identity of custom and belief in succeeding centuries. Vincent of Lerins had said that the catholic faith was what had "always been believed." And although medieval histories of the world, from that of Peter Comestor to that of Vincent of Beauvais, always allowed for a succession of different ages before Christianity appeared, it was generally believed that, after the establishment of Christianity, no fundamental changes of belief and custom had occurred. This idea of adherence to the belief and customs of former centuries was directly inherited from the moralists of pre-Christian Rome. And in proportion as the Roman Church became the centre of the organization of all the Latin Churches, so unchanging sameness of belief and custom came to be accepted both as a fact and as an ideal. Unity was contrasted not merely with the diversity of local customs, but with differences between one century and another. Thus, it was easy enough for medieval Emperors to play the part of the Caesars, without knowing very exactly who the Caesars were; and it was easy for St. Peter, the Galilean fisherman, to be imagined and depicted in the costume of a medieval Pope. History in the eighth century, and for many centuries after, was treated as a chronicle of events and the names of persons, without any reference to changes in institutions or in the climate of opinions.

Such was the theory of the facts—the generally accepted idea of what had actually occurred. In practice, however, quite obviously the medieval system in north-western Europe did not cover the whole world. The claims of the admirers of the Roman Empire, even in its best days, were unfounded. They arose out of ignorance of Chinese and Indian civilizations, and of undiscovered continents.

[1] As in letters of Gregory the Great and in Illa unitas quae pax vocatur. Aquinas, *Summa Theol.* i, ii, q. cv. 1 ad 3, multitudo regum magis est data ad poenam quam ad eorum perfectum.

Even under the Roman Empire civilization was wrongly imagined to be peculiar to men who lived, as Plato says, like frogs round the pool of the Central Sea. But the conception that the whole world was included in the catholicity of north-western Europe in the Middle Ages, was even more absurd than the earlier Roman belief. After the eighth century this "catholic" whole world excluded the Mohammedans and even the "Greeks," as members of the Greek-speaking Churches were called. The medieval imagination was so strong, that it could claim for the Latin Churches and the kingdoms to which those Churches had given moral authority, a universality which all educated men must have known was a fiction. But the universality which did not exist in fact, remained as an ideal, inherited from the ignorance which adorned the Roman Empire with divine attributes.

Similarly, the unity which was supposed to exist between the beliefs and practices of the first and the fifth and later centuries, was a fiction. What remained the same was only a form of words; and the same words can indeed continue to be used in succeeding ages with entirely different senses, or better still, with no sense at all. Clearly, the bishops mentioned in the New Testament were quite unlike the bishops of the fifth century; and these latter would certainly have been astonished to meet the princely bishops of the ninth century. The kings of the barbarian tribes in the fifth century were quite unlike the "Lord's anointed" of the ninth century. And there is no trace in the fifth century of kings and emperors going to battle, supported by the relics of saints, as in the eighth and later centuries. This is not the place to discuss the changes which occurred in theological ideas; but clearly the position of the Virgin Mary in heaven had not been generally recognized, before the fifth century, to be what it was during the Middle Ages. Ritual did, indeed, remain the same for many centuries after the fifth; and the preservation of Latin as a ritual language assisted in the maintenance of certain words or phrases in the expression of belief from one generation to another. But under the surface of traditional rituals and verbal forms, the current of thought and emotion during the Middle Ages was setting towards the great changes of the sixteenth century.

As for the medieval conception that the generally accepted beliefs and practices, affecting social organization, *ought* to be the same in all parts of the world and in succeeding ages—such an ideal was the natural result of the social confusion which followed the collapse of the Roman Empire. To men of that time, variety of custom and belief seemed to be barbarism, as compared with the unity of the Roman world; and the uncertainty of life from year to year was contrasted with the supposed eternity of Rome. The medieval ideal, therefore, was the reflection of the needs and the hopes of a chaotic society. But obviously different forms of government are suitable in different climates and different stages of social development. And, in any case, it is impossible to establish or maintain medieval kingship and the absolute control of opinion by the clergy, in a community whose members can read and write and think for themselves. A new form of universal belief (*catholica fides*) has indeed been achieved in the acceptance of the same truths of science in all parts of the world. But the "*catholica fides*" of the sciences is the result of independent observation and experiment of individuals in all nations, and is not derived from the authority of any one organized group of persons.

The medieval ideal of unity of doctrine and practice in succeeding ages is even more misleading. The conception that the knowledge of facts or the estimate of values *ought* to remain the same in later ages as it was in more primitive times, was due to a misunderstanding of the nature of experience. As experience changes, new facts are brought to light, and new values in morality and religious custom and belief are discovered. The continuity of an individual's experience from birth to death does not involve his acceptance of his childhood as if it provided the test of truth or of moral excellence. And in the succession of generations, the changes which take place in the generally accepted view of man and the world are to be welcomed rather than lamented—even when the whole of an earlier system of thought is displaced by later discoveries, as when the Copernican took the place of the Ptolemaic astronomy. But the conception that religious or theological statements do not conform to the rule of any other body of knowledge, is due to the theory of "revelation," which will be discussed elsewhere. It is enough to note here that social institutions in the Middle Ages were greatly affected by the belief in "revealed" truths which were different in their source and their subject-matter from the truths discovered by ordinary methods of knowledge. The idea of "revelation" itself was probably due to the fact that nothing was known in the early centuries of the Christian era about the sources or the age of the Hebrew scriptures. These writings, therefore, appeared to be exceptionally independent of such ordinary experience as was known to be the source of "Homer" or of the works of Plato. Also the authors of the Hebrew scriptures made claims which would have seemed preposterous to the more prudent writers of Greece and Rome. The Hebrews claimed to be directly informed by their God. But although Homer and Hesiod professed knowledge about *their* Gods, they never claimed to have learnt it by special communications from the Gods themselves. From the earliest stages of medieval thought, however, any opinion which was asserted to be of divine origin was readily accepted. Thus the Sybils became as authoritative as "David" in the "Dies Irae." The belief that a day of judgement was to come, was based upon the words of the Sybil and of David;[1] and therefore, in the last versions of medievalism which affected the arts, Michelangelo painted the Sybils to balance the Hebrew prophets on the ceiling of the Sistine Chapel. Thus the books of the Old Testament became authoritative as guides to the duties of kings and bishops, not by argument from evidence, but because they were believed to contain special instructions on the art of government, given directly by God. And this belief became the basis of a social ideal which established the practices of primitive Semitic tribes as models for the Christian kingdoms and Churches of medieval Europe. The ideal of government, both civil and ecclesiastical, in the Middle Ages was monarchical; and whether mistaken or not, this ideal had its origin in the very limited experience of the centuries between the fifth and the ninth, under the

---

[1] Dies irae, dies illa
Solvet seclum in favilla,
Teste David cum Sybilla.

influence of an uncritical study of the Hebrew Scriptures. But unity of doctrine and practice, which involves confining the development of social relations within the narrow limits of the beliefs and customs of a primitive society, is an absurdity.

In the pursuit of a mistaken social ideal, the effort to preserve unity of custom and belief from generation to generation, had an important effect upon social institutions. It was the chief bulwark of an established order, and, therefore, of vested interests. The continuance of a tradition may be due to the effects of unconscious imitation, as when a child copies an adult. Such continuance is natural and may be harmless. But the conscious and deliberate maintenance of ancient customs and belief, especially by those who derive benefit from them, can only cramp the intelligence and narrow the emotions. Enforced unity in faith and morals from age to age is atavism; and it makes public policy in Church and State merely applied archaeology. It was perhaps useful in a time of social experiment, such as the early Middle Ages, to control the ·emotions, even at some cost to the intelligence. The emotions connected with moral standards and religious practices were certainly refined and elevated during the early Middle Ages by those who strove to maintain unity; for the chief emotions current from the fifth and ninth centuries should be compared historically, not with the serenity of Marcus Aurelius, nor with the aloofness of an eighteenth-century philosopher, but with the childish fears and hopes which disturbed the minds of the majority in the last days of the Roman Empire in the West. A new civilization could not have come into existence unless fears and hopes had been canalized. Emotions thus controlled keep men together and are necessary for social stability in times of violence and uncertainty. But to continue as an ideal for all time what was an unfortunate necessity in past ages is obviously a mistake. In practice it is a refusal to bring into the open air—"day's garish eye"—what appears to be more impressive in a "dim religious light." And if the restraint placed upon the tendency to change is organized by a clergy and civil rulers who are owners or controllers of large amounts of land or other wealth, the result is not so much purity of doctrine as security of despotism. It should not be forgotten that the Latin Churches, which stood for the preservation of the same standard of morals from generation to generation, had become by the ninth century owners of immense properties in all parts of western Europe. The chief bishops and abbots were administrators of these properties; and, as the records show, they had a keen sense of the advantages of wealth and power. Obedience and trust in bishops—the *ecclesia docens*—are virtues which have proved to be convenient for vested interests in every age. Uncorrected by other and more adult virtues, they preserve unity at the cost of liberty.

The Other World

The third dominant idea of the First Europe was that of an "other world." It was generally believed that, besides the world of sight and sound, of hills and rivers and living men, there was another, consisting of heaven above the blue sky, hell under the earth, and purgatory placed uncertainly between them. Heaven and hell were believed to be inhabited by persons called angels and devils, who had not lived in the ordinary world, and also by all those who had so lived during the four thousand years since creation. Most of the well-known persons of pre-Christian history were living in torture in hell—Socrates, Plato and Seneca, together with the Emperors Nero and Claudius. Trajan had had a special reprieve as a result of the prayers of Gregory the Great. All this was taken quite literally by Christian teachers and the majority of Europeans between the fifth and the fifteenth centuries. The language used about it was not metaphorical or symbolic. It was intended as a statement of fact. And beliefs concerning facts of this kind deeply affected social institutions and the relations between men in society.

This is not the place to discuss the philosophy or the view of the universe implied in the medieval conception of an other world. For the purpose of the argument here only the relation between these beliefs and the social institutions of the First Europe is relevant. And the most important characteristics of this relation are: first, the effect which actual social institutions had upon the way in

which the "other world" was conceived; and secondly, the effect
of conceptions of the "other world" upon social institutions after
the fifth century. For example, the situation in heaven and hell was
conceived in terms of the Roman Empire and its ecclesiastical institutions; and, on the other hand, the belief that the "other
world" was ruled by an absolute Authority, infallible and immune
from criticism, supported the view that the ideal form of government on earth was monarchical dictatorship.

Here also the contrast between theory and practice is obvious.
In theory the "other world" was entirely different from the actual
world of daily experience. The dualism which affected all medieval
thinking had the same effects in the theory of an other world as it
had in the theory of the soul. In theory, the soul was entirely distinct
from the body; but in practice the soul was conceived as a faded
reproduction of the body. It had sight and other senses. As Claudianus
Mamertus explains in his treatise on the character of the soul (*De
Statu Animae*), the soul cannot see the internal organs of the body,
only because they are material. But without the body the soul can
see what is not material.[1] Pictures of souls from the earliest
Egyptian painting to the latest of medieval Europe, are always
pictures of bodies; and this was not regarded as mere symbolism.
It was a reproduction of what visionaries claimed to have actually
seen. Similarly the conception of the "other" world was only a
pale reproduction of certain characteristics of the social situation in
a Christian Empire.

The worship of rulers has already been referred to in the third
chapter, where it was shown that the Roman Emperors adopted,
for the increase of their prestige, certain connections with sun-
worship. The nimbus or halo is the best example of this. And in
this case it may seem that an absolute ruler adopted the characteristics of God. But in the fifth century, quite obviously, the
Christian God or Christ and his Saints, were conceived as a ruler
and his Court. They derived the halo which became the sign of
sanctity in heaven from the use made of it in representations of the
Roman Emperors. Similarly the ordinary official title of a Roman

---

[1] Claudianus Mamertus, *De Statu Animae*, iii, 9. *Pat. Lat.*, 53.

Emperor after Constantine was "Our Lord" (*Dominus noster*) which became the usual title of Christ.[1]

As Duchesne says: "The conception of the celestial court was influenced far less by the Olympus of the poets than by the sight which lay open before their own eyes, that of the earthly kingdom of the Emperor and his immediate attendants; attendants whose favour availed against the laws, often mitigated their severity and ensured to those to whom it extended the accomplishment of their desires. None the less the distribution of the divine implied in the cultus of the Blessed, did correspond in some degree to a mode of regarding the relations of the Divinity with men which was common enough among the pagans. A particular saint protected more particularly this or that country, showed himself helpful in particular circumstances, healed this or that disease. Benefit was to be derived from invoking him near his tomb or in a sanctuary which was specially dedicated to him."[2] For the purpose of the argument here, however, the connection between the Pagan Heroes and Christian Saints is less important than the fact that the persons of the "other" world were conceived to be merely reproductions of those in the real world who had power or influence.

Again, the choir of heaven is obviously a reproduction of the circle (*corona*) of the clergy on either side of their bishop, or of bishops in council, or, at a somewhat later date, of monks or nuns singing "divine office." Thus Pope Leo the Great, in his address to his clergy after his election as bishop of Rome, says that, when he saw the splendid vestments and jewels, he almost thought that he was among the angels in heaven.[3] The "divine work" (*opus divinum*), which in the rule of St. Benedict means the singing of psalms and canticles, was conceived in the Middle Ages to be continued for ever in heaven. That part of the life of monks and nuns in which, no doubt, they felt the greatest joy, was to continue in heaven without the distasteful necessity of manual or other labour for food and clothing. The heaven of the Middle Ages was mainly

[1] "The lord" was originally the sun-god, to whom the Lord's Day or Sunday was dedicated. For "Dominus noster" see Bury's ed. of *Gibbon*, vol. ii, app. 10.
[2] Duchesne, *History of the Christian Church*, Eng. trans., 1924, vol. iii, p. 9
[3] Leo, *Sermo*, ii, 2. (*Pat. Lat.*, 54.)

the ideal of celibates; and therefore its joys are entirely sexless.[1] The most striking contrast is to be found in the Mohammedan conception of a desirable eternity in the skies with houris in attendance. Finally, the blessed in heaven were conceived to be for ever removed from change, disorder, or the effect of what had happened on earth after their deaths. This was not quite consistent with the other medieval idea of the saints in heaven as persons continually helping their clients on earth. As early as the fifth century the medieval idea had begun to develop that the severity of God might be warded off by a member of the heavenly Court who had direct access to him. And even as late as the sixteenth century in Italy, where medieval ideas still affected painting, Giorgio Vasari describes how he painted a picture of the heavenly Father about to send plagues upon the earth; and of St. Roch protecting the people from these plagues.

As for hell, the sufferings of the damned were believed to be regarded with equanimity and even pleasure by the blessed. It has been noted in the second chapter that St. Augustine felt a certain moral hesitation concerning the idea of eternal punishment; but he persuaded himself that revenge was justifiable as an act of God. Again, about two hundred years later, in the *Dialogues* of Gregory the Great, the difficulty is urged that "No judge that loves justice takes pleasure in cruelty; and the purpose of a just master in punishing a wicked servant, is the amendment of his wickedness." But if the wicked in hell are never to be made any better by their torture, what is the purpose of such torture? To this Gregory replies that God does not take pleasure in the torments of hell, but maintains them in order that the blessed may appreciate more keenly the joys of heaven when they see the torments they have escaped. "And as Christians during their lives do not pray for the devils already damned, so when they are in heaven they do not oppose what God pleases to do."[2] The sentiments of St. Augustine and St. Gregory survived throughout the Middle Ages and later in the doctrines of the Calvinists. The conception that a ruler who used

[1] In the book of *Revelation* (xiv. 4) there are said to be in heaven one hundred and forty-four thousand "who have not been contaminated with women, for they are virgins" (παρθένοι).   [2] Gregory, *Dialogues*, iv, 44.

punishment for everlasting revenge, and not for the improvement of those who suffered, was worthy of worship, is an indication of the primitive state of the idea of justice in the Middle Ages. It is well known that the visions of the other world and the details of its tortures which Dante used seven hundred years later, were first clearly expressed in the *Dialogues* of Gregory the Great.[1] In the same book also is the first expression of the medieval conception of purgatory as a place of punishment which is curative and not merely revengeful. This is indeed a sign that the idea of justice was affecting the original belief in eternal damnation. But Gregory attempts to prove the existence of purgatory from the metaphorical language in St. Paul's Epistle to the effect that a man may be saved "yet so as by fire."[2]

The practices believed to be followed by the ruler of heaven were obviously derived from the experience of rulers on earth. It must be remembered that the world in which these conceptions developed was familiar with the torture and burning of slaves or political opponents of the ruler. Early Christians had been burnt and tortured; and soon after the days of Gregory the Great it became an established custom of Roman Emperors in Constantinople to have the eyes of rebels burnt out and their tongues slit.[3] The most Christian Empress, Irene, at the end of the eighth century, who had the approval of the reigning Pope because of her orthodoxy in the matter of images, directed the blinding of her own son, the Emperor Constantine, in order to secure herself in power. The practice of blinding and other maiming spread in the ninth century to the barbarian kingdoms of the West, and to the Court of the Pope himself. It was in these terms that men conceived the actions of the ruler of heaven.

As for the effects of the medieval conceptions of heaven and hell upon social institutions, these may be summarized under three headings. The generally accepted idea of an "other" world supported absolute monarchy in State and Church; it supported the desire for

---

[1] Especially in *Dialogues*, iv, 36 and 37.
[2] Gregory, *Dialogues* iv, 39, quoting 1 Cor. iii. 11–15.
[3] The usual method of blinding was by holding a red-hot brazen plate in front of the eyes of the victim.

"glory," as the purpose of public policy, and it gave a divine example for the persecution of heretics. Monarchy was supported by the idea that heaven was a kingdom ruled by a king, who was, as the clergy were always reminding the civil Authorities, like Melchizedek, also a priest. The idea of the king as a kind of Christ, "the anointed one," has been already discussed in an earlier chapter. But the divine example of government did more than confer prestige upon one warrior as compared with others on earth. It also gave to the king a certain moral authority over the making of law and the administration of justice, which in practice violated the tradition of government, both among the Romans and the barbarians. Laws among the barbarians were statements of traditional custom, not the commands of kings; and in the Roman tradition law was not conceived to have its origin in the will of a ruler until Roman Law was in decay. But the conception of the ruler of heaven, subordinating all nature and all men to his will, greatly increased the tendency to absolutism in the Middle Ages. Thus monarchy came to be regarded as the best form of government by Thomas Aquinas, who wrote that "kingship is the best government of a people, if it is not corrupted."[1] And thus also, even in modern times, the political science of the early ninth century was expressed in the idea of kingship, by the institution of the feast of Christ the King in the encyclical of Pope Pius XI, dated December 11, 1925 (*Quas primas*). This encyclical says that the "essentials of lordship" are supreme power in legislation, justice and executive action, which is the theory of government implied in the Capitularies of the Frankish kings from about A.D. 750 to about A.D. 830—a theory since generally abandoned. Probably, therefore, the "divine right of kings" originally meant something more than absolute power derived from God. It may even have meant the power of a God-king.

Secondly, the conception that God had created the world, not for any advantage which it might derive from existence but for his own "glory," affected the public policy of kings and others who

[1] Thomas Aquinas, *Summa Theol.*, i, ii ae. 9, 105, art. 1 ad 2. But in *Summa Theol.*, ii, ii ae. qu. 50, art. 1 ad 2. *Regnum* is used for "government" including all the best forms.

aimed at "glory." The phrase in the New Testament "Glory in the highest" was, no doubt, the expression of the sense of the sublime in the contemplation of the heavens; but the Roman imperial coins inscribed "Gloria Romanorum," indicate the connection of the word "glory" with what is now called prestige. The crown and other decorations of kings were clearly intended to express this kind of glory; but unfortunately glory also meant the power of attracting attention especially by victory in war. Thus, although some kings in the first fervour of conversion to Christianity might resign their kingship, as many kings in England did in the seventh and eighth century, in the ninth century kings were much more inclined to imitate David and Solomon. And glory, as the chief purpose of a ruler following the lessons of heaven, has remained one of the most disastrous purposes of public policy.[1]

Thirdly, the conception of hell supported the punishment of heretics or other opponents of the established order. If God could punish by all forms of torture those who opposed him, a king or other ruler felt justified in following the divine example. The punishment of heretics by torture and death was not so much directed against errors in doctrine as against disturbers of social peace, destroyers of that unity which it was essential for the public Authorities to maintain. It was feared that God would punish the whole community for any defect which was allowed to persist in it.

Finally, the conception of an other world in which there was neither time nor change, obstructed the development of social institutions, because the ideal social situation was believed to be one which remained always the same. Eternity, as an ideal type of existence, was already expressed in the pre-Christian conception of "eternal Rome"; and when heaven became, in the fifth century, "Rome in the skies" (*Roma caelestis*), as it was for Prudentius, the influence of the eternity of this new Rome reinforced the stability of established authority on earth in a time of social confusion; but it also prevented the natural growth of new forms of government

[1] See Anatole France, *L'Ile des Pingouins* (ed. 1908), p. 172. Of Trinco (Napoléon): "lors de sa chute, il ne restait dans notre patrie que les bossus et les boiteux dont nous descendons. Mais il nous a donné la gloire."—"Il vous l'a fait payer cher!"—"La gloire ne se paye jamais trop cher, répliqua mon guide."

in Church and State. As Professor Whitehead has written: "Change-less order is conceived as the final perfection, with the result that the historic universe is degraded to a status of partial reality. . . . We should beware of philosophies which express the dominant emotions of periods of slow social decay. Our inheritance of philo-sophic thought is infected with the decline and fall of the Roman Empire, and with the decadence of eastern civilization. It expresses the exhaustion following upon the first three thousand years of advancing civilization."[1]

The conception of ideal existence as timeless or changeless, which misled Plato, affected, not only the Christian idea of the immor-tality of the soul, but also the policy of Christian writers and preachers who used it to support the maintenance of any established order and the vested interests connected with it.

The Establishment of Medieval Christendom

In spite of mistaken theories and defective practice, the work done during the four centuries following the collapse of the Roman Empire in western Europe laid the foundations for the establish-ment of medieval Christendom. The troubles of the ninth and tenth centuries, during which the second barbarian invasions occurred, put a severe strain upon the social institutions which had already come into existence. Fears and hopes in a time of social disturbance grew to monstrous proportions. But the new institutions survived— bishoprics, kingdoms, monasticism and new systems of customary law. And these became the foundations of a new civilization—that of the First Europe. The characteristics of some of these social institutions have been already discussed in earlier chapters; but it may be useful to give a short summary of the whole design. The building has been added to, in part destroyed, in part reconstructed; but the general plan of its earliest foundations can be discerned.

The establishment of medieval Christendom involved, first, *the unity of Europe*. This unity was an expression of an intellectual out-look and emotional reaction to experience which was common to all the peoples of the West. It was not a political unity, and it never

[1] Whitehead, *Modes of Thought* (1938), p. 109.

became one in spite of attempts to make it so. But out of that "spiritual" unity has come modern science and modern music; and it has survived the decline of the social institutions which first supported it. The unity of medieval Christendom depended upon the Latin Churches. It was Christian and Roman and, therefore, cosmopolitan and not international. That is to say, it disregarded or treated as trivial all differences of race and language. It assumed, as the later Roman Empire had assumed, and as it is implied in the words of St. Paul, "neither Jew nor Greek," that the individual person was united chiefly as a Roman and a Christian with all other individuals. But this obviously was true only so long as nations and national literatures, in the modern sense of those words, did not exist. Secondly, the unity of medieval Christendom depended largely upon the use of the Latin language by all those who were able to read and write. But this divided the learned from the common experience of the majority of their fellows, from which alone the development of the sciences, the arts, and religion receives its sustenance. As Condorcet wrote, at the end of the eighteenth century, "If it was impossible to make Latin a vulgar tongue common to all Europe, the custom of writing on the sciences in Latin would have only a transient utility for the scientists; and the existence of a scientific language which was the same in all nations, while the people of each nation spoke a different tongue, would only separate men into two classes, perpetuate among common folk their prejudices and errors, put an obstacle to true equality, to the equal use of the same reasoning and an equal knowledge of necessary truth; and, by thus putting a stop to the progress of the mass of humanity, would end, as in the East, by destroying that of the sciences themselves."[1]

Secondly, medieval Christendom showed that *moral authority unites* men more effectually than force or fear. The Churches never maintained armed forces. The schools and universities, which formed part of the spiritual power (*studium et ecclesia*), stood somewhat outside the exercise of government and the organization of production. And western civilization depends, not upon any

[1] Condorcet, *Esquisse d'un tableau historique* (Paris, 1866), tome i, p. 173.

system of production or of government, but upon religion and morality; that is to say, a certain attitude towards what is worthy of worship, and the acceptance of certain moral standards. These were expressed or embodied in new institutions after the fall of the Roman Empire. The kindliness, clemency and providence (*pietas, clementia, providentia*) claimed for the Roman Emperor on coins and monuments became the characteristics of the Church, acting in the name of Christ.

Thirdly, medieval Christendom proved in practice *the impossibility of a dualism* which divides the material from the spiritual—the body from the soul, the facts of life from the standards of moral value. In spite of the efforts of abstract thinkers and idealists, misled by Oriental influences in Manichaeanism and monasticism, European or western civilization has never accepted in practice the disregard for the use of natural forces and material advantages often associated with Eastern "wisdom." Europe has always maintained that your house could be improved as well as your character. Western civilization, for this reason, has been able to reduce disease by improved drainage; and this, so far from exhausting the power to use the highest human faculties, has been accompanied by a splendid development of the arts in architecture, music and painting, and a wide extension of human knowledge. All this was made possible in the establishment of medieval Christendom by the subordination of wealth and power to the moral authority which directed the use of them. If the best men and women from the fifth to the ninth century had cut themselves off from the use of wealth and power, Christianity itself might have disappeared.

Conclusion

Two general questions remain to be noticed, the answers to which affect every estimate of the importance of the history studied in this book: first, what was the relation of "Christianity" to the moral standards and social institutions of the early Middle Ages? Secondly, what is the place of tradition in the history of any one type of civilization?

No attempt can be made here to define the meaning of the word

"Christianity," especially as there is no agreement on the subject, even among professed Christians. But there are certain current ideas concerning the true nature of Christianity which have obviously not been accepted in the preceding pages. Some writers seem to imagine that there is an original "pure Christianity," expressed in the New Testament, which was later "corrupted" by the worship of relics and the establishment of the Papacy. Certainly the Christianity of St. Boniface in the eighth century was not the same as that of St. Augustine in the fifth or that of St. Paul's Epistles. But an oak is nothing like an acorn; and there is no reason to suppose that the acorn has been "corrupted" when it has grown into an oak. The conception that Christianity is "real" or "pure" only when it is the religion of the writers and first readers of the documents collected in the New Testament, implies that Christianity is not directly concerned with the greater part of human activities. The religion of the New Testament is that of small communities without influence or interest in the art of government, in the processes of production and trade, in the sciences or the arts of their day. The existence of these small communities was made possible by Roman Law, Roman roads, and the Roman control of land and sea. The writing of the documents which they used was made possible by centuries of labour and genius in the development of language and literature. But with all this the early Christians were not concerned. In the fourth and later centuries, however, a large number of men and women became Christians, who were aware of the problems of government, of industry, of science and the arts. They knew that the preaching of Christianity had been made possible by the maintenance of peace in the Roman Empire; and they thought that it was not unchristian to preserve and develop the institutions which had made the growth of Christianity possible. They faced the problem of the use of armed force, of the control of labour and of the promotion of learning, none of which had been faced by such Christian writers as Tertullian, who repudiated the whole system upon which his life and his writings depended. It is hardly reasonable, therefore, to condemn Gregory the Great or Boniface for accepting responsibility for the maintenance of peace and justice, merely because the first Christians were unaware of any such responsibility. Whatever may be the definition of Christianity, the Christianity of the ninth century must be treated by the historian as genuine Christianity, although its social setting, its language, its outlook and its customs were indeed very different from those expressed in the New Testament. On the other hand, the Christianity of St. Augustine, of Gregory the Great, and of St. Boniface— each of them different from the other—cannot be accepted as the only real Christianity, even if medieval Europe thought it was. Some writers and preachers in the sixteenth and seventeenth centuries repudiated the worship of relics and the supremacy of the Pope, and continued to call themselves Christian; while others maintained that if Christendom in the First Europe was really Christian, there could be no other Christianity than that of scholastic philosophers who, not unnaturally, had misunderstood Aristotle. The changes which have occurred in European or western civilization, have indeed been caused partly by different interpretations of Christianity, or by the selection of different texts, differently interpreted, from its sacred books. But the extension of knowledge and the improvement of moral standards, especially in the later stages of the history of western Europe, were also in part caused by ideas and activities entirely different from those of Christianity, and in some cases definitely opposed to it, or at least to the beliefs and customs of those who professed to be Christians. Christianity, indeed, is only one thread in the pattern of European civilization; and in the history of social institutions it is subordinate in importance to the influence of the Roman system of law and government, and to that of the Greek-Roman civilization of the Mediterranean countries. From the fifth to the ninth century at least, the Christian Churches were chiefly engaged in conveying into a new form of civilization the traditions of government and the arts which they had learnt under the Roman Empire. And indeed, it was not until the Churches had repudiated or forgotten the social irresponsibility of the earlier Christian communities that they were able to act as civilizing agents among the barbarians of the North. Religious doctrine and ritual could hardly have survived without ecclesiastical

661

organization; and that organization, throughout the Middle Ages, was Roman in origin and spirit.

To say, however, that the Christianity of medieval Christendom was as truly "Christian" as that of the first Christians, does not imply that everyone who claimed to be Christian in any age, had a right to do so. The bishops and priests of the early Middle Ages who supported the blinding of their rivals, were not "Christian" in any reasonable sense of that much-abused term; nor were the nobles who struggled chiefly for private wealth and power. They were not merely bad Christians; they were not Christians at all. Christianity in every age is a way of life, involving the acceptance in practice of certain moral standards. The way of life among the first Christians in small sheltered communities, without responsibility for peace or for justice outside their membership, was not the same as the way of life for men and women who were responsible for law and government. But, in both cases, it involved the same tradition. Similarly, the Christianity of the fifth century was that of adults, and the Christianity of the eighth that of children. There is a great difference between the cures of cancer and gout at baptism, as recorded by St. Augustine,[1] and the cure of Constantine's leprosy, described in the *Donation of Constantine* in the eighth century, because St. Augustine implies that the cure was the result of the virtues of the sufferer, and for the later writer baptism was merely magic. But the Christianity of children was still Christianity, even if credulity could be misused for private gain.

This raises the question of the place of tradition in the history of civilized life. Those who had most influence upon thought and emotion, in the arts and in government as well as in religion, during the early Middle Ages, were well aware of their dependence upon the past. After the collapse of the Roman system in western Europe, throughout the Middle Ages, and perhaps as late as the eighteenth century, the guides and leaders of European communities studied and quoted either the Fathers of the Church or the great writers of Athens and Rome. In the earlier years of the First Europe

[1] Augustine, *De Civ. Dei*, xxii, 8. Even St. Augustine is simple-minded. Black boys, who were really devils, jumped on the gouty foot to prevent the good man going to his baptism.

it was indeed natural that men and women, surrounded by real dangers and the terrors of the imagination, should look back with regret and admiration to earlier times. The remains of Roman architecture were the more impressive when the knowledge and skill which had made it possible were lost. The fragments of Roman literature and the earliest Christian records were more notable because few could read or write. Isidore of Seville, for example, in the sixth century, must have had an extensive library from which to draw his encyclopaedia (*Origines* or *Etymologiae*). But by the ninth century hardly anything was left except the works of Isidore himself, for the interpretation of inherited ideas. The chief aim of Isidore was the presentation of acquired knowledge—not its extension. The same purpose dominated the work of Hrabanus Maurus, abbot of Fulda, and afterwards archbishop of Mainz (A.D. 847–856). Similarly the copying of the manuscripts of ancient books was even more important after the collapse of the Roman system, than the writing of new books; and from Cassiodorus in the sixth century, in southern Italy, to Alcuin at Tours at the end of the eighth century, the copying of manuscripts was one of the chief means of preserving tradition. As the barbarian invaders of the fifth century had sought, not to destroy the Roman Empire, but to have a share in its wealth and power, so the descendants of those barbarians and of the populations they looted, sought in the ninth century, not to replace the Roman civilization and culture, but to preserve as much as they could find among its ruins. The loss of technical skill, of the arts and of knowledge, after the collapse of the Roman system, was disastrous enough; but the disaster would have been even greater if nothing of the past had remained in the First Europe.

On the other hand, the attempt to preserve tradition may succeed only in embalming a corpse. The Latin of the medieval Church was a dead language. It had been saved from the confusion of popular speech in the eighth century, out of which grew Italian, French and Spanish; and among the people who spoke Germanic and Celtic tongues, it was unintelligible except to a few, even in the sixth and seventh centuries. Churchmen and scholars used Latin because their thoughts moved among the dead. Similarly, the vestments of the Church were only the fashionable dress of the upper class in the early sixth century under the Roman Empire; but by the ninth century the fashions of the dead had become the symbols of sacred office. Indeed the dead haunted the Middle Ages, not merely in the language of its scholars, and the clothing of its priests, but also in the ideas and policies which dominated the lives of all. For example, in the oldest Roman tradition the authority of the aged was embodied in the right of the father (*paterfamilias*) to condemn the members of his family to death. Under the medieval system, the Roman tradition was preserved in the title of "father" (*padre, père* and Holy Father) to express the authority of the priest. And it was believed that the Holy Father and the bishops, "our fathers in God," had the right to condemn their children to hell. The effort to preserve the past was more often than not like a search for a gospel in a graveyard, where it discovered only ghosts. The greatest of these was the ghost of Rome.

The fundamental problem was never understood in the Middle Ages. That problem is how to distinguish what is living from what is dead among the ideas and customs which each generation inherits. And the distinction can be made only if tradition is critically examined. But the critical mind had never been Roman. It was Athenian. And not until the Renaissance did Europe re-discover the Athenians. Indeed, the ghost of Rome has injured civilization in Europe, precisely because in it survived the uncritical Roman admiration for the past. There could be no greater contrast in the history of civilization than this contrast between Rome and Athens: Rome looked to the old world and Athens to the new. As an expression of the Roman spirit, the words of Ennius, quoted by Cicero, are repeated with Cicero's comment by St. Augustine: "The old ways and the men of old make Rome stand firm."[1] The Roman Church preserved the same worship of the past as the pre-Christian teachers of Rome had preached. On the other hand, the spirit of Athens has been traditionally recognized in the statement

[1] Augustine, *De Civitate Dei*, ii, 21, quoting Ennius: "Moribus antiquis res stat Romana virisque."

in the Acts of the Apostles that the Athenians always sought to know "What is new."[1] The *"aliquid novi"* of the Vulgate translation, became the very symbol of heresy in the Middle Ages, for the same reason that led the Romans to call revolution *"res novae."*[2] What was new, was to the Athenians a birth to be welcomed: to the Romans it seemed subversive, devilish, like the fruit of the tree of knowledge which God had forbidden to man. The ghost of Rome thus brought to the First Europe both good and evil—good, in the effort to preserve tradition; evil, in the uncritical acceptance of what happened to be preserved.

The attempt to preserve tradition implies, further, the domination of certain ideas about the past; but the past in the minds of any generation is a reconstruction which is largely the work of the imagination. In the life of an individual the memory of childhood depends partly upon the survival of impressions which happen to have been vivid and may not have been important. But it depends also upon a selection and re-arrangement of episodes. This selection is due to the needs and the hopes of later life. Similarly, in the history of generations, the past which dominates the mind of any age is partly the result of the accidental survival of ruins and fragmentary records, but partly also a work of the imagination. And in the early Middle Ages when, as it has been pointed out above, the imagination was strong and uncritical, the past was reconstructed in fantastic shapes. The result was a conception of the early Church and of the Roman Empire, which in the ninth century was unconsciously dominated by the needs and the hopes of a period of social confusion. And, in addition to the unconscious work of the imagination upon ruins and records, there was a deliberate creation of an unreal past in such documents as the *Donation of Constantine* and the False Decretals for the support of one policy or another. Thus, the effort to preserve tradition was by no means, in practice, a careful adaptation of later ideas and institutions to ancient models.

[1] In the Authorized Version (Acts xvii. 21): "And the Athenians and strangers which were there, spent their time in nothing else but either to tell or to hear some new thing."

[2] "Novus homo," the Roman phrase for an "outsider," is almost the same as the heretic in the eyes of Catholic orthodoxy. "Tabulae novae" meant a repudiation of debt.

It was much more often and more generally an imaginative reconstruction of the past to suit the needs and the hopes of the Authorities in Church and State, in any given situation. If it was convenient to appeal to tradition, there was no hesitation in composing documents, charters or official letters, which supported the claims of this or that writer.

But clearly, the distinction between old and new is not the same as the distinction between true and false, or that between good and evil. To welcome what is new implies not merely the expectation of more experience and more knowledge, but also confidence in one's ability to distinguish truth from falsehood, whatever its age. This ability is the power of reason. The Roman reliance on what is old was, indeed, a confession of inability to think. But the patron of Athens was "Reason." The dominant word in the Roman tradition was "*lex*," and law is conservative. The dominant word in Athens was "*logos*"—the Word, Thought, Reason. But the men and women of the First Europe were committed by the accident of history to the Roman tradition, and although the critical intelligence revived from time to time, it was never powerful enough until it finally shattered the medieval system at the Renaissance. Plato's doctrine that "we must go where the argument (λόγος) carries us," was never wholly forgotten.[1] Boethius, in the sixth century, sought consolation, not in any sacred writings, but in Reasoning. In the ninth century Scotus Erigena, an Irishman trained in Greek thought, boldly expressed the principle of criticism in his statement that "genuine authority is not opposed to correct reasoning, nor correct reasoning to genuine authority":[2] the authority of Scripture is to be followed; but the meaning of its words discovered by reasoning.[3] Such a plain statement scandalized the devout; and, worse still, it appeared to endanger vested interests in the established order. Erigena was condemned. And not until Abelard (A.D. 1079–1142) produced his essay called "Yes and No" (*Sic et Non*), with its collection of glaring contradictions between equally authoritative texts, was the attempt again made to escape from the bondage of

[1] Plato, *Rep.*, iii, 394d.
[2] Erigena, *De Divisione Naturae*, i, 66. (*Pat. Lat.*, 122.)   [3] Ibid., col. 509.

the uncritical Roman tradition. The medieval mind was unwilling to face the fact that contradictory statements could be found in equally authoritative sources. It attempted to cover the nakedness of logical contradiction in terms with the fig-leaf of mystery. But there is no mystery about a contradiction in terms. It arises out of the attempt to unite in one system of thought, or one system of moral principles, the very different expressions of different poets and preachers, who lived in widely separated ages. But for the Middle Ages there was no fundamental difference between the book of *Genesis* and the book of *Revelation*, or between the teaching of the Bible and that of St. Augustine or of Gregory the Great. Abelard was condemned as Erigena had been; but they were not typical of the men of their time. The critical intelligence was not indeed suppressed. It had not yet arisen in adequate strength.

And now the medieval mind survives only in sheltered corners, which the keen air of Athens has not yet reached. The twentieth century owes a debt of gratitude to those men and women of the First Europe, who kept a light shining in dark ages, who built a home for the spirit out of the ruins among which they lived. But a later age need not repeat the mistake of simple and timid minds, making their way for the first time into a new world. We should not hesitate to leave behind us the path cut through the wilderness of the First Europe. We have reached higher and clearer ground.

INDEX

I. SUBJECTS

ABBOTS: as civil administrators, 298, 407; as ambassadors, 446; prestige increases with wealth of monasteries, 406; functions of, in Rule of St. Benedict, 385; bishops subordinate to, in Ireland, 286.

ABSOLUTISM: in Church and State supported by accepted idea of the other world, 654.

AFRICA: and the Empire in the sixth century, 244; Vandal conquest of, 133; Vandal persecutions in, 204; Mohammedan conquest of, 250, 264.

AGRICULTURE: Roman, 417; Medieval, 405, 433, 440 sq.

ANOINTMENT: 261, 283, 291, 304.

APPEASEMENT: Empire's policy of, towards Barbarians, 62, 143; a cause of loss of prestige, 145.

ARIANISM: dominant in Barbarian kingdoms of fifth century, 196; cause and effects of this, 182; traditions of Roman Empire opposed to, 168; conversion of Visigoths from, 257; also mentioned, 133, 180, 185, 202, 215.

ARISTOCRACY: Roman and Medieval compared, 462.

ARCHAISM: its influence on First Europe, 37, 307, 346, 485.

ASCETICISM: in West, 368; in fifth century, highly regarded, 375.

BAPTISM: 157, 238, 591.

BARBARIANS: general description of, 31, 273; of diverse and mutually hostile tribes, 423; infiltration into service of Empire, 102; their contribution to development of New Europe, 273; not opposed to or desirous of destroying Roman civilization, 34; earlier raids, 60; their settlements, A.D. 400–600, 463, 469.

BARBARIAN KINGS: their kingship originated in Roman recognition, 194; the title rex, 192, 209, 304; in fifth century mostly Arians, 196; a cause of internal weakness, 198; did not rely on mercenaries, 227: influence of Old Testament on their position, 303; compelled to use Roman administrative experience, 195; their Council, 361; legislation by, 360.

BARBARIAN KINGDOMS: general results of their creation, 221; relations of Church and State in, 298; of Burgundians, 206; of English, 273, 284; of Franks, early period, 207; Gaul becomes France, 276; Carolingians' policy, 580; in Italy, 587 sq.; of Ostrogoths (in Italy), 208, 218; of Vandals, 204; of Visigoths, 199; and see Charles the Great, Laws.

BISHOPS: Latin, and Roman Empire, 183; sources of power, 198, 232; theory of their functions in eighth century, 311; kings, and — in Spain in sixth century, 256; in Gaul, 277; in England, 287; in Ireland, 292; different types of, 173, 278; appointments controlled by Frankish kings, 277; moral authority of Roman Empire passes to bishops, 148; in the fifth century become "dictators," 88; and chief officials and representatives of Churches, 159; and take over many civil functions, 184; examples of their taking part in resistance to barbarian raids, 177; subordinate to abbots in Ireland, 286.

SUBJECTS

"Defeatism": religious in fifth century, 64, 371.
Deification: of Emperors, 118.
Democracy: influence of Christianity in forming modern, 25.
Depopulation: caused by slavery, 93; and the Roman poll-tax, 452.
"Dictatorship": of Roman Emperor, 168, 318; of the Papacy, 493; of bishops, 88.
Discipline: dominant position of Roman Church regarding, 536.

Emperor, the "Play" (Charles the Great): reasons why title desired—prestige of Imperial Rome, 572; and of Christian Rome, 574; reasons why Roman Church established new Emperor, 575; the title and its meaning, 605; sources of information, 578; general conclusions, 611.
Europe, the First: formation of, 23; transition from Roman system to, summarized, 36; analogies with the present-day transition, 54; during period conditions in North and South very different, 270; dominant ideas in, —; the Two Powers (Spiritual and Temporal), 629; a Catholic Church, 643; the Other World, 653; no conception of social justice, 51; unity of classes a characteristic of, 455.

Fugitive slaves: and manual workers, 90, 328; *and see* Refugees.

Germans and Romans: conflict between one type of barbarism and one type of civilization, 29.
Germany: conversion to Christianity, 294; English monks in, 393.
Greek language: original language of early Christian Churches, 126, 501; unknown to majority of bishops of West, 229; thus, a source of division, 243, 501.

Heaven: medieval conception of, 652; Mohammedan, 584, 653.
Heaven and Hell: effect on social institutions of medieval conception of, 654.
Hell: medieval conception of, 653.
Historians: their limitations, 42.
History: uses of, 53.
Holy Roman Empire: *see* Emperor.
"Home Guard": none behind Roman frontiers, 460; organized in ninth century, 475.
Homosexuality: 334, 348, 352, 370.

Iconoclasm: causes, 588, 596; leads to final breach between Roman Church and Empire, 550; Charles the Great supports, 311.
Ireland: influence of, on learning, etc., 292; monasticism in, 286, 378.
Italy: Empire and Church after destruction of Gothic power, 252.

Jews: position under early Empire, 153; merchants, 446; object to image-worship, 585; persecutions of, in Spain, 260, 335; believed to be connected with Mohammedans, 622.

671

KEYS: of St. Peter, 505, 507, 534; magical efficacy of keys containing fragments of St. Peter's chains, 257, 534.
KINGSHIP: in seventh and eighth centuries, theory of, 312.

LATIN LANGUAGE: supplanted by Greek as official language, 169, 243; its retention in West by the learned: divides West from East, 169, 245, 327, 641 n.; unites West across borders of kingdoms, 52, 185, 297, 298, 403, 658; tends to make clergy a separate caste, 315, 403, 504, 658; increases prestige of bishops of Rome, 501, 504; preserves ritual from change, 646.
LAW: supremacy, of recognized, 485; "Natural," 363.
LAW, ENGLISH: compared with continental systems, 357; early, 287, 331, 357.
LAW, ROMAN: 323; Codex Theod., 325; summaries of, by barbarian kings: Edict of Theodoric, 329; Breviarium Alarici, 330; Roman Law of Burgundians, 206, 330; use of, allowed to "Roman" subjects of barbarian kings, 323, 329, 337; no such class in England, 357; also mentioned, 122, 206, 215, 225, 317.
LAWS AND CANONS: compared as to origin, etc., 317, 322.
LAWS OF BARBARIANS: 319, 331; judicial procedure, 338; — oaths, 338; ordeal, 340; legislation, 360; of Alamanni, 337; Bavarians, 337; Burgundians, 337; Franks, 335; capitularies of Frankish kings, 309, 319, 341; Lombards, 337; Visigoths, 330, 333; other tribes, 337.
LOCALIZATION IN NEW EUROPE OF: administration of justice, 434; production, 456; defence, 475; reason why centralization impossible, 486.
LORDS OF THE LAND (MEDIEVAL): the Roman villa, 465; barbarian settlements introduce new types of landowners, 469; nobles against kings, 471; localization of power under, 457, 461; attempts at centralization, 464, 473; methods of warfare influence formation of lordships, 476; social position of, 478; theory of position of, 482; general review, 485.

MAGIC: sense in which word used, 158; Christian rituals, relics, etc., associated with, 158, 445; as a source of power, 235; examples of belief in, 236, 285, 473, 637.
MANUAL WORK: new conception of, introduced by monasticism, 405.
MEDITERRANEAN: safety of, essential to Empire, 123, 128.
MERCHANTS: Syrians or Jews, 446.
MILITARY SERVICE: early Christian views regarding, 84; organization of Roman, in fifth century, 452; local—see Home Guard.
MINTS: 447.
MOHAMMEDAN: religion, 266, 583; conquest of Africa, 242, 251; other conquests, 242, 584; invasions of France, 472, 581; piracy, 621.
MONASTERIES: centres of culture, 381, 402; copying of manuscripts in, 390; help to build up a rural civilization, 405; an instance of corporate ownership, 408.
MONASTICISM: a new social experiment, 367; early, in East, 537; early, in West, 233, 374, 537; Irish, 292, 378; St. Benedict, 382; Benedictines, 386; reforms, 395; relations with State, 396; and with Church, 399; influences leading to spread of, different in North and South, 389; women in, 374, 391.
MORAL AUTHORITY: what it is, 116; the fundamental problem with which this book is concerned, 57; change in nature in passing from Imperial authorities to bishops, 148; — of Roman Empire: attempts to increase it by religious means, 114, 120; its decline, 56; causes, 125, 145; and stages, 129, 138, 140; — acquisition of, by Churches through: bishops, 148, 232; monks and nuns,

II. NAMES, TITLES, ETC.

676